POLITICAL PARTIES OF EUROPE

The Greenwood Historical Encyclopedia of the World's Political Parties

Five reference guides to the world's significant political parties from the beginnings of the party system in eighteenth-century England to the present. Each guide provides concise histories of the political parties of a region and attempts to detail the evolution of ideology, changes in organization, membership, leadership, and each party's impact upon society.

Political Parties of the Americas: Canada, Latin America, and the West Indies
Edited by Robert J. Alexander

The Greenwood Historical Encyclopedia of the World's Political Parties

POLITICAL PARTIES OF EUROPE

Albania-Norway

Edited by Vincent E. McHale
Sharon Skowronski, Assistant Editor

GREENWOOD PRESS
Westport, Connecticut • London, England

Library of Congress Cataloging in Publication Data

Main entry under title:

Political parties of Europe

(The Greenwood historical encyclopedia of the world's
political parties)
  Bibliography: p.
  Includes index.
  Contents: v. 1. Albania-Norway — v. 2. Poland-
Yugoslavia.
  1. Political parties—Europe—History—Handbooks,
manuals, etc. I. McHale, Vincent E., 1939-
II. Skowronski, Sharon. III. Series.
JF2011.P595   1983   324.24'002'02   83-15408
ISBN 0-313-21405-0 (lib. bdg. : set)
ISBN 0-313-23804-9 (lib. bdg. : v. 1)
ISBN 0-313-23805-7 (lib. bdg. : v. 2)

Library of Congress Catalog Card Number: 83-15408
ISBN: 0-313-21405-0 (set)
      0-313-23804-9 (v. 1)

First published in 1983

Greenwood Press
A division of Congressional Information Service, Inc.
88 Post Road West
Westport, Connecticut 06881

Printed in the United States of America

10 9 8 7 6 5 4 3 2 1

CONTENTS

TABLES

PREFACE

POLITICAL PARTIES OF EUROPE is the second in an encyclopedic series covering the history and development of political party activity across the world. The purpose of this series is to provide a comprehensive reference guide to all significant political parties in various world regions through brief biographical sketches, covering such bases as date and circumstances of foundation; evolution of ideology and program; evolution of organization, including splits, mergers, associations, and alliances; and impact on government and society. While the series is designed partly for those in need of accurate information on modern party formations, emphasis has also been placed on relevant historical developments in order to chart continuities and discontinuities of parties and party systems over time and thus locate contemporary partisan phenomena within a broader longitudinal framework.

The European study aims to be comprehensive in several important ways. First, Europe as a region has been defined in the widest possible geographical sense. It is inclusive of both eastern Europe, where extensive party development occurred during the interwar years (1918-1939), and the Soviet Union (historical Russia), whose brief experience with a multiparty system was limited to the period of the *Duma* (1905-1917). Although the contemporary communist party-states of eastern Europe exhibit little deviation from the dominant, single-party mold, coverage of their pre-communist political experiences illustrates the rich and varied tradition of European political life and extends the scope of this volume beyond that of a narrow, western European focus.

Second, size was not a limiting factor in determining system coverage. The material gathered in this study is based upon a universe of 39 distinct party systems ranging from European "ministates" such as Andorra and Monaco, where modern parties have only recently evolved from factional associations, to the directly elected European Parliament, where novel forms of transnational party organization are beginning to take shape. Also, certain locally self-governing systems, such as the Faroe Islands, Greenland, and Northern Ireland, are treated under the metropolitan systems of Denmark and the United Kingdom respectively.

For each system, the inclusion rule for partisan organizations was to provide information on every party that secured at least one seat in the national parliament or governing assembly. In most cases, we have attempted to furnish coverage for virtually all parties, past or present, of all political hues, for which we have reliable information, however sparse it might be. In several systems where extraparliamentary groupings have had a significant impact on the nation's sociopolitical culture, as in Spain or Italy, these groupings have also been mentioned.

Finally, we have chosen to include as separate chapters the three formerly independent Baltic states of Estonia, Latvia, and Lithuania in order to complete our coverage of Europe. Although these countries are now constituent parts of the Soviet Union, their brief periods of independence in the 1920s and 1930s gave rise to distinctive party systems which represented an amalgam of ideologies and organizational styles drawn from the political cultures of central, northern, and western Europe. Within the Soviet Union chapter, we have included capsule descriptions of the parties that formed in response to the fleeting independence of the Ukraine (1918-1920).

With the sole exception of the chapter dealing with the European Parliament, this reference is organized along individual country lines. Only Germany has been subdivided into three chapters: Historical Germany, covering the period up to 1945, and the contemporary states of East and West Germany. Each chapter contains an introductory statement of varying length which describes salient features of that nation's political and social setting and provides background commentary on the history and development of party activity. The contours of the present party system are fully outlined with information current, in most instances, up to 1982. The major governing institutions in each country are identified and described in relation to the structure and functioning of the party system. Attention is also given to the rules of party competition as defined by the mechanics of the electoral system and the operation of the assembly or national legislature. Each introduction concludes with a bibliography of selected background sources, including some in the vernacular where suitable material in English is unavailable.

In each chapter, the introduction and bibliography are followed by an alphabetical listing of party entries, including English and vernacular names as well as party acronyms. Complete biographical information can be found under the main entry, identified by the official or standard English name for that party. Alternate forms of party names—English, vernacular, or acronym—have been cross-referenced to the main entry within that chapter. Internal cross-references throughout the volume are also provided. Within a party biography, a cross-reference to any other party for which information is provided *within the same chapter* is noted either by an asterisk (*) following the first appearance of the party name, which directs the reader to that main entry, or by a parenthetical notation in lower case print: (*see* Liberal National Party). A cross-reference to a party for which information is provided *in a separate chapter* is identified by a parenthetical notation in which the appropriate chapter title appears as upper-case print: (*see* UNITED KINGDOM). In some cases, additional citations of source material have been appended to the individual party biographies under the subheading of *Further Reference*.

With the exception of Albania and East Germany, each chapter is accompanied by tabular data on electoral history. This information details fluctuating party representation over time in the assembly or national legislature and, in most instances, also outlines the pattern of governing party coalitions where appropriate. Beginning dates for these tables vary according to the establishment of meaningful competitive elections in each system. Also, the reporting of seats won by individual parties may show some slight discrepancies from other sources, depending upon when the seat count was taken and the degree of party switching by elected representatives once in the assembly. The figures presented in this volume represent a consensus based upon our consultation of several reliable sources. Tables have been footnoted to indicate party mergers, electoral alliances, and, where necessary for clarification, changes in party names from one election to another.

Appendix materials in the form of party genealogies and country chronologies have been arranged to refine and complement the biographical information. The genealogies provide a concise summary of party development in each system, with dates of origins, splits, mergers, and name changes clearly identified for each party. Electoral alliances are also included. The country chronologies are not meant to be exhaustive but are designed to highlight certain political events and dates in the history of each system.

In completing a project of this scope and magnitude, we have incurred many debts along the way. We are grateful to Greenwood Press for entrusting us with the task of organizing this volume and bringing it to fruition. We offer special thanks to Marilyn Brownstein, Cynthia Harris, and Mildred Vasan for their unflagging confidence, generous assistance, and long-suffering patience during all stages of this undertaking.

We wish to thank all of our contributors, whose cooperation and enthusiasm were essential to the successful completion of this project. Many agreed to be part of this effort before they realized the extent of their commitment, and they later found themselves laboring through several revisions and repeated requests for additional information or clarification. They did it all cheerfully and in the spirit of making the final product a superb reference work.

We also wish to recognize the assistance of others who, although not contributors in the formal sense, did provide us with data or various forms of support. Included here are our thanks to the unnamed staff members of various embassies and foreign delegations who responded graciously to our requests for information. For institutional support, we are grateful to the Dean's Office of Western Reserve College, Case Western Reserve University for office space and typing assistance, and also to the Dean's Office of the School of Liberal Arts and Sciences, St. John's University for their support of Tadeusz Cieplak's research on Poland.

Our final thanks go to our friends and colleagues at Case Western Reserve University, especially the members of the Political Science Department (Jack DeSario, Kenneth Grundy, Maurice Klain, and Daniel Minns), whose tolerance, understanding, and vigorous encouragement helped to smooth over many rough spots along the way. Elsie Finley of Freiberger Library offered helpful bibliographic advice, and Hatem S. Abu-Lebdeh assisted us in tracking down various factual data.

This volume represents the end product of a truly collaborative effort in which editorial responsibility was broadly shared, especially as the project matured. Although the division of labor was blurred for the most part, Vincent McHale assumed responsibility for the initial development and overall management of the academic side of the project. He wrote the introduction, the chapters on the Baltic states, compiled most of the tabular material, and assisted in the revisions of several chapters. Sharon Skowronski wrote the chapter on Luxembourg, compiled the party genealogies and the bulk of the country chronologies, and shared in chapter revisions. In addition, she assumed responsibility for quality control by typing and copy-editing several drafts of the manuscript. Both editors collaborated in the writing of the chapter on the European Parliament.

Vincent E. McHale
Sharon Skowronski
June 1982

ABOUT THE CONTRIBUTORS

MARC BAER (United Kingdom) is assistant professor of history at Frostburg State College. He received his Ph.D. from the University of Iowa in 1976. Having published on aspects of British political history in *Albion* and the *Journal of Urban History*, Dr. Baer is presently completing a study of the political structure of Victorian London.

JOSEPH B. BOARD (Sweden) is the Robert Porter Patterson Professor of Government at Union College. He received degrees in jurisprudence from Oxford University and then the Ph.D. from Indiana University in 1962. Dr. Board's work on Scandinavia has appeared in the *Swedish Journal of Political Science*, *Scandinavian Studies*, and the *American Political Science Review*. He is also the author of *The Government and Politics of Sweden* (1970).

TADEUSZ N. CIEPLAK (Poland) is associate professor of government at Saint John's University, New York. He received the LL.M. and Ph.D. degrees from McGill University in 1955 and 1962 respectively. Extensive writings by Dr. Cieplak on aspects of Polish politics have appeared in the *Polish Review* and *Canadian-American Slavic Studies*. He is also the editor of *Poland since 1956* (1972).

A. S. COHAN (Ireland) is senior lecturer in politics at the University of Lancaster, United Kingdom. He received his Ph.D. from the University of Georgia in 1970. Dr. Cohan's articles on Irish politics have appeared in the *British Journal of Politics* and *Comparative Politics*. Also, he is the author of *The Irish Political Elite* (1972) and *Theories of Revolution* (1975).

VAN COUFOUDAKIS (Cyprus) is associate professor of political science at Indiana University-Purdue University, Fort Wayne. He received his Ph.D. from the University of Michigan in 1972. The Cyprus questions have been the subject of Dr. Coufoudakis's writings for European and American publications. He is the editor of *Essays on the Cyprus Conflict* (1976).

JAMES A. DUNN, JR. (Belgium) is associate professor of political science at Rutgers University, Camden. He received his Ph.D. from the University of Pennsylvania in 1970. His research on Belgian politics has appeared in *Comparative Political Studies*, *Comparative Studies in Society and History*, and the *Western Political Quarterly*. Dr. Dunn is also the author of *Miles to Go: European and American Transportation Policies* (1981).

ERIC S. EINHORN (Norway) is associate professor of political science at the University of Massachusetts, Amherst. He received the Ph.D. from Harvard University in 1972. His studies on the politics of the Nordic countries have appeared in *Polity*. Dr. Einhorn is also the author of *Security Policy and International Politics in a Small State: The Case of Denmark* (1971).

TROND GILBERG (Romania) is professor of political science and associate director of the Slavic and Soviet Language and Area Center, Pennsylvania State University. He received the Ph.D. from the University of Wisconsin in 1969. His articles have appeared in *Eastern European Quarterly* and *Problems of Communism*. Dr. Gilberg is also the author of *The Soviet Communist Party and Scandinavian Communism* (1973) and *Modernization in Romania since World War II* (1975).

MICHAEL HODGES (Gilbraltar, Malta) is associate professor and chairman of international relations, Lehigh University. He received his Ph.D. from the University of Pennsylvania in 1973. Dr. Hodges is the author of *Multinational Corporations and National Government* (1975), and editor of *European Integration* (1972) and *Economic Divergence in the European Community* (1981).

ANTHONY JAMES JOES (Italy) is professor of politics and director of international relations at Saint Joseph's University. He received the Ph.D. from the University of Pennsylvania in 1970. Having published in *Comparative Political Studies* and *Orbis*, Dr. Joes is also the author of *Fascism in the Contemporary World* (1978) and *Mussolini* (1982).

ERIC A. JOHNSON (Historical Germany) is associate professor of history at Central Michigan University. He received his Ph.D. from the University of Pennsylvania in 1976. He research on German history has appeared in the *Journal of Interdisciplinary History*, the *Journal of Social History*, and *Social Science History*.

D. GEORGE KOUSOULAS (Yugoslavia) is professor of political science at Howard University. He received the Ph.D. from Syracuse University in 1976. Studies of Balkan politics by Dr. Kousoulas have appeared in *Orbis* and the *Yearbook of International Communist Affairs*. He is the author of *Revolution and Defeat: The Story of the Greek Communist Party* (1973) and *On Government and Politics* (1982).

MARTIN J. E. KRÁL (Austria) is a Ph.D. candidate in political science at the University of Washington. His research interests include the persistence of party machines and the role of Slavic minorities in Austrian politics.

H. PETER KROSBY (Finland) is professor of history at the State University of New York, Albany. He received his Ph.D. from Columbia University in 1967. Dr. Krosby's articles on Nordic affairs have appeared in *Current History, American Historical Review, Political Science Quarterly*, and the *Western Political Quarterly*. He is the author of *Finland, Germany, and the Soviet Union, 1940-1941: The Petsamo Dispute* (1968).

JOSEPH P. MASTRO (Soviet Union) is associate professor of political science at North Carolina State University. He received his Ph.D. from Pennsylvania State University in 1972. Dr. Mastro is the author of several papers on political leadership in the Soviet Union.

GERALD R. McDANIEL (Denmark) is professor of government at California State University, Sacramento. He received his Ph.D. from the University of California, Berkeley, in 1963. Having published in the *American-Scandinavian Review*, he is currently completing a study of government and politics in Denmark.

WALTER C. OPELLO, JR. (Portugal) is assistant professor of political science at the University of Mississippi. He received his Ph.D. from the University of Colorado in 1973. His research on Portuguese politics has appeared in *Comparative Politics, Legislative Studies Quarterly*, and *West European Politics*.

JAMES S. PACY (Hungary) is associate professor of political science at the University of Vermont. He received the Ph.D. from American University in 1967. Dr. Pacy has written extensively on the subject of diplomats in *Asian Affairs, East European Quarterly*, the *Foreign Service Journal*, and *World Affairs*.

RICHARD D. PARTCH (East Germany, West Germany), formerly an assistant professor of political science at Niagara University, is currently a sociologist with the United States Department of the Interior. He received his Ph.D. from the University of Pennsylvania in 1976. German political parties has been the subject of Dr. Partch's work appearing in *German Studies Review, Quality and Quantity*, and *Zeitschrift für Soziologie*.

DAVID W. PAUL (Czechoslovakia) is assistant professor of political science at the University of Washington. He received the Ph.D. from Princeton University in 1973. Dr. Paul's articles have appeared in *Problems of Communism, Slavic Review*, and the *International Studies Quarterly*. He is also the author of *Czechoslovakia: Profile of a Socialist Republic at the Crossroads of Europe* (1981).

KENNETH J. PITTERLE (Switzerland) is currently a research specialist in international affairs at the Wharton School of the University of Pennsylvania. He received his Ph.D. from Pennsylvania in 1980. His doctoral research focused on the dynamics of the Swiss party system.

JOSEPH H. ROGATNICK (Andorra, Liechtenstein, Monaco, San Marino) is professor of international management at Boston University. He received his Ph.D. from the University of Pennsylvania in 1976. Dr. Rogatnick has had a distinguished career as an international business executive and as senior economic and diplomatic officer of the United States government.

MICHAEL ROSKIN (Spain) is associate professor of political science at Lycoming College. He received his Ph.D. from American University in 1972. Dr. Roskin's studies of Spanish politics have appeared in *Foreign Policy* and the *Political Science Quarterly*. He is also the author of *Other Governments of Europe* (1977) and *Countries and Concepts: An Introduction to Comparative Politics* (1982).

NIKOLAOS A. STAVROU (Albania, Bulgaria) is professor of political science at Howard University. He received his Ph.D. from George Washington University in 1970. Extensive writings by Dr. Stavrou on the politics of the Balkan states have appeared in *World Affairs* and *The Outlook*.

RICHARD F. TOMASSON (Iceland) is professor of sociology at the University of New Mexico. He received his Ph.D. from the University of Pennsylvania in 1960. His work has appeared in *American-Scandinavian Review, Current History,* and *Comparative Studies in Society and History*. Dr. Tomasson is the author of *Sweden: Prototype of a Modern Society* (1970) and *Iceland: The First New Society* (1980).

FRANK L. WILSON (France) is associate professor of political science at Purdue University. He received the Ph.D. from the University of California, Los Angeles, in 1969. Having published on various aspects of French politics in *Comparative Politics, Western Political Quarterly,* and in *World Politics,* Dr. Wilson is also the author of *The French Democratic Left* (1971) and coauthor of *The Comparative Study of Politics* (1979).

STEVEN B. WOLINETZ (Netherlands) is associate professor of political science at Memorial University, Newfoundland. He received his Ph.D. from Yale University in 1973. His research on Dutch political parties has appeared in *West European Politics* and in several book chapters.

POLITICAL PARTIES
OF EUROPE

INTRODUCTION

Politics is essentially a bundle of processes concerned with the allocation of power, authority, and values for a society. Because of its distributive aspects, the political life of a nation is determined by the interactions of several environmental conditions. Physical geography often affects the socioeconomic milieu, which in turn may shape the system of values and cultural norms of the society's people. The dynamics of contemporary political life must also be viewed as an outgrowth of historical experience as embodied in those evolutionary trends involved in developmental change.

These observations are especially appropriate for an understanding of political parties and party systems. Parties have come to represent the central link between society and government. As such, they are one of the most important and universal features of political life in the 20th century. Political parties reflect the excitement and dynamism of Man's political experience, for they give life and animation to the otherwise static formal institutions of government.

Despite their acknowledged importance and virtual universality in the contemporary world, political parties defy precise definition or classification. The term *party* is derived from the old French word *partir* (to divide). Hence political parties are made up of individuals who have organized into groups for the purpose of representing the diversified and usually divisive values of political ideologies. Generally, in competitive systems, parties operate to aggregate various societal interests into an array of policy proposals. Parties are also motivated by the common goal of seeking to control the establishment and operation of governmental institutions and thus to participate directly in the decision-making process. Therefore, they must attempt to generate sufficient mass support for the purpose of installing a set of decision makers who are committed to using the previously aggregated policies as a basis for governance. Aside from this commonality, however, parties tend to exhibit a wide array of rationales, orientations, organizational structures, and behavioral styles. Moreover, some parties within a given system may aggregate societal interests more effectively than others. These are usually the larger, managerial-type parties that seek to form majoritarian governments.

Political parties can be distinguished from other mass political organizations largely by the scope of their respective activities and their claim to governance.

The major difference between parties and interest groups is that the latter rarely, if ever, seek control of government in their own right but function instead to influence policy outcomes that directly or indirectly affect their members. Pseudo- or protoparties, such as political clubs, citizen lobbies, and various political movements, are generally more ephemeral in nature and tend to wax and wane in political importance. On an organizational continuum, they lie somewhere between parties and interest groups. Nevertheless, pseudo-parties have weighed heavily on political development in many countries by providing the impetus for restructuring various social and economic interests into new partisan forces.

European political parties trace their origins to loosely organized elite factions and court cliques which began to coalesce around the monarch or other governing nobility at various times during European history. However, their phenomenal growth in importance, starting in the latter half of the 19th century, was the direct result of the diffusion of liberal democracy as an organizing mode of political life. Liberal democratic government, in contrast to traditional elitist and authoritarian forms, was predicated upon the notions of a rational citizenry controlling government through representative institutions and a firm belief that the masses could be organized effectively for political action. The political party then emerged as a new, multifunctional, organizational entity, whose primary tasks were the development and refinement of programs and policies, usually around some set of fundamental beliefs, vague or explicit; and the mobilization of the citizenry in support of political elites who were committed to the translation of their respective partisan programs into government action.

Of course, the early definitions of "rational citizenry" were limited as to which segments of the population were regarded as qualified—whether through social status, wealth, or educational levels—to make rational decisions. Therefore, the development of political parties in Europe was also tied to another facet of liberal democratic ideology: electoral reform. The impetus for electoral reform was to improve the representative character of governmental institutions through an expansion of the suffrage to include groups newly defined as qualified to make sound political decisions. Electoral reform also sought the establishment of greater equity in the representation of political forces within national decision-making institutions. Although the nature and timing of electoral reform varied according to society, in most cases the reforms resulted in an increase rather than a diminution of the number of political parties making claims on the governmental system.

Hence, from the very beginning, European parties were faced with a dual and often conflicting role. They were not only expected to articulate, organize, and represent group interests from a chaotic mass public, but they were also expected to unite themselves into larger political aggregations for the purpose of effective governance. Thus parties must not only provide a focus for political division in order to justify their existences and maintain their constituencies, but they must also foster consensus among the mass public and broaden their support if they are to be successful contenders for power. The organizational and behavioral reaction to these conflicting imperatives has led to a diversity of parties and party systems in the European context.

In most European countries, the nature and depth of various social cleavages has exerted the dominant influence on the evolution of the party system. Cleavage lines also define the limits of political aggregation. In those European countries where deep and antagonistic cleavages have existed among religious, ethno-linguistic, or regional subcultures, the party system is strained to adjust a fragmented political culture to the needs of a stable political order. Where such cleavages are nonexistent or muted, the party system tends to operate in a less conflictual manner and has more aggregation potential.

Several specific dimensions of sociopolitical cleavage have played and continue to play singular roles in the structuring of European party systems. Early divisions in northern Europe (for example, in Scandinavia and the United Kingdom) tended to be urban-rural or regional in nature and found expression in the Conservative and Liberal parties of the 19th century. Although these parties originally pitted traditional economic interests against those of the rising middle classes, they gradually evolved into managerial organizations that were prompted to seek broad-based majorities across economic lines in their respective societies.

In other systems, especially those of southern Europe (as in Italy, France, Spain), religious controversy between clericals and anticlericals formed the principal basis for partisan divisions. The persistence of socioreligious antagonisms over time was often aided by a configuration of separate socialization channels, embodying the various religious tenets, many of which were able to transmit divisive political communications through the parties into the political system. By providing a continual focus for political conflict, religious quarrels in these societies served to intensify other sociopolitical divisions, particularly those surrounding the nature of the regime itself. Religious controversy tended to peak toward the end of the 19th century and has subsided since 1945. Parties with religion-based programs, however, continue to play a major role in Austria, Belgium, France, Italy, the Netherlands, Switzerland, and West Germany.

The social turmoil growing out of the processes of developmental change in Europe has often aligned one sector of the society against another. Conflicting class orientations and the issue of labor versus capital ultimately led to the emergence of socialist parties toward the end of the 19th century. As a result of the 1917 Bolshevik Revolution in Russia, Europeans have also been sharply divided in their attitudes toward communism and the role of the communist party in their respective political systems. While the socialist parties gradually adopted a reformist stance, the communists have stressed class warfare and have advocated replacement of existing republican institutions. In eastern Europe, where communist parties have come to power, they have abandoned the competitive party system for a hegemonic regime dominated by the communist party. However, like other political ideologies, communism has experienced internal disputes regarding interpretations of ideology and the various means by which to achieve specified goals. In recent years, European communist parties have been fractured by differences first between Chinese- versus Moscow-oriented factions and later between doctrinaire ideological conservatives versus moderate elements willing to cooperate on a limited basis with other political groups.

Ethno-linguistic and regionalist parties have also reemerged in recent years, largely as a reaction to developmental change and the increasing centralization of political and social life in which subcultural interests tend to be overshadowed by national issues. In many European countries, the cleavages represented by these groups are mutually reinforcing; and when they are congruent, with sharp variations in economic development (as in Belgium), they have had the effect of disrupting stable patterns of party activity by making national consensus more difficult to achieve. Similar trends have been evidenced in eastern Europe, especially in Czechoslovakia and Yugoslavia, where restless minorities have pressed for greater decentralization.

New sources of political division have emerged in Europe with the formation of pseudo-parties related to movements for governmental reform, ecology, and women's rights. The nature of their demands appears to have little relationship to the structure of existing partisan differences. Although on the surface such pseudo-parties appear minuscule and unimportant, we cannot dismiss their potential for mobilizing important sectors in the society around new and emergent cleavages. There are numerous instances in European history where pseudo-parties and extraparliamentary groups have had to be reckoned with by the major party formations.

While political parties may be reflective of societal divisions, not every societal cleavage finds expression in the party system. This is because party systems are molded by the institutional frameworks and rules under which parties must operate. For example, various types of electoral arrangements act either to facilitate or inhibit the organization of political differences within a given society and thereby play a critical role in determining the character and type of party behavior. Europe has experimented with a variety of voting systems (including proportional representation, majority vote per district, party-list voting, transferable votes, and so forth). Historically, the expansion of the suffrage and alterations in voter eligibility have had important effects on both numbers and types of parties operating within a particular system.

Scholars have been divided as to the actual impact of the electoral system on political parties. Politicians, however, have been keenly aware of the strategic importance of electoral contrivance. The electoral system has often been viewed as a key element in the struggle for control of the state and its decision-making apparatus. Other types of institutional parameters have served to benefit or penalize parties in terms of their share of representation in the institutions of governance. All of the eastern European communist party-states have quotas which limit the share of assembly seats that can be obtained by the noncommunist groups. There are also restrictions as to the number of candidates permitted to contest elections. In western Europe, parties are governed by legislation involving registration, finance, access to media, and minimum percentages of the total vote required to seat representatives. In some countries, there are also rules which establish a minimum number of seats for the formation of parliamentary groups. This latter device works against smaller parties by giving added voice to the dominant political formations.

The establishment of transnational party formations represents a new chapter in European political development. Transnational party organization first became evident in eastern Europe with the installation of hegemonic communist party systems after World War II. While the ruling communist parties were national in form, with the exception of Yugoslavia, they were linked across national boundaries to an international system of like-minded parties known as the world communist movement. The movement itself has included both ruling and nonruling communist parties and at one time attempted to provide a monolithic organizational structure for worldwide political action. Eurocommunism is a step in this direction, but conflict persists as to the allocation of organizational and ideological leadership in the international movement.

The advent of direct elections to the European Parliament has created new opportunities and incentives for transnational party development in western Europe. By directly involving the masses in European affairs at the supranational level, transnational party formations are likely to reflect an entirely new set of political issues which cut across national boundaries. Several extraparliamentary transnational party federations have been organized to complement existing parliamentary groups. If this trend continues and full-fledged transnational parties take shape, it could result in heightened awareness of supranational political and policy issues among the national electorates and in turn raise new demands for an expansion of the decision-making responsibility of the Parliament in the European Community. It may also disrupt the stability of national party systems by injecting divisive transnational issues (such as regional inequalities) into the aggregation process at the domestic level. Many transnational issues are difficult to process within the organizational and political framework of national societies.

Europe has served as the cradle of political parties, and the development of parties elsewhere in the world owes much to the European political heritage. Not only do parties have a long history in Europe, but they are still in the process of evolution and transformation. In both East and West, the growing complexity and interdependence of modern life, coupled with the need to balance equity against effective system performance, has thrust parties into the role of system managers, in which they are charged with the formation of *pragmatic* alternative policies and the widest possible bases for governance. In eastern Europe, these same forces have prompted more political pluralism, if only within the confines of the hegemonic communist party.

The prospects for the future of European party systems are mixed. Party stability is likely to be attainable only in those circumstances where divisive historical cleavages have been eroded and where economic growth remains undisturbed by domestic constraints or international crises. However, the development of broad-based parties capable of building and maintaining an expanding consensus may be difficult, if not impossible, to achieve in many countries, and failures in the party system may lead to future political crises and possibly to regime changes.

Bibliography

The literature on European parties and party systems is fairly large. Citations concerning specific party systems or individual parties are listed in the bibliographies following each chapter introduction or appear under the subheading of *Further Reference* at the end of a party entry. The material listed below covers comparative aspects of parties and party systems in general, as well as related phenomena such as electoral systems.

Belloni, Frank, and Dennis Beller. *Faction Politics: Political Parties and Factionalism in Comparative Perspective.* Santa Barbara, Calif.: Clio Press, 1978.

Butler, David, Howard R. Penniman, and Austin Ranney, eds. *Democracy at the Polls: A Comparative Study of Competitive National Elections.* Washington, D.C.: American Enterprise Institute, 1981.

Carstairs, Andrew McLaren. *A Short History of Electoral Systems in Western Europe.* Winchester, Maine: Allen & Unwin, 1980.

Dahl, Robert A., ed. *Political Oppositions in Western Democracies.* New Haven, Conn.: Yale University Press, 1966.

Duverger, Maurice. *Political Parties.* Translated by Robert and Barbara North. New York: Wiley, 1954.

Epstein, Leon D. *Political Parties in Western Democracies.* New York: Praeger, 1967.

Fischer-Galati, Stephen, ed. *The Communist Parties of Eastern Europe.* New York: Columbia University Press, 1981.

Hand, Geoffrey et al. *European Electoral Systems Handbook.* London: Butterworth, 1979.

Henig, Stanley, and John Pinder, eds. *European Political Parties.* London: Allen & Unwin, 1979.

Herman, V. *Parliaments of the World.* London: Macmillan, 1976.

Huntington, Samuel P., and Clement H. Moore, eds. *Authoritarian Politics in Modern Society: The Dynamics of Established One-Party Systems.* New York: Basic Books, 1970.

Irving, R.E.M. *The Christian Democratic Parties of Western Europe.* Winchester, Maine: Allen & Unwin, 1979.

Janda, Kenneth. *Political Parties: A Cross-National Survey.* New York: Free Press, 1980.

Keesing's Contemporary Archives. London: Keesings Publications, annual volumes.

Lange, Peter, and Maurizio Vannicelli, eds. *The Communist Parties of Italy, France and Spain: Postwar Change and Continuity.* Winchester, Maine: Allen & Unwin, 1981.

La Palombara, Joseph, and Myron Weiner, eds. *Political Parties and Political Development.* Princeton, N.J.: Princeton University Press, 1966.

Lawson, Kay. *The Comparative Study of Political Parties.* New York: St. Martin's Press, 1976.

Lipset, Seymour M., and Stein Rokkan, eds. *Party Systems and Voter Alignments.* New York: Free Press, 1967.

Mackie, Thomas T., and Richard Rose. *The International Almanac of Electoral History.* London: Macmillan, 1974.

Merkl, Peter, ed. *Western European Party Systems: Trends and Prospects.* New York: Free Press, 1980.

Michels, Robert. *Political Parties.* Translated by Eden and Cedar Paul. Glencoe, Ill.: Free Press, 1949.

Newmann, Sigmund, ed. *Modern Political Parties.* Chicago, Ill.: University of Chicago Press, 1956.

Ostrogorski, M. *Democracy and the Organization of Political Parties.* London: Macmillan, 1902.

Patterson, William E., and Alastair H. Thomas, eds. *Social Democratic Parties in Western Europe.* New York: St. Martin's Press, 1977.

Pederson, Mogens N. "The Dynamics of European Party Systems: Changing Patterns of Electoral Volatility." *European Journal of Political Research* 7 (1979): 1-26.

Pridham, Geoffrey, and Pippa Pridham. *Transnational Party Cooperation and European Integration.* Winchester, Maine: Allen & Unwin, 1981.

Rogger, Hans, and Eugen Weber, eds. *The European Right: A Historical Profile.* Berkeley: University of California Press, 1965.

Rokkan, Stein, and Jean Meyriat, eds. *International Guide to Election Statistics.* The Hague: Mouton, 1969.

Rose, Richard, ed. *Electoral Behavior: A Comparative Handbook.* New York: Free Press, 1974.

Sartori, Giovanni. *Parties and Party Systems: A Framework for Analysis,* vol. 1. London: Cambridge University Press, 1976.

Shoup, Paul S. *The East European and Soviet Data Handbook.* New York: Columbia University Press, 1981.

Smith, Gordon. *Politics in Western Europe,* 3d ed. New York: Holmes & Meier, 1980.

Starr, Richard F., ed. *Yearbook on International Communist Affairs.* Stanford, Calif.: Hoover Institution Press, annual volumes.

Urwin, Derek W. "Political Parties, Societies and Regimes in Europe: Some Reflections on the Literature." *European Journal of Political Research* 1 (1973): 179-204.

Vincent E. McHale

ALBANIA

The SOCIALIST PEOPLE'S REPUBLIC OF ALBANIA (*Republika Popullore Socialiste ë Shqipërisë*) is a small European country, the size of Maryland, bordered by Yugoslavia to the north and east, Greece to the south, and the Adriatic Sea to the west. Isolated and mountainous, Albania remains one of the least developed of the European states. Of the 2.6 million inhabitants, only 34 percent can be classified as urban dwellers. The population is composed of two ethnically and linguistically distinguishable groups of Albanian stock—Ghegs and Tosks—and a sizable Greek minority. During the reign of King Zog, a Gheg, his dialect was the official language of government and business; since 1945, Tosk has been used. Historically, the population has been predominantly Muslim with a small proportion of Christian sects, although the constitution emphatically declares Albania to be an atheist state.

The People's Republic of Albania was formally established on January 11, 1946, following elections in 1945 which resulted in a communist-dominated assembly. A new constitution was adopted in 1976, renaming Albania as a Socialist People's Republic and designating the Labor Party of Albania* as the sole political force in the country. Supreme governmental power is nominally vested in a single chamber, the People's Assembly, which is composed of 264 deputies (one for every 8,000 inhabitants). Deputies are elected by direct universal suffrage (starting at age 18) for four-year terms, on the basis of a single list of candidates proposed by the Democratic Front.* No opposition is tolerated in Albania's elections. The People's Assembly meets very briefly, acting only to ratify decisions made by higher governmental organs. The Assembly elects a smaller governing body, the Presidium, whose president acts as head of state, and a Council of Ministers responsible for daily governmental operations. The chairman of the Council of Ministers serves as prime minister. There is a high degree of correspondence between positions in the hierarchies of government and those in the Labor Party of Albania.

Albania became an independent entity at the onset of the Balkan wars, after nearly 450 years of Turkish rule. On November 28, 1912, a small group of Albanian patriots, representing several religious sects and regions of their nation, assembled in the city of Vlona amid a rising nationalistic fervor and declared the independence of their country from the collapsing Ottoman Empire. Ismail Qemal Vlora, a prominent Albanian emigré from Constantinople who for years had been involved in efforts to gain freedom for his nation, assumed the leadership of a provisional government and proceeded with the enormous task of building a unified nation-state under adverse external and internal conditions. As a first step, Vlora requested immediate recognition of his government by the major European powers, and he solicited their assistance in delineating the borders of the new state in such a way as to encompass within them the entire Albanian nation.

The fragile political entity which Vlora and his compatriots created in Vlona faced the immediate hostility of neighboring states who had their own designs on Albania's territory, and Vlora faced the suspicions of the major powers whose mistrust of each other gave rise to the politics of Balkanization. In the name of national unity and the realities of war, competitive party politics were avoided. The Albanian patriots presented a domestic united front in the hopes that this would secure the recognition of their country. However, most of the signers of Albanian independence engaged in partisan politics in the 1920s and provided the cadres for the two parties that contended for political power: the Popular Party* and the Progressive Party.* Yet "normal" party life in the new Albanian state was retarded by the external limitations of a prescribed political system imposed upon the nation's sovereignty.

On December 16, 1912, less than one month after the declaration of independence and through the efforts of England and Germany, the Ambassadors' Conference of London placed the Albanian question on its agenda and in principle recognized the country's independence. On March 22, 1913, a border commission delineated the territory of the new state, which has remained unchanged to this day. In addition, the Ambassadors' Conference agreed that Albania should be "an autonomous principality, sovereign and hereditary," with her independence guaranteed by six European powers. A prince was to be selected from one of the royal houses of Europe. No mention of political freedom or a competitive party system was made in the formal documents related to the creation of the Albanian "hereditary principality."

On March 7, 1914, Prince Wilhelm of Wied arrived in the port city of Durazzo to assume his duties. The foreign-born and foreign-appointed ruler arrived amid internal conflicts and general resentment. Under normal conditions, the national coalition constructed by Vlora could have evolved into the prototype of a national party. But resentment of a foreign prince, domestic clan conflicts, and the outbreak of World War I temporarily halted any movement toward partisan politics. Following an internal rebellion, Prince Wilhelm left the country, only weeks after his arrival, without renouncing his title or the right to return.

For the duration of World War I, Albania was administered by several powers—Greece, Serbia, Italy, and France—but this temporary state of affairs did not negate the gains from the Ambassadors' Conference. Albania, however, labored under a continuous threat of partition. Italy, once a proponent of Albanian independence, sought to reduce the size of postwar Albania and negate de facto the 1913 borders; Yugoslavia, who already had a substantial number of Albanians within her prewar borders, sought additional territory; and Greece demanded Epirus, the southern part of Albania, which is still inhabited by ethnic Greeks. In this rather critical juncture, President Woodrow Wilson of the United States fervently supported self-determination and specifically insisted upon Albania's sovereignty.

Amid internal disunity and external threats, but encouraged by Wilson's support, prominent Albanian leaders convened in the city of Ljushna on January 21, 1920, and formed a Regency Council composed of leaders of the country's four religious sects—Suni, Bektashi, Orthodox, and Catholic. The Council assumed the functions of government, assisted by a 30-member, nonpartisan Senate. Within a year, a parliament was elected by indirect vote on a ratio of one deputy per 12,000 inhabitants, but the candidates did not carry a partisan label. The government, which established Tirana as its capital, stabilized the country; and on December 19, 1920, Albania was admitted to the League of Nations. With the first parliament as a laboratory, the first Albanian political parties appeared with Western-sounding names and ideologies. But normal party life was interrupted by the emergence of Ahmet Zogu (who in 1928 proclaimed himself King Zog I of Albania), the Italian occupation of the country, and World War II. In 1944 the communists seized power under the banner of the National Liberation Front and formed a provisional government. Since then, all competitive party activity has been terminated.

Bibliography

Islami, Selim, and Frasheri Christo. *Historia ë Shqipërisë* (History of Albania). Tirana: Naim Frasheri, 1960.

Pano, Nicholas C. *The People's Republic of Albania*. Baltimore: Johns Hopkins Press, 1968.

Prifti, Peter R. *Socialist Albania since 1944: Domestic and Foreign Developments*. Cambridge, Mass.: MIT Press, 1978.

Shpuza, Selim. *Revolucioni Demokratikoborgeze ë Shqipërisë i Qershorit 1924* (The Democratic-Bourgeois Revolution of Albania of June 1924). Tirana: Ministrija e Aresimit, 1959.

Skendi, Stavro. *Albania*. New York: Praeger, 1958.

———. *The Political Evolution of Albania 1912-1924*. New York: Mid-European Studies Center, 1954.

Vokopola, Qemal. "Albania." In *Government, Law and Courts in the Soviet Union and Eastern Europe*, edited by Vladimir Gsovski and Kazimierz Grzybowski. London: Atlantic Books, Stevens and Sons, 1959.

Political Parties

COMMUNIST PARTY OF ALBANIA (*Partia Komuniste ë Shqipërisë*: PKSh). Considerable controversy surrounds the origin and history of the Albanian Communist Party. Prior to 1941, one cannot speak of a distinctive Albanian communist movement. To the extent that Albanian nationals played any role in the movement, they did so in the name of internationalism and as agents of the Third Communist International (Comintern). The party was founded in Tirana on November 7, 1941, with the assistance of two emissaries (Miladin Popovic and Dusan Mungosa) of Josip Broz Tito, leader of the Yugoslav partisans, and under the sponsorship of the Comintern. Current leaders of the party claim that credit for the creative leadership and successes of the PKSh belongs to them and not to Tito or the Comintern. More specifically, Albanian party historians attribute the party's formation to the "correct leadership" of its first and, up to now, only secretary-general, Enver Hoxha. With equal persistence, Yugoslav historians argue that their guidance was instrumental in creating the Albanian Communist Party during the dark days of Italian occupation.

Approximately 60 members, representing self-proclaimed party cells from Korcha, Shkodra, Tirana, and the Koçova, participated in the founding congress of the PKSh. What brought them together were Germany's attack against the Soviet Union and the instructions sent by the Comintern to its national sections to prepare for total war against the Germans in order to alleviate the military pressure "against the fatherland of socialism." Popovic and Mungosa remained in Albania for the duration of the war, and on occasion they were assisted in their efforts to maintain unity and fighting spirit among the Albanian communists by Zvetozar Vukmanovic-Tempo, who later became chief of staff of the Yugoslav Army. The PKSh assumed political power at the end of the war; and by intimidation and terror, the party eliminated all challenges to its authority.

The PKSh assumption of political power in 1944 was facilitated by the party's exploitation of Albanian nationalism and by the failure of the Western Allies to support an effective noncommunist alternative. From the founding of the party until liberation, the Albanian communists were shielded under the banner of the National Liberation Front. This movement had broad nationalist appeal throughout Albania.

Despite its total control of Albanian society after 1944, the PKSh was beset from its inception by both internal divisions and external interference. Serious conflict surfaced after World War II when Koçi Xoxe, a key party member and minister of interior, sought to remove several of his competitors from political power. Xoxe had the support of the Yugoslav government which, in its growing dispute with the Soviet Union, was eager to retain influence over Albania. After the Tito-Stalin rift in 1948, Xoxe was removed from authority. Arrested and executed as a "titoist," Xoxe's removal precipitated major purges in the Albanian party ranks.

The Second Party Congress in 1948 was called to define the party line following the Yugoslav-Soviet break. At that congress, the PKSh was renamed the Labor Party of Albania, * in order for its title to "reflect the state of development of the society and the classes it served." Enver Hoxha became the undisputed leader, with Mehmet Shehu second in command. Since 1948, these two individuals have effectively ruled Albania with little opposition and with widespread terror.

DEMOCRATIC FRONT (*Fronti Demokratik*). A mass electoral organization with compulsory membership for all Albanians 18 years of age and above, the Front's function is to sponsor electoral lists for national and local elections. As a rule, such lists are prepared by the Labor Party of Albania. *

FASCIST PARTY OF ALBANIA (*Partia Fashismit ë Shqipërisë*: PFSh). The Albanian Fascist Party made its appearance in 1938, a time when fascism was fashionable throughout Europe. Patterned after its Italian counterpart and directly controlled from Rome, the PFSh featured Mussolini-type insignia and a paramilitary youth organization. There are no precise figures on its actual membership, but there is little evidence that the PFSh was popular among responsible Albanian leaders—they viewed it as an additional sign of Italian encroachment upon their country's independence and sovereignty, which had been gained only 15 years earlier. During the Italian occupation, the Albanian Fascist Party played a political role by providing coerced mass support for the cabinets of Xhafer Ypi, a former Zogu supporter, and Shefqët Verlaci, who was made premier by a powerless Albanian Constituent Assembly.

Further Reference. Tomori (Albanian daily newspaper), particularly years 1938-1940.

FRONTI DEMOKRATIK. *See* DEMOCRATIC FRONT.

LABOR PARTY OF ALBANIA (*Partia ë Punës ë Shqipërisë*: PPSh). The Communist Party of Albania* was renamed the Labor Party of Albania at the Second Party Congress in 1948. The party has continued to face a number of difficulties in dealing with world events and their relationship to international communism. Following the Tito-Stalin rift, a crisis occurred in the party after the Twentieth Congress of the Communist Party of the Soviet Union (see SOVIET UNION) in 1956 when Nikita Khrushchev pressed for the elimination of the "cult of personalities" and "rehabilitation of the victims of the Stalinist era." Leaders Enver Hoxha and Mehmet Shehu, viewing Khrushchev's criticism as an attack on their leadership style, took advantage of the Sino-Soviet rift and shifted their ideological allegiances to the People's Republic of China.

Eventually the Albanians broke all ties with the Soviet Union and the other European communist parties. For more than ten years, the Albanian communist leadership behaved as an ideological appendage to the Chinese Communist Party and adopted most of its practices, including the Cultural Revolution. However, relations between the PPSh and China became strained following President Richard Nixon's 1972 visit to Peking and the general improvement in Sino-American relations. Following Mao Zedong's death in 1976, the PPSh terminated all party-to-party relations with Peking.

The basic ideological differences stressed by the Albanian party are related to the theory of the "three worlds," which the PPSh views as a ploy to facilitate China's ambitions to acquire superpower status. Thus in the Seventh Party Congress, China was openly criticized; and Enver Hoxha placed a claim to the international leadership of the "correct and true Marxist-Leninist parties" of the world (of which 28 such parties had sent representatives to this 1977 Seventh Party Congress).

The structure and organization of the PPSh is similar to that of other ruling communist parties. Theoretically the Party Congress is the highest legislative body; but in practice the Politburo, which is currently made up of 12 members, controls all power and governmental decisions. The total PPSh membership of 101,500 of 1981, including candidates, represented only four percent of the Albanian population. The party is managed by a vast bureaucracy controlled by a 72-member Central Committee and a Secretariat, of which Enver Hoxha is first secretary. A persistent criticism among rank and file of the party is that it has failed to rejuvenate itself. All of the higher organs remain in the hands of a group of wartime comrades and their relatives, making the PPSh one of the most nepotistic communist parties in the world.

Further Reference. Labor Party of Albania, *Dokumenta Kryesorë të Partisë së Punës së Shqipërisë* (Principal Document of the Labor Party of Albania), vols. 1, 2 (Tirana, 1961); Stavrou, Nikolaos A., "Albanian Communist Party: Origin, Seizure of Power, Past and Present Contradictions" (Master's thesis, George Washington University, 1965).

PARTIA Ë PUNËS Ë SHQIPËRISË. *See* LABOR PARTY OF ALBANIA.

PARTIA FASHISMIT Ë SHQIPËRISË. *See* FASCIST PARTY OF ALBANIA.

PARTIA KOMUNISTE Ë SHQIPËRISË. *See* COMMUNIST PARTY OF ALBANIA.

PARTIA PERPARIMTARE. *See* PROGRESSIVE PARTY.

PARTIA POPULLORE. *See* POPULAR PARTY.

PFSh. *See* FASCIST PARTY OF ALBANIA.

PKSh. *See* COMMUNIST PARTY OF ALBANIA.

POPULAR PARTY (*Partia Popullore*: PP). The Popular Party was formed in 1921 among the deputies of the first indirectly elected parliament. The emergence of the PP (as well as that of its ideological counterpart, the Progressive Party*) followed the formation of a regency council and a unity government at the Congress of Ljushna. Under the influence of Wilsonian principles, the unity government created the proper political atmosphere and legal framework which facilitated a competitive and unhindered party system. While the title of the Progressive Party was merely euphemistic, the Popular Party became known almost immediately as the party of reform and social progress.

Similar to party systems in the other Balkan countries, the PP did not have a permanent organization nor long-lasting internal cohesiveness. It was essentially a personality-centered political aggregate influenced by the progressive ideology of its top leaders, and initially it was dominated by Western-educated intellectuals. The nominal leader of the Popular Party was Harvard-educated Bishop Fan S. Noli of Durazzo, who sought to introduce American democratic principles into a society which had just emerged from more than four centuries of Ottoman rule.

In addition to Noli, several prominent personalities representing diverse interests and regions joined forces under the umbrella of the PP and for three years (1921-1924) dominated the political life of the country. Among those personalities were Ahmet Zogu, a Gheg chieftain with considerable local following; Xhafer Ypi; and Eshref Frashëri. During this three-year period, five cabinets were formed and brought down as a result of shifting loyalties within the party. The number of cabinets during this short period is indicative of the disunity which plagued the PP from its inception. Specifically, two issues eroded party effectiveness: an ideological cleavage between emigré and domestic leaders concerning the pace of reforms and their divergent views about "law and order." The domestic leaders such as Zogu and Ypi favored a gradual approach to modernization, while Noli espoused more radical and somewhat unrealistic methods (unrealistic given Albania's stage of development).

In 1922, following an attempted coup, the Noli-led radical wing of the PP withdrew its support from the Ypi government, of which Zogu was minister of the interior, and declared themselves to be the government's opposition. This was a clever ploy, having the impact of weakening the government without abandoning the party or compromising its ideology by joining the actual opposition, the Progressives. In June 1924, following the assassination of one of its young members, Avni Rustemi, Noli's parliamentary opposition staged a mass demonstration in Tirana and precipitated the intervention of the military on Noli's behalf. The Ypi cabinet resigned, Noli became prime minister, and Zogu fled to Belgrade. Zogu returned to Albania seven months later with the help of the Yugoslav General Staff, and he led an army composed of Ghegs and the remnants of General Wrangel's White Russian troops. Noli, who was prime minister for only seven months and who had unrealistically tried to implement drastic reforms, fled to Italy with some of his followers, who later provided the nucleus of the Communist Party of Albania.*

In 1925, Zogu was elected president by a controlled parliament, and he commenced an authoritarian rule which mixed important reform with strong-handed tactics. Three years later, Zogu was proclaimed King Zog I of Albania—a post he held until his departure, forced by the Italian occupation army in April 1939. Competitive party life was seriously retarded during Zogu's 14-year rule as president and king, but it was never completely suspended.

PP. *See* POPULAR PARTY.

PPSh. *See* LABOR PARTY OF ALBANIA.

PROGRESSIVE PARTY (*Partia Perparimtare*). The Progressive Party was the ideological counterpart of the Popular Party.* It, too, emerged in 1921 after Albania secured its independence. Contrary to its name, however, the Progressive Party opposed all major reforms promoted by the Popularists and instead sought to defend the economic and social privileges of the major landowners, who dominated the Progressives from their inception.

The Progressive Party was a loosely organized coalition of southern landowners and northern conservatives who realized that Albania could not easily overcome four centuries of Ottoman traditions and social norms. Like the Popular Party, the Progressives were a parliamentary organization and made no attempt to formalize their existence among the masses. The nominal party leader, Mehdi Frashëri, was a respected intellectual; but actual power rested with Shefqët Verlaci, a Tosk landlord, who played a dominant and often negative role in Albanian politics for almost 20 years. Other than defense of class privileges and opposition to "modernistic ideas," the Progressives failed to develop a viable political ideology. However, given the divisions in the ranks of the Popular Party, the Progressives often held the balance of power by providing tacit support to competing personalities, including Ahmet Zogu. The party declined after Zogu became king of Albania, but several of its founders assumed leadership positions during the 1930s. Frashëri became prime minister under Zogu in 1935, and Verlaci was appointed to that post by the Italian occupation authorities in 1939.

Nikolaos A. Stavrou

ANDORRA

The VALLEYS OF ANDORRA (*Valls d'Andorra*, Catalan; *Les Vallées d'Andorre*, French) or the PRINCIPALITY OF ANDORRA (*Principado de Andorra*, Spanish) is a very small co-principality (180 square miles) located in the Pyrenees Mountains, wedged between France and Spain. Formerly an isolated pastoral community, Andorra's population (about 28,000 in 1980) has developed in recent years into a relatively affluent commercial society whose principal economic activities are catering to tourists and manning the hundreds of duty-free shops that have sprung up as a result of the country's taxless regime.

Andorra's executive and legislative powers rest jointly with the president of France and the bishop of Seo de Urgel (Spain) who, as co-princes, enact legislation and conduct the country's affairs such as defense, the judiciary, and foreign relations through their respective and appointed resident representatives: the French Prefect of the Pyrenees-Orientales department (locally titled the *Viguier Français*), and the Spanish Vicar-General of Urgel Diocese (locally titled the *Veguer Episcopal*). This unusual form of government dates from 1278 and is a result of the settlement (*Paréage*) of a dispute over Andorran suzerainty between the French count of Foix, who owned a large area of terrain to the north of Andorra, and the bishop of Urgel, whose principal domain abutted on the southern border of the Pyrenean enclave. The 1278 agreement split the rule of the disputed land between the bishop and the count. Through inheritance, the sovereign powers on the French side passed to the kings of Navarre, then to the kings of France, and eventually to the presidents of France. Today, whoever is elected to the French presidency automatically becomes the French co-prince; whomever the pope appoints to the bishopric of Urgel likewise automatically becomes the episcopal co-prince. Catalan is the official Andorran language, but French and Spanish are also widely used.

As a result of its medieval form of government, Andorra has no formal constitution. However, a co-princely reform enacted in 1866 created a 24-member, single-chamber General Council of the Valleys of Andorra (*El Consell General de las Valls d'Andorra*). It is an administrative rather than a representative body, although it has functioned to submit motions and proposals to the resident delegations of the co-princes. Four councilors are elected from each of the country's six parishes. They serve four-year terms, with half of the Council seats up for election every two years. Suffrage is universal for all Andorrans who have reached the age of 21 years. Women were enfranchised in 1970 and were granted the right to stand for public office in 1973. Turnout for Council elections is generally about 80 percent of the Andorran electorate (approximately 3,200).

The decisions of the General Council are implemented by a Syndic (or manager, Syndic Procureur General) and a SubSyndic, each chosen by the Council. Customarily, the Syndic has been chosen from among the Council membership, while the SubSyndic has been selected from outside that body. Syndics serve three-year terms and may be reelected just once. They have no discretionary powers. Policy decisions must be approved by the Council as a whole, which meets at regular, established intervals and at special sessions as required by the work load. Local government functions through parish councils of ten members each, and they are assisted by advisory lower-level communal bodies. Both are elected by universal suffrage.

In recent years, Andorrans have begun to compare their ancient form of government with those of other western European countries; and although they are firmly rooted in the concept of the co-principality, the Andorrans have considered the possibility of drafting a formal constitution. Proposals have also been discussed for instituting popular election of the syndics.

Andorra has no institutionalized party system. Historically, candidates for seats on the General Council have run as independents. However, various political factions have long existed in Andorran society and, starting in the early 1970s, began to coalesce into loosely organized groupings to contest both local government and Council elections. Andorran law technically forbids political parties. The two principal groupings have been a conservative pro-Spanish faction and a liberal pro-French faction. Liberal-reformist elements have campaigned under the labels of "Democracy and Progress" and "Moderates." In late 1976, these latter groupings merged into a new quasi-political party, the Andorran Democratic Association.* Following the 1977 election, the conservative faction lost its majority position on the General Council, with an equal number of seats going to the conservatives and the Andorran Democratic Association (see table 1).

Bibliography

Bélinguier, Bertrand. La Condition juridique des Vallées d'Andorre. Paris: Editions A. Pedone, 1970.

Brutails, J. A. La Coutume d'Andorre. 2d ed. Andorra la Vella: Editorial Casal i Vall, 1965.

Frisch, Max. Andorra. London: Methuen, 1964.

Sacotte, Jean Charles. "Les Vallées d'Andorre." Notes et Études Documentaires, no. 4087. Paris: La Documentation Française, 1974.

U.S. Department of State. "Andorra." Background Notes Series, no. 8578. Washington, D.C.: Government Printing Office, October, 1975.

Vidaly Guitart, José Mariá. *Instituciones Politicas y Sociales de Andorra*. Madrid: Instituto Francisco de Vitoria, 1949.

Political Party

ANDORRAN DEMOCRATIC ASSOCIATION. Founded in 1976 by the merger of two reformist groups (the "Democracy and Progress" faction and the "Moderates" faction), the Andorran Democratic Association is the only quasi-political "party" in Andorra. In 1977 the grouping secured 12 seats on the General Council. The Association's principal goal is to establish broad-based democratic government in Andorra through a series of institutional reforms. Specific reforms proposed have included proportional representation to the General Council, based upon national electoral lists instead of the current system of allocating four seats per parish, and direct election of the syndics. However, a referendum held on January 16, 1978, dealing with these and other reforms proved to be inconclusive, with the Association's proposals supported by only 31 percent of the electorate. The Andorran Democratic Association was dissolved in May 1980 and replaced by the Democratic Association of Andorra.

Joseph H. Rogatnick

TABLE 1. Distribution of Seats by Faction in the General Council of Andorra, 1975-1977

	Partial Elections	
Faction	1975	1977
"Conservatives"	14	12
"Democracy and Progress"	6	—
"Moderates"	4	—
Andorran Democratic Association*	—	12
Total	24	24

Note: Total number of seats increased to 28 in December 1979.

*The Andorran Democratic Association was dissolved in May 1980 and replaced by the Democratic Association of Andorra.

AUSTRIA

The FEDERAL REPUBLIC OF AUSTRIA (*Bundesrepublik Österreich*) is a central European country whose southern and western regions are situated in the Alps and whose eastern area is dominated by the Danube River basin. This Alpine republic of 32,376 square miles is inhabited by approximately 7.5 million (1979 estimate) German-speaking descendants of the multiethnic Habsburg Empire. Therefore, citizens' surnames are almost as often Slavic, Italian, or Hungarian as they are German. Austrian dialects are closely related to Bavarian and Swiss German. Still, two other ethnic communities persist—about 20,000 Slovenes in southern Carinthia and nearly 40,000 Croats in Burgenland, both groups indigenous to these areas but separated from their cultures through historical accident. Although Austria's population is 90 percent Roman Catholic, the commitment to this traditionally conservative, rural-based faith is weakening: only 36 percent are regular church-going believers, and the rest may follow certain religious traditions but spend more time communing with others in local inns and cafes than in the pews. The social transformation of Austrian society since imperial times makes agnosticism and iconoclastic political practices seem less foreign now than in the past.

While Austrian history reaches back to Charlemagne's efforts to defend his empire against eastern Slavic and Asiatic invasions, Austria's nationalism and political system are of much more recent vintage. Once the center of the far-flung Habsburg Empire, Austria is now a small federal republic and permanently neutral. The devolution from world power to Alpine tourist oasis has been hard on Austria's psyche—vestiges of the old order coexist (or compete) with more dynamic influences attributable to the country's enduring economic boom and sociopolitical developments. Contemporary Austria consists of nine provinces, called *Länder*: Vorarlberg, Tirol, Salzburg, Upper Austria, Lower Austria, Carinthia, Styria, Burgenland, and Vienna (which is also the nation's capital). Although each *Land* in the federation theoretically administers its own affairs, there is little doubt that provincial autonomy is circumscribed.

Austrian political history was dominated for centuries by the Habsburg dynasty and its hereditary claim to the Holy Roman Empire. As the protector of much of central Europe against 15th- and 16th-century Turkish invasions, Austria and the Habsburgs became the most powerful territorial rulers, bringing regions such as Hungary under their influence during the 16th and 17th centuries. Also, as a part of the fledgling Germanic empire, Austria emerged as the most powerful entity in the collection of various sovereign Germanic states called the German Confederation, 1815-1866. (See HISTORICAL GERMANY). Content with its position of authority, however, Austria did not heed the pan-German, nationalistic tendencies that were gathering strength in the first half of the 19th century. Prussia (see HISTORICAL GERMANY), under the leadership of Otto von Bismarck, soon usurped Austria as the Germanic authority by activating unification forces. As a result, in 1866 Austria was defeated by Prussia in a short but decisive war. Preferring exclusion rather than subservience, Austria then separated itself from the growing German empire, a move unopposed by Prussia.

On the home front, the Habsburgs had maintained absolute control over Austrian political and governmental life. In 1848, however, the March Revolution served notice that the monarchy could not remain absolute much longer. In 1861, Emperor Franz Josef I permitted an Austrian *Reichsrat* (Imperial Council) to be formed, with the unicameral council composed of delegates from the traditional *Landtage* (state assemblies) in the hereditary provinces. While confronted with internal pressures for participatory government, Austria also was faced with autonomist sentiments from the long-subdued Hungarian dependents. After seven years of negotiations with the Hungarians, and just one year after defeat by the Prussians, Austria finally agreed to the compromise (*Ausgleich*) that established the Austro-Hungarian Empire. The 1867 *Ausgleich* created a dual monarchy that permitted Hungary independence in internal affairs; but the most important functions in the empire were still discharged in Vienna, the capital of the Austro-Hungarian Empire (*see also* HUNGARY). The *Reichsrat* was then reorganized into a bicameral legislature, somewhat on the British model, with an upper House of Lords (*Herrenhaus*) and a lower chamber, the House of Deputies (*Haus der Abgeordneten*). Originally, the lower house was elected by various social classes in Austrian society. Following suffrage reform in 1907, the membership was selected on the basis of direct universal manhood suffrage.

It was the lower house that would serve as the cradle of Austrian political parties. Its deputies more often than not represented ethnic, cultural, philosophical, or sectarian interests; coalitions and memberships were fluid, if not outright illusory. Deputies tended to form "clubs" or associations for the discussion of public issues and for voting alignments in the *Reichsrat*. For some time, German liberals (mostly found in the Constitutional Party*) were the major force in the parliament. The more radical elements among the German liberals sought greater democratization, a limited government, and social welfare measures, while the emperor and his court only reluctantly yielded to the forces of modernization. When in 1879 the imperial prime minister, Count Edward Taaffe, found he could no longer count on a coalition of German liberals, clerical groups, and conservative circles, he created another coalition in the *Reichsrat* composed mostly of Slavic and agrarian groupings and known as the "Iron Ring." Though subject to frequent disagreement and personality conflicts, this coalition remained intact and supported the emperor's cabinet for nearly 20 years.

In the 1880s, three disillusioned German liberals became the founding fathers of the *Lager* (or camps) into which the Austrian party system is commonly divided. The clerico-reformist elements under Karl Lueger's effective direction formed the Christian-Social Party,* marxists were organized by Victor Adler into the Social-Democratic Party,* while German nationalists and the radical right wing of Austria's political spectrum joined forces under Georg Schönerer. Although the German nationalist movement would continue to be split into many groups, the Schönerer-led League of German Nationalists* for some time was the center of pan-Germanism. Eventually, ethnic discord in the *Reichsrat* contributed to that council's impotence, and the emperor and his cabinet resorted to emergency decrees and autocratic methods after pan-German and Slavic deputies made a shambles of parliamentary procedure in 1897. At the same time, the Christian-Social and Social-Democratic parties grew into modern mass parties, forces to be reckoned with in the last years of the empire. Furthermore, the step-by-step expansion of suffrage hastened Austria's transformation from an atomized party system, based on narrow curia and ethnic representation, to a well-defined bi- (sometimes tri-) polar constellation.

In the aftermath of World War I, an Austria was created that was a shadow of its former self. Gone were the empire and the Habsburgs, an unwanted federal republic was established in 1918 through Allied Powers intervention, the economy was in ruins (and remained that way well into the 1930s), and relatively peaceful competition among the *Lager* soon turned into nasty, violent strife. The new constitution went into effect on November 10, 1921. It provided for a bicameral legislature with a 50-member upper house, the *Bundesrat*, whose seats were filled by the provincial assemblies, and a 165-member lower house, the *Nationalrat*, whose seats were filled by proportional representation (*see* table 2).

Economic weakness, coupled with bitter political and social dissatisfaction, caused deep rifts in the Austrian polity. The result was a tripartite sociopolitical cleavage of clerical-conservative, socialist, and pan-German groups. The reactionary Home Defense League (*see* Homeland Bloc) became a private army for antimarxists, and the Republican Defense League (*see* Social-Democratic Party) one for the Social-Democrats. After initial cooperation from 1918 to 1920, the major parties of that time formed antagonistic, vertically integrated polities: government was firmly in the hands of the conservative Christian-Socials, who were aided at times by the Pan-German People's Party* and the Agrarian League*; and at the same time, the Social-Democrats under Otto Bauer pursued a provocative policy of baiting right-wingers with Austromarxist, quasi-revolutionary sloganeering while securing their redoubts in Vienna, Linz, and other industrial centers. A Jewish party contested elections in Vienna, parties of the Slovene minority in Carinthia; the Burgenland Croats sought local representation; and profascist or ultranationalist organizations rose to challenge these alien elements and the system at large. In the late 1920s, the drift toward authoritarian rule in

Austria was speeded by the establishment of Austrian nazi and fascist organizations. Relations among the parties deteriorated so badly that civil war ensued in 1934. The nazi and marxist parties were outlawed; and in the end, all parties were incorporated in a fascist unity front. This "corporate state" (*Ständestaat*), created after the assassination of Chancellor Engelbert Dollfuss in July 1934, was short-lived—nazi subversion from within (*see* National Socialist German Workers' Party) and from across the borders (*see* NATIONAL SOCIALIST GERMAN WORKER'S PARTY, HISTORICAL GERMANY) effectively counteracted the government's belated effort to rally the population to an Austrian national consciousness. In 1938 the long-sought *Anschluss* (union) with the German Reich was effected, and the "republic that no one wanted" crumbled.

The Second Republic that arose from the rubble of World War II is a creation of political parties, not of peace treaties. The lessons taught by the disastrous interwar period were learned well. Although Austria was "liberated" from nazi oppression, for ten years the country was occupied by Allied troops. The politicians of the three approved parties—the Austrian People's Party,* the Socialist Party of Austria,* and the Communist Party of Austria,* as the *Lager* parties are now called (*see* table 4)—for once pooled their forces in an effort to maintain Austrian independence. When the Communist Party (never influential, even in the Soviet-occupied zone) left the national unity government in 1947, the two equally strong remaining parties formed their Grand Coalition (*see* table 3). Much has been written about its *Proporz* (proportional representation) system in every level of administration. The *Lager* mentality weakened only imperceptibly during the 1940s and 1950s. To the Allied occupiers, the party leaders presented a unitary front, but one which frequently failed to conceal the wrangling off-stage. When opportune, the major parties played on the fears of partisanship: here the spector of a "red" popular front (Socialist-Communist coalition), there the image of unscrupulous capitalist and robber barons.

On May 15, 1955, Austrians celebrated the signing of the state treaty that would remove all foreign troops from their soil and permit them to function once more as a permanently neutral, sovereign state. There was little interest in *Anschluss* at that point, nor in the pan-Germanism of the past. Though the national *Lager* (camp) was reconstituted with the founding of the League of Independents* and its successor, the Freedom Party of Austria,* electoral and emotional appeal of such organizations was, and remains, low. Austrians have grown to cherish the concept of a separate identity; moreover, the Grand Coalition partners have coopted many of the *Lager's* interests. Also, the Catholic Church is no longer involved in political affairs as it had been in the past. Nevertheless, Austria remains a highly politicized country where *Proporz* led to a balancing of Red (leftist) and Black (rightist) forces: a "Red" president, a "Black" chancellor; a "Black" school principal, a "Red" vice-principal; and so on. Austria also has a well-entrenched patronage system and extraordinarily high party memberships. In a country where fractions of one percent determine electoral outcomes, there is no room for independents.

In 1966 the Grand Coalition between the People's Party and Socialist Party had run its course, and the conservative People's Party (ÖVP) received an absolute majority in the legislative elections of that year. Four years later, it was the Socialists' turn; and the Austrian Socialist Party (SPÖ) under Bruno Kreisky has been the dominant party in national politics since. Underneath, little of the system has changed. The conservative character of Austrian culture has perpetuated the *Proporz* in a fashion. Less ideology and much more pragmatism is noticeable. The SPÖ has broadened its appeal in the provinces, while the ÖVP is receiving support from former German nationalists and socialists.

Although the president is the head of state, as in most parliamentary governments the prime minister (here, chancellor) directs governmental affairs. The chancellor's cabinet ministers and department heads may belong to the same party, but subordinate posts are staffed with adherence to precedence. Some ministries and organizations are traditionally peopled by SPÖ members, other are hereditary ÖVP fiefs; and this partisan delineation extends deep into the substructure of Austrian society. Within today's bicameral parliament—the upper-house *Bundesrat* (Federal Council) and the 183-member lower-house *Nationalrat* (National Council)—party directive often overrules individual initiative. In the *Proporz* years, the lower-house factions did little more than give formal endorsement to what had been negotiated and decided in the party headquarters some time before. Today, provincial legislatures, communal councils, district committees, and municipal governments function in much the same way.

Apart from the segmented pluralism of the *Lager*, the most striking feature of the Austrian party system is its concentration. Although the Austrian Freedom Party (FPÖ) sees itself as potential tie-breaker, the two major parties (ÖVP and SPÖ) have only toyed with the idea of forming a coalition with this FPÖ "midget." Regardless of the FPÖ's program of the moment, Austria has been moving toward a two-party system since 1920: in that year, 78 percent of the vote went to the Christian-Socials and Social-Democrats; in 1949 the vote rose to 83 percent, with the Christian-Socials being replaced by the People's Party and the Social-Democrats replaced by the Socialist Party; and in 1970 these latter two parties together received 93 percent of the national vote. The SPÖ and ÖVP can today point to one of the highest party memberships (relative to vote) in the world, and national elections attract up to 97 percent of the electorate (92 percent, approximately 5,187,000, in 1979), even though only the presidential election is compulsory. Suffrage is now universal, starting at 19 years of age. The electoral laws, to be sure, have tended to favor the large parties. The modified d'Hondt system permits the division of remaining votes after the basic figure has been reached by a party in a given electoral district. This system has frustrated Communist, Freedom Party, and other minor party efforts to obtain mandates.

Although partisanship in Austria is still a form of secular religion, there are signs that the *Lager* consciousness is weakening. It is clear that most Austrians belong to a major party as much for philosophical or symbolic reasons as for material rewards. Manifest political behavior is no longer a clearly party-sponsored one; citizen initiatives and independent popular movements indicate that extraparty influences have arisen, although voter independence has not translated into support for third parties. Moreover, the personalities of the political leaders are becoming more important than their party identifications. For instance, the Socialist Party's Bruno Kreisky turned the 1979 *Nationalrat* elections into a contest of statesmanship, as though the Socialists' freewheeling spending and string of scandals did not matter. As public opinion saw it, Kreisky won by a landslide, while his party barely succeeded in receiving the mandate to govern.

Bibliography

Barker, Elisabeth. *Austria 1918-1972.* London: Macmillan, 1973.

Berchtold, Klaus, ed. *Österreichische Parteiprogramme 1868-1966.* Munich: Oldenbourg Verlag, 1967.

Blecha, Karl, Rupert Gmoser, and Heinz Kienzl. *Der Durchleuchtete Wähler.* Vienna: Europaverlag, 1964.

Bluhm, William T. *Building an Austrian Nation: The Political Integration of a Western State.* New Haven, Conn.: Yale University Press, 1973.

Diamant, A. "The Group Basis of Austrian Politics." *Journal of Central European Affairs* 18 (July 1958): 134-155.

Engelmann, Frederick. "Austria: The Pooling of Opposition." In *Political Opposition in Western Democracies*, edited by Robert Dahl. New Haven, Conn.: Yale University Press, 1966.

Fischer, Heinz, ed. *Das Politische System Österreichs.* Vienna: Europaverlag, 1974.

Gerlich, Peter, Georg Ress, and Rodney Stiefbold. *Nationalratswahl 1966: Österreichisches Wahlhandbuch*, vol. 4. Vienna: Österr. Bundesverlag, 1968.

Hölzl, Norbert. *Propagandaschlachten: Die Österr. Wahlkämpfe 1945 bis 1971.* Vienna: Geschichte und Politik, 1974.

Lehmbruch, Gerhard. *Proporzdemokratie: Politisches System und Politische Kultur in der Schweiz und in Österreich.* Tübingen: J.C.B. Mohr, 1967.

Nassmacher, Karl-Heinz. *Das Österreichische Regierungssystem: Grosse Koalition oder Alternierende Regierung?* Cologne: Westdeutscher Verlag, 1968.

Pelinka, Anton, and Manfried Welan. *Demokratie und Verfassung in Österreich.* Vienna: Europaverlag, 1971.

Pulzer, Peter G. J. "The Legitimizing Role of Political Parties: The Second Austrian Republic." *Government and Opposition*, vol. 4, no. 3 (1969): 324-344.

Steiner, Kurt, ed. *Modern Austria.* Palo Alto, Calif.: SPOSS, Inc., 1981.

——. *Politics in Austria.* Boston: Little, Brown and Co. 1972.

Stiefbold, Rodney. "Segmented Pluralism and Consociational Democracy in Austria: Problems of Political Stability and Change." In *Politics in Europe*, edited by Martin O. Heisler. New York: David McKay, 1974.

Stiefbold, Rodney et al., eds. *Wahlen und Parteien in Österreich.* 3 vols. Vienna: Österr. Bundesverlag, 1966.

Sully, Melanie. *Political Parties and Elections in Austria.* New York: St. Martin's Press, 1981.

Political Parties

AGRARIAN LEAGUE (*Landbund*). The Agrarian League was formed in 1925 as successor to the pre-World War I German Agrarian Party and the National Party. The League united numerous local groups and organizations that were dissatisfied with the strong clerical bent of the Christian-Social Party.* The Agrarians' preoccupation with rural and agricultural affairs limited its appeal. The League also competed with the Pan-German People's Party* for the nationalist vote but, with so many political organizations in the same corner, found the going difficult. When the Pan-Germans broke out of the governing coalition, the Agrarians replaced them in the so-called *Schoberblock*. Agrarian leaders, like Vinzenz Schumy, saw themselves as representatives of a corporate state (*Ständestaat*) prototype, and therefore they fit easily into the Fatherland Front* of the 1930s.

AUSTRIAN FARMERS' PARTY. *See* PAN-GERMAN PEOPLE'S PARTY.

AUSTRIAN PEOPLE'S PARTY(*Österreichische Volkspartei*: ÖVP). Although by now it differs considerably from its predecessor, the Austrian People's Party acknowledges its political links to the Christian-Social Party.* The conservative camp (*Lager*) party of the Second Republic was formed already in informal, secret discussions of conservative activists during 1944 and early 1945, although the official ÖVP founding date is April 17, 1945. The early party statutes note that the ÖVP "is a Christian-democratic party based on principles of social integration and federalism," but the ÖVP has made a determined break with the past in avoiding strong, direct links with the Catholic Church (a major political flaw of the old Christian-Social Party).

A union of economic and cultural associations, the People's Party was decentralized from the start. Its early leaders represented the "corporate" (*Stände*) ideal of the First Republic: Leopold Figl, the party chairman and federal chancellor, guided the farmers; Julius Raab, an ex-*Heimwehr* (*see* Homeland Bloc) activist, represented the business interests; while Leopold Kunschak had been an organizer of the Catholics and workers already in 1892 under Karl Lueger's Christian-Social Party. Determined not to repeat the divisive, at times violent, Christian-Social politicking which had led to dictatorship and nazi rule, these People's Party leaders formed a coalition agreement in 1946 with their opponents in the Socialist Party of Austria.* As one of the three democratic political parties permitted to operate in post-World War II Austria, the People's Party made every effort to limit communist influence, mindful of what was happening in neighboring countries. After the last remaining cabinet member representing the Communist Party of Austria* resigned his post in 1947, the People's and Socialist parties engineered a Grand Coalition that was to last until 1966.

Although the ÖVP had, in the citizens' eyes, continued the traditional identification of the conservative *Lager* with the status of *the* governing party, the preeminence of the ÖVP was frequently in doubt. The party failed to court the pan-German nationalists, hewing firmly to *Austrian* nationalism, and therefore lost votes and mandates to the new German-nationalist League of Independents.* But the lesson was learned; and as German nationalism of a less radical sort had become acceptable again, the ÖVP encouraged defections from the right of Austria's political spectrum. Many formerly compromised members of the Nazi Party (*see* National Socialist German Workers' Party) and Homeland Bloc activists were now accepted into the ÖVP.

While the People's-Socialist Grand Coalition played on, the People's Party itself was rocked by embarrassing scandals in the late 1950s. A new generation of party leaders, exemplified by Hermann Withalm and Josef Klaus, emerged over the next five years. The ÖVP looked to the successful Christian Democratic Union (*see* WEST GERMANY) for inspiration, and Chancellor Julius Raab and Economy Minister Reinhard Kamitz engineered an economic course following the West German example. The result was a somewhat belated "economic miracle," grist for the party propaganda mill in subsequent elections where the party posted increases in popular votes and number of mandates. In 1966 the Raab-led cabinet resigned early over budgetary conflicts with the Socialist coalition partner, and the ÖVP chose to run alone in the next election. The ÖVP succeeded with surprising ease. The Socialists had been split by the Democratic Progressive Party,* and the Socialists had blundered by not expressly disavowing the Austrian Communist Party's guarantee of support. The ÖVP had resurrected the "popular front" scare quite effectively.

Although ÖVP presidential candidates had been unsuccessful in the 1963 and 1965 elections, Josef Klaus, the new chancellor, appeared to have the marks of a winner. But the party became overconfident and during the next four years gambled away its easy victory. In the 1970 elections, Klaus was narrowly defeated by the Socialist Party's Bruno Kreisky, and Klaus went into sullen retirement. The following year, the Socialists achieved an absolute majority with 93 seats (50 percent) to the ÖVP's 80 seats; furthermore, the ÖVP presidential candidate, Kurt Waldheim, lost to Vienna mayor Franz Jonas. The former ÖVP defense minister, Karl Schleinzer, a popular and able politician, then attempted to bring order into the party's affairs.

With the People's Party now in the unaccustomed position as government critic and "loyal opposition," many of its tactics are directed at salvaging what is left of past support. There was some hope that the party could regain its seats in the 1975 elections. Only six weeks before the fall elections, however, ÖVP leader Schleinzer died in a tragic automobile accident; and his successor, a young banker named Josef Taus, failed to turn the party around. Taus's popularity was consistently lower than that of the party; and despite great effort, his bland and unassuming nature could not measure up to the magic of the reigning Socialist, Bruno Kreisky. Belatedly recognizing this, the party leadership convinced Taus to yield his chairmanship to Alois Mock, a more attractive and engaging career politician. Since his election in 1980, Mock has engineered a course which steers clear of direct confrontation with Kreisky while assailing the Socialist Party's performance as the ruling party.

The People's Party had been plagued with an image problem throughout the 1970s. Its political advertising was inept, and it has been unable to gauge the shift in citizen concerns. Like the Communist Party, the ÖVP chases the illusion that popular support for the reigning Socialist Party is merely a temporary infatuation. The 1979 elections proved otherwise: while both the Socialist Party and Freedom Party of Austria* gained *Nationalrat* seats, the ÖVP not only fell to 77 seats but also lost heavily in Lower Austria, usually an ÖVP fiefdom.

Part of the ÖVP's problem stems from its inability to develop a coherent philosophy. The ÖVP would like to be known as "the party of the progressive center" (Salzburg Program, November 30, 1972), yet it cannot sever completely its sectarian ties with a conservative Catholicism. The ÖVP avers commitment to multiparty democracy and a social-market economy, but it has not yet articulated how its rule would benefit an already prosperous Austria. The ÖVP's decentralized membership system could be blamed for the malaise—it takes a skillful manager to engineer a consensus among the party's five political organizations (the *Bünde*) and their provincial counterparts. For a long time, one became a member of the ÖVP not by simply joining, but by a more indirect route: depending on one's vocation, one could join the *Bauernbund* (423,000 farming members), the *Wirtschaftsbund* (141,000 business owners), the *Österreichischer Arbeiter- und Angestelltenbund* (270,000 workers), an organization for women (70,000 members), and one for youth (61,000 members). As many ÖVP activists belong to more than one such organization, even the party has to guess at its own membership. Each organization jealously guards its bailiwick, and intraparty harmony is only a sometime thing.

In good Austrian fashion, compromise solutions are hammered out at each level in the ÖVP hierarchy. Ostensibly, the triennial National Party Conference is designated the supreme body of the party, but the chairman and central secretary hold the most influential posts. Provincial governors and the *Bünd* presidents serve as advisers, although frequently they are at odds with the central party leadership. The People's Party has not been able to duplicate the Socialist Party's social and economic organizations, but the ÖVP seeks to compensate through a well-entrenched patronage system. The ÖVP is still strong in western Austria, particularly in the rural areas, and the party appeals to the religiously devout; to farmers; to nonunion, middle-class wage earners; to businessmen; and to well-educated conservatives. Demographic and socioeconomic shifts among Austria's population have, however, eroded party support among these strata.

Further Reference. Heindl, G., *Wie Wir Wurden: Der Weg der Österreichischen Volkspartei* (Vienna: Bundesparteileitung, 1965); Mock, Alois, ed., *Die Zukunft der Volkspartei: Eine Kritische Selbstdarstellung* (Vienna: Verlag Fritz Moden, 1971); Reichhold, J., *Geschichte der ÖVP* (Graz: Styriaverlag, 1975).

BURGENLAND FARMERS' LEAGUE. *See* PAN-GERMAN PEOPLE'S PARTY.

BURGENLÄNDISCHER BAUERNBUND. *See* PAN-GERMAN PEOPLE'S PARTY.

CARINTHIAN ELECTORAL UNION. *See* CARINTHIAN UNITY LIST.

CARINTHIAN FARMERS' LEAGUE. *See* PAN-GERMAN PEOPLE'S PARTY.

CARINTHIAN UNITY LIST (*Kärntner Einheitsliste; Koroška enotna lista:* KEL). The Carinthian Unity List has reestablished the active participation of regional, ethnic organizations in Austrian politics. Though limited in its appeal to those portions of Carinthia where there persists an influential Slovene-speaking population, the KEL's leaders (among them Pavel Apovnik, Karel Smolle, and Filip Warasch) have sought to develop a broader-based opposition to the three major parties.

The antecedents of these regional organizations were locally successful Slovene electoral groupings in the late 1940s. More recently, in 1965, Slovene conservatives campaigned for seats in the *Landtag* as the Carinthian Electoral Union (*Kärntner Wahlgemeinschaft; Koroška volilna skupnost*) but received only 4,272 votes. After similarly limited successes in local elections, the Union faded from the Austrian political scene. The abandonment of Slovene minority rights issues by the major parties during the 1970s, exacerbated by ethnic discord in Carinthia, led to the creation of the KEL in 1975. A hard core of about 4,500 voters—Slovenes, progressives, and disaffected straight-party voters—help shore up the contention that an alternative to the mass-party monopoly exists. The KEL platform seeks economic well-being for the traditionally poor border region, more cultural programs in behalf of the minority, and the implementation of existing minority rights.

CHRISTIAN-SOCIAL PARTY (*Christlich-Soziale Partei*). The Austrian Christian-social movement, seen as an upstart in the 1880s, soon grew to wield a formidable political influence and now forms the core of the conservative *Lager* (camps) in Austrian politics. In the 1870s, Karl von Vogelsang was active in Catholic reform circles and eventually formed the United Christian Party. However, Vogelsang's party was considered merely one of several clerical groupings, and its following was limited to liberals, social activists, and the enlightened clergy. It was Vogelsang's student, Dr. Karl Lueger, a former member of the Club of German Progressives,* who developed a mass following for the movement. In 1889, Lueger—along with Prince Alois Liechtenstein, Monsignor Josef Scheicher, Monsignor Franz Schindler, and others—transformed the grouping into the Christian-Social Party that was to set the tone of conservative politics for the next century.

An able orator and sometime demagogue, Lueger offended the political and clerical establishment. In building the Christian-social movement on the support of largely disenfranchised lower classes, the party was not considered respectable (even when Lueger's criticism of Imperial mismanagement and unrestrained capitalist exploitation rang true). Lueger's brand of populism, generously spiced with anti-Semitic remarks and pan-German sentiments, was welcomed by Vienna's petite-bourgeoisie. Soon Lueger was elected mayor of Vienna, but Emperor Franz Josef I would not sanction the appointment. The mayoral race aroused political passions, with Viennese voters later approving the first election by even greater margins and the emperor unyielding in his opposition. Through papal intervention, Franz Josef finally relented; and in 1897, Lueger and his Christian-Socials took over the administration of Vienna. During his tenure, the city experienced a much-needed renovation, and its social services and transportation improvements were worthy of imitation. The Christian-Socials also gained support in the provinces, and other clerical and conservative groups linked up with the new mass party. By 1907 the Christian-Social Party had gained respectability and emerged as the major partner in the national government coalition.

The Christian-Social leadership floundered after Lueger's death in 1910. Party disunity and growing conservative-clerical tendencies within the movement, coupled with a sudden leadership vacuum, led to considerable losses in the 1911 *Reichstag* elections. The Social-Democratic Party* took over Vienna's administration, and the Christian-Socials maintained their stature in the national government only because of the onslaught of World War I.

In 1918 the Christian-Social Party was reconstituted as the leading conservative party in Austria. Having shifted from its original interests and proletarian support base to a party representing the concerns of the countryside, business, and the clergy, the Christian-Social Party of the interwar years became a class-based, clerico-fascist government party, unable to halt Austria's slide toward authoritarian rule. Under Monsignor Ignaz Seipel, the dominant clerical wing of the party displayed a fierce antimarxism that was to poison Christian-Social relations with the Social-Democrats and lead to the demise of the First Republic. Unable to sustain an absolute majority in elections, the Christian-Socials formed an antimarxist, bourgeois coalition (*Bürgerblock*) with the Pan-German People's Party* and the Agrarian League.* This coalition grappled with ever-present crises while denying the Social-Democrats any opportunity to help resolve this state of affairs.

During the late 1920s, the Christian-Socials drifted ever more to the right. Cooptation of nationalist, protofascist, and revisionist elements (from the nobility to the Homeland Bloc*), the influence of Hungarian and Italian forms of fascism, and of German naziism, forced the party away from any compromise with its Social-Democratic rival. Violent clashes between Austria's socialists and fascists, resulting in the 1927 Vienna riots at Justizpalast, made the radical-right Home Defense League (*see* Homeland Bloc) respectable; thereafter, the League became the paramilitary arm of the Christian-Social Party.

The Christian-Socials found it increasingly difficult to restrain their extremist elements, particularly as it appeared that the Christian-Socials were limping behind more aggressive forces. While in the 1927 general elections the party had received 49 percent of the vote, the candidature of the Nazi Party (*see* National Socialist German Workers' Party) and the Homeland Bloc in 1930 reduced

Christian-Social popularity considerably (to 36 percent). Monsignor Seipel's successor, Engelbert Dollfuss, tried to check the drift. But the private armies had a mind of their own, and random violence was the order of the day. Persistent efforts to disarm the socialists incited civil war, and banning the Nazi Party provoked the abortive July 1934 uprising in which Dollfuss lost his life. His successor, Kurt Schuschnigg, then completed the transformation to full-fledged dictatorship. The Christian-Social Party had no place in a *Ständestaat* (corporate state); and for the short life of corporatism, the party became the major component in the Fatherland Front* and disappeared along with the First Republic after the union with Germany during World War II.

Further Reference. Diamant, Alfred, *Austrian Catholics and the First Republic: Democracy, Capitalism, and the Social Order, 1918-1934* (Princeton: Princeton University Press, 1960); Knoll, Reinhold, *Zur Tradition der Christlich-Sozialen Partei* (Vienna: Hermann Böhlau, 1973).

CHRISTLICH-SOZIALE PARTEI. *See* CHRISTIAN-SOCIAL PARTY.

CLUB OF GERMAN PROGRESSIVES (*Klub der Deutschen Fortschrittspartei*). Austrian progressive liberalism never developed into a *Lager* (camp) as did other prevailing political movements. In the sectarian Imperial Council, however, it was a force to be reckoned with. The progressive movement had its beginnings in the Constitutional Party* and in several parliamentary clubs enamored with classic liberalism and scientific rationalism. The movement's first independent organization, the Progressive Club (*Fortschrittsklub*, 1873-1879), sought a broad program of labor legislation and social-administrative reforms. In time, the club's members developed a radical pan-German orientation. Their anti-Hungarian, anti-Imperial bias made the Progressives unwelcome in ruling circles, while efforts to push tax reform and to exert control over the bureaucracy gained them no friends in the administration.

The Progressives at one time included nearly all founding fathers of the Austrian political spectrum: Victor Adler, founder of the Social-Democratic Party*; Karl Lueger, father of the Christian-Social Party*; and Georg Schönerer, leader of the League of German Nationalists.* Constant squabbling within the Progressives, however, had its deleterious effects, and the movement lost influence in the 1890s.

In 1897 a parliamentary crisis brought forth a *Klub der Deutschen Fortschrittspartei*, led mostly by Sudeten German Progressives like Josef Redlich, Gustav Gross, and Josef Kopp. For a while, the party was a voice of reason, compared to the cacophony in the *Reichsrat*. The enlargement of suffrage, however, weakened the Progressives' cause. Its support had come from influential urban and upper-class elements; in an era of mass parties and strident pan-Germanism, the German Progressives saw their prize programs being coopted by larger parties. The remnants of the Progressives merged with the League of German Nationalists in 1910, and the liberal cause reemerged only after 1955 in the form of the Freedom Party of Austria.*

COMMUNIST PARTY OF AUSTRIA (*Kommunistische Partei Österreichs*: KPÖ). Of all contemporary Austrian parties, only the KPÖ can claim a continuous organizational history dating back to the dawn of the republic. On November 3, 1918, left-wing members of the Social-Democratic Party* attempted to engineer a general strike, eventually broke away from the parent party, and founded the KPÖ. Longevity, however, does not equal success. After the heady days of Red Brigades and soviets, the KPÖ found itself isolated. Not only would the Social-Democrats not join a marxist solidarity front, but they cooperated with conservative forces in opposing the KPÖ.

During the period between the world wars, the Communist Party of Austria acted like (and was) an insignificant, esoteric sect. Intensely concerned with internal party affairs, the KPÖ received, at most, one percent of the vote in general elections. Even the *Bürgerblock* (the bourgeois party coalition) did not view the Communists as dangerous, and the KPÖ was permitted to operate until all marxist organizations were banned in May 1933. The Social-Democratic Party was banned along with the KPÖ, and although the two parties shared a common fate, there was little cooperation even in the underground. Social-Democratic leader Otto Bauer was careful to draw a line of separation, and Communist efforts to recruit left-wing socialists from the Revolutionary Socialists (Austria)* party were largely unsuccessful. The KPÖ leadership and its cadres were scattered—the lucky ones escaping to London or the Soviet Union, the less fortunate ending up in concentration camps.

The Communist leaders returned to Austria with the Allied forces in Spring 1945, at which time Johann Koplenig and his band of Muscovites (including Franz Honner and Ernst Fischer) resurrected the Communist Party of Austria. With the Soviet Red Army controlling nearly half of Austria, the KPÖ thought that the "National Front" takeover-pattern would succeed as well in Austria as it had in eastern Europe. Certainly the Allied insistence on a democratic unity government comprised of the KPÖ, the Socialist Party of Austria,* and the Austrian People's Party* indicated to Koplenig that the Communists were to play a leading role in the Second Republic. With most of Austria's right-wing elements compromised, Allied authorities fell back on bona fide antifascists to fill administrative and police posts. Communists dominated the security services and major industries administered by the Soviets. However, in the creation of a tripartite government, no one KPÖ official could enact independent policies, though the KPÖ vainly believed that the November 1945 elections would affirm its new status. Despite its advantageous situation, the KPÖ received only 174,000 votes (5.4 percent), while the two other parties split the rest (ÖVP-50 percent, SPÖ-44 percent). Gone was the dream of rapid transformation, and the Communist Party of Austria has never recovered from the trauma.

For the next two decades, the KPÖ labored under the illusion of being a potent force, while in the minds of Austrians the party was identified with Russian occupation and stalinist subversion. After failing to win at the ballot box or in dividing the Socialist Party camp, KPÖ officials called for a general strike in 1947 and in September 1950 attempted to initiate a coup. The Austrian government was well prepared for such tactics and held firm, as did the Austrian populace. Unexpectedly, the Soviet Union provided little direct support, and the KPÖ failed.

Even worse was that proletarian support for the Communist Party was waning, despite desperate efforts to consolidate the Austrian political left. The KPÖ's absorption of the Left Socialists* and the Independent Democratic Union* could not halt the decline, no matter under what label the KPÖ campaigned. In 1949 only 5.1 percent of the electorate voted for the Communists under the Left Bloc (*Linksblock*) label; in 1953, 5.3 percent voted Communist under the name of the Electoral Organization of Austrian People's Opposition (*Wahlgemeinschaft Österreichische Volksopposition*); in 1956 only 4.4 percent for the Communists and Left Socialists (*Kommunisten und Linksozialisten*); then the vote fell to 3.3 percent in 1959; and so on. In the 1970s, the KPÖ received barely one percent of the popular vote in national elections. Since 1959 the party has been without representation in parliament and since 1970 without mandates in the provincial *Landtags*. However, Communists still hold a few city council seats in Lower Austria and in trade union or enterprise committees.

The steady erosion of Communist Party support stems in part from the KPÖ's unwavering adherence to Moscow directives. Old-line stalinists are in firm control of the KPÖ: the party defended Soviet actions in the 1956 Hungarian Revolt and is adept at imitating the course of action of the Communist Party of the Soviet Union (*see* SOVIET UNION). The KPÖ has been faced with two ideological crises: in 1963 pro-Chinese Communists broke away from the KPÖ to form the Marxists-Leninists of Austria (MLÖ)* party. Then in 1968 the reformist sentiment swept the KPÖ. Communist leaders imprudently applauded the Czechoslovak Experiment with marxist humanism. As in Czechoslovakia, however, there followed a purge; and Ernst Fischer, the KPÖ's renowned intellectual and publicist, was expelled from the KPÖ along with 27 of 87 Central Committee members.

The KPÖ is organized much as any other communist party. In 1965 the octogenarian Johann Koplenig stepped aside, and Franz Muhri, then 43, became party chairman. The KPÖ finances itself through membership fees and operation of about 300 East-West trade firms. Its publications, the *Volksstimme* (daily) and *Weg und Ziel* (a theoretical monthly), barely sustain their own operating costs. Party membership has continually fallen from a high of 155,000 in 1947 to approximately 18,000 today, and the party's rank and file are the sclerotic and unrepentant hard-liners who have never supported any other party. Furthermore, the average age within the Communist Party is 61 years. The KPÖ not only fails to attract young people but went so far as to disband its youth organizations after the 1968 digression. The Communist Party of Austria now resembles very much the KPÖ of the First Republic.

Further Reference. Fürnberg, Friedl, *Geschichte der KPÖ: 1918-1955* (Vienna: Globus, 1977); Steiner, Herbert, *Die KPÖ von 1918-1938* (Meisenheim am Glan: Anton Hain, 1968); Toch, Josef, "Enklave KPÖ," in *Bestandaufnahme Österreich*, edited by Jacques Hannak (Vienna: Forum Verlag, 1963).

COMMUNISTS AND LEFT SOCIALISTS. *See* COMMUNIST PARTY OF AUSTRIA.

CONSTITUTIONAL PARTY (*Verfassungspartei*). After the Austro-Hungarian Compromise of 1867 and the establishment of the Imperial Council, this catch-all party served as the emperor's loyal legislative representation until the party's demise in the 1880s. In 1879 the Constitutional Party fell out of favor and was replaced by Count Taaffe's "Iron Ring" coalition of Slavic and agrarian parties.

The Constitutional Party supported classic liberal principles but shied away from the anticlerical and strongly pro-German platforms of its more radical deputies. The party soon divided into Old Liberal and Progressive wings, a split which eventually initiated further fractionalization and the party's impotence. Some of the Constitutional Party's less timid social reform proposals became part of the Linz Program in 1882. This program stressed national and social questions, including a union of all German-speaking Austrian lands and the institution of German as the state language.

DEMOCRATIC PARTY OF AUSTRIA (*Demokratische Partei Österreichs: DPÖ*). Founded in July 1945 by Franz Knappitsch, the DPÖ was a short-lived, right-wing party. Its only notable showing occurred in the 1945 provisional government elections (5,972 votes). In January 1946, it was banned by the occupation powers who feared a rightist revival. Poorly organized and unfocused, supported mostly by monarchists and minor officialdom, the DPÖ's activities were eclipsed by the rapid formation of the Grand Coalition between the Austrian People's Party* and the Socialist Party of Austria.* In 1949 the DPÖ received only five votes, most of its supporters having joined the League of Independents.*

DEMOCRATIC PROGRESSIVE PARTY (*Demokratische Fortschrittliche Partei: DFP*). More a one-person protest movement than a party, the DFP was founded in June 1965 by the former interior minister from the Socialist Party of Austria,* Franz Olah. Accused of diverting trade union funds and of challenging the Socialist Party leadership, Olah was forced to resign from party, trade union, and governmental posts in late 1964. The DFP developed a populist program, calling for enlargement of political rights, the elimination of partisan loyalty in parliament, and for bureaucratic reforms.

As popular head of the trade union federation, Olah could count on sympathy from rank-and-file trade unionists and dismayed socialists. He received little support from liberal or progressive circles when he employed ultranationalist (and even anti-Semitic) appeals in an effort to expand his base of support within the middle classes. Austria's major daily newspaper, the *Kronenzeitung*, had received some of the trade union federation funds and served as Olah's mouthpiece. In the 1966 general elections, however, the DFP failed to gain a mandate, even though it received 148,528 (3.3 percent) votes and inadvertently aided the Austrian People's Party* in gaining an absolute majority. The DFP never developed a national following and contested only a few local elections in 1967 and 1968, all with disappointing results. In the 1970 national elections, the DFP received only 15,000 votes and thereafter faded into insignificance.

DEMOKRATISCHE FORTSCHRITTLICHE PARTEI. *See* DEMOCRATIC PROGRESSIVE PARTY.

DEMOKRATISCHE PARTEI ÖSTERREICHS. *See* DEMOCRATIC PARTY OF AUSTRIA.

DFP. *See* DEMOCRATIC PROGRESSIVE PARTY.

DPÖ. *See* DEMOCRATIC PARTY OF AUSTRIA.

EFP. *See* EUROPEAN FEDERALIST PARTY.

ELECTORAL ORGANIZATION OF AUSTRIAN PEOPLE'S OPPOSITION. *See* COMMUNIST PARTY OF AUSTRIA.

ELECTORAL PARTY OF INDEPENDENTS. *See* LEAGUE OF INDEPENDENTS.

EUROPÄISCHE FÖDERALISTISCHE PARTEI. *See* EUROPEAN FEDERALIST PARTY.

EUROPEAN FEDERALIST PARTY (*Europäische Föderalistische Partei*: EFP). The EFP was founded on October 21, 1960, by Otto Molden, a publisher, and by other liberal intellectuals. The European Federalists see themselves as local representatives of an inevitable United Europe, and the party is the political outgrowth of an annual European Forum conference held at Alpbach, Tirol. The EFP claims a national, not a partisan, perspective. As a member of the Federated International of European Federalist Parties, the EFP also adheres to that organization's political program, which decries the growth of state capitalism and big business, as well as the perpetuation of nationalistic conflict. The EFP platform paints an optimistic picture of Europe's future.

At the ballot box, however, the European Federalists have had little success in developing a following within Austria. In the 1962 elections, the EFP received 535 votes, while in the 1967 presidential elections, the EFP candidate received only four percent of the national vote. Since then, the party has failed to generate any enthusiasm for more than mere symbolic participation in Austrian politics.

FATHERLAND FRONT (*Vaterländische Front*). The Fatherland Front (also known as the Patriotic Front) was organized in 1933 by the Christian-Social Party* chancellor, Engelbert Dollfuss, to counter the danger from extreme left and right elements and to protect Austrian independence. Partly to appease Italy's Mussolini, Dollfuss worked to make the Front the primary organization of the *Ständestaat* (corporate state). The Front consolidated all organizations and vocational groups supporting the Dollfuss regime, most notably the *Bürgerblock* (coalition) parties and the Home Defense League (*see* Homeland Bloc). With the passage of Dollfuss's 1934 constitution, all political parties ceased to exist in Austria, and the Front served as the *Ständestaat's* conduit to the masses. From 1934 to 1938, the Front sought to instill, belatedly, an Austrian national consciousness while clinging to the clerical and quasi-monarchical traditions of the old bourgeois parties.

FORTSCHRITTSKLUB. *See* CLUB OF GERMAN PROGRESSIVES.

FPÖ. *See* FREEDOM PARTY OF AUSTRIA.

FREEDOM PARTY OF AUSTRIA (*Freiheitliche Partei Österreichs*: FPÖ). The FPÖ was founded on October 17, 1955, by Anton Reinthaller, an Upper Austrian ex-minister of the Austrian Nazi Party (*see* National Socialist German Workers' Party). The FPÖ's ranks soon swelled with a mixture of German nationalists; conservative libertarians; former members of the nationalist Homeland Bloc,* League of Independents,* and Nazi organizations; and those who found unpalatable the Grand Coalition between the Austrian People's Party* and the Socialist Party of Austria.*

With the withdrawal of Allied supervision, ten years after the end of World War II, the FPÖ continued the League of Independents' (VdU) defense of the Third Reich experience, but the FPÖ also stressed its role as the only effective alternative to the monopoly of the *Proporz* parties. Reinthaller hoped to increase the nationalists' share of parliamentary seats in the 1956 general elections; instead, the new party received only half of the 1953 VdU vote and had to console itself with six mandates. It became clear that many of the VdU's supporters had found a haven in the two major parties of the Grand Coalition. If it hoped to survive, the FPÖ had to shift closer to the People's Party. In the 1957 presidential election, the People's Party and the FPÖ did cooperate in proposing a supraparty candidate, Dr. Wolfgang Denk. The surgeon lost, a victim of Austrian concern over balancing the leadership, but the FPÖ had at least become respectable.

In 1958 an ex-SS man and fellow Upper Austrian, Friedrich Peter, took the reins of the Freedom Party and endeavored to enlarge the FPÖ beyond its Alpine base (Carinthia, Styria, Salzburg, Vorarlberg, and part of Upper Austria) while also attempting to broaden party appeal to entice blue-collar workers and farmers. As the party could distribute little patronage, the strategy ultimately failed. (Even today, the FPÖ is endemically poverty-stricken; unlike the larger parties, only ten percent of FPÖ supporters are dues-paying members.) In the early 1960s, the Socialist Party leader, Franz Olah, supplied Peter with party funds in hopes of forging a Socialist-Freedom coalition in the next election. The two parties did cooperate in the celebrated Habsburg case in 1963, preventing the "pretender," Dr. Otto Habsburg (son of Karl IV, who had abdicated in 1918), from entering the country. But this dalliance did not sit well with the conservative People's Party who, when they were victorious in the 1966 elections, claimed never to have considered a much talked-about coalition including the Freedom Party. The FPÖ suffered losses in all electoral districts that year, and Peter's career seemed at a crisis point.

However, the national elements within the FPÖ stood behind Peter. Although the party had lost one-third of its support in the ten years of his leadership, Friedrich Peter received a vote of confidence. In 1970 the FPÖ and Socialist Party again talked about the possibility of a minority coalition; but, in the end, the FPÖ conservatives turned down the Socialist offer. Yet the Socialists went ahead on their own and scored an epic electoral victory.

More recently, the Freedom Party's penchant for ultranationalist causes (South Tirol, the Carinthian-Slovene dispute, German war victims) has led the party into its deepest crises. The increasingly outspoken, heavily ex-Nazi nationalist wing of the party has offended the sensibilities of moderate and libertarian FPÖ members by incautious anti-Semitic and pro-Hitler outbursts. This lack of innerparty control has proved fatal for Friedrich Peter. In 1975, Simon Wiesenthal, the Nazi hunter, announced that in World War II Peter had served in an SS murder brigade on the Eastern Front. Despite frequent denials, the public believed that the FPÖ leader probably had participated in the manhunts. The party could not abide the thought that it was led by a mass murderer and continued to protect its leader, at least until the public furor had died down and a more amenable chairman could be found. When the FPÖ mayoral candidate won the 1975 elections in Graz (Austria's second-largest city) and did even better in Spring 1978, the party had found its man. Alexander Götz, a photogenic, urbane young politician with impeccable credentials, took over the party until an even more ambitious leader of the libertarian wing of the party, Norbert Steger, toppled him barely two years later. Steger has developed a genuine following among all but the most intransigent right-wing elements and in popularity polls stands equal with the new People's Party head, Alois Mock. Due to changes in Austrian electoral laws, the FPÖ now sends 11 deputies to the *Nationalrat*, though it still receives only about 5.5 percent of the popular vote. However, recent local elections and the results of the May 1979 general election indicate that the FPÖ is gaining in popular esteem.

Like the larger parties, the Freedom Party derives its consistent support from members of associated economic interest groups (*Verbande*) for farmers, workers, and entrepreneurs, as well as from cultural and student organizations. The average FPÖ member is a middle-class, urban, better-than-average-educated official or businessman. Through its student organization, the FPÖ replenishes itself with recruits from the German nationalist fraternities. The party has undergone considerable change in its ideological underpinnings and no longer rejects Austrianism as it had in the past. It understands that there is no place for a pan-German movement in modern Austria and that the Freedom Party can only hope to be of some influence when the major parties have reached an impasse.

Further Reference. Riedlsperger, Max E., *The Lingering Shadow of Nazism: The Austrian Independent Party Movement Since 1945* (Boulder, Colo.: East European Quarterly, 1978).

FREIHEITLICHE PARTEI ÖSTERREICHS. *See* FREEDOM PARTY OF AUSTRIA.

GdVP. *See* PAN-GERMAN PEOPLE'S PARTY.

GERMAN AGRARIAN PARTY. *See* AGRARIAN LEAGUE.

GERMAN NATIONAL LEAGUE. *See* CLUB OF GERMAN PROGRESSIVES.

GRM. *See* GROUP OF REVOLUTIONARY MARXISTS.

GROSSDEUTSCHE VOLKSPARTEI. *See* PAN-GERMAN PEOPLE'S PARTY.

GROUP OF REVOLUTIONARY MARXISTS (*Gruppe Revolutionärer Marxisten*: GRM). The trotskyite wing of the communist movement in Austria is represented by the GRM. These communists were expelled from the pro-Chinese Marxists-Leninists of Austria (MLÖ)* in 1972 after vehement objections to the MLÖ's maoist theorizing and unwillingness to allow differences of opinion within that party. The GRM members, mostly university students, have had little success in advancing their cause outside of universities. Hampered by traditional Austrian conservatism (even among avowed marxists) and frequently found feuding with other radical-left factions, the GRM receives few votes in local elections. The trotskyites were also damaged by identification with anarchist or terrorist groups aligned with elements in West Germany. In the 1979 general elections, the GRM received less than 1,000 votes, and it is unlikely to widen its base of support.

GRUPPE REVOLUTIONÄRER MARXISTEN. *See* GROUP OF REVOLUTIONARY MARXISTS.

HEIMATBLOCK. *See* HOMELAND BLOC.

HEIMWEHR. *See* HOMELAND BLOC.

HITLERBEWEGUNG. *See* NATIONAL SOCIALIST GERMAN WORKERS' PARTY.

HITLER MOVEMENT. *See* NATIONAL SOCIALIST GERMAN WORKERS' PARTY.

HOME DEFENSE LEAGUE. *See* HOMELAND BLOC.

HOMELAND BLOC (*Heimatblock*). The Homeland Bloc constituted the only effort by the Home Defense League (*Heimwehr*) to form a legal political organization. In the 1930 general election, the Bloc received 227,000 votes (6.2 percent), and its eight deputies participated in the *Bürgerblock* coalition with the Christian-Social Party* and Pan-German People's Party.* The coalition was the height of cynicism, for in May of that year the *Heimwehr* met at Korneuburg and swore that it rejected Western democracy and the Austrian state. In subsequent local elections, Bloc candidates boasted of an inevitable coup. A feeble effort was mounted in 1931, but the government quickly disarmed the participants.

Actually, the Homeland Bloc was never as significant as the *Heimwehr* itself. The *Heimwehr* was a private army that had arisen out of groups of right-radical German bands roving Austria after World War I. Under the leadership of Ernst Starhemberg and Major Emil Fey, the *Heimwehr* formed a 300,000-member paramilitary force, ostensibly to protect Austria from Slavic encroachment from without and marxist subversion from within. The *Heimwehr*'s corporatist beliefs were derived from Othmar Spann, its authoritarian ideals from Imperial Austria, and its antimarxist stance from Christian-socialism. *Heimwehr* funding, however, came from Germany, Italy, Hungary, and local conservatives. The *Heimwehr* was, for most part, poorly led by vain and ambitious warlords—the Christian-Social Party leaders enjoyed the army's protection; but when Starhemberg's men sought to overthrow the Christian-Social government, Chancellor Engelbert Dollfuss defanged the *Heimwehr* by incorporating its units into the Fatherland Front.* In 1936, Chancellor Kurt von Schuschnigg broke with the erratic, impetuous Starhemberg and integrated what was left of the *Heimwehr* into the regular military. Of course, with the demise of the *Heimwehr* went the political activity of the Homeland Bloc.

Further Reference. Jedlicka, Ludwig, "The Austrian Heimwehr," *Journal of Contemporary History*, vol. 1, no. 1 (1966): 127-144; Whiteside, Andrew, "Austria," in *The European Right: A Historical Profile*, edited by Hans Rogger and Eugen Weber (Berkeley: University of California Press, 1965).

INDEPENDENT DEMOCRATIC UNION (*Unabhängige Demokratische Union*: UDU). The UDU was founded on December 12, 1945, by Richard Lodron and Josef Dobretsberger. The Union drew its support from the ranks of disgruntled

Revolutionary Socialists (Austria)* and from the Communist Party of Austria.*
The UDU campaigned in the 1949 elections, received 12,167 votes, and then
joined the Communist-led Leftist Bloc. The UDU members were integrated into
the Electoral Organization of Austrian People's Opposition (see Communist
Party of Austria) in later elections until the Democratic Union was officially
dissolved in 1971.

KÄRNTNER BAUERNBUND. See PAN-GERMAN PEOPLE'S PARTY.

KÄRNTNER EINHEITSLISTE. See CARINTHIAN UNITY LIST.

KÄRNTNER WAHLGEMEINSCHAFT. See CARINTHIAN UNITY LIST.

KEL. See CARINTHIAN UNITY LIST.

KLUB DER DEUTSCHEN FORTSCHRITTSPARTEI. See CLUB OF GER-
MAN PROGRESSIVES.

KOMMUNISTEN AND LINKSOZIALISTEN. See COMMUNIST PARTY
OF AUSTRIA.

KOMMUNISTISCHE PARTEI ÖSTERREICHS. See COMMUNIST PARTY
OF AUSTRIA.

KOROŠKA ENOTNA LISTA. See CARINTHIAN UNITY LIST.

KOROŠKA VOLILNA SKUPNOST. See CARINTHIAN UNITY LIST.

KPÖ. See COMMUNIST PARTY OF AUSTRIA.

LANDBUND. See AGRARIAN LEAGUE.

LANDBUND FÜR ÖSTERREICH. See PAN-GERMAN PEOPLE'S PARTY.

LAND LEAGUE FOR AUSTRIA. See PAN-GERMAN PEOPLE'S PARTY.

LEAGUE OF GERMAN NATIONALISTS (Verband der Deutschnationalen).
The League of German Nationalists was the flagship of the pan-German Schönerer
Movement in the late 1800s. Georg Ritter von Schönerer, a wealthy Bohemian
member of the Progressive Club (see Club of German Progressives), split with
those more moderate German nationalists and formed the League in 1885. The
League and its successors (such as the Pan-German People's Party*) adopted a
reformist program which sought improvement of living standards and endeav-

ored to establish honest, fair government. However, the populist and anti-Semitic elements of the Schönerer Movement soon began to predominate the League.

Schönerer's strident anticlerical, anti-Habsburg rabble-rousing won him few friends among workers and farmers. The League's major base of support was found in the lower middle classes, large estate owners, German student fraternities, and in ethnically mixed areas. The Schönerer Movement provoked ethnic conflict throughout the empire, with the populace feeling that the League must be held responsible for the tumultuous *Reichstag* meetings and gradual breakdown of democratic institutions in Austrian Cisleithania. The pan-Germans scored their greatest triumph in 1901, but Schönerer's dictatorial and arrogant manner brought him into conflict with more flexible party figures, such as Karl Wolf. The pan-Germans sent only five deputies (out of 516) to the 1907 *Reichstag*, and the party receded into insignificance upon its mentor's retirement. Schönerer's influence on young Adolf Hitler—and on the development of German nationalism—surpassed by far his contribution to Austrian parliamentarism.

LEAGUE OF INDEPENDENTS (*Verband der Unabhängigen*: VdU). The League of Independents was founded on July 22, 1949, by two Salzburg journalists, Herbert Kraus and Dr. Victor Reimann. In the politicized Austrian society of postwar Allied occupation, there were citizens who could not, or would not, choose from among the three Allied-approved parties (the Austrian People's Party, * the Communist Party of Austria, * and the Socialist Party of Austria*). The League of Independents was to serve as a catch basin for the uncommitted and also the newly enfranchised voter.

At the time of the League's creation, large numbers of German prisoners of war were being released from Soviet detention camps; coincidentally, about 500,000 former members of the Nazi Party (National Socialist German Workers' Party*) were permitted to engage in political activity again. Under the tacit sponsorship of Socialist Party leaders, the VdU was granted permission by occupation authorities to campaign in eastern Austria as the Electoral Party of Independents (*Wahlpartei der Unabhängigen*: WdU). The Socialist Party hoped to channel such potential People's Party voters away from that conservative camp. However, the WdU/VdU soon adopted the platforms, if not the strident militancy, of the prewar national *Lager* (camps). The party's libertarian principles attracted much less attention than its defense of pan-Germanism and of the nazi experience.

The WdU/VdU won 16 seats in the 1949 elections, with its strength in former Nazi Party strongholds. The increasing influence of Nazi members within the VdU led to an inevitable split. The independent voters found refuge in one of the major parties, while the libertarians, the pan-German nationalists, and the ardent Nazis grappled for control of the VdU. Thus disunited, the VdU suffered reverses in general and in local elections.

In November 1955, the VdU linked up with the followers of Anton Reinthaller to form the Freedom Party of Austria. * VdU leaders Kraus and Reimann denounced the neonazi course that the new party was taking, and they resigned. On April 7, 1956, the VdU was officially dissolved.

LEFT BLOC. *See* COMMUNIST PARTY OF AUSTRIA.

LEFT SOCIALISTS (*Linksozialisten:* LS). When Erwin Schärf, prominent leader of the Socialist Party of Austria,* was expelled from that party for pro-communist agitation, he founded the LS as an alternative to what he perceived as a drift to the right by the Socialist Party. Drawing its support largely from radical Socialists and members of pro-Soviet circles, the LS joined the Communist Party of Austria* one year later in the 1949 electoral grouping of the Left Bloc (*see* Communist Party of Austria). Thereafter, the LS was absorbed by the Communists' Electoral Organization of Austrian People's Opposition, although the Communists continued to advertise themselves as a coalition of Communists and Left Socialists (*see* Communist Party of Austria) in electoral campaigns.

LIBERALE PARTEI ÖSTERREICHS. *See* LIBERAL PARTY OF AUSTRIA.

LIBERAL PARTY OF AUSTRIA (*Liberale Partei Österreichs:* LPÖ). One of the more ephemeral postwar parties, the LPÖ claimed to be a successor to the liberal parties in the old *Reichsrat*. Founded by Otto Häussler and Karl Kobler, the LPÖ received only 1,571 votes in the 1966 elections and vanished during the early 1970s.

LINKSBLOCK. *See* COMMUNIST PARTY OF AUSTRIA.

LINKSOZIALISTEN. *See* LEFT SOCIALISTS.

LPÖ. *See* LIBERAL PARTY OF AUSTRIA.

LS. *See* LEFT SOCIALISTS.

MARXISTEN-LENINISTEN ÖSTERREICHS. *See* MARXISTS-LENINISTS OF AUSTRIA.

MARXISTS-LENINISTS OF AUSTRIA (*Marxisten-Leninisten Österreichs:* MLÖ). The escalation of the Sino-Soviet ideological conflict after 1960 led to a severe rift in the small Communist Party of Austria (KPÖ).* Eventually, a group of dissenters led by Franz Strobl and Alfred Jocha split away from the KPÖ and formed the pro-Chinese MLÖ on June 12, 1965. The new party contested the 1966 elections in one Vienna district but received only 486 votes. The MLÖ leaders lambasted the revisionism of Soviet and Austrian communists and extolled the virtues of maoist and Albanian orthodoxy. However, growing discord between trotskyite and maoist wings of this small party led to a split in 1972.

The maoists expelled the rival faction, which in turn formed the Group of Revolutionary Marxists.*

Today, the MLÖ has a small following among radical university students and disenchanted marxists. However, the party has not been active in national elections since the 1960s.

MLÖ. See MARXISTS-LENINISTS OF AUSTRIA.

NATIONAL DEMOCRATIC PARTY (Nationaldemokratische Partei: NDP). Austria's National Democratic Party is closely linked with the National Democratic Party of Germany (NPD). (See WEST GERMANY). The Austrian party was founded at the height of German NPD success, in 1966, by Dr. Norbert Burger, an Innsbruck professor and supporter of South Tirolean terrorist activities. While at first the Austrian NDP directed its attention to the Tirolean issue, the party soon adopted additional causes, from securing German culture along the Yugoslav border to demanding the full rehabilitation of Nazi (National Socialist German Workers' Party*) figures.

Unlike the nationalistic Freedom Party of Austria,* the NDP is a militant organization, and its 200-odd activists cherish their storm-trooper image. National Democratic groups engage in frequent skirmishes with left-wing organizations, and the NDP was very active in the Carinthian-Slovene disputes of the 1970s. Like its West German counterpart, the NDP is vociferously antimarxist and, as befits its nazi constituency, defends the achievements of the Third Reich, rejects economic liberalism, and praises German culture and the Teutonic soil. However, for practical reasons, the NDP does not desire Anschluss (union) with Germany at this time.

Although party leader Burger claims a following of over 4,000, the National Democrats have failed miserably in provincial and national elections. The party appeals mostly to former Nazis and to ultranationalists; the NDP youth groups have fared poorly, suffering frequent defections and attracting only a few recruits.

NATIONALDEMOKRATISCHE PARTEI. See NATIONAL DEMOCRATIC PARTY.

NATIONAL PARTY. See AGRARIAN LEAGUE.

NATIONAL SOCIALIST GERMAN WORKERS' PARTY (Nationalsozialistische Deutsche Arbeiterpartei: NSDAP). Although close ties were formed between the radical-right movements in Austria and Germany during the immediate post-World War I era, the German NSDAP (see NATIONAL SOCIALIST GERMAN WORKER'S PARTY, HISTORICAL GERMANY) did not establish a formal Austrian branch until 1926. The local leader, Walter Riehl, had been a companion of Adolf Hitler but was rather independent-minded. Consequently, the Austrian NSDAP (also called the Hitler Movement, or Hitlerbewegung) was directed from Bavaria by Theo Habicht, whose policies grew more radical and dangerous as time went on. The Nazis (a shortened name taken from the vernacular pronunciation of *National* and *Sozialist*) were only marginally successful in achieving respectability during the *Bürgerblock* coalition years (1921-1930). In the 1927 national elections, the Austrian NSDAP netted only 705 votes. However, by 1930 the Nazis received 111,627 votes (though failed to get a mandate). Subsequent local and provincial elections confirmed that the Hitler Movement appeared to grow more quickly than had been anticipated. In the 1932 Vienna municipal elections, the NSDAP won 15 out of 100 seats (the ruling Christian-Social Party* won only four more). The Nazis capitalized on the anti-Semitic, pan-German, and antimarxist sentiments of conservative Austrians; but they fared badly in nationalist circles over Hitler's South Tirol policy, which sought autonomy for the province from Italy, Austria's principal patron of that time.

Habicht's influence soon led to the purge of Riehl, and the Nazis turned to violence and unchecked terror to push Austria to the brink of chaos. Backed by the radical-right Home Defense League (*see* Homeland Bloc), Austria's chancellor, Engelbert Dollfuss, answered the terror and German propaganda barrages by banning the NSDAP. However, forcing the party underground did little to dampen its enthusiasm for conflict. On July 25, 1934, Nazi shock troops attempted an uprising. The operation was bungled badly, but a squad managed to assassinate Chancellor Dollfuss. The perpetrators of the uprising were apprehended, tried, and executed or convicted. Still, the "Illegals" were undeterred. During the 1934-1938 period, the NSDAP created an enormous underground movement. The *Anschluss* (union) with Germany of 1938 was viewed by the Austrian Nazis as the ultimate reward for their struggle, and many of them achieved positions of great responsibility within the *Reich* administration.

NATIONAL SOCIALIST PARTY. *See* PAN-GERMAN PEOPLE'S PARTY.

NATIONALSOZIALISTISCHE DEUTSCHE ARBEITERPARTEI. *See* NATIONAL SOCIALIST GERMAN WORKERS' PARTY.

NATIONALSOZIALISTISCHE PARTEI. *See* PAN-GERMAN PEOPLE'S PARTY.

NAZI PARTY. *See* NATIONAL SOCIALIST GERMAN WORKERS' PARTY.

NDP. *See* NATIONAL DEMOCRATIC PARTY.

NSDAP. *See* NATIONAL SOCIALIST GERMAN WORKERS' PARTY.

ÖSTERREICHISCHES BAUERNPARTEI. *See* PAN-GERMAN PEOPLE'S PARTY.

ÖSTERREICHISCHE VOLKSPARTEI. See AUSTRIAN PEOPLE'S PARTY.

ÖVP. See AUSTRIAN PEOPLE'S PARTY.

PAN-GERMAN PEOPLE'S PARTY (Grossdeutsche Volkspartei: GdVP). While the Pan-German People's Party had genuine links to the radical German heritage of the Schönerer Movement (see League of German Nationalists), the GdVP was less the party of the people than of the bureaucracy, business elements, and the urban middle class.

The GdVP was founded in 1920 as the union of 17 other smaller, mostly insignificant parties, including the Austrian Farmers' Party (Österreichische Bauernpartei), the Carinthian Farmers' League (Kärntner Bauernbund), the National Socialist Party (Nationalsozialistische Partei), the Land League for Austria (Landbund für Österreich), and the Burgenland Farmers' League (Burgenländischer Bauernbund). For much of its existence, the GdVP functioned as an invaluable member of the Bürgerblock (bourgeois) coalition. Franz Dinghofer and several holdovers from the Schönerer era sought to broaden GdVP appeal, but there was little congruence between the leadership and its followers. The party sought Anschluss (union) with Germany, yet cooperated with the Christian-Social Party* which by that time was expressing Austrian nationalistic sentiments. The GdVP sponsored German nationalism, but consistently less effectively than the Home Defense League (see Homeland Bloc), the local Nazis (see National Socialist German Workers' Party), or the other members of the government coalition. The GdVP's most illustrious representative, Vienna's police chief, Johann Schober, had disdained all party memberships but eventually joined the GdVP in 1930. Later, Pan-German and Nazi leaders forged an alliance to bring an end to the Kurt Schuschnigg regime (see Christian-Social Party); in so doing, the GdVP signed its own death warrant.

PATRIOTIC FRONT. See FATHERLAND FRONT.

REPUBLICAN DEFENSE LEAGUE. See SOCIAL-DEMOCRATIC PARTY.

REPUBLIKANISCHER SCHUTZBUND. See SOCIAL-DEMOCRATIC PARTY.

REVOLUTIONÄRE SOZIALISTEN (ÖSTERREICHS). See REVOLUTIONARY SOCIALISTS (AUSTRIA).

REVOLUTIONARY SOCIALISTS (AUSTRIA) (Revolutionäre Sozialisten [Österreichs]: RS[Ö]). When Chancellor Engelbert Dollfuss (of the Christian-Social Party*) banned Austria's marxist parties in 1933, the Social-Democratic Party* went underground. By the next year, activists formed a conspiratorial cell organization, headquartered in Brno, Czechoslovakia. This "Foreign Bureau" was directed by Otto Bauer and other Social-Democratic leaders who were able to escape the post-civil war mass arrests. The RS(Ö) continued to publish Social-Democratic newspapers and proceeded to set up illegal organizations within Austria. Hampered by frequent arrests (the regime maintained excellent files on party members), the RS(Ö) went through several changes in leadership without, however, faltering in its antigovernment agitation. Under Josef Buttinger, the party organized a clandestine network, funneling money and members in and out of the country. With the 1938 *Anschluss* (union) with Germany, all such activity was stopped and the RS(Ö) cells disbanded, for the Germans' Gestapo was known to be much more efficient than the Austrian police. RS(Ö) functionaries fled abroad and helped set up the Austrian resistance and the nucleus of the postwar Socialist Party of Austria.*

Further Reference. Buttinger, Josef, *In the Twilight of Socialism: A History of the Revolutionary Socialists of Austria* (New York: Praeger, 1953).

RS(Ö). *See* REVOLUTIONARY SOCIALISTS (AUSTRIA).

SOCIAL-DEMOCRATIC PARTY (*Sozialdemokratische Partei*). The Hainfeld Congress of 1889 marked the beginning of the social-democratic movement in Austria. Despite persistent judicial repression against all socialist groups, the movement turned into a party and grew very quickly under the able leadership of Victor Adler. Adler, like many of the other Social-Democratic Party leaders, came from a prosperous Jewish background and had earlier been associated with the Club of German Progressives.* Aligned with the Second International (one of whose leaders Adler had become), the Social-Democratic Party nevertheless was organized into national wings representing the major ethnic groups in the empire.

The Social-Democrats competed with Lueger's Christian-Social Party* for support from the "little man." Expansion of suffrage in 1897 gave the Social-Democrats 14 seats in the *Reichstag*. With the introduction of universal male suffrage ten years later, there were 87 Social-Democratic deputies in the legislature. As with social-democratic parties of other countries, the Austrian party was split into at least three wings. The centrist and right wings, headed by Karl Renner and Adler, were not as antagonistic toward the monarchy as was the left wing, whose doctrinaire marxists were fond of calling Adler the "Court Councillor of the Revolution"; indeed, Adler tried to develop a compromise within the imperial context. At the 1899 Brünn Congress, the Social-Democrats endorsed the proposal to transform the empire into a federation. Far from marxist revolution, Austrian socialists developed Austromarxism to serve as a local variant of the international plan.

By 1911 the Social-Democratic Party had grown to a formidable size, and its national factions voted as a bloc in the *Reichstag*. The party defeated the Christian-Socials in Vienna and elsewhere. By 1914 the Social-Democrats constituted the largest party in Austria, though still in opposition; and had it not been for World War I, there is little doubt that the Social-Democratic Party would have assumed the mantle of the government party. However, the Social-Democrats were frustrated in their endeavors by conservative opposition, and the party turned toward defining its own theoretical underpinnings and toward making Vienna, the "Red Fortress," a model of socialist communal planning.

After the war's end, the Social-Democrats and the rival Christian-Socials emerged as the largest political organizations in the new republic. Following a brief, uncomfortable coalition period (1918-1920), the Social-Democrats went into opposition. Although very popular in urban and industrial centers, the party had difficulty establishing a foothold in the conservative, nationalist, and strongly Catholic countryside. After hopes of a union with Red Germany and Soviet Hungary faded with the onset of the "White Terror" (monarchist reaction), the new Social-Democratic leader, Otto Bauer, sought to protect the party from its numerous enemies by forming the Republican Defense League (*Republikanischer Schutzbund*), a paramilitary grouping, in answer to the protofascist Home Defense League (*see* Homeland Bloc), which eventually became associated with the Christian-Social Party. Relations between the *Lager* worsened steadily; and the growing hate between Bauer and the Christian-Social Party's Ignaz Seipel limited an Austrian voter's choice to that between "the Kingdom of Heaven, and the Marxist Paradise of the Classless Society on Earth."

The Social-Democratic Party consistently received over 40 percent of the popular vote and had between 68 and 72 representatives in the *Nationalrat*, but it was isolated through various *Bürgerblock* coalitions (notably those between the Christian-Socials and the Pan-German People's Party*). In 1927 the acquittal of Home Defense League rowdies led to the torching of the Palace of Justice and unrestrained rioting. The result was ever-worsening repression and street violence, and extremists in both the Home Defense League and the Social-Democratic Party held sway. In line with the radical program adopted by the Social-Democrats in Linz in 1926, Bauer stressed the revolutionary aspects of marxism, which provoked the conservatives even more. In 1933, Chancellor Engelbert Dollfuss (of the Christian-Social Party) sought to disarm the Social-Democrats' Republican Defense League, but not the Christian-Socials' Home Defense League, and he met with determined resistance. Incautious actions on both sides led to the brief 1934 civil war in which over 300 lives were lost. This was the pretext Dollfuss needed to declare the Republican Defense League and the entire Social-Democratic Party illegal. Insofar as its members were not arrested, the Social-Democrats went underground, joined its offshoot party, the Revolutionary Socialists (Austria), * or abstained from political activity entirely. Karl Renner retired to the country, resuming political activity in 1945 when directed by the arriving Soviet Red Army to form a provisional government. At that time, Renner helped to found the Socialist Party of Austria.*

Further Reference. Bauer, Otto, *The Austrian Revolution* (London: Leonard Parsons, 1925); Leser, Norbert, "Austro-Marxism: A Reappraisal," *Journal of Contemporary History*, vol. 1, no. 2 (1966).

SOCIALIST PARTY OF AUSTRIA (*Sozialistische Partei Österreichs:* SPÖ). When the first phalanx of Soviet Red Army troops entered Austria in late March 1945, its officers soon encountered the 74-year-old retired patriarch of the Social-Democratic Party,* Karl Renner. Renner was asked to form a provisional government; at the same time, other Social-Democratic leaders returned from exile in Great Britain, Sweden, and the United States, or from hiding, from concentration camps, and from military service. They established the Socialist Party of Austria on April 14, 1945.

Initially, the SPÖ was founded as the "Socialist Party of Austria (Social-Democrats and Revolutionary Socialists)." However, the parenthetical appellation was soon dropped since the party was headed mostly by moderate socialists (like the patrician Imperial Army general Theodor Körner, Dr. Adolf Schärf, and Oskar Helmer, who was to play an important role in wresting control of the police apparatus from the Communist Party of Austria*). Realizing that the times demanded more pragmatic policies and less provocative posturing, the SPÖ cooperated with the erstwhile archenemies in the conservative camp throughout the occupation years. SPÖ leaders refused Communist Party entreaties to form a popular marxist front and instead negotiated the first of many coalition agreements with the conservative Austrian People's Party.*

The November 1945 elections proved the Socialists correct—the Communists were no threat, despite so many conditions in their favor; but the conservatives would continue to be the Socialists' rivals. The SPÖ, now coequal with the Austrian People's Party, gradually broke out of its Austromarxist ideological ghetto, though not without some hesitation—SPÖ leaders feared defections from their left (*see* Left Socialists) and from the Revolutionary Socialists (Austria)* components if the SPÖ disassociated itself from anticlericalism and class-struggle slogans too quickly. After Dr. Renner became the country's first president, and after the Communist Party of Austria lost electoral support because of its subversive tactics and close relations with the occupying Soviet Red Army, the SPÖ and the Austrian People's Party formed the "Grand Coalition" with its attendant features of *Proporz* proportional representation and patronage. The Socialists habitually played a quasi-opposition role, even during the ten years of occupation, because of the Austrian People's Party's greater strength in the lower house which permitted that party to fill influential state posts.

In 1958 the SPÖ sought to broaden its appeal by courting disaffected Austrian People's Party voters. The new SPÖ program toned down the Social-Democrats' language and goals. Socialism and religious practice no longer were viewed as being incompatible. Influenced by the success of the British Labour Party (*see* UNITED KINGDOM) and the German Social Democratic Party (*see* WEST GERMANY), the SPÖ engineered a pragmatic course which was to nibble away at People's Party strength in the provinces.

In the early 1960s, however, it was the SPÖ that was in trouble. The party was plunged into its deepest crisis by the unimaginative leadership of SPÖ party functionary Bruno Pittermann (whose campaign slogan, "Every man for Pittermann,

Pittermann for every man," was turned into "Every man for Pittermann, bitter then for every man"). The Olah Affair (see Democratic Progressive Party), the Habsburg problem (see Freedom Party of Austria), a citizens' initiative supported by the People's and Freedom parties, and internal SPÖ disputes—all contributed to SPÖ decline.

With new leaders in 1966, the People's Party won the absolute majority it sought, and the Socialists found themselves really out of power. The SPÖ's electoral disaster produced an internal shake-out—Pitterman yielded, despite desperate efforts by him and other leaders like Anton Benya, to prevent Dr. Bruno Kreisky from becoming party chairman. The 1967 "Extraordinary Congress" became a pivotal event for the Socialists as the new party chief brought fresh life into the organization. Kreisky, who had earlier represented the provinces' faction, formed a team of 1,400 experts to prepare detailed plans for Austria's future. He made the provincial organs feel less peripheral by changing party statutes and by recruiting heavily from among their memberships. There was also a sense of excitement, youthfulness, and adventure in the party. In 1970 the SPÖ reversed its defeat of 1966. Although the Socialists held only a relative majority (and there was talk that a Socialist-Freedom Party coalition might have to be formed), Kreisky knew that the People's Party was demoralized. He called for a special election in 1971, and on October 10 the Socialists attained an absolute majority: they had hoped to increase their lead in the *Nationalrat* by perhaps six seats (from 81); instead they gained 12 seats. The SPÖ has been Austria's ruling party ever since.

Nevertheless, there has been trouble in the Socialist Party. The independent and pro-People's Party press has investigated and publicized a never-ending stream of SPÖ scandals during the 1970s. At a local level, the 70-year control of Vienna's city government has made the Socialist city administrators arrogant, careless, and corrupt. Public outcry over financial mismanagement, graft, poor planning, and collusion between party and city officials and developers has been a continual embarrassment to the SPÖ, although the party continues to defend Vienna's city hall. Of greater importance are the national scandals: the aristocratic Socialist defense minister, Karl Lütgendorf, was found to be dealing illegally in arms with Syria; the SPÖ abandoned its Carinthian-Slovene constituency over a special census issue; and Kreisky became embroiled in the Simon Wiesenthal nazi-hunt case against Freedom Party leader Friedrich Peter. Kreisky, who grew up in unproletarian, prosperous, Jewish-Moravian surroundings, came to Peter's defense, in spite of evidence linking Peter with SS extermination commandos of World War II. For these and other reasons, the Socialist Party was considered to be very vulnerable in 1975 and 1979, though Kreisky turned the May 6, 1979, election into a personal triumph, as well as a party victory.

Kreisky consistently has been the moving force in the party. He fancies himself an elder statesman and clearly relishes his self-anointed role as Mideast peace negotiator. He is as unruffled by the "Austrian Watergate"—the controversies surrounding the building of Vienna's General Hospital and its attendant kickbacks, bribes, and charges of mismanagement—as by recent announcements that he is on Palestine terrorist hit lists. At the same time, he has been affected personally by the unauthorized challenge of protegé and Vice Chancellor Mannes Androsch during 1980. Androsch, also serving as economics minister, made the error of becoming embroiled in the General Hospital scandal and failed to note that a conflict of interest existed between his ministerial position and a private venture. This permitted Kreisky to shunt Androsch into a comfortable, nonpolitical post; currently, the "Sun King," always a crafty and deliberate strategist, appraises party policies and potential successors in the twilight of his rule.

The SPÖ is a member of the Socialist International. The party organization, revised in 1967, makes a 54-member National Party Committee the central policymaking organ. The party's Control Commission, elected from among the National Party Committee membership, oversees administrative and financial affairs. The SPÖ receives about 64 percent of its funding through membership dues and party-owned enterprises, such as the major-circulation daily *Arbeiter-Zeitung*. Furthermore, Socialists have long been famous for their welfare programs involving services such as day-care centers, tuition reimbursements, health spas, discount stores, travel agencies, sports clubs, retirement homes, and non-Catholic funeral facilities. While the party has maintained a steady enrollment of about 730,000 (up from 360,000 in 1945), the SPÖ can rely on the majority of Austrian trade unionists in the ÖGB Federation of Trade Unions for electoral support. There has been some effort to imitate the People's Party interest-group organizations, but the Socialist farmers' and business leagues are still relatively unimportant.

Presently, the SPÖ's greatest asset may be Bruno Kreisky himself. He has emerged as Austria's premier statesman of modern times. While it may seem quixotic to have a well-to-do, glib, bourgeois Jew lead a socialist movement, Austrian socialism had known others before him—Victor Adler (*see* Social-Democratic Party) and Otto Bauer come to mind. An energetic corps of party lieutenants oversees an army of 70,000 functionaries, many of whom also hold responsible administrative positions. The SPÖ's public relations and electoral campaigns are very effective, particularly since the revision of ideological tenets in 1958. Increasingly, the SPÖ's appeal reaches hereditary People's Party voters, and only 56 percent of SPÖ supporters are blue-collar workers or wage earners. The SPÖ has secured a stronghold in Carinthia and the Burgenland, both traditionally anticlerical (yet rural) provinces. The Socialists now threaten People's Party majorities in Upper Austria and Salzburg, and in the 1979 elections the SPÖ also won heavily in Lower Austria. Although only six percent of Socialists admit regular church attendance, the party and the Catholic Church have come to an understanding which has made party membership acceptable among the faithful. Apart from a bothersome chorus of young Socialist idealists, who see the SPÖ moving from Austromarxism to Austro-opportunism, the Socialist Party now is a coherent, potent force in Austrian politics.

Further Reference. Austrian Socialist Party (SPÖ), *Rote Markierungen: Beitrage zur Ideologie und Praxis der Österreichischen Sozialdemokratie* (Vienna: Sozialistische Partei, 1972); Porta, Hans T., *Die SPÖ 75 Jahre Nach Hainfeld* (Vienna: Wedl, 1965); Secher, Herbert P., "The Socialist Party of Austria: Principles, Organization, and Policies," *Midwest Journal of Political Science* 3 (1959): 277-299; Shell, Kurt L., *The Transformation of Austrian Socialism* (New York: State University of New York Press, 1962).

SOCIALIST PARTY OF AUSTRIA (SOCIAL-DEMOCRATS AND REVOLUTIONARY SOCIALISTS). *See* SOCIALIST PARTY OF AUSTRIA.

SOZIALDEMOKRATISCHE PARTEI. *See* SOCIAL-DEMOCRATIC PARTY.

SOZIALISTISCHE PARTEI ÖSTERREICHS. *See* SOCIALIST PARTY OF AUSTRIA.

SPÖ. *See* SOCIALIST PARTY OF AUSTRIA.

UDU. *See* INDEPENDENT DEMOCRATIC UNION.

UNABHÄNGIGE DEMOKRATISCHE UNION. *See* INDEPENDENT DEMOCRATIC UNION.

UNITED CHRISTIAN PARTY. *See* CHRISTIAN-SOCIAL PARTY.

VATERLÄNDISCHE FRONT. *See* FATHERLAND FRONT.

VdU. *See* LEAGUE OF INDEPENDENTS.

VERBAND DER DEUTSCHNATIONALEN. *See* LEAGUE OF GERMAN NATIONALISTS.

VERBAND DER UNABHÄNGIGEN. *See* LEAGUE OF INDEPENDENTS.

VERFASSUNGSPARTEI. *See* CONSTITUTIONAL PARTY.

WAHLGEMEINSCHAFT ÖSTERREICHISCHE VOLKSOPPOSITION. *See* COMMUNIST PARTY OF AUSTRIA.

WAHLPARTEI DER UNABHÄNGIGEN. *See* LEAGUE OF INDEPENDENTS.

WdU. *See* LEAGUE OF INDEPENDENTS.

Martin J. E. Král

TABLE 2. Distribution of Seats in Austria's *Nationalrat* under the First Republic, 1919-1930

Party	1919	1920	1923	1927	1930
Agrarian League	—	—	5	9	9
Christian-Social Party	69	85	82	73	66
Homeland Bloc	—	—	—	—	8
Pan-German People's Party*	26	28	10	12	10
Social-Democratic Party	72	69	68	71	72
Total	167	182	165	165	165

*In 1919, a summation of mandates for several pan-German parties; Pan-German People's Party officially founded in 1920.

TABLE 3. Ruling Coalitions in Austria since 1918

First Republic, 1918-1934

1918-1920	Christian-Social Party Social-Democratic Party
1920	*Proporz* government without chancellor
1920-1927	Christian-Social Party Pan-German People's Party *Bürgerblock*
1927-1932	Christian-Social Party Pan-German People's Party Agrarian League *Bürgerblock*
1932	Christian-Social Party Agrarian League *Bürgerblock*
1932-1934	Christian-Social Party Agrarian League Homeland Bloc *Bürgerblock*
1934-1938	Fatherland Front dictatorship

Second Republic, 1945-present

1945-1947	Austrian People's Party Socialist Party Communist Party
1947-1966	Austrian People's Party Socialist Party Grand Coalition
1966-1970	Austrian People's Party
1970-	Socialist Party

Note: First-named party is dominant coalition party.

TABLE 4. Distribution of Seats in Austria's *Nationalrat* under the Second Republic, 1945-1979

Party	1945	1949	1953	1956	1959	1962	1966	1970	1971	1975	1979
Austrian People's Party	85	77	74	82	79	81	85	78	80	80	77
Communist Party[*]	4	5	4	3	0	0	0	6	0	0	0
Freedom Party[**]	—	16	14	6	8	8	6	6	10	10	11
Socialist Party	76	67	73	74	78	76	74	81	93	93	95
Total	165	165	165	165	165	165	165	165	183	183	183

[*] Known as the Left Bloc in 1949, as the Electoral Organization of Austrian People's Opposition in 1953, as the Communists and Left Socialists in 1956.

[**] Known as the League of Independents prior to 1956.

BELGIUM

The KINGDOM OF BELGIUM (*Royaume de Belgique*, French; *Koninkrijk België*, Dutch; *Das Königtum Belgien*, German) is located at the crossroads of Europe between Britain, France, Germany, and the Netherlands. This small (11,781 square miles) but densely populated (9.7 million) land has long been one of the world's most highly industrialized countries. Two major ethnic-linguistic groups make up the bulk of the population: the Dutch-speaking Flemish, about 56 percent of the total population, occupy the northern provinces; the French-speaking Walloons, 44 percent of the total, inhabit the south. Both languages are officially spoken in the capital city of Brussels, but French is more widespread there. A very small German-speaking group is found in the eastern cantons on the border with West Germany. Belgium's location and population structure have insured that it is influenced by most of the major European trends, but the country's own political institutions have proved quite durable and adaptable in the years since Belgium became independent.

Belgium was, like most of the Low Countries, under the rule of the dukes of Burgundy for most of the later Middle Ages. The area then, like most of central Europe, came into the realm of the Habsburgs for several centuries, first under the Austrian house (beginning in the late 1400s); then the Spanish (1556-1713), when the Belgium region was known as the "Spanish Netherlands"; and then becoming the "Austrian Netherlands" as part of compensation to the Habsburgs when the Spanish crown passed to the Bourbons. A period of French control followed, beginning in 1795 with Napoleon's early military ventures. Upon Napoleon's defeat, the major European powers realigned national boundaries at the Congress of Vienna (1815), at which time Belgium was given to the Kingdom of the Netherlands to strengthen the northern European buffer against France. The Belgians, however, being greatly discriminated against in political, religious, and economic affairs, revolted against the Dutch and declared independence on October 4, 1830. Though Belgian independence was not officially recognized by the Dutch until 1839, the Belgian revolt marked the first permanent breach in the 1815 Vienna settlement.

The Belgian constitution of 1831, still the nation's basic charter, organized the Belgian political system as a constitutional monarchy and a parliamentary system. The bicameral Belgian legislature consists of the Chamber of Representatives (*Chambre des Représentants; Kamer van Volksvertgenwoordigers*) and the Senate (*Sénat; Senaat*), with 212 and 179 members respectively. Elections to parliament are based upon a direct system of proportional representation (d'Hondt system) with universal, compulsory suffrage for Belgians 21 years of age. (Unjustified absence from the polls warrants a fine of 400 francs.) The current electorate is approximately 6.8 million, and women acquired full suffrage equality in 1948. Although the electoral law fixes the ratio of seats to population at one seat for every 45,750, some minor maldistribution exists. Elections to the Senate are complicated by procedures which stipulate that only a portion may be directly elected (a number equal to one-half of the Chamber membership), 48 are elected by the nine provincial councils, and a number equal to one-half the provincial senators is selected by the Senate body itself. Executive authority resides with the reigning monarch (currently King Baudouin), but in actual practice is exercised by a prime minister and cabinet responsible to the bicameral legislature.

The Belgian constitution makes no mention of political parties, but over the years they emerged to become crucial elements in Belgian political life, linking mass participation to elite leadership. The key to the development of the Belgian party system is found in the relationship between party formation and the three great social cleavages that have divided Belgium in modern times: the religious-philosophical cleavage, the economic-ideological cleavage, and the ethnic-linguistic cleavage.

Both the Liberal Party (1846-1961)* and the Catholic Party* were formed in the 19th century during religious-philosophical conflict over the role of the Catholic Church in society and education. This dispute between supporters of the church and anticlerical seculizers reached its peak in the "school war" of 1879-1884. The "war" ended with a Catholic electoral victory, and the Catholics then took control of Belgian politics, winning absolute majorities in parliament until 1919 (*see* table 5). They continue to be the strongest political family in Belgium today, constituting the Christian People's Party*-Christian Social Party* federation (*see also* CVP-PSC and table 6). The Liberals, a classic cadre party, managed to hold onto a place in the party system thanks only to the introduction of proportional representation in 1900.

Political mobilization around the economic-ideological cleavage began in the 1880s. The extension of universal manhood suffrage (1893)—tempered by a system which allowed the wealthy and well-educated to cast up to three votes—resulted in the growth of a democratic-socialist party linked to a strong trade union movement and a host of allied organizations. Since the abolition of plural voting in 1919, the Belgian Socialist Party* has been the second-largest political formation in Belgium. In 1921 the Communist Party of Belgium* split off from the Socialists (at that time, the Belgian Workers' Party*), but the Communists have always represented only a small minority of the Belgian left, with the exception of a few years immediately following World War II. The interwar period saw the three "traditional" parties—Catholics, Liberals, Socialists—and their respective networks of groups and organizations settle down to fairly stable relations. Much of Belgian public life was politicized along party lines, but partisan conflict was kept from getting out of hand by the tradition of elite accommodation practiced by the leaders of the three parties.

The ethnic-linguistic cleavage, while perhaps beginning in the subjugation of Belgium to the Netherlands during the early 19th century, first began to have an impact on the Belgian party system in the period between the world wars. Long-dormant Flemish protests against Francophone domination in a unitary Belgium generated Flemish nationalist parties, which sought federal autonomy for Flanders or even reunion with the Netherlands. But World War II and then the struggles over the Royal Question and the school issue set back the electoral progress of Flemish nationalism. In the 1960s, however, the Flemish nationalist People's Union* increased its votes dramatically, reaching a peak of nearly 19 percent of the votes in Flanders in 1971. This forced the Flemish wings of the traditional parties to become more independent of their Francophone allies—to the point where the Catholic and Liberal parties, in particular, have virtually split along ethnic-linguistic lines. Flemish success also stimulated the formation of Francophone federalist parties in Brussels and Wallonia aimed at protecting the rights of French-speakers in those regions.

In the early 1970s, lengthy negotiations among leaders of the traditional and federalist parties led to agreements on constitutional and institutional changes to permit greater cultural autonomy for each ethnic group and more decentralized decision making for each region. By December 1970, constitutional amendments were passed by which Belgium was officially divided into three linguistic regions of French-speaking Wallonia, Flemish- or Dutch-speaking Flanders, and bilingual Brussels. In July 1971, cultural councils were established to deal with matters of French and Flemish interest, and a German cultural council was added in June 1973. This reduced the political gap between the traditional and federalist parties to the point where federalist parties from both ethnic-linguistic communities agreed to participate in the government together.

The late 1970s, however, saw great conflict over the specific design of a federalized, devolutionized Belgium. The government resulting from the April 17, 1977, parliamentary elections was again led by the Flemish Christian People's Party (CVP), in coalition with the Francophone Christian Socials (PSC), the Flemish Socialists (BSP), the Francophone Socialists (PSB), the Democratic Front of Francophones,* and the (Flemish) People's Union (see table 7). By March 1978, this government had secured preliminary agreement from parliament on the Egmont Pact.

The Egmont Pact proposed to establish, in effect, four governments for Belgium (the current central government, plus one each for Wallonia, Flanders, and Brussels) and eight legislative assemblies (the central Chamber of Representatives and Senate, three cultural councils [the current French, Flemish, German], and a directly elected regional assembly for each of the linguistic areas of Wallonia, Flanders, and Brussels). Dissent has arisen from some parties that believe so many governmental bodies will create more conflict than small Belgium can accommodate. Furthermore, some factions (particularly the Flemish CVP and BSP) support the devolution of national power into only two regional assemblies, one French-speaking and one Dutch-speaking, with the capital city of Brussels remaining open to both communities and without separate regional status. This issue stems from the fact that 85 percent of the Brussels population is French-speaking; allowing Brussels its own regional assembly would, in effect, give Belgium's Francophones control of Brussels as well as of Wallonia, thereby allocating two-thirds of Belgium's regional powers to the French-speakers, even though the French-speakers represent only 44 percent of the national population.

The Egmont Pact controversy greatly contributed to the resignation of Prime Minister Léo Tindemans on October 11, 1978. In July 1978, parliament had reconsidered the constitutionality of the Egmont Pact. Tindeman's own party (the Flemish CVP) argued that making Brussels a separate regional administration would mean that the Flemish parliament would have to meet in a city in Flanders, not in Brussels as they would wish. As a result of Tindemans's resignation, parliament was dissolved on November 15, and new elections were scheduled for December 17, 1978. The election campaigns focused on the Egmont Pact. By April 1979 the new government was formed, led by Prime Minister Wilfried Martens (CVP), in coalition with the PSC, PSB, BSP, and FDF. However, the CVP's continued opposition to establishment of full regional parity for Brussels led to the FDF's withdrawal from the governing coalition by January 1980.

On April 9, 1980, the governing coalition was again dissolved, after Prime Minister Martens's two failures to obtain the needed two-thirds Senate approval for the establishment of the three regional powers. Acting contrary to his party's wishes, Martens announced the new coalition government on May 18: the CVP, PSC, PSB, BSP, the Flemish-liberal Party of Liberty and Progress,* and the newly formed and French-speaking Reformist and Liberal Party.* With this government, Martens proposed in the same month that Flanders and Wallonia progress toward regional autonomy but that the issue of Brussels' regional status be temporarily postponed. By July-August 1980, both houses of parliament agreed to this proposal, and Flanders and Wallonia were instructed to establish their directly elected regional councils by October 1982.

With the devolution issue temporarily settled, Belgian politics have focused recently on economic questions. On October 4, 1980, the Flemish liberals (PVV) and Francophone liberals (PRL) resigned from the coalition government over Martens's proposals to ease Belgium's balance-of-payments problem (a $4 billion deficit in 1979) by cutting government spending in all departments by 2.2 percent. It appears, however, that the ethnic-linguistic cleavage will continue to shape Belgian politics, since the increasingly complicated solutions proposed seem to generate as much controversy as they resolve.

Bibliography

Centre de Recherche et d'Information Socio-Politique (CRISP). *Courrier Hebdomadaire du C.R.I.S.P.* (Brussels, biweekly).

Frognier, André-Paul. "Parties and Cleavages in the Belgian Parliament." *Legislative Studies Quarterly* 3 (February 1978): 109-132.

Frognier, André-Paul, Vincent McHale, Dennis Paranzino. *Vote, Clivages Socio-Politiques et Développement Regional en Belgique*. Louvain: Vander, 1974.

Hill, Keith. "Belgium: Political Change in a Segmented Society." In *Electoral Behavior: A Comparative Handbook*, edited by Richard Rose. New York: Free Press, 1974, pp. 29-107.

Hugget, Frank E. *Modern Belgium*. London: Pall Mall Press, 1969.

Institut Belge de Science Politique. *Res Publica*. (Brussels, quarterly).

Lorwin, Val R. "Belgium: Religion, Class, and Language in National Politics." In *Political Oppositions in Western Democracies*, edited by Robert A. Dahl. New Haven, Conn.: Yale University Press, 1966, pp. 147-187.

————."Linguistic Pluralism and Political Tensions in Modern Belgium." *Canadian Journal of History* 5 (March 1970): 1-23.

Rowies, Luc. *Les partis politiques en Belgique*. 2d ed. Brussels: Centre de Recherche et d'Information Socio-Politique, 1977.

Political Parties

BELGIAN SOCIALIST PARTY (*Parti Socialiste Belge*: PSB; *Belgische Socialistische Partij*: BSP). The Belgian Workers' Party,* abolished by the Germans during World War II, was reconstituted in 1945 as the Belgian Socialist Party. Indirect membership via trade unions was abolished. By the 1970s, the party claimed nearly 250,000 dues-paying members.

Electorally, the Socialists remain the second-largest Belgian party after the Christian People's Party,* with the Socialist vote having stabilized at the 26 to 28 percent level since 1965. In the postwar period, the Socialists have been members of the government more often than not, and they have held the prime ministership three times: under Paul Henri Spaak throughout the late 1940s, under Achille Van Acker in the mid-1950s, and under Edmond Leburton in 1973-1974.

Socialist voters are predominantly workers and salaried employees. The PSB-BSP electoral bastions are the Walloon industrial areas and Antwerp. The party has been losing many of its former supporters in Brussels. The Socialists retain slightly more anticlerical tendencies than had the Liberal Party (1846-1961),* for example, on the abortion issue. The PSB-BSP platform on economic policy calls for more social control over key sectors of industry and more worker participation in decision making, but not for large-scale nationalization.

The Socialists long retained a greater degree of national unity in the face of the ethnic-linguistic problem than did the other two traditional political families, the Catholics (*see* CVP-PSC) and the Liberals. The Socialists adopted a policy of absolute linguistic parity in national party offices, going so far as to institute a system of two linguistic co-presidents in 1971 and permitting the running of separate party lists in election campaigns. However, the Brussels party branch split into two linguistic factions in the 1970s; and on October 28, 1978, the national party, unable to resolve differences over the allocation of regional responsibilities under the Egmont Pact (*see* Belgium introduction), split into a Francophone wing (the PSB) led by André Cools and a Flemish wing (the BSP) under Karel Van Miert. The PSB has supported the Egmont Pact. The BSP, however, though initially agreeing with the PSB, as of the 1978 elections announced it would prefer that Brussels be regarded not as a region but as a city, open to both Flemish and Francophones. Both the PSB and BSP have served in the most recent governing coalitions of 1980.

Further Reference. Abs, Robert, *Histoire du parti socialiste belge* (Brussels: Institut Emile Vandervelde, 1974); Kramer, S. P., "Belgian Socialism at the Liberation: 1944-1950," *Res Publica*, no. 1 (1978): 115-139.

BELGIAN WORKERS' PARTY (*Parti Ouvrier Belge*: POB; *Belgische Werkliedenpartij*: BWP). The predecessor of the Belgian Socialist Party,* the POB was founded in 1885 and was a member of the Second International. It was called the Workers' Party because the founders believed that the word "Socialist" would alienate many potential supporters. From the beginning, the majority of POB leaders were committed to working for change within the system rather than to violent revolution. They concentrated their early efforts on winning the right to vote for the workers and improving social services. This revisionist position was spelled out in the so-called Quaregnon Charter, published just before the first universal male suffrage election in 1894. Between 1894 and 1919, the Socialists were generally third in the number of seats won in parliament, after the Catholic Party* and Liberal Party (1846-1961).* After abolition of the plural vote system in 1919, the Belgian Workers' Party took over second place and remained there until 1940.

The first POB participation in the national government came during World War I when party president Emile Vandervelde was brought into the cabinet, then meeting in exile in France. At the end of the war, in 1921, a small minority of leftist radicals split from the POB to form the Communist Party of Belgium.* This further strengthened the reformist tendencies within the Workers' Party; and in the interwar years, the POB participated in governmental coalitions nearly half the time, usually in national union cabinets with the Liberals and Catholics. During the depression, the party moved further to the right, adopting the explicitly nonmarxist Plan of Labor of Hendrik de Man, who became party president in 1939 and had the misfortune to preside over the dissolution of the Belgian Workers' Party in 1940 on orders from the occupying Germans.

BELGISCHE SOCIALISTISCHE PARTIJ. *See* BELGIAN SOCIALIST PARTY.

BELGISCHE WERKLIEDENPARTIJ. *See* BELGIAN WORKERS' PARTY.

BSP. *See* BELGIAN SOCIALIST PARTY.

BWP. *See* BELGIAN WORKERS' PARTY.

BRUSSELS RALLY. *See* DEMOCRATIC FRONT OF FRANCOPHONES.

CATHOLIC PARTY (*Parti Catholique; Katholieke Partij*). The Catholic Party is the historical and organizational ancestor of the Christian People's Party* and the Christian Social Party,* Belgium's contemporary Christian-democratic parties. The term "Catholic Party" is sometimes used to refer to supporters of the church in the early decades of Belgian independence; but the party as such was not organized until 1884, when the many Catholic school committees formed during the "school war" were transformed into local sections of the party. Although it held the majority of seats in parliament until 1919, it remained a loosely organized federation of Catholic groups. In 1921 the party, renamed the Catholic Union, was restructured to give official recognition to its four major organizational and sociological components: the Federation of Catholic Circles and Associations, the League of Christian Workers, the Flemish Farmers Association, and the League of the Middle Classes. The rise of Flemish nationalism led to another restructuring in 1936. The party's new name was the Bloc of Catholics, and it was divided into two linguistic wings: the Flemish Catholic People's Party (*Katholieke Vlaamsche Volkspartij*) in Flanders and the Social Catholic Party (*Parti Catholique Social*) in Francophone areas. After World War II, these linguistic divisions were retained in the surviving Christian parties, respectively the Christian People's Party and the Christian Social Party.

Further Reference. Simon, Alois, *Le parti catholique belge* (Brussels: Notre Passé, 1958).

CHRISTELIJKE VLAAMSE VOLKSUNIE. *See* PEOPLE'S UNION.

CHRISTELIJKE VOLKSPARTIJ. *See* CHRISTIAN PEOPLE'S PARTY.

CHRISTIAN PEOPLE'S PARTY (*Christelijke Volkspartij*: CVP). As a successor to the old Catholic Party,* the CVP was founded in 1945 as the Flemish wing of the Christian-democratic CVP-PSC federation.* Since 1968, however, the Christian People's Party has been virtually autonomous. Ostensibly a grouping for those of Christian inspiration but shorn of church ties, the CVP supports state subsidies to Catholic schools and opposes abortion. On socioeconomic issues, the CVP is more progressive than the (Francophone) Christian Social Party (PSC)* but more moderate than the Belgian Socialist Party.* On ethnic-linguistic issues, the CVP takes a strong stance in favor of cultural autonomy for Flanders and on limiting the expansion and powers of the predominantly Francophone Brussels region. On the question of creating new regional institutions (*see* Egmont Pact, Belgium introduction), the CVP's Wilfried Martens (prime minister December 1978-   ) has been instrumental in helping to resolve the conflict by securing parliamentary agreement to postpone the establishment of full regional autonomy for Brussels, though progressing with such plans for Wallonia and Flanders.

The Christian People's Party leads all other parties in Flanders in the number of votes received. CVP support comes mainly from practicing Catholics in the small towns and countryside and from that portion of the Flemish working class organized in the Christian trade union movement. The CVP always had greater weight in the national Christian-democratic federation than the Francophone PSC because two-thirds of the federation's total votes came from Flanders. The CVP has been the leading party in the Belgian state as well. Its recent shares of the vote in parliamentary elections was 26.19 percent in 1977 and 26.13 percent in 1978. Also, four CVP leaders—Gaston Eyskens, Théo Lefèvre, Léo Tindemans, and Wilfried Martens—have held the post of Belgian prime minister during most of the 23 years of the 1958-1981 period.

CHRISTIAN SOCIAL PARTY (Parti Social Chrétien: PSC). As the Francophone wing of the Christian-democratic federation, the CVP-PSC,* the Christian Social Party was founded in 1945 as a successor to the old Catholic Party.* The PSC generally places second or third in votes received in Wallonia. Nationally, the party secured 9.75 percent of the vote in 1977 and 10.13 percent in 1978 (in the latter election, placing fifth in percentage of votes behind the Christian People's Party [CVP],* the Flemish and Francophone wings of the Belgian Socialist Party,* and the Flemish-liberals of the Party of Liberty and Progress*). PSC supporters are mainly rural Catholics and some middle- and upper-class urban Catholics. Consequently, PSC policy positions tend to be more conservative than those of the (Flemish) Christian People's Party.

Since the 1968 crisis over the transfer of the Francophone section of the Catholic University of Louvain out of the Flemish language area, the PSC has operated as an autonomous party, although it cooperates with the CVP on many issues and has been included in the recent CVP-led governmental coalitions. The PSC (under party leader Charles-Ferdinand Nothomb) initially defended the controversial Egmont Pact (see Belgium introduction) as originally written. However, by Summer 1980 (under party leader Paul Vanden Boeynants, who had served as interim prime minister after the October 1978 resignation of the CVP's Léo Tindemans), the PSC had agreed to the government proposal that the decision on regional autonomy for Brussels be temporarily postponed.

COMMUNIST PARTY OF BELGIUM (Parti Communiste de Belgique: PCB; Kommunistische Partij van België: KPB). The PCB was founded in 1921 under the direction of Joseph Jacquemotte, who led a dissident faction of the Belgian Workers' Party.* The Communists elected their first deputies to parliament in 1925, though they remained a splinter group until just after World War II. Because of their role in the resistance, the Communists were invited to participate in the coalition governments of the immediate postwar period. In 1946 the party did well enough at the polls to become temporarily the third-largest party in Belgium. But Cold War tensions soon forced the Communists out of the government. The party's voting support dropped off sharply in the late 1940s and early 1950s and has never recovered—the PCB received only 2.71 percent of the vote in the 1977 elections and 3.25 percent in 1979, mostly from the French-speaking areas of Wallonia and Brussels.

The pro-Moscow PCB program calls for the nationalization of all public services and utilities, reduction of unemployment, and redistribution of income through higher taxes on wealth and a guaranteed minimum income. Like the Belgian Socialist Party,* the Belgian Communists support full intraparty ethnic parity and have established three party-presidential offices: a national president (currently held by Louis van Geyt), a French-speaking president (Jean Terfve), and a Dutch-speaking president (Jef Turf). A three-region federal system (the Egmont Pact, see Belgium introduction) is the party's prescription for Belgium's ethnic-linguistic problem, and in foreign policy the Communists call for a reduction of military spending and the dissolution of military blocs.

CVP. See CHRISTIAN PEOPLE'S PARTY.

CVP-PSC. The national Christian-democratic federation, the CVP-PSC consists of the (Flemish) Christian People's Party (CVP)* and the (Francophone) Christian Social Party (PSC).* The federation had been established in 1945 as successor to the old Catholic Party.* Since 1968, however, each of these component parties has acted autonomously, holding separate party congresses, electing their own party officers, and adopting their own party policy positions. The post of president of the national federation has been vacant since 1972, although the federation still maintains in Brussels a secretariat that provides services to both the PSC and CVP.

DEMOCRATIC FRONT OF FRANCOPHONES (Front Démocratique des Francophones: FDF). Founded in 1964 in response to national linguistic laws that seemed to favor the Flemish in Brussels, the Democratic Front of Francophones (FDF) rapidly grew into the largest party in the Brussels region, measured in terms of votes in national elections. Its sister organization on the local level, the Brussels Rally (Rassemblement Bruxellois), was the leading party in local elections. The FDF was structured explicitly in a pluralist manner to attract support from former Catholics, socialists, and liberals. In 1968 the FDF formed a national federation with the economics-oriented Walloon Rally*; each party preserved its own structure but cooperated with the other on platform and parliamentary matters.

Regarding the controversial issue of regional institutions (see Egmont Pact issue, Belgium introduction), the FDF opposes linguistic parity in public bodies in Brussels, calling instead for proportionality. It favors making Brussels an equal partner in a Belgium federated into three regions, with the limits of the Brussels region to be democratically determined by plebiscite, not fixed by an act of the national parliament in which the Flemish have the majority.

The FDF joined in a government coalition for the first time in April 1977. Then, as a result of the December 1978 elections in which the FDF received 4.25 percent of the national vote, the Democratic Front in April 1979 again entered the government coalition led by the (Flemish) Christian People's Party (CVP).* However, the CVP's continued advocacy of only partial, not full regional autonomy for the predominantly French-speaking capital city of Brussels led to the FDF's withdrawal from the government by January 1980. The FDF's withdrawal (particularly of its three cabinet members) cast into doubt the legitimacy of the government since Article 86 of the Belgian constitution requires cabinet parity between the number of French-speakers and Dutch-speakers; hence Prime Minister Wilfried Martens (CVP) replaced the three FDF ministers with members of the (Francophone) Christian Social Party.*

Under party leader Antoinette Spaak, the FDF has continued to support Brussels parity with the other regional groupings of Wallonia and Flanders. Furthermore, the FDF has criticized those Francophone parties (particularly the Christian Socials and the Francophone wing of the Belgian Socialist Party* and the Reformist and Liberal Party*) of having abandoned Brussels in their July-August 1980 agreement to the CVP proposal to postpone a decision on the Brussels issue.

DEMOCRATIC UNION FOR THE RESPECT OF LABOR. See RESPECT FOR LABOR AND DEMOCRACY/DEMOCRATIC UNION FOR THE RESPECT OF LABOR.

FDF. See DEMOCRATIC FRONT OF FRANCOPHONES.

FLEMISH BLOC (Vlaams Bloc). In preparation for the December 1978 parliamentary elections, the Flemish Bloc was formed as an electoral alliance between the Flemish People's Party (Vlaamse Volkspartij: VVP) and the Flemish National Party (Vlaams Nationale Partij: VNP). The VVP had been established in 1977 when Lode Claes, a senator representing the People's Union,* defected from that party. In the 1978 elections, the new Flemish Bloc won one seat in the Chamber of Representatives, filled by Karel Dillen of the old VNP. The VVP-VNP electoral alliance was sealed in May 1979 when the Flemish Bloc was constituted as a formal political party.

FLEMISH CATHOLIC PEOPLE'S PARTY. See CATHOLIC PARTY.

FLEMISH CHRISTIAN PEOPLE'S UNION. See PEOPLE'S UNION.

FLEMISH NATIONAL LEAGUE (Vlaamsch Nationaal Verbond: VNV). A Flemish nationalist group, the Flemish National League united several smaller parties and had its greatest electoral success during the period between the world wars. By 1939 the VNV was the fourth-largest party in parliament, holding 17 seats out of 202. But the VNV took on the cryptofascist style of its leader, Staf De Clercq, and openly collaborated with the Germans during the World War II occupation. At the liberation the party was dissolved, and many of its members were convicted of treason.

FLEMISH NATIONAL PARTY. *See* FLEMISH BLOC.

FLEMISH PEOPLE'S PARTY. *See* FLEMISH BLOC.

FRONT DÉMOCRATIQUE DES FRANCOPHONES. *See* DEMOCRATIC FRONT OF FRANCOPHONES.

GERMAN-SPEAKERS' PARTY. *See* PARTY OF BELGIAN GERMAN-SPEAKERS.

KATHOLIEKE PARTIJ. *See* CATHOLIC PARTY.

KATHOLIEKE VLAAMSCHE VOLKSPARTIJ. *See* CATHOLIC PARTY.

KOMMUNISTISCHE PARTIJ VAN BELGIË. *See* COMMUNIST PARTY OF BELGIUM.

KPB. *See* COMMUNIST PARTY OF BELGIUM.

LIBERAAL PARTIJ. *See* LIBERAL PARTY (1846-1961).

LIBERAL PARTY (1846-1961) (*Parti Libéral; Liberaal Partij*). Founded in 1846, the first Liberal Party constituted the first formally organized political party in Belgium. A group of bourgeois freethinkers and anticlericals, the Liberal Party was determined to secularize the Belgian state and all its organs, especially the schools. The Liberals reached the peak of their importance from 1878 to 1884 when they carried out the "school war" against the Catholic Church's influence in education. Thereafter, the organization of the Catholic Party,* universal suffrage, and the rise of the socialist Belgian Workers' Party* brought about the Liberals' decline. Hanging on in the 20th century as the indispensable coalition partner in a system where no party had a majority, in 1961 the Liberal Party formed the basis for a new grouping, the Party of Liberty and Progress.*

Further Reference. De Clerck, Jacques, *Histoire du parti libéral* (Brussels: Centre Paul Humans, 1974).

LIBERAL PARTY (1974-1979) (*Parti Libéral:* PL). The second of Belgium's Liberal parties was established in 1974 as a reconstituted, Brussels-based splinter of the Party of Liberty and Progress (PLP)*; the PL readopted the name of the PLP's parent grouping, the Liberal Party (1846-1961).* In the 1974 parliamentary elections, the PL had been associated in an electoral alliance with the Brussels-based Democratic Front of Francophones* and won three seats; but in 1977 the PL elected two representatives running as a separate list and elected one representative in 1978. In 1979 the PL merged with the Party of Walloon Reforms and Liberty* (another PLP splinter) to form a new grouping, the Reformist and Liberal Party.*

PARTEI DER DEUTSCHSPRACHIGEN BELGIER. *See* PARTY OF BELGIAN GERMAN-SPEAKERS.

PARTI CATHOLIQUE. *See* CATHOLIC PARTY.

PARTI CATHOLIQUE SOCIAL. *See* CATHOLIC PARTY.

PARTI COMMUNISTE DE BELGIQUE. *See* COMMUNIST PARTY OF BELGIUM.

PARTI DE LA LIBERTÉ ET DU PROGRÈS. *See* PARTY OF LIBERTY AND PROGRESS.

PARTI DES RÉFORMES ET DE LA LIBERTÉ WALLON. *See* PARTY OF WALLOON REFORMS AND LIBERTY.

PARTIJ VOOR VRIHHEID EN VOORTUITGANG. *See* PARTY OF LIBERTY AND PROGRESS.

PARTI LIBÉRAL. *See* LIBERAL PARTY (1846-1961) and (1974-1979).

PARTI OUVRIER BELGE. *See* BELGIAN WORKERS' PARTY.

PARTI POUR LA RÉFORME ET LA LIBERTÉ. *See* REFORMIST AND LIBERAL PARTY.

PARTI RÉFORMATEUR ET LIBÉRAL. *See* REFORMIST AND LIBERAL PARTY.

PARTI SOCIAL CHRÉTIEN. *See* CHRISTIAN SOCIAL PARTY.

PARTI SOCIALISTE BELGE. *See* BELGIAN SOCIALIST PARTY.

PARTY FOR REFORM AND LIBERTY. *See* REFORMIST AND LIBERAL PARTY.

PARTY OF BELGIAN GERMAN-SPEAKERS (*Partei der Deutschsprachigen Belgier*: PDB). The PDB, also called more simply the German-Speakers' Party, is a small political grouping that was formed in 1972 to advance the special needs of the German-speaking population, particularly in Belgium's eastern cantons. The PDB has thus far failed to secure any representation in the Chamber or Senate.

Belgium's German-speaking minority has had special governmental consideration since June 1973, in the form of a German cultural council. However, the German-speakers have feared the implications of the Egmont Pact (see Belgium introduction) for their own interests. Under the pact's provisions, the administration of the nation's eastern cantons, where most of the German minority reside, would fall under control of the French-speakers of Wallonia, though the Germans would be represented by two seats on the Wallonia regional assembly. Hence in the campaigns for the December 1978 parliamentary elections, the PDB ran with the slogan "We want to remain Belgians but not to become Walloons." The PDB leaders are Reiner Pankert and Michel Louis.

PARTY OF LIBERTY AND PROGRESS (Parti de la Liberté et du Progrès: PLP; Partij voor Vrijheid en Vooruitgang: PVV). Under the leadership of Omer Van Audenhove, the old Liberal Party (1846-1961)* was reorganized and renamed in 1961 to form the Party of Liberty and Progress. This entailed abandoning the earlier party's traditional anticlericalism and reinforcing a conservative stance on socioeconomic policy in order to attract conservative Catholics unhappy with the progressivism of the CVP-PSC* Christian-democratic federation. The operation had a spectacular success in the 1965 elections, in which the PLP-PVV increased the Liberal share of the votes from 12.3 percent to 21.6 percent. Since then, however, Belgium's ethnic-linguistic cleavage has been splintering the party's unity, and its voting support has slipped in every subsequent election.

In the 1970s the party's national organs tended to be overshadowed by the regional wings of the party. The Flemish PVV wing went its own way on ethnic-linguistic matters. The Walloon PLP wing in 1977 merged with several factions of the Walloon Rally* to form the Party of Walloon Reforms and Liberty.* Also, the liberals of Brussels split into several different groups and tendencies, including one that readopted the name of the old Liberal Party (see Liberal Party [1974-1979]) and then merged with the Party of Walloon Reforms and Liberty to form the Reformist and Liberal Party.*

With the Walloon PLP wing having departed, the Flemish PVV wing contested separately the December 1978 parliamentary elections and won 10.33 percent of the national vote. PVV support continues to be primarily from the middle and upper classes. The PVV has rejected the Egmont Pact (see Belgium introduction) as making Belgium ungovernable with so many administrative bodies. However, on May 18, 1980, the PVV entered the government coalition led by Prime Minister Wilfried Martens (of the Christian People's Party*), following the collapse of the previous coalition over the issue of devolution of power to new regional institutions. At that time, the PVV agreed to Martens's proposal to progress on the establishment of regional autonomy for Flanders and Wallonia but to postpone a decision on the status of Brussels. This proposal was accepted by both houses of parliament in July-August 1980. On October 4, 1980, however, the PVV resigned from the coalition government over economic and defense issues.

PARTY OF WALLOON REFORMS AND LIBERTY (*Parti des Réformes et de la Liberté Wallon:* PRLW). The PRLW was initiated in 1977, prior to that year's parliamentary elections, by a large dissident segment of the Walloon Rally* that opposed that party's leftward drift. These dissidents were joined by the Francophone wing of the liberal Party of Liberty and Progress,* under the leadership of André Damseaux. The PRLW is a pluralist and reformist party. Though supporting the concept of a federalized Belgium, the PRLW has opposed the specific details of the Egmont Pact (*see* Belgium introduction) as ungovernable.

The PRLW won 18.8 percent of the votes in Wallonia in the 1977 parliamentary elections, making it the third-largest party in that region. In the 1978 elections, the PRLW retained its 14 seats in the Chamber of Representatives. However, in an attempt to strengthen the Francophone-liberal position in Belgian politics, in 1979 the PRLW merged with the Liberal Party (1974-1979)* of Brussels (also a splinter from the Party of Liberty and Progress) to establish the Reformist and Liberal Party,* a grouping that briefly entered the government coalition in 1980.

PCB. *See* COMMUNIST PARTY OF BELGIUM.

PDB. *See* PARTY OF BELGIAN GERMAN-SPEAKERS.

PEOPLE'S UNION (*Volksunie:* VU). Beginning as a Flemish splinter from the Christian People's Party,* the VU was originally called the Flemish Christian People's Union (*Christelijke Vlaamse Volksunie*). After the 1954 parliamentary elections, however, the party deemphasized its clerical connections and became simply the *Volksunie.* As the principal Flemish nationalist party of the post-World War II period, the VU's platform calls for cultural autonomy in a federalized Belgium: Flemish must be the only language in Flanders, and it must have equality with French in the Belgian national government and in the Brussels area. The adamancy of the party's linguistic position is exemplified by a September 29, 1980, demonstration in Camines in which some 3,000 VU members clashed with police over the local government's refusal to construct a separate Dutch school in this predominantly French-speaking area. With regard to the issue of devolution of national governmental powers, the VU has supported the original Egmont Pact (*see* Belgium introduction), including the stipulation that Brussels be made into a third regional component of the federation.

Although amnesty for wartime Flemish collaborators was a major point in its early platforms, the People's Union has been at pains to avoid the label of a right-wing party. On nonethnic issues, the party has often adopted rather progressive positions, such as calling for the nationalization of the Belgian energy sector, more government control of conglomerates, more worker participation in management of business firms, and so on. The VU's electoral successes kept pressure on the Flemish wings of the traditional parties (such as, the Catholic Party, * the Liberal Party [1846-1961], * and the Belgian Socialist Party*) to move toward greater autonomy for Flanders. Much of the VU's early program has been enacted into law, so much so that in 1977 the VU was able to enter into a government coalition committed to further extension of the decentralization process.

The VU's electoral support increased in the 1960s, peaking in 1971 with nearly 19 percent of the vote in Flanders (11.1 percent nationally). The VU declined to 10.04 percent in the 1977 elections and to 7.02 percent in 1978.

PL. *See* LIBERAL PARTY (1974-1979).

PLP. *See* PARTY OF LIBERTY AND PROGRESS.

POB. *See* BELGIAN WORKERS' PARTY.

PRL. *See* REFORMIST AND LIBERAL PARTY.

PRLW. *See* PARTY OF WALLOON REFORMS AND LIBERTY.

PSB. *See* BELGIAN SOCIALIST PARTY.

PSC. *See* CHRISTIAN SOCIAL PARTY.

PVV. *See* PARTY OF LIBERTY AND PROGRESS.

RAD-UDRT. *See* RESPECT FOR LABOR AND DEMOCRACY/DEMOCRATIC UNION FOR THE RESPECT OF LABOR.

RASSEMBLEMENT BRUXELLOIS. *See* DEMOCRATIC FRONT OF FRANCO-PHONES.

RASSEMBLEMENT WALLON. *See* WALLOON RALLY.

REFORMIST AND LIBERAL PARTY (*Parti Réformateur et Libéral:* PRL). The PRL was established on May 19, 1979, during a special joint-party congress of the reformist-federalist Party of Walloon Reforms and Liberty* and the Brussels-based Liberal Party (1974-1979).* At this congress, Jean Gol, a former leader of the Walloon grouping, announced that the new party would seek cooperation with the Party of Liberty and Progress.* The latter is the parent grouping from which both the Brussels and Walloon liberal parties had emerged in 1974 and 1977 respectively. Also at the May congress, the new formation was initially named the Party for Reform and Liberty (*Parti pour Réforme et la Liberté*: PRL); however, upon its formal constitution as a recognized political party on June 23, 1979, the official name was registered as the Reformist and Liberal Party. Jean Gol was elected as PRL chairman.

The PRL entered the government coalition formed on May 18, 1980, under Prime Minister Wilfried Martens (of the Christian People's Party*), after the collapse of the previous coalition over the issue of devolution and the Egmont Pact (*see* Belgium introduction). With the devolution issue temporarily settled in July-August 1980, however, the PRL resigned from the government on October 4, 1980, over economic and defense issues.

RESPECT FOR LABOR AND DEMOCRACY/DEMOCRATIC UNION FOR THE RESPECT OF LABOR (*Respect voor Arbeid en Democratie/Union Démocratique pour le Respect du Travail*: RAD-UDRT). A small grouping, Respect for Labor and Democracy won one seat in the 1978 Chamber of Representatives. Led by Robert Hendrick, the RAD-UDRT advocates total economic freedom and a drastic reduction of taxation.

RESPECT VOOR ARBEID EN DEMOCRATIE/UNION DÉMOCRATIQUE POUR LE RESPECT DU TRAVAIL. *See* RESPECT FOR LABOR AND DEMOCRACY/DEMOCRATIC UNION FOR THE RESPECT OF LABOR.

REX. Founded by the dynamic, young Léon Degrelle in 1936, Rex was the one significant "flash party" in Belgian history. Rex capitalized on economic depression and political scandals to win 11.5 percent of the votes in the 1936 parliamentary elections, with appeals based on a potpourri of nationalism, anticommunism, anti-Semitism, and Catholicism (*Christus Rex*). In 1937, Degrelle forced a by-election in which he challenged Prime Minister Van Zeeland (of the Catholic Party*) head-to-head. Socialists and liberals united behind Van Zeeland, who won with over 80 percent of the votes. Electorally, Rex never recovered from this humiliation. Politically, the grouping was ruined by the flagrant collaboration of Degrelle with Hitler during World War II. In 1945, Degrelle fled into exile in Spain.

Further Reference. Stengers, J., "Belgium," in *The European Right: A Historical Profile*, edited by H. Rogger and E. Weber (Berkeley: University of California Press, 1965).

RW. *See* WALLOON RALLY.

SOCIAL CATHOLIC PARTY. *See* CATHOLIC PARTY.

UDRT. *See* RESPECT FOR LABOR AND DEMOCRACY/DEMOCRATIC UNION FOR THE RESPECT OF LABOR.

UNION DÉMOCRATIQUE POUR LE RESPECT DU TRAVAIL. *See* RE-SPECT FOR LABOR AND DEMOCRACY/DEMOCRATIC UNION FOR THE RESPECT OF LABOR.

VLAAMSCH NATIONAAL VERBOND. *See* FLEMISH NATIONAL LEAGUE.

VLAAMSE VOLKSPARTIJ. *See* FLEMISH BLOC.

VLAAMS NATIONALE PARTIJ. *See* FLEMISH BLOC.

VNP. *See* FLEMISH BLOC.

VNV. *See* FLEMISH NATIONAL LEAGUE.

VOLKSUNIE. *See* PEOPLE'S UNION.

VU. *See* PEOPLE'S UNION.

VVP. *See* FLEMISH BLOC.

WALLOON RALLY (*Rassemblement Wallon:* RW). Founded in 1967 by uniting several smaller Walloon parties, the Walloon Rally is strongly federalist. But unlike the other federalist parties—the People's Union* and the Democratic Front of Francophones (FDF)*—the RW always has been more interested in the economic aspects of decentralization than in the linguistic or cultural aspects. Its program calls for the creation of regional decision-making institutions to stimulate investment and growth in the economically troubled region of Wallonia. After its success in the 1968 parliamentary elections, the RW formed an alliance with the FDF but retained its organizational autonomy. Its vote peaked in 1971 with 21.2 percent of the votes cast in Wallonia.

In 1974, the RW became the first federalist party to accept participation in the government. It did this without its FDF ally, which created tension between the two parties and within the Walloon Rally itself. The RW leadership sought to reestablish the Rally as a left-wing grouping, but this move was opposed by the party's centrist faction that wanted to remain committed to "ideological pluralism." Hence on November 24, 1976, the Walloon Rally officially split: the centrist grouping, led by François Perin and Jean Gol, left the RW and by early 1977 had joined with the Liberal Party (1974-1979)* to form the Party of Walloon Reforms and Liberty.* The remaining RW members, led by Paul-Henri Gendebien, turned the Walloon Rally more to the left. The RW was excluded from the government in 1977 and suffered a severe electoral defeat that same year, losing about half of its votes and securing only five seats in the Chamber of Representatives. The 1978 elections resulted in a further reduction to four Chamber seats.

James A. Dunn, Jr.

TABLE 5. Distribution of Seats in Belgium's Chamber of Representatives, 1894-1939

Party	1894	1900	1912	1919	1921	1925	1929	1932	1936	1939
Catholic Party[a]	104	86	101	73	80	78	76	79	63	73
Communist Party of Belgium	—	—	—	—	—	2	1	3	9	9
Belgian Workers' Party	21	32	18	70	68	78	70	73	70	64
Flemish National League	—	—	—	—	4	6	11	8	16	17
Liberal Party (1846-1961)	12	33	22	34	33	23	28	24	23	33
Liberal-Socialist Cartel[b]	15	—	43	—	—	—	—	—	—	—
Rex	—	—	—	—	—	—	—	—	21	4
Independents and others[c]	0	1	2	9	1	0	1	0	0	2
Total	152	152	186	186	186	187	187	187	202	202

[a] Known as the Catholic Party, 1884-1921; the Catholic Union, 1921-1936; the Bloc of Catholics, 1936-World War II. (*See also* Christian People's Party and Christian Social Party, table 6.)

[b] A coalition of Liberal Party elements and the Belgian Workers' Party.

[c] Daenist Group in 1900 and 1921; in 1919, includes Ex-Servicemen (2 seats), the Flemish Nationalists (5 seats), National Renovation (1 seat), and the Middle Class Party (1 seat).

TABLE 6. Distribution of Seats in Belgium's Chamber of Representatives, 1946-1981

Party	1946	1949	1950	1954	1958	1961	1965	1968	1971	1974	1977	1978	1981
Belgian Socialist Party (BSP-Flemish wing) [a]	69	66	77	86	84	84	64	59	61	59	62	26	26
Belgian Socialist Party (PSB-Francophone wing)												32	35
Christian People's Party (CVP-Flemish wing) [b]	93	105	108	95	104	96	77	69	67	50	56	57	43
Christian Social Party (PSC-Francophone wing)										22	24	25	18
Communist Party of Belgium	23	12	7	4	2	5	6	5	5	4	2	4	2
Democratic Front of Francophones [c]	—	—	—	—	—	—	5	0	0	0	10	11	6
Flemish Bloc [d]	—	—	—	—	—	—	—	—	—	—	—	1	1
Liberal Party (1974-1979)	—	—	—	—	—	—	—	—	—	3	2	1	—
Party of Liberty and Progress [e]	17	29	20	25	21	20	48	47	34	30	17	22	28
Party of Walloon Reforms and Liberty	—	—	—	—	—	—	—	—	—	—	14	14	—

73

TABLE 6. (Continued)

Party	1946	1949	1950	1954	1958	1961	1965	1968	1971	1974	1977	1978	1981
People's Union[f]	0	0	0	1	1	5	12	20	21	22	20	14	20
Reformist and Liberal Party[g]	—	—	—	—	—	—	—	—	—	—	—	—	24
Respect for Labor and Democracy	—	—	—	—	—	—	—	—	—	—	—	1	3
Walloon Rally	—	—	—	—	—	—	—	12	24	22	5	4	2
Independents and others	0	0	0	1	0	2	0	0	0	0	0	0	4
Total	202	212	212	212	212	212	212	212	212	212	212	212	212

[a] Before 1945, known as Belgian Workers' Party (*see* table 5); during 1945-1978, comprised a federation, which then split into the two linguistic wings as noted above.

[b] Originally known as the Catholic Party (*see* table 5); during 1945-1968, comprised the CVP-PSC federation, which then split into the two linguistic wings as noted above.

[c] Figure for 1965 represents seats obtained by minor Walloon parties which later formed the Democratic Front of Francophones; in 1981, ran a joint electoral list with the Walloon Rally.

[d] Formed in 1978 as an electoral alliance between the Flemish People's Party and the Flemish National Party (previously unrepresented in parliament); became formal political party in 1979.

[e] Prior to 1961, known as the Liberal Party (1846-1961); starting in 1977, figures represent only seats obtained by the Flemish wing (PVV) of the party after the Francophone wing (PLP) split off to merge with dissident factions of the Walloon Rally to form the Party of Walloon Reforms and Liberty.

[f] Prior to 1954, known as the Flemish Christian People's Union.

[g] Formed by the 1979 merger of the Liberal Party (1974-1979) and the Party of Walloon Reforms and Liberty.

TABLE 7. Ruling Coalitions in Belgium since 1944

Years	Coalition
1944-1945	Christian People's Party/Christian Social Party Belgian Workers' Party Liberal Party (1846-1961) Communist Party of Belgium
1945	Belgian Socialist Party Christian People's Party/Christian Social Party Liberal Party (1846-1961) Communist Party of Belgium
1945-1947	Belgian Socialist Party Liberal Party (1846-1961) Communist Party of Belgium
1947-1949	Belgian Socialist Party Christian People's Party/Christian Social Party
1949-1950	Christian People's Party/Christian Social Party Liberal Party (1846-1961)
1950-1954	Christian People's Party/Christian Social Party
1954-1958	Belgian Socialist Party Liberal Party (1846-1961)
June 1958-Nov. 1958	Christian People's Party/Christian Social Party
1958-1961	Christian People's Party/Christian Social Party Liberal Party (1846-1961)
1961-1966	Christian People's Party/Christian Social Party Belgian Socialist Party
1966-1968	Christian Social Party/Christian People's Party Party of Liberty and Progress
1968-1973	Christian People's Party/Christian Social Party Belgian Socialist Party
1973-1974	Belgian Socialist Party Christian People's Party/Christian Social Party Party of Liberty and Progress

TABLE 7. Continued.

Years	Coalition
1974-1977	Christian People's Party/Christian Social Party Party of Liberty and Progress Walloon Rally
Apr. 1977-Oct. 1978	Christian People's Party/Christian Social Party Belgian Socialist Party Democratic Front of Francophones People's Union
Oct. 1978-Dec. 1978	Christian Social Party/Christian People's Party Belgian Socialist Party Democratic Front of Francophones People's Union
Dec. 1978-Apr. 1979	Christian People's Party/Christian Social Party Belgian Socialist Party
Apr. 1979-Jan. 1980	Christian People's Party/Christian Social Party Belgian Socialist Party Democratic Front of Francophones
Jan. 1980-	Christian People's Party/Christian Social Party Belgian Socialist Party

Note: First-named party is dominant coalition party.

BULGARIA

The PEOPLE'S REPUBLIC OF BULGARIA (*Narodna Republika Bulgariya*) was formally established on December 4, 1947. Bulgarian constitutional development dates from 1879; and following major amendments in 1893 and 1911, Bulgaria remained a constitutional kingdom until the World War II era. On September 8, 1946, a republic was proclaimed, following a Soviet-dictated popular referendum which rejected the monarchy.

Bulgaria is somewhat smaller than New York State and consists of a fertile plateau in the north, plains on the Black Sea coast, and a mountain range stretching across the southwest regions. Bulgaria shares borders with states belonging to three different political groupings: to the north is Romania, a Warsaw Treaty Organization member; to the west is Yugoslavia, a nonaligned state; and to the south are Greece and Turkey, both NATO members. For almost 200 miles, the Danube River defines Bulgaria's borders with Romania and provides an inland navigation route for both nations.

Bulgaria has a population of nearly nine million, approximately 60 percent of which lives in urban centers. The capital city, Sofia, is the largest urban center with a population just under one million and a growing industrial capacity which provides employment for the majority of its inhabitants.

Bulgaria derives its name from the Bulgars, an Asiatic group that migrated to the area during the 7th century A.D. By the 9th century the more numerous Slavs in the area absorbed the new settlers, who had by then adopted the Orthodox Christian religion and gradually perceived themselves as an extension of the Slavic nation rather than as an ethnically distinct group. In the early medieval period, a powerful Bulgarian Kingdom dominated the Balkan peninsula and became a major source of trouble for the Byzantine Empire. Today, the Bulgarian people speak a Slavic language with heavy Russian influence, reflective of the long Greek and Turkish domination over the area.

Bulgarian national revival followed the same general pattern as that of neighboring Balkan states, to a great extent precipitated by the self-determination movement unleashed by the French Revolution. However, almost 500 years of Ottoman rule had set the tone of the country's subsequent internal development and its rather stormy record in international affairs.

Fostered by its Orthodox clergy and free-roaming monks, Bulgarian nationalism increasingly took the form of savage popular uprisings, usually put down by even more savage Ottoman interventions. An autonomous Bulgarian state emerged after the Russo-Turkish War of 1877-1878, which itself was caused by the Bulgarian uprising of 1876. Yet the external constraints placed upon the newly founded Balkan entity had reduced it de facto to a Russian foster child. The birth of an "independent Bulgaria" by the 1878 Treaty of San Stefano was a painful experience for Bulgarian nationalists, for later that year Bulgaria was drastically reduced at the Berlin Congress by the insistence of western European powers who feared Russian dominance over the post-Ottoman Balkan vacuum. Restoration of Bulgarian gains achieved at San Stefano became a national goal for almost all Bulgarian statesmen and political movements following the Berlin Congress. Their desire to achieve that goal has colored the history of Bulgaria's development for the past 70 years and partially explains the pro-Russian sentiment among its people today. Because of the persistent drives to gain control, of at least Macedonia and Thrace, Bulgaria has acquired the much-deserved reputation of being a volatile and unstable Balkan state.

Part of Bulgaria's international reputation is derived from her unfortunate choice of allies in most conflicts of the 20th century. She seemed always destined to side with the losers. Thus in the final round of the Balkan wars, Bulgaria had to forfeit substantial territorial gains to Romania and Turkey; her defeat as an ally of the Central Powers at the end of World War I probably cost her a much-sought outlet to the Aegean Sea, as well as other territories disputed among Bulgaria, Yugoslavia, and Greece.

The Treaty of Neuilly (1919) seemed to have sealed the future size and borders of modern Bulgaria. In an effort to negate the treaty's provisions, Bulgaria allied with the Axis Powers in World War II, only to suffer a rebuff by the Allies in a last-minute peace overture in 1944. However, the peace treaty of 1947 proved to be favorable to Bulgaria. At the insistence of the Soviet Union, who dominated the area, Bulgaria regained Dobrudja from Romania and otherwise retained her prewar borders. Despite demands from Yugoslavia, Greece, and Turkey for border adjustments, Bulgaria assumed an aggressive posture with Soviet backing and initiated a massive expulsion of the Turkish population, thus coming close to making Bulgaria a monoethnic community. (The almost 800,000 Turks remaining in the country have been declared Muslim Bulgarians, thus negating any claim to separate ethnicity.) At the same time, Bulgaria rejected Yugoslavia's demands for the recognition of a Macedonian minority within the Bulgarian borders and in turn laid occasional claims to the Macedonia Republic of Yugoslavia on the historically false grounds that that republic's population is an extension of the Bulgarian nation.

Political parties first emerged in Bulgaria in 1879 with the formation of a National Assembly (*Narodna Sobranie*) under the terms of the Tirnovo Constitution (1879). With Russian approval and sponsorship, the Tirnovo Constitution endowed the new state with a constitutional monarchy far more liberal than that of its Russian counterpart. A strong parliament (*Sobranie*) was elected by universal manhood suffrage starting at 21 years of age, with one deputy for every 10,000 inhabitants. Guarantees of civil and political liberties and provisions for social welfare were among the constitution's distinguishing features. Technically a tributary principality until 1909, Bulgaria stood out among its east European neighbors as the proud possessor of the most liberal constitution. In terms of domestic politics, Bulgaria's constitution was a major achievement of the National Liberal Party,* which under the strong and enlightened leadership of Stefan Stambolov remained in power until 1894.

During its 65-year existence, the Tirnovo charter fought losing battles for survival owing to structural deficiencies of the document itself, the strains resulting from Bulgaria's many wars, the personal ambitions of monarchs and politicians, and the country's occasional adventures into trading democratic rule for expansionist ventures. Yet under the general auspices of this early manifestation of liberalism, the Tirnovo document provided the framework within which the political life of Bulgaria unfolded. Since 1879 approximately 15 political structures fulfilling most, if not all, of the characteristics of the political party concept were active in the domestic scene. The Tirnovo Constitution's utility and popularity is attested by the fact that it remained the guiding national charter until its abrogation by the new communist order in 1946 and its replacement by the Dimitrov Constitution.

The emergence of constitutionalism in Bulgaria, and the nation's adoption of liberal Western practices much earlier than most of her northern neighbors, should not obscure the fact that Bulgaria had a foreign-supported monarchy much like those in Greece and Yugoslavia. The Bulgarian royal house was not always above politics; on numerous occasions, it manipulated party alliances for the purpose of augmenting its own share of power.

The first ruler of modern Bulgaria was Prince Alexander of Battenberg, Prince of Hess and nephew of Alexander II of Russia. An impetuous young man, Prince Alexander brought with him some of the authoritarian habits of his cultural upbringing. He quarrelled with Stambolov's National Liberals; temporarily suspended the constitution; and to curry favor with the supernationalists, he championed Bulgaria's cause against his benefactor, the Russians, by fostering a liberal-conservative front which he de facto led. Finally, he accommodated himself to let the Liberals govern. In 1886 he was forced to abdicate by a combination of external (primarily Russian) intrigues and domestic dissatisfaction.

The throne remained vacant until another German prince, Ferdinand-Saxe Coburg-Gotha, was selected to rule Bulgaria against Russian preferences. Stambolov, who was sensitive to Russia's intrigues and future ambitions, maneuvered a constitutional amendment to permit the new king to marry a Roman Catholic without the requirement that he bring up his children in the Orthodox faith. It was a symbolic gesture by which the new king and Stambolov put distance between themselves and Moscow. In 1908, in another show of independence, Ferdinand took advantage of Austria's annexation of Bosnia-Herzegovina to proclaim himself "Tsar of the Third Bulgarian Kingdom." This was Ferdinand's stepping-stone to his bringing Bulgaria into World War I on the side of the Axis Powers. He abdicated in 1918 in favor of his son, Boris III.

Boris was equally a "political king" and involved himself in numerous partisan conspiracies. A military-political coup staged in 1923 set the course for political irregularities that resulted in royal involvement in the formation of political alliances and weak coalition governments. Similarly, a coup on May 19, 1934, contributed significantly to the eclipse of constitutionalism and paved the way for an era of profascism in Bulgarian politics. Boris died suddenly in 1943, and his elder son, Simeon III, came to the throne at the age of six. A regency managed the affairs of state in Simeon's name until the communist-dominated Fatherland Front,* with assistance of the remnants of the 1923 and 1934 military conspiracies, staged a coup as soon as the Soviet troops crossed the Danube in September 1944. With the proclamation of the communist republic in 1946, King Simeon went into exile and the monarchical era of Bulgarian politics came to an end.

Bulgaria's political parties prior to World War I had reflected the agrarian nature of its society and a tendency toward fragmentation, even though class was never the sole criterion for party allegiances. Complicating the process of party formation were ideological questions, such as pan-Slavism versus Westernism and the ever-present irredentist ambitions over Macedonia. Economic issues, as usual, were crucial in determining party affiliation and political coalitions, but factionalism weakened the parties that had emerged after the adoption of the Tirnovo Constitution in 1879. Unresolved regime questions, a drift toward authoritarianism by the king, and parochialism characterized the party life of Bulgaria. The country's societal structure was, in many respects, responsible for the relative ease with which allegiances shifted from one party to another. Being a predominantly agrarian country, prewar Bulgaria was essentially egalitarian: the peasants owned their own plots of land, and the merchants were not an exploitative class. In such a setting, militant politics had at best a narrow base, particularly among the small foreign-trained intelligentsia. But in the final analysis it was militancy, not majority, that decided the course of Bulgarian politics.

In 1879 two major political groupings predominated: conservatives and the National Liberals. From 1879 to 1918, however, the National Liberals were the strongest political group in Bulgaria. They governed the country for 20 years and produced seven prime ministers. Nevertheless, the upper hand in politics belonged to King Ferdinand, who skillfully exploited the factional splits within the parties. From 1894 until the outbreak of World War I, Bulgaria experienced some 12 changes of government, with some nine political parties competing for power.

Following Stambolov's resignation over a minor issue in 1894, the National Liberals under conservative Konstantin Stoilov held power until 1900. Thereafter, the government was in the hands of one or another of the proliferating liberal factions. The Liberal Vasil Radoslavov steered Bulgaria into supporting King Ferdinand's entry into World War I on the side of the Central Powers, and Radoslavov remained in office until his resignation in June 1918.

In the period between the two world wars, Bulgaria, in common with several other European countries, underwent phases of revolutionary disturbance, democratic experimentation, and finally reaction, as shown by the distribution of seats in the *Sobranie* (*see* table 9). From 1919 until 1923, center stage belonged to the powerful Bulgarian National Agrarian Union* (*see* table 8) and its leader, the controversial Alexander Stamboliiski. Virtually the only prominent politician to reject nationalist aims in favor of improving the lot of the peasantry, Stamboliiski antagonized the restive Macedonians, the military, the civil service, and—owing to his evident republican leanings—the royal family. The coup in June 1923 toppled his party from power and cost his life. The so-called Democratic Alliance,* headed by Alexander Tsankov, instituted harsh repressive measures against the Agrarians. An ineffectual coup in September 1923, led by the Bulgarian Communist Party,* was easily suppressed, and ensuing Communist terror tactics led to the temporary suppression of that party in 1925.

In 1926 another Democratic Alliance coalition, headed by Andrei Liapchev (a member of the Democratic Party*) and Atanas Burov (a man of conservative outlook and who led the Populist Party*), took office and survived until 1931. Real power, however, remained with Ivan Volkov, minister of war, who had been political boss of the Military League,* the main instrument of the 1923 coup.

Bulgarian politics during the 1920s were sharply polarized. The opposition parties represented social classes or groups—peasants, industrial workers, and middle-class intellectuals—any two of which found it impossible to cooperate solidly for mutual electoral advantage. Cutting across all political boundaries were the increasingly disruptive Macedonians, whose political arm, the Internal Macedonian Revolutionary Organization,* was notorious for its terroristic traits. Overshadowing parliamentary politics was the growing authoritarian trend embodied in the activities of the king, the Military League and its successor (*Zveno**), and a number of conservative or protofascist politicians.

Bulgaria's last free elections took place in 1931. At that time, a coalition named the People's Bloc* (consisting of members of the reemerging Agrarian Party [*see* Bulgarian National Agrarian Union], the Democratic Party, the Radical Party,* and some National Liberal factions) formed a government under the Democrats Alexander Malinov and Nikola Mishanov until 1934. In May of that year, a coup led by Colonel Damian Velchev, one of the leaders of the Military League, ended normal parliamentary politics in Bulgaria. Moderating the effect of the actions was the monarchical opposition to Velchev and dissentions within the Military League. The government that resulted from the coup was headed by retired Colonel Kimon Georgiev and included other members of *Zveno* (the political arm of the League). By October 1935, King Boris was able to assert his own control and ruled as dictator in all but name until his death in 1943.

Although Bulgaria during World War II was technically at war with both Britain and the United States, King Boris had limited her participation in the war to the occupation of Macedonian and Thracian territory, which he intended to annex after the war. Shrewdly, he never declared war against Russia. Even so, the approach of the Soviet Red Army in the summer of 1944 sent shock waves throughout the Balkans.

Pro-Russian sympathies in Bulgaria led to the union of Communist Party-led detachments and other opposition elements in the Fatherland Front,* an overall resistance organization. On September 4, 1944, the regency appointed Konstantin Muraviev, of the Agrarians of Gichev,* to form a pro-Western government. The next day, however, the USSR declared war on Bulgaria and entered the country unopposed. Meanwhile, Muraviev had asked in vain for an armistice and had declared war on Germany. On September 8, Colonels Velchev and Georgiev seized power in Sofia in the name of the Fatherland Front. A government headed by Georgiev included four Communists, as well as the *Pladne**agrarian G. M. Dimitrov (not to be confused with Georgi Dimitrov of the Communist Party). Following the triumphant entry of the Red Army into Sofia on September 16, the Bulgarian forces, whom the Russians kept intact, fought alongside the Russians and Yugoslavians until the end of hostilities in 1945. In the process, the relationship between Bulgaria and Yugoslavia was complicated in that during the previous three years, Yugoslav partisans had been fighting *against* the very same Bulgarian army.

Events thereafter followed the general east European pattern of communist takeover. From the establishment of the first Fatherland Front government in 1944 to the Fifth Congress of the Bulgarian Communist Party in December 1948, the Communists consolidated their ruling monopoly by means of terror and intimidation. The first phase of this process (1944-1945) was marked by the four strongest parties of the 1931 elections (all anticommunists) being prohibited from engaging in organized political activity. Next (in 1945-1946) came the elimination of all opponents within the governmental apparatus. Disillusioned former allies of the Fatherland Front, including many Agrarians and members of the Bulgarian Social Democratic Party,* were forced outside the Front and into a temporarily tolerated opposition. Simultaneously, Communist influence within the Fatherland Front continued to grow. A controlled plebiscite on September 8, 1946, abolished the monarchy and led to the proclamation of a People's Republic. The general elections of October 27, 1946, for a Grand National Assembly (a constituent assembly) found the opposition Agrarians and Social Democrats winning some 30 percent of the popular vote and 99 deputies, with the Communist Party winning 277 deputies. This ushered in the third phase of Communist takeover (1947-1948) in which the opposition was liquidated. In 1947 opposition leader Nikola Petkov (Agrarian) was tried on trumped-up charges and hanged. By July 1948, the Agrarian Union and the Social Democratic Party had been formally disbanded.

Thus in December 1948, Communist Party Leader Georgi Dimitrov could declare at the Fifth Party Congress that the dictatorship of the proletariat had come into being and that Bulgaria was on its way to socialism. By this time, the only political entity other than the Communists was an emasculated Agrarian

Union, the shell of which was preserved to facilitate the political control and mobilization of the peasantry. Henceforth, the political history of Bulgaria is coterminous with that of the Bulgarian Communist Party.

Bulgaria's political system today, as defined and directed by the Bulgarian Communist Party (BKP), makes Bulgaria a one-party state. In the February 1950 words of Vulko Chervenko, the country's notorious stalinist dictator, "the party shares power with no one. . . . No institution, organization, or person can be above the Politburo and the Central Committee of the Party." The dominance of the BKP in all facets of life is reflected in the country's socialist practices and legal system. Bulgarian law confirms the party's role as follows: "The Bulgarian Communist Party cannot be classed as an association because it is the guiding force in the structure of the people's democratic state, and cannot be controlled by the state which is one of its transmission belts." Hence the Bulgarian Communist Party has become since 1945 a structure placed above both the law and the state. Despite recent efforts to adopt principles of socialist legality and to eliminate the harmful effect of the cult of personality, the BKP leadership has retained its earlier stalinist outlook.

The governing structures of contemporary Bulgaria are similar to other socialist systems in eastern Europe. A unicameral National Assembly, composed of 400 members, is elected every five years by universal adult suffrage, beginning at 18 years of age. Candidates drawn from the BKP, the Bulgarian National Agrarian Union, and other approved organizations are placed on the ballot under the guidance of the Fatherland Front. Candidates are elected by simple majority in single-member districts. The National Assembly, in turn, elects a Council of State and a Council of Ministers, which function as legislative and executive bodies. Currently, the distribution of groups and seats in the National Assembly is: Bulgarian Communist Party, 272; Bulgarian National Agrarian Union, 100; and nonparty organizations, 28.

Bibliography*

Black, Cyril E. *The Establishment of Constitutional Government in Bulgaria.* Princeton, N.J.: Princeton University Press, 1966.

Brown, E. F. *The New Eastern Europe: The Khrushchev Era and After.* New York: Praeger, 1966.

Dellin, L. A. *Bulgaria.* New York: Praeger, 1957.

Ionescu, Ghita. *The Politics of European Communist States.* New York: Praeger, 1967.

Lang, David Marshall. *The Bulgarians: From Pagan Times to the Ottoman Conquest.* Boulder, Colo.: Westview Press, 1976.

Nenoff, Dragomir. *The Bulgarian Communist Party.* New York: National Committee for a Free Europe, 1951.

*I wish to thank Professor F. Jackson Piotrow for his preliminary bibliographical research, which he generously made available to this writer.

Oren, Nissan. *Bulgarian Communism: The Road to Power, 1934-1944*. New York: Columbia University Press, 1971.

―――. *Revolution Administered: Agrarianism and Communism in Bulgaria*. Baltimore: Johns Hopkins University Press, 1973.

Pundeff, Mari, and Ivan Zlatin. "Bulgaria." In *Government, Laws and Courts in the Soviet Union and Eastern Europe*, edited by Vladimir Gsovski and Kazimier Grzybovski. London: Atlantic Books, 1959.

Rothchild, Joseph. *The Communist Party of Bulgaria: Origins and Development 1883-1926*. New York: Columbia University Press, 1959.

Political Parties

AGRARIAN PARTY. *See* BULGARIAN NATIONAL AGRARIAN UNION.

AGRARIANS OF GICHEV (*Vracha*). The Agrarians of Gichev was the moderate wing within the Bulgarian National Agrarian Union (BNZS).* The grouping received its name after one of its most prominent leaders, Dimitur Gichev; the party's nickname came from the address of its headquarters, Vracha 1 (or "Sparrow 1").

Initially, the *Vracha* was a wing within the BNZS. Under the leadership of Gichev, Konstantin Muraviev, and Vergil Dimov, the *Vracha* remained a relatively cohesive group during the years of the BNZS's illegality that followed the 1923 coup and assassination of Alexander Stamboliiski, leader of the then-powerful BNZS. The *Vracha*, in fact, dominated the Iron Bloc* coalition that had successfully contested the 1927 elections. When the BNZS reemerged legally in 1931 as the Agrarian Party, the *Vracha* wing provided the core influence for the People's Bloc* coalition.

However, during the 1930s the Gichev wing came under severe attacks from the left wing of the Agrarian movement for its "compromising policies." The leftist Agrarians, who organized their own grouping under the name *Pladne*,* drifted in the direction of the Bulgarian Communist Party,* leading to the formal split of the Gichev and *Pladne* groups into separate parties in 1941.

The Gichev Agrarians initially maintained their separate existence with some success. On September 4, 1944, in the chaos of World War II, the royal regency selected *Vracha* leader Konstantine Muraviev to form a pro-West government. Muraviev immediately asked, in vain, for an armistice with the Allies, and he also declared war on Germany. Nevertheless, the next day, on September 5, Russian troops entered Bulgaria unopposed. And finally, on September 8, the Communist-dominated Fatherland Front,* with the muscle of the Military League,* staged a coup that toppled the short-lived Muraviev government.

Following the 1944 coup, both the Gichev and *Pladne* groups were being systematically purged by the power-assuming Communist Party. The *Pladne* group, in particular, had earlier cooperated with the Communists and was infiltrated in the Communists' attempt to eliminate *Pladne* leadership. Therefore, in a final effort to stay afloat, the *Vracha* and *Pladne* parties reunited in 1945 under the old BNZS name and contested the 1946 elections with some success. After the elections, a reorganized BNZS was formed by the Communists and remains in existence today, albeit under control of the Bulgarian Communist Party.

ALEXANDER STAMBOLIISKI PEASANT UNION. *See* PLADNE.

BKP. *See* BULGARIAN COMMUNIST PARTY.

BNZS. *See* BULGARIAN NATIONAL AGRARIAN UNION.

BROAD SOCIAL DEMOCRATIC PARTY. *See* BULGARIAN SOCIAL DEMOCRATIC PARTY.

BRP. *See* BULGARIAN WORKERS PARTY.

BSDP. *See* BULGARIAN SOCIAL DEMOCRATIC PARTY.

BULGARIAN AGRARIAN UNION. *See* BULGARIAN NATIONAL AGRARIAN UNION.

BULGARIAN COMMUNIST PARTY (*Bulgarska Komunisticheska Partiia*:BKP). Bulgarian communism traces its origins to the founding of the Bulgarian Social Democratic Party* in 1891. The most significant leader of Bulgarian marxism, Dimitur Blagoev, formed the first-known marxist circle in Russia in 1883-1884 while studying at Saint Petersburg. Several other leading Bulgarian socialists, later to become communists, drew spiritual sustenance from their semiconspiratorial experiences in tsarist Russia.

In 1903 the Bulgarian Social Democrats split into "Narrow" and "Broad" factions, with the future communists rallying behind the Narrow ideology of promoting industrialization and developing a revolutionary proletariat. The Narrow Social Democratic Party (*see* Bulgarian Social Democratic Party) appealed largely to intellectuals, disgruntled civil servants, students, and militant trade unionists. The industrial proletariat as such was minuscule. With Dimitur Blagoev's 1919 election to the executive committee of the new Communist International, the Narrow Social Democratic Party changed its name to the Bulgarian Communist Party (BKP). The BKP gained 25 percent of the popular vote in the 1919 election, thus taking second place only to the Bulgarian National Agrarian Union* in the nation's politics and emerging in the first rank of east European communist parties.

The BKP failed to support the Agrarians against the Military League* in the June 1923 coup that toppled the Agrarians from government power. As a result, the Bulgarian Communists were goaded by Moscow into staging a completely ineffectual coup of their own in September of that same year. The rightist victors (see Democratic Alliance) then unleashed anti-Bolshevik reprisals, which the Bulgarian Communists answered with acts of terror. In April 1925, a bomb set by the BKP, in an effort to slay the king and his members of government, killed scores of important Bulgarian citizens in the Sofia Cathedral. Communist leaders—including Georgi Dimitrov, Vasil Kolarov, and Vulko Chervenkov—fled under sentences of death to the Soviet Union, there to become utterly dependent upon Stalin. Dimitrov's career in exile was noteworthy for his brilliant testimony at the Reichstag "fire trial" in Leipzig in 1933, followed by his elevation to the secretary-generalship of the Comintern.

Bulgarian authorities banned the BKP in 1925, but the party reemerged in 1927 under the legal cover of the Bulgarian Workers Party* and enjoyed some success at the polls until the 1934 total ban of political parties. In response to the dictatorial regime of 1934, the Communists helped form the People's Constitutional Bloc.*

During World War II, the BKP, closely watched and directed by Moscow, distributed propaganda in Bulgaria and organized a small partisan movement in the countryside after the German invasion of the Soviet Union. In June 1942, Dimitrov engineered from Moscow the formation of the Fatherland Front,* initially functioning as a resistance organization. The Front came to political power on September 8, 1944, in a coup d'état masterminded by the Military League just three days after the Soviets declared war on Bulgaria and entered the country unopposed. The Fatherland Front in 1944 set the stage for Communist activity on a mass scale. In the first Front government, the BKP (with four members) was in a minority; nevertheless it held the key ministries of interior and justice. From then until 1947, the BKP consolidated its power inexorably. Stalin's agents in this process were Dimitrov and other Bulgarian Communists who returned from Moscow in November 1945. To Dimitrov belongs the credit for replacing the Bulgarian police with a Communist militia backed by the Soviet Red Army, thus circumventing the minister of defense, General Velchev of the Military League.

Stalin's notorious anti-Tito purge marked the next important stage of BKP development. In the course of the purge, all elements of the BKP suspected of anything less than total subservience to the USSR were eliminated physically or politically. The outstanding victim was Traicho Kostov, considered a leading candidate to succeed Dimitrov. Kostov was executed in December 1949 for harboring titoist tendencies.

In the wake of the Tito affair and the post-Stalin evolution of the Communist Party of the Soviet Union (see SOVIET UNION), the BKP leadership underwent important changes. Dimitrov died during a visit to Moscow in July 1949. After a brief interregnum with Vasili Kolarov as head of party and government, Vulko Chervenkov became BKP first secretary in January 1950. The leading figures in Chervenkov's regime were Anton Yugov, former minister of the interior, who was named premier in 1950; and Todor Zhivkov, who entered the Politburo in 1952 and became first secretary in 1954.

Destalinization in the mid-1950s led to Chervenkov's demotion and finally to his expulsion from the BKP in 1962. Named premier (chairman of the State Council) in 1962 was Todor Zhivkov, who has since maintained his position as unrivaled head of the BKP collective leadership. He presided over the posthumous "rehabilitation" of the 1940s purge victims, including that of Kostov, and has since pressed forward with efforts to raise living standards and to bring Bulgaria up to the "higher levels of Soviet-model socialist development." Except for a 1965 conspiracy among a small circle of army officers, Zhivkov's regime has been notably free of factional opposition or internal dissent. Of all the east European countries, with the possible exception of the German Democratic Republic, postwar Bulgaria has bowed most completely to Soviet dictates in virtually every aspect of domestic and foreign affairs.

With over 800,000 members in 1981, the BKP accounts for nine percent of the country's population. In terms of social composition, about 41 percent of BKP members are workers, only 23 percent are peasants, and some 36 percent are white-collar employees and intelligentsia. Since 1958, party membership has grown by more than 300,000, with bureaucrats and blue-collar workers accounting for the major part of the increase. Communist strength in the Bulgarian National Assembly had grown to 272 in 1976, although the party achieved its highest plurality in 1966 when its deputies numbered 280.

At the top of the BKP structural pyramid stand three interlocking bodies: the Politburo, the Secretariat, and the Central Committee. In theory, the fountain of authority within the BKP is the Party Congress, to which some 1,500 deputies are chosen and which meets by statute every five years. Among its prescribed functions, the Congress elects the 250-odd members, voting and nonvoting, of the Central Committee. Nominally, the Central Committee also elects the nine-member Secretariat, headed by the first secretary, and the Politburo with its 11 full and six candidate members. The Politburo and Secretariat members are not always set by statutes, nor are members prohibited from holding multiple offices. The Secretariat supervises the implementation of party policy, whereas the Politburo sets policy and makes decisions on all important matters that come before the party leadership.

Various mass organizations, acting as auxiliaries of the BKP, are used by the party hierarchy to exert and maintain control over the population. The most important of these organizations, each headed by loyal BKP members, is the Fatherland Front, as well as the Central Council of Trade Unions and the Communist Youth League.

The Central Council of Trade Unions (*Tsentralen Suvet Profesionalni Suiuz*) consists of 13 separate trade unions, each of which accepts the leading role of the BKP in the determination of all economic questions. The Council's function is to ensure the mobilization of labor for fulfillment of the national economic plan. Total membership of the Council in 1973 was about 2.6 million.

The Dimitrov Communist Youth League (*Dimitrovski Komunistcheski Mladezhki Suiuz*, or *Komsomol*) is patterned in all important respects after the Soviet

Komsomol and the parent communist parties of both organizations. Membership in the Komsomol is supposedly limited to Bulgarians from 14 to 24 years of age. Total membership in the early 1970s was about one million. The Komsomol directs much of its energies toward overcoming the youth alienation which Zhivkov described as "the main problem for the young" in his "Youth Theses" of December 1967. Children too young to join the Komsomol are steered into the Pioneers (or Young Septembrists).

In addition to the creation of mass organizations and the colonization of all political groups and labor associations in the civilian society, the BKP paid particular attention to the Bulgarian Army. The work of the party in the armed forces is considered crucial; and after the 1965 conspiracy among a few army officers, the party's control of the military has increased considerably. This control is exercised by the Central Political Administration of the People's Army in accordance with Article 55 of BKP bylaws.

Financially, the Bulgarian Communist Party is self-sustaining. Everyone admitted, after careful screening and sponsorhip, is expected to pay one percent of his/her monthly salary as an initial admission fee and thereafter a percentage of monthly earnings ranging from 0.5 to three percent.

The current BKP leadership appears to be relatively united. First Secretary Todor Zhivkov managed to eliminate the last of probable opponents in 1977 with the removal from the Politburo and Central Committee of Boris Velchev. Velchev's removal precipitated a substantial rejuvenation of the highest party organ, with the net result of reducing the average age of the Politburo to 58 years and that of the Central Committee to 54 years. Yet despite the elevation of younger people to political centers, there is no evidence to this date that the BKP intends to chart its own course in domestic or foreign affairs. One of the party's weaknesses, which could potentially cause serious dissensions, is the scale of nepotism and "political double-dipping" among its more powerful leaders. At least 19 members of the Politburo, Party Secretariat, and Control Commission hold more than one key governmental position; several members of Zhivkov's own family have been elevated to positions of power, including his daughter, Ludmi Pa, who until her premature death in July 1981 held memberships in the Central Committee and the Politburo and was chairperson of the Council of Culture.

BULGARIAN NATIONAL AGRARIAN UNION (*Bulgarski Naroden Zemedelski Suiuz*: BNZS). The BNZS is probably the longest-surviving political structure of modern Bulgaria. Currently an auxiliary of the Bulgarian Communist Party,* the BNZS is Bulgaria's only other legal political formation and is recognized in the nation's 1971 constitution as "united" in purpose with the Communists. The continuation of the BNZS perpetuates the mythology, initiated by Communist leader Georgi Dimitrov in 1946, that the Communists had no intention of eliminating all political parties from the public life of the country. At the time of signing the peace treaty with Russia and the Allies after World War II, Dimitrov seized the opportunity to characterize "allegations that we Communists are preparing to expel the opposition from the Grand National Assembly [as] stupid and inconsistent." Four years later his successor, Vulko Chervenko, defined the relationship of the BNZS as being one of a "transmission belt" of the Communist Party's policies, even though the two structures were pro forma and granted similar prerogatives in fielding candidates for public office.

The Bulgarian Agrarian Union or Agrarian Party (two names by which the BNZS is also known) was founded in 1879 by Dimitur Dragiev, and initially it was referred to as an association aimed at improving the lot of the peasantry. Rapidly, it evolved into a full-fledged political party and played a leading role in the coalitions that governed Bulgaria immediately after World War I. In the elections of April 1923, the Agrarians received 53 percent of the popular vote and formed a strong independent government.

The leading BNZS personality was the innovative Alexander Stamboliiski, whose objectives were to initiate broader welfare programs to aid the peasantry and to establish a peasant republic tied to the Green International through cooperation with neighboring countries. In so doing, Stamboliiski acquired an array of fatal enemies across the political spectrum. A June 1923 coup masterminded by the semisecret Military League* overthrew the Agrarians and contributed to the murder of Stamboliiski. Eight years later, the BNZS reemerged from illegality as the Agrarian Party and became a senior partner in a coalition called the People's Bloc,* formed to combat the Democratic Alliance* that had governed Bulgaria since the 1923 coup. The new People's Bloc governed from 1931 until the next Military League coup of 1934. Although the Bloc government was formally headed by the Democratic Party,* the Bloc adopted the Agrarian philosophy; and its leaders during the period of coalition politics were Dimitur Gichev, Konstantin Muraviev, and Vergil Dimov, leaders of the BNZS moderate wing known as the Agrarians of Gichev.*

In 1941 the Agrarians split into two groups: the Agrarians of Gichev, which continued to pursue earlier and by then seemingly outdated politics; and the *Pladne** group, which had drifted toward the left and Communist Party control under the People's Constitutional Bloc* and then the Fatherland Front.* The Fatherland Front and the Military League were behind the September 1944 coup that overthrew the short-lived Gichev Agrarian government of Konstantine Muraviev. In 1945, in an attempt to maintain existence in the face of Communist purges, both Gichev's Agrarians and the *Pladne* group reunited and revived the old BNZS name under the leadership of Nikola Petkov. But by then the party's ideology did not matter, for the Soviet Red Army had become the arbiter of Bulgarian political life. For the last time, the Agrarians contested the 1946 election and received one-third of the popular vote. The BNZS was dissolved after Petkov's arrest and execution (see Fatherland Front), but the BNZS was soon reconstituted as a full subservient to the Communist Party.

In its present form, the BNZS boasts a membership of about 130,000, the majority of whom are farmers. The BNZS organizational structure mirrors that of the Bulgarian Communist Party. A national Party Congress convenes every four years and elects an executive Council, which roughly corresponds to the Central Committee of the Communist Party. A standing committee of the Council serves as the main link with the Communist Party organizations and manages the day-to-day affairs of the BNZS. The Agrarians' current chairman, Georgi Traykov, has nominal power in state affairs, even though in theory the BNZS is the senior governmental partner, sharing seats in parliament with the Communists. Usually, a percentage of National Assembly seats is reserved for BNZS candidates (100 seats in the 1976 election), and some BNZS elected officials occupy state positions. But for all intents and purposes, the BNZS has indeed become a transmission belt of Bulgarian Communist Party policies at all levels of political activity.

Further Reference. Miller, Marshall Lee, *Bulgaria during the Second World War* (Stanford, Calif.: Stanford University Press, 1975); Oren, Nissan, *Revolution Administered: Agrarianism and Communism in Bulgaria* (Baltimore: Johns Hopkins University Press, 1973); Sipkov, Ivan, ed., *By-Laws of the Bulgarian Communist Party* (Washingtion, D.C.: Library of Congress, 1980).

BULGARIAN SOCIAL DEMOCRATIC PARTY (*Bulgarska Socialdemokraticheska Partiia*: BSDP). The BSDP was founded in 1891, along with several other parties that influenced the course of Bulgarian politics for almost 50 years. Initially, the BSDP preferred to be called a movement and reflected the influences of similar phenomena in western Europe and Russia. By the 1900s, the party became domesticized and reflected more accurately the peculiarities of Bulgarian society.

In 1903 the BSDP split into two factions, the "Narrow" and the "Broad" Social Democratic parties. The split, which came only one year after the Russian Social Democratic Workers' Party (*see* SOVIET UNION) divided into Bolsheviks and Mensheviks, was caused by differences among the BSDP leaders concerning the proper role of the peasantry. The Broad faction, under the leadership of Janko Sakazov, was inclined to expand the base of participation in the party by utilizing the peasantry as the primary force for social reform. The Narrows, on the other hand, under the leadership of Dimitur Blagoev, preferred a tightly knit organization, well disciplined, and based solely on the minuscule Bulgarian working class and intelligentsia. With Blagoev's election in 1919 to the Executive Committee of the new Communist International, the Narrow Social Democratic Party changed its name to the Bulgarian Communist Party.*

In 1927 the BSDP developed several factions in response to the Democratic Alliance (DS),* the then-ruling rightist coalition that had succeeded to governmental power following the 1923 coup d'état led by the Military League.* A few BSDP elements responded to the DS's call for peacemaking and to the Alliance's suppression of the Communists, and in the 1927 elections these few Social Democrats supported the DS, which continued to govern Bulgaria until 1931. Most BSDP elements instead joined the Iron Bloc* coalition that opposed the DS and that was led by the Agrarians of Gichev,* themselves another target of DS repression.

During World War II, the BSDP feared Nazi Germany (see HISTORICAL GERMANY) more than they feared the Communists. Therefore, in 1942 the BSDP joined forces with the Bulgarian Communists and the left-wing Pladne* splinter from the Bulgarian National Agrarian Union* to form a resistance organization called the Fatherland Front.* The Front, however, soon took control of the Bulgarian government after the 1944 coup. At the war's end, the Social Democrats were systematically purged by the power-assuming Communists (see Fatherland Front), thus by 1948 completing the circle that had started in 1891.

BULGARIAN WORKERS PARTY (Bulgarska Rabotnicheska Partiia: BRP). The BRP was a legal front organization, established to contest the 1927 elections on behalf of the Bulgarian Communist Party,* which had been outlawed in 1925. Parallel to the Workers Party, the Independent Workers and Professional Union was created, which provided grass-roots support for the party's programs.

Throughout its existence, the Workers Party managed, under the pretext of being a bona fide organization, to increase its following among the peasants and workers. However, the power of deciding the course of BRP policies was retained by the illegal Bulgarian Communist Party and the Comintern. In September 1934, four months after a military coup against the government, all political parties were banned. Following the ban, the BRP was absorbed by the Communist Party since the BRP was useful only when it operated in the open, and it made no sense to maintain two underground organizations that had the same goals. However, during its seven years of legal existence, the Workers Party had been able to develop a genuine domestic following, which could have potentially developed into a more nationalistic brand of communism. Historians of the Bulgarian communist movement view this possibility as the main reason for the absorption of the Workers Party by the Communist Party in 1935. In fact, the suspicion prevailed in Moscow at the time that most of Georgi Dimitrov's followers were within the Workers Party, rather than within the illegal Communist Party operating from Russian soil. Stalin, as evidenced from his treatment of the Yugoslav Communists (see COMMUNIST PARTY OF YUGOSLAVIA [1919-1952], YUGOSLAVIA), could not tolerate divided loyalties or parties not effectively under his own control. Nevertheless, a faction of the Workers Party existed until 1948, when it was "reorganized" and formally merged into the Bulgarian Communist Party.

BULGARSKA KOMUNISTICHESKA PARTIIA. See BULGARIAN COMMUNIST PARTY.

BULGARSKA RABOTNICHESKA PARTIIA. See BULGARIAN WORKERS PARTY.

BULGARSKA SOCIALDEMOKRATICHESKA PARTIIA. *See* BULGARIAN SOCIAL DEMOCRATIC PARTY.

BULGARSKI NARODEN ZEMEDELSKI SUIUZ. *See* BULGARIAN NATIONAL AGRARIAN UNION.

DEMOCRATIC ALLIANCE (*Demokraticheska Sgovor*: DS). The Democratic Alliance was the outgrowth of the People's Alliance (also known as the Democratic Entente), a coalition of small rightist parties that had carried out the successful 1923 coup against Alexander Stamboliiski's government under the Bulgarian National Agrarian Union.* The core membership of the People's Alliance consisted of the royalist Military League,* including Generals Ivan Rusev and Ivan Volkov, and Lieutenant Colonels Damian Velchev, Kimon Georgiev, and Nikola Rachev. Some of these military men played a key role in subsequent military coups (1934, 1944), and others served as the king's viceroys within the Bulgarian political parties.

On the civilian side, the People's Alliance was led by the respected professor, Alexander Tsankov, who had succeeded in attracting to himself prominent politicians from the Democratic Party.* Tsankov assumed the premiership in June 1923 and immediately set out to create a viable, broader political party out of the People's Alliance. The outcome of his efforts was the creation of the Democratic Alliance, which successfully contested the 1927 elections and ruled Bulgaria until it was displaced by the opposition People's Bloc* in 1931. The DS implemented a program of political pacification, though primarily achieved through repression of the Agrarians and of the Bulgarian Communist Party.* Also, Tsankov himself never recovered from the accusation that he had contributed to the murder of Alexander Stamboliiski, who, as the years passed, had acquired mythical qualities.

Being a loosely defined coalition of parties with substantial political talent, the Democratic Alliance provided Bulgaria with several prime ministers. Because the DS did not suffer from any serious ideological divisions, the king utilized the party's leaders to form cabinets with relative ease. Tsankov was the primary force behind the DS, and he headed the government during 1923-1926. However, in fact the structure was always under the de facto leadership of a troika made up of Tsankov, Andrei Liapchev (a Democrat), and Atanas Burov (founder of the Populist Party*); the latter two men headed the Bulgarian DS government during 1926-1931.

Participants in this rather heterogeneous coalition—besides members of the Military League, the centrist Democrats, and the conservative Populists—were the nationalistic National Liberal Party,* dissident segments of the Bulgarian Social Democratic Party,* the ethnonationalistic Internal Macedonian Revolutionary Organization,* and several other minor groups.

DEMOCRATIC ENTENTE. *See* DEMOCRATIC ALLIANCE.

DEMOCRATIC PARTY (*Demokraticheska Partiia*: DP). The DP was formed in the 1890s by Petko Karavelov following his break with Alexander Stamboliiski's Bulgarian National Agrarian Union.* Throughout its existence, the DP remained a consistent supporter of national independence, and it played a significant role in the development of pluralistic political life in modern Bulgaria.

Like most other Bulgarian parties, the Democratic Party was by and large a personality-oriented political structure without nationwide organization. Its membership could be determined only by the number of votes received during electoral contests. Being a somewhat right-of-center party and having set a political agenda aimed at the maximization of national independence, the Democrats were called upon repeatedly to save the country when Bulgaria's international position was compromised by inept decisions and a tendency by the kings to enter world conflicts on the side of the losers. The DP played a key role in the formal declaration of independence of Bulgaria from Great Power tutelage in 1908, and the party assumed the task of helping to provide an orderly political life thereafter. In the course of its rule, the DP substantially reduced tensions between various militant political factions and set the foundations of middle and higher Bulgarian education. In 1919, as in 1908, the Democratic Party was called upon to help salvage Bulgarian interests at the end of World War I and from the chaos that ensued from the fact that Bulgaria was declared an enemy country of the Allies.

Alone or in various coalitions, the Democrats ruled Bulgaria for 13 years; and, in spite of an often fragmented body, it always managed to have a respectable representation in the National Assembly. DP member Andrei Liapchev was part of the Democratic Alliance* government of 1926-1931. From 1931 to 1934, the DP participated in the People's Bloc* and provided two prime ministers, Alexander Malinov and Nikola Mishanov. The DP was also represented in the 1944 coalition government under Konstantin Muraviev, a member of the Agrarians of Gichev* who led Bulgaria's last democratic government. Muraviev, however, was overthrown by the Fatherland Front* in September 1944; and with the advent of rule by the Bulgarian Communist Party,* the DP was extinguished in 1944.

DEMOKRATICHESKA PARTIIA. *See* DEMOCRATIC PARTY

DEMOKRATICHESKA SGOVOR. *See* DEMOCRATIC ALLIANCE.

DP. *See* DEMOCRATIC PARTY.

DS. *See* DEMOCRATIC ALLIANCE.

FATHERLAND FRONT (*Otechestven Front*: OF). The Fatherland Front is today a mass organization that performs some elementary functions usually performed by political parties. The Front's origins are traceable to World War II, and its growth and current role follow the patterns of similar structures in eastern Europe.

Conceived in Moscow in 1942, the OF was the brainchild of Georgi Dimitrov, the secretary-general of the Comintern. During World War II, the Front served as the umbrella for resistance organizations fighting against the German occupation and their domestic collaborators. The existence of the OF was formally announced in 1942, and initially it operated underground directly under control of the Bulgarian Communist Party.* Among the early Front participants were *Pladne** (a left-wing faction of the Bulgarian National Agrarian Union*), radical elements of *Zveno** (the political arm of the royalist Military League*), the Bulgarian Social Democratic Party,* the leftist Radical Party,* and several other minor organizations and parties opposed to nazi rule. The Bulgarian Communist Party, however, had captured the OF's leadership from the outset and upon liberation proceeded to cleanse the OF ranks of unreliable elements.

In conjunction with radical elements of the Military League, the OF staged a coup d'état on September 8, 1944, against the government of Konstantin Muraviev of the Agrarians of Gichev.* Upon completion of the coup, the Front formed the government, headed by Kimon Georgiev of the Military League and including the leader of the *Pladne* Agrarians, Dr. G. M. Dimitrov (not to be confused with Georgi Dimitrov, the Comintern agent). Dr. Dimitrov, however, opposed the dominant role of the Communist Party in the governing Front on the grounds that the Communists were a minority force in Bulgarian politics. In 1945, Dr. Dimitrov was accused of "sabotaging" the OF and its policies, and he went into exile. By 1945 the *Pladne* and Gichev Agrarians had reunited in an attempt to ward off Communist purges. Dr. Dimitrov's successor as leader of the reunited Bulgarian National Agrarian Union (BNZS) was Nikola Petkov, and he was squeezed out by a Communist-sponsored splinter group led by A. Obbov within the BNZS. Following Petkov's removal, the Agrarians were "reorganized" by the Communist regime and reduced to the status of a Communist Party instrument. However, with the removal and subsequent execution of Petkov, the Fatherland Front had forfeited all claims that it represented the majority of the Bulgarian people. Petkov remained a popular figure, and his reputation was immensely enhanced by the kangaroo court that convicted him.

Following the settling of scores with the Agrarians, the Communists next turned their attention to the Bulgarian Social Democrats. They, too, were purged of unreliable elements, and a Communist-controlled faction of the Social Democratic Party under Dimitur Keikov staked the claim that they were the "true socialists" and were consequently permitted to remain in the Front, being completely absorbed into the Communist Party by 1948.

Zveno's turn came in 1945, and it was purged in a ruthless manner by the newly reformed ministry of the interior. General Velchev, leader of the 1944 coup by the Military League, was accused of collaboration with Draža Mikhailovitch, the Serbian nationalist, and for being a reactionary in having masterminded the 1923 coup against Alexander Stamboliiski's Agrarian government. Velchev's police force was replaced by a Communist-controlled militia.

By 1949 all remnants of OF component parties were either throughly eliminated or directly absorbed into the OF. Following the completion of purges, the
Fatherland Front was reorganized and reduced to the level of a mass organization
whose activities are closely controlled by the Bulgarian Communist Party. Currently, the Front boasts a membership of about 130,000, and it is the formal
organization that fields candidates for the National Assembly and other elective
offices. However, this is simply a formality since all candidates must be screened
and approved by local Communist Party organizations. The Front's most useful
task in the electoral process is that it provides a forum where candidates and
noncontroversial issues are discussed and approved. In the course of its development, the Fatherland Front has been given a few additional responsibilities,
such as supervision of public enterprises, municipal services, and collective labor
bargaining.

Further Reference. Seton-Watson, Hugh, *Nationalism and Revolution: 1946-63* (New
York: Praeger, 1964).

IMRO. *See* INTERNAL MACEDONIAN REVOLUTIONARY ORGAN-
IZATION.

INTERNAL MACEDONIAN REVOLUTIONARY ORGANIZATION
(*Vutreshna Makidoniski Revoliutsionna Organizatsiia:* VMRO; known most commonly by its English acronym: IMRO). The IMRO originated in the 1890s as a
secret organization, composed of fierce nationalists whose original aim was two-
fold: to liberate Macedonia from Ottoman rule, and to form an independent
state. The movement never transformed itself into a political party. Yet it
influenced the domestic and foreign policies of Bulgaria and contributed significantly to the country's reputation of being a troublemaker in the Balkans. From
1923 to 1934, the IMRO engaged in massive domestic terror aimed at altering
the country's conciliatory policies toward Yugoslavia. IMRO members participated in Bulgarian conservative governments as individuals, under the auspices
of the rightist Democratic Alliance.* During the German occupation of Bulgaria, the IMRO expanded its terrorist activities in Yugoslav Macedonia and
occupied Thrace. By the end of World War II, however, the IMRO's influence
dissipated in Bulgaria under the advent of undisputed communist rule. (Some
IMRO branches in other European nations are still in existence. For example,
see INTERNAL MACEDONIAN REVOLUTIONARY ORGANIZATION,
YUGOSLAVIA.)

IRON BLOC (*Zhelezen Bloc*). The Iron Bloc was the name given to the coalition, dominated by the Agrarians of Gichev,* that contested the 1927 general
elections in opposition to the rightist Democratic Alliance (DS).* The DS was
the incumbent government sponsored by the Military League,* which had been
responsible for the 1923 coup against the Agrarian government of Alexander
Stamboliiski (*see* Bulgarian National Agrarian Union). Other participants in
the Iron Bloc were the Bulgarian Social Democratic Party*; a rather ephemeral

artisans group; and members of the recently established *Zveno*,* the public political arm of the semiclandestine Military League. *Zveno* infiltrated political groupings and assisted in promoting the League's conspiracies until the mid-1940s.

LINK. *See* ZVENO.

MILITARY LEAGUE (*Voena Liga* or *Voena Suiuz*). The Military League was formed after World War I, though historians argue that such an informal organization within the Bulgarian Army was active as early as 1893. The League's principal aim was to keep politicians on their toes. When it appeared to the League that governments were damaging national interests (as perceived by the League), or were inefficient and corrupt, the League did not hesitate to intervene and remove these governments. In this way, the Military League acted as the watchdog of the king and eliminated parties and persons who threatened the dominancé of the throne.

The Military League masterminded three major coup d'états. The first was in June 1923, bringing an end to rule by the Bulgarian National Agrarian Union* and the murder of the Agrarians' influential leader, Alexander Stamboliiski. The League subsequently sponsored (unofficially) the right-wing Democratic Alliance,* which governed Bulgaria from 1923 to 1931. The Democratic Alliance was displaced by the Agrarian-dominated People's Bloc* coalition in the election of 1931. In response, the Military League's second coup in 1934 put an end to parliamentary rule and began a ban on all political party activity in Bulgaria. In the chaos of World War II, the Bulgarian regency appointed a new government, against whom the third coup was led by the League's recognized leader, the superintendent of the Sofia Military Academy, Colonel Damian Velchev. Velchev led the communist-dominated Fatherland Front* and the *Zveno** group in the September 8, 1944, coup against the pro-West, Agrarian (*see* Agrarians of Gichev) government of Konstantin Muraviev. This final coup paved the way for the nation's takeover by the Bulgarian Communist Party.*

Since it had never declared itself to be a political party, preferring to remain nonpublic, the Military League organized the *Zveno* group in 1923. Via *Zveno*, the League entered the Bulgarian political arena in 1927 with *Zveno*'s participation in the Agrarian-led Iron Bloc* coalition. Ironically, the Iron Bloc hoped to displace the Democratic Alliance government that was sponsored by the Military League.

During World War II, *Zveno* participated in the resistance under the banner of the Fatherland Front and in so doing contributed to the Front's popularity. Following the 1944 coup, Colonel Velchev assumed the ministry of defense and war in the first Fatherland Front government, only to be accused months later of antiparty activities and collaboration with the enemy. Like the other Front participants—the Agrarians and the Bulgarian Social Democratic Party*—*Zveno*, too, was "reorganized" and formally reduced to one of the components of the

Fatherland Front. With *Zveno*'s demise went the existence of the Military League.

NARODEN BLOC. *See* PEOPLE'S BLOC.

NARODEN KONSTITUTSIONEN BLOC. *See* PEOPLE'S CONSTITUTIONAL BLOC.

NARODNITSI PARTIIA. *See* POPULIST PARTY.

NARODNOLIBERALNA PARTIIA. *See* NATIONAL LIBERAL PARTY.

NARROW SOCIAL DEMOCRATIC PARTY. *See* BULGARIAN SOCIAL DEMOCRATIC PARTY.

NATIONAL LIBERAL PARTY (*Narodnoliberalna Partiia*: NLP). The NLP was one of the two oldest political parties of Bulgaria (the other being the Bulgarian National Agrarian Union*). Both parties were formed at the time of the constituent assembly which produced the Tirnovo Constitution of 1879 (*see* Bulgaria introduction). Following the adoption of that charter, the National Liberals grew in influence and strength and, along with the Agrarians, represented the overwhelming majority of the Bulgarian electorate.

The NLP provided Bulgaria with several prime ministers during the 1879-1918 period, and the party contributed immensely to the growth of a viable free-enterprise system. Its rank and file, however, was never homogeneous or guided by firmly held ideological principles. Radicals, nihilists, intense nationalists, and national revisionists found a home in the National Liberal Party.

Among the outstanding achievements of the NLP, primarily under the leadership of Stefan Stambolov, were the Tirnovo Constitution and its successful policy of putting distance between the fledgling Bulgarian state and Russia, home of Bulgaria's first ruler (Prince Alexander) and a country that contemplated the annexation of Bulgaria. Among the party's failures was its association with the Central Powers during World War I, which in fact contributed to the frustration of Bulgaria's efforts to obtain long-cherished goals, such as the incorporation of Macedonia into the Bulgarian national fold. The NLP participated in the nationalistic Democratic Alliance* during 1927-1931; and some NLP elements, discontented with the Democratic Alliance, joined the opposition People's Bloc* during 1931-1934. With this disintegration into several political factions, the National Liberal Party ended as a political influence by 1934.

NLP. *See* NATIONAL LIBERAL PARTY.

OF. *See* FATHERLAND FRONT.

OTECHESTVEN FRONT. *See* FATHERLAND FRONT.

PEOPLE'S ALLIANCE. *See* DEMOCRATIC ALLIANCE.

PEOPLE'S BLOC (*Naroden Bloc*). The People's Bloc was the coalition that facilitated the comeback of the Agrarian Party (*see* Bulgarian National Agrarian Union) in the 1931 elections. Led by Alexander Malinov, a Democrat, the People's Bloc was composed of Malinov's own Democratic Party*; the Radical Party* led by Stoian Kosturkov; a wing of the National Liberal Party* led by G. Petrov; and the Agrarians of Gichev,* a moderate wing of the Bulgarian National Agrarian Union, with the latter now reappearing as the Agrarian Party for the first time since the 1923 coup which had overthrown the Agrarian government. Although Malinov led the coalition, it was the Agrarians who provided the muscle, the masses, and the success at the polls. The Democrats provided the government leadership under Alexander Malinov and Nikola Mishanov. The immediate effect of the Bloc's appearance was the intensification of tensions and the introduction of the spoils system at all levels of government. The People's Bloc-supported government was overthrown by the May 1934 coup d'état staged by the Military League.*

PEOPLE'S CONSTITUTIONAL BLOC (*Naroden Konstitutsionen Bloc*). Formed in 1936, the People's Constitutional Bloc may very well be considered as the precursor of the Fatherland Front* (which, before its total takeover by the Bulgarian Communist Party,* had been organized to oppose nazi occupation). The People's Constitutional Bloc emerged during the period of united front policy announced by the Comintern; and it consisted of Communists, the *Pladne** agrarians, some members of the Democratic Party,* and the *Petorska** group. The Bloc was formed in reaction to the 1934 coup by the Military League* that had resulted in a suspension of all political party activity in Bulgaria. Until the disruption brought by World War II, the Bloc fought for restoration of the constitution and the return of parliamentary rule.

PEOPLE'S UNION ZVENO. *See* ZVENO.

PETORSKA. The *Petorska* (or "Quintet") was an informal organization formed after the 1934 coup against the Bulgarian government by the Military League.* The *Petorska* was composed of five leaders (thus the name Quintet), theoretically representing five political parties, among them the Agrarians of Gichev,* the Radical Party,* and elements of the then-defunct Democratic Alliance.* One of the *Petorska's* noteworthy acts was to petition the king for restoration of the constitution and for holding free elections at the time when fascism was on the rise in Bulgaria and elsewhere. In 1936 the *Petorska* continued to promote its view by joining the People's Constitutional Bloc.*

PLADNE. The *Pladne* was the radical leftist wing of the Bulgarian National Agrarian Union (BNZS).* After the 1923 coup which overthrew the Agrarian government and resulted in the assassination of Agrarian leader Alexander Stamboliiski, the BNZS was abolished by Bulgarian authorities and maintained its existence clandestinely until 1931. At that time, however, the new BNZS, now under the name of the Agrarian Party, experienced internal conflicts between its leftists and the more moderate Agrarians of Gichev* wing. Therefore, in 1932 the leftists formed the "Alexander Stamboliiski Peasant Union," commonly known as the *Pladne* (or "Zenith," the name of its newspaper). Although remaining officially within the Agrarian Party at that time, the *Pladne* faction participated in the 1936 People's Constitutional Bloc* and was one of the founders of the communist-controlled Fatherland Front.*

Due largely to the *Pladne*'s drift toward close cooperation with the Bulgarian Communist Party,* in 1941 the *Pladne* and Gichev Agrarians formally split into two separate parties. *Pladne* representatives, including party leader Dr. G. M. Dimitrov, participated in the first Fatherland Front government formed after World War II liberation. However, by then the Communists had systematically eliminated the *Pladne* leadership and derailed its program from what the *Pladne*, attempting to pursue Stamboliiski's goals, had had in mind. In 1945, in an attempt to save both of their existences, the *Pladne* and the Agrarians of Gichev reunited to reconstitute the Bulgarian National Agrarian Union, which remains in existence today albeit under control of the Bulgarian Communist Party.

POPULIST PARTY (*Narodnitsi Partiia*). The Populist Party was a minor grouping led by Atanas Burov, who joined the Democratic Alliance* in 1925 and played a role in its life thereafter. Ideologically, the Populists were considered to be the right-wing faction of the Alliance, and the Populist Party remained throughout its existence as a "personality party," with limited grass-roots support. Burov was co-leader of the Democratic Alliance government that ruled Bulgaria during 1926-1931.

QUINTET. *See* PETORSKA.

RADICAL PARTY (*Radikalna Partiia*). In 1903 the Radical Party was formed by dissidents of the centrist Democratic Party.* The Radicals were led by the respected politician Naicho Tsanov and received support from leftist intellectuals and even from nihilists. The party participated in various coalition governments, including the People's Bloc,* and was also a member of the *Petorska** grouping after the 1934 coup that ended parliamentary rule. The Radical Party leader during the 1940s, Stefan Kosturkov, brought the grouping into the Fatherland Front* in 1942 and, therefore, under control of the Bulgarian Communist Party.* In 1949 the Radical Party was formally merged into the Fatherland Front.

RADIKALNA PARIIA. *See* RADICAL PARTY.

SPARROW. *See* AGRARIANS OF GICHEV.

VMRO. *See* INTERNAL MACEDONIAN REVOLUTIONARY ORGAN-
IZATION.

VOENA LIGA. *See* MILITARY LEAGUE.

VOENA SUIUZ.*See* MILITARY LEAGUE.

VRACHA. *See* AGRARIANS OF GICHEV.

VUTRESHNA MAKIDONISKI REVOLUTISIONNA ORGANIZATSIIA. *See*
INTERNAL MACEDONIAN REVOLUTIONARY ORGANIZATION.

ZEMEDELSKI PARTIIA. *See* BULGARIAN NATIONAL AGRARIAN PARTY.

ZENITH. *See* PLADNE.

ZHELEZEN BLOC. *See* IRON BLOC.

ZVENO. *Zveno* (or "Link") was established in 1923 as the public political arm of
the royalist and semiclandestine Military League.* Informally, the *Zveno* participated in several coalitions while it continued its conspiratorial role, including
infiltration into the Iron Bloc,* a group opposing the Democratic Alliance*
government supported by the Military League after its 1923 coup d'état. The
Zveno also assisted the League in the 1934 coup against constitutional government. However, the League's officers' corps came to be suspicious of the group,
and so did the king. Hence the government cabinet formed after the 1934 coup
reformed *Zveno*'s course and undertook some radical steps to curb the activities
of the terrorist Internal Macedonian Revolutionary Organization* and to attempt to normalize relations with Yugoslavia. The *Zveno* joined the communist-
led Fatherland Front* in 1942 and masterminded the coup that overthrew the
Agrarians of Gichev* government of Konstantine Muraviev in September 1944.
Thus *Zveno* and the Military League perhaps unwittingly prepared the way for a
regime acceptable to the Russians and to the Bulgarian Communist Party.*
Officially reorganized under the name "People's Union Zveno," the party merged
with the Fatherland Front in 1949. However, most of the *Zveno* leaders who had
participated in the resistance and the 1944 coup were ultimately executed,
exiled, or disgraced by the Communists.

Nikolaos A. Stavrou

TABLE 8. Ruling Parties or Coalitions in Bulgaria since 1879

Years	Party or Coalition
1879-1919	National Liberal Party
1919-1923	Bulgarian National Agrarian Union
1923-1931	Democratic Alliance
1931-1934	People's Bloc: Democratic Party Bulgarian National Agrarian Union (Gichev wing) National Liberal Party (Petrov wing) Radical Party
1934-1935	*Zveno* (Military League)
1935-1944	Nonpartisan (king-controlled)
1944-1945	Fatherland Front: Bulgarian Communist Party Bulgarian Social Democratic Party *Pladne* Radical Party *Zveno*/Military League (though all parties purged or absorbed by the Communist Party by 1949)
1945-	Bulgarian Communist Party

Note: First-named party is dominant coalition party.

TABLE 9. Distribution of Seats in Bulgaria's *Sobranie*, 1919-1931

Party	1919	1920	Apr. 1923	Nov. 1923	1927	1931
Bulgarian Communist Party[a]	47	50	16	1	3	31
Bulgarian National Agrarian Union[b]	85	110	212	33	46*	72**
Bulgarian Social Democratic Party	38	9	2	29	10*	5
Democratic Alliance[c]	—	—	—	142	168	64
Democratic Party				17 }	12	42**
Populist Party[d]	66[f]	60	15	14 }	2	—
Radical Party				8	16	7**
National Liberal Party[e]			0			—
National Liberal Party (Petrov wing)					—	29**
National Liberal Party (Smilov wing)					—	14
Artisans group					5*	—
Macedonian group					11	8
Independents and others	0	0	0	3	0	2**
Total	236	229	245	247	273	274

Note: Since 1948, the composition of the 400-seat Bulgarian *Sobranie* is determined prior to each election. For the 1976 election, 25 percent of the seats were allocated to the Bulgarian National Agrarian Union, 7 percent to nonparty organizations, and 68 percent to the Bulgarian Communist Party.

[a] Banned in 1925; contested 1927 and 1931 elections under the name of the Bulgarian Workers Party, a legal front organization, which was reabsorbed into the Communist Party in 1935.

[b] Composed of the *Pladne* and Agrarians of Gichev wings; continues to exist as an auxiliary of the Bulgarian Communist Party.

[c] Known as the People's Alliance prior to the 1927 elections; consisted primarily of the Military League and included rightist dissidents of several other parties (of the Democratic Party, National Liberal Party, Bulgarian Social Democratic Party, Internal Macedonian Revolutionary Organization [not to be confused with the "Macedonian group" listed above], and the Populist Party), though the bulk of most of these additional groups did not affiliate with the Military League and the Alliance.

[d] Merged into the Democratic Alliance in 1923.

[e] Split into two factions (Petrov and Smilov) in 1931.

[f] Prior to November 1923 elections, the Democratic, Populist, Radical, and National Liberal parties formed the "Bourgeois Coalition." The National Liberal Party ran independently in April 1923.

[*] These parties constituted the Iron Bloc coalition in 1927 (61 seats), which unsuccessfully opposed the Democratic Alliance; also included *Zveno*, which at that time was the public political arm of the semiclandestine Military League that infiltrated political parties to promote the League's rightist policies.

[**] These parties constituted the People's Bloc coalition in 1931 (152 seats), which succeeded in defeating the Democratic Alliance.

CYPRUS

The REPUBLIC OF CYPRUS (*Dimokratia Kyprou*, Greek; *Kibris Cumhuriyeti*, Turkish) is an island in the eastern Mediterranean, located approximately 40 miles south of Turkey and 90 miles west of the Lebanon and Syrian coasts. The island's bicommunal population of 630,000 (1980 estimate) consists of 82 percent Greek Cypriots and 18 percent Turkish Cypriots, according to the 1960 census. A small number of other minorities, such as Maronites and Armenians, also inhabit the island, but they are counted as part of the Greek Cypriot population. Thus the recent history of Cyprus and its political development cannot be discussed without examining the impact of the bicommunal character of the republic, and the external interventions and occupations of the strategically located island that have occurred over the years by various powers that have dominated the eastern Mediterranean.

Despite diverse conquests and interventions, Cyprus has retained the Hellenic personality it acquired in antiquity. But the Ottoman conquest in 1570-1571 altered the demographic pattern of the island by transplanting there a population different from the Greek Cypriot native element by culture, ethnic origin, language, and religion. The Ottoman conquest also had the unanticipated effect of revitalizing the Orthodox Church of Cyprus. Under the *Millet* system of Ottoman administration, the Church of Cyprus became the unchallenged spokesman for Greek Cypriot political, social, educational, and religious affairs.

Britain controlled Cyprus from 1878 to 1960, when independence was granted to the island. Upon assuming control, Britain found the Greek Cypriot community already mobilized under the leadership of the Orthodox Church in pursuit of *enosis*, that is, the union of Cyprus to Greece. The second half of the 19th century was one of intense Greek nationalism under the impact of the Megali Idea, the movement to liberate and unify the unredeemed sections of the Hellenic world to the newly independent Greek state. Most of the territories involved were under Ottoman domination, and the unification movement had a great impact on the Greek Cypriots.

The British unwillingness to recognize the seriousness and depth of Greek Cypriot nationalism, and the British pattern of administration in treating each community as a natural extension of Greece and Ottoman Turkey, served only to formalize the ethnic divisions that had previously been bonded under the

Ottoman Empire. These factors eventually led to the organized opposition of the minority Turkish Cypriot community.

National-level politics were virtually absent from colonial Cyprus, given the concentration of power in the British administration. The limited political activity of the Greek Cypriot community was determined by the quest for *enosis* and, consequently, the degree (or lack) of cooperation with the British governor. More extensive was the political activity at the local level in municipal elections. The Orthodox Church, however, in addition to guiding the *enosis* quest, directed considerable activity toward combatting the influence of communism, which first appeared on the island in 1923 with the creation of the Communist Party of Cyprus, and continued through its successor, the Progressive Party of the Working People (AKEL). * The success of the communists in the local elections of 1946 greatly alarmed both the church and the Cypriot conservative middle class. The church possessed the wealth, influence, and organization to combat communism; and the nationalist middle class, lacking organization, offered its support to the church leadership.

The Greek Cypriot middle and upper classes also channelled some of their political activity through the Cypriot National Party (KEK) *; but aside from the KEK's temporary successes in the municipal elections of 1949, the party did not exert much influence in Cypriot politics.

Up until the early 1950s, the political consciousness of the Turkish Cypriots grew slowly, and from then on it developed largely in proportion to the dynamism of the *enosis* movement of the Greek Cypriot community. The Turkish Cypriots saw in Britain the basic protection of their rights and so remained loyal to the British governor and opposed *enosis*.

Strategic considerations motivated Britain's refusal to yield to the demands of the Greek Cypriot nationalists in the early 1950s. Consequently, while Greece raised the issue of Cyprus at the United Nations in 1954, the Greek Cypriots set up the National Organization of Cypriot Fighters (*Ethniki Organosis Kyprion Agoniston*: EOKA) to lead an armed liberation struggle against the British. However, as communist activity had been prohibited in Greece, the Cypriot communists were excluded from the EOKA, and this organization never obtained the characteristics of a revolutionary movement. Instead, until independence, the EOKA remained a conservative, nationalist, anticolonial organization.

Nevertheless, in turn Britain encouraged Turkey's claims on Cyprus in an attempt to blunt the Greek and Greek Cypriot demands. Britain also encouraged the formation of the Turkish Defense Organization (*Türk Mukavemet Teskilati*: TMT), a millitant opponent to the EOKA. Furthermore, in 1955 Dr. Fazil Kuchuk established a Turkish Cypriot political party, the Cyprus Turkish National Union, * to promote the political aims of the Turkish Cypriots. In both ethnic communities, conservative elements dominated the political scene and the militant organizations, and, consequently, other forms of political action along class or communal lines were effectively neutralized.

Five years of aborted negotiations started in 1954, as well as violence against the British and an increasing degree of intercommunal friction among the Cyp-riots. In the Spring of 1959, negotiations closed between Greece and Turkey in Zurich, and between Greece, Turkey, Britain, and representatives of the two Cypriot communities in London. As a result, Cyprus became an independent republic and was given a constitution in 1960.

Postindependence political activity in Cyprus was colored by several factors, the foremost being continued political segregation of the two ethnic communi-ties. The republic's very constitutional structure prevented integration in that the Greek Cypriots elected a Greek Cypriot president, while the Turkish Cyp-riots elected a Turkish Cypriot vice-president (who primarily possessed veto powers). Elections to the 50-member, unicameral Cypriot House of Representa-tives were also along communal lines, on a 70:30 ratio (35 Greeks and 15 Turks, with all members serving five-year terms).

Consequently, the political parties that emerged following independence ap-pealed exclusively to their own ethnic groups. Parties, such as the communist AKEL, whose ideologies encouraged cooperation across communal lines, quickly came under considerable intimidation, especially from the Turkish Cypriot lead-ership and its militant organizations. As a result of continued division, political violence became evident in both communities. Often supported by sources outside of Cyprus, such violence was intended to intimidate the opposition; and political parties were known to informally maintain their own militias, number-ing from a few to several hundred men.

After 1960, the new political parties in Cyprus (see table 11) developed mostly among the Greek Cypriots, who had gained with independence a politi-cal infrastructure and a political elite in favor of independence. Enosis continued to have an emotional appeal, becoming in the long run a source of division and instability among the Greek Cypriots, as well as a source of friction between the two ethnic communities. Yet this process of political development was strength-ened by a more realistic understanding among the Greek Cypriots of their economic, cultural, and political differences from mainland Greece. In addi-tion, the Greek Cypriot majority viewed the 1960 constitution as an externally imposed document, depriving them of their rights. The Turkish Cypriots, on the other hand, saw the constitution as the minimum guarantee of their con-cerns. Moreover, because of their minority status, the Turkish Cypriots were not (and still are not) able to display much independence from mainland Turkey.

The years of conflict, both before and after independence, have made foreign policy and intercommunal issues dominant in Cypriot politics, thus relegating domestic ideological differences and socioeconomic policy to a secondary posi-tion. Furthermore, Cypriot parties tend to be personality-type groupings. Only the communist AKEL and the social-democratic Unified Democratic Union of the Center* in the Greek Cypriot community can be described as ideological parties. The leading personality of the Greek Cypriots was Archbishop Makarios, who dominated from the early 1950s until his death on August 3, 1977. This charismatic leader directed the Greek Cypriots as ethnarch, archbishop, and president in a unique display of his personal influence and that of the Church of Cyprus in the life of the island. In this political role, Makarios acted as the great conciliator among the many political tendencies within the Greek Cypriot community. The Turkish Cypriots have not yet experienced a leader of Makarios's stature.

The circumstances and terms of Cypriot independence had increased bicommunal rivalry and led to problems in the implementation of the 1960 constitution. On November 30, 1963, President Makarios presented a number of proposals for constitutional change which, if adopted, would have removed obstacles from the functioning of postindependence state machinery and would have provided for a unified Cypriot state. But Turkey and the Turkish Cypriots rejected Makarios's proposals. Numerous intercommunal incidents occurred during Christmas 1963, as a result of which the Turkish Cypriots withdrew from the government, which has since remained in Greek Cypriot hands. Intermittent violence and threats of Turkish intervention during Spring 1964 led to the placement on Cyprus of a United Nations peacekeeping force.

Various attempts at negotiation under American and/or United Nations auspices failed to produce a resolution of the intercommunal differences. The Greek Cypriots remained suspicious of the Turkish Cypriot federalist proposals as covers for partition of Cyprus, a goal advocated by both Turkey and the United States since the mid-1950s. In contrast, the Turkish Cypriots feared the Greek Cypriot proposals for a unitary republic as a cover for Greek Cypriot domination and eventual union of Cyprus to Greece. Attempts at resolving the constitutional breakdown were complicated by the involvement of Greece, Turkey, and the United States in various overt and covert ways. The junta that ruled Greece from 1967 to 1974 actively sought the destabilization of Makarios's government; and with American support, the Greek government undertook secret negotiations with Turkey, culminating in the June 1971 consensus to partition Cyprus.

Despite these developments, the intercommunal 1968-1974 negotiations under United Nations auspices had nearly produced a settlement. However, on July 15, 1974, the Greek Cypriot National Guard (officered by mainland Greek military personnel) staged a coup against President Makarios and temporarily removed him from office. Makarios was replaced by Nicos Sampson, leader of the Progressive Party. * Although constitutional order was restored in Cyprus within a few days, the coup provided the legal justification for Turkish military intervention and the subsequent occupation of 40 percent of the territory of Cyprus.

With support from Turkey, the Turkish Cypriots established the so-called Turkish Federated State of Cyprus in the northern half of the island on February 13, 1975. They proceeded to approve by referendum a new constitution for their region and to elect their own president and parliament in 1976. (The Turkish Cypriot parliament is composed of 40 members elected for five-year terms; see table 10.) Without denying that this action may be a first step toward a unilateral declaration of independence, the Turkish Cypriots are now calling for the restructuring of the Cypriot Republic along bicommunal and bizonal confederal lines.

Raouf Denktash of the National Unity Party* became the first elected president of the Turkish Federated State of Cyprus, having previously served as president of the Turkish Cypriot Communal Chamber under the original 1960 constitution of Cyprus, and as Turkish Cypriot interlocutor in the intercommunal talks of 1968-1974. Although the Greek Cypriot government enjoys international recognition as the government of the Republic of Cyprus, it has not exercised jurisdiction over the area occupied by the Turkish Army since 1974.

Intermittent negotiations since 1974 have failed to break the deadlock over the outstanding territorial and constitutional issues, despite the meeting between President Makarios and Raouf Denktash in 1977, and between President Kyprianou and Denktash in 1979, which resulted in two agreements with guidelines for the intercommunal negotiations. While Turkey and the Turkish Cypriots are seeking a solution to legitimize the outcome of their Summer 1974 military operations in Cyprus, the Greek Cypriots are unwilling to accept solutions imposed by force and amounting to the partition of their country.

Today, both ethnic communities enjoy a multiparty system. All Cypriot parties, though particularly those of the Greek Cypriot community, finance, publish, or are closely affiliated with some of the major newspapers of the island in order to inform and mobilize public opinion. Although the parties of the two communities differ on domestic policy matters, they generally maintain a unified, ethnocentric position on the issue of how to restructure the Cypriot Republic. In addition, despite the philosophical similarity among the left-of-center parties of both communities, these parties have yet to prove able to break the communal barrier. Cyprus then remains divided, with rather dim prospects for reversing the trend toward partition within the near future.

Bibliography

Adams, Thomas W. AKEL: The Communist Party of Cyprus. Stanford, Calif.: Hoover Institution Press, 1971.

Coufoudakis, Van. "U.S. Foreign Policy and the Cyprus Question: An Interpretation." Millennium, vol. 5, no. 3 (Winter 1976-1977): 245-268.

Crouzet, François. Le Conflit de Chypre, 1946-1959. 2 vols. Brussels: Établissements Émile Bruylant, 1973.

Denktash, Raouf R. The Cyprus Problem. Nicosia: Public Information Office of the Turkish Cypriot Administration, 1974.

Foley, Charles, ed. The Memoirs of General Grivas. New York: Praeger, 1965.

Hill, Sir George. A History of Cyprus. 4 vols. Cambridge: At the University Press, 1940-1952.

Kyriakides, Stanley. Cyprus Constitutionalism and Crisis Government. Philadelphia: University of Pennsylvania Press, 1968.

Loizos, Peter. The Greek Gift-Politics in a Cypriot Village. New York: St. Martin's Press, 1975.

Markides, Kyriakos C. *The Rise and Fall of the Cyprus Republic.* New Haven and London: Yale University Press, 1977.

Polyviou, Polyvios G. *Cyprus in Search of a Constitution: Constitutional Proposals and Negotiations, 1960-1975.* Nicosia, Cyprus: Nikolaou and Sons, 1976.

Political Parties

AKEL. *See* PROGRESSIVE PARTY OF THE WORKING PEOPLE.

ANORTHOTIKON KOMMA ERGAZOMENOU LAOU. *See* PROGRESSIVE PARTY OF THE WORKING PEOPLE.

CENTER UNION PARTY (Greek Cypriot, *Enosis Kentrou:* EK). The EK was formed in late 1980 by Tassos Papadopoulos, a centrist politician who was elected in 1976 as an independent. He had supported the Democratic Party (DEKO)* and had served briefly as Greek Cypriot interlocutor in the intercommunal talks until his dismissal in 1978. Papadopoulos broke with the Democratic Party due to personal differences with President Spyros Kyprianou, who had remained leader of the DEKO following his election to the presidency.

In the 1981 parliamentary elections, the EK ran a distant sixth among the contesting seven parties, receiving only 2.7 percent of the vote. The party's founder also failed to get elected. Some of the reasons for the EK's failure are to be found in the similarity of its platform to that of the Democratic Party and thus the EK's failure to offer a real alternative to the centrist voter. Also, the EK did not have time to establish an effective organization on the island prior to the elections.

COMMUNAL LIBERATION PARTY (Turkish Cypriot, *Toplumcu Kurtulus Partisi:* TKP). Founded in 1976 by Alpay Durduran, a Turkish-educated engineer, the TKP won six of the 40 seats in the new Turkish Cypriot parliament in the 1976 elections. By Summer 1980, the party's parliamentary strength had risen to seven seats as a result of a defection from the Populist Party.*

The Communal Liberation Party advocates social-democratic principles and social justice within the context of the principles of Kemal Atatürk of Turkey. Consequently, the party is highly critical of the economic philosophy and policy of the ruling National Unity Party (UBP),* and the TKP views the issue of the economy as the chief problem facing the Turkish Cypriots. Opposed to the favoritism shown to big capital by the UBP, the TKP has supported civil servants and other workers in strikes which are considered to result from the absence of policies beneficial for the working classes and for a planned economy. Also, arguing that a capitalist economy creates external dependence, exploitation, and waste of resources, and that it increases social injustice, the TKP calls for a peaceful social revolution that will place economic management and con-trol of the means of production in worker-run public enterprises and cooperatives.

Although the TKP has supported the November 1976 resolution adopted by the new Turkish Cypriot parliament on how to resolve the Cyprus problem, the party has joined other opposition parties in challenging National Unity's han-dling of the problem. The Communal Liberation Party opposes the presence of foreign military bases on Cyprus; opposes the partition of the island; and rejects the unilateral declaration of independence advocated by Turkish Cypriot and UBP leader, Raouf Denktash. Rather, the TKP stands for an independent, bizonal, federal, demilitarized, and nonaligned Republic of Cyprus. The party advocates more contacts between the two Cypriot communities and has pledged to seek an "early" solution of the Cyprus problem when it gains power.

By Spring 1978, a degree of cooperation had emerged between the TKP and the other two major opposition parties (the Republican Turkish Party* and the Populist Party*) against the ruling UBP on all major policy issues. A sign of the TKP's growing popularity was its performance in the 1980 local elections, in which the party received more than a third of the votes cast in the Turkish-held section of Cyprus. This figure compares to 1976 when the TKP received about 21 percent of the overall vote.

Ziya Rizki, the party's candidate for the presidency of the Turkish Federated State of Cyprus, received 30.4 percent of the vote in the 1981 elections, run-ning second to the incumbent Raouf Denktash of the UBP. More striking was the TKP's performance in the 1981 parliamentary elections, where its strength more than doubled compared to 1976. As a result, the TKP is now the second-largest party, controlling 13 of the 40 seats in the Turkish Cypriot parliament. It also has a strong possibility of becoming the major partner in a coalition gov-ernment with the Democratic People's Party* and Republican Turkish Party* if the UBP-led coalition does not receive a parliamentary vote of confidence.

COMMUNIST PARTY OF CYPRUS. *See* PROGRESSIVE PARTY OF THE WORKING PEOPLE.

CTP. *See* REPUBLICAN TURKISH PARTY.

CUMHURIYETCI TÜRK PARTISI. *See* REPUBLICAN TURKISH PARTY.

CYPRIOT NATIONAL PARTY (Greek Cypriot, *Kypriakon Ethnikon Komma:* KEK). Founded in 1944, the Cypriot National Party formally dissolved in 1960, although it had been inactive since 1955 in the midst of the anticolonial strug-gle. The KEK was particularly known for the personality of its leader, Dr. Themistocles Dervis, rather than for its ideological foundation.

With a membership primarily of professionals, doctors, lawyers, and upper-middle-class people, the Cypriot National Party was strongly anticommunist, and it became the gathering place of the Cypriot right and extreme right. The

KEK was the "nationalist" party that attempted to counter communist influence in Cyprus. But given the absence of national-level politics, the KEK's concerns were mainly with mayoral elections in urban areas.

The KEK did not make any special efforts to attract labor, farmers, or rural residents into its ranks and so did not receive support from these groups. According to some observers, the KEK received the backing of the Orthodox Church of Cyprus as part of church policy to combat communist influence on the island. The KEK also strongly endorsed *enosis* (the union of Cyprus to Greece). Despite its loose organizational structure, in the 1949 local elections the KEK was able to elect 11 of the 15 mayors in the major urban centers of Cyprus, including the capital city of Nicosia. However, because of its conservative character, the KEK was accused of pro-British sympathies and cooperation with the colonial administration. Under the conditions of the anticolonial struggle in Cyprus and the creation of an independent republic, instead of continuing advocacy for union with Greece, the party dissolved. Most of the KEK members followed Dervis when he assumed leadership of another right-wing party, the Democratic Union of Cyprus. *

CYPRUS IS TURKISH PARTY. *See* CYPRUS TURKISH NATIONAL UNION.

CYPRUS TURKISH NATIONAL UNION (Turkish Cypriot, *Kibris Milli Türk Birligi*: KMTB). Founded in 1955, the KMTB is the successor of a political organization known as the Cyprus Is Turkish Party. Both groupings were the creation of Dr. Fazil Kuchuk, and their primary aim was the protection and promotion of Turkish Cypriot rights. Prior to independence, the KMTB advocated the partition of Cyprus as the method of protecting the Turkish Cypriots from the *enosis* aspirations of the Greek Cypriots. Following independence, however, the KMTB advocated the full implementation of the London and Zurich agreements which had led to the 1960 Cypriot constitution.

Under the leadership of Kuchuk, who became the vice-president of the Cypriot Republic, the Cyprus Turkish National Union won all 15 seats allocated to the Turkish Cypriots in the 1960 elections to the House of Representatives. The party subscribed to anticommunist and conservative principles. However, the KMTB deputies withdrew from the republic's legislature following the intercommunal incidents of 1963, and these deputies continued to legislate by themselves for the small portion of the Turkish Cypriot community under their control. The KMTB broke apart in 1973, and most of its members provided the foundation on which the new Turkish Cypriot political parties were established in the aftermath of the 1974 coup and the Turkish military intervention in Cyprus.

DEK. *See* DEMOCRATIC UNION OF CYPRUS and DEMOCRATIC NATIONAL PARTY.

DEKO. *See* DEMOCRATIC PARTY.

DEMOCRATIC NATIONAL PARTY (Greek Cypriot, *Demokratikon Ethnikon Komma*: DEK). The Democratic National Party was founded by Dr. Takis Evdokas in the aftermath of Cyprus' 1968 presidential election. The DEK was staunchly conservative. It was in clear opposition to President Makarios's handling of the bicommunal problem, and the party saw *enosis* as the only viable alternative for Cyprus, as well as the guarantee against communist influence on the island. Although the DEK received 9.8 percent of the Greek Cypriot vote in the 1970 legislative election, the party did not gain any seats as it was excluded from the collaborative arrangements that distributed legislative seats among the major Greek Cypriot parties.

In establishing the Democratic National Party, Dr. Evdokas attempted to fill the vacuum left by other right-wing parties (that is, the Cypriot National Party* and the Democratic Union of Cyprus*) which had thus far failed to offer substantial opposition to the more liberal government. With support from various young professionals, scientists, some businessmen, and from farmers, Evdokas first tested Makarios's political strength in the 1968 presidential elections. But Evdokas received only two percent of the vote. The DEK's platform had criticized the Makarios government for creating a new class of leaders whose only criterion for their part in government had been their participation in the anticolonial struggle. In addition, the DEK opposed the government on grounds of corruption, nepotism, political oppression, and terrorism against its critics; its nonaligned foreign policy; and for creating an anti-Hellenic climate in Cyprus. Instead, the DEK had urged cooperation with Greece and the West to resolve the Cyprus problem and had called for building an effective defense for Cyprus. For his criticisms of the government, Evdokas was fined and temporarily jailed in 1970, but he was allowed to come out of jail and take part in the 1970 legislative elections.

Despite Evdokas's efforts to attract "clean" conservatives into the party ranks and to avoid the use of violence against the government, Evdokas found it difficult to cope with the Greek-sponsored subversion of the Cypriot government in the post-1967 period and with the extremism of the right-wing National Organization of Cypriot Fighters (*see* Cyprus introduction). Under these circumstances, the Democratic National Party became inactive in 1972. Evdokas resigned from the party in 1973, just before the presidential election, and he remained committed to change by dialogue, not violence.

In the two years following the 1974 Turkish intervention on Cyprus, the DEK rejected the principle of *enosis* as a viable solution for the island's problems and called instead for a truly independent and democratic republic. In 1976 the DEK formally dissolved, and most of its members—except its founder—joined the rightist Democratic Rally.*

DEMOCRATIC PARTY (Greek Cypriot, *Demokratiko Komma*: DEKO). The Democratic Party was established in 1976 as a result of the political realignment that occurred in the Greek Cypriot community in the aftermath of the 1974 coup, the Turkish intervention, and the divisions that emerged among President Makarios's former supporters. The Democratic Party can best be described as a coalition of liberal, center, and moderate Greek Cypriot political forces. Ranged on the political spectrum, the DEKO would have the Democratic Rally* on its right, and on its left the communist Progressive Party of the Working People* and the social-democratic Unified Democratic Union of the Center.* The DEKO founder was Spyros Kyprianou, a close Makarios associate since the days of the anticolonial struggle. A British-educated lawyer, Kyprianou also served for 12 years as the first foreign minister of Cyprus. He succeeded Makarios to the presidency following the latter's death on August 3, 1977.

In the legislative elections of 1976, the Democratic Party won 21 of the 35 Greek Cypriot seats in the Cypriot House of Representatives, although its strength has been considerably reduced by defections prior to the 1981 parliamentary elections. Those defectors formed or joined centrist or liberal parties such as the Center Union Party,* the New Democratic Front,* and the Pancyprian Renewal Front,* though they failed to get elected. Others joined the Democratic Rally. The DEKO, because of its makeup, enjoys support from a wide segment of the Greek Cypriot population, both urban and rural, and all its socioeconomic strata (including the business community, as a result of the party's preference for free enterprise). In its foreign policy and the problem of Cyprus, the DEKO has attempted to remain close to Makarios's principles of an independent, bicommunal, sovereign, territorially integrated, and nonaligned federal Republic of Cyprus. As of late, preference has also been expressed for the demilitarization of Cyprus.

Despite the preference for nonalignment and the criticisms directed toward the West for its role in Cyprus, the Democratic Party cannot be characterized as anti-Western. In seeking a negotiated settlement, the party emphasizes the implementation of United Nations resolutions; maintains that internationalization and ties with the Third World and Eastern bloc will assist in such a resolution; and the party views Turkey as the country with which the Cyprus government must deal to resolve the problems of the island. The DEKO also sees the necessity of close cooperation with the democratically elected mainland Greek government in reaching such a settlement. The party has been openly critical of Glafcos Clerides (founder of a DEKO rival, the Democratic Rally), who turned into a government critic after having been a former supporter of President Makarios. The Democratic Party has successfully cooperated with the Progressive Party of the Working People (AKEL) and the Unified Democratic Union of the Center (EDEK) in selecting DEKO founder Kyprianou as president of Cyprus and maintaining a common minimum foreign policy line, despite differences over the handling of domestic issues.

But in late Spring 1980, the DEKO came under attack, not only from its rival on the right (the Democratic Rally), but also from its allies on the left, the EDEK and AKEL. This clash indicated a breakdown in the three parties' previous consensus on foreign policy issues, as well as on Kyprianou's inability to perform as conciliator in the tradition of the late President Makarios. While the

EDEK has continued its qualified support of the overall foreign policy of the government, it has strongly criticized performance on issues such as the purge of the public service, the police, and the armed forces of those involved with the Greek junta and the 1974 coup in Cyprus, and the revelations of corruption in the agricultural cooperative movement which involved many DEKO supporters. The AKEL, in addition to these issues, late in May 1980 accused President Kyprianou of mishandling foreign policy and of being "inferior to the circumstances." Consequently, the AKEL officially declared that it withdrew its confidence and dissociated itself from the government.

In the 1981 parliamentary election, in which Greek Cypriot parties had not concluded a pre-election cooperation agreement, the DEKO ran third among the seven parties that participated in the elections, obtaining eight of the 35 seats. Postelection analyses indicated that many of the disenchanted DEKO voters may have voted for Clerides's Democratic Rally. But despite the defections suffered by the DEKO, the party survived and remains the main force in the center of Cypriot politics. Its candidate for speaker of the House of Representatives, George Ladas, won with the support of the AKEL.

DEMOCRATIC PEOPLE'S PARTY (Turkish Cypriot, *Demokratik Halk Partisi:* DHP). The DHP's founder is Nejat Konuk, former leader of the National Unity Party (UBP)* and first prime minister of the Turkish Federated State of Cyprus. Founded in 1979 by UBP defectors, the Democratic People's Party held five seats and was the third-largest party in the Turkish Cypriot parliament. The party's first actual electoral test was in the 1980 local elections, where the DHP ran a distant fourth against the UBP, the Republican Turkish Party,* and the Communal Liberation Party* in the three major towns of the Turkish-held section of Cyprus. Just prior to the 1981 elections, the DHP absorbed the Populist Party,* whose leader, Alper Orhon, became the DHP's sixth deputy.

In the 1981 parliamentary elections, both the UBP and the DHP were affected by popular dissatisfaction with the conservative parties, and therefore the DHP's strength was reduced to three seats. Osman Orek, a founder of the DHP, and Alper Orhon, both leading members of the party, failed to get elected. The DHP presidential candidate, Husamettin Tanyar, ran a distant fourth, receiving only 4.8 percent of the vote. Although the DHP is now the fourth-largest party in the Turkish Cypriot parliament, its leader, Nejat Konuk, was elected speaker with UBP support. The DHP's secretary-general is Ismet Kotat, who also served under the UBP as minister of labor, cooperatives, and rehabilitation.

The Democratic People's Party maintains that the Turkish Cypriots are an "inseparable and unbreakable part of the great Turkish nation." Philosophically, the DHP classifies itself as a social-democratic party, believing in equality, freedom, interdependence, unity, and solidarity. It upholds the principles of nationalism, revolutionism, populism, and secularism as defined by Turkey's Kemal Atatürk, and the party is against all forms of exploitation and colonialism. Finally, the DHP is against state monopolies and intervention in the economy, preferring policies that strengthen the private economic sector and promote confidence in it.

DEMOCRATIC RALLY (Greek Cypriot, *Demokratikos Synagermos:* DS). The Democratic Rally is the latest party to be formed by Glafcos Clerides. (About Clerides's earlier involvement in Greek Cypriot political parties, *see* Patriotic Front and Unified Party.)

Formed prior to the 1976 legislative elections, the DS became the rallying point of the most conservative and right-wing elements in Cyprus that have advocated nonviolent opposition to the government. Upon the Rally's formation, it was joined by members of Clerides's defunct Unified Party, as well as by former members of the also-conservative Democratic National Party.* Under the collaborative party arrangements during the 1976 elections the DS received no seats, despite the fact that it polled 25 percent of the Greek Cypriot vote. Clerides, former speaker of the Cypriot House of Representatives and Greek Cypriot interlocutor in the intercommunal talks, failed to get elected.

But after the 1976 elections, President Makarios instituted an advisory body in which all major party leaders, including Clerides, participated. Clerides resigned from this council in 1978 in disagreement with the policies of the next president, Spyros Kyprianou of the Democratic Party, and has since called for the president's resignation. Clerides is opposed to the electoral system as applied in the past and charged the collaborating parties with undermining the Cypriot political system.

In the absence of collaborative party arrangements in the 1981 parliamentary elections, the Democratic Rally won 12 of the 35 seats in the Cypriot House of Representatives. In the popular vote, Clerides's party ran a close second to the communist Progressive Party of the Working People (AKEL),* receiving 31.9 percent of the vote, and thus consolidating its position as the major conservative party in Cyprus and as the parliamentary opposition to the government of President Spyros Kyprianou. The increase in the share of votes claimed by the DS can be attributed to a shift by disaffected voters from the Democratic Party.*

The high percentage of votes cast for the DS and AKEL may indicate an emerging polarization in Cypriot politics. It may also indicate a shift among the voters toward parties that have adopted a softer line in the handling of intercommunal talks with the Turkish Cypriots.

The Democratic Rally is clearly the most conservative, free-enterprise, and pro-Western of the Greek Cypriot parties at this time. In facing the Cyprus problem, Clerides (since his 1976 dismissal as Greek Cypriot interlocutor in the intercommunal talks) has openly disagreed with the government's handling of the problem, despite his former years of support for government policies. He rejects Makarios's neutralism on the grounds that it has not protected Cypriot interests; nor, he believes, can reliance on the United Nations be seen as offering any help to Cyprus. Without ignoring the Third World or the Eastern bloc, Clerides now advocates working with the Western powers and close cooperation with Greece to resolve the Cyprus problem; he calls for increasing the defensive capabilities of Cyprus; and seeks a negotiated settlement at the shortest possible time. In contrast to the liberal forces in Cyprus, the Democratic Rally is against the suggestion to "cleanse" the Cypriot state of those who had collaborated with the Greek junta up to 1974. Finally, the DS is against any form of cooperation with the communists on the grounds that they will ultimately betray parliamentary democratic principles.

Clerides's formation of the DS marked a turning point in his progressive shift to the right of Greek Cypriot politics. The incorporation into the DS of most conservative and right-wing political forces is also indicative of the emerging polarization in Greek Cypriot politics which was not evident in earlier years. Clerides's conservatism, his pro-Western preferences, and his handling of important issues since 1974 have raised accusations from other Greek Cypriot parties that he and the DS may be serving Western interests in Cyprus, a charge vehemently denied by Clerides and other DS leaders.

DEMOCRATIC UNION OF CYPRUS (Greek Cypriot, *Demokratiki Enosis Kyprou*: DEK). This DEK was another in the sequence of Greek Cypriot right-wing parties that functioned from 1959 to 1968 in the Cypriot political arena. (*See also* Democratic National Party, *Demokratikon Ethnikon Komma*, DEK.) The Democratic Union was established by John Clerides, father of Glafcos Clerides who founded the Patriotic Front* in 1960. Following John Clerides's death, the DEK was chaired by Dr. Themistocles Dervis, founder of the Cypriot National Party (KEK).* Actually, most of the KEK's leading members followed Dervis into the DEK.

The Democratic Union, much like the KEK, was a personality party with no serious organizational structure. The DEK's main objective was to warn the Greek Cypriots of the dangers posed by the independence agreements signed by President Makarios in London in 1959. The DEK's founder ran against Makarios in the 1960 presidential election; and with support from the communist Progressive Party of the Working People,* John Clerides received nearly 33 percent of the Greek Cypriot vote. It should be noted that Glafcos Clerides worked against his father's candidacy by supporting Makarios.

Also much like the KEK, the Democratic Union failed to appeal either to labor or to farmers, who were clearly Makarios's supporters. The DEK accused Makarios of creating personality-cult politics and of undermining the achievements of General Grivas and his National Organization of Cypriot Fighters (*see* Cyprus introduction) in the struggle for independence. Still further, the Makarios government was accused of being behind the terrorism faced by many of the DEK's leading members (such as the kidnapping of its newspaper editor and assassination attempts against the party's vice-chairman, Dr. Polydorides).

Given the involvement of Western powers in Cypriot politics and problems, the DEK remained critical of these powers, despite the DEK's conservative and anticommunist character.

The Democratic Union broke apart in 1968 with the deaths of many of its original members and the discrediting of the Cypriot right wing by its association with the pre-1974 Greek junta.

DEMOKRATIK HALK PARTISI. *See* DEMOCRATIC PEOPLE'S PARTY.

DEMOKRATIKI ENOSIS KYPROU. *See* DEMOCRATIC UNION OF CYPRUS.

DEMOKRATIKO KOMMA. *See* DEMOCRATIC PARTY.

DEMOKRATIKON ETHNIKON KOMMA. *See* DEMOCRATIC NATIONAL PARTY.

DEMOKRATIKOS SYNAGERMOS. *See* DEMOCRATIC RALLY.

DHP. *See* DEMOCRATIC PEOPLE'S PARTY.

DS. *See* DEMOCRATIC RALLY.

EDEK. *See* UNIFIED DEMOCRATIC UNION OF THE CENTER.

EK. *See* CENTER UNION PARTY.

ENIEA DEMOKRATIKI ENOSIS KENTROU. *See* UNIFIED DEMOCRATIC UNION OF THE CENTER.

ENIEON. *See* UNIFIED PARTY.

ENOSIS KENTROU. *See* CENTER UNION PARTY.

EOKA. *See* CYPRUS INTRODUCTION.

ETHNIKI ORGANOSIS KYPRION AGONISTON. *See* CYRPUS INTRO-DUCTION.

HALKCI PARTI. *See* POPULIST PARTY.

HP. *See* POPULIST PARTY.

IRP. *See* REFORMATION AND WELFARE PARTY.

ISLAHAT REFAH PARTISI. *See* REFORMATION AND WELFARE PARTY.

KEK. *See* CYPRIOT NATIONAL PARTY.

KIBRIS MILLI TÜRK BIRLIGI. See CYPRUS TURKISH NATIONAL UNION.

KKK. See PROGRESSIVE PARTY OF THE WORKING PEOPLE.

KMTB. See CYPRUS TURKISH NATIONAL UNION.

KYPRIAKON ETHNIKON KOMMA. See CYPRIOT NATIONAL PARTY.

MHP. See NATIONAL GOAL PARTY.

MILLI HEDEF PARTISI. See NATIONAL GOAL PARTY.

NATIONAL GOAL PARTY (Turkish Cypriot, *Milli Hedef Partisi*: MHP). Formed in 1981 prior to the elections in the Turkish-controlled section of Cyprus, the MHP is headed by Faik Basharan. In the presidential elections, the MHP endorsed Raouf Denktash of the National Unity Party* for being a leader in the freedom struggle of the Turkish Cypriot community and as a proponent of Turkism. In the elections for the Turkish Cypriot parliament, the MHP ran only in the Famagusta district, appealing almost exclusively to the Turkish mainland settlers inhabiting primarily in that area. However, the MHP performed poorly, receiving 0.35 percent of the vote in the Famagusta district and 0.13 percent of the total vote.

The National Goal Party is a Turkish nationalist party whose platform is a less developed version of that of the Turkish Union Party (TBP).* Like the TBP, the MHP stands for economic self-sufficiency, advocates independence from foreign countries, considers the Turkish Cypriot community as undetachable from the Turkish nation, and is one more example of the penetration of the Turkish Cypriot community by right-wing Turkish mainland political forces.

NATIONAL ORGANIZATION OF CYPRIOT FIGHTERS. See CYPRUS INTRODUCTION.

NATIONAL SOLIDARITY. See NATIONAL UNITY PARTY.

NATIONAL UNITY PARTY (Turkish Cypriot, *Ulusal Birlik Partisi*: UBP). The National Unity Party was founded in September 1975 by Raouf Denktash, president of the Turkish Federated State of Cyprus, former president of the Turkish Cypriot Communal Chamber, and Turkish Cypriot interlocuter in the 1968-1974 intercommunal talks. The UBP is the outgrowth of a political organization led by Denktash known as National Solidarity (*Ulusal Dayanisma*) that had participated in the 1970 Turkish Cypriot communal elections.

In the first legislative elections that were held in the Turkish Federated State of Cyprus in June 1976, the National Unity Party won 30 of the 40 seats in the new Turkish Cypriot parliament. The UBP also won eight of the 11 major mayoralties and nearly half of the elected village headmen in the 1976 local elections. However, by Summer 1978 the party's parliamentary strength had been reduced to 26 deputies; and by Summer 1980, the UBP sat only 23 deputies, following defections generated by ideological reasons, the inability of the party to cope with the problems of the Turkish Cypriot economy, and accusations of corruption in the leadership ranks. Five of these lost seats were held by members of the Democratic People's Party,* founded by former UBP leader Nejat Konuk in 1979. The other two former UBP deputies became independents.

The declining appeal of the UBP was also shown in the 1980 local elections. While in 1976 the party had received nearly 53 percent of the overall votes cast, that vote was down to about 40 percent of the total in 1980. The Communal Liberation Party* seems to have been the primary beneficiary of the UBP losses. It should be noted, however, that in 1976 much of the UBP opposition was not yet well organized and did not participate fully in the local elections; this organizational problem was overcome by 1980, and the opposition's greater electoral successes illustrate the UBP's actual declining support.

The 1981 parliamentary and presidential elections in the Turkish Cypriot community confirmed the electorate's shift away from the conservatives. Running against four other candidates, Raouf Denktash was reelected president of the Turkish Federated State of Cyprus. But his share of the vote had been reduced to 51.7 percent. The UBP also suffered a major setback in the parliamentary elections, obtaining only 18 of the 40 seats, thus losing its control of the parliament. As a result of these elections, the Turkish Cypriot community has entered a period of coalition or even minority governments. At the time of this writing, the efforts for a UBP coalition with the Democratic People's Party (a UBP splinter) and the Turkish Union Party* (for a total of 21 of the 40 seats) had not produced results.

The National Unity philosophy is close to that of the Justice Party of mainland Turkey, that of a conservative party emphasizing its loyalty to the principle of social justice and reforms undertaken in Turkey by Kemal Atatürk. The UBP has tried to appeal to all Turkish Cypriots. On the Cyprus problem, the party stresses the quality of the two ethnic communities in an independent, bizonal, nonaligned federal Cypriot Republic. Consequently, the UBP recognizes the government of the Republic of Cyprus as only the administrative organ of the Greek Cypriot community; refuses to recognize the validity of United Nations resolutions on Cyprus; supports the active involvement of Turkey and Greece in the negotiations for a solution to the Cyprus problem; and sees the presence of the Turkish Army in Cyprus as a basic safeguard for the Turkish Cypriot community.

In the economic sphere, the National Unity Party advocates the coexistence of public and private sectors, with strong preference shown for the private sector. The UBP maintains an active organizational structure throughout the area under Turkish Army jurisdiction. The party leadership consists primarily of lawyers, and in the UBP ranks one finds most major political figures active in Turkish Cypriot politics since the end of World War II, with the notable exception of Dr. Fazil Kuchuk, founder and leader of the Cyprus Turkish National Union.*

NEA DEMOKRATIKI PARATAXI. *See* NEW DEMOCRATIC FRONT.

NEDEPA. *See* NEW DEMOCRATIC FRONT.

NEW DEMOCRATIC FRONT (Greek Cypriot, *Nea Demokratiki Parataxi*: NEDEPA). The NEDEPA was formed late in 1980 by Alekos Michaelides, a centrist businessman/politician and defector from the Democratic Party (DEKO).* Michaelides had served as speaker of the House of Representatives following the election of the DEKO's Spyros Kyprianou to the presidency. Because of his position as speaker, and because he served as acting president during Kyprianou's overseas travels, this relatively unknown newcomer to Cypriot politics gained prominence in Cyprus and abroad. Michaelides was considered by many as the future leader of the DEKO. His defection from the party was due to personal differences with President Kyprianou, who retained the leadership of the party after his election to the presidency.

   The NEDEPA's platform is essentially similar to that of the Democratic Party. In the 1981 parliamentary elections, the NEDEPA ran last among the seven parties that contested the Greek Cypriot elections, receiving 1.9 percent of the vote. Alekos Michaelides failed to get elected.

PAME. *See* PANCYPRIAN RENEWAL FRONT.

PANCYPRIAN RENEWAL FRONT (Greek Cypriot, *Pankyprio Anorthotiko Metopo*: PAME). The PAME was formed late in 1980 by Dr. Chrysostomos Sofianos, the popular minister of education who had served under both Presidents Makarios and Kyprianou. Frequently accused by Cypriot conservatives of being a communist, Sofianos's defection from the Kyprianou (Democratic Party*) government was due to both personal and ideological reasons. Kyprianou possesses neither Makarios's charismatic personality, nor the ability to balance diverse forces. Moreover, after his election to the presidency, Kyprianou maintained his leadership of the Democratic Party.

   Ideologically, the PAME is a liberal-democratic party, sharing many of the social and political ideas of the Unified Democratic Union of the Center (EDEK).* Sofianos, despite his popularity and name recognition, failed to get elected to the Cypriot House of Representatives in the 1981 elections. His party ran a distant fifth among the seven parties contesting those elections, receiving 2.79 percent of the vote. (It should be noted, however, that the PAME received the largest vote among the three parties that were formed by defectors from the Democratic Party coalition.) The PAME's failure can be explained by the fact that in competing for a place in the left-center of the Cypriot political arena, it did not possess the strength, organizational structure, and ideological fervor and appeal of parties such as the EDEK and the communist Progressive Party of the Working People.* Dr. Sofianos received nearly 14 percent of the vote in his home district of Paphos, defeating Alekos Michaelides of the New Democratic Front* (another Democratic Party splinter). But in the process, Sofianos hurt the EDEK the most by taking away that party's democratic-socialist voters. Two themes dominated Sofianos's campaign: the threat posed by the resurgence of right-wing forces in Cyprus through the legitimacy given to them by the Democratic Rally,* and the Cypriot rather than the Greek identity of the Greek Cypriot community.

PANKYPRIO ANORTHOTIKO METOPO. See PANCYPRIAN RENEWAL FRONT.

PATRIOTIC FRONT (Greek Cypriot, *Patriotikon Metopon*: PM). Founded in 1960, the Patriotic Front was a loose coalition of Greek Cypriot nationalists supporting President Makarios. It was headed by Glafcos Clerides, an Oxford-trained lawyer and speaker of the Cypriot House of Representatives. The PM had no particular social base or clear ideology. It thus encompassed all extremes of Greek Cypriot politics, except the communist Progressive Party of the Working People (AKEL).* Clerides's staunch anticommunism was notably evident in 1960 when he opposed the presidential candidacy of his father, John Clerides (founder of the Democratic Union of Cyprus*), who ran his campaign with support from the AKEL.

The PM, being a loose coalition, allowed considerable individual expression among its members. Initially successful, in the 1960 elections to the Cypriot House of Representatives the PM won 30 of the 35 seats allocated to the Greek Cypriots by the constitution. But in the late 1960s, as Clerides attempted to bring the party under his personal control, the PM split apart and thus provided the founding members for the new political parties that emerged in Greek Cypriot politics.

The overall foreign policy of the Patriotic Front was based on the principles of an independent, sovereign, unitary, nonaligned Republic of Cyprus. *Enosis* was only a distant goal of the party in the aftermath of independence. Following the breakdown of the Cypriot republic in 1963 and the withdrawal of the Turkish Cypriot legislative representatives from the affairs of the republic, the Patriotic Front provided President Makarios with the necessary legislative backing to pursue his policy of "unfettered independence" for Cyprus and later to engage in negotiations with the Turkish Cypriots for restructuring the Cypriot state.

In other policy areas, the PM displayed primarily a pro-business attitude and attempted not to antagonize Greece or the West. The party thus received wide support from such groups as the middle class, the business community, and professionals. The association of many cabinet members with the PM gave the party additional influence, particularly in the rural areas of Cyprus. The breakup of the Front was due largely to Clerides's inability to bring the party under his control and to the pressures exerted against the Cypriot government by the junta that seized control of the mainland Greek government in 1967.

After the dissolution of the Patriotic Front, many members were attracted to the Progressive Front,* and the PM's social democrats formed the Unified Democratic Union of the Center.* Clerides continued in Greek Cypriot politics by founding the Unified Party* in 1969 and later the Democratic Rally* in 1976.

PATRIOTIKON METOPON. See PATRIOTIC FRONT.

PK. See PROGRESSIVE PARTY.

PM. See PATRIOTIC FRONT.

POPULIST PARTY (Turkish Cypriot, Halkci Parti: HP). Founded in 1975 by Alper Orhon, a Turkish-educated economist, the Populist Party won two seats in the 1976 Turkish Cypriot parliamentary elections. In 1977 the HP suffered a defection of one of its original two deputies to the Communal Liberation Party.* Then, just prior to the 1981 elections, the Populist Party merged into the Democratic People's Party (DHP),* with Alper Orhon becoming the DHP's sixth parliamentary deputy. In the setback suffered by the DHP in the 1981 elections, however, Orhon failed to get reelected.

The Populists were dedicated to social-democratic principles. The party was considered left-of-center and was seen by many as an extension of mainland Turkey's Republican Party. Much like the other opposition parties of the Turkish Cypriot community, the HP endorsed the November 1976 resolution of the Turkish Cypriot parliament on the Cyprus problem. The Populists advocated close cooperation with Turkey in the handling of the Cyprus issue and had often stated that if Turkey was to depart from its support of an independent, non-aligned, bizonal, federal Republic of Cyprus, then the HP would follow Turkey's lead on the matter. The Populists frequently condemned the Turkish Cypriot leadership and the ruling National Unity Party* for their inept handling of the Cyprus problem and for the lack of consultation with the opposition parties in preparation of the negotiating proposals that have been submitted.

Along with the other opposition parties (the Communal Liberation Party and the Republican Turkish Party), the HP criticized National Unity for lack of economic planning; the preferential treatment given to select members of the private sector; and National Unity's inability to deal with corruption, unemployment, and inflation. The Populist Party therefore supported strikes by civil servants and other workers. The party was also critical of the dependence on Turkey for the economic development of the northern (Turkish Cypriot) part of the island, which has brought into Cyprus the economic instability of Turkey. Although the HP accepted that private enterprise has a place in the economy, the party warned against excessive profits and domination of the economy by the private sector. The Populists showed preference for popularly controlled, state-run economic enterprises; for the participation of workers and their organizations in development planning; and for the democratization of economic life. Thus the Populist Party was against any form of political or economic exploitation and stood firm on the principles of Turkey's Kemal Atatürk. In addition, the HP was critical of the cooperation between the National Unity Party's right wing and mainland Turkey's Justice Party and Nationalist Action Party. Consequently, the Populists joined the other Turkish Cypriot opposition parties against the philosophy and policies of the ruling National Unity Party.

PP. *See* PROGRESSIVE FRONT.

PROGRESSIVE FRONT (Greek Cypriot, *Proodeftiki Parataxis*: PP). The Progressive Front was established in 1970 and won seven of the 35 seats allotted to the Greek Cypriots in the legislative elections of that year. The PP was founded by Dr. Odyseas Ioannides and Andreas Azinas, the director of Cyprus' agricultural cooperatives. The party drew its strength from the *Panagrotike Enosis Kyprou* (PEK), the right-wing farmers' union; and the PP attracted many disappointed members of the defunct Patriotic Front* and Unified Party* who had not found adequate influence in those groupings led by Glafcos Clerides. Actually, in the 1970 elections the PP was the Unified Party's primary rival on the right. The Progressive Front attempted to appeal to the same conservative constituency as the Unified Party, though the PP never succeeded in becoming a serious threat. The primary difference between the two parties was not ideological but their bases of support, with the PP seeking the rural vote and PEK's support, but even there having a difficult time competing against the Unified Party.

Given its right-wing orientation, the Progressive Front faced serious internal dissension soon after the 1970 election. The right wing of Cypriot politics, with the support of the mainland Greek junta, had attempted to subvert the Cypriot government and eventually staged the 1974 coup against President Makarios. On this issue, the PP's rightist membership found itself torn apart. Members such as Azinas supported Makarios; while others, such as Ioannides and his coalition partner, Nicos Sampson (*see* Progressive Party), supported the *enosis* activities of the right-wing dissidents. Following the 1974 coup in Cyprus, Sampson was appointed president of the island by the military who had seized control of the government for a few days. Ioannides became Sampson's minister of health. Under the impact of the 1974 coup and the subsequent Turkish intervention, the Progressive Front fell apart and was officially disbanded in 1976.

PROGRESSIVE PARTY (Greek Cypriot, *Proodeftiko Komma*: PK). The Progressive Party was the personal grouping of Nicos Sampson, created for the sole purpose of promoting his candidacy in the 1970 legislative elections. The PK is now defunct in the aftermath of the 1974 coup staged by the Cypriot National Guard with support from the mainland Greek junta.

During the anticolonial struggle, Sampson was a well-known member of the National Organization of Cypriot Fighters (EOKA: see Cyprus introduction), and he was made famous by his terrorist actions. After independence, Sampson remained committed to the cause of *enosis* (union of Cyprus to Greece), leading his attack against President Makarios through his own newspaper, *Machi*. Sampson also offered the support of his private militia to the Progressive Front,* giving political muscle to that party. Much of Sampson's criticism of Makarios was largely due to Sampson's being left out of an influential position in the government. Also, Sampson and his party were staunchly anticommunist and opposed Makarios's neutralism toward that ideology.

When the July 15, 1974, coup was carried out in Cyprus, Sampson was appointed president to replace Makarios. Lasting for only a few days in that position, Sampson was eventually arrested and tried in 1976. He was convicted for his participation in the coup; and after serving more than three years of his term, he was allowed to leave for western Europe for "medical reasons."

PROGRESSIVE PARTY OF THE WORKING PEOPLE (Greek Cypriot, *Anorthotikon Komma Ergazomenou Laou*: AKEL). The AKEL is clearly the oldest and largest political party in Cyprus. Founded in 1926 as the Communist Party of Cyprus (KKK), the grouping joined the Comintern in 1928 and was banned by the British colonial administration in 1933. With its current name of the AKEL, the party was restructured in 1941 and has since been headed by Ezekias Papaionnou.

Much of AKEL's power base comes from the close control exerted by the party on the Pan-Cypriot Federation of Labor, which represents some 50 percent of the unionized workers in Cyprus. In the 1960 legislative elections, the AKEL claimed five of the 35 seats allocated to the Greek Cypriots by the constitution. Its representation in the 1970 and 1976 elections increased to nine seats. However, the AKEL has often claimed that it has accepted a lower number of seats in the Cypriot House of Representatives, especially in the 1960 elections, than its actual membership warrants. Also, the AKEL has expressed preference for a proportional representation system, instead of the collaborative arrangement allocating seats among the cooperating parties. In the absence of such collaborative party arrangements in the 1981 elections, the AKEL emerged as one of the two largest Greek Cypriot parties, commanding 32.8 percent of the vote and winning 12 of the 35 seats in the Cypriot House of Representatives.

The AKEL has been set up to promote the interests of the working class of Cyprus. It is a communist party, based on the teachings of marxism-leninism, proletarian internationalism, and scientific socialism. The AKEL thus considers itself to be the only true marxist-leninist party in Cyprus, and it has been accused by its opponents, within and outside of Cyprus, of being subservient to Moscow even at the time of Eurocommunism. The AKEL has attempted to appeal to all working people in Cyprus, including workers, farmers, artisans, professionals, and the intelligentsia, and the party maintains a disciplined organization.

Although it disagrees with the government's social policy, the AKEL (until 1980) supported the government's foreign policy, given the urgency of the problems facing the republic. The communists have also cooperated with the other major parties in supporting a common minimum foreign policy program. The primacy of foreign policy issues has forced the AKEL to deemphasize the party's domestic objectives, and this has brought considerable criticism from the social democrats of the Unified Democratic Union of the Center.*

The AKEL stands for social and agricultural reform; advocates purging the state apparatus and the armed forces of right-wing elements; and has promoted a rapprochement with the Turkish Cypriots. The AKEL believes in an independent, nonaligned, demilitarized, federal, bicommunal Republic of Cyprus, under international guarantees, and along the lines of the 1977 Makarios-Denktash agreement and the 1979 Kyprianou-Denktash agreement (*see* Cyprus introduction). The party supports the intercommunal talks as the method of resolving the internal aspects of the Cyprus problem (such as constitutional, territorial), while it calls for an international conference to deal with external aspects (demilitarization, withdrawal of foreign forces, termination of the 1960 Treaties of Alliance and Establishment, international guarantees). This view is also shared by the Soviet Union.

In the pre-independence period, the AKEL found itself caught between the dogmatism of its platform and the political power exerted in Cypriot society and politics by the Orthodox Church of Cyprus. The church led the fight for *enosis* (union of Cyprus to Greece), an objective of wide appeal among the Greek Cypriots. Yet given the legal prohibition of all communist activity in mainland Greece and Greece's total commitment to the West in the post-World War II period, the AKEL found itself lukewarm, if not opposed, to *enosis*. Instead, the AKEL quietly favored self-determination for Cyprus, thus creating suspicion, if not also friction, with the nationalists. As a result, the communists were not allowed to participate openly in the anticolonial struggle of the popular National Organization of Cypriot Fighters (*see* Cyprus introduction) and were excluded from the grand coalition of the Patriotic Front.*

In the 1960 elections, the AKEL opposed President Makarios's candidacy, instead offering its support to John Clerides of the Democratic Union of Cyprus,* but the party soon concluded a truce with the president and received five of the 35 seats in the Greek Cypriot side of the House of Representatives. Upon Makarios's death in August 1977, the communists cooperated with the social-democratic Unified Democratic Union of the Center and with the Democratic Party* to select the latter's founder, Spyros Kyprianou, as the next president of the republic. Until recently, the AKEL had fully supported the government and enjoyed full freedom of action (especially because of Makarios's distrust of the right wing and the discrediting of the rightists in the post-1967 period in Cyprus).

However, on March 3, 1980, the AKEL addressed a memorandum to President Kyprianou outlining its views on major policy issues in an attempt to preserve political unity and to maintain the common policy agreed upon earlier.

Dissatisfied with the president's response, the party's Plenum and Central Committee adopted and made public on May 30, 1980, a lengthy statement by which it withdrew its confidence in the government.

Expressing concern about the deadlock in the intercommunal talks, the AKEL statement attributed this stalemate not only to Western imperialism and Turkish as well as Turkish Cypriot chauvinism, but for the first time also blamed the "unsuitable handlings, lack of daring and determination" on the part of the president. In addition, the statement declared the AKEL's opposition to: the government's handling of issues relating to the purge of the public service, police, and armed forces from those cooperating in the 1974 coup; taxation; the corruption in the agricultural cooperative movement; and the slow implementation of the rapprochement policy with the Turkish Cypriot community.

The party's decision to "dissociate" itself from the Kyprianou government was justified on the grounds of "protecting the general interests of the struggle for salvation and vindication of our cause." The communists went on to call for a spirit of compromise on the part of the government in an attempt to resume the intercommunal negotiations, and for the strict adherence to the 1977 Makarios-Denktash agreement and the 1979 Kyprianou-Denktash agreement.

Since the ideological debate that broke out between the AKEL and the Unified Democratic Union of the Center (EDEK) in 1979, signs were evident that the foreign policy consensus developed by the AKEL, EDEK, and the moderate Democratic Party was coming apart. However, the withdrawal of the AKEL's confidence in the government represented a dramatic step that some noncommunist political observers attributed to a policy change originating in Moscow. The EDEK has even gone further to suggest that the AKEL had accepted the partition of Cyprus and had indirectly become an ally of the rightist Democratic Rally* and Western imperialism. With the reopening of the intercommunal negotiations late in 1980, President Kyprianou's planned trip to Moscow in Fall 1981, and the outcome of the 1981 elections, the AKEL once more extended its support to the government and provided the votes that elected the Democratic Party candidate as speaker of the House of Representatives. Therefore, one of the most important aspects of Cypriot politics in the years ahead will be how the AKEL utilizes its political power, now that it has formally emerged as one of the two largest Greek Cypriot political parties.

Further Reference. Adams, Thomas W., *AKEL: The Communist Party of Cyprus* (Stanford, Calif.: Hoover Institution Press, 1971).

PROODEFTIKI PARATAXIS. *See* PROGRESSIVE FRONT.

PROODEFTIKO KOMMA. *See* PROGRESSIVE PARTY.

REFORMATION AND WELFARE PARTY (Turkish Cypriot, *Islahat Refah Partisi:* IRP). The IRP was founded in 1979 by a retired noncommissioned officer, Mr. Ozer Ergene. The party represents another example of Turkey's ideological penetration into the Turkish Cypriot community. The IRP ideology is identical to that of Professor Necmettin Erbakan's traditionalist National Salvation Party (MSP) in Turkey.

The IRP platform calls for a professional volunteer army; the abolition of "meaningless" taxes, including those on salaries, wages, and profits of the working people; limiting the size of the government bureaucracy and establishing a "scientific and moral" administration. As an anticommunist party, the IRP calls for legislation "to give a definite end to the extremist ideological doctrines and moves bent on toppling the people's freedom through the abuse of such freedoms." The IRP also calls for an eight-year compulsory education system based on the teaching of Islam, ethics, and ways of recognizing "extremist and perverse" ideologies. Much like the MSP of Turkey, the IRP emphasizes a return to traditional Islamic values as a means of resisting the onslaught of modernization and Westernization, and the party sees Turkey's salvation in the non-Soviet East. Consequently, a good case can be made that such beliefs constitute a rejection of Atatürkism.

The IRP currently holds no seats in the Turkish Cypriot parliament, having not yet competed in any parliamentary elections. But in the 1980 local elections, the party ran last in the three major towns of the Turkish-held section of Cyprus.

Appealing to the extreme right of the Turkish Cypriot community, the IRP has attempted to incorporate into its ranks many of the settlers brought into Cyprus from the Turkish mainland since the 1974 Turkish invasion. Because of these actions, the IRP has been strongly criticized by the Communal Liberation Party* and the Republican Turkish Party.* These two latter parties have also expressed fears that the political violence prevailing in Turkey will be imported into northern Cyprus by parties such as the IRP.

REPUBLICAN TURKISH PARTY (Turkish Cypriot, *Cumhuriyetci Türk Partisi*: CTP). Founded in 1970 by A. M. Berberoglu, the Republican Turkish Party has been headed since 1976 by Ozker Ozgur, a Turkish-educated teacher and a parliamentary representative. Berberoglu ran unsuccessfully against Raouf Denktash (of the National Unity Party*) for the presidency of the Turkish Federated State of Cyprus in 1976. In that year's parliamentary elections, the party won only two of the 40 seats in the new Turkish Cypriot parliament.

In the 1981 presidential elections in the Turkish Cypriot community, Ozker Ozgur ran a distant third against Raouf Denktash of National Unity and Ziya Rizki of the Communal Liberation Party,* receiving 12.75 percent of the vote. But in the parliamentary elections, the CTP's strength increased to five seats as a result of the voters' shift away from the conservative parties.

The Republican Turkish Party is a social-democratic party, and it is clearly at the extreme left of the Turkish Cypriot political spectrum, identifying closely with the Republican Party in mainland Turkey. Although the CTP has endorsed the Turkish Cypriot parliament's November 1976 resolution on the principles for a settlement of the Cyprus problem, the CTP has gone beyond this resolution by advocating removal of the British sovereign bases from Cyprus; openly opposing the partition of Cyprus; accusing "British-American imperialism" for much of the problem of Cyprus; and characterizing Denktash's threats of unilateral independence by the Turkish Cypriots as the first step toward partition. With these qualifications, the Republican Turkish Party stands for an independent, nonaligned, federal Republic of Cyprus, set up on a geographic basis.

The CTP is the most outspoken of the Turkish Cypriot parties in favor of rapprochement with the Greek Cypriots. The party has repeatedly advocated the "unification of our divided country," and has emphasized its faith in intercommunal negotiations as the means of resolving the Cyprus problem. The CTP is strongly supported by the Turkish Cypriot trade union, DEV-IS. Because of its ideological positions, the party has been accused by the ruling National Unity Party (UBP) of being the representative of the Greek Cypriot's communist Progressive Party of the Working People (AKEL)* in the northern section of Cyprus. It should be noted that both the AKEL and the social-democratic Unified Democratic Union of the Center* (also a Greek Cypriot party) have repeatedly applauded CTP leader Ozgur for his political courage.

In the domestic sector, the social-democratic character of the CTP is reflected in its attack on the economic policy of the ruling UBP, which is seen as leading to profiteering and corruption by government officials, while failing to bring land reform and to deal with unemployment and inflation. The CTP has also condemned the UBP's and Denktash's rule as dictatorial, and has supported strikes by civil servants and other workers due to the government's failure to adopt a planned economy and to implement measures to assist the working classes. The Republicans' platform can be summarized as antifascist, anticapitalist, and antidictatorial.

The Republicans, since Spring 1978, have sought to cooperate with the other liberal opposition parties to bring down the UBP government. If in the aftermath of the 1981 elections the UBP is unable to form a new government, the Republicans are expected to attempt to join in a coalition with the Communal Liberation Party to form a government commanding 21 of the 40 seats in the Turkish Cypriot parliament.

SAP. *See* SOCIAL JUSTICE PARTY.

SOCIAL JUSTICE PARTY (Turkish Cypriot, *Soysal Adelet Partisi*: SAP). The SAP was formed just prior to the 1981 elections in the Turkish-controlled section of Cyprus by Turkish mainland settlers and some Turkish Cypriots. Because its founder, Salaheddin Oztokatli, has not yet qualified for citizenship in the Turkish Federated State of Cyprus, the party is run by a committee that includes Mehmet Kurumanastirli and Oktay Serbulent.

The SAP ran only in the Famagusta district, where Turkish mainland settlers are primarily concentrated. However, the party made a poor showing in the parliamentary elections, receiving only 0.24 percent of the vote in the district and 0.09 percent of the overall vote. In the presidential election, the SAP supported Raouf Denktash of the ruling National Unity Party.*

The SAP is ideologically similar to the Turkish Union Party* and competes for the same electorate of Turkish mainland settlers. With a limited platform, the party is pro-Turkish, nationalist, and conservative. The SAP stresses socio-economic justice and an eight-year, free and compulsory education system with emphasis on technical education. On the Cyprus problem, the party has declared its support for the November 5, 1976, resolution adopted by the Turkish Cypriot parliament. The SAP is one more example of the ideological penetration into the Turkish Cypriot community by right-wing mainland Turkish political forces.

SOYSAL ADELET PARTISI. *See* SOCIAL JUSTICE PARTY.

TBP. *See* TURKISH UNION PARTY.

TKP. *See* COMMUNAL LIBERATION PARTY.

TMT. *See* CYPRUS INTRODUCTION.

TOPLUMCU KURTULUS PARTISI. *See* COMMUNAL LIBERATION PARTY.

TÜRK BIRLIGI PARTISI. *See* TURKISH UNION PARTY.

TURKISH DEFENSE ORGANIZATION. *See* CYPRUS INTRODUCTION.

TURKISH UNION PARTY (Turkish Cypriot, *Türk Birligi Partisi*: TBP). Founded in 1979 by retired army officers, the TBP is an example of the ideological penetration of the Turkish mainland into the Turkish Cypriot community. The Turkish Union Party, which is still organizing its structure and platform, is the counterpart of Colonel Alparslan Türke's Nationalist Action Party (MHP) in Turkey, which has been accused of being a fascist party.

Calling itself a national socialist party, the TBP's philosophy is based on racialism and advocacy of the incorporation of the whole of Cyprus into Turkey. The party has attempted to bring into its ranks the extreme right of the Turkish Cypriot political spectrum, particularly the Turkish mainland settlers brought into Cyprus since the 1974 Turkish invasion. Its first electoral test was in the 1980 local elections, where it suffered a major setback. In the 1981 presidential election, the TBP supported Raouf Denktash of the ruling National Unity Party.* In the parliamentary elections of that year, the party's leader, Ismail Tezer, was elected as the TBP's only deputy, and he was elected from the Famagusta area where most Turkish mainland settlers are concentrated. (Tezer, a retired Turkish Airforce colonel, currently operates a hotel in the Turkish-controlled area of Cyprus.) Being the eldest deputy in the Turkish Cypriot parliament, Tezer acted as its temporary speaker at the opening session. Even though he is the party's only deputy, as a result of the 1981 election outcome Tezer's vote will be sought by any conservative government coalition, thus increasing the party's influence.

Because of its extremist ideology and its ties to the MHP in Turkey, the TBP has been attacked by both the Communal Liberation Party* and the Republican Turkish Party* for threatening the peace and cohesion of the Turkish Cypriot community, and for importing into the northern section of Cyprus the political violence practiced by Colonel Türke's "commandos" in the Turkish mainland. Both parties have also accused the ruling National Unity Party of tolerating, if not also encouraging, such political extremism of the TBP.

TÜRK MUKAVEMET TESKILATI. See CYPRUS INTRODUCTION.

UBP. See NATIONAL UNITY PARTY.

ULUSAL BIRLIK PARTISI. See NATIONAL UNITY PARTY.

ULUSAL DAYANISMA. See NATIONAL UNITY PARTY.

UNIFIED DEMOCRATIC UNION OF THE CENTER (Greek Cypriot, *Eniea Demokratiki Enosis Kentrou*: EDEK). Founded in 1969 by Dr. Vassos Lyssarides—confidant, advisor, and physician of the late President Makarios—the EDEK represents the moderate-left democratic-socialist forces in Cyprus. In the 1970 legislative elections, the party commanded only two of the 35 seats allocated to the Greek Cypriots by the constitution, but its strength increased to four seats in the 1976 elections.

In the absence of collaborative party arrangements in the 1981 elections, the EDEK ran a distant third, receiving 8.2 percent of the vote and three seats in the Cypriot House of Representatives, a loss of one seat compared to the 1976 elections. In the process, the deputy party leader, Takis Hadjidimitriou, failed to get elected.

The EDEK's key elements and supporters were first politically active in the Patriotic Front,* the loose, pro-Makarios coalition party. As Glafcos Clerides attempted to transform the Patriotic Front into a disciplined and conservative party, the progressives and democratic socialists split off to form the EDEK in 1969, soon after Clerides dissolved the Patriotic Front and formed the Unified Party.* The EDEK attempts to appeal to all working strata in Cyprus, including farmers, peasants, small businessmen, as well as the Cypriot intelligentsia and scientists. The party maintains an active organization throughout the free areas of the republic and claims to have in its ranks the only "progressive forces" that have been active in the anticolonial struggle (a clear reference to the inactivity of the communist Progressive Party of the Working People [AKEL]* during that period).

The EDEK's platform is based on the fundamental assumption that Cyprus started as a semi-independent state and today is a semioccupied state (that is, occupied by Turkey since 1974). Consequently, the first priority was and remains the liberation of Cyprus from foreign domination, dependence, and occupation; and until this is achieved, socioeconomic reform cannot be implemented. For these reasons, the EDEK has been described by some as having the characteristics of a national liberation-front movement. In practice, the EDEK maintains strong ties with such movements around the world, as well as with various socialist states. The party leader, Dr. Lyssarides, was one of the founders of the Afro-Asian People's Solidarity Organization in 1962. In this manner, he has been able to strengthen Cyprus' diplomatic position, given his ties and influence among the nonaligned and Third World nations.

In the domestic arena, the EDEK again calls for the conscription of people and resources to the national liberation struggle; proposes land reform; supports the expansion of a planned economic sector; advocates the nationalization of the country's banks and mineral resources; promotes the expansion of free education and of the national health program; and is committed to the equality of women. Although close to the communist AKEL in its economic policy, the EDEK—in addition to participation in the anticolonial struggle—differs from the AKEL over that party's support of the Soviet Union. The EDEK has also accused the AKEL of accepting a "middle-class life-style" of complacency and bureaucratization. Fearing that imperialist forces are instigating internal strife in Cyprus, the EDEK has consistently supported both President Makarios and his successor, President Kyprianou. Although it differs with the government over domestic policy, the EDEK expresses satisfaction that the party's general foreign policy is reflected in that of the republic. Since the Spring of 1980, the EDEK has become more vocal in its criticism of the government's performance on such domestic issues as the corruption in the agricultural cooperative movement, and the purge of the public service, police, and armed forces of those that supported the Greek junta and the 1974 coup in Cyprus. The EDEK has also openly criticized the handling of specific aspects of the Cyprus problem by the government, accusing it of departing from Makarios's foreign policy principles, failing to pursue the internationalization of the Cyprus problem, and the implementation of the United Nations resolutions on Cyprus.

An even more significant development has been the growing rift and ideological warfare that broke out early in June 1979 between the EDEK and the AKEL over the latter's commitment to the struggle for the liberation of Cyprus. The EDEK has interpreted the AKEL's withdrawal of confidence in the government, and the latter's calls for "bold steps" on the part of the Greek Cypriots in the intercommunal talks, as implying the acceptance of the fait accompli of Turkish occupation, the weakening of Cyprus, and of the AKEL's becoming an ally of the Democratic Rally* in the legalization of imperialist schemes against Cyprus.

As a result, the EDEK and the AKEL have engaged since then in major debates on these subjects through their newspapers, in parliament, and in public rallies.

The EDEK supports the principle of an independent, nonaligned, demilitarized Cyprus through the intercommunal talks and the implementation of United Nations resolutions on Cyprus. The party also advocates rapprochement with the Turkish Cypriots and has applauded the Turkish Cypriot's Republican Turkish Party* for its commitment to the same cause. In addition to its message of friendship to the Turkish Cypriots, the EDEK has called for a common struggle against the threat posed to all Cypriots by foreign occupation and imperialism. With the primacy of the liberation struggle, the EDEK calls for strong defenses against Turkey's threats, seeks the support of all who fight imperialism, and actively advocates the establishment of a Cypriot militia to guard against the recurrence of fascism in Cyprus. This dynamic party finds strength and influence not so much in its numbers, but in its activist and internationally recognized leadership and good organization.

UNIFIED PARTY (Greek Cypriot, *Enieon*). The Unified Party was established in 1969 by Glafcos Clerides, an Oxford-trained lawyer, speaker of the House of Representatives, and Cypriot interlocutor in the 1968-1974 intercommunal talks. Following the breakup of Clerides's Patriotic Front,* the Unified Party incorporated into its ranks the Front's conservative forces. In the 1970 legislative elections, the Unified Party received some 26 percent of the Greek Cypriot vote and 15 of the 35 seats allocated to the Greek Cypriots by the constitution. Refusing campaign support from the communist Progressive Party of the Working People,* Clerides was reelected speaker of the House with the support of the right-wing Progressive Front.*

The Unified Party became the vehicle for promoting the interests of the business community and the urban middle class. It was definitely a pro-Western party, committed to the principles of a free enterprise economy and private ownership. The party, up until the early 1970s, clearly supported President Makarios and defended the Hellenic character of an independent Cypriot state in which the Turkish Cypriots would enjoy guaranteed rights. By the time the party was established, union with Greece was seen as only a distant goal. And with the worsening of the crisis between the Greek junta and the Cypriot government, Clerides softened his criticism against Athens. In his many capacities as speaker of the House and chief interlocutor for the Greek Cypriots, he was accused by the liberals of being "soft" toward the Turks and the Greek junta. The party and Clerides himself came under severe pressures from within Cyprus following his temporary assumption of the Cypriot presidency in the aftermath of the collapse of the junta that briefly ruled Cyprus during Summer 1974.

In 1976, Clerides was dismissed as interlocutor because of his handling of negotiations with the Turkish Cypriots after Turkey's invasion. As a result, Clerides became a critic of President Makarios and his government. The combination of these problems and the upheaval within Cyprus caused by the 1974 Turkish invasion brought about the demise of the Unified Party in 1976. Many of its members joined the Progressive Front,* while others joined Clerides in forming yet another rightist party, the Democratic Rally.*

Van Coufoudakis

TABLE 10.   Distribution of Seats in Turkish Federated State of Cyprus' National Council since 1975 Establishment

Party	1976	1981
Communal Liberation Party	6	13
Democratic People's Party	—	3
National Unity Party	30	18
Populist Party	2	—
Republican Turkish Party	2	5
Turkish Union Party	—	1
Total	40	40

TABLE 11. Distribution of Seats in Cyprus' House of Representatives since 1960 Independence

Party	1960	1970	1976	1980[a]	1981
Greek Cypriot					
Democratic Party	—	—	21	19	8
Democratic Rally	—	—	0	1	12
Patriotic Front	30	—	—	—	—
Progressive Front	—	7	—	—	—
Progressive Party of the Working People	5	9	9	9	12
Unified Democratic Union of the Center	—	2	4	4	3
Unified Party	—	15	—	—	—
Independents	0	2	3	4	0
Total	35	35	37	37	35
Turkish Cypriot					
Cyprus Turkish National Union	15	b	c	—	—
Total (Greek & Turkish Cypriot)	50	35	37	37	35

[a] Elections were not held at this time. These figures reflect House composition as of Summer 1980 after party defections.
[b] The Turkish Cypriot representatives withdrew from the House in 1963 and did not participate in the 1970 elections.
[c] The Turkish Federated State of Cyprus was established February 13, 1975. First elections were held in 1976. See table 10.

CZECHOSLOVAKIA

The CZECHOSLOVAK SOCIALIST REPUBLIC (*Československá Socialistická Republika*) is a small industrialized state roughly the size of North Carolina. It is located in central Europe, surrounded by Poland, the two Germanies, Austria, Hungary, and the Soviet Union. Of the country's 15.25 million inhabitants (1979 estimate), about 64 percent are Czech and 30 percent Slovak. Hungarians, living mostly in Slovakia, represent the largest of several ethnic minorities. Approximately 70 percent of the people profess to be Roman Catholic, 15 percent belong to various Protestant denominations, and the remainder have no religious affiliation. Since 1969, Czechoslovakia has officially been a binational federal state composed of the Czech and Slovak Republics. Both Czech and Slovak are official languages.

Formal political life is centered in the Federal Assembly (*Federální shromáždění*), a bicameral body made up of a 200-member Chamber of the People (*Sněmovna lidu*), elected by proportional representation; and a 150-member Chamber of Nationalities (*Sněmovna národů*), with 75 seats for the Czechs and 75 seats for the Slovaks. Elections to both houses are held every five years, with universal suffrage beginning at 18 years of age. The current electorate is about 10.6 million.

Political activities throughout the land are organized and controlled by the National Front,* which incorporates many political and quasi-political organizations including several minor parties (for example, Czechoslovak People's Party,* Czechoslovak Socialist Party,* Party of Freedom,* Party of the Slovak Revival*). However, in matters of actual power and policy-making authority, the system is dominated by the Communist Party of Czechoslovakia (KSČ)* and its subsidiary, the Communist Party of Slovakia (KSS).*

Notwithstanding the one-party rule characterizing the current political system, Czechoslovakia has a rich and colorful party tradition reaching back to pre-independence days. Prior to the establishment of modern Czechoslovakia in 1918, the territories belonged to the Austro-Hungarian Empire. In the provinces of Bohemia, Moravia, and Silesia, a lively and pluralistic political development had taken place in the late 19th century, as Austrian rule encouraged the formation of parties among both the Czech and German ethnic communities. In the territories of Slovakia and Ruthenia, governed from Budapest under the Dual Monarchy, the more autocratic Hungarian rule discouraged political activism among the non-Hungarian nationalities; nevertheless, political grouping began to take place among the Slovaks between 1900 and 1914, and a few Slovak candidates were elected to the Hungarian parliament during this time. The founders of the Czechoslovak Republic therefore drew upon an already substantial political tradition as they laid the foundations of their new state (*see* table 12).

The First Republic (1918-1938) was a unitary state built upon a liberal, Western-style constitution. A bicameral parliament elected the president of the republic, who appointed the prime minister and cabinet. The powers of the chief executive were enhanced in practice by the republic's first president, Tomáš G. Masaryk, and his successor, Edvard Beneš. The sociopolitical atmosphere was generally quite libertarian, and strong emphasis was placed on individual rights. Although the population was ethnically diverse, the constitution accorded no corporate rights or privileges to ethnic or national groups. As a result, the state system was persistently challenged by secessionist and autonomist movements growing not only out of the large German minority, but also from within the substantial Slovak ultranationalist movement and the disaffected Hungarian minority.

The party system of the First Republic was pluralistic to the point of fragmentation. Party lines formed around ethnic, religious, and social-class identities, with crosscutting constituencies and splinter groups adding to the assortment. There were, for example, four socialist parties (including the KSČ and the German Social Democratic Party*), two ultranationalist Slovak parties (one Catholic and one Protestant), and various parties representing no fewer than seven ethnic constituencies (Czech, Slovak, German, Hungarian, Polish, Ukrainian, and Jewish). The total number of parties that came into being at one time or another is hard to determine, but as many as 29 offered candidates for election to the National Assembly in one single year (1925). Many parties proved to be ephemeral, but at least eight Czech and Slovak parties and three German parties were of national significance. No party ever approached majority status in the National Assembly; government coalitions were always composed of four or more parties (*see* table 13).

A combination of domestic and international factors caused the fall of the First Republic. Internally, the polity was weakened by intensified unrest on the part of German ultranationalists (*see* Sudeten German Party), stimulated and abetted by Hitler's regime across the borders. The Germans were joined by extremists in the Slovak People's Party* who demanded autonomy for Slovakia. Externally, Czechoslovakia came under increasing pressure from Nazi Germany and was abandoned by her French, British, and Russian allies. The Munich Agreement of September 1938 dictated the cession of the Sudetenland to Germany and compelled radical changes in Czechoslovakia's internal political structure. The resulting Second Republic granted autonomy to Slovakia and greatly restricted party activity, while curtailing democracy and civil liberties. Within six months this system gave way as Hitler's army occupied Bohemia and Moravia; Slovakia seceded to form a separate state allied with Germany, and sizable territories in the border regions were taken by Hungary and Poland. These events, occurring in March 1939, were the prelude to the political order of World War II; legitimate political parties ceased to exist in the Protectorate of Bohemia and Moravia, while Slovakia was ruled through a one-party system under the puppet dictatorship of Monsignor Jozef Tiso. Most of the major political leaders of the First Republic escaped into exile, but large numbers of their active followers and cohorts were incarcerated during the war.

Upon the war's end, the returned exile leaders and those who had survived the prison camps set about to reconstruct the polity on the basis of a limited, pluralist democracy. Their efforts were facilitated by the expulsion of the troublesome German minority. For the first time, the Communists agreed to participate in a coalition with other parties, and they played a crucial role in the reconstruction of the Czechoslovak state. In the new system, the former parties of the right were outlawed, and those parties allowed to regroup were brought together loosely within the framework of a National Front. Only four parties were allowed to organize in the Czech lands (the Communists, Socialists, People's Party, Czechoslovak Social Democratic Workers' Party*), and four in Slovakia (the Communists, the Labor Party,* the Party of Freedom, and the Democratic Party*). Edvard Beneš returned from exile to resume the presidency in this new system, now called the Third Republic.

This situation was not destined to last long. The coalition government, seriously divided on a range of questions both domestic and international, was rendered further unstable by the pressures of the Soviet Union. The state that had occupied and liberated most of Czechoslovakia in 1945 had a strong interest in the postwar political situation of its new ally and played an important, if mostly indirect, role in the Czechoslovak Communists' ascent to total power. This they accomplished in February 1948 in a bloodless coup d'état that ended the limited pluralism of the Third Republic and began the development of what is, in effect, a one-party monopoly.

In their drive to consolidate their power following February 1948, the Communist Party disposed of their political rivals in various ways. The Social Democrats were forced to merge with the Communist Party, while the Socialist and People's parties were statutorily compelled to limit their membership and functions to the point of impotence. The Slovak Democratic Party was disbanded and replaced by the insignificant Party of the Slovak Revival. The Party of Freedom had no real social basis in the beginning and was simply allowed to continue its essentially meaningless existence in perpetuity. The Slovak Labor Party, similarly weak, disintegrated. The National Front, established in 1945 as an overarching institution for regulating and coordinating the parties of the

Third Republic, was coopted by the KSČ in 1948 and has been under the Communists' strict control ever since.

In 1968 a short-lived reform government came into power under the leader-ship of Alexander Dubček (as first secretary of the KSČ), Oldřich Černík (as prime minister), and others. The reform government considered numerous pro-posals for change in the system of political participation; these included sugges-tions for revitalizing the National Front, giving increased importance to the minor parties, and allowing the return of an independent Social Democratic Party. However, before these issues could be resolved, Czechoslovakia was in-vaded by her allies, led by the Soviet Union. After some months of diplomatic pressure and domestic political uncertainty, the reformist leaders were replaced by a coalition of conservative and hard-line forces led by Gustáv Husák. In the resulting, so-called normalization of the political atmosphere, the single-party monopoly has been reaffirmed and the discussion of radical political alternatives forcibly prohibited.

Bibliography

Graham, Malbone W. "Parties and Politics." In Czechoslovakia, edited by Robert J. Kerner. Berkeley and Los Angeles: University of California Press, 1940.

Hapala, Milan E. "Political Parties in Czechoslovakia, 1918-1938." In Czechoslovakia Past and Present, edited by Miloslav Rechcígl, Jr., vol. 1. The Hague and Paris: Mouton, 1968.

Hoch, Charles. "The Political Parties in Czechoslovakia." Czechoslovak Sources and Doc-uments, no. 9. Prague: Orbis, 1936.

Korbel, Josef. Twentieth-Century Czechoslovakia. New York: Columbia University Press, 1977.

Kusin, Vladimir V. Political Grouping in the Czechoslovak Reform Movement. London: Macmillan, 1972; New York: Columbia University Press, 1972.

Kusin, V. V., and Z. Hejzlar. Czechoslovakia 1968-1969: Annotation, Bibliography, Chro-nology. New York: Garland, 1974.

Mamatey, Victor S., and Radomír Luža, eds. A History of the Czechoslovak Republic 1918-1948. Princeton, N.J.: Princeton University Press, 1973.

Paul, David W. The Cultural Limits of Revolutionary Politics: Change and Continuity in Socialist Czechoslovakia. Boulder, Colo., and New York: East European Quarterly and Columbia University Press, 1979.

Skilling, H. Gordon. Czechoslovakia's Interrupted Revolution. Princeton, N.J.: Princeton University Press, 1976.

Taborsky, Edward A. Communism in Czechoslovakia 1948-1960. Princeton, N.J.: Princeton University Press, 1961.

Ulč, Otto. Politics in Czechoslovakia. San Francisco: W. H. Freeman, 1974.

Political Parties

"AGAINST FIXED-ORDER LISTS." See NATIONAL FASCIST COM-MUNITY.

AGRARIAN PARTY. *See* REPUBLICAN PARTY OF FARMERS AND PEASANTS.

BUND DER LANDWIRTE. *See* GERMAN LEAGUE OF FARMERS.

ČESKOSLOVENSKÁ NÁRODNĚ-SOCIALISTICKÁ STRANA. *See* CZECHO-SLOVAK NATIONAL SOCIALIST PARTY.

ČESKOSLOVENSKÁ SOCIALNĚDEMOKRATICKÁ STRANA DĚLNICKÁ. *See* CZECHOSLOVAK SOCIAL DEMOCRATIC WORKERS' PARTY.

ČESKOSLOVENSKÁ STRANA LIDOVA. *See* CZECHOSLOVAK PEOPLE'S PARTY.

ČESKOSLOVENSKÁ STRANA NÁRODNĚ-DEMOKRATICKÁ. *See* CZECHO-SLOVAK NATIONAL DEMOCRATIC PARTY.

ČESKOSLOVENSKÁ STRANA SOCIALISTICKÁ. *See* CZECHOSLOVAK SOCIALIST PARTY.

COMMUNIST PARTY OF CZECHOSLOVAKIA (*Komunistická strana Československa*: KSČ). Czechoslovakia's Communist Party was founded in 1921 as the result of a split in the Czechoslovak Social Democratic Workers' Party.* With the support of the Communist International (Comintern), the left wing of the Social Democrats, led by Bohumír Šmeral, left the older party and formed the KSČ. The Communists quickly developed an electoral base within the now-factionalized working class, and in addition the party gained support from numerous groups among the more disaffected ethnic minorities who identified with the Communists' antipathy toward the political structure of the First Republic.

The new party soon found itself further divided over questions of revolution-ary strategy and was criticized by the Comintern in the mid-1920s for its alleg-edly insufficient appreciation of the class struggle. Continuing intraparty conflict culminated in the election of Klement Gottwald to the party's top position in 1929. The victory of Gottwald climaxed the rise of the left, and the new leadership proceeded immediately to carry out what it called the "bolsheviza-tion" of the KSČ: a weeding out of cadres and an increase in the polemical, revolutionary tone of the party's rhetoric. Yet another turn of policy was to come with the acceptance of the Comintern line on united-front tactics, coinciding with the signing of a mutual defense treaty between the Soviet Union and the Czechoslovak Republic in 1935. Although the KSČ made no attempt to enter a government coalition on the pattern of the French Popular Front (*see* FRANCE INTRODUCTION), the KSČ's rhetoric moderated at this time, and Gottwald himself led the party into a position of tacitly supporting the bourgeois regime. Indeed, the Communists proved later to be courageous defenders of the nation, publicly criticizing the Munich Agreement of 1938 and the Hácha government of the Second Republic. With the German occupation of Bohemia and Moravia, the Communists fell victim to political persecution, and many of them were imprisoned. In Slovakia the party was forced underground, and many Communists played a leading role in the resistance movement. Having separated from the KSČ in 1939 for tactical reasons, the now-illegal Slovak Communist Party joined other underground forces in fighting a guerilla war against the Tiso regime, culminating in the valiant but abortive Slovak National Uprising of 1944 (see Communist Party of Slovakia [KSS]).

The party's image of wartime resistance—a valid image, despite the fact that many of the top leaders escaped into exile, including Gottwald—enhanced the Communists' popular appeal in the immediate postwar years. Meanwhile, Gottwald developed a close relationship with Stalin during his wartime exile in the Soviet Union; this relationship was a key element in the pattern of the Czechoslovak-Soviet alliance, developed before the end of the war, and the eventual entry of Czechoslovakia into the Soviet camp. Returning to Prague in 1945, Gottwald led the KSČ into a coalition government under the auspices of the National Front.* In 1946 parliamentary elections were held in which the Communists openly and fairly won a plurality of the vote (38 percent, including the KSS vote in Slovakia). Although it must be borne in mind that this plurality was won in a field of parties that had been greatly reduced in comparison to the elections of the First Republic, it nonetheless represented an impressive gain over the KSČ's consistent tally of ten to 12.7 percent in the three elections between 1925 and 1935. As a result of the 1946 elections, Gottwald was appointed prime minister; in his cabinet, Communists held several strategically important portfolios, notably the ministries of agriculture, information, internal trade, finance, and the interior (including responsibility for the police and civil administration). From these vantage points they were able to manipulate a wide range of politically important functions, creating a solid base of social control even before their accession to total power.

The power takeover occurred in February 1948 following nearly a year of growing conflict within the National Front. In protest against the Communists' attempt to dominate and use the internal security forces for their own political benefit, most of the non-Communist cabinet members resigned in the hope that President Beneš would dissolve the government and form a new one on a basis less favorable to the Communists. Beneš vacillated, however, and communications between him and the non-Communist ministers broke down. The Communists now seized the broadcasting services, closed down noncommunist newspapers and party offices, and arrested a number of opposition leaders. The trade unions, also under Communist Party control, threatened a general strike. Gottwald now demanded that a new government be appointed in conformance with his wishes, and President Beneš complied. From this moment on, the Communists' control over the instruments of political power solidified. In June, the Social Democratic Party merged with the KSČ, and three months later the

Slovak Communist Party was formally brought back into the structure of the central party. The National Front quickly declined, becoming merely an extension of the KSČ.

From 1948 to 1968, the KSČ ruled Czechoslovakia unchallenged, following a general pattern of organization and rule modeled rather closely after that of the Communist Party of the Soviet Union (CPSU, see SOVIET UNION), to whose leaders the Czechoslovak Communists frequently turned for support and advice. Between 1950 and 1954, a massive purge was carried out on the urging of the CPSU, resulting in the removal of an estimated 550,000 people from party membership and the imprisonment of many hundreds of party members; some prominent Communist leaders, including the one-time first secretary, Rudolf Slánský, were executed for alleged crimes of treason and conspiracy. Political arrests spread throughout society as the secret police unleashed a wave of terror. The political violence that took place during these years was not unlike that occurring in other countries of the Soviet bloc, although many educated estimates suggest that the scope and intensity of the terror was greater in Czechoslovakia than in any other country of eastern Europe. The atmosphere of fear and insecurity produced by these events continued to pervade society for many years after the terror subsided.

The Communists' ruling policies followed lines similar to those of the CPSU, emphasizing the revolutionary transformation of the social and economic order, the leveling of incomes and class structure, the systematic reorientation of citizens' political values, and the mobilization of all productive forces for the building of socialism. Early statistics in the economic sectors seemed to indicate success in terms of gross production targets, but by the early 1960s the economy had fallen seriously out of balance and sunk into a state of stagnation. Subsequently, other problems became apparent: unrest among intellectuals, disillusionment among the youth, tension between Czechs and Slovaks, indications of incompetency throughout the ranks of party and government, and a growing sense of public alienation from the polity and its leaders. These factors prompted the changes in party leadership and the search for new political and economic policies that were undertaken in 1968.

The reforms of 1968, however, proved to be only a short-lived deviation from the more standard policy lines; the party's relaxation of social controls encouraged the activation of political forces outside the Communist Party, thereby seeming to threaten the KSČ's previously unchallenged authority and bringing on the intervention of Czechoslovakia's socialist allies. The policies that followed in the 1970s, therefore, were in large part motivated by an official desire to return to strict party control and stamp out all tendencies toward pluralism. As of this writing, the party has succeeded once again in eliminating all serious challenges to its rule. This it has done at the cost of a generalized public demoralization; despite the rise of organized dissent in the mid-1970s, centering in the Charter 77 movement, the regime's opponents have been prevented from enlisting the active support of the working masses.

The basic unit of KSČ organization is the party cell, or primary unit, organized mostly in local workplaces. The members of each primary unit, meeting in plenary session, elect a committee to direct the work of the party organization. The committee, in turn, elects a chairman, who is the most influential person on the local level. Connecting these primary organizational units to the top party levels are precinct units (in large cities), city or rural subdistrict units, district and regional organizations. At each of these levels, the members are nominally elected by the units immediately below, although the candidates are carefully screened from above. Again at each level, plenary sessions elect a committee that is given a wide array of functions; the committee elects a Bureau as its executive organ and a Secretariat to keep records and administer membership policies. These smaller bodies are very powerful for they have the authority to supervise and control all party activities at their respective levels. Of particular importance is the role of the Secretariat, which at each level of organization oversees the nomination of candidates for official positions within the party.

Above the regional organizations are those of the central party apparatus. (It should be mentioned that the Communist Party of Slovakia occupies a peculiar position between the regional party units in Slovakia and the central party institutions.) At the top level of the KSČ, the Party Congress is officially designated as the supreme party institution. It meets every four years, but the Central Committee is authorized to call an extraordinary congress between regular meetings of the Party Congress. (One notable extraordinary congress was called in Prague immediately following the Soviet invasion in 1968; the delegates met secretly to discuss the party's response to the occupation of their country.) The Party Congress elects a Central Committee, which according to party statutes is the most authoritative body operating between sessions of the Party Congress. However, actual power tends to concentrate in the Presidium of the Central Committee and the Secretariat, both of which are in theory elected by the Central Committee but in practice are self-appointing. In the mid-1970s, the Presidium numbered 11 full members and two candidate members, the Secretariat had six members, and the Central Committee had approximately 120 full members and 50 candidate members. At the top of the KSČ leadership at the time of this writing was Gustáv Husák, occupying the position of general secretary since replacing Alexander Dubček in April 1969.

In 1981 the party's total membership numbered 1,532,000 (including candidate members), or about 10 percent of the country's entire population. The KSČ is therefore a mass party, as it has been rather consistently since 1945. This was not always the case; from its original base of some 350,000 members in 1921, membership figures dropped off during the 1920s. Then, in keeping with Gottwald's desire to build a streamlined leninist party, the membership plummeted to just over 30,000 in the early months of the "bolshevization" drive; this figure increased to over 70,000 thereafter, but the mass base of the earlier years was not attained again until after World War II. The membership leaped to more than 2.5 million in the months following the February coup of 1948, but by the end of the purges the figure had fallen to less than 1.5 million. More recently, a major fluctuation occurred between January 1969 and December 1970 as the party's membership declined by more than 25 percent; this resulted primarily from the leadership's efforts to oust all those who had been implicated in what were officially termed "counterrevolutionary" activities in 1968.

Further Reference. Korbel, Josef, *The Communist Subversion of Czechoslovakia* (Princeton, N.J.: Princeton University Press, 1959); Král, Martin J. E., "Functions and Characteristics of Candidate Presidium Members of the Czechoslovak Communist Party" (Master's thesis, University of Washington, 1974); Skilling, H. Gordon, "The Formation of a Communist Party in Czechoslovakia," *American Slavic and East European Review* 14 (October 1955): 346-358; and "The Comintern and Czechoslovak Communism: 1921-1929," *American Slavic and East European Review* 19 (April 1960): 234-247; and "Gottwald and the Bolshevization of the Communist Party of Czechoslovakia, 1929-1939," *Slavic Review* 20 (December 1961): 641-655; Toma, Peter, "The Communist Party of Czechoslovakia," in *The Communist Parties of Eastern Europe*, edited by Stephen Fischer-Galati (New York: Columbia University Press, 1979); Wightman, G., and A. H. Brown, "Changes in the Levels of Membership and Social Composition of the Communist Party of Czechoslovakia, 1945-73," *Soviet Studies* 27 (July 1973): 396-417; Zinner, Paul E., *Communist Strategy and Tactics in Czechoslovakia, 1918-1948* (New York: Praeger, 1963).

COMMUNIST PARTY OF SLOVAKIA (*Komunistická strana Slovenska:* KSS). The KSS was founded as a party separate from the Communist Party of Czechoslovakia (KSČ)* in 1939 as a result of the political division of Czechoslovakia following the German occupation of Bohemia and Moravia. During World War II, the KSS led a strictly illegal existence, nevertheless playing an important role in the armed resistance that developed in the Slovakian hinterlands. During that time, the KSS was largely cut off from the exiled leaders of the KSČ, a factor that contributed to a certain espirit de corps among the Slovak Communists which was to persist after the war as well. Many Communists fought bravely in the Slovak National Uprising after the German occupation of Slovakia in 1944, and the memory of that unsuccessful uprising is honored today as a heroic part of Slovakia's national heritage.

Between 1945 and 1948, the KSS continued to be organized as a separate political party in the reunified Czechoslovakia, albeit in close alliance with the KSČ. In the 1946 elections, the KSS proved to be a rather weak partner, capturing only 30.4 percent of the votes cast throughout Slovakia and running a distant second to the right-wing Democratic Party.* Seven months after joining in the coup d'état of 1948, the KSS formally became a part of the KSČ, although maintaining a separate organizational structure within the parent body. Thus the KSS today has a special identity that is officially recognized. (There is no parallel organizational structure for the party in the Czech lands.)

During the purges of the early 1950s, the KSS suffered a particular form of political persecution as many Slovak Communists were punished for alleged crimes of "bourgeois nationalism." Several of the most prominent KSS leaders fell into this category and were imprisoned (for example, Gustáv Husák and

Ladislav Novomeský); and Vladimír Clementis, a former minister of foreign affairs, was executed. In the course of subsequent developments, the position of the KSS became increasingly weak, while the governmental and administrative institutions that had been set up in Slovakia in the immediate postwar years were similarly diminished in scope and importance.

These efforts at establishing vigorous central control over Slovakia engendered resentment among many Slovak Communists. Powerless to challenge political reality in the 1950s, they began a slow rise to prominence in the 1960s and ultimately sparked a wide-ranging discussion within the KSČ about the political and economic status of Slovakia. One spokesman for the Slovak viewpoint, Alexander Dubček, became first secretary of the KSČ and a leader of the 1968 reform government. He was succeeded in 1969 by an even more outspoken proponent of the Slovak cause, Gustáv Husák, who thus climaxed a startling political comeback by reaching the very pinnacle of power. From the 1968 discussions of the "Slovak problem" emerged a plan for the federalization of the republic; this was achieved after the Soviet-led invasion and went into effect on January 1, 1969, reorganizing Czechoslovakia into the present two, constituent republics. Separate administrative and judicial structures in the Czech Republic and Slovak Republic were given wide-ranging responsibilities. Both in design and in practice, the federal system has failed to live up to the hopes of the most ardent Slovak federalists. The Communist Party was not similarly federalized, despite much discussion of such a possibility in 1968, and therefore the preeminently powerful political organization within the country retains its centrally structured pattern of authority.

The Communists were traditionally weaker in Slovakia than in the Czech lands, owing largely to the lower level of social and economic development, the relative weakness of the working class, and the strength of religious beliefs in what was, until recently, a predominantly peasant society. In the First and Third Republics, the Communists consistently attracted a smaller percentage of votes in Slovakia than in Bohemia and Moravia; the strength of the Communist vote in the districts of Slovakia tended to correlate positively with the proportion of ethnic minorities in the population, particularly Hungarians and Ukrainians. At the time of the Communist takeover, the party's membership was only 210,222, compared to 1,329,450 members in the KSČ of Bohemia and Moravia; thus the KSS accounted for only 13.7 percent of the Communists' total membership in Czechoslovakia at that time. Since then, the general tendency has been toward an increase in the KSS membership in both relative and absolute terms. In 1976 the KSS numbered approximately 310,000 members or roughly 22.4 percent of the total within the KSČ.

Further Reference. Lipták, L'ubomír, *Slovensko v 20. storočí* (Bratislava: Vydavatel'stvo politickej literatúry, 1968); Steiner, Eugen, *The Slovak Dilemma* (Cambridge: At the University Press, 1973).

ČSL. *See* CZECHOSLOVAK PEOPLE'S PARTY.

ČSS. *See* CZECHOSLOVAK SOCIALIST PARTY.

ČSSD. *See* CZECHOSLOVAK SOCIAL DEMOCRATIC WORKERS' PARTY.

CZECHOSLOVAK NATIONAL DEMOCRATIC PARTY (*Československá strana národně-demokratická*). The National Democrats, a right-wing party in the First Republic, traced their ancestry to the rise of modern Czech nationalism in the political order of the Austro-Hungarian Empire. Their immediate forebears, called the Young Czech Party, had emerged in the 1860s as a radical offshoot of the National Liberal Party (the "Old Czechs"); the latter was a conservative group that disintegrated and disappeared in the latter decades of the 19th century.

In 1918 the Young Czechs and several smaller groups merged to form what was first called the Czech State-Rights Party but which changed its name in 1919 to the Czechoslovak National Democratic Party. Several very important leaders of the Czech independence movement and, after 1918, the first (provisional) Czechoslovak government belonged to this party. Among them were Karel Kramář, the republic's first prime minister, and Alois Rašín, the first finance minister. In the parliamentary elections of 1920, however, the party's sixth-place finish signaled a weakness in its social base, which consisted primarily of large industrial and financial interests; in 1925 the party fell to tenth place with only four percent of the total vote. Thereafter the party turned ever more toward the right, espousing Czech nationalism and very conservative social policies. In 1935, Kramář (by then hostile to the government) led his party into an alliance with the National Fascist Community.* The resulting movement was called the National Union.* After World War II, the National Democrats were not allowed to reorganize.

CZECHOSLOVAK NATIONAL SOCIALIST PARTY (*Československá národně-socialistická strana*). Founded in 1897 in reaction to the internationalism of the Czech Social Democratic Party (*see* Czechoslovak Social Democratic Workers' Party), the National Socialist Party was a nonrevolutionary socialist party that focused its attention on domestic, Czechoslovak problems. An important party of the center-left in the First and Third Republics, the National Socialists were a consistent partner in government coalitions and the party with which the republic's second president, Edvard Beneš, was affiliated. The party was reduced to a subservient role in 1948, however, when it was renamed the Czechoslovak Socialist Party.*

CZECHOSLOVAK PEOPLE'S PARTY (*Československá strana lidova*: ČSL). The ČSL has been a minor party since 1948, existing within the National Front* as a nominal representative of Czechoslovakia's Roman Catholics. It publishes an official newspaper, *Lidova demokracie*. Like the Czechoslovak Socialist Party,* the ČSL is organized only in Bohemia and Moravia, and its membership and functions are strictly controlled.

The ČSL has a long history, formed in 1904 and emerging after 1918 as a centrist Roman Catholic union based on several pre-independence groups. Its early leader, Monsignor Jan Šrámek, was an influential figure in the First Republic. The party's base among Roman Catholics was diminished by the 1922 split that developed between Czech and Slovak groupings, resulting in the reestablishment of a separate Slovak People's Party. *

The ČSL participated in the National Front system between 1945 and 1948, but the party was quickly and ruthlessly reduced to puppet status following the communist takeover. Amid the democratic stirrings throughout society in 1968, the question of revivifying the ČSL was discussed. However, despite a relatively rapid increase in the party's membership, the subject was not resolved by the time of the Soviet-led invasion that stopped all discussion of new political alternatives.

CZECHOSLOVAK SOCIAL DEMOCRATIC WORKERS' PARTY (Československá socialnědemokratická strana dělnická: ČSSD). A "Czechoslav" branch of the Austrian Social-Democratic Party (see AUSTRIA) was founded in the Czech lands in 1878, and a Slovak wing of the Hungarian Social Democratic Party (see HUNGARY) emerged in 1905. Both were affiliated with the Second International. Although each was in theory committed to the international working-class movement, both developed nationalistic tendencies and moved close to the nationality movements in the Austro-Hungarian Empire. Upon Czechoslovakia's independence, the two branches merged into one party and for a short time became the most powerful political force in the new state.

Following the party's plurality (25.7 percent of the vote) in the 1920 parliamentary elections, ČSSD leader Vlastimil Tusar became prime minister. The party's preeminence was short-lived, however, as the left wing split off to form the Communist Party of Czechoslovakia (KSČ) * in 1921. Thereafter the Social Democrats lost considerable ground, falling to 8.9 percent of the popular vote in 1925. By the end of the interwar period, the party had regained some of its earlier strength (13 percent in 1929, 12.6 percent in 1935) but never again reached the position it had held in 1920. Nevertheless, the ČSSD was a frequent participant in the coalition governments of the First Republic.

The party's electoral base was centered in the working class, and indeed there developed a keen rivalry between the ČSSD and the KSČ for influence among the trade unions. Except for the 1925 elections, the ČSSD generally attracted more votes than did the KSČ; and throughout the interwar period, the larger percentage of trade unions were affiliated with the ČSSD. The party's ideological position, reflecting a moderate socialist stance, seemed more appealing to the Czech and Slovak workers than the strident revolutionary ideology of the KSČ; and the ČSSD's attitude of cooperation with the government of the First Republic was similarly more popular than the Communists' generally antipathetic position.

The Social Democrats suffered very great losses during World War II as the party's leadership in the Czech lands was quickly and relentlessly persecuted by the German occupying forces. In Slovakia the party went underground and merged with the Communist Party of Slovakia* in 1944. The ČSSD that emerged following liberation was a truncated party, operating only in the Czech lands and having lost the best part of its previous leadership.

In the period leading up the the Communists' 1948 coup, a fatal split developed again within the ČSSD—the left wing (led by Zdeněk Fierlinger) moved closer to the KSČ, anticipating a partnership with the Communists, while the right wing (led by Bohumil Laušman) opposed the Communists' effort to gain power through illegal means. At the moment of the coup, the left managed to gain control over the party and announced its solidarity with the Communists. Four months later, the ČSSD was formally absorbed by the KSČ.

In the 1968 discussions of political reform, a number of former Social Democrats raised the question of reviving their defunct party. A preparatory committee was formed, and negotiations took place with certain KSČ leaders. The Communists, however, steadfastly rejected the proposal to allow the revival of an independent ČSSD—a prospect that Czechoslovakia's socialist-bloc allies found particularly objectionable—and no such development had occurred by the time of the Soviet-led invasion.

Further Reference. Horak, Jiri, "The Czechoslovak Social Democratic Party 1938-1945" (Ph.D. diss., Columbia University, 1960); Nedvěd, Jaroslav, "Cesta ke sloučení sociální demokracie s Komunistickou stranou v roce 1948," *Rozpravy Československé akademie věd* 78 č. 8 (1968).

CZECHOSLOVAK SOCIALIST PARTY (*Československá strana socialistická:* ČSS). A minor party within the National Front* system of contemporary Czechoslovakia, the ČSS has been systematically limited in its political role since 1948. In contrast, its predecessor, the Czechoslovak National Socialist Party,* had been an influential force in the political system of the First Republic; a consistent partner in coalition governments; and the party with which the republic's second president, Edvard Beneš, was affiliated.

The National Socialists reorganized within the National Front in 1945, but the party (renamed the Czechoslovak Socialist Party after the communist coup) was forced into a subordinate position after February 1948. The party's leaders made an unsuccessful attempt in 1968 to enhance the ČSS's position in the political order. Today, the party's role is that of a puppet organization. Its main contact with the public is maintained through the publication of the party's strictly controlled newspaper, *Svobodné slovo*. The ČSS has no organization in Slovakia.

CZECH STATE-RIGHTS PARTY. *See* CZECHOSLOVAK NATIONAL DEMOCRATIC PARTY.

DEMOCRATIC PARTY (*Demokratická strana:* DS). The DS arose in Slovakia in 1944 as a coalition of centrist and rightist groups that had opposed the wartime

Tiso regime. As a part of the postwar National Front* system, the DS caused some controversy among its coalition partners in 1946 by allying itself with Slovak Catholic spokesmen, some of whom had been associated with the newly-outlawed Slovak People's Party.* In the 1946 elections, the Democratic Party received a big majority in Slovakia—62 percent—though the party's vote total (just under one million) represented only about one-seventh of the tally in the republic as a whole. Because of its obvious strength in Slovakia, the party was quickly attacked by the communists following the 1948 coup; the DS was effectively dissolved and was replaced by the impotent Party of the Slovak Revival.*

DEMOKRATICKÁ STRANA. See DEMOCRATIC PARTY.

DEUTSCHE SOZIALDEMOKRATISCHE PARTEI. See GERMAN SOCIAL DEMOCRATIC PARTY.

DS. See DEMOCRATIC PARTY.

GERMAN LEAGUE OF FARMERS (*Bund der Landwirte*). An important minority party of the First Republic, the League of Farmers became the first German group to adopt an "activist" (meaning "cooperative") stance vis-à-vis the Prague government. The party's leader, Franz Spina, served in governments continuously between 1926 and 1938.

GERMAN SOCIAL DEMOCRATIC PARTY (*Deutsche Sozialdemokratische Partei*). Initially, the German Social Democratic Party was organized as the Sudeten branch of the Social Democratic Party of Germany (SPD) (*see* HISTORICAL GERMANY). The strongest party of the German minority prior to the rise of the Sudeten German Party,* the German Social Democrats in Czechoslovakia occupied an ideological position on the left, similar to that of the Czechoslovak Social Democratic Workers' Party.* On the national question, the Sudeten SPD initially favored secession, but the party shifted its position dramatically in the course of the 1920s to one of staunch loyalty to the Czechoslovak republic; the party's leader, Ludwig Czech, served in First Republic governments from 1929 to 1938. Like the Czechoslovak Social Democratic Workers' Party, the Sudeten SPD split into two groups in 1921, the left wing joining the Communist Party of Czechoslovakia.*

HLINKA'S SLOVAK PEOPLE'S PARTY. See SLOVAK PEOPLE'S PARTY.

HLINKOVA SLOVENSKÁ L'UDOVA STRANA. See SLOVAK PEOPLE'S PARTY.

HSL'S. See SLOVAK PEOPLE'S PARTY.

KOMUNISTICKÁ STRANA ČESKOSLOVENSKA. See COMMUNIST PARTY OF CZECHOSLOVAKIA.

KOMUNISTICKÁ STRANA SLOVENSKA. See COMMUNIST PARTY OF SLOVAKIA.

KSČ. See COMMUNIST PARTY OF CZECHOSLOVAKIA.

KSS. See COMMUNIST PARTY OF SLOVAKIA.

LABOR PARTY (Strana práce). An ephemeral group organized in 1946 by right-wing social democrats in Slovakia, the Labor Party attracted 3.1 percent of the Slovakian vote in the 1946 parliamentary elections (0.7 percent of the total votes cast in Czechoslovakia).

NÁRODNÍ FRONTA. See NATIONAL FRONT.

NÁRODNÍ OBEC FAŠISTICKÁ. See NATIONAL FASCIST COMMUNITY.

NÁRODNÍ SJEDNOCENÍ. See NATIONAL UNION.

NATIONAL FASCIST COMMUNITY (Národní obec fašistická). Formed in 1927 under the leadership of General Rudolf Gajda, the National Fascist Community was an ultranationalist Czech fringe party. Running under the label "Against Fixed-Order Lists" in the 1929 parliamentary elections, the Fascists received slightly less than one percent of the total vote. They joined with the Czechoslovak National Democratic Party* in 1935 to form the National Union*; the latter was dissolved in 1937. The Fascists attempted to make a comeback during the German occupation of Bohemia and Moravia, and they played a brief role in the wartime government. However, because of their strident Czech nationalism, the German occupation authorities did not trust them, and their role was limited to a minor one. The National Fascist Community was dissolved and outlawed at the end of the war.

Further Reference. Havránek, Jan, "Fascism in Czechoslovakia," in Native Fascism in the Successor States, 1918-1945, edited by Peter F. Sugar (Santa Barbara, Calif.: ABC Clio, 1971); Zacek, Joseph F., "Czechoslovak Fascism," in Native Fascism in the Successor States, 1918-1945, edited by Peter F. Sugar (Santa Barbara, Calif.: ABC Clio, 1971).

NATIONAL FRONT (Národní fronta: NF). Shortly before the end of the war in 1945, the leaders of six Czechoslovak parties in exile agreed to join in a broad coalition of the left that would set up the postwar government and begin the process of reconstruction. The parties involved were the Communist Party of Czechoslovakia (KSČ),* the Communist Party of Slovakia,* the Czechoslovak Social Democratic Workers' Party,* the Czechoslovak National Socialist Party,* the Czechoslovak People's Party,* and the (Slovak) Democratic Party.* The former parties of the right as well as the minority parties were not allowed to reorganize on the grounds that some or all of their leaders had become tainted by collaboration with the Germans.

Between 1945 and 1948 the NF attempted to coordinate the policies of the constituent parties. The NF program was a moderate-to-radical social reform platform, advancing the nationalization of large industry, redistribution of agricultural holdings, a mixed economy guided by short-term plans, and a system of local government reorganized around so-called national committees. The constitution of the First Republic was essentially retained, albeit with few changes such as the granting of a limited autonomy to Slovakia. It soon became apparent that the NF was unable to withstand the conflicts developing among its constituent parties; and with the Communists' move toward total power in 1948, the coalition collapsed.

Under Communist rule, the NF became subordinate to the KSČ and was turned into a highly structured umbrella under which all mass organizations throughout the country were obliged to find their home. Leadership with the NF is drawn from the top representatives of the various organizations operating under its supervision (such as the trade unions; youth movements; women's societies; and other institutions organized around professional, service, and recreational interests). Thus in addition to its directly political functions—which include the supervision of elections organized on the basis of a single slate of candidates certified by the NF—the Front has become a major intermediary between the Communist Party and the society. All social organizations must be approved and registered by the NF, and any that provoke official disapproval can be disbanded by the Front.

In 1968 the discussions concerning reforms in the system of political participation centered on the role of the NF. Many proposals were raised for a revitalization of the Front, and the possibility of a multiparty system within NF auspices was put forward. The Soviet-led invasion put an end to these discussions, and since then the NF has continued its role as an instrument of the ruling party's (KSČ's) control system.

NATIONAL LIBERAL PARTY. See CZECHOSLOVAK NATIONAL DEMOCRATIC PARTY.

NATIONAL UNION (Národní sjednocení). The National Union was an alliance formed in 1935 by the National Fascist Community,* the Czechoslovak National Democratic Party,* and some smaller fringe groups. The National Union received 7.6 percent of the vote in the 1935 parliamentary elections. The Union was dissolved in 1937.

NF. See NATIONAL FRONT.

OLD CZECHS. See CZECHOSLOVAK NATIONAL DEMOCRATIC PARTY.

PARTY OF FREEDOM (*Strana slobody*). The Party of Freedom was organized in Slovakia in 1946. It was never more than a splinter party with a total membership of fewer than 1,000. In 1946 the party received 3.7 percent of all votes cast in Slovakia (0.9 percent of those in Czechoslovakia).

PARTY OF NATIONAL UNITY. *See* SLOVAK PEOPLE'S PARTY.

PARTY OF THE SLOVAK REVIVAL (*Strana slovenské obrody*). Following the 1948 dissolution of the Democratic Party,* the Party of the Slovak Revival was established within the National Front.* Organized only in Slovakia, the party has no substantial social base, and its membership has never surpassed 1,000. Although the party has no effective political power, it publishes an official newspaper, *L'ud*.

REPUBLICAN PARTY OF FARMERS AND PEASANTS (*Republikánská strana zemědělského a malorolnického lidu*). The Republican Party of Farmers and Peasants, also called the Agrarian Party, was founded in 1922 when two older parties, the Czech Agrarian Party and the Slovak National Republican and Peasant Party, merged. The resulting political organization became the strongest party of the First Republic, appealing to both large and small farmers among Czechs and Slovaks alike. At no time did the party's share of the total vote exceed 15 percent; however, the Agrarians were represented in every government coalition during the lifetime of the First Republic. The party's founder, Antonín Švehla, served twice as prime minister and was one of the most influential politicians in the republic until his death in 1929. Despite the moderate, right-centrist character of the party's ideological position, a number of its leaders gravitated toward the far right in the late 1930s, and some eventually fell into collaboration with the German occupational forces. For this reason, the Agrarians were not allowed to resume their activities in 1945, and the party was outlawed.

Further Reference. Paleček, Anthony, "Antonín Švehla: Czech Peasant Statesman," *Slavic Review* 21 (December 1962): 699-708.

REPUBLIKÁNSKÁ STRANA ZEMĚDĚLSKÉHO A MALOROLNICKÉHO LIDU. *See* REPUBLICAN PARTY OF FARMERS AND PEASANTS.

SdP. *See* SUDETEN GERMAN PARTY.

SLOVAK NATIONAL REPUBLICAN AND PEASANT PARTY. *See* REPUBLICAN PARTY OF FARMERS AND PEASANTS.

SLOVAK PEOPLE'S PARTY (*Slovenská l'udova strana*: SL'S). Also known as Hlinka's Slovak People's Party (*Hlinkova slovenská l'udova strana*: HSL'S). The Slovak People's Party was founded in 1913 under the leadership of Father Andrej

Hlinka, whose name was added to that of the party in 1925. Following the 1920 parliamentary election, the SL'S entered into an alliance with the Czechoslovak People's Party*; this ended in 1922 with the Slovak group's disgruntlement over the Czech group's cooperation with the centralist government. The SL'S/HSL'S thereafter pursued a policy of opposition to the unitary state, consistently calling for a constitutional change granting autonomous powers to Slovakia. The HSL'S briefly participated in a government coalition (1927-1929) but thereafter returned to a position of increasingly hostile opposition.

The HSL'S attracted right-wing Slovak nationalists, ranging from clericalist-conservatives to fascists. Hlinka himself favored Slovak autonomy within the Czechoslovak Republic, but some extremist elements within the HSL'S preferred secession. Shortly before his death in 1938, Hlinka flirted with the ultranationalist Sudeten German Party*; however, it was left to his successor, Monsignor Jozef Tiso, to carry this move further. Tiso became prime minister of autonomous Slovakia during the ephemeral Second Republic; and upon Nazi Germany's occupation of Bohemia and Moravia, he became ruler of the new Slovak Republic, nominally independent but in reality a closely controlled satellite of the Third Reich. At this point, the party's name was officially changed to the Party of National Unity, but it continued to be referred to in common parlance as the HSL'S.

In power, the party monopolized political life in Tiso's clerical-fascist dictatorship. Its two paramilitary wings, the Hlinka Guards and the Hlinka Youth, were modeled to a great extent after the SS and the *Hitler-Jugend*. Upon the collapse of the Slovak Republic and the 1945 reestablishment of a unified Czechoslovak state, the party was outlawed.

SLOVENSKÁ L'UDOVA STRANA. *See* SLOVAK PEOPLE'S PARTY.

SL'S. *See* SLOVAK PEOPLE'S PARTY.

SMALL TRADERS' PARTY. *See* TRADESMEN'S PARTY.

STRANA PRÁCE. *See* LABOR PARTY.

STRANA SLOBODY. *See* PARTY OF FREEDOM.

STRANA SLOVENSKÉ OBRODY. *See* PARTY OF THE SLOVAK REVIVAL.

SUDETENDEUTSCHE HEIMATFRONT. *See* SUDETEN GERMAN PARTY.

SUDETENDEUTSCHE PARTEI. *See* SUDETEN GERMAN PARTY.

SUDETEN GERMAN HOMELAND FRONT. *See* SUDETEN GERMAN PARTY.

SUDETEN GERMAN PARTY (*Sudetendeutsche Partei*: SdP). The Sudeten German Party had been founded in 1933 under the name of the Sudeten German Homeland Front (*Sudetendeutsche Heimatfront*). Its name was changed in 1935. The SdP was an extremist organization that based its support on nationalistic impulses within the German minority. The rise of the SdP within the German community was phenomenal; at first expressing loyalty to the constitutional structure of the First Republic, the party successfully attracted more than two-thirds of the German vote in 1935 and, indeed, emerged from the elections with the largest tally of any party in Czechoslovakia (1,249,530 votes: 15.2 percent of the total). In subsequent years, the SdP was instrumental in whipping up separatist sentiment among its followers, becoming a fifth column in the Czechoslovak Republic. Konrad Henlein, the party's founder and leader, drew into a close alliance with Adolf Hitler (*see* HISTORICAL GERMANY) and helped precipitate the international crisis that led to the demise of Czechoslovakia in 1938-1939.

Further Reference. Bruegel, J. W. *Czecholovakia before Munich* (Cambridge: At the University Press, 1973); Lemberg, Eugen, and Gotthold Rhode, eds., *Das deutsch-tschechische Verhältnis seit 1918* (Stuttgart: Kohlhammer, 1969).

TRADESMEN'S PARTY (*Živnostenská strana*). Also called the Small Traders' Party and organized in 1920 as a splinter from the Czechoslovak National Democratic Party,* the Tradesmen's Party represented the specific class interests of independent retailers and craftsmen. The party's ideological position was right of center, and it tended to cooperate with the Republican Party of Farmers and Peasants* in parliament. Its high-water mark was reached in the 1935 elections when the party won 5.4 percent of the vote and 17 seats in the lower house. Disbanded during the war, the Tradesmen's Party was not allowed to reorganize afterward.

YOUNG CZECH PARTY. *See* CZECHOSLOVAK NATIONAL DEMOCRATIC PARTY.

ŽIVNOSTENSKÁ STRANA. *See* TRADESMEN'S PARTY.

David W. Paul

TABLE 12. Distribution of Seats in Czechoslovakia's *Snemovna Lidu* during the Czechoslovak Republic, 1920-1946

Party	1920	1925	1929	1935	1946
Communist Party of Czechoslovakia	—	41	30	30	114
Czechoslovak National Democratic Party[a]	19	13	18	17	—
Czechoslovak National Socialist Party	24	28	32	28	55
Czechoslovak People's Party	21	31	25	22	46
Czechoslovak Social Democratic Workers' Party	74	29	39	38	37
German League of Farmers	13	24	16	5	—
German Social Democratic Party	31	17	21	11	—
Republican Party of Farmers and Peasants[b]	40	46	46	45	—
Slovak People's Party[c]	12	23	19	22	48
Sudeten German Party	—	—	—	44	—
Tradesmen's Party	6	13	12	17	—
German minority parties[d]	26	30	29	6	—
Hungarian minority parties[d]	10	4	9	9	—
Independents and others	5	1	4	6	5
Total	281	300	300	300	305

[a] In 1935, fused with the National Fascist Community to form the National Union.
[b] The 1920 results include the Czech Agrarian Party, the Slovak National Republican and Peasant Party.
[c] After 1925, known as Hlinka's Slovak People's Party.
[d] Based on designated ethnic constituencies permitted to elect representatives to the legislature.

TABLE 13.   Ruling Coalitions in Czechoslovakia since 1918

Years	Coalition
1918-1919	All-party coalition
1919-1920	Czechoslovak Social Democratic Workers' Party Czechoslovak National Socialist Party Republican Party of Farmers and Peasants Czechoslovak National Democratic Party
1920-1921	Nonpartisan government
1921-1922	Czechoslovak National Democratic Party Czechoslovak Social Democratic Workers' Party Republican Party of Farmers and Peasants Czechoslovak People's Party Independents
1922-1925	Republican Party of Farmers and Peasants Czechoslovak National Democratic Party' Czechoslovak Social Democratic Workers' Party Czechoslovak People's Party
1925-Mar. 1926	Republican Party of Farmers and Peasants Czechoslovak National Democratic Party Czechoslovak Social Democratic Workers' Party Czechoslovak People's Party Tradesmen's Party
Mar. 1926-Oct. 1926	Nonpartisan government
1926-1928	Republican Party of Farmers and Peasants Slovak People's Party Tradesmen's Party German League of Farmers German Christian Social Party
1928-1929	Republican Party of Farmers and Peasants German League of Farmers German Christian Social Party Slovak People's Party Czechoslovak National Democratic Party
1929-1932	Republican Party of Farmers and Peasants Czechoslovak National Democratic Party Czechoslovak Social Democratic Workers' Party Czechoslovak People's Party

TABLE 13. (*Continued*)

Years	Coalition
	German League of Farmers
	German Social Democratic Party
	Tradesmen's Party
1932-1935	Republican Party of Farmers and Peasants
	Czechoslovak People's Party
	Slovak People's Party
	Czechoslovak Social Democratic Workers' Party
1935-1938	Republican Party of Farmers and Peasants
	Czechoslovak People's Party
	Slovak People's Party
	Czechoslovak Social Democratic Workers' Party
	Tradesmen's Party
	German Christian Social Party
1939-1945	Dismemberment and military occupation
1945-1948	"National Front"—Communist Party of Czechoslovakia
	Czechoslovak Social Democratic Workers' Party
	Czechoslovak National Socialist Party
	Czechoslovak People's Party
	(Slovak) Democratic Party
Feb. 1948-	Communist Party of Czechoslovakia

Note: First-named party is dominant coalition party.

DENMARK

The KINGDOM OF DENMARK (*Kongeriget Danmark*) is one of the few remaining constitutional monarchies in Europe. Despite its small size (16,631 square miles), with a 1979 population of 5,125,000, and notably lacking in raw materials for industry, Denmark has become recognized for its development of a highly efficient system of agriculture and the production of high-quality manufactured goods. As a result, the society is one of the top half-dozen wealthiest in the world as measured in per capita gross domestic product.

Approximately 95 percent of Denmark's population belongs to the Evangelical Lutheran Church, a state-supported institution. Denmark's relatively homogeneous society has a long tradition of political stability, despite a parliamentary representation in the 20th century of not fewer than four main political parties, a number increasing to ten or more in the unicameral parliament (the *Folketing*) after 1973. No single Danish party has had a majority in parliament in this century (*see* tables 14 and 15); thus one-party minority government or a coalition is traditional.

The current *Folketing* membership is 179, with elections scheduled every four years, subject to early dissolution. Suffrage is universal at 18 years of age, with a modified proportional representation system in effect. The eligible electorate in 1979 was approximately 3.7 million. The bulk of the *Folketing* membership (139, including two seats elected by the Faroe Islands and two seats elected by Greenland) is mandated on a constituency basis, and the remaining 40 seats are used to even out party representation among those groups that receive at least two percent of the total vote.

In 1848, Denmark achieved a peaceful transition from a benign but formally absolutist monarchy (dating back to the Middle Ages) to a more democratic constitutional system with extensive male suffrage and competitive political factions. A coalition of traditional elites, aristocrats, large landowners, and the leaders of large businesses maintained control of government until near the end of the century, although that control was seriously challenged in the 1870s by the growing power of small farmers, rural religious groups, intellectuals, and the organized working class. Parliamentarism was affirmed in 1901; and the Liberal Party* was joined by the Social Democratic Party of Denmark,* the Radical Liberals,* and, in 1915, a liberalized Conservative People's Party* to become the four "old" parties that have been the core of the Danish political system since that time, regularly accounting for 80 to 90 percent of the parliamentary representation until 1973.

A constitutional change in 1915 institutionalized a proportional representation electoral system that has been significant for the fairness of its distribution of mandates, especially after 1953, to those parties that are able to meet a minimum requirement of two percent of the popular vote. With the exception of wartime governments, the Social Democrats either alone or in formal alliance have led the regime for 43 of the years 1924 to 1981 (*see* table 16). The Liberal and Conservative parties have cooperated in parliament since the mid-1920s, forming their first government in 1951-1953 and later, with the Radical Liberals, in 1968-1971. The Liberals have had government by themselves in 1926-1929, 1945-1947, and 1973-1975. An unprecedented coalition of the Social Democrats and Liberals governed Denmark from August 1978 to September 1979.

The Danish monarchy is now completely neutral in the political system, its last significant interjection being in the financial-political crisis of early 1920. The monarchy remains popular, particularly after 1953 when female succession was permitted. Queen Margrethe II took the throne in 1972.

Denmark was neutral during World War I but regained in 1920 a portion of Schleswig lost to Prussia in 1864, a border question that has long rankled in Danish politics. After occupation by Germany in World War II, Denmark joined NATO in 1949; the five-nation Nordic Council in 1952; and in 1972, after a bitter campaign, Denmark approved membership in the European Economic Community (EEC) (*see* EUROPEAN PARLIAMENT). Despite majority support for its NATO alliance, Danish policy has sought a minimal military expenditure, preferring to harbor its resources for domestic needs. The financial crises that have developed since the early 1970s—including inflation, unemployment, a large foreign debt, and a formidable balance-of-payments deficit—have reemphasized the need for continuous government supervision of the Danish economy.

The main economic interest groups—especially the trade unions, the Employer's Association, and the agricultural organizations—tend to coordinate their needs with government through extensive bureaucratic as well as political linkages. Danish society is thoroughly organized into a competitive, pluralistic structure of groups.

Beginning in the early 1970s, a growing public dissatisfaction with government policies, particularly high taxation, led to the "earthquake" election of December 1973. This election resulted in sharp reductions for the old parties and a doubling of the number of parties represented in the *Folketing*. Although some minor parties returned (including the Communist Party of Denmark,* which had been out since 1960), the most significant development was the advent of a populist antitax, antibureaucracy, antiwelfare protest grouping, the Progress Party,* which attained the second-largest representation that year. Subsequent elections have sustained both the Progress Party and the other minor parties, although the drastic losses of the Social Democrats have largely been regained. Even so, from an 84 percent share of the popular vote in 1971, the four old parties had been reduced by 1977 to only 61.1 percent, though the 1979 elections saw a rise to 68.7 percent.

Both before and after 1973, Danish politics has been an excellent example of the politics of compromise, where, of necessity, the traditional political forces have never pushed their views to extremes but have sought accommodation. This tradition is being challenged by the fractionalization of the 1970s and tested by the continuance of difficult economic conditions; but Denmark retains an essential stability, a high level of democratic participation, and general respect for human welfare and dignity.

The FAROE ISLANDS (*Faerøerne*) in the North Sea have been under Danish administration since 1380 but have had extensive local self-government since the 1850s. The population of approximately 40,000 (1978) speaks an old Norse dialect and is supported mostly by fishing and sheep-raising (*faer* means "sheep"). The Islands elect two representatives (there was only one such seat until 1949) to the Danish parliament, where the Faroese have usually maintained neutrality vis-à-vis Danish internal politics. However, in the last 20 years there has been more open involvement.

Since 1920, three parties have been most successful in electing Faroese representatives to the *Folketing*. Of these, the Union Party* has had a general political affiliation and programmatic sympathy with the Danish Liberals, while the Faroese Social Democrats have had an obvious association with their Danish counterpart. The third-most-represented Faroese grouping, the People's Party,* was founded in 1945 and stands for Faroese self-government and complete sovereignty. The Social Democrats have had a single representative since 1947 (but not 1957-1960); the Union Party has had one seat from 1950-1960 and since 1977. The People's Party, currently unrepresented in the *Folketing*, had one seat in 1947-1950, 1957-1960, and 1964-1973. A newer advocate of Faroese independence, the Republican Party,* elected a candidate in 1973-1977. Other parties contesting elections in recent years have included the Old Home Rule* and the Progressive and Fishermen's Party.* Nonparty candidates have frequently drawn nearly as many votes as those from the major parties.

The Faroese also elect members to their own 32-seat parliament (the *Lagting*). A half-dozen political parties contest these elections (*see* table 17), in general divided into two groups—one supportive of maintaining the union with Denmark; the other, with varying degrees of militancy, advocating complete independence. This issue, while a continuous one, is now not of major proportions.

GREENLAND (*Grønland*), the world's largest island at 840,000 square miles, contains approximately 50,000 inhabitants (1979) who are mostly Eskimo and support themselves by fishing and seal-hunting. Greenland had been a Danish colony since 1721. Its colonial status was ended in 1953, and its voters were allowed to elect two representatives to the Danish parliament. Organized parties have not been a feature of elections in Greenland, although there is evidence of change as the island moves toward greater self-rule. The Greenlandic Social Democrats elected one candidate during 1964-1973 and again in 1979, while a loose grouping of younger voters oriented more toward the Danish Forward Party* chose a representative during 1971-1977. In 1977 an association called the Feeling of Community* elected a Greenland member with a neutral party program, and in 1979 one Greenlandic candidate joined the *Folketing* group of the (Danish) Socialist People's Party.*

Most recently, there has been an independence and self-rule thrust to Greenlandic politics. The increasing strategic importance of Greenland and its actual and potential store of natural resources has strengthened the hand of Greenlanders seeking self-government. In 1978, with permission from the Danish government, a local referendum overwhelmingly (70.1 percent) approved the establishment of a local government system, although ties with Denmark remain.

While the parties in Greenland's politics have been little more than regional and interest group associations, most voters have generally been either nonpartisan or of a leftist orientation. The first general elections for the newly created Greenlandic assembly (the *Landsting*) were held on April 4, 1979, and the 21 seats were contested by 92 candidates. The Forward Party won 13 seats, and the Feeling of Community obtained the remaining eight seats (*see* table 18). Four other parties and several independents also contested these elections.

Bibliography

Borre, Ole. "Recent Trends in Danish Voting Behavior." In *Scandinavia at the Polls*, edited by Karl H. Cerny. Washington, D.C.: American Enterprise Institute, 1977.

Damgaard, Erik. "Stability and Change in the Danish Party System over Half a Century." *Scandinavian Political Studies* 9 (1974).

Denmark: An Official Handbook. 15th ed. Copenhagen: Ministry of Foreign Affairs, 1974.

Einhorn, Eric S. "Denmark's Stormy Passage." *Current History*, vol. 70, no. 415 (April 1976).

Jones, W. Glyn. *Denmark.* London: Ernest Benn, 1970.

Miller, Kenneth E. *Government and Politics in Denmark.* Boston: Houghton Mifflin Co., 1968.

Møller, Poul, ed. *De politiske partier.* Albertslund: Det Danske Forlag, 1974.

Thomas, Alastair H. *Parliamentary Parties in Denmark, 1945-1972.* Occasional Paper no. 131. Glasgow: Survey Research Center, University of Strathclyde, 1973.

Thorsen, Svend et al. "Rigsdagen og partierne." In *Den Danske Rigsdag, 1849-1949*, edited by Julius Bonholt et al, vol. 3. Copenhagen: J. H. Schultz, 1953.

West, John F. *Faroe: The Emergence of a Nation.* London: C. Hurst and Co., 1972.

Political Parties

AGRARIAN PARTY (*Bondepartiet*). The economic depression of the early 1930s led to a Danish agricultural protest movement that caused the founding of the Agrarian Party in May 1934 under the original title of the Free People's Party (*Frie Folkeparti*). Three Liberal Party* parliamentary members defected to represent the new grouping; and in the 1935 election, the Free People's Party received 3.2 percent of the vote and five seats. The party program became increasingly rightist and militantly pro-small farmer so that in 1939 the Agrarian title was adopted. In that year's election, the party maintained its strength. But following the German occupation of World War II, the Agrarians gave their support to the Danish Nazi Party (*see* National Socialist Worker's Party of Denmark); and as a result, the Agrarians lost half their seats in 1943 and were eliminated in 1945 with the arrest of their leaders.

ATASSUT. *See* FEELING OF COMMUNITY.

BONDEPARTIET. *See* AGRARIAN PARTY.

CD. *See* CENTER DEMOCRATS.

CENTER DEMOCRATS (*Centrum-Demokraterne*: CD). One of the recent protest parties, the CD was founded in November 1973 by Erhard Jacobsen, a right-wing member of the Social Democratic Party of Denmark* who continues as the CD's primary personality. Jacobsen's defection from the Social Democrat government's increases of taxes on homeowners precipitated the election of December 1973. As the long-time mayor of a large Copenhagen suburb, Jacobsen had become the spokesman for white-collar workers and had decried the Social Democratic dependence in the early 1970s on the more radical Socialist People's Party.*

The 1973 election brought the CD 7.8 percent of the vote and 14 seats (though one of those seats was actually won by the CD's electoral coalition partner, the Schleswig Party*). Popular support has since varied, dropping to 2.2 percent in 1975, rising to 6.4 percent in 1977, and dropping to 3.2 percent in 1979. Despite its favoring of lower property and many other taxes and for a slowing of the government's expenditures on social welfare programs, the CD has consistently joined the Liberal Party* and Social Democratic Party governments in the various crisis compromises that have highlighted Danish politics since 1973. (Even the CD's splinter, the Trade and Business Party [1979],* provided support for the Social Democrat-Liberal government of 1978-1979.) As long as Jacobsen retains his position as a gadfly critic of government and as long as the party holds to the center, it is likely that a small CD representation will be retained.

CENTRUM-DEMOKRATERNE. *See* CENTER DEMOCRATS.

CHRISTIAN PEOPLE'S PARTY (*Kristeligt Folkeparti*: KrF). Given the increasing secularization of Danish life after World War II and the decline in importance of the state-supported Lutheran Church, the KrF is something of an anomaly. Founded in April 1970, the KrF articulates a concern among some Danes, especially in the rural and more church-oriented populace of the Jutland region, at the greater evidence of moral permissiveness as seen in the 1969 elimination of prohibitions against all printed pornography and the later institution of free abortion. From the beginning, the KrF has been supportive of a social-liberal view toward welfare programs, yet favoring a conservative support for a less-secularized politics and for a return to a more traditional moral code.

The earliest KrF head was Jacob Christensen, and the most recent and best-known leader is Jens Møller. The party contested the 1971 election but barely failed to get representation, receiving just under two percent of the vote. In 1973, following a series of internal party struggles and factional divisions, the KrF attained a four percent voter support and seven seats in the *Folketing*. The party vote rose to 5.3 percent in 1975, declined to 3.4 percent in 1977, and in 1979 dropped even further to 2.6 percent.

COMMUNIST PARTY OF DENMARK (*Danmarks Kommunistiske Parti*: DKP). The DKP was organized in November 1919 as the Left Socialist Party of Denmark (*Danmarks Venstre Socialistiske Parti*, not to be confused with the modern Left Socialists*). The Left Socialist Party was joined by earlier organized socialist and syndicalist parties such as the Socialist Labor Party (*Socialistisk Arbejderparti*) and the Independent Social Democracy (*Uafhaengige Socialdemokrati*). The DKP title was approved by the Communist International in 1920.

During its early years, the Danish Communist Party suffered continual internal problems and gained less than one percent of the vote in elections. By 1932, however, the DKP had a forceful chairman in Aksel Larsen and gained its first two seats in the *Folketing* with 1.1 percent of the vote. The DKP grew slowly until its prohibition under German occupation during World War II, but militant and successful underground resistance by Communist Party members so increased the party's public support that after the war its main leaders were taken into the first all-party government. In the following election, the DKP reached its all-time high of 12.5 percent of the vote and 18 *Folketing* seats; but already in 1947 the growing perception of a Soviet threat reduced DKP support by half, and a slow reduction followed until 1960 when it received only 1.1 percent of the vote and, under the 1953 two-percent-minimum requirement, lost all representation. This loss was primarily because of the party's expulsion of Larsen, its leader for 26 years, who in 1958 had begun an opposition to Moscow's dominance of the party and proposed a greater Danish national communism. (Larsen went on to found the Socialist People's Party,* a grouping that in recent years has been credited with winning over Communist voters and thereby reducing the DKP's parliamentary representation.) Until 1973 the DKP never received more than 1.4 percent of the vote; but in the 1973 election, support jumped to 3.6 percent, to 4.2 percent in 1975, and to 3.7 percent in 1977. In 1979, however, the Communists fell to only 1.9 percent, thus again losing any *Folketing* representation.

The Danish Communists developed a more moderate course after 1960, and its leader until his 1978 death, Knud Jespersen, was a popular figure. The initial return of the DKP to greater popularity in the 1970s, despite other competition on the left of the political spectrum, stemmed from a general decrease in the perceived threat from the USSR and a willingness by the DKP to take a strong nationalistic, anti-EEC, pro-Nordic neutrality line. The 1979 loss of support is credited to the rise of the less extreme Socialist People's Party and the Left Socialists. Also, the DKP has suffered further internal conflict, as evidenced by the pre-1979 election formation of the Communist Workers' Party (*Kommunistiske Arbejdersparti*), a maoist grouping that secured only 0.4 percent of the 1979 vote. The current DKP chairman is Jørgen Jensen.

Further Reference. Rohde, Peter H., "Communist Party of Denmark," in *The Communist Parties of Scandinavia and Finland*, edited by A. F. Upton (London: Weidenfeld, 1972).

COMMUNIST WORKERS' PARTY. *See* COMMUNIST PARTY OF DENMARK.

CONSERVATIVE PARTY. *See* CONSERVATIVE PEOPLE'S PARTY.

CONSERVATIVE PEOPLE'S PARTY (commonly called simply the Conservative Party, *Konservative Folkeparti*: KF). Since its ideological change in 1915 from a traditional, elitist party called "The Right" (*Højre*), the KF has been that "old" party most strongly representing the urban and suburban middle class, large landowners, and the interests of private business and employers. The party has prided itself on outspoken patriotism and a belief in national defense, and it has been a clear proponent for Denmark's inclusion in the European Economic Community (EEC) (*see* EUROPEAN PARLIAMENT). While opposing policies of the Social Democratic Party of Denmark* for a broader welfare state, the KF has accepted the social regulatory policies earlier established and did little to lessen them while in government in the early 1950s and late 1960s. From 1920 to 1973, the Conservatives' popular vote was always 16 to 21 percent. In 1973 it dropped sharply to nine percent, fell to 5.5 percent in 1975, made a recovery to 8.5 percent in 1977, and increased further to 12.5 percent in 1979, making the KF tied with the Liberal Party* as Denmark's currently second-largest political party.

The "tax revolt" of 1973 led many KF voters to defect to the Progress Party,* but the decline also coincided somewhat with a leadership vacuum after the death of strong parliamentary leader Poul Sørensen in 1970. Recently, the party has presented a more forceful image under the leadership of Poul Schlütter and Ib Stetter, enhanced to some extent by the Conservatives' becoming the main center-right party in opposition after the Liberal Party joined the government in 1978. Since its founding, the KF has probably suffered less from internal fractionalization than any major party; although badly divided over the Schleswig problem after both world wars, no permanent splits occurred. In 1938 a naziist KF member left to form the National Union (*see* National Socialist Worker's Party of Denmark). In 1976 a KF *Folketing* member, Hans Jørgen Lembourn, formed the Moderate Party, but it failed to qualify for the 1977 election and did not return.

DANISH INTERNATIONAL LABOR ASSOCIATION. *See* SOCIAL DEMOCRATIC PARTY OF DENMARK.

DANISH NAZI PARTY. *See* NATIONAL SOCIALIST WORKER'S PARTY OF DENMARK.

DANISH PEOPLE'S PARTY. *See* NATIONAL SOCIALIST WORKER'S PARTY OF DENMARK.

DANISH UNION (*Dansk Samling:* DS). Another example of a party that primarily owed its existence to the vigor and attractiveness of a single individual, the Danish Union featured its founder, Arne Sørensen, a West Jutland teacher, who organized the party in 1936. Similar to the Christian People's Party, * the Progress Party, * and the Independent Party, * the DS under Sørensen's leadership combined protests against the welfare policies of the Social Democratic Party of Denmark* with a call for more individual initiative in meeting social problems, a religious and moral revival, stronger national defense, and a now-forgotten urge for a Scandinavian federal union.

Despite allegations of nazi sympathies (*see* National Socialist Worker's Party of Denmark), after the German occupation of World War II Sørensen and his followers joined the Danish resistance, a move that increased DS voter support to 2.2 percent in 1943 and to 3.1 percent in 1945. Sørensen became a minister in the postwar coalition government, but he resigned his party position before the 1947 election, given the failure of his party's demands for territorial expansion in Schleswig at Germany's expense. In 1947 the Danish Union lost all its *Folketing* seats and never returned, despite small efforts as late as 1964.

DANMARKS KOMMUNISTISKE PARTI. *See* COMMUNIST PARTY OF DENMARK.

DANMARKS NATIONALSOCIALISTISK ARBEJDERSPARTI. *See* NATIONAL SOCIALIST WORKER'S PARTY OF DENMARK.

DANMARKS RETSFORBUND. *See* JUSTICE PARTY OF DENMARK.

DANMARKS VENSTRE SOCIALISTISKE PARTI. *See* COMMUNIST PARTY OF DENMARK.

DANSK FOLKEPARTI. *See* NATIONAL SOCIALIST WORKER'S PARTY OF DENMARK.

DANSK SAMLING. *See* DANISH UNION.

DKP. *See* COMMUNIST PARTY OF DENMARK.

DNSAP. *See* NATIONAL SOCIALIST WORKER'S PARTY OF DENMARK.

DR. *See* JUSTICE PARTY OF DENMARK.

DS. *See* DANISH UNION.

ERHVERVSPARTI. *See* TRADE AND BUSINESS PARTY (1917-1924) and (1979).

ESKIMO MOVEMENT (Greenlandic, *Inuit Ataqatigiit*). Greenland's Eskimo Movement is a marxist-leninist group that has supported complete independence from Denmark and has advocated restricting Greenlandic citizenship to those having at least one Eskimo parent. In the pre-autonomy general elections of 1979, the Eskimo Movement received only four percent of the Greenlandic vote.

F. *See* PROGRESS PARTY.

FARMER'S PARTY (*Landmanspartiet*). P. C. Poulsen, a large landowner, formed the Farmer's Party in 1924 as an alternative to the Liberal Party. * Poulsen urged better government support for farmers, while opposing increased government expenditures in general. The Farmer's Party served only to weaken the Liberal vote in the 1924 election, received only 0.9 percent itself, and never contended again.

FEELING OF COMMUNITY (Greenlandic, *Atassut*). The *Atassut* is one of the two major political formations in Greenland (the other major grouping being the Forward Party*). The Feeling of Community is basically a moderate grouping that has favored a continuation of Greenland's ties to the European Economic Community. In the 1979 pre-autonomy general elections, the *Atassut* won eight seats in Greenland's *Landsting*. The party leader, Lars Chemnitz, had been chairman of the pre-autonomy council (the *Landsraad*).

FF. *See* PEOPLE'S PEACE POLICY PARTY.

FOLKEFLOKKEN. *See* PEOPLE'S PARTY.

FORWARD PARTY (Greenlandic, *Siumut*). The socialist Forward Party is one of the two major political formations in Greenland (the other major grouping being the Feeling of Community*). The *Siumut* has opposed Greenland's ties to the European Economic Community and has urged withdrawal unless special concessions are made. In the 1979 pre-autonomy general elections, the Forward Party won 13 seats in Greenland's *Landsting* and formed a government under the direction of Jonathan Motzfeldt, the party leader.

FREDSPOLITISK FOLKEPARTI. *See* PEOPLE'S PEACE POLICY PARTY.

FREE PEOPLE'S PARTY. *See* AGRARIAN PARTY.

FREE SOCIAL DEMOCRACY (*Frie Socialdemokrati*). Founded in March 1920 by C. E. Marott, a former *Folketing* representative of the Social Democratic Party of Denmark,* the Free Social Democracy particularly favored a return of Flensborg to Denmark in the Schleswig referendum. The party elected no candidates in any of the three elections of the 1920s, and the party disappeared from contention.

FREMSKRIDTS-OG FISKERFLOKKEN. *See* PROGRESSIVE AND FISHER-MEN'S PARTY.

FREMSKRIDTSPARTIET. *See* PROGRESS PARTY.

FRIE FOLKEPARTI. *See* AGRARIAN PARTY.

FRIE SOCIALDEMOKRATI. *See* FREE SOCIAL DEMOCRACY.

GAMMEL SELVSTYRE. *See* OLD HOME RULE.

HØJRE. *See* CONSERVATIVE PEOPLE'S PARTY.

INDEPENDENT PARTY (*Uafhaengige Parti*: U). First formed in September 1953 by former Liberal Party* prime minister, Knud Kristensen, the Independent Party sought a constituency to the farthest "responsible right" in the Danish political spectrum. The party barely failed to gain representation in both 1953 and 1957, peaked with 3.3 percent of the votes and six seats in 1960, and declined to 2.5 percent of the vote in 1964. Thereafter, U failed to secure a sufficient percentage for representation, but it has maintained its organization for lobbying purposes.

Initially, the Independents rallied around Kristensen's opposition to the 1953 constitutional revision, but U was also characterized by the rural and small-town adherence to traditionalist religious views that later formed the base for the Christian People's Party.* The Independent Party opposed the welfare state in general, except for government aid to farmers and fishermen, and it supported NATO, giving a particular expression of concern for the Danish minority in

German Schleswig. Kristensen never returned to the *Folketing*, and the primary parliamentary leader was Ivar Poulsen, who himself later broke with the party.

INDEPENDENT SOCIAL DEMOCRACY. *See* COMMUNIST PARTY OF DENMARK.

INUIT ATAQATIGIIT. *See* ESKIMO MOVEMENT.

JUSTICE PARTY OF DENMARK (*Danmarks Retsforbund:* DR). Typical of several other Danish parties that have combined a seemingly inconsistent agenda of policy supports, the Justice Party has managed to stay alive for some 60 years by appealing to a cross section of voters. The DR (also known as the Single-Tax Party) is one of the few successful Henry Georgist or single-tax parties in the world, although that particular issue no longer is the DR's rallying point. In the early part of the century, several groups formed to discuss and promote the taxation and social ideas of the United States economist, Henry George. The complete tax on land and its value, with the returns to benefit all, appealed to the laboring class, while support for laissez-faire trade and strong opposition to the state's intervention in the rights of the individual drew voters from the center and right of the political spectrum.

Formally founded in 1919 by a number of writers, intellectuals, and clergy-men, the Justice Party has won voter support since its first contest in 1924. The DR gained parliamentary seats already in 1926 and was represented continuously until 1960, when it suffered such a sharp decline that it did not return to the *Folketing* until 1973. DR voter support has swung between 0.7 percent and 8.2 percent, averaging 2.7 percent. The most successful period was 1947-1960, and in 1957 the DR was drawn into a governing coalition with the Social Democratic Party of Denmark* and the Radical Liberals.* This coalition, however, proved destructive to the Justice Party because of the DR's need to accept many programs that it traditionally opposed while getting little of its own programs supported in return. From 1960 to 1973, the Justice Party lost all representation; but in 1973 it gained five seats, lost them all in 1975 (having won only 1.8 percent of the vote), but regained six seats (with 3.3 percent) in 1977. The 1979 elections brought a reduction to 2.6 percent of the vote and five seats.

The DR has pursued an erratic center-right course since 1973, with its most notable opposition being toward Danish participation in the European Economic Community. The present party leader in parliament is Ib Kristensen.

KF. *See* CONSERVATIVE PEOPLE'S PARTY.

KOMMUNISTISKE ARBEJDERSPARTI. *See* COMMUNIST PARTY OF DENMARK.

KONSERVATIVE FOLKEPARTI. *See* CONSERVATIVE PEOPLE'S PARTY.

KrF. *See* CHRISTIAN PEOPLE'S PARTY.

KRISTELIGT FOLKEPARTI. *See* CHRISTIAN PEOPLE'S PARTY.

LANDMANSPARTIET. *See* FARMER'S PARTY.

LC. *See* LIBERAL CENTER.

LEFT. *See* LIBERAL PARTY.

LEFT SOCIALIST PARTY OF DENMARK. *See* COMMUNIST PARTY OF DENMARK.

LEFT SOCIALISTS (*Venstresocialisterne*: VS). In 1967 six members of the parliamentary group of the Socialist People's Party (SF)* established the Left Socialists and were immediately supported by a number of SF adherents. The point of dissension was the SF's support for the wage policies of the government then led by the Social Democratic Party of Denmark.* Ascribing more to a collective leadership, the Left Socialists decried authoritarianism in both the Communist Party of Denmark* and its splinter, the Socialist People's Party. Also, the Left Socialists have believed themselves to be more purely and aggressively socialist than either of these other two leftist parties. (Indeed, the new Left Socialists adopted the name of the Left Socialist Party of Denmark, predecessor to the Danish Communist Party, perhaps harking to an earlier day of Communist Party purity.)

Already in 1968, the Left Socialists attracted four percent of the vote and won four seats in the *Folketing*, but the party was itself given to factionalism that halved its strength in 1968. By 1971 it failed to gain any seats (with only 1.6 percent of the vote) and did not return until 1975. At that time, the party received 2.1 percent, gaining slightly in 1977 to 2.7 percent, and to 3.7 percent in 1979 (thereby helping in this last election to unseat the Communists from *Folketing* representation). Thus the Left Socialists are ideologically in the narrow space between the Communist Party and the Socialist People's Party, and the Left Socialists have only a tenuous hold on political representation. Yet the Left Socialists continue to draw voter support, particularly among younger voters, radical intellectuals, and dissatisfied Communist, SF, and Social Democratic voters. The Left Socialists' program resembles much of the agenda put forward by the other two leftist parties, including strong opposition to NATO and to the European Economic Community.

LIBERAL CENTER (*Liberalt Centrum*: LC). The Liberal Center was founded in late 1965 by two defecting members of the Liberal Party* *Folketing* group (Niels Westerby and Børge Diderichsen). However, the grounds for the new Liberal Center party were formed earlier in the 1960s by a growing debate within the

Liberal Party, especially among the Copenhagen membership, that the old party was becoming too conservative and should seek more accommodation with the social-reform-seeking Radical Liberals* and the Social Democratic Party of Denmark.* Once formed, the LC drew enough voter support in 1966 (2.5 percent of the vote) to win four seats, but the LC's only real influence was to move the Liberal Party to absorb a number of LC proposals. Therefore, by 1968 the LC lost its representation and therefter disappeared. Prophetically, the LC pointed toward the Liberal coalition with the Radical Liberals and the Conservative People's Party* in the 1968 government and toward the more dramatic Social Democratic-Liberal coalition of 1978.

LIBERALE PARTI. *See* LIBERAL PARTY.

LIBERAL PARTY (*Liberale Parti*; most commonly known in the vernacular as *Venstre*: V). The oldest continuous political party in Denmark, the Liberal Party was formally organized in 1870 when several groups opposing the conservative regime came together. The term *Venstre* means "Left," and at the time of its founding V was indeed a leftist grouping, standing for a large number of democratic, social, and business reforms, and especially for greater aid to that majority of the society that was dependent on the land for its livelihood. The Liberal Party was never attracted to socialism, and it has remained a moderate liberal party with much of its voter support primarily in the rural, church-supporting populace of Jutland.

In its moderateness, the Liberal Party has experienced a number of dissents. The first occurred in 1905 when a V faction pushed for even greater and faster social reforms and left the party to become the Radical Liberals,* a grouping that has since proved a considerable competitor for V votes. Opposing the Liberals' moderateness from the right of the political spectrum were those who split from V in 1934 to form the Free People's Party (which later became the Agrarian Party*) and those who followed V leader Knud Kristensen in establishing the Independent Party* in 1953. But then, again from the left, the Liberals' moderate economic policies of the mid-1960s resulted in dissent from those who advocated greater spending on social welfare programs and who defected from V to establish the Liberal Center.*

Despite these internal conflicts, and after winning its struggle for democratic parliamentarism in 1901, V became a dominant political force for most of the next 30 years. Essentially, V governments held power during 1901-1909, 1910-1913, 1920-1924, and 1926-1929. After 1920, when it received 34 percent of the vote, the Liberal Party declined slowly but dropped below 18 percent only once (in 1935) until 1971 when voter support declined to 15.6 percent. Not until the latter part of the 1930s did V and the Conservative People's Party* begin to heal their mutual antagonism and form a more "bourgeois" bloc. The 1945 election gave the Liberals enough support so that a government under Knud Kristensen was formed, but this lasted just two years. During 1951-1953 a Liberal-Conservative government led by Erik Eriksen realized passage of a new constitution; but from September 1953 until 1968, V was in opposition again, returning in the Radical Liberals-Liberal-Conservative coalition with V leader, Poul Hartling, as foreign minister.

Since 1971, the Liberal Party has been subjected to wide swings of political activity. Reduced to 12.3 percent support in the 1973 election, V still was that "old" party that fared best, and Hartling led a one-party regime with such success that in the January 1975 election V's support almost doubled to 23.3 percent. Despite this increase, Hartling could not put together a coalition, and he relinquished the reins to the Social Democratic Party of Denmark. *

In 1977 the Liberals lost all of their earlier gains and returned to a 12 percent support. With this loss blamed on ineffective leadership, Hartling soon left his party position. After considerable intraparty discussion, a new and younger leader, Henning Christophersen, led V into an unprecedented government coalition with the Social Democrats in August 1978. This surprising association at first permitted V to push its program of less government spending on social welfare, reduction of the foreign debt, and increased association with the European Economic Community (the last because of the benefits to agricultural interests). By September 1979, however, the Social Democrat-Liberal coalition had eroded over questions of economic policy and over the Social Democrats' proposals to establish worker co-ownership of industry. Therefore, after the October 1979 elections, the government was again formed only by the Social Democrats.

With an effective party organization, frequently strong and popular leaders, and the most widespread party press, the Liberal Party in the 1979 *Folketing* elections maintained its earlier share of the vote (12.5 percent). However, V's previous role as head of Denmark's center-right parties is now threatened by the Conservatives, who in 1979 also won 12.5 percent of the vote, thereby tying with the Liberals for the position as Denmark's current second-largest party.

LIBERALT CENTRUM. *See* LIBERAL CENTER.

MODERATE PARTY. *See* CONSERVATIVE PEOPLE'S PARTY.

NATIONALE GENREJSNINGSPARTI. *See* NATIONAL SOCIALIST WORKER'S PARTY OF DENMARK.

NATIONAL PEOPLE'S PARTY. *See* NATIONAL SOCIALIST WORKER'S PARTY OF DENMARK.

NATIONAL RESURRECTION PARTY. *See* NATIONAL SOCIALIST WORKER'S PARTY OF DENMARK.

NATIONAL SOCIALIST WORKER'S PARTY OF DENMARK (or Danish Nazi Party, *Danmarks Nationalsocialistisk Arbejdersparti*: DNSAP). Danish support for the German nazi movement (*see* NATIONAL SOCIALIST GERMAN WORKER'S PARTY, HISTORICAL GERMANY) began in the 1920s with particular concentration in the German minority area of South Jutland. The formal DNSAP was not organized until May 1932, and the main Danish Nazi Party leader from 1933 until his 1944 resignation was Fritz Clausen. The DNSAP program followed the main lines of Hitler's party, but voter support was too low in 1932 and 1935 to win parliamentary mandates. In 1939 the DNSAP received 1.8 percent of the national vote and three *Folketing* seats. Despite the German occupation of Denmark in early 1940, Clausen gained little personal or official status. Furthermore, the DNSAP could not increase its popular support, winning only 2.1 percent and three seats in 1943. Clausen soon left the party, which itself was outlawed with the end of the war and its members punished in various ways.

After 1940, several pro-DNSAP factional parties organized but received little support. The National Resurrection Party (*Nationale Genrejsningsparti*) was founded in July 1940 by Svend E. Johansen, a former member of the Justice Party of Denmark.* In 1941, Johansen and T. M. Andersen formed the Danish People's Party (*Dansk Folkeparti*) as a nazi-inspired opponent of the DNSAP, but in 1943 Andersen split to form the National People's Party (*Nationalt Folkeparti*). The National Union (*Nationalt Samvirke*) had been organized in 1938 with Victor Pürchel, a prominent former Conservative People's Party* member, as the main leader. As a right-wing, antiparliamentary party, the National Union received one percent of the vote in 1939; however, the National Union joined the Danish Union,* then eventually split off again to become part of the Danish People's Party.

Since the end of World War II, Danish naziism continues more as a "cause," sporadically supported by only a few individuals and without political importance.

NATIONALT FOLKEPARTI. *See* NATIONAL SOCIALIST WORKER'S PARTY OF DENMARK.

NATIONALT SAMVIRKE. *See* NATIONAL SOCIALIST WORKER'S PARTY OF DENMARK.

NATIONAL UNION. *See* NATIONAL SOCIALIST WORKER'S PARTY OF DENMARK.

OLD HOME RULE (Faroese, *Gammel Selvstyre*). The Old Home Rule is a minor Faroe Islands grouping which has advocated severing links with Denmark. The party has been represented in the Islands' *Lagting* assembly by two parliamentary seats. In the past two elections, 1974 and 1978, Old Home Rule has polled approximately 7.2 percent of the vote.

PENSIONER'S PARTY (*Pensionistspartiet*). Spokesmen for the particular problems of pensioners qualified this party for the 1977 election. However, the

Pensioner's Party received only 0.9 percent of the vote after what was considered to be an ineffective campaign. The Pensioner's Party did not contest the 1979 elections.

PENSIONISTSPARTIET. *See* PENSIONER'S PARTY.

PEOPLE'S PARTY (Faroese, *Folkeflokken*). The People's Party is the third-most-important political grouping on the Faroe Islands. The party was founded in 1945 and advocates complete sovereignty for the Islands. Averaging approximately 20 percent of the Faroe Islands vote, the People's Party is currently represented by six seats in the Islands' *Lagting*. The party has been in coalition with the Faroese branch of the Social Democratic Party of Denmark* and with the (Faroese) Republican Party.*

PEOPLE'S PEACE POLICY PARTY (*Fredspolitisk Folkeparti*: FF). Pacifists and opponents of military alliances, especially of NATO, founded the FF in December 1963. In March 1964, a member of the Socialist People's Party* in the *Folketing* left that party and claimed representation for the FF. In the May 1964 election, the FF received only 9,070 votes (0.4 percent) and lost even its one seat. The FF has nominated no candidates since, but it continues as an informational and lobbying group.

PROGRESSIVE AND FISHERMEN'S PARTY (Faroese, *Fremskridts-og Fiskerflokken*). The Progressive and Fishermen's Party is a minor political grouping that has contested Faroe Islands *Lagting* elections. It has opposed the maintenance of close links with Denmark. The party's strength increased from two to six percent between 1974 and 1978, and it is currently represented by two members in the Faroese *Lagting*.

PROGRESS PARTY (*Fremskridtspartiet*: F). The traditional stability of Danish voters has meant that new political parties seldom have quick success or a long life. The phenomenal breakthrough of the Progress Party, founded only in 1972, proved the notable exception. The party's originator, continuing leader, and "strong man" is Mogens Glistrup, a wealthy lawyer who in 1971 had begun a general criticism of the Danish tax system, of government expenditures on welfare, and of the expanding civil service.

Glistrup capitalized on a growing public frustration with economic conditions and high taxes, and in the 1973 election the Progress Party became Denmark's second-largest party with 15.9 percent of the vote and 28 seats. In the succeeding two elections, F lost only slightly (achieving 13.6 and 14.6 percent of the vote) and appears to have established itself as a rather permanent protest party on the right of Denmark's political spectrum, not least because it receives support from certain working-class voters as well as from the traditional middle class and conservatives.

Glistrup's initially sweeping program of a radical cut in welfare costs, a halving of the civil service, and virtual elimination of the military has since been modified, but the basic themes remain. Being against most government policies (although strongly favoring Danish participation in the European Economic Community) has caused F to reject virtually all alliance arrangements, although a few have been offered. Despite a 1978 conviction and heavy financial penalty for tax evasion, Glistrup, who contended the case was one of political vengeance, remains a popular figure and dominant Progress Party leader. Some internal party opposition developed in 1979 by an F faction that advocated modification of the party line in order to promote F cooperation with other parties. However, a September 1979 party congress narrowly approved the continuation of Glistrup's isolated policy. It is likely that this internal dissension contributed to the Progress Party's loss of support in the October 1979 elections, declining to 11 percent of the vote and dropping F to the position of Denmark's fourth-largest party (after the Social Democratic Party of Denmark, * the Liberal Party, * and the Conservative People's Party*). Nevertheless, as long as conditions in Denmark permit F to be a viable party, it appears that the traditional four- or five-party, two-bloc structure will stay splintered, and weak minority or unstable coalition governments will be the rule.

Further Reference. Neilsen, Hans Jørgen, "The Uncivic Culture: Attitudes towards the Political System in Denmark, and Vote for the Progress Party 1973-1975," *Scandinavian Political Studies* 11 (1976).

RADICAL LEFT. *See* RADICAL LIBERALS.

RADICAL LIBERALS (also known as the Radical Left, *Radikale Venstre*: RV). Defectors from the Liberal Party* (unhappy with the effect of new tax reforms on small farmers, in opposition to increased defense expenditures, and advocating more rapid electoral reform) founded the RV in 1905. Then, as later, the RV attracted a number of urban intellectuals, as well as the rural vote.

Already in 1909, the Radical Liberals formed their first government under C. Th. Zahle, who also headed a wartime regime from 1913 to 1920, during which many RV proposals were enacted. Opposition to an expanded Schleswig acquisition plus national economic difficulties cut RV support in 1920 from 32 to 15 *Folketing* seats. The party declined steadily until the mid-1960s, dropping from a high of 13 percent of the vote in 1924 to 5.3 percent in 1964. Even so, the party's belief in social reforms and its centrist position in the Danish political spectrum permitted either formal or informal alliance with the Social Democratic Party of Denmark, * notably in coalition governments during 1929-1940 and 1957-1964. Thus the Radical Liberals, at least until the 1970s, have exercised considerably more influence than their actual numbers might suggest, especially in the fields of education, government reform, and foreign and military policy.

In the 1960s, the RV's opposition to the Social Democrats' growing interest in leftist support led to a coolness that strengthened a new RV alliance with the

Liberal Party and Conservative People's Party.* This culminated in the RV, led by Hilmar Baunsgaard, heading a tripartite government after the 1968 election. The Radical Liberals had surged back to 15 percent of the vote and had doubled its representation; but in 1971, although the RV retained 14.4 percent support, both the Liberals and Conservatives lost and the ministry returned to Social Democrat control.

A new decline then began for the RV that by 1977 had reduced the party to a voter support of only 3.6 percent, though support rose slightly to 5.4 percent in 1979. The ascent of new center parties (the Center Democrats* and the Christian People's Party*), the retirement of several veteran leaders, and a renewal of traditional intraparty strife are among the causes for the current RV debacle. Despite the decline, the Radical Liberals are unlikely to disappear because the party continues to have the most even support of any party from all elements of Danish society. The role of a "balance-of-power" party is significant in Danish politics, and this tends to help preserve centrist groups. Even so, the RV has never had strong organization, and it has long had opposing factions within itself. Ambivalence remains over Danish neutrality and military defense positions, despite at least implicit support for NATO in recent years and a reluctant favoring of membership in the European Economic Community. The RV's support of social reforms has weakened in the 1970s with the maintenance of its alliance with the Liberals and Conservatives.

RADIKALE VENSTRE. See RADICAL LIBERALS.

REPUBLICAN PARTY (Faroese, *Tjodveldisflokken*). The Republican Party, the second-largest party contesting elections on the Faroe Islands, has been an advocate of independence for the Islands. Averaging over 20 percent of the local vote, the party is currently represented by six members in the Islands' *Lagting* as a result of elections in 1978. The Republicans are currently in coalition with the local branch of the Social Democratic Party of Denmark* and the People's Party.*

RIGHT. See CONSERVATIVE PEOPLE'S PARTY.

RV. See RADICAL LIBERALS.

SAMBANDSFLOKKEN. See UNION PARTY.

SAMFUNDSPARTIET. See SOCIETY PARTY.

SCHLESWIG PARTY (*Slesvigske Parti*: SL). The SL has represented the small German minority population in Schleswig, that part of South Jutland that voted in 1920 to return to Danish rule. To permit its candidates to compete, the SL has not been required to fulfill the usual requirements for forming a recognized party. As a result, although it never had more than 0.9 percent of the total vote, with an average of approximately 9,000 votes in 16 elections, the SL elected one representative in the South Jutland area during 1920-1939 and 1953-1960. This person, especially Pastor Johannes Schmidt (1920-1939), spoke for protection of the German culture but, although often critical of Danish policies, stayed neutral in party politics despite giving support during 1939-1945 to the nazi movement (see National Socialist Worker's Party of Denmark).

After World War II, the Schleswig Party pledged its loyalty to Denmark; nevertheless, it did not win a seat until the new constitution was adopted in 1953. The party's failure to elect a candidate after 1960 did not mean a loss of concern for the German minority, whose interests are handled by a special all-party committee headed by the Danish prime minister.

In the elections of 1973, 1975, and 1977, one SL candidate was elected to the *Folketing* by running in the South Jutland district on the Center Democrats ticket. However, the SL withdrew from this electoral coalition prior to the 1979 elections when the Center Democrats accused the SL candidate of having been a German SS member during World War II. As a result, the Schleswig Party did not run candidates in 1979. (For additional information on Schleswig concerns, see DANISH PARTY, HISTORICAL GERMANY; and SOUTH SCHLESWIG VOTER'S LEAGUE, WEST GERMANY.)

SD. See SOCIAL DEMOCRATIC PARTY OF DENMARK.

SELF-GOVERNMENT PARTY (*Selvstyrepartiet*). Founded in 1926 by Cornelius Petersen, the Self-Government Party was predominantly a South Jutland grouping that advocated self-rule for that region, a devaluation of the currency, and limiting the vote to landowners. In 1926 the party offered some candidates only in South Jutland. However, the party received no seats and did not appear again.

SELVSTYREPARTIET. See SELF-GOVERNMENT PARTY.

SF. See SOCIALIST PEOPLE'S PARTY.

SINGLE-TAX PARTY. See JUSTICE PARTY OF DENMARK.

SIUMUT. See FORWARD PARTY.

SL. See SCHLESWIG PARTY.

SLESVIGSKE PARTI. See SCHLESWIG PARTY.

SOCIAL DEMOCRATIC PARTY OF DENMARK (*Socialdemokratiet i Danmark: SD*). Since 1924, the SD has been the largest party in Denmark in terms of voter support. Consequently, it has led the government alone or in coalition some 43 years by 1981, not counting the wartime all-party regimes. Social Democrat leaders and programs have had the greatest domestic impact on Danish public policy.

Typical of other European socialist parties, Denmark's SD was organized outside of parliament, initially as the Danish International Labor Association. The Association's birth dated from July 1871 when Louis Pio, Harold Brix, and Paul Geleff began a socialist newspaper and agitated for reforms along marxist lines. Official repression of the Association and its leaders did not deter organization of labor unions. Therefore by 1884, the party, now entitled the Social Democrats, could elect its first two members to parliament. Steady growth followed as the party broadened its voter base to attract rural workers, and by 1913 the SD had the largest representation in parliament, though the party avoided forming a government until 1924.

The historically most prominent SD leader, Thorvald Stauning, party chairman of 1910-1939, was a minister in the union government during World War I; he headed his own ministry during 1924-1926 and during the "golden age" of SD rule, the regimes of 1929-1940, which saw immense programs of social legislation put into being. From 1929 to 1964, the SD averaged just over 41 percent of the popular vote for the *Folketing* but could never win a majority of its own. From 1966 to 1977, the Social Democrats fell to an average of 33.7 percent of the vote. Hans Hedtoft led governments during 1947-1950 and 1953-1955; followed by H. C. Hansen, 1955-1960; Viggo Kampmann, 1960-1962; Jens Otto Krag, 1962-1968 and 1971-1972; and Anker Jørgensen, 1973 and since 1975.

Lacking their own majority, Social Democrat leaders have, of necessity, been required to compromise and to seek alliances wherever possible. The traditional association with the Radical Liberals* faded after 1966, and the 1960s dependence on the Socialist People's Party* has slackened since 1973. The paradoxical coalition with the nonsocialist and moderate Liberal Party* from August 1978 to September 1979 is typical of the SD's pragmatic effort to seek a broad basis for governing, especially during difficult economic times. Almost from the first, the SD abjured a revolutionary tone, and at least since World War II the party has almost completely moved away from a doctrinaire socialist program. The party's neutrality beliefs were abandoned in the late 1940s, after occupation by Germany during World War II, and the SD has been a supporter of NATO and EEC membership, although preferring a larger Scandinavian alliance.

Despite the close ties between the Social Democrats and the primary labor union organization (*Landsorganisationen De Samvirkende Fagforbund:* LO), when in government the SD leaders have consistently, if reluctantly, interfered in contract negotiations to prevent or to lessen major labor conflicts. As a result of its pragmatism and opportunism, the SD has tended to lose ideologically leftist members to the more radical parties (the Socialist People's Party* and Left Socialists*); yet the Social Democrats' unwillingness to reduce the financial burden of government social programs has, in the 1970s, cost it support from its more conservative wing and even from some of the frustrated or affluent working class who in protest have gone to the Progress Party* or to the SD's own splinter, the Center Democrats.* Consequently, in 1973 the SD dropped precipitously to 25.6 percent of the vote. But the Social Democrats recovered to a level of 37 percent in 1977; and in 1979 the party rose to 38.3 percent, a level not enjoyed since 1966. The August 1978, unprecedented governing coalition with the Liberal Party* had come apart by September 1979 over economic policy issues. In particular, the Liberals protested the SD's proposals to establish worker co-ownership of industry as a means of securing trade union acceptance of wage restraints toward the goal of curbing inflation. Hence, after the October 1979 elections, the SD alone formed a minority government once again.

Although it has suffered a deterioration in its previously strong organization, a reduction of its party press, and an increasing conflict with its allies in the LO, the Social Democratic Party's flexible and popular leaders and its historic drive to head the government make it likely that the SD will continue to be the most significant and productive party in Danish politics for the foreseeable future.

Further Reference. Thomas, Alastair H., "Social Democracy in Denmark," in Social Democratic Parties in Western Europe, edited by William E. Paterson and Alastair H. Thomas (New York: St. Martin's Press, 1977).

SOCIALDEMOKRATIET I DANMARK. See SOCIAL DEMOCRATIC PARTY OF DENMARK.

SOCIALISTISK ARBEJDERPARTI. See COMMUNIST PARTY OF DEN-MARK.

SOCIALISTISK FOLKEPARTI. See SOCIALIST PEOPLE'S PARTY.

SOCIALIST LABOR PARTY. See COMMUNIST PARTY OF DENMARK.

SOCIALIST PEOPLE'S PARTY (Socialistisk Folkeparti: SF). Another instant success among recent Danish parties has been the SF, which has profited by filling an ideological gap between the Communist Party of Denmark* and the Social Democratic Party of Denmark* and, above all, because it was initially the creation of long-time Communist Party leader Aksel Larsen. Larsen, in parliament since 1932, was expelled by the Communists in 1958 when he urged a more nationalistic line similar to the Yugoslavian, thus in opposition to Moscow's influence.

The Socialist People's Party was formally organized in 1959 and drew immediate support from defecting Communist Party members, radical Social Democrat voters, and especially from a large number of university students. In the 1960 election, the SF blossomed with 6.1 percent of the vote, reached 10.9 percent in 1966, but by 1977 had dropped to 3.9 percent (posting an average of 6.6 percent in eight Folketing elections). The SF strength after 1966 led to its being courted by Social Democrat governments, and, while no formal coalition developed, the SF became a vital support for many Social Democrat proposals. This connection led to both disaffection among the more radical SF members and strong opposition from the center-right parties. Larsen's death in 1972 and rejuvenated Communist and Left Socialists* parties (the Left Socialists being an SF splinter of 1967) cut the SF's appeal, although in 1979 the party rose to 5.9 percent of the vote, helping in that year to unseat the Communists from *Folketing* representation.

The main SF party leader since 1972 has been Gert Pedersen. The party has consistently featured a number of traditional socialist proposals, opposition to capitalism, nationalization of financial and industrial institutions, and a leading role by workers in management. The SF favors neutrality for Denmark, elimination of military arms, a nuclear-free central Europe and Scandinavia, and the SF has strongly opposed membership in the European Economic Community.

SOCIETY PARTY (*Samfundspartiet*). The Society Party was a church-oriented grouping founded in 1932. It drew support from former Liberal Party* members dissatisfied with that party's lack of concern for religious interests and from those elements of Danish society in general opposition to the class conflict found among the various parties. The Society Party offered only a few candidates in the election of 1935; the party won no seats and disappeared.

SULISSARTUT. *See* WAGE-EARNERS PARTY.

TJODVELDISFLOKKEN. *See* REPUBLICAN PARTY.

TRADE AND BUSINESS PARTY (1917-1924) (*Erhvervsparti*). The first Danish party named Trade and Business Party was founded in 1917 to represent business organizations and the middle-class voter. The party won one parliamentary seat in 1918 and four seats in the election of 1920. An effort to broaden the party's appeal in 1922 led to a split that saw two representatives leave to form another group. This so weakened both groupings that both failed to win seats in 1924 and had no further electoral activity. (*See also* Trade and Business Party [1979].)

TRADE AND BUSINESS PARTY (1979) (*Erhvervsparti*). The second Danish party named Trade and Business Party existed in 1979 only in the form of its founder, Asger Lindinger, a Center Democrats* *Folketing* representative who split with that party in 1978. Since then, Lindinger proved important in providing the single vote necessary for the Social Democratic Party of Denmark*-Liberal Party* government (1978-1979) to attain a majority, especially for that government's drastic economic proposals of 1979. (*See also* Trade and Business Party [1917-1924].)

U. *See* INDEPENDENT PARTY.

UAFHAENGIGE PARTI. *See* INDEPENDENT PARTY.

UAFHAENGIGE SOCIALDEMOKRATI. *See* COMMUNIST PARTY OF DENMARK.

UNION PARTY (Faroese, *Sambandsflokken*). In the 1978 elections to the Faroe Islands' *Lagting*, the Union Party became the dominant political grouping, capturing over 26 percent of the vote and eight seats. These seats were retained in the 1980 election. The party has advocated the maintenance of close links between Denmark and the Faroe Islands. The Union Party has been in opposition to the coalition of the Faroese branch of the Social Democratic Party of Denmark,* the People's Party,* and the Republican Party.*

V. *See* LIBERAL PARTY.

VENSTRE. *See* LIBERAL PARTY.

VENSTRESOCIALISTERNE. *See* LEFT SOCIALISTS.

VS. *See* LEFT SOCIALISTS.

WAGE-EARNERS PARTY (Greenlandic, *Sulissartut*). Greenland's Wage-Earners Party was created by the Trade Union Federation as a vehicle for contending the pre-autonomy general elections of June 1979. The Danish government had denied the Federation permission to run a joint list of candidates with the Forward Party,* and a separate political formation was insisted upon. The Wage-Earners Party won five percent of the votes but obtained no seats.

Gerald R. McDaniel

TABLE 14. Distribution of Seats in Denmark's *Folketing*, 1918-1943

Party	1918	1920	1920	1920	1924	1926	1929	1932	1935	1939	1943
Agrarian Party*	—	—	—	—	—	—	—	0	5	4	2
Communist Party	—	—	—	—	0	0	0	2	2	3	—
Conservative People's Party	22	28	26	27	28	30	24	27	26	26	31
Danish Union	—	—	—	—	—	—	—	—	—	0	3
Justice Party	—	—	—	—	0	2	2	4	4	3	2
Liberal Party	44	48	51	51	44	46	44	38	28	30	28
National Socialist Worker's Party	—	—	—	—	—	—	—	0	0	3	3
Radical Liberals	33	17	16	18	20	16	16	14	14	14	13
Schleswig Party	—	—	—	1	1	1	1	1	1	1	0
Social Democratic Party	39	42	42	48	55	53	61	62	68	64	66
Trade and Business Party (1917-1924)	1	4	4	3	0	—	—	—	—	—	—
Total	139	139	139	148	148	148	148	148	148	148	148

*Known as the Free People's Party in 1932 and 1935.

TABLE 15. Distribution of Seats in Denmark's *Folketing*, 1945-1979

Party	1945	1947	1950	1953	1953	1957	1960	1964	1966	1968	1971	1973	1975	1977	1979
Center Democrats[a,b]	—	—	—	—	—	—	—	—	—	—	—	14	4	11	6
Christian People's Party	—	—	—	—	—	—	—	—	—	—	0	7	9	6	5
Communist Party	18	9	7	7	8	6	0	0	0	0	0	6	7	7	0
Conservative People's Party	26	17	27	26	30	30	32	36	34	37	31	16	10	15	22
Danish Union	4	0	0	0	0	0	0	0	—	—	—	—	—	—	—
Independent Party	—	—	—	—	—	0	6	5	0	0	0	—	—	—	—
Justice Party	3	6	12	9	6	9	0	0	0	0	—	5	0	6	5
Left Socialists[c]	—	—	—	—	—	—	—	—	—	4	—	—	4	5	6
Liberal Center	—	—	—	—	—	—	—	—	4	—	—	—	—	—	—
Liberal Party	38	49	32	33	42	45	38	38	35	34	30	22	42	21	22
Progress Party	—	—	—	—	—	—	—	—	—	—	—	28	24	26	20
Radical Liberals	11	10	12	13	14	14	11	10	13	27	27	20	13	6	10
Schleswig Party[a]	0	0	0	0	1	1	1	0	0	0	0	—	—	—	—
Social Democratic Party	48	57	59	61	74	70	76	76	69	62	70	46	53	65	68
Socialist People's Party[c]	—	—	—	—	—	—	11	10	20	11	17	11	9	7	11
Total	148	148	149	149	175[d]	175	175	175	175	175	175	175	175	175	175

[a] In 1973, 1975, and 1977, seats won by Center Democrats include one seat held by Schleswig Party.

[b] In 1978, one member of Center Democrats split off to form the Trade and Business Party (1979).

[c] In December 1967, six deputies of Socialist People's Party split off to form the Left Socialists.

[d] Reflects Danish total in unicameral *Folketing* established in new constitution of 1953. In addition, the Faroe Islands and Greenland each elects two deputies for a *Folketing* total of 179. See separate tables for Faroe Islands and Greenland.

181

TABLE 16. Ruling Parties or Coalitions in Denmark since 1920

Years	Party or Coalition
Mar.-May 1920	Nonpartisan civil servant government
May 1920-1924	Liberal Party
1924-1926	Social Democratic Party
1926-1929	Liberal Party
1929-1940	Social Democratic Party Radical Liberals
1940-1945 *	Social Democratic Party Radical Liberals Liberal Party Conservative People's Party
May-Nov. 1945	Union government of all parties
Nov. 1945-1947	Liberal Party
1947-1950	Social Democratic Party
1950-1953	Liberal Party Conservative People's Party
1953-1957	Social Democratic Party
1957-1960	Social Democratic Party Radical Liberals Justice Party
1960-1964	Social Democratic Party Radical Liberals
1964-1968	Social Democratic Party
1968-1971	Radical Liberals Liberal Party Conservative People's Party
1971-1973	Social Democratic Party
1973-1975	Liberal Party
1975-1978	Social Democratic Party
1978-1979	Social Democratic Party Liberal Party
1979-	Social Democratic Party

Note: First-named party is dominant coalition party.
* From late August 1943 to early May 1945, the four-party government did not function.

TABLE 17. Distribution of Seats in the Faroe Islands' *Lagting*, 1970-1980

Party	1970	1974	1978	1980
Old Home Rule	1	2	2	3
People's Party	5	5	6	6
Progressive and Fishermen's Party	1	1	2	2
Republican Party	6	6	6	6
Social Democratic Party (Faroese)	7	7	8	7
Union Party	6	5	8	8
Total	26	26	32	32

TABLE 18. Distribution of Seats in Greenland's First *Landsting*, 1979

Party	1979
Eskimo Movement	0
Feeling of Community	8
Forward Party	13
Wage-Earners Party	0
Independents	0
Total	21

EAST GERMANY

The GERMAN DEMOCRATIC REPUBLIC (*Deutsche Demokratische Republik*) comprises the eastern half of historical Germany, formed as a result of territorial divisions enacted after World War II. The country consists of 41,770 square miles with nearly 17 million inhabitants (1981 estimate). Soviet occupation facilitated the installation of communist rule in the early postwar years and sponsored the formation of the German Democratic Republic on October 7, 1949. The 1949 constitution was similar to the Weimar Constitution of 1919 (*see* HISTORICAL GERMANY). A new constitution promulgated in 1968 formalized the establishment of the republic as an independent socialist state. East Germany is closely tied to the socialist bloc—particularly to the Soviet Union—in political, ideological, economic, military, and most other matters.

East Germany has a multiparty system. Since 1947, however, competitive elections have not been held between the political parties. Like some other east European states (including Bulgaria, Czechoslovakia, and Poland), East Germany's party system is best described as hegemonic. Several parties are permitted, but only one party (the Socialist Unity Party of Germany*) dominates politics at all levels and does so without formal or actual organized competition.

Supreme power is vested in the unicameral People's Chamber (*Volkskammer*), which in turn elects the Council of State. The People's Chamber is composed of 434 delegates who are elected for five-year terms by universal suffrage (beginning at age 18). Election is on the basis of a single list drawn from among a limited number of political parties and "mass organizations." Voters may cross out the names of candidates they do not favor; however, only a small number exercise this option. The process of selection is controlled by the National Front of Democratic Germany (*Nationale Front des Demokratischen Deutschlands*). Organized into some 220 regional and nearly 17,000 local offices, the National Front is not itself a political party, nor does it send delegates to the legislature. What makes the National Front important, insofar as East German electoral politics are concerned, is that it has the responsibility for allocating, prior to an election, how many seats each party and mass organization will receive in the *Volkskammer*.

Once the National Front has decided on the allotment of seats, each of the five political parties and four mass organizations permitted representation in East

Germany then determines the individual candidate from each party or organization who will fill that particular vacancy. Since there usually has been only one candidate for each seat, there is no real contest. Ballots are cast by the East German electorate (approximately 11.4 million in 1976) either to approve or disapprove the official list. (Note that East Berlin, unlike West Berlin, does not enjoy a constitutional status separate from the German Democratic Republic, and the city is represented by 66 nonvoting National Front members.) Recently, more candidates have been nominated than there are seats to be filled. The result, however, is not electoral competition. The excess number simply serve as alternates on a reserve list. In 1976, for example, 591 candidates were on the ballot—434 were elected; 157 were placed on the reserve list.

Irrespective of these activities, the result of *Volkskammer* elections has little to do with the distribution of real political power in East Germany. The legislature is little more than a facade. Effective power is held by the top echelons of the ruling communist party, the Socialist Unity Party of Germany. The primary role of the *Volkskammer* is not to represent the people, as one would find among Western parliamentary democracies, but to represent the state to the people.

Bibliography

Bothe, Michael. "The 1968 Constitution of East Germany." *American Journal of Comparative Law*, vol. 17, no. 2 (1969): 268-291.

Childs, David. *East Germany*. New York: Praeger, 1969.

Dahrendorf, Ralf. *Society and Democracy in Germany*. Garden City, N.Y.: Doubleday, 1969.

Dornberg, John. *The Other Germany*. Garden City, N.Y.: Doubleday, 1968.

Hanhardt, Arthur, Jr. *The German Democratic Republic*. Baltimore: Johns Hopkins University Press, 1968.

Heidenheimer, Arnold J. *The Governments of Germany*. 3d ed. New York: Thomas Y. Crowell, 1971.

Ludz, Peter Christian. *The Changing Party Elite in East Germany*. Cambridge, Mass.: MIT Press, 1972.

———. *The German Democratic Republic from the Sixties to the Seventies*. Cambridge, Mass.: Harvard University Center for International Affairs, 1970.

Roskin, Michael. *Other Governments of Europe*. Englewood Cliffs, N.J.: Prentice-Hall, 1977.

Smith, Jean Edward. *Germany Behind the Wall*. Boston: Little, Brown & Co., 1967.

Political Parties

CDU. *See* CHRISTIAN DEMOCRATIC UNION.

CHRISTIAN DEMOCRATIC UNION (*Christlich Demokratische Union*: CDU). Licensed in 1945 to operate within the eastern zone, the Christian Democratic

Union initially functioned autonomously of the East German state, more or less as independently as most political parties in the western zone. During this period, the CDU established itself to be representative of middle-class interests and put itself under the same broad banner of Christianity as its counterpart in West Germany (see CHRISTIAN DEMOCRATIC UNION/CHRISTIAN SOCIAL UNION, WEST GERMANY). In the national election of October 1946, which was prior to the establishment of the two Germanies and therefore competitive, the combined returns for the Christian Democrats and the Liberal Democratic Party of Germany* equalled the vote for the amalgam of the Communist Party of Germany-Social Democratic Party of Germany (see WEST GERMANY).

Autonomy for all of the East German noncommunist elements was short-lived. As the Iron Curtain closed off the countries of eastern Europe from the west, the communist party in East Germany (the Socialist Unity Party of Germany*) began to consolidate power methodologically. Pressure was applied against the Christian Democrats beginning in 1947. Those leaders who disapproved of the changes were either removed or suppressed. Jacob Kaiser left in 1947, while Ernst Lemmer waited until 1949 before fleeing to the West. They and others were replaced with new party leaders who could better accommodate themselves to the communist elements. This new leadership included Otto Nuschke and August Bach, responsible in the early years for moving the CDU into alignment with Socialist Unity Party policy. The movement of the CDU was concluded under the leadership of Gerald Götting.

Prior to the showdown with the communists in 1947, the CDU membership in East Germany was estimated at 200,000. Since that time, the Christian Democrats have suffered declines, and more recent estimates place party membership well below half the 1947 figure. The CDU is represented in the Volkskammer.

CHRISTLICH DEMOKRATISCHE UNION. See CHRISTIAN DEMOCRATIC UNION.

COMMUNIST PARTY OF GERMANY. See SOCIALIST UNITY PARTY OF GERMANY.

DBD. See DEMOCRATIC PEASANTS' PARTY OF GERMANY.

DEMOCRATIC PEASANTS' PARTY OF GERMANY (Demokratische Bauernpartie Deutschlands: DBD). The DBD is an artifact of the Socialist Unity Party of Germany (SED).* The DBD has never had an independent status. The party was created in April 1948 to improve the SED position among East German farmers and specifically to help in the collectivization of agriculture.

From the beginning, the DBD has been led by tested and true communists such as Ernst Goldenbaum, whose membership in the Communist Party of

Germany (see HISTORICAL GERMANY and WEST GERMANY) dates back to 1923. On the other hand, from time to time the DBD has criticized agricultural policy in the Democratic Republic but never to the point of questioning the underlying principles and rationale of that policy. Estimates of DBD membership have hovered over the years at around 70,000. The DBD is represented in the *Volkskammer*.

DEMOCRATIC WOMEN'S LEAGUE OF GERMANY (*Demokratische Frauenbund Deutschlands*: DFD). The DFD is not a political party as such, but it is one of four mass organizations which sends delegates to the *Volkskammer*. The DFD is closely affiliated with the Socialist Unity Party of Germany,* operating largely as a transmission belt by seeking to promote greater acceptance of official East German policy. Reported DFD membership is above three million women.

DEMOKRATISCHE BAUERNPARTEI DEUTSCHLANDS. See DEMOCRATIC PEASANTS' PARTY OF GERMANY.

DEMOKRATISCHE FRAUENBUND DEUTSCHLANDS. See DEMOCRATIC WOMEN'S LEAGUE OF GERMANY.

DEUTSCHER KULTURBUND. See GERMAN CULTURAL FEDERATION.

DFD. See DEMOCRATIC WOMEN'S LEAGUE OF GERMANY.

DK. See GERMAN CULTURAL FEDERATION.

FDGB. See FREE GERMAN TRADE UNION FEDERATION.

FDJ. See FREE GERMAN YOUTH.

FREE GERMAN TRADE UNION FEDERATION (*Freier Deutscher Gewerkschaftsbund*: FDGB). The FDGB is one of four official mass organizations which performs certain quasi-political functions in the Democratic Republic and, accordingly, is given representation in the national assembly. Besides representing workers' interests in the *Volkskammer*, it more importantly seeks to promote greater acceptance of official policy among East German workers. The FDGB also strives to bond relations between East Germany and workers in West Germany. Membership is estimated at about 6.7 million workers.

FREE GERMAN YOUTH (*Freie Deutsche Jugend*: FDJ). The Free German Youth was founded in Spring 1946. It was quickly taken under control by the communists. Like other mass organizations in East Germany, the FDJ is closely affiliated with the Socialist Unity Party of Germany.* The FDJ is the only organization in the Democratic Republic today permitted to represent youth interests.

The Free German Youth provides its members with a variety of services, including indoctrination in communist policy. Members in the FDJ may be no older than 26 years of age, although this restriction does not apply for FDJ leadership. Including its affiliated organization for younger children, age six to 14 years, the Free German Youth has about 3.5 million members. Membership is drawn from the military, schools, local neighborhoods, and among employed youth. The FDJ is given representation in the *Volkskammer*.

FREIE DEUTSCHE JUGEND. *See* FREE GERMAN YOUTH.

FREIER DEUTSCHER GEWERKSCHAFTSBUND. *See* FREE GERMAN TRADE UNION FEDERATION.

GERMAN CULTURAL FEDERATION (*Deutscher Kulturbund*: DK). A number of German intellectuals formed the German Cultural Federation immediately after World War II, ostensibly for nonpartisan purposes. Initially the DK operated in both West and East Germany, but it was soon declared illegal in West Germany. The Federation continued to function in East Germany and was given representation as a mass organization to the *Volkskammer*. The group has been used by the Socialist Unity Party of Germany* to help propagate official cultural policy. Membership is estimated at over 100,000 persons.

LDPD. *See* LIBERAL DEMOCRATIC PARTY OF GERMANY.

LIBERAL DEMOCRATIC PARTY OF GERMANY (*Liberal Demokratische Partei Deutschlands*: LDPD). The LDPD began as the counterpart to the Free Democratic Party of West Germany (*see* WEST GERMANY). From its inception and through the first national election held in 1946, the LDPD was a viable alternative to the socialist-communist amalgam. In the 1946 election, the Liberals stood for individual initiative and private ownership.

Beginning in 1949, the LDPD came up against the same intense pressure that was already being applied against the Christian Democratic Union.* The Liberals were slower to succumb; nevertheless, the LDPD was forced to backpedal so that by 1952 its position, too, conformed to official policy. Although the party to this day has continued to follow a "correct" ideological path, some LDPD segments still harbor nonmarxist views toward socialism.

Financial support for the LDPD comes primarily from membership dues and proceeds from party publications, including *Der Morgen*, which is published in Berlin. At its inception, the LDPD was the second-largest party in East Germany with about 200,000 members. As the party lost its autonomy, support declined. In 1978 its membership was estimated at well below 100,000. The LDPD is currently represented in the *Volkskammer*.

Further Reference. Kulback, R., and H. Weber, *Parteien im Blocksystem der DDR: Aufbau und Funktion der LDPD und der NDPD* (Cologne: West Deutschen Verlag, 1969).

LIBERAL DEMOKRATISCHE PARTEI DEUTSCHLANDS. *See* LIBERAL DEMOCRATIC PARTY OF GERMANY.

NATIONAL DEMOCRATIC PARTY OF GERMANY (*National Demokratische Partei Deutschlands*: NDPD). (This National Democratic Party should not be confused with the party of the same name which exists in West Germany.) The NDPD is an extension and creation of the Socialist Unity Party of Germany (SED)* and was established in 1948 for the purpose of integrating and building support for the SED regime among former nazi and military elements then living in East Germany. The party seeks to build support from among these groups by appealing to patriotism and nationalism.

Since its inception, the NDPD has been tightly controlled by the SED. The NDPD leadership consists only of those who have in the past demonstrated loyalty to the communist cause. For example, the first National Democratic leader, Lothar Bolz, dates his membership in the Communist Party of Germany (*see* HISTORICAL GERMANY and WEST GERMANY) back to 1933. Bolz spent the war years not in Germany but in the Soviet Union.

In mid-1949, membership in the NDPD was estimated at below 17,000. More recently, party membership was estimated at over 115,000. The NDPD is allocated a portion of seats in the *Volkskammer*.

NATIONAL DEMOKRATISCHE PARTEI DEUTSCHLANDS. *See* NATIONAL DEMOCRATIC PARTY OF GERMANY.

NATIONALE FRONT DES DEMOKRATISCHEN DEUTSCHLANDS. *See* EAST GERMANY INTRODUCTION.

NATIONAL FRONT OF DEMOCRATIC GERMANY. *See* EAST GERMANY INTRODUCTION.

NDPD. *See* NATIONAL DEMOCRATIC PARTY OF GERMANY.

SED. *See* SOCIALIST UNITY PARTY OF GERMANY.

SOCIALIST UNITY PARTY OF GERMANY (*Sozialistische Einheitspartei Deutschlands*: SED). Examining the distribution of political power in the Democratic Republic, one finds the SED in a hegemonic position and that the SED dominates politics in the country. The party was formed in April 1946 as the result of a merger within the Soviet zone of the Social Democratic Party of Germany and the Communist Party of Germany (*see* HISTORICAL GERMANY and WEST GERMANY). The new SED amalgam was organizationally patterned after the Communist Party of the Soviet Union (*see* SOVIET UNION).

Both the Social Democratic Party and the Communist Party had agreed prior to amalgamation that the leadership of each party was to be given an equal vote within the new SED. Both parties agreed to operate under the notion of parity. Communists and Socialists were thus appointed in pairs to the all-important Central Secretariat: Wilhelm Pieck, Walter Ulbricht, Anton Ackermann, and Franz Dahlem for the Communist Party; and Otto Grotewohl, Paul Fechner, Erich Gniffke, and Otto Meier for the Social Democratic Party. Yet hardly two years passed before the Socialist position began to erode. In January 1949, a massive purge of Socialists eliminated most non-Communist elements from the SED.

Over the past eight years, the regime of Erich Honecker has moved to relax controls a bit within the SED and in the Democratic Republic in general. Nevertheless, the principle of "democratic centrism" is still basic to SED organization. The essence of Walter Ulbricht's regime remains intact.

In formal terms, the highest party organ is the Party Congress. In reality, however, power is more centralized, with nearly all important decisions made at higher levels. The primary function of the Party Congress, which meets every four years, is actually to approve policy decisions made by the top party members.

Compared to the Party Congress, the Central Committee is much smaller (about 100 to 150 members). Formally, the Committee elects members to the Politburo and Secretariat. Actually, the Central Committee provides a pool of potential candidates for cooptation to the highest party levels. The Central Committee also has the responsibility of transmitting and helping to implement at lower party levels decisions made by the Politburo.

The real locus of political power in East Germany is found in the Politburo. Virtually all important political decisions are made here. The Secretariat is slightly smaller in size than the Politburo, and it is second in importance. It numbers just below a dozen members and is the administrative arm of the SED. The Secretariat oversees party activity, the state bureaucracy, and all other major organizations in the Democratic Republic.

Membership in the SED has vacillated between one and two million persons. The 1981 estimated membership was 2,130,671. Most members are workers, although party statisticians include within this category salaried persons, as well as the intelligentsia. Slightly less than half actually may be considered industrial blue-collar workers. An increasing proportion of party members, at all levels of responsibility, have a technical background and expertise. As East Germany continues to modernize, strictly ideological considerations should become decreasingly important.

SOZIALISTISCHE EINHEITSPARTEI DEUTSCHLANDS. *See* SOCIALIST UNITY PARTY OF GERMANY.

Richard D. Partch

FINLAND

The REPUBLIC OF FINLAND (*Suomen Tasavalta*, Finnish; *Republiken Finland*, Swedish) is officially a bilingual country, and public institutions and political parties have both Finnish and Swedish names. Finland is one of Europe's largest (130,128 square miles) and least densely populated (4.8 million) countries, and it is a land of lakes, forests, and tundras straddling the arctic circle. Less than 13 percent of Finns live in the two northernmost provinces, which have almost half of the land area. Of the economically active population, industry and construction employ 34 percent, services 31 percent, commerce 15 percent, agriculture and forestry 12 percent, and transport and communication eight percent. Finland's democratic system of government is a mixture of parliamentarism and a strong presidency. There has been universal suffrage for men and women since 1906 (the voting age is now 18), responsible cabinet government since 1917, and a republican form of government since 1919. The main constitutional laws are the Form of Government Act of 1919 and the Parliament Act of 1928 (which updated the original act of 1906).

Finland's president is elected for a six-year term by an electoral college of 300 members chosen by the voters, and the president may be reelected for an unlimited number of terms. Exceptional procedure may also be used, requiring special legislation. Six of the 14 presidential elections since 1919 have been conducted under such procedures, most recently in 1974 when the parliament extended the incumbent's term for four years.

Supreme executive power is vested in the president. He is commander-in-chief of the armed forces, can dissolve parliament and call new elections, shares with parliament the right to initiate and repeal legislation, and is preeminently responsible for the conduct of foreign relations. A presidential veto can be overridden by parliament only after new elections.

Parliament (*Eduskunta; Riksdagen*), comprised of 200 members elected for four-year terms, reflects the population distribution extremely closely. On the other hand, under the d'Hondt method of proportional representation used in Finland, the cost of individual seats may vary greatly, and small parties with nationwide rather than concentrated regional support are often shortchanged. For example, the Social Democratic League of Workers and Smallholders[*] got only two seats for 100,396 votes (= 50,198 per seat) in the 1962 election, while the Swedish People's Party* got 14 seats for 147,950 votes (= 10,568 per seat). Electoral alliances of two or more parties may overcome the problem, but it is an unpredictable ploy which often backfires. It paid off handsomely, however, for the Social Democratic League in 1966 when it formed an electoral alliance with the Finnish People's Democratic League* and emerged with seven seats for 61,274 votes (= 8,753 per seat).

The historical evolution and present character of the Finnish party system reflect uniquely Finnish experiences and circumstances. From the 12th century to 1808, Finland belonged to Sweden and was governed from Stockholm. Ceded to Russia in 1809, Finland was an autonomous grand duchy under the tsar and was governed largely from Helsinki until 1917 independence. But six centuries of Swedish rule had left a permanent legacy of Swedish cultural traditions and a Swedish-speaking political, economic, and social elite which continued to dominate the country's affairs. The mid-19th-century Finnish national awakening was deliberately promoted by that elite as a means of warding off the potentially overpowering Russian influence. The effort succeeded and soon led to a serious linguistic cleavage in Finnish society, a split which produced the first party groupings.

Late 18th-century autocratic Swedish constitutional laws, abandoned in Sweden in 1809, survived in Finland throughout the Russian period. The country's affairs were administered by a Finnish government council, named the Senate for Finland since 1816, and presided over by a Russian governor-general representing the tsar. The Estates Diet, summoned in 1809 to sanction the new arrangements, was not called again until 1863, signalling the beginning of a new era of legislative and political activity. A loosely organized Finnish Party* emerged at that point, dedicated mainly to the primacy of the Finnish language and culture. A Swedish Party (see Swedish People's Party) evolved in the 1870s and 1880s as Swedish-speakers organized in defense of their privileges and interests. A labor movement grew up in the 1880s, leading to the formation of a political party (see Finnish Social Democratic Party) at the end of the following decade. In the 1890s, the Finnish Party split into conservative and liberal groupings.

The threat of Russification, turning into a full-fledged campaign after 1899, moved the linguistic issue into the background as the parties responded to Russian oppressive measures. In 1905, with Russia weakened by war with Japan and massive internal turmoil, a general strike in Finland brought Russian concessions. In November the tsar empowered the Finnish Senate to prepare proposals for legislative reforms. The result was the Parliament Act of 1906 and full democratic freedoms. And the Agrarian Union (see Center Party) was formed as the nation prepared for the parliamentary election of 1907, the first to be conducted on the basis of universal suffrage.

But another decade of Russian oppression began in 1907, a decade during which Finland went through eight parliamentary elections (for the composition of the parliament during this period, see table 19), its Senate was reduced to impotence, and some of its leaders were consigned to Siberian exile. World War

I aroused hopes of independence, and Russia's military collapse and the Bolshevik revolution provided the opportunity. On December 6, 1917, the Senate proclaimed Finland independent. Civil war followed seven weeks later.

The bloody Civil War of 1918 reflected long-standing economic and social inequities, and it pitted the Red (communist-supporting) majority of the working class against the White (tsarist) farmers and urban bourgeoisie in an uncompromising struggle for control of the newly independent state. The Whites won and promptly took brutal vengeance. Thousands of Reds died in postwar concentration camps. This trauma deepened already existing social cleavages and was to have a decisive impact on Finnish politics for at least two generations. (Table 20 shows the effect on the makeup of the legislature.) Not only was the Finnish Communist Party* driven underground after a decade of official—and not entirely undeserved—harassment, but even the Finnish Social Democratic Party was considered too leftist and unfit for government participation during the period between the world wars. And there was a strong right-wing trend during much of the 1930s, including a fascist fringe movement.

World War II brought renewed trauma. Attacked by the Soviet Union in 1939, Finland joined Germany in attacking the Soviet Union in 1941, only to emerge defeated in 1944 and deprived of some 10 percent of its territory. Finland escaped occupation, but a Soviet-controlled Allied Control Commission resided in Helsinki until 1947, a nearly crippling war indemnity had to be paid, and there were massive problems of reconstruction and refugee resettlement. Most importantly, the Finnish Communist Party was restored to full political activity, and Finland was required to develop and maintain a foreign policy that posed no threat to Soviet security. That policy, developed by President Juho Kusti Paasikivi (1946-1956) and refined and extended by President Urho Kaleva Kekkonen (1956-), is generally referred to as the Paasikivi-Kekkonen line.

Perhaps ironically, defeat and the imperative of surviving next door to the Soviet Union forced the completion of extending full democratic and political rights to all segments of Finland's population, notably the left wing. (For the distribution of legislative seats, see table 21.) The Finnish Communist Party resurfaced as soon as the war ended, and together with dissident left-wing Social Democrats formed the Finnish People's Democratic League,* a permanent electoral alliance or pseudoparty under whose banner these groups have contested all elections since 1945. Joining the Social Democrats and Agrarians in a Red-Green coalition, this League served in three successive governments from 1944 to 1948 and had the prime ministry from 1946 to 1948. Kept out of all governments for 18 years thereafter, it has since participated in most cabinets from 1966 to 1970 and from 1975 to the present.

Finnish governments are traditionally short-lived, having averaged just over 12 months each since 1917. The longevity record was established by Toivo Kivimäki's bourgeois coalition which held office from December 1932 to October 1936. Multiparty coalitions are the rule rather than the exception in Finland (see table 22). Only seven of the 61 cabinets since 1917 have been single-party ones; nine have been more or less nonpolitical presidial, or caretaker, cabinets; and 45 have been coalitions of two to six parties. This gives an obvious advantage to parties of the center, which can align themselves more easily with other parties in either direction. Not surprisingly the Agrarians, who occupy the center of the Finnish political spectrum (and changed their name in 1965 to the Center Party), have served in more governments than any other party, including all but one of the coalitions.

Since the mid-1960s, there has been a marked trend toward the center in Finnish politics, a trend which has left four large parties predominant. But it has also caused a number of minor and miniparties to be spun off as dissidents refused to follow the majority. An attempt to brake this party fragmentation—which is by no means a novel phenomenon in Finnish politics—was made with the Election Act of 1969. Fully implemented since 1972, it requires all parties to be registered with the ministry of justice, and any party that fails to win parliamentary representation in two successive elections is automatically deregistered, thus losing its party status. New parties can obtain official recognition by presenting a petition signed by at least 5,000 eligible voters. Only recognized parties may now nominate candidates, and no candidate may stand for election in more than one district.

Although the centripetal trend is not unique to Finland, one uniquely Finnish circumstance may well have served to accelerate the trend there since World War II. Because of the imperative of subscribing to the Paasikivi-Kekkonen line in foreign policy, no political party that fails to give that policy its unqualified support, or that is adjudged suspect on that point by the Soviet Union, can assume cabinet responsibility without causing problems for Finnish-Soviet relations. This does not mean that Finnish parties must be either pro-Soviet or procommunist, nor indeed that they may not be anticommunist; but it does mean that they may not be anti-Soviet if they wish to be eligible for government participation. This requirement is rooted in Soviet memories of the Finnish-German attack in 1941 and the strong anti-Soviet attitude of Finnish parties after 1918. Thus the Social Democratic Party, anathema to Moscow after the Finnish civil war, had recurrent problems with the Soviet Union until it purged the last survivors of the post-1918 leadership in 1963. That left the National Coalition Party* as the only major party still under a cloud of Soviet suspicion, and it has been excluded from all cabinets since 1966.

Except for this prudent self-limitation produced by history and confined to the realm of foreign affairs, there are no restrictions on political activity or democratic freedoms in Finland. That the parties and parliament have lost some of their normal power and influence to the president is due to a combination of abdication on their part and the exceptional abilities and acuity of President Kekkonen. Most of the parties have been beset by internal strife and external competition and have evidenced an often appalling unwillingness to accept responsibility for major political decisions. This has left the stage to Kekkonen, whose willingness to take charge has never been conspicuously lacking. There are strong signs, however, that the parties are now moving to correct this imbalance and restore parliament to its full constitutional role, perhaps through constitutional reforms restricting the presidential powers.

Bibliography

Allardt, Erik, and Pertti Pesonen. "Cleavages in Finnish Politics." In *Party Systems and Voter Alignments: Cross-National Perspectives*, edited by Seymour M. Lipset and Stein Rokkan. New York: Free Press, 1967.

Berglund, Sten, and Ulf Lindström. *The Scandinavian Party System(s)*. Lund: Student-litteratur, 1978.

Borg, Olavi. "Basic Dimensions of Finnish Party Ideologies: A Factor Analytical Study." *Scandinavian Political Studies* 1 (1966): 94-117.

Krosby, H. Peter. "Finland: The Politics of Economic Emergency." *Current History* 70 (1976): 173-176, 184.

Kuusisto, Allan A. "Parliamentary Crises and Presidial Governments in Finland." *Parliamentary Affairs* 11 (1958): 341-349.

Nousiainen, Jaakko. *The Finnish Political System*. Cambridge, Mass.: Harvard University Press, 1971.

Pesonen, Pertti. *An Election in Finland: Party Activities and Voter Reactions*. New Haven, Conn.: Yale University Press, 1968.

Rantala, Onni. "The Political Regions of Finland." *Scandinavian Political Studies* 2 (1967): 117-140.

Törnudd, Klaus. "Composition of Cabinets in Finland, 1917-1968." *Scandinavian Political Studies* 4 (1969): 58-70.

———. *The Electoral System of Finland*. London: Hugh Evelyn, 1968.

Political Parties

AGRARFÖRBUNDET. *See* CENTER PARTY.

AGRARIAN PARTY OPPOSITION. *See* CENTER PARTY.

AGRARIAN UNION. *See* CENTER PARTY.

AGRARPARTIETS OPPOSITION. *See* CENTER PARTY.

AHVENANMAAN KOKOOMUS. *See* ÅLAND COALITION.

ÅLAND COALITION (*Ahvenanmaan Kokoomus; Åländsk Samling:* ÅL.SAML.). The Åland Islands, an archipelago of thousands of islands in the Baltic Sea off the southwestern tip of mainland Finland, were demilitarized by international convention in 1856 and by the League of Nations in 1921. The population (22,500) is 96 percent Swedish-speaking and has a history of separatism, but efforts to join Sweden were rebuffed after World War I. The League of Nations confirmed Finland's sovereignty over Åland but also guaranteed Åland's status as an autonomous province. Finland assumed that guarantee unilaterally in 1951, thus preserving Åland's Swedish character in perpetuity. Åland is allotted one member of the Finnish parliament, who invariably joins forces with the Swedish People's Party. *

The Åland Coalition is an electoral organization embracing all noncommunist groups, a total of six in 1979. It has participated in all elections since 1948, always receiving over 90 percent of the Åland vote (98.5 percent in 1979).

ÅLÄNDSK SAMLING. See ÅLAND COALITION.

ÅL.SAML. See ÅLAND COALITION.

AP. See FINNISH COMMUNIST PARTY and FINNISH SOCIAL DEMO-CRATIC PARTY.

ARBETARNAS OCH SMÅBRUKARNAS PARTI. See FINNISH COMMU-NIST PARTY.

ARBETARNAS OCH SMÅBRUKARNAS SOCIALDEMOKRATISKA FÖRBUND. See SOCIAL DEMOCRATIC LEAGUE OF WORKERS AND SMALLHOLDERS.

ASSF. See SOCIAL DEMOCRATIC LEAGUE OF WORKERS AND SMALL-HOLDERS.

CENTERPARTIET. See CENTER PARTY.

CENTER PARTY (Keskustapuolue: KP; Centerpartiet: CP). The KP was originally founded as the Agrarian Union (Maalaisliitto; Agrarförbundet) in October 1906, although its political program was not definitively settled until late 1908. The Agrarian Union was essentially an offshoot of the late 19th-century Finnish movement (see Finnish Party), with the Union's separate existence made practicable by the introduction of universal suffrage. A strongly nationalistic party, the Union was also imbued with the peasant romanticism of its founder, Santeri Alkio, a shopkeeper and popular writer of rustic tales. But the party's main political purpose was to represent the interests of the small farm owners of northern and eastern Finland against the overweening influence of the big landowners, urban bourgeoisie, and state bureaucracy.

At the time of its founding, the Center Party was perhaps more genuinely democratic than any other political group in Finland. There was also a streak of radicalism in the party, as seen most clearly in its flirtation with the Finnish Social Democratic Party (SDP) * on the eve of Finland's independence. Since the civil war, in which the peasantry provided the bulk of tsarist manpower, the KP has been both antisocialist and anti-big business, although it has never hesitated to align itself with either in government coalitions. The KP has served in coalitions including the National Coalition Party* on 20 occasions, all but three of them prior to 1944, and with the SDP 29 times (including three "nonpolitical" presidial cabinets) since 1937. Cooperation between the KP and the SDP has, in fact, been the most consistent ingredient in Finland's postwar political stability, albeit a cooperation punctuated by vigorous rivalry.

For the Center Party, this sort of opportunism, or pragmatism, is born of necessity. Strictly an agrarian party in the beginning—the name change from Agrarian Union to Center Party did not occur until 1965—its popular base has been dwindling steadily, especially since Finland's belated industrial revolution after World War II accelerated the population shift from rural to urban areas. This forced the party not only to change its name in a so-far-not-very-successful effort to broaden its electoral appeal, but also to take positions on national issues of little immediate concern to its agrarian clientele. For example, the KP has sought to present itself as the chief custodian of the Paasikivi-Kekkonen foreign policy line, a claim not entirely without merit though deeply resented by other parties. The Centrists stand for the sanctity of private property and free-enterprise capitalism, but only regarding relatively small-scale enterprises—industrial, commercial, or agricultural—evenly distributed throughout the country. And the KP favors the nationalization of large industries which fail to serve the general national interest. The KP also advocates central state planning of all production.

Essentially, the Center Party's broad-based program is designed to stem the population flow away from the countryside, and perhaps to reverse it. For the fact is that the KP remains today a party for the small farmers of northern and eastern Finland. It has failed to make significant inroads among the voters of heavily populated south and southwest Finland, and its relative strength among the parties is declining. Popular KP support in parliamentary elections grew slowly from 5.8 to 12.4 percent in the pre-independence period, then jumped dramatically after the civil war. From 1919 to 1966, the KP was Finland's second-largest party; and during three parliamentary periods (1929-1930, 1948-1951, 1962-1966), it was the largest party. Since 1970, however, the KP has stood third, its electoral support a stable 16 to 17 percent, and it seems destined to slip to fourth place.

Like other major Finnish parties, the KP has suffered from internal personality and policy conflicts, and its various turns toward left or right in order to stay in the center have caused dissidents to split off and form rival parties. This has been particularly true in the postwar period of government cooperation with the Social Democrats. For example, an Agrarian Party Opposition (*Maalaisliton Oppositio; Agrarpartiets Opposition*) fielded its own candidates in the 1958 election but drew only a few thousand votes and disappeared. That was not the case, however, with the Finnish Rural Party,* another 1958-1959 spin-off that eventually became a major threat to the KP and probably contributed significantly to the decline of its parent party. The Finnish Center Party (*Suomen Keskustapuolue; Finlands Centerparti*), which made its brief and utterly unsuccessful appearance in the 1962 election, was actually a KP trial balloon intended to test the party's potential appeal to urban voters.

Even if the KP fails in its efforts to gain new voters outside of its traditional agrarian base, the party's role as a major Finnish political force seems secure, and the KP will probably continue to be a necessary pivot of Finnish coalition cabinets. Ably led since World War II by V. J. Sukselainen (1945-1964) and Johannes Virolainen (1965-1980), the Centrists are now under the energetic chairmanship of Paavo Väyrynen. Born in 1946, Väyrynen is a veteran member of parliament and several governments, and he is the brightest of a handful of very young Finnish political stars. Already the KP has provided Finland with three presidents—Lauri Relander (1925-1931), Kyösti Kallio (1937-1940), and Urho Kekkonen (1956-   )—and more cabinet ministers than any other party.

CHRISTIAN WORKERS' PARTY (*Kristillinen Työväenpuolue; Kristliga Arbetarpartiet*). Opposed to the marxist revolutionary radicalism of the Finnish Social Democratic Party* before the civil war, the Christian Workers' Party contested all parliamentary elections from 1907 to 1919, gaining 1.5 to 2.7 percent of the vote, and winning one or two seats in all but two of those nine elections.

CONSTITUTIONAL FINNISH-MINDED PARTY. See FINNISH PARTY.

CONSTITUTIONAL PEOPLE'S PARTY (*Perustuslaillinen Kansanpuolue*: PKP; *Konstitutionella Folkpartiet*: KFP). The PKP was organized in 1973 by right-wing defectors from other bourgeois parties, notably the National Coalition Party* and the Swedish People's Party.* Originally named the Finnish Constitutional People's Party (*Suomen Perustuslaillinen Kansanpuolue; Finlands Konstitutionella Folkparti*), the PKP took its present name in 1976.

Occupying the extreme right wing in Finnish politics, the PKP is militantly anticommunist and still views the 1918 civil war as a war of independence. It maintains that Finland's foreign policy is slanted toward the Soviet Union and calls for a balanced—though not ideologically neutral—policy of neutrality, a strong defense, and closer ties to Scandinavia. The party seeks to preserve and strengthen the Swedish language and culture of Finland. It has been vigorously critical of President Kekkonen and advocates radical constitutional reform aimed at the supremacy of parliament over the president. The PKP social policy stresses prevention rather than welfare.

Led since 1974 with a strong hand by Georg Ehrnrooth (who represented the Swedish People's Party in parliament from 1958 to 1974), the PKP has been torn by dissension and defections. Ehrnrooth retained his seat on the PKP ticket in the 1975 election but lost it in 1979 in spite of a large individual vote (he got more votes than 14 of the 20 successful candidates in Helsinki). The party ran its own candidate in the 1978 presidential election, but he won only six of the 300 electoral college members. If the PKP manages to stay intact and to concentrate its electoral support around a few candidates, it is likely to regain parliamentary representation.

CP. *See* CENTER PARTY.

DEMOKRATISKA FÖRBUNDET AV FINLANDS FOLK. *See* FINNISH PEOPLE'S DEMOCRATIC LEAGUE.

DFFF. *See* FINNISH PEOPLE'S DEMOCRATIC LEAGUE.

FFEP. *See* FINNISH PEOPLE'S UNITY PARTY.

FFR. *See* PATRIOTIC PEOPLE'S MOVEMENT.

FINLANDS ARBETARPARTI. *See* FINNISH COMMUNIST PARTY and FINNISH SOCIAL DEMOCRATIC PARTY.

FINLANDS CENTERPARTI. *See* CENTER PARTY.

FINLANDS FOLKS ENHETSPARTI. *See* FINNISH PEOPLE'S UNITY PARTY.

FINLANDS KOMMUNISTISKA ARBETARPARTI. *See* FINNISH COMMUNIST PARTY.

FINLANDS KOMMUNISTISKA PARTI. *See* FINNISH COMMUNIST PARTY.

FINLANDS KONSTITUTIONELLA FOLKPARTI. *See* CONSTITUTIONAL PEOPLE'S PARTY.

FINLANDS KRISTLIGA FÖRBUND. *See* FINNISH CHRISTIAN LEAGUE.

FINLANDS LANDSBYGDSPARTI. *See* FINNISH RURAL PARTY.

FINLANDS SMÅBONDEPARTI. *See* FINNISH RURAL PARTY.

FINLANDS SOCIALDEMOKRATISKA PARTI. *See* FINNISH SOCIAL DEMOCRATIC PARTY.

FINLANDS SOCIALISTISKA ARBETARPARTI. *See* FINNISH COMMUNIST PARTY.

FINNISH CENTER PARTY. *See* CENTER PARTY.

FINNISH CHRISTIAN LEAGUE (*Suomen Kristillinen Liitto*: SKL; *Finlands Kristliga Förbund*: FKF). Founded in 1958 in reaction to the moral secularization of Finnish society, the SKL is considered to be a right-wing party. Its primary purpose is the creation of a society built on a "Christian world view," and it advocates close collaboration between state and church to that end. The League wants to strengthen religious instruction in public schools and considers that the arts should serve conservative national values and Christian faith and morals. It favors a free-enterprise economy but wants to keep productive units small and dispersed. The SKL position on social welfare is that society is responsible for the poor, infirm, and incapacitated, but not the indolent. On the latter point, the party program cites Saint Paul: "If any would not work, neither should he eat." The SKL supports the Paasikivi-Kekkonen foreign policy line and calls for increased economic aid to developing countries.

The SKL was not formally registered as a party until 1972, although it contested the parliamentary elections of 1966 and 1970, winning one seat in the latter. Since then it has enjoyed remarkable success for a small party, raising its parliamentary representation to four seats in 1972 and nine in 1975. It retained these seats in 1979 when it won 4.8 percent of the vote, thus equalling the Swedish People's Party* and surpassing the Finnish Rural Party (SMP),* although Raimo Westerholm, the SKL chairman since 1973, lost the seat he first won in 1970. The SKL now has ten seats, having gained one lost by the SMP through the death of one of its members. SKL voters are distributed fairly evenly throughout the country, except the far north, with a certain concentration in the southeastern and south-central provinces.

FINNISH COMMUNIST PARTY (*Suomen Kommunistinen Puolue*: SKP; *Finlands Kommunistiska Parti*: FKP). The SKP was founded in Moscow in August 1918 by leaders of the Finnish Social Democratic Party (SDP)* who had fled Finland at the end of the civil war. The original SKP program abjured the parliamentary process and democratic tactics, insisting that only violent armed revolution could achieve the "iron dictatorshiop of the workers." When the SKP joined the Comintern, Finnish courts immediately ruled the party a criminal organization. The SKP remained in exile until September 1944, operating from Moscow and Stockholm. Most of the party's top figures fell victim to the Soviet purges of the 1930s; the only notable survivor was Otto Wille Kuusinen, who made a brilliant career in the Comintern and the Communist Party of the Soviet Union (*see* SOVIET UNION).

Returning surreptitiously to Finland in Spring 1919, Kuusinen found conditions unsuitable for renewed revolution. Improvising, in violation of his instructions, he tried instead to recapture the Social Democratic Party. When the attempt failed, being narrowly defeated at the SDP national convention in December, Kuusinen built a new party around the captured SDP Helsinki organization. In May 1920, that group reconstituted itself as the Finnish Socialist Workers' Party (*Suomen Sosialistinen Työväenpuolue*: SSTP; *Finlands Socialistiska*

Arbetarparti: FSAP), but it was broken up by police when it voted to join the Comintern. It regrouped in June under the same name but without joining the Comintern. The SSTP won 14.8 percent of the vote and 27 seats to the 1922 Finnish parliament, its greatest electoral success in four outings under that and other labels.

Faithfully obeying Finnish Communist Party directives, the SSTP's parliamentary contingent indulged in violently revolutionary oratory—once even moving that the constitution be abrogated and a soviet republic established, thus provoking increased police harassment and calls for the party's suppression. Realizing the danger, the SSTP in May 1923 changed its name to the Finnish Workers' Party (*Suomen Työväenpuolue*: STP; *Finlands Arbetarparti*: AP, not to be confused with an earlier Finnish Workers' Party under Social Democratic auspices) and toned down its extremism. Even so, in August the party's leadership, parliamentary representatives, newspaper editors, and other officials were arrested, eventually to be convicted and imprisoned after a dubious political trial. In March 1925, the Finnish Supreme Court declared the STP illegal.

Yet overt political activity continued. Under various electoral guises, generally if inaccurately referred to as the Workers' and Smallholders' Party (*Työväen ja Pienviljeläin Puolue*; *Arbetarnas och Småbrukarnas Parti*), the Finnish Communists and their allies won 18 seats to the 1924 parliament, 20 in 1927, and 23 in 1929 when their vote reached 13.5 percent. But no new public party was created. The Finnish Communist Party had found it difficult to control the STP, whose leaders viewed the emigrés in Moscow as being out of touch with realities in Finland and hence tended to go their own ways. It was easier to control the individual parts of an amorphous movement, and the SKP tried to do so through an underground network of reliable party organizers and agitators. Special attention was paid to the trade unions, whose central organization the SKP had captured in 1920.

The police struck again in Spring 1928, and the entire SKP underground leadership was arrested. Further setbacks came in 1929 when the Social Democratic Party pulled its trade unions out of the Communist-dominated central federation and set up its own, while leading members of the SKP parliamentary group broke away and formed the Left Group of Finnish Workers (*Suomen Työväen Vasemmistoryhmä*).

At the same time, the rabidly anticommunist Lapua movement (*see* Patriotic People's Movement) sprang up, quickly assuming nationwide proportions and fascist characteristics. In June 1930, Lapua hooligans kidnapped two Communist members of parliament, whereupon the police arrested the rest, parliament was dissolved, and new elections were called. Due to violent Lapua intimidation, only 11,504 votes were cast for Communist Party candidates, none was elected, and in October the new parliament prohibited all Communist activity. By 1935 most Communist activists had been imprisoned, and the work of the SKP in Finland was effectively crippled—except at the "Communist University" within the walls of the Tammisaari prison, a prime source of post-World War II party leaders.

After 1935, the Finnish Communist Party disbanded what remained of its underground network in Finland and concentrated without much success on the creation of antifascist popular fronts. On December 1, 1939, following its invasion of Finland, the Soviet Union set up a "Finnish People's Government" under Kuusinen's premiership, quietly shelving it a few weeks later when it met with no positive response among Finnish workers. During the Finnish-Soviet war of 1941-1944, the SKP organized small partisan bands on Finnish territory, a futile venture which produced some 20 martyrs to the cause but no disruption of the Finnish war effort.

Two points might be made about SKP activities between 1918 and 1944. First, the emigré leadership, slavishly obedient to Comintern directives, pursued a course which reflected shifting Soviet priorities and ignored the real concerns of Finnish workers, who felt that even the Social Democrats after 1918 had sold out to the bourgeoisie. Second, the SKP was never a threat to Finnish independence during those years; the violent reaction to its pronouncements and illicit activities reflected perceptions as unrealistic as those of the SKP itself. The only genuine threat to Finnish democracy came from the right.

The Finnish-Soviet armistice agreement of September 19, 1944, lifted the prohibition on communist activity, and the SKP was registered as a political party in late October. At the same time, on the initiative of left-wing Social Democratic dissidents, the SKP joined in the formation of the Finnish People's Democratic League (SKDL), * a permanent electoral alliance through which the SKP has contested all postwar elections. Thus it is difficult to measure precisely the mass support of the SKP itself, except by the fact that the great majority of successful SKDL candidates always has been Communist. But this may be misleading as an indicator, for it seems probable that the bulk of votes cast for the SKDL has remained a protest vote against the Social Democratic Party. Perhaps symptomatically, SKP membership since the war has stood at 40,000 to 50,000, while SKDL membership has been in the 140,000 to 170,000 range.

Not surprisingly, the Finnish Communist Party experienced some problems adjusting to postwar life as a legal party in a democratic system, although it has demonstrated a greater doctrinal and tactical flexibility than in prewar years. In October 1944, its leaders, newly emerged from prison or hiding, resolved to adopt a constitutional rather than revolutionary course and to seek mass support at the polls. But the SKP Central Committee, which would survive almost intact for over two decades, was composed of loyal stalinists such as Aimo Aaltonen (chairman, 1944-1966), Ville Pessi (secretary-general, 1944-1969), and Hertta Kuusinen (the fiery and personable daughter of Otto Kuusinen). For three years, until the September 1947 ratification of the Finnish-Soviet peace treaty, the SKP no doubt profited from the presence in Helsinki of a Soviet-dominated Allied Control Commission. When Yrjö Leino, Hertta Kuusinen's husband, became minister of the interior in April 1945, the Finnish Communists took a vigorous lead in implementing those armistice stipulations that required the proscription of "fascist-type" organizations and the prosecution of "war criminals." The party's arrogance in those years left it vulnerable when the Control Commission departed and anticommunist sentiments resurfaced, reinforced by international events of 1947-1948 and by unsubstantiated rumors of SKP coup plans in March-April 1948. In May, Leino was censured by parliament for malfeasance in office, and he was removed from the cabinet. The Agrarians (see Center Party) and Social Democrats dissolved their Red-Green bloc agreement with the SKP for government collaboration, and the voters administered a rebuke to the Communists in the July 1948 election when the SKDL lost 13 seats (including two gained when Social Democratic defectors had jumped to the SKDL after the 1945 election). The new government had no Communist Party ministers.

Inexperience and arrogance brought on the 1948 debacle. By the time the SKP was readmitted to cabinet responsibility in 1966, a new generation of moderate leaders had started to push the 1944 generation and its ideas out of the party leadership. Showing their muscle in 1965, the new leaders defeated Hertta Kuusinen for a top SKDL post in favor of a non-Communist; and in 1966 they put in their own man, Aarne Saarinen, as SKP chairman. The revolt was completed in 1969 when Pessi was replaced as secretary-general in favor of Arvo Aalto, and the Central Committee membership was thoroughly revamped. The defeated stalinists formed a new party, the Finnish Communist Workers' Party (*Suomen Kommunistinen Työväenpuolue; Finlands Kommunistiska Arbetarparti*), but Soviet intervention prevented an open split. The opposition, led by Taisto Sinisalo, set up a full-fledged political organization but did not register it as a party. A superficial reconciliation, effected on the eve of the March 1970 election, nonetheless proved a major setback for the SKP. The SKDL got only 16.6 percent of the vote, down from 21.2 in 1966, and was lucky to elect 36 representatives (including 19 SKP reformers, 15 SKP traditionalists, and two non-Communists).

Since then the Sinisalo faction, popularly known as Taistoites, has increased its attacks on SKP majority leaders and policies, thus defying party discipline which requires democratic decision making and absolute solidarity once decisions have been made. While clearly enjoying Soviet favor, the minority has been driven back gradually, and Sinisalo himself lost his seat in parliament in 1979. Saarinen now appears ready for a showdown. In October 1979, he described the stalinists' "extremist attitudes" as outdated and irrelevant, an "unnecessary ballast" which the party must jettison. The 1981 party congress failed to resolve this issue. Instead, a compromise was fashioned with the election of Saarinen as party chairman and Sinisalo as deputy chairman.

The current SKP program, adopted by the Fifteenth Party Congress in 1969, espouses the "Finnish road to socialism," described as peaceful and democratic, requiring the support of a popular and parliamentary majority. The experience of existing socialist countries offers useful models, but uniquely Finnish traditions and characteristics are considered equally important. The transition to socialism would involve extensive nationalization of the means of production, but private ownership of small- and medium-sized enterprises, especially already existing producer and consumer cooperatives, would be permitted if they are not exploitive. All economic activity would be subject to central state planning. Full employment, stable prices, and rent control would be maintained. The social security system would be completed, industrial democracy fully developed, and the police and armed forces democratized. Other political parties enjoying the support of "the working people" would be free to function, but the development of socialism must be led by a "workers' party guided by the lodestar of scientific socialist theory created by Marx, Engels, and Lenin."

In the area of foreign policy and security, the Finnish Communist Party supports the Paasikivi-Kekkonen line, promotes nuclear-free zones and the limitation of nuclear arms, partial as well as general disarmament, collective security in Europe, and a reduction of the Finnish armed forces. The SKP stresses friendship with the Soviet Union and peaceful coexistence among states with different social systems.

Further Reference. Hodgson, John H., *Communism in Finland: A History and Interpretation* (Princeton, N.J.: Princeton University Press, 1967), and "Finland: The SKP and Electoral Politics," in *Communism and Political Systems in Western Europe*, edited by David E. Albright (Boulder, Colo.: Westview Press, 1979); Upton, A. F., "The Communist Party of Finland," in *Communism in Scandinavia and Finland: Politics of Opportunity*, edited by A. F. Upton (Garden City, N.Y.: Anchor Books/Doubleday, 1973); Wagner, Ulrich, *Finnlands Kommunisten: Volksfrontexperiment und Parteispaltung 1966-1970* (Stuttgart: Verlag W. Kohlhammer, 1971).

FINNISH COMMUNIST WORKERS' PARTY. *See* FINNISH COMMUNIST PARTY.

FINNISH CONSTITUTIONAL PEOPLE'S PARTY. *See* CONSTITUTIONAL PEOPLE'S PARTY.

FINNISH PARTY (*Suomalainen Puolue*; *Finska Partiet*). The historic root from which several of Finland's modern parties grew, the Finnish Party emerged rather amorphously from the Diet of 1863, gradually assuming a more distinctive organizational form and surviving in various shapes until 1918. Its primary raison d'être was the promotion of Finnish language and culture at the expense of Swedish, on the assumption that only an indigenous Finnish mass culture could evoke the national spirit necessary to resist eventual assimilation by Russia. Led by the historian Yrjö Sakari Yrjö-Koskinen until his death in 1903, the party was responsible for the establishment of Finnish-language schools, the introduction of Finnish as a coequal administrative language, and the rise of Finnish-language literature and Finnish-oriented historiography.

Yrjö-Koskinen's single-minded dedication to the promotion of Finnish, a cause he equated with patriotism, not only forced the Swedish-speaking elite to start its own party (*see* Swedish People's Party) but also spawned groups within his own party whose concerns transcended his. A Liberal Club led by Leo

Mechelin emerged in 1877-1878 and in 1880 published a Liberal Party Program that urged that promotion of Finnish-language education take a backseat to such causes as economic liberalism and democratic reform. Denounced by Finnish nationalists, most of these early liberals soon joined the Swedish Party (*see* Swedish People's Party). A liberal academic group emerged in the late 1880s in response to increased Russian pressure on autonomous Finnish institutions. These Young Finns remained faithful to the Finnish Party's cultural program but were willing to work with Swedish elements against the threat of Russification.

After 1899, when the Russification campaign shifted into high gear, the Young Finns, led by Jonas Castrén, adopted a policy of passive resistance in defense of Finnish constitutional rights. They organized the Constitutional Finnish-Minded Party (1902), which in 1906 was transformed into the Young Finnish Party (*Nuorsuomalainen Puolue; Ungfinska Partiet*). The conservative wing of the Finnish Party, known since the early 1890s as the Old Finns (*Vanhasuomalaiset; Gammalfinnarna*) and led since 1903 by Johan Danielson-Kalmari, chose a course of partial compliance with Russian decrees designed to save something rather than risk losing everything.

Thus by 1906 the two wings of the Finnish Party stood as wholly separate entities, ready to contest the first democratic parliamentary election in 1907. The Old Finns proved the stronger, winning 59 seats to 26 for the Young Finns. But while the latter maintained a stable support level during the ensuing decade, the Old Finns, due to their increasingly unpopular compliance policy, declined steadily to a low of 33 seats in 1916. In the 1917 election, the last before Finland's independence, both Finnish parties and a liberal splinter group, the People's Party (*Kansanpuolue; Folkpartiet*, not to be confused with a People's Party* of a later time), joined in an antisocialist bourgeois electoral alliance, the United Finnish Parties, which won 61 seats (Old Finns, 32; Young Finns, 24; People's Party, five).

The definitive division and demise of the Finnish Party came in 1918 as newly independent Finland weighed the issue of a monarchist versus a republican form of government. Most Old Finns were conservative and monarchist; the small People's Party was liberal and republican; and the Young Finns were badly split between monarchists, led by Pehr Evind Svinhufvud, and republicans, led by Kaarlo Ståhlberg. In the end, the Young Finn Ståhlberg faction and the People's Party, joined by the small Old Finn republican minority, on December 8 founded the National Progressive Party (*see* Liberal People's Party), while the Old Finn majority and the Young Finn Svinhufvud faction formed the National Coalition Party* the next day.

FINNISH PEOPLE'S DEMOCRATIC LEAGUE (*Suomen Kansan Demokraattinen Liitto:* SKDL; *Demokratiska Förbundet av Finlands Folk:* DFFF). This permanent electoral alliance, or pseudoparty, was founded on October 29, 1944, by dissidents of the Finnish Social Democratic Party (SDP)* and the Finnish Communist Party (SKP)* who hoped to build a broad antifascist popular front of left-of-center groupings. That hope was dashed when the SDP by a close vote decided to stay out, but more than 100 SDP local chapters and several other political and cultural associations did join. In 1946 the left-wing socialists organized the Socialist Unity Party (*Socialistinen Yhtenäisyyspuolue; Socialistiska Enhetspartiet*), which was a component part of the SKDL during the Unity Party's nine-year existence.

In 11 postwar parliamentary elections, the SKDL has averaged one-fifth of the vote, with peaks of 23.5 percent in 1945 and 23.2 percent in 1958 when it outpolled all other parties and won 50 seats. The SKDL is the only party capable of giving the Center Party* a close race in economically depressed northern Finland. The Soviet invasion of Czechoslovakia, coupled with a rift in the SKP, caused the SKDL its great election setback of 1970, at which time it fell to 16.7 percent of the vote and 36 seats. It has not been able to make a significant recovery since then.

Although the Finnish Communist Party accounts for less than one-third of the total SKDL membership, the Communists' superior organization and discipline have made it the dominant SKDL force since the beginning. Except for 1945, when ten of 49 SKDL seats were won by non-Communists, 90 to 95 percent of the successful SKDL candidates in all parliamentary elections have been Communists. Yet the SKP consistently has refused to take open control of the organization, in spite of recurring demands from within its own rank to do so. Apparently, the SKDL's usefulness as an electoral front would be forfeited if a merger or takeover were effected.

But that assumption also creates a strong negotiating position for the non-Communist elements in the SKDL, although they failed to take advantage of it until the mid-1960s. The election of Ele Alenius as secretary-general in February 1965, and then as chairman in 1967, started a new and increasingly democratic trend in the SKDL, a trend which may have influenced the coincidental Communist Party evolution as much as reflected it. By 1975, Alenius had become the target of strident Soviet criticism that the SKDL under him was leading the SKP rather than the other way around. The SKP majority responded by giving Alenius its most resounding support.

The elevation of Alenius to the SKDL chairmanship coincided with the adoption of a new party program which reflected his ideas. It recognized that Finnish society had undergone major structural changes since 1944, was more affluent and democratic than ever before, and that even the working class was moving toward the center of the political spectrum. The SKDL saw as its task to further that trend by working for increased economic equality, industrial democracy, social justice and security, a higher minimum wage and more equitable taxation, nationalization of monopoly enterprises and more effective utilization of natural resources through central planning, and the separation of church and state. The program offered "a democratic and socialist alternative" for Finland's further economic and democratic development and extended an invitation to the "forces of the center" to collaborate in its implementation. And it stressed that the means employed must always be democratic. The Paasikivi-Kekkonen foreign policy line was, as in the past, given unqualified support.

The draft of a revised program, published in April 1979, went farther along the same lines, but the nationalization of monopoly enterprises was now described as a last resort, to be adopted only if public control agencies failed to keep them in line. The draft program also called for a constitutional amendment making parliament the supreme organ of state authority. Two months later, at the SKDL's Twelfth Party Congress, Alenius noted that socialism remained the party's goal, but not a socialism tied to marxist-leninist philosophy. There was no conflict, he said, between SKDL-type socialism and a consumer society. SKP Chairman Aarne Saarinen echoed Alenius's statements. The SKDL, he said, must continue to move toward the center. Kalevi Kivistö, a non-Communist who succeeded Alenius as chairman at the end of the congress, hailed what he called "a humanistic socialism in blue and white"—the colors of the Finnish flag. In sum, the SKDL seems firmly launched on "the Finnish road to socialism," a concept of which Alenius has been the main theoretician.

FINNISH PEOPLE'S PARTY. See LIBERAL PEOPLE'S PARTY and PEOPLE'S PARTY.

FINNISH PEOPLE'S UNITY PARTY (Suomen Kansan Yhtenäisyyden Puolue: SKYP; Finlands Folks Enhetsparti: FFEP). The SKYP emerged in 1972-1973 when 13 of the 18 members of parliament for the Finnish Rural Party (SMP)* broke away as a consequence of policy differences and deep personality conflicts with the SMP chairman. Led from 1973 to 1979 by Eino Haikala, the SKYP lost all but one of its seats in the 1975 election, in which it received 1.6 percent of the vote. That percentage was cut in half in the 1978 presidential election—Haikala failed to win a single elector. In 1979 the SKYP was eliminated from parliament with a vote of 0.3 percent, and a Gallup Poll at the end of that year showed continued decline. Recovery is not expected.

FINNISH PRIVATE ENTREPRENEURS' PARTY (Suomen Yksityisyrittäjäin Puoluejärjestö: SYP; Privateföretagarnas Partioganisation i Finland: PPF). Founded in 1972 under the chairmanship of Reijo Tamminiemi, the SYP hoped to represent small businessmen. Its conservative program exalted private property rights and free-enterprise capitalism and called for a strong defense, careful scrutiny of welfare expenditures, tax reforms, and patriotism. With 0.4 and 0.04 percent of the votes in the 1975 and 1979 elections, the party failed to win representation and was deregistered.

FINNISH RURAL PARTY (Suomen Maaseudun Puolue: SMP; Finlands Landsbygdsparti: FLP). A perennial phenomenon in Finnish politics has been the alienation of the smallholders, torn among the Center Party (KP),* the Finnish Communist Party,* and the Finnish Social Democratic Party.* From time to time, separate smallholders' parties have been formed (*see* Finnish Smallholders' Party), but they have had little success at the polls.

The exception has been the SMP, a KP splinter group which originated in 1958 when Veikko Vennamo, a KP member of parliament, broke away and in 1959 formed the Finnish Small Farmers' Party (*Suomen Pientalonpoikien Puolue; Finlands Småbondeparti*). Although this party won nearly 50,000 votes (2.2 percent) in the 1962 election, it failed to win parliamentary representation. A splinter group, the Small Farmers' Party Opposition (*Pientalonpoikien Oppositio; Småbondepartiets Opposition*), with 6,329 votes, also failed and disappeared from the scene. Vennamo regained his seat in 1966, the only successful SMP candidate that year, and the party subsequently took its present name.

The Finnish Rural Party's spectatular breakthrough came in the 1970 election, when it won 10.5 percent of the votes and 18 seats. It maintained parliamentary representation in 1972, although its vote slipped to 9.2 percent. Personality conflicts and policy differences split the SMP's parliamentary delegation shortly thereafter, and 13 members left to form the Finnish People's Unity Party* in 1972-1973. The 1975 election reduced the SMP to two seats (although its 3.6 percent of the vote should have given it seven), but it came back in 1979 with seven seats and 4.6 percent of the votes.

The Rural Party is the closest to a populist party that Finland has seen since the 1930s; and Vennamo, its strongman leader until 1979 when he was succeeded by his son Pekka, had all the qualities of an accomplished demagogue. His absolute control of the party machinery and his unilateral decisions were directly responsible for the 1972 split, which followed a revolt against his decision to seek government collaboration with the Social Democrats and the communist-dominated Finnish People's Democratic League.* Religiosity is traditionally a strong feature of Finnish agrarian populist movements, and SMP voters were outraged by the idea of political collaboration with socialists and communists. According to its 1967 program, the SMP is based on the principles of Christian morality.

The SMP maintains that the democratic rights of Finnish citizens, though constitutionally guaranteed, have been eroded by the power of big capital, religious and political intolerance, bureaucratic high-handedness, and social injustice. The party opposes any concentration of political and economic power, and it calls for decentralization of state agencies, a more even geographical distribution of economic enterprises, and stress on small units of production, commerce, and farming. It supports the Paasikivi-Kekkonen foreign policy line, but Vennamo was a consistently vigorous critic of President Kekkonen's application of that line.

Above all, the Finnish Rural Party offers a highly detailed program for the social and economic improvement of small farmers, for whose allegiance the SMP competes mainly with the Center Party. Symptomatically, the SMP's electoral breakthrough followed the Centrists' decision to change their name (from the Agrarians) and to seek support among the urban population, a decision expertly exploited by Vennamo. Whether the SMP can maintain the level of support regained in 1979 remains to be seen. Pekka Vennamo, while not a dynamic demogogue, appears to be more democratic than his father and thus less likely to alienate SMP supporters.

Further Reference. Matheson, David, and Risto Shänkiaho, "The Split in the Finnish Rural Party: Populism in Decline in Finland," *Scandinavian Political Studies* 10 (1975): 217-223; Sänkiaho, Risto, "A Model of the Rise of Populism and Support for the Finnish Rural Party," *Scandinavian Political Studies* 6 (1971): 27-47.

FINNISH SMALL FARMERS' PARTY. *See* FINNISH RURAL PARTY.

FINNISH SMALLHOLDERS' PARTY (*Suomen Pienviljelijäin Puolue; Finska Småbrukarpartiet*). This small agrarian party contested the parliamentary elections of 1929 through 1954. It won one seat in 1930 and 1936, two in 1939 when it contested as the Smallholders' and People's Party (*Pienviljelijäin ja Maalaiskansan Puolue; Småbrukar- och Folkpartiet*), and three seats in 1933 (its best election with 37,544 votes, 3.4 percent). The Smallholders declined sharply after 1945 and disappeared after the 1954 election in which the party barely attracted 1,000 votes. The core of Smallholders' support was in the northern province of Ouly, which more recently has also been the heart of Finnish Rural Party* support.

FINNISH SOCIAL DEMOCRATIC PARTY (*Suomen Sosialidemokraattinen Puolue*: SDP; *Finlands Socialdemokratiska Parti*: SDP). The first Finnish workers' association was founded in Helsinki in 1883 by Viktor Julius von Wright, and others soon followed. Loosely organized and led by bourgeois reformers dedicated to the improvement of working conditions, these associations were at first subordinate to the two wings of the Finnish Party.*

The Finnish labor movement grew more revolutionary in the mid-1890s, leading to Wright's resignation in 1896. He was succeeded by Nils af Ursin, a marxist, and in 1899 a Finnish Workers' Party (*Suomen Työväenpuolue*: STP; *Finlands Arbetarparti*: AP) was formed under his leadership. (This STP should not be confused with a later party of the same name. *See* Finnish Communist Party.) In 1903 the present SDP name was adopted, as well as a purely socialist program calling for a unicameral parliament, universal suffrage, prohibition, and an eight-hour workday. The program's revolutionary character was implicit: these goals were to be pursued by "all means appropriate and consistent with the people's sense of justice." Not until 1952, when a new program was adopted, did the SDP formally enshrine the principle that "democratic and parliamentary methods shall be observed in all political activity."

The Social Democratic Party was Finland's driving force for democratic reform up to 1917. A massive labor strike in 1905 forced the radical government reforms of 1906, accepted by the established classes with considerable misgivings. Those misgivings turned to alarm when the SDP won 80 seats in the 1907 election and kept increasing its representation until 1916, when it won 103 seats and an absolute majority in parliament.

Previously stymied by renewed Russian oppression after 1907 and by a nonsocialist majority, the SDP was stymied again after its great 1916 election victory. Although the 1917 coalition government was headed by a Social Democrat, Oskari Tokoi, the impact of the Russian Revolution overtook Finland, and parliament was dissolved against SDP opposition. In the October election, the SDP lost 11 seats and its majority. Accumulated bitterness made the Bolshevik Revolution an attractive example for Finnish labor, and even as independence was proclaimed in December, both Red Guards and White (tsarist) Guards were forming in Finland. On January 28, 1918, civil war broke out when both sides, by a remarkable coincidence, took simultaneous action. Most of the SDP leaders became involved on the Red side. When the war was lost, they fled to Russia and founded the Finnish Communist Party. Tokoi went to the United States.

Väinö Tanner reassembled the shattered pieces of the SDP. He had been a member of the Tokoi cabinet and a right-winger who had disavowed the party's revolutionary slide and refused to run in the 1917 election. He became party chairman in 1918 and intermittently held the post until retiring, at the age of 82, in 1963. Although he could be petty toward rivals and merciless with enemies, it is probably fair to say that Tanner more than anyone else kept Finland on the road to democracy prior to World War II. Salvaging Finland's largest political party and keeping it on a democratic course through the turbulent interwar period was a remarkable achievement in itself. Tanner also led the fight against the Lapua movement (*see* Patriotic People's Movement) and against the communists, earning the enduring enmity of the Soviet Union for himself and for the SDP.

A pragmatic man not given to abstractions or ideologies, Tanner's main concerns were Finland's independence, strengthening its democratic system, and social and economic reform. He meant to achieve the latter through collaboration with the bourgeois parties, but they were slow to respond. Although the SDP won 80 seats in the 1919 election, and although Tanner was able to keep an SDP minority cabinet in office for a year in 1926-1927, it was not until 1937 that the party became an accepted and regular partner in coalition governments. The party remained suspect, to be sure, but Tanner himself had won the respect of the other parties. Except for a nine-month period in 1940-1941 when Soviet pressure kept him out, Tanner served in all Finnish governments from March 1937 to August 1944. The SDP had 85 seats in the wartime parliament.

Old divisions in the SDP resurfaced during the 1941-1944 Finnish-Soviet war. Six members of parliament who opposed Tanner's firm support for the war policy were expelled from the SDP, convicted of treason, and imprisoned until the war's end. Even so, a "peace opposition" emerged within the party soon thereafter and grew to major proportions by 1943-1944. After the war, when Tanner refused to relinquish party control and an electoral alliance with the Finnish People's Democratic League (SKDL)* was rejected, much of the opposition defected to the Communist-dominated SKDL. In the April 1945 election, the SDP won 50 seats; but two members subsequently switched to the SKDL, giving that party a plurality of 51 seats to 49 for the Center Party* and 48 for the SDP. Those three parties formed a Red-Green bloc, the core of Finnish coalition governments until 1948.

Tanner was imprisoned from February 1946 to November 1948, convicted with seven other wartime leaders of "war responsibility" in a trial forced by the Soviet Union. But his hold on the Social Democratic Party continued, secured by a new generation of right-wing Social Democrats led by Väinö Leskinen. Returned to parliament in 1951, Tanner regained the SDP chairmanship in April 1957 in a close contest with Karl-August Fagerholm, an opposition man who served as prime minister in 1948-1950, 1956-1957, and 1958-1959. All of Fagerholm's governments had problems with the Soviet Union, the last of which was forced out by intense Soviet pressure. In the 1956 presidential election, Fagerholm lost to Urho Kekkonen by a vote of 151 to 149.

Tanner's refusal to stand aside had far-reaching consequences. It was the underlying cause of several Finnish-Soviet crises, the most serious of which occurred in 1958-1959 and 1961. It also played into the hands of the Finnish Communist Party in the early postwar period and probably enabled the Finnish People's Democratic League to become a more significant element in Finnish politics than otherwise might have been possible. And it created divisions within the SDP that haunted and weakened the party for two decades. The group that left in 1944-1945 was irretrievably lost. After the June 1946 party congress, which elected Emil Skog chairman and Leskinen secretary, a formal opposition led by Fagerholm constituted itself within the SDP until a compromise was reached in 1947. However, as Skog moved toward the SDP's left wing, Leskinen engineered Skog's ouster at an extraordinary party congress in April 1957, when Tanner won by one vote over Fagerholm. Soviet warnings followed promptly, the Fagerholm government fell, and the Skog faction organized an internal party opposition which openly defected after the 1958 election to form the Social Democratic League of Workers and Smallholders* in 1959. Having won 48 seats in that election, the SDP was reduced to 37 seats after the split. Fagerholm's ill-fated third cabinet was formed in July, but a Soviet trade embargo forced it out by the end of the year.

Yet the Social Democrats continued on their suicidal course. In 1961, together with the National Coalition Party* and other right-wing elements, the SDP formed an alliance to promote a conservative candidate against the Center Party's Kekkonen in the 1962 presidential election, thus bringing on another grave Finnish-Soviet crisis and a crushing SDP defeat in the 1962 parliamentary election (only 38 Social Democrats were elected). That disaster ended Tanner's influence in the party. In June 1963, he was succeeded by Rafael Paasio, under whose leadership the SDP set a new course, regained its natural following, and was rewarded with 55 seats in the 1966 election. In four subsequent elections, the party's representation has been a stable 52 to 55 and its share of the vote

23.4 to 25.8 percent. In 1975, Paasio relinquished the chairmanship to Kalevi Sorsa. The SDP has participated in all but one of the nine Finnish coalition governments since 1966, and Social Democrats have headed six of them. Mauno Koivisto, prime minister in 1968-1970 and again since 1979, is the overwhelming popular favorite to succeed Kekkonen as president in 1984.

While the 1952 SDP program remains in effect, actual party policy tends to be more up-to-date and pragmatically flexible. The program stresses the inability of a free-market economy controlled by big capital to respond to national and individual needs, and calls for central state planning and selective nationalization. In practice, however, the emphasis has been almost wholly on planning, but not central state planning. Since the late 1960s, "incomes-policies" agreements among labor, management, and the government have covered everything from wages, welfare, and working conditions to prices, taxes, education, and the environment. There is no longer much talk of nationalization. The SDP is more concerned with consumer protection, full social security, and adequate day-care services. Full employment and industrial democracy remain important goals. The party gives its unqualified support to the Paasikivi-Kekkonen foreign policy line and has since the late 1960s challenged the Center Party's self-appointed custodianship of that line. In the early 1970s, the "kiddie gang" of young SDP intellectuals sought to radicalize the party and promoted closer relations with the Soviet Union in both foreign and defense policy. Their impact was slight, and most of them drifted away to the Finnish People's Democratic League.

Further Reference. Helenius, Ralf, "The Finnish Social Democratic Party," in *Social Democratic Parties in Western Europe,* edited by William E. Paterson and Alastair H. Thomas (London: Croom Helm, 1977).

FINNISH SOCIALIST WORKERS' PARTY. *See* FINNISH COMMUNIST PARTY.

FINNISH WORKERS' PARTY. *See* FINNISH COMMUNIST PARTY and FINNISH SOCIAL DEMOCRATIC PARTY.

FINSKA FOLKPARTIET. *See* LIBERAL PEOPLE'S PARTY and PEOPLE'S PARTY.

FINSKA PARTIET. *See* FINNISH PARTY.

FINSKA SMÅBRUKARPARTIET. *See* FINNISH SMALLHOLDERS' PARTY.

FKF. *See* FINNISH CHRISTIAN LEAGUE.

FKP. *See* FINNISH COMMUNIST PARTY.

FLP. *See* FINNISH RURAL PARTY.

FOLKPARTIET. *See* FINNISH PARTY and PEOPLE'S PARTY.

FOSTERLÄNDSKA FOLKRÖRELSEN. *See* PATRIOTIC PEOPLE'S MOVEMENT.

FRISINNADES FÖRBUND. *See* LIBERAL LEAGUE.

FSAP. *See* FINNISH COMMUNIST PARTY.

GAMMALFINNARNA. *See* FINNISH PARTY.

IKL. *See* PATRIOTIC PEOPLE'S MOVEMENT.

INDEPENDENT SOCIAL DEMOCRATS. *See* SOCIAL DEMOCRATIC LEAGUE OF WORKERS AND SMALLHOLDERS.

ISÄNMAALLINEN KANSANLIIKE. *See* PATRIOTIC PEOPLE'S MOVEMENT.

KANSALLINEN EDISTYSPUOLUE. *See* LIBERAL PEOPLE'S PARTY.

KANSALLINEN KOKOOMUS. *See* NATIONAL COALITION PARTY.

KANSANPUOLUE. *See* PEOPLE'S PARTY and FINNISH PARTY.

KESKUSTAPUOLUE. *See* CENTER PARTY.

KFP. *See* CONSTITUTIONAL PEOPLE'S PARTY.

KK. *See* NATIONAL COALITION PARTY.

KOK. *See* NATIONAL COALITION PARTY.

KOKOOMUS. *See* NATIONAL COALITION PARTY.

KONSTITUTIONELLA FOLKPARTIET. *See* CONSTITUTIONAL PEOPLE'S PARTY.

KP. *See* CENTER PARTY.

KRISTILLINEN TYÖVÄENPUOLUE. *See* CHRISTIAN WORKERS' PARTY.

KRISTLIGA ARBETARPARTIET. *See* CHRISTIAN WORKERS' PARTY.

LAPUA MOVEMENT. *See* PATRIOTIC PEOPLE'S MOVEMENT.

LEFT GROUP OF FINNISH WORKERS. *See* FINNISH COMMUNIST PARTY.

LFP. *See* LIBERAL PEOPLE'S PARTY.

LIBERAALINEN KANSANPUOLUE. *See* LIBERAL PEOPLE'S PARTY.

LIBERALA FOLKPARTIET. *See* LIBERAL PEOPLE'S PARTY.

LIBERAL CLUB. *See* FINNISH PARTY.

LIBERAL LEAGUE (*Vapaamielisten Liitto; Frisinnades Förbund*). In 1951, when the National Progressive Party transformed itself into the Finnish People's Party (*see* Liberal People's Party), its more conservative elements refused to go along and instead formed the Liberal League. The League ran candidates in the parliamentary elections of 1951 through 1962, winning one seat in the latter election through an electoral alliance with the National Coalition Party.* The League's popular vote ranged from 0.27 to 0.34 percent. In 1965 it merged with the Finnish People's Party to form the Liberal People's Party. The League advocated unregulated free enterprise, reduction of farm subsidies, and a conservative social policy of very limited welfare.

LIBERAL PEOPLE'S PARTY (*Liberaalinen Kansanpuolue*: LKP; Liberala Folkpartiet: LFP). The LKP has operated under a profusion of names since its origins as the liberal wing of the Finnish Party.* When that party broke up in 1918, the liberal elements—most of whom had been Young Finns (*see* Finnish Party)—were joined by the 1917 People's Party (*see* Finnish Party) on December 8 and formed the National Progressive Party (*Kansallinen Edistyspuolue; Nationella Framstegspartiet*). The National Progressives split in 1951, with the majority continuing its main traditions as the Finnish People's Party (*Suomen Kansanpuolue; Finska Folkpartiet*), constituted on February 3 (and not to be confused with an earlier party of the same name. *See* People's Party.). The minority of the National Progressives formed the Liberal League.* On December 29, 1965, these two groups reunited under the present LKP name.

These frequent name changes, the internal divisions and formal splits, and the electoral history of steady decline are, of course, typical of modern liberal parties resting on ideology rather than social class or vested interest. Before independence, when the Finnish Party championed the cause of Finnish constitutional rights in the face of Russian violations, the party had a stable and reliable constituency. This carried over to the 1919 election when the party, now under the National Progressive label, won 12.8 percent of the vote and 26 seats in parliament and its leader, Kaarlo Ståhlberg, was elected as the republic's first president (1919-1925). In the 1922 election, the party's vote slipped to 9.2

percent, beginning a gradual decline marked by lows of 5.6 percent in 1929, 4.8 percent in 1939, and 3.9 percent in 1948.

The 1951 name change and program revision brought the combined Finnish People's Party-Liberal League up to 7.9 percent in 1954, after which it remained steady at about six percent until 1970. Then came renewed and rapid decline. In 1979 the LKP got 3.7 percent of the vote and four seats in parliament. As a small party, it has also been a consistent victim of the d'Hondt method of proportional representation, regularly receiving three or four seats less than its proportion of the popular vote should have yielded. Nonetheless, as a party of the center the LKP has been a frequent participant in coalition cabinets. From 1917 to 1944, Liberals served in all but five of the 27 cabinets of that period, and they have served in 18 of 34 postwar cabinets.

According to its 1971 program, the Liberal People's Party identifies itself as "a liberal reform party of the political center" whose ideological cornerstone is social liberalism based on individual liberty, national self-determination, and the equality and common responsibility of all citizens. The LKP favors a pluralistic and tolerant society, and it opposes all concentration of political, economic, or spiritual power. To those ends the LKP promotes full freedom of information and direct democracy to the fullest practicable extent, including industrial democracy, abolition of bureaucracy, decentralization of state authority and dispersal of state agencies, increased emphasis on local and regional government, decision making by referendum, and fair distribution of parliamentary seats based on the percentage of the national vote obtained by each party. The LKP regards both capitalism and socialism as outdated and alien to interests of the individual. Most recently, the party has come out strongly against building or planning any more nuclear power stations in Finland. It supports the Paasikivi-Kekkonen foreign policy line, an effective defense, closer relations with Scandinavia, and greater supranational authority for the United Nations, which the LKP sees as the only organization capable of solving global problems.

Founded by the "father" of Finland's 1919 constitution, Ståhlberg, the LKP has always remained faithful to the constitutionalist principles of its Young Finn predecessors. The LKP's popular image is that of a party of (and for) intellectuals, and it tends to draw its leaders from university faculties. Ståhlberg himself was a professor of administrative law and chief justice of the Supreme Administrative Court. Recent party chairmen include Beli Merikoski (1958-1968), a professor of theoretical physics. The current chairman is Jaakko Itälä, a political scientist.

LKP. *See* LIBERAL PEOPLE'S PARTY.

MAALAISLIITTO. *See* CENTER PARTY.

MAALAISLITON OPPOSITIO. *See* CENTER PARTY.

NATIONAL COALITION PARTY (*Kansallinen Kokoomus*: KK; *Nationella Samlingspartiet*: SAML). Founded in December 1918 to carry on the main ideals of the Finnish Party,* the KK—commonly referred to as *Kokoomus*, or KOK—is Finland's main conservative party and identifies itself abroad as the National Coalition (Conservative) Party.

The KK began its career as the advocate of lost causes. It was led by Pehr Evind Svinhufvud, a hero of the pre-independence anti-Russification activists, head of the 1917-1918 independence government, and regent of Finland in 1918. The National Coalition Party comprised those elements of the former Finnish party that had advocated a monarchical form of government and had engineered the election of a German prince to Finland's throne, which was effectively nullified by Germany's defeat in World War I.

The KK lost the republican forces in 1919, winning only 28 seats in that year's parliamentary election. Also, the KK's candidate for the presidency was overwhelmingly defeated by Kaarlo Ståhlberg of the National Progressive Party (*see* Liberal People's Party), which was the liberal faction of the old Finnish Party from which the KK had also originated. The KK recovered quickly, however, and won 19 percent of the vote and 38 seats in 1929. But the next year, due to its championship of anticommunist legislation, the National Coalition won 42 seats, its greatest electoral success until 1979. In 1931, Svinhufvud was elected president on a nationalistic and antisocialist platform, and he kept the Finnish Social Democratic Party* out of all governments until he lost his bid for reelection in 1937. In three elections between 1933 and 1939, the KK lost much of its vote to the right-wing Patriotic People's Movement,* dropping to 10.4 percent and 20 seats in the 1936 election. Svinhufvud remained pro-German until his death in 1944.

A frequent partner in pre-1944 governments, the National Coalition Party has been included in only three governments since then (and four "nonpolitical" presidial cabinets). Through the 1960s, the party's electoral support stood at around 15 percent, with a high of 17 percent and 33 seats in the 1948 election, and lows of 12.8 percent and 24 seats in 1954 and 13.8 percent and 26 seats in 1966. The Coalition then began to move away from its rigid conservative positions. Under the chairmanships of Juha Rihtniemi (1965-1971) and Harri Holkeri (1971-1979), the KK gradually became a moderate conservative party of the political center, abandoned its anti-Soviet stance, and embraced the foreign policy line of President Kekkonen, whose candidacy for reelection the KK supported in 1974 and 1978. While this caused right-wing elements to defect to new parties such as to the Constitutional People's Party* and the Finnish Christian League,* it also brought the KK new voters and electoral successes in the 1970s. This trend culminated in the spectacular victory of 1979 when the KK won 21.7 percent of the vote and 47 seats, becoming Finland's second-largest party.

Under Ilkka Suominen, elected chairman in 1979, the KK is continuing the course set by Rihtniemi and implemented by Holkeri. The National Coalition may soon reemerge as a government party, although Holkeri's attempt to form a cabinet after the 1979 election failed. According to Suominen, the KK aspires to take over the center position in Finnish politics (that is, from the Center Party*), and recent Gallup Polls indicate that the KK may be succeeding: at the end of 1979, popular KK support stood at 22.7 percent.

The general aim of the KK, according to its ideological program of 1970, is "the consolidation of Finnish independence and the safeguarding and development of the democratic political and legal system, based on individual liberty and security." The KK exalts patriotism and those religious and moral values which "help build Finnish society." The party advocates a free-market economy based on private ownership, but it also accepts the need for public enterprise so long as it is profitable and does not become a burden on society. The family is the central social unit, and all citizens should enjoy equality of rights, opportunities, and obligations. Democracy should be based on "either direct decision-taking or election of decision-takers."

The political action program of the KK, adopted in 1972, elaborates on these principles, emphasizing the party's concept of a "social choice economy" in which all decisions should consider the effect on the individual, especially the ethical and social effects of economic activity. Production and consumption and the supply of goods, services, and job opportunities should be so arranged that "the opportunities for individual choice are as wide as possible." A political-action draft program approved by the party board in 1979 reiterates this concept but also adds new emphasis on the quality of life, a statement favoring trade unions and the right to strike, and a call for the judicious exploitation of natural resources in order to assure a balance between the consumption and production of renewable resources. The program supports Finland's existing constitution but suggests that presidential elections be direct, with a run-off between the two top candidates if neither wins a first-round majority. The KK supports the Paasikivi-Kekkonen foreign policy line, closer relations with Scandinavia and the Soviet Union, and an effective defense.

NATIONAL COALITION (CONSERVATIVE) PARTY. See NATIONAL COALITION PARTY.

NATIONAL PROGRESSIVE PARTY. See LIBERAL PEOPLE'S PARTY.

NATIONELLA FRAMSTEGSPARTIET. See LIBERAL PEOPLE'S PARTY.

NATIONELLA SAMLINGSPARTIET. See NATIONAL COALITION PARTY.

NUORSUOMALAINEN PUOLUE. See FINNISH PARTY.

OLD FINNS. See FINNISH PARTY.

PATRIOTIC PEOPLE'S MOVEMENT (*Isänmaallinen Kansanliike*: IKL; *Foster-ländska Folkrörelsen*: FFR). A violent anticommunist demonstration in Lapua in late 1929 triggered the fast-growing Lapua Movement, a fascist-inspired superpatriotic crusade against communism and socialism which found ready national support in bourgeois and military circles. The Movement was directly responsible for the enactment of Finland's anticommunist laws in 1930, but the Movement's strong-arm methods of political kidnappings, beatings, and murder cost it its initial semiofficial support and led to its being outlawed in 1932. Resurfacing the same year as the Patriotic People's Movement, a black-shirted fascist party, the IKL contested three elections. It won 14 seats in 1933 through electoral alliances with the National Coalition Party,* 14 seats again in 1936, and eight in 1939. The IKL had one minister in Jukka Rangell's 1941-1943 coalition government. In September 1944, under the terms of the Finnish-Soviet armistice agreement, the IKL was banned as a fascist-type organization.

Further Reference. Rintala, Marvin, *Three Generations: The Extreme Right Wing in Finnish Politics* (Bloomington: Indiana University Press, 1962); Upton, A. F., "Finland," in *European Fascism*, edited by S. J. Woolf (London: Weidenfeld and Nicolson, 1968).

PEOPLE'S PARTY (*Kansanpuolue; Folkpartiet*). A party using the name People's Party contested the 1917 parliamentary election (*see* Finnish Party) and had joined in forming the National Progressive Party (*see* Liberal People's Party). Another, actually called the Finnish People's Party (*Suomalainen Kansanpuolue; Finska Folkpartiet*), appeared in the election of 1933 (winning 0.8 percent of the vote and two seats) and in 1936 (winning 0.6 percent and one seat). In the 1951 election, the People's Party label was resurrected by the National Coalition Party* for use as a spurious electoral ally designed to lure votes from the newly established Finnish People's Party (*see* Liberal People's Party) through the similarity of their names.

PERUSTUSLAILLINEN KANSANPUOLUE. *See* CONSTITUTIONAL PEOPLE'S PARTY.

PIENTALONPOIKIEN OPPOSITIO. *See* FINNISH RURAL PARTY.

PIENVILJELIJÄIN JA MAALAISKANSAN PUOLUE. *See* FINNISH SMALLHOLDERS' PARTY.

PKP. *See* CONSTITUTIONAL PEOPLE'S PARTY.

PPF. *See* FINNISH PRIVATE ENTREPRENEURS' PARTY.

PRIVATEFÖRETAGARNAS PARTIORGANISATION I FINLAND. *See* FINNISH PRIVATE ENTREPRENEURS' PARTY.

RADICAL PEOPLE'S PARTY. *See* SWEDISH PEOPLE'S PARTY.

RADIKAALINEN KANSANPUOLUE. *See* SWEDISH PEOPLE'S PARTY.

RADIKALA FOLKPARTIET. *See* SWEDISH PEOPLE'S PARTY.

RKP. *See* SWEDISH PEOPLE'S PARTY.

RUOTSALAINEN KANSANPUOLUE. *See* SWEDISH PEOPLE'S PARTY.

RUOTSALAINEN PUOLUE. *See* SWEDISH PEOPLE'S PARTY.

RUOTSALAINEN VAPAAMIELINEN PUOLUE. *See* SWEDISH PEOPLE'S PARTY.

RUOTSALAINEN VASEMMISTO. *See* SWEDISH PEOPLE'S PARTY.

SAML. *See* NATIONAL COALITION PARTY.

SAP. *See* SOCIAL DEMOCRATIC LEAGUE OF WORKERS AND SMALL-HOLDERS.

SDP. *See* FINNISH SOCIAL DEMOCRATIC PARTY.

SFP. *See* SWEDISH PEOPLE'S PARTY.

SKDL. *See* FINNISH PEOPLE'S DEMOCRATIC LEAGUE.

SKL. *See* FINNISH CHRISTIAN LEAGUE.

SKP. *See* FINNISH COMMUNIST PARTY.

SKYP. *See* FINNISH PEOPLE'S UNITY PARTY.

SMÅBONDEPARTIETS OPPOSITIO. *See* FINNISH RURAL PARTY.

SMÅBRUKAR- OCH FOLKPARTIET. *See* FINNISH SMALLHOLDERS' PARTY.

SMALL FARMERS' PARTY OPPOSITION. *See* FINNISH RURAL PARTY.

SMALLHOLDERS' AND PEOPLE'S PARTY. *See* FINNISH SMALLHOLDERS' PARTY.

SMP. *See* FINNISH RURAL PARTY.

SOCIAL DEMOCRATIC LEAGUE OF WORKERS AND SMALLHOLDERS (*Työväen ja Pienviljelijäin Sosialidemokraattinen Liitto*: TPSL; *Arbetarnas och Småbrukarnas Socialdemokratiska Förbund*: ASSF) Following the stormy congress of the Finnish Social Democratic Party (SDP)* in April 1957, the defeated left wing organized an internal party opposition, the Independent Social Democrats. In September, four members of this group, by then known as the Social Democratic Opposition (*Sosialidemokraattinen Oppositio; Socialdemokratiska Oppositionen*), accepted ministries in the coalition government formed by V. J. Sukselainen, chairman of the Center Party,* and the group was promptly expelled from the SDP. In the 1958 parliamentary election, the Social Democratic Opposition won three seats, and 11 members of parliament elected on the SDP ticket subsequently defected to the Opposition group. In 1959 the Opposition formed a new party, the Social Democratic League of Workers and Smallholders (TPSL), under the chairmanship of former SDP chairman Emil Skog.

The Social Democratic Party split was reflected in trade union organizations. The Skog faction controlled the Confederation of Finnish Trade Unions (SAK) at the time of the split; and in 1960 a rival organization, Finland's Trade Union Organization (SAJ), was formed by unions loyal to the Social Democratic Party. After 1963, when the right wing lost control of the SDP, efforts to heal the trade union rift were begun, leading eventually to the founding of a new SAK in 1969.

Within the TPSL, too, there was a growing desire for reconciliation, especially after the party lost all but two of its parliamentary seats in the 1962 election in spite of a large popular vote (100,396 = 4.4 percent). Skog himself favored reconciliation, as a result of which he was replaced as party chairman by Aarre Simonen. The Skog faction began a slow drift back to the SDP, and the Simonen group initiated TPSL cooperation with the communist-dominated Finnish People's Democratic League (SKDL).* Through successful electoral alliances with the SKDL in the 1966 election, the TPSL won seven seats in spite of a sharp decline in its popular vote (to 2.6 percent). Simonen became minister of justice in the coalition cabinet led by Rafael Paasio of the SDP from 1966 to 1968.

In the elections of 1970 and 1972, the TPSL was reduced to 1.4 and one percent of the vote respectively and no seats, causing the majority to dissolve the TPSL and remerge with the SDP. A small TPSL minority formed the Socialist Workers' Party (*Sosialistinen Työväenpuolue*: STP; *Socialistiska Arbetarpartiet*: SAP), chaired by Simonen until his death in 1977. The STP failed to win any seats in the elections of 1975 and 1979 (with 0.3 and 0.1 percent of the vote) and was deregistered. It is not likely to return.

SOCIAL DEMOCRATIC OPPOSITION. *See* SOCIAL DEMOCRATIC LEAGUE OF WORKERS AND SMALLHOLDERS.

SOCIALDEMOKRATISKA OPPOSITIONEN. *See* SOCIAL DEMOCRATIC LEAGUE OF WORKERS AND SMALLHOLDERS.

SOCIALISTISKA ARBETARPARTIET. *See* SOCIAL DEMOCRATIC LEAGUE OF WORKERS AND SMALLHOLDERS.

SOCIALISTISKA ENHETSPARTIET. *See* FINNISH PEOPLE'S DEMO-CRATIC LEAGUE.

SOCIALIST UNITY PARTY. *See* FINNISH PEOPLE'S DEMOCRATIC LEAGUE.

SOCIALIST WORKERS' PARTY. *See* SOCIAL DEMOCRATIC LEAGUE OF WORKERS AND SMALLHOLDERS.

SOSIALIDEMOKRAATTINEN OPPOSITIO. *See* SOCIAL DEMOCRATIC LEAGUE OF WORKERS AND SMALLHOLDERS.

SOSIALISTINEN TYÖVÄENPUOLUE. *See* SOCIAL DEMOCRATIC LEAGUE OF WORKERS AND SMALLHOLDERS.

SOSIALISTINEN YHTENÄISYYSPUOLUE. *See* FINNISH PEOPLE'S DEM-OCRATIC LEAGUE.

SSTP. *See* FINNISH COMMUNIST PARTY.

STP. *See* FINNISH COMMUNIST PARTY and FINNISH SOCIAL DEMO-CRATIC PARTY and SOCIAL DEMOCRATIC LEAGUE OF WORKERS AND SMALLHOLDERS.

SUOMALAINEN KANSANPUOLUE. *See* PEOPLE'S PARTY.

SUOMALAINEN PUOLUE. *See* FINNISH PARTY.

SUOMEN KANSAN DEMOKRAATTINEN LIITTO. *See* FINNISH PEOPLE'S DEMOCRATIC LEAGUE.

SUOMEN KANSANPUOLUE. *See* LIBERAL PEOPLE'S PARTY.

SUOMEN KANSAN YHTENÄISYYDEN PUOLUE. *See* FINNISH PEOPLE'S UNITY PARTY.

SUOMEN KESKUSTAPUOLUE. *See* CENTER PARTY.

SUOMEN KOMMUNISTINEN PUOLUE. *See* FINNISH COMMUNIST PARTY.

SUOMEN KOMMUNISTINEN TYÖVÄENPUOLUE. *See* FINNISH COMMUNIST PARTY.

SUOMEN KRISTILLINEN LIITTO. *See* FINNISH CHRISTIAN LEAGUE.

SUOMEN MAASEUDUN PUOLUE. *See* FINNISH RURAL PARTY.

SUOMEN PERUSTUSLAILLINEN KANSANPUOLUE. *See* CONSTITUTIONAL PEOPLE'S PARTY.

SUOMEN PIENTALONPOIKIEN PUOLUE. *See* FINNISH RURAL PARTY.

SUOMEN PIENVILJELIJÄIN PUOLUE. *See* FINNISH SMALLHOLDERS' PARTY.

SUOMEN SOSIALIDEMOKRAATTINEN PUOLUE. *See* FINNISH SOCIAL DEMOCRATIC PARTY.

SUOMEN SOSIALISTINEN TYÖVÄENPUOLUE. *See* FINNISH COMMUNIST PARTY.

SUOMEN TYÖVÄENPUOLUE. *See* FINNISH COMMUNIST PARTY and FINNISH SOCIAL DEMOCRATIC PARTY.

SUOMEN TYÖVÄEN VASEMMISTORYHMÄ. *See* FINNISH COMMUNIST PARTY.

SUOMEN YKSITYISYRITTÄJÄIN PUOLUEJÄRJESTÖ. *See* FINNISH PRIVATE ENTREPRENEURS' PARTY.

SVENSKA FOLKPARTIET. *See* SWEDISH PEOPLE'S PARTY.

SVENSKA FRISINNADE PARTIET. *See* SWEDISH PEOPLE'S PARTY.

SVENSKA PARTIET. *See* SWEDISH PEOPLE'S PARTY.

SVENSKA VÄNSTERN. *See* SWEDISH PEOPLE'S PARTY.

SWEDISH LEFT. *See* SWEDISH PEOPLE'S PARTY.

SWEDISH LIBERAL PARTY. *See* SWEDISH PEOPLE'S PARTY.

SWEDISH PARTY. *See* SWEDISH PEOPLE'S PARTY.

SWEDISH PEOPLE'S PARTY (*Ruotsalainen Kansanpuolue*: RKP; *Svenska Folkpartiet*: SFP). The sole purpose of the RKP since its origins a century ago has been to defend the interests of the Swedish ethnic minority in Finland. The transfer of Finland to Russian rule in 1809 did not end the predominance of Swedish political, economic, and cultural traditions established during the previous six centuries, and the privileged social elite remained almost entirely Swedish.

When the Swedish elite's dominance was threatened by the activities of the Finnish Party* in the 1860s and 1870s, a Swedish Party (*Ruotsalainen Puolue; Svenska Partiet*) was formed. Loosely organized at the 1877-1878 session of the Estates Diet, the Swedish Party developed into an effective interest party in step with the acceleration of the Finnish language into the country's institutions of education and administration. Until the Diet's demise in 1906, the Swedish minority retained its control of the Estates of the Nobility and Burgesses, while the Finnish majority controlled the Estates of the Clergy and Farmers. It was natural, therefore, that the Swedish Party faced the parliamentary reforms of 1906 with apprehension and preferred a bicameral parliament whose upper house might preserve some of the privileges of the Swedish minority.

Reconstituted as the Swedish People's Party in 1906, the party won 24 seats in the 1907 election, the first to the new unicameral parliament. The RKP managed to maintain this level of representation with minor variations through 1936, when it won 21 seats. Thereafter, its strength declined steadily in step with the proportional decline of Finland's Swedish-speaking population. From 11.2 percent of the vote in 1936, the RKP has slipped through all subsequent elections to 4.6 percent and nine seats in 1979 (plus one seat for the RKP's ally, the Åland Coalition*).

Although it has been a minor party for the past four decades, the RKP has avoided the underrepresentation normally suffered by small parties. This is because the Swedish-speaking population, up to 80 percent of whom vote for the RKP, is concentrated within five electoral districts; and the party normally does not contest parliamentary elections in the other ten districts, including the Åland Islands where the RKP is nevertheless guaranteed one seat through the Åland Coalition.

The RKP initially sought to avoid divisive political issues not directly related to its ethnic mission. However, this proved unrealistic in view of the economic concerns of the party's rural voters and the split of its urban voters between conservative and liberal orientations. The RKP took a position of bourgeois centrism and agrarian conservatism, resulting in permanent tension and pendular swings that spun off defectors and splinter parties. In 1918, when the RKP strongly backed a monarchy, the liberal republican wing formed the Swedish Left (*Ruotsalainen Vasemmisto; Svenska Vänstern*), which a decade later became an electoral rival and contested three elections, winning one seat in 1930 and again in 1945.

The Swedish Left was succeeded by the Swedish Liberal Party (*Ruotsalainen Vapaamielinen Puolue; Svenska Frisinnade Partiet*), also called the Radical People's

Party (*Radikaalinen Kansanpuolue; Radikala Folkpartiet*), which attracted a few votes in 1948 and 1951 but then disappeared. In the 1960s, as the RKP swung to the left, its conservative wing rebelled. Many joined the Finnish Christian League* in the ensuing years, and a sizable bloc departed in the early 1970s to join in the formation of the Constitutional People's Party. *

Yet the liberal course staked out by the RKP under such chairmen as Jan-Magnus Jansson (1966-1973), Kristian Gestrin (1973-1974), and Carl-Olof Tallgren (1974-1977) continues under Pär Stenbäck, chairman since 1977. The current RKP program, adopted in 1974, retains the original emphasis on maintaining the separate cultural and linguistic identity of the Swedish-speaking minority and presents the party as the natural bridge to neighboring Scandinavia, but it also takes moderately liberal positions on most current issues in Finnish politics. The RKP advocates an egalitarian evolution of Finnish democracy with stress on the individual's rights and well-being, an equitable distribution of income, and free health care for all. It favors a competitive market economy oriented toward the consumer, but within a centrally planned framework. Industrial development should be regionally balanced and respect the environment and quality of life. The RKP also pays homage to "positive" Christian and humanistic values and supports religious instruction in the schools. In the area of foreign policy, the RKP backs the Paasikivi-Kekkonen line, calls for more attention to foreign aid, wants the United Nations strengthened, considers détente in Europe a step toward world peace, and advocates further integration of the Nordic states.

SYP. *See* FINNISH PRIVATE ENTREPRENEURS' PARTY.

TAISTOITES. *See* FINNISH COMMUNIST PARTY.

TPSL. *See* SOCIAL DEMOCRATIC LEAGUE OF WORKERS AND SMALL-HOLDERS.

TYÖVÄEN JA PIENVILJELÄIN PUOLUE. *See* FINNISH COMMUNIST PARTY.

TYÖVÄEN JA PIENVILJELIJÄIN SOSIALIDEMOKRAATTINEN LIITTO. *See* SOCIAL DEMOCRATIC LEAGUE OF WORKERS AND SMALL-HOLDERS.

UNGFINSKA PARTIET. *See* FINNISH PARTY.

UNITED FINNISH PARTIES. *See* FINNISH PARTY.

VANHASUOMALAISET. *See* FINNISH PARTY.

VAPAAMIELISTEN LIITTO. *See* LIBERAL LEAGUE.

WORKERS' AND SMALLHOLDERS' PARTY. *See* FINNISH COMMUNIST PARTY.

YOUNG FINNISH PARTY. *See* FINNISH PARTY.

YOUNG FINNS. *See* FINNISH PARTY.

H. Peter Krosby

TABLE 19. Distribution of Seats in Finland's *Eduskunta*, 1907-1917

Party	1907	1908	1909	1910	1911	1913	1916	1917
Agrarian Union	9	9	13	17	18	18	19	26
Christian Workers' Party	2	2	1	1	1	0	1	0
Finnish Party[*]	59	54	48	42	43	38	33	32
Finnish Social Democratic Party	80	83	84	86	86	90	103	92
People's Party[*]	—	—	—	—	—	—	—	5
Swedish People's Party	24	25	25	26	26	26	21	21
Young Finnish Party[*]	26	27	29	28	28	28	23	24
Total	200	200	200	200	200	200	200	200

[*] These three parties (Finnish Party, People's Party, and Young Finnish Party) formed the United Finnish Parties coalition in 1917. (*See also* National Coalition Party and the National Progressive Party, table 20.)

TABLE 20.   Distribution of Seats in Finland's *Eduskunta*, 1919-1939

Party	1919	1922	1924	1927	1929	1930	1933	1936	1939
Agrarian Union	42	45	44	52	60	59	53	53	56
Christian Workers' Party	2	—	—	—	—	—	—	—	—
Finnish People's Party	—	—	—	—	—	—	2	1	—
Finnish Smallholders' Party[a]	—	—	—	—	0	1	3	1	2
Finnish Social Democratic Party	80	53	60	60	59	66	78	83	85
National Coalition Party[b]	28	35	38	34	28	42	18	20	25
National Progressive Party[c]	26	15	17	10	7	11	11	7	6
Patriotic People's Movement	—	—	—	—	—	—	14	14	8
Swedish Left	—	—	—	—	—	1	—	—	0
Swedish People's Party	22	25	23	24	23	20	21	21	18
Workers' and Smallholders' Party[d]	—	27	18	20	23	0	—	—	—
Total	200	200	200	200	200	200	200	200	200

[a] Known as the Smallholders' and People's Party in 1939.
[b] A merger of the Old Finn majority in the Finnish Party with the monarchist (Svinhugvud) faction in the Young Finnish Party. (*See also* Finnish Party and Young Finnish Party, table 19.)
[c] A merger among the Old Finn republican minority in the Finnish Party, the republican (Ståhlberg) faction in the Young Finnish Party, and the People's Party. (*See also* table 19.)
[d] Finnish Communist Party until 1920; used various labels for campaigning purposes. (*See also* Finnish People's Democratic League, table 21.)

TABLE 21. Distribution of Seats in Finland's *Eduskunta*, 1945-1979

Party	1945	1948	1951	1954	1958	1962	1966	1970	1972	1975	1979
Agrarian Union[a]	49	56	51	53	48	53	49	37	35	35	36
Åland Coalition[b]	—	1	1	1	1	1	1	1	1	1	1
Constitutional People's Party										1	0
Finnish Christian League	—	—	—	—	—	—	0	1	4	9	9
Finnish People's Democratic League[c]	49	38	43	43	50	47	41	36	37	40	35
Finnish People's Unity Party										1	0
Finnish Rural Party[d]	—	—	—	—	—	0	1	18	18	2	7
Finnish Smallholders' Party	0	0	0	0							
Finnish Social Democratic Party	50	54	53	54	48	38	55	51	55	54	52
Liberal League[e]	—	—	0	0	0	1	—	—	—	—	—
National Coalition Party	28	33	28	24	29	32	26	37	34	39	47
National Progressive Party[f]	9	5	10	13	8	13	9	8	7	9	4
Social Democratic League of Workers and Smallholders[g]	—	—	—	—	3	2	7	0	0	—	—
Swedish Left[h]	1	0	0	—	—	—	—	—	—	—	—
Swedish People's Party	14	13	14	12	13	13	11	11	9	9	9
Total	200	200	200	200	200	200	200	200	200	200	200

a Renamed as the Center Party in 1965.

b Represents Åland Islands; usually affiliates with the Swedish People's Party.

c Permanent electoral alliance since 1944 consisting of the Finnish Communist Party and left-wing dissidents of the Finnish Social Democratic Party (calling themselves the Socialist Unity Party).

d Known as the Finnish Small Farmers' Party, 1958-prior to 1966 election.

e A dissident conservative element which split from the National Progressive Party in 1951. It merged with its parent grouping in 1965 to become the Liberal People's Party (see National Progressive Party).

f Known as the Finnish People's Party, 1951-1965; in 1965, absorbed the Liberal League and became the Liberal People's Party.

g Known as the Social Democratic Opposition, 1957-1959.

h Known as the Swedish Liberal Party after 1945 election.

TABLE 22. Ruling Coalitions in Finland since 1917

Formation Date	Coalition
Apr. 1917	Finnish Social Democratic Party
Oct. 1917	National Progressive Party Agrarian Union Swedish People's Party Old Finns
1919	National Progressive Party Agrarian Union Swedish People's Party
1921	National Progressive Party Agrarian Union
May 1922	Presidial government
Sep. 1922	National Progressive Party Agrarian Union
1924	National Progressive Party Agrarian Union National Coalition Party Swedish People's Party
1925	National Progressive Party National Coalition Party Swedish People's Party
1926	Finnish Social Democratic Party
1927	Agrarian Union National Progressive Party Swedish People's Party
1928	National Progressive Party National Coalition Party
1929	Agrarian Union National Progressive Party
1930	National Coalition Party Agrarian Union National Progressive Party Swedish People's Party
1931	Agrarian Unioin National Coalition Party National Progressive Party Swedish People's Party
1936	Agrarian Union National Coalition Party National Progressive Party

TABLE 22. (*Continued*)

Formation Date	Coalition
1937	National Progressive Party Agrarian Union Finnish Social Democratic Party
1939	National Progressive Party Agrarian Union Finnish Social Democratic Party Swedish People's Party
1940	National Progressive Party Agrarian Union Finnish Social Democratic Party Swedish People's Party National Coalition Party
1941	National Progressive Party Agrarian Union Finnish Social Democratic Party Swedish People's Party National Coalition Party Patriotic People's Movement
1943	National Coalition Party National Progressive Party Agrarian Union Swedish People's Party Finnish Social Democratic Party
1944	National Progressive Party Swedish People's Party Agrarian Union Finnish Social Democratic Party Finnish People's Democratic League
1946	Finnish People's Democratic League Agrarian Union Swedish People's Party Finnish Social Democratic Party
1948	Finnish Social Democratic Party
1950	Agrarian Union National Progressive Party Swedish People's Party
Jan. 1951	Agrarian Union Swedish People's Party National Progressive Party Finnish Social Democratic Party

TABLE 22. (*Continued*)

Formation Date	Coalition
Sep. 1951	Agrarian Union Swedish People's Party Finnish Social Democratic Party National Coalition Party
July 1953	Agrarian Union Swedish People's Party
Nov. 1953	Presidial government
May 1954	Swedish People's Party Agrarian Union Finnish Social Democratic Party
Oct. 1954	Agrarian Union Finnish Social Democratic Party
1956	Finnish Social Democratic Party Finnish People's Party Swedish People's Party Agrarian Union
May 1957	Agrarian Union Finnish People's Party
Nov. 1957	Presidial government
Aug. 1958	Finnish Social Democratic Party Agrarian Union Finnish People's Party Swedish People's Party National Coalition Party
1959	Agrarian Union
1962	Agrarian Union Swedish People's Party Finnish People's Party National Coalition Party
1963	Presidial government
1964	Agrarian Union Swedish People's Party Finnish People's Party National Coalition Party
1966	Finnish Social Democratic Party Center Party Finnish People's Democratic League
1968	Finnish Social Democratic Party Finnish People's Democratic League

TABLE 22. (*Continued*)

Formation Date	Coalition
1968 cont.	Liberal People's Party Swedish People's Party Center Party
May 1970	Presidial government
July 1970	Center Party Swedish People's Party Liberal People's Party
1971	Presidial government
Jan. 1972	Finnish Social Democratic Party
Aug. 1972	Finnish Social Democratic Party Center Party Swedish People's Party Liberal People's Party
1975	Center Party Finnish Social Democratic Party Swedish People's Party Liberal People's Party Finnish People's Democratic League
1976	Center Party Liberal People's Party Swedish People's Party
1977	Finnish Social Democratic Party Center Party Liberal People's Party Finnish People's Democratic League Finnish Communist Party
1979	Finnish Social Democratic Party Center Party Finnish People's Democratic League Swedish People's Party

Note: First-named party is dominant coalition party.

FRANCE

The FRENCH REPUBLIC (*République Française*) is the largest nation in western Europe geographically, with over 211,000 square miles and an estimated 54 million (1981) inhabitants. It is, however, still small by American standards, as it is less than the size of Texas. Metropolitan France is bounded on the north by the English Channel, Belgium, Luxembourg, and West Germany; to the east by Switzerland and Italy; Spain and the Mediterranean Sea are to the south; and the Atlantic Ocean is to the west. The island of Corsica in the Mediterranean is also considered to be part of metropolitan France.

France is divided into units of subnational administration called departments. Metropolitan France, including Corsica, consists of 96 departments. Once holding extensive colonies, France still maintains jurisdiction over several areas throughout the world. Five of these areas are regarded as overseas departments (*départements d'outre mer*) and elect representatives to the French parliament: Guadeloupe and Martinique (in the West Indies), Réunion (in the Indian Ocean), French Guiana (South America), and the joint department of Saint Pierre and Miquelon (off Newfoundland, Canada). Four other areas are referred to as overseas territories (*territoires d'outre mer*) but also have representation in the French parliament: New Caledonia, French Polynesia, and the jointly administered Wallis and Futuna islands (all in the South Pacific), and Mayotte (an island off the African coast).

France has passed through a succession of political forms and electoral arrangements since the overthrow of the monarchical system by the French Revolution (1789-1793). The 1958 constitution of the Fifth Republic, as revised in 1962, provides for a president elected by universal suffrage, beginning at age 18. The term of office is seven years. Presidential election requires an absolute majority of the votes cast, with provision for a run-off election, if required, between the top two vote-getters. The president appoints the prime minister and has the power to dissolve the parliament and call for new elections. The president may also propose referenda dealing with specific issues; and under Article 16 of the constitution, he may rule by decree for limited periods under a state of national emergency.

Parliament is a bicameral body consisting of the Senate (*Sénat*) and the National Assembly (*Assemblée Nationale*). The two chambers are equal in power, except that the lower-house National Assembly has priority in budgetary matters and that the cabinet is responsible only to the lower house. The members of the upper-house Senate (currently 283) are elected indirectly by electoral colleges composed of local and departmental councillors and members of the National Assembly. Senators are elected for nine years, with one-third of the Senate membership being renewed every three years. Of the total Senate membership, 264 senators are elected from metropolitan France, 13 from the overseas areas, and six from French nationals living abroad.

The 491 deputies of the National Assembly are elected from single-member constituencies for five-year terms under direct universal suffrage in a two-ballot system. In each electoral district, a candidate is declared elected on the first ballot if he or she obtains an absolute majority of the votes cast. This is rarely achieved. In 1981, for example, only 156 of the 491 seats (or 31.5 percent) were filled on the first ballot. If no one is elected at this stage, a run-off election is held two weeks later among those candidates that had received on the first ballot votes equal to 12.5 percent of that district's number of registered voters. (In 1958, the cut-off for second-ballot eligibility had been five percent of the first-ballot votes, amended to ten percent of the eligible electorate in 1967, and further amended to the current level as of 1976.) On the second ballot, where the number of candidates is generally reduced to two or perhaps three, only a plurality is needed to be elected. Seventeen of the Assembly deputies are elected by overseas areas.

The two-ballot system leads to political maneuverings among the French parties. Electoral agreements will be made among parties of similar outlook to withdraw their candidates from the second ballot in order to limit competition against a remaining candidate who has the best-perceived chance of winning the election. This is a primary reason why the number of candidates on a district's second ballot is usually reduced to two or three.

The history of France, as of many other European nations, begins politically with the Roman Empire. The Romans called the French area Gaullia. With the fall of the Roman Empire, France began to develop a feudalism that was more permeating than elsewhere in Europe. The strong feudalism, with local supremacy of vassals, limited the central powers of the monarch throughout most of the Middle Ages. The provinces had their own bodies, called Estates, which assembled representatives of the clergy, nobility, and peasants to determine local administration. Through the centuries, however, the French monarchy had been slowly centralizing its authority, starting with the Capet dynasty in A.D. 987 and ruling for some 350 years, then followed by the Valois dynasty for the next 250 years. By the 14th century, while the English monarchy, for example, had become limited, the French monarchy had been transformed from limited to absolute. Also by the 14th century, the provincial Estates led to the development of an equivalent body to advise the king—the Estates-General—but this body was restricted in its authority and met only upon summons from the king.

The first king of the Bourbon dynasty was Henry of Navarre, ruling as Henry

IV from 1589 to 1610. The succeeding Bourbons, in particular, strengthened the absolute monarchy in France. Henry's successor, Louis XIII (ruling 1610-1643), and his minister, Cardinal Richelieu, stripped the French nobility of an important political task by transferring the supervision of local administration to royal *intendants*, appointed from among the commoners. These *intendants* were then elevated to a type of nobility, thus broadening that class but also dividing its ranks by differing self-interests. Moreover, the Estates-General met in 1614 but would not be summoned again until 1789.

Louis XIV (ruling 1643-1715) succeeded in national unification of France's diverse groups (such as the Alsatians, Burgundians, Normans). He did this, in part, by eliminating local autonomy and abolishing municipal elections in 1692. Louis XV (1715-1774) appointed and dismissed ministers on whim. Louis XVI (1774-1792) was particularly stubborn and, until forced by the French Revolution, did little to curb France's ever-increasing financial problems and socioeconomic conditions left over, in great part, from feudalism.

The elite of the Catholic Church, which had comprised the First Estate of the old Estates-General, made up less than one percent of France's population yet held exensive property. (It should be noted, however, that common priests were poor and as part of the Third Estate received little financial support from their ecclesiastical superiors.) The church was exempt from taxation and in turn levied its own tithe on local peasants. The nobility, forming the Second Estate, comprised less than two percent of the population but controlled approximately 20 percent of the landholdings. They, too, were exempt from taxation but levied their own manorial taxes on the peasants. Finally, the commoners, or the Third Estate, formed about 98 percent of the population. Most of these were peasants, though the bourgeoisie was included. In addition to paying church tithes and manorial taxes, the commoners also bore the full burden of income, property, and poll taxes to the French crown. But rising prices, small landholdings, and drought brought impossible conditions to these peasants by the 1780s.

In 1788, King Louis XVI attempted to curb the economic problem by raising new loans and increasing taxation. Meeting immediate defeat, Louis summoned the Estates-General to meet the following spring, thus attempting to revive an institution that had been essentially dead for 175 years. However, the elected members of the 1789 Estates-General, convening on May 5, insisted on procedural changes from those traditionally used.

Previously, each Estate deliberated issues separately, and passage of a measure required consent of two Estates and the crown. In 1789, however, the Third Estate insisted that the entire assembly deliberate as a whole, with each deputy having one vote. Meeting opposition, on June 17 the Third Estate broke from the body and proclaimed itself the National Assembly. Louis's commands for the return of the Third Estate were refused. On June 27, the king succumbed—wishing to expedite a solution to his economic problems, regardless of the name of the body—and ordered the First and Second Estate deputies to join the

National Assembly. Thus began the body which now constitutes the lower house of the French legislature.

On August 26, 1789, the National Assembly finalized its "Declaration of the Rights of Man," a document that promised a constitution would be written to guarantee individual rights of property and liberty. The Assembly also abolished tithes and manorial taxes, instead instituting an income tax to be paid by all. In November, in an attempt to curb the still-growing national debt, the Assembly seized all church lands and larger estates of the nobility, intending to sell them. In 1791 the Assembly produced a written constitution, guaranteeing individual rights and devising a system of national administration. France was divided into 83 departments of approximately equal size. Each department was further divided into districts and communes, with each department and commune to have elected councils and officials. The franchise was limited, however, to males who paid a minimum amount of income taxes, and thus the vote was denied to about one-third of France's adult male population. Despite such attempts to reform French government, continuing socioeconomic problems had radicalized French society into revolution, one that had already begun with popular uprisings in July 1789, such as the historic seizure of the Bastille and comparable revolts throughout the rest of the country.

Volumes of material have been written on the French Revolution, a topic too extensive to be included here. Suffice to say that the revolution abolished the Bourbon monarchy and led to the establishment of the short-lived First Republic in 1792. Following a military coup in 1799, the republic was transformed into the First Empire under Napoleon Bonaparte in 1804. The First Empire collapsed under the stress of military defeat, following Napoleon's attempt to conquer all of western and central Europe. From 1814 to 1830, the Bourbon monarchy was restored under Charles X. Revolutionary events in the Summer of 1830 once again ousted the Bourbons and led to the transference of the throne to Louis Philippe of the Orleanist branch of the Bourbon dynasty. In 1848 another revolution introduced a presidential system and universal manhood suffrage under the Second Republic (1848-1851).

Although France was among the first countries to adopt universal manhood suffrage (in 1848), French political parties did not begin to take form until the second half of the 19th century with the inception of the Third Republic (1875-1940). Under the National Assembly of the Second Republic, the political struggle was between loosely organized factions of republicans and conservatives. The former supported a secular, republican form of government; the latter stood for clerical privileges and a restoration of the monarchy. Following the coup of Louis Napoleon (nephew of Napoleon Bonaparte) in 1851 and the installation of the Second Empire, partisan divisions were muted and did not reappear until 1870 when France suffered defeat in the Franco-Prussian War.

The collapse of the Second Empire led to a return of the embryonic partisan divisions which had been manifested under the Second Republic. In 1871 a National Assembly was elected to create a new government for France, but the

Assembly soon became hopelessly divided. Although heavily monarchist in sentiment, the Assembly was actually composed of mutually antagonistic groups who were ill-organized and exhibited no real degree of cohesion. The result was the Third Republic in 1875, which was to have the longest life of any French regime to date.

At the inception of the Third Republic, the monarchists were divided into Legitimists, who supported the principle of absolutism and the restoration of the Bourbon dynasty; Bonapartists or Imperialists, who sought the return of Louis Napoleon based upon the "will of the people"; and the Orleanists, whose goal was to return the line of succession to the Orleanist branch (Louis Philippe) of the Bourbon family (see also Monarchists). The death of the Count of Chambord in 1883, who left no legitimate heir, deprived the Legitimists of their claims to the French throne. The Orleanist candidature eventually passed to the Count of Paris, who came to be regarded as the pretender to the French throne. After 1875, the monarchists began to be known as reactionaries or simply "the right." Those who were not pledged to the monarchy but preferred strong centralized government became known as conservatives or moderate republicans after 1881, and finally as progressives after 1898.

The republicans were also divided into several major groupings. The extreme left was organized into the Radical Party (see Radical-Socialist Party) of Léon Gambetta. It had considerable success in the Assembly between 1879 and 1893. Following the death of Gambetta in 1881, it broke apart, with one group remaining Radical and the other constituting the core of the French socialist movement (see Socialist Party). Other groupings of republicans were organized into the left and the center-left by Jules Grèvy and Adolph Thiers respectively. French socialist elements also appeared in 1871 that took on partisan form by 1879. French socialists at this time, however, were divided internally into several competing ideological factions (marxists, Blanquists, Reformists, Possibilists; see Socialist Party), which weakened their ability to act in a concerted way.

French governments during the early years of the Third Republic were dominated by various coalitions of Radicals and republicans. Coalition ministries of Radicals or moderate elements were formed to counter royalists or conservatives; or in some cases, republicans formed alliances with conservatives in opposition to other republicans. This pattern continued to 1914. Parties remained factionalized and undisciplined until the first decade of the 20th century. They rarely voted as a unit in the Assembly, and personal interests were of paramount importance.

The history of modern French parties begins around the turn of the century with the consolidation of older groups, such as the Radicals in 1901, and the emergence of new political forces, such as the Christian democrats and socialists. (For Third Republic parties appearing in the Chamber at this time, see table 23.) Parties also began to develop extensive extraparliamentary organizations for the mobilization of support. The encyclical, Rerum Novarum, of Pope Leo XIII, led to a new political attitude on the part of progressive Catholics in France. No longer tied to monarchical restoration, progressive Catholics formed organizations known as the Conservative Rallies (*Conservateurs Ralliés* or *Ralliément*) that were pledged to support the republican form of government. As a result, a new conservative grouping, the Popular Liberal Action Party (*see* Popular Republican Movement), was formed in 1899 to reconcile Catholic interests with republicanism. A more liberal Christian democratic grouping developed into the Popular Democratic Party in 1924 and ultimately became the foundation for the Popular Republican Movement after World War II.

Other secular conservative elements formed the Democratic Alliance* under Adolph Carnot in 1901, which later evolved into the Republican-Democratic and Social Party (*see* Democratic Alliance) of Raymond Poincaré in 1920. As the various moderate or progressive groupings began to lose power with the emergence of the new parties, they, too, reorganized into the Republican Federation of France* in 1903.

Various attempts to consolidate French socialism during this period culminated in the founding of a unified party in 1905 (*see* Socialist Party). This unity, however, was short-lived. The French political left, including the Socialists, divided over World War I and the Bolshevik Revolution in Russia (*see* SOVIET UNION). The issue of the war resulted in the formation of national-oriented socialist parties, while the latter event in Russia led to the creation of the French Communist Party.*

Important developments occurred on the extreme political right that would have a menacing influence in post-World War I France. Extreme nationalist sentiment and a desire for revenge against Germany led to the formation of various patriotic leagues, of which the League of French Action (1905) was the most important (*see* Extreme Right). At first these groups were monarchist in nature; but after World War I, they were transformed into quasi-fascist movements, as represented by the French Popular Party and the French Social Party (*see* Extreme Right).

During the World War I years (1914-1919), partisan conflict was at a low ebb in France. Broad multiparty cabinets were formed under a basically conservative governing coalition known as the Sacred Union (*Union Sacrée*). The Union was ruptured in 1917 by the defection of the Socialist Party, and it was later destroyed by the formation of the French Communist Party. The period following the armistice saw a return to the old parties, as well as the emergence of yet newer groups with reformist platforms. Some of the older parties suffered losses in support during the war years—the Socialists through party fragmentation; the Radicals through electoral shifts. After 1918 the Radicals were essentially reduced to a rural middle-class party.

In the early 1920s, French parties displayed a tendency to form large blocs of various ideological hues. On the right was formed the National Republican Bloc (*Bloc National Républicain*), composed of the Republican Federation of France, the Democratic Alliance, and the Popular Liberal Action Party. Between 1920 and 1924, the Bloc constituted almost two-thirds of the Assembly seats. In 1924 the Radicals and Socialists formed the Left Bloc (*Cartel des Gauches*) as a parliamentary organization to combat the influence of the National Bloc. The Cartel exercised considerable influence until 1928, when the political center was returned to power.

The period between 1929 and 1932 was one of cabinet instability that ended with the formation of the National Union government in 1934. The deepening economic depression led to falling industrial production, unemployment, budget deficits, and various scandals. The rising threat of fascism, coupled with general riots and strikes, eventually led to the formation of the Popular Front (a coalition of Communists, Socialists, and Radicals under Socialist direction) as a means of consolidating the strength of the republican left. The Popular Front collapsed one year later, and Socialist leader Léon Blum was replaced by the Radical notable Eduoard Daladier in 1938. The Daladier government ordered the dissolution of the Communist Party on September 26, 1939.

The German invasion of France in Summer 1940 ended the Third Republic. On July 10, 1940, the National Assembly voted 569 to 80 to abrogate the constitution of 1875 and to give full powers to Marshal Philippe Pétain, an aging World War I hero, who proceeded to set up a government of unoccupied France in the city of Vichy under the terms of a German armistice. Pétain declared himself head of the French state, ended the parliamentary regime, and constructed a governmental system based upon personal rule. Although no official ban was placed on political parties, most continued to function only clandestinely. Only the parties of the extreme right, especially the French Social Party and French Popular Party, openly rallied in support of the Vichy regime and the corporative idea (see Extreme Right).

With the liberation of France in 1944, a new political era began. Few wished to revive the Third Republic that had collapsed in 1940, and the Vichy constitution was totally unacceptable. The immediate postwar period was dominated by the personality of General Charles de Gaulle (see Gaullists), a popular, national, World War II hero. Initially, de Gaulle had no political party of his own and ruled without restraint. His policy was to forge a broad coalition of political forces that would be representative of France as a whole.

The political parties that emerged in the post-World War II period had their roots in the defunct Third Republic. The Communists could point to a distinguished resistance record, and they managed to dominate the General Confederation of Labor (Confédération Generale du Travail: CGT), France's largest labor union. The Socialists and Radicals were much reduced in strength. The former was split into various wings; the latter was charged with the failure of 1940. The various parties of the right were associated with collaborationism and the Vichy regime. The one new party was the Popular Republican Movement (MRP), which had developed out of the small prewar Christian democratic group. The MRP advocated social reforms and a policy of European unity.

Elections to the 1945 constituent assembly resulted in a victory for left-wing forces, which were determined to return France to an assembly-type of government. A split developed between de Gaulle and the leftist parties, and on

January 20, 1946, de Gaulle resigned as head of the French government. On June 2, 1946, the first draft constitution of the Fourth Republic was rejected in a nationwide referendum. A second constituent assembly was elected; and after several changes, including the addition of a second legislative chamber (the Senate), the second draft was approved on October 13, 1946. Over eight million Frenchmen abstained. Although the Third Republic had begun on an even slimmer margin of support, it had lasted for 70 years; the Fourth Republic would end in 1958 after only 12 years of existence.

The 12 years of the Fourth Republic represented a period of parliamentary dominance. Governments were overthrown with ease, and the electoral system virtually denied the possibility of a solid majority (see table 24). Governing coalitions were extremely fragile and subject to dissolution under the slightest stress. Problems in the economy and foreign affairs seemed to require different coalitions. However, after each crisis and dissolution, very often the same groups attempted to form the new governments (see table 25). As government crises worsened over the war in Indochina and the demands for Algerian independence, cynicism and disenchantment with the institutional arrangements of the Fourth Republic grew in intensity.

The end of the Fourth Republic was brought about by a military revolt in Algeria in May 1958 on the part of the French army, whose leaders feared abandonment by the Paris government. The civilian government had proved to be incapable of resolving the impasse and securing the obedience of the French military. In an attempt to prevent the possible outbreak of civil war, President René Coty declared Charles de Gaulle as premier-designate; and on June 1, 1958, de Gaulle and his cabinet were formally invested as the government of France by the National Assembly. The Assembly also approved the drafting of a new constitution. It was submitted to a referendum on September 28, 1958, and received overwhelming approval (82.5 percent) by the electorate. In addition, de Gaulle offered the overseas territories the option of choosing their form of association with France. A no vote would mean instant independence. Only Guinea made this choice. Algeria was denied this option since it was, technically, part of metropolitan France. Thus began the Fifth Republic (1958-).

At the end of his first seven-year term of office, de Gaulle contested the presidency in 1965 and secured victory over his challenger, François Mitterrand (see Convention of Republican Institutions), the candidate of the united left. On April 27, 1969, de Gaulle abruptly resigned the presidency following the defeat of his referendum on regional decentralization and reform of the Senate. He was succeeded by interim president Alain Poher (see Democratic Center). In June 1969, former Gaullist Prime Minister Georges Pompidou was elected as de Gaulle's successor. Pompidou's death on April 2, 1974, once again opened the presidency and pitted François Mitterrand (who had not run in 1969 and in 1971 had joined the Socialist Party) against Valéry Giscard d'Estaing, former Gaullist minister of finance who was the founder of the Republican Party. * Although Mitterrand won the most votes on the first ballot (43.3 percent), he lost the second round to Giscard d'Estaing in a very close race (50.8 percent to 49.2 percent). The two candidates were separated by about 400,000 votes. The 1981 presidential election (April 26-May 10) once again pitted Mitterrand against Giscard d'Estaing. This time the result was a victory for Mitterrand (51.7 percent) on the second ballot, and he became the first Socialist president since the Fourth Republic.

The legislative elections of the Fifth Republic (see table 26) revealed a rise and then a decline of Gaullism. Gaullism peaked in 1968 (June elections); but in 1973 and 1978, the left came close to victory. With the 1981 election of Mitterrand to the presidency, the left, for the first time during the Fifth Republic, secured both that office and the Assembly and hence the government leadership (see table 27).

The structural and institutional changes introduced by de Gaulle at the beginning of the Fifth Republic played a major role in transforming and simplifying the French party system. One of the chief instruments was the electoral system, which between 1875 and 1958 had been changed nine times. Then there were modifications to the methods of presidential election (1962), and the 1967 and 1976 provisions raising the minimum first-ballot vote required for eligibility to compete in the run-offs for the legislative elections. It is significant that only the method of presidential election is fixed by the constitution (Article 7, as amended in 1962), while the electoral law applicable to parliament is governed by ordinary legislation.

Throughout French history, different electoral systems have served either to benefit or penalize certain political groups in terms of their parliamentary representation. The parties of the left, as well as splinter groups, have generally favored a system of proportional representation. Conservative forces have preferred a system which, in effect, would isolate the Communist Party and weaken the parliamentary strength of the left.

The Fourth Republic operated under two fundamentally different electoral systems. Proportional representation was in effect for the constituent assembly in 1945 and the first post-World War II legislative elections in November 1946. The rules were changed to accommodate a majoritarian list system for the 1951 and 1956 elections, although proportional representation continued in effect for certain large towns. Tactical alliances were permitted so that parties could count the votes of all their affiliates in the final distribution of Assembly seats. Such alliances were designed to increase the parliamentary strength of the moderate left and reduce the representation of the Communist Party.

The electoral system of the Fifth Republic appears to have facilitated a fundamental change in traditional party practices and behavior. The single-member, two-ballot system does tend to encourage party factionalization on the first ballot. Yet the reward of political victory for less-than-majority contenders can only be achieved on the second ballot through a policy of party alliances or regroupment. Similarly, the provisions of direct election of the president (1962) worked against narrow, factionalizing tendencies so common in the French tradition. Party lines have been greatly simplified over the course of the Fifth Republic as the parties have demonstrated their adaptability to the new institutional arrangements.

Another important influence on the party system has been the nationalization of political life in France since 1958. In the past, local notables (mayors and other elected city officials, as well as opinion leaders such as schoolteachers, doctors, businessmen, farm leaders, and clergy) had played an important part in French politics. They interpreted national politics for the citizenry of the small towns or villages. They often controlled electoral outcomes in rural areas where voters were uninformed and sometimes uninterested in national politics. With the advent of television, even the most rural of voters can now watch directly as national leaders discuss national concerns.

Nationalization of politics has also led to increasing centralization of French political life. Centralized campaigns first became evident in the 1967 legislative elections, with issues and strategies handed down from the central party offices in Paris. The Gaullists employed a professional public relations firm that conducted seminars for the party's candidates and provided them with speeches, detailed socioeconomic data on their districts, and suggested campaign plans. Although the left generally scorned this marketing approach to politics, it had its own gimmicks: badges, self-answering phones with recorded messages, and so forth. All of these were nationally distributed. In addition, the left's strategy of internal unity instead of alliance with the center was imposed on candidates by refusing the party label to those unwilling to accept the new strategy. In 1973 and 1978, there was less gimmickry, but the campaigns were equally centralized. Issues and strategies were again handed down from the central party offices. Only candidates willing to accept these guidelines were able to get the investiture of the national party. Since voters increasingly tended to vote for candidates who had endorsement of the national parties, the central party office's control over the use of label enhanced the power of the party over even well-entrenched candidates. Hence the nationalization of politics has resulted in the penetration of the major parties into all areas of France.

French party organizations appear to be healthy. Membership in all major parties has risen significantly since the early 1970s. The parties are successful in getting voters out to the polls, and party units at the grass-roots level have been revitalized and operate on a year-round basis. They appear to be successful in mobilizing their members for a variety of partisan activities and in maintaining internal unity and discipline. Voting cohesion in the National Assembly rose steadily during the first decade of the Fifth Republic and has remained high.

The current political scene in France is dominated by only four or five major parties. The system is further simplified by the grouping of these major parties into two remarkably durable and cohesive coalitions. The Gaullists and Giscardians formed an alliance in 1962 that dominated French politics until 1981. Since 1969, most centrist and moderate conservative groups have joined this former majority coalition. The earlier opposition—the Socialists, Communists, and left-wing Radicals—have formed a Union of the Left* that dates back to 1965. These two coalitions virtually monopolize the political scene. The result has been the emergence of a bipolar party system made up of fairly stable multiparty coalitions. Parties outside these coalitions have either rallied to one of the alliances or have been relegated to the sidelines of French politics.

This is not to say that relations among the partners in both major coalitions have not been sometimes strained. Within each coalition, the constituent parties compete for votes and members from similar social categories. Also, the parties struggle for leadership positions: Gaullists and Giscardians contend for dominance of the majority, and Socialists and Communists seek the leadership of the left. The tensions have been especially great in the Union of the Left as the electoral balance shifted after 1974, giving the Socialist Party more votes than the Communist Party for the first time since World War II. Despite the tensions, the two coalitions persist because the two-ballot electoral system makes cooperation essential for the run-off second ballot. Typically, the second-ballot contests are duels between a single majority candidate and a single left-wing candidate. Failure to agree to cooperation on the second ballot would bring the risk of significant losses in a party's parliamentary delegation.

Presidental elections by universal suffrage provide another incentive for the formation of broad coalitions. In the past, parties might hope to influence politics by winning a few seats in parliament and then by taking part in the often lengthy negotiations that were required to produce a government. Under the Fifth Republic, the emergence of a powerful, popularly elected president who could dominate politics presented an important new political prize. To win this prize, parties had to develop broad coalitions in order to achieve the nationwide majority required to elect a president. The Union of the Left was the product of an effort to elect a left-wing president in 1965, and the Gaullist-Giscardist coalition absorbed the former opposition centrists in 1969 and 1974 in order to preserve its presidential majority coalition.

There is some evidence that France has moved toward the establishment of party government with the advent of a stable government majority system. In the Fourth Republic, the voters had only the choice between supporting the antiregime oppositions of the extreme left or extreme right, or the center parties which by necessity had to govern. Now the electorate can choose between the distinctly different Gaullist-Giscardists and the socialist left, both of which are capable of forming a stable government. The voter's choice is more rational, and the citizen through making this choice is more directly linked with government. The French parties have thus been restructured to resemble the British model of responsible governmental parties and are providing the democratic linkage between the people and government.

Bibliography

Barron, Richard. *Parties and Politics in Modern France.* Washington, D.C.: Public Affairs Press, 1959.

Bon, Frédéric. *Les Elections en France: Histoire et Sociologie.* Paris: Seuil, 1978.

Borella, François. *Les Partis politiques dans la France d'aujourd'hui.* Paris: Seuil, 1977.

Bourgin, Georges, Jean Carrère, and André Guerin. *Manuel des Partis politiques en France.* Paris: Les Editions Rieder, 1928.

Campbell, Peter. *French Electoral Systems and Elections since 1789,* 2d ed. London: Faber, 1965.

Charlot, Jean. *Les Partis politiques.* Paris: Armand Colin, 1971.

———. *Répertoire des publications des partis politiques français, 1944-1967.* Paris: Armand Colin, 1970.

Corcos, Ferdinand. *Catéchisme des Partis Politiques.* Paris: Editions Montagne, 1932.

Frears, J. P. *Political Parties and Elections in the French Fifth Republic.* New York: St. Martin's Press, 1977.

Goguel, François, and Alfred Grosser. *La Politique en France.* Paris: Armand Colin, 1975.

Kraehe, Rainer. *Le Financement des partis politiques.* Paris: Presses Universitaires de France, 1972.

Laponce, Jean. *The Government of the Fifth Republic: French Parties and the Constitution.* Berkeley: University of California Press, 1961.

Penniman, Howard R., ed. *France at the Polls: The Presidential Election of 1974.* Washington, D.C.: American Enterprise Institute, 1975.

———. *The French National Assembly Elections of 1978.* Washington, D.C.: American Enterprise Institute, 1980.

Soltau, Roger H. *French Parties and Politics, 1871-1921.* London: Oxford University Press, 1930.

Political Parties

ACTION FRANÇAISE. *See* MONARCHISTS.

ACTION NATIONALISTE. *See* EXTREME RIGHT.

ACTION RÉPUBLICAINE ET SOCIALE. *See* GAULLISTS.

AGRARIAN PARTY. *See* MODERATES.

AJS. *See* TROTSKYITES.

ALGERIE FRANÇAISE. *See* EXTREME RIGHT.

ALLEMANISTS. *See* SOCIALIST PARTY.

ALLIANCE COMMUNISTE. *See* SOCIALIST PARTY.

ALLIANCE DÉMOCRATIQUE. *See* DEMOCRATIC ALLIANCE.

ALLIANCE DES JEUNES POUR LE SOCIALISME. *See* TROTSKYITES.

ALLIANCE OF YOUTH FOR SOCIALISM. *See* TROTSKYITES.

ALLIANCE RÉPUBLICAINE DÉMOCRATIQUE. *See* DEMOCRATIC AL-LIANCE.

ALLIANCE RÉPUBLICAINE POUR LES LIBERTÉS ET LE PROGRÈS. *See* EXTREME RIGHT.

ALTERNATIVE '81. *See* UNIFIED SOCIALIST PARTY.

ANARCHIST COMBAT ORGANIZATION. *See* ANARCHISTS.

ANARCHIST FEDERATION. *See* ANARCHISTS.

ANARCHISTS (*Anarchistes*). Anarchist political formations in France can be traced to the revolutionary socialist doctrines espoused by Pierre Joseph Proudhon (1809-1865). Anarchists are opposed to all forms of government authority and instead advocate a political system in which small voluntary communities replace the institutions of the modern state. They tend to reject any institutionalized form of participation, including voting, and many believe that social justice can be accomplished only through the use of revolutionary violence.

Anarchists can be divided into three basic groupings: pure individualists, who reject leadership and organization and engage in spontaneous acts of violence; syndicalists, who seek to destroy the state and rebuild the political system around labor unions; and communist libertarians, who seek a communist society on the basis of the soviet. Anarchist organizations have been part of the French political scene since the early 1900s. In the post-World War II period, the years 1956 and 1968 were high points in the emergence of French anarchist groupings.

Since the mid-1950s, various local anarchist organizations have been loosely coordinated by the Anarchist Federation (*Fédération Anarchiste*) and its publication, *Le Monde Libertaire* (The Libertarian World). Rejecting any form of electoral participation as a "fraud," the Federation has functioned largely as a propaganda vehicle for anarchist views. Its avowed political goal is direct worker control of the economy.

Several anarchist groups emerged during the turmoil of May-June 1968. Some were syndicalist in nature, such as the Revolutionary Anarchist Organization (*Organisation Révolutionnaire Anarchiste*: ORA). Others were based upon groups of student militants, such as the Black and Red (*Noir et Rouge*) and the Movement of March 22d (*Mouvement du 22 Mars*); the latter was dissolved in June 1968. Other such groupings were also short-lived, with members drifting to other anarchist or ultraleftist formations.

In 1976 a group of dissidents broke from the Anarchist Federation to form the Anarchist Combat Organization (*Organisation Combat Anarchiste*: OCA) and proceeded to establish cells in various French cities. Another Federation splinter group formed the Union of Libertarian Communist Workers (*Union des Travailleurs Communistes Libertaires*: UTCL) in 1978, with promises to fashion a revolutionary alternative to existing political formations on both the right and left. None of the recent groups has taken part in French elections. Membership in France's anarchist organizations has been estimated to be several thousand.

APC. *See* REGIONAL AUTONOMIST PARTIES.

ARLP. *See* EXTREME RIGHT.

ARS. *See* GAULLISTS.

ASSOCIATION NATIONALE RÉPUBLICAINE. *See* REPUBLICAN FEDERATION OF FRANCE.

ASSOCIATION OF CORSICAN PATRIOTS. *See* REGIONAL AUTONOMIST PARTIES.

ASSOCIU DI PATRIOTI CORSI. *See* REGIONAL AUTONOMIST PARTIES.

AUJOURD'HUI L'ÉCOLOGIE. *See* ECOLOGY POLITICAL MOVEMENT.

AUTONOMOUS SOCIALIST PARTY. *See* UNIFIED SOCIALIST PARTY.

BLACK AND RED. *See* ANARCHISTS.

BLANQUISTS. *See* SOCIALIST PARTY.

BLOC RÉPUBLICAIN NATIONAL. *See* FRANCE INTRODUCTION.

BONAPARTISTS. *See* FRANCE INTRODUCTION.

BOULANGISTS. *See* FRANCE INTRODUCTION.

BRETON AUTONOMIST AND SOCIALIST SELF-RULE FRONT. *See* REGIONAL AUTONOMIST PARTIES.

BRETON DEMOCRATIC UNION. *See* REGIONAL AUTONOMIST PARTIES.

BRETON LIBERATION FRONT. *See* REGIONAL AUTONOMIST PARTIES.

CAMELOTS DU ROI. *See* EXTREME RIGHT and MONARCHISTS.

CARTEL DES GAUCHES. *See* FRANCE INTRODUCTION.

CCA. *See* TROTSKYITES.

CD. *See* DEMOCRATIC CENTER.

CDP. *See* DEMOCRATIC CENTER.

CDS. *See* DEMOCRATIC CENTER.

CENTER FOR DEMOCRACY AND PROGRESS. *See* DEMOCRATIC CENTER.

CENTER OF PROGRESS AND MODERN DEMOCRACY. *See* DEMOCRATIC CENTER.

CENTER OF SOCIAL DEMOCRATS. *See* DEMOCRATIC CENTER.

CENTRE DÉMOCRATIQUE. *See* DEMOCRATIC CENTER.

CENTRE DE PROPAGANDE DES RÉPUBLICAINS NATIONAUX. *See* EXTREME RIGHT.

CENTRE DES DÉMOCRATES SOCIAUX. *See* DEMOCRATIC CENTER.

CENTRE DU PROGRÈS ET DE LA DÉMOCRATIE MODERNE. *See* DEMOCRATIC CENTER.

CENTRE MARXISTE-LENINISTE DE FRANCE. *See* MAOISTS.

CENTRE NATIONAL DES INDÉPENDANTS. *See* NATIONAL CENTER OF INDEPENDENTS AND PEASANTS.

CENTRE NATIONAL DES INDÉPENDANTS ET PAYSANS. *See* NATIONAL CENTER OF INDEPENDENTS AND PEASANTS.

CENTRE NATIONAL DES RÉPUBLICAINS SOCIAUX. *See* GAULLISTS.

CENTRE POUR DÉMOCRATIE ET PROGRÈS. *See* DEMOCRATIC CENTER.

CENTRE RÉPUBLICAIN. *See* REPUBLICAN CENTER.

CERCLE TOCQUEVILLE. *See* CONVENTION OF REPUBLICAN INSTITUTIONS.

CHOISIR. *See* CHOOSE.

CHOOSE (*Choisir*). Created in March 1978 as an outgrowth of the women's movement, Choose was designed to be a political vehicle for female candidates in the 1978 national legislative elections. The party was led by Gisèle Halimi, who, along with Andrée Michel and Genevieve Pastre, fashioned a platform based on women's rights issues. Choose sponsored 43 candidates but polled only a little over 32,000 votes. No Choose candidates were elected. The party did best in Bordeaux and the Paris region.

CHRISTIAN DEMOCRACY. *See* POPULAR REPUBLICAN MOVEMENT.

CIR. *See* CONVENTION OF REPUBLICAN INSTITUTIONS.

CITIZENS 60. *See* CONVENTION OF REPUBLICAN INSTITUTIONS.

CITOYENS 60. *See* CONVENTION OF REPUBLICAN INSTITUTIONS.

CLUB JEAN MOULIN. *See* CONVENTION OF REPUBLICAN INSTITUTIONS.

CLUB OF JACOBINS. *See* CONVENTION OF REPUBLICAN INSTITUTIONS.

CLUBS POLITIQUES. *See* CONVENTION OF REPUBLICAN INSTITUTIONS.

CNI. *See* NATIONAL CENTER OF INDEPENDENTS AND PEASANTS.

CNIP. *See* NATIONAL CENTER OF INDEPENDENTS AND PEASANTS.

CNRS. *See* GAULLISTS.

COLLECTIVE ECOLOGY '78. *See* ECOLOGY POLITICAL MOVEMENT.

COMITÉ DE RASSEMBLEMENT NATIONAL. *See* EXTREME RIGHT.

COMITÉS COMMUNISTES POUR L'AUTOGESTION. *See* TROTSKYITES.

COMMITTEE OF THE NATIONAL RALLY. *See* EXTREME RIGHT.

COMMUNIST ALLIANCE. *See* SOCIALIST PARTY.

COMMUNIST COMBAT ORGANIZATION. *See* TROTSKYITES.

COMMUNIST COMMITTEES FOR SELF-MANAGEMENT. *See* TROTSKY-ITES.

COMMUNIST LEAGUE. *See* TROTSKYITES.

COMMUNIST MOVEMENT OF FRANCE: MARXIST-LENINIST. *See* MAOISTS.

CONSERVATEURS RALLIÉS. *See* POPULAR REPUBLICAN MOVEMENT.

CONSERVATIVE RALLIES. *See* POPULAR REPUBLICAN MOVEMENT.

CONVENTION DE LA GAUCHE CINQUIÈME RÉPUBLIQUE. *See* LEFT-WING GAULLISTS.

CONVENTION DES INSTITUTIONS RÉPUBLICAINES. *See* CONVENTION OF REPUBLICAN INSTITUTIONS.

CONVENTION OF REPUBLICAN INSTITUTIONS (*Convention des Institutions Républicaines*: CIR). Forums for debate, in the form of "clubs," have existed in France since the Second Republic, although these early forums generally concerned themselves with social and moral issues. Eventually, as social policy entered the realm of politics and government, such clubs began to debate political issues. Even these associations, however, remained extraparty and maintained a focus on intellectual stimulation rather than direct action.

The phenomenon of political clubs (*clubs politiques*) saw a great proliferation in the early 1960s, when at least 120 such groupings were organized, primarily in Paris but also in France's other large cities. These clubs generally had a leftist political bias. Many were formed by individuals who wanted to become involved in politics but who found the existing parties of the left too rigid and archaic. Other clubs of the 1960s were simply miniparties, composed of political figures who had left larger parties and who wanted to retain their followings. The clubmen, drawn largely from young intellectuals and upper-middle-class employees, were often left-wing Catholics who were repelled by the anticlericalism of the traditional leftist parties. Initially continuing to separate themselves from party politics, these clubs hoped to provide forums for debate of issues such as constitutional reform, republicanism and democracy, and France's role in developing a greater Europe. Club memberships numbered about 500 to 1,000 each.

The club movement of the early 1960s was generally led by those clubs that had achieved prominence at an earlier time. The Club of Jacobins (*Club des Jacobins*) had originated during the Fourth Republic and initially was composed of defectors from the Radical-Socialist Party.* Citizens 60 (*Citoyens 60*) evolved out of the Socialist Party.* Miscellaneous clubs included the *Club Jean Moulin*, which grew out of the World War II resistance movement; the Tocqueville

Circle (*Cercle Tocqueville*), centered in Lyons; the New Democracy (*Démocratie Nouvelle*), centered in Marseilles; the Young Republic (*Jeune République*), dating to 1911 and made up of leftist Catholics (*see* Popular Republican Movement); and the League of the Rights of Man (*Ligue des Droits de l'Homme*), founded in 1898 and devoted to individual liberties.

In the early 1960s, many of the more politically committed clubs became concerned over attempts by the French Communist Party* to ally itself with groupings of France's noncommunist left. Charles Hernu, leader of the Club of Jacobins, conferred with François Mitterrand, then leader of the Democratic and Socialist Union of the Resistance (UDSR).* Under Mitterrand's influence, Hernu agreed to assemble the various political clubs in an attempt to help unify the noncommunist left. At a June 6, 1964, meeting, attended by the clubs mentioned above and some 30 to 35 of the newer political clubs, it was decided that a federation of clubs would be formed. Hence in October 1964, the Convention of Republican Institutions (CIR) was established.

By 1965 the CIR claimed to represent 50 to 60 clubs, but many clubs active in left-wing politics remained apart from it. In that year, Mitterrand's UDSR also joined the CIR, giving the Convention a distinct political-party flavor. With Mitterrand elected as the new CIR leader, the Convention supported his candidacy in the 1965 presidential election. Furthermore, in September 1965, the CIR became a constituent element in the Federation of the Democratic and Socialist Left (FGDS),* an electoral coalition including the Socialists and Radical-Socialists. Other political clubs associated with the FGDS but maintained their independence from the CIR. A few clubs, like the *Club Jean Moulin*, refused to join the FGDS. The CIR, more committed to partisan politics, actively contested the 1967 parliamentary election, winning 16 seats as part of the FGDS.

The FGDS collapsed in 1968, although the CIR continued to exist under Mitterrand until 1971, when he merged the Convention into the Socialist Party. By this time, most of the other clubs had dissolved or had withdrawn from the political scene, returning to their intended purpose of providing local forums for intellectual research and debate.

Further Reference. Wilson, Frank L., "The Club Phenomenon in France," *Comparative Politics* 3 (July 1971): 517-526.

CONVENTION OF THE LEFT FIFTH REPUBLIC. See LEFT-WING GAULLISTS.

CONVERGENCE FOR SELF-DETERMINATION. See UNIFIED SOCIALIST PARTY.

CONVERGENCE POUR L'AUTOGESTION. See UNIFIED SOCIALIST PARTY.

CORSICAN NATIONAL LIBERATION FRONT. See REGIONAL AUTONOMIST PARTIES.

COURANT B. *See* TROTSKYITES.

CROIX DE FEU. *See* EXTREME RIGHT.

CURRENT B. *See* TROTSKYITES.

DCF. *See* POPULAR REPUBLICAN MOVEMENT.

DEMOCRATIC ALLIANCE (*Alliance Démocratique*). Founded in May 1901 by Adolphe Carnot, the Democratic Alliance was intended as a federation of various conservative but not reactionary groupings. The party's program was quite similar to that of the Republican Federation of France,* and both parties constituted the major part of the National Republican Bloc (*see* France introduction) in the 1920s and 1930s.

Supported mainly by industrial and commercial classes, the Alliance was closer to the political center than the Republican Federation. It differed with the Federation on the religious question by its advocacy of state neutrality and its opposition both to clericalism and anticlericalism. The Alliance accepted taxation on incomes and business but stood opposed to collectivist measures. The party was open in the sense that its members could also belong to other political organizations. Among the important leaders of the Alliance were Raymond Poincaré, Jules Siegfried, P. Waldeck-Rousseau, and Pierre Flandin.

The Alliance was reorganized several times. It had become the Republican Democratic Alliance (*Alliance Républicaine Démocratique*) in 1911, and the Republican-Democratic and Social Party (*Parti Républicain-Démocratique et Social*) in 1920. It was last reorganized in 1936. An attempt to revive the Alliance following World War II failed because of divisive personal conflicts among the leadership. In 1945, remaining elements of the Alliance became associated with the Republican Party of Liberty.*

DEMOCRATIC AND SOCIALIST UNION OF THE RESISTANCE (*Union Démocratique et Socialiste de la Résistance*: UDSR). The UDSR was a minor, though important party of the Fourth Republic. The Union originated in several noncommunist resistance movements that had split off from France's main resistance organization in January 1945 over the issue of cooperation with the French Communist Party.* At first, the UDSR remained a loose federation of various regional groupings, and it was originally allied with the Socialist Party* for the general election of October 1945. Breaking with the Socialists shortly thereafter, when the Socialists cooperated with the Communists on adoption of a draft constitution, the UDSR became an organized political party in 1946 under the leadership of René Pleven. After 1951, the UDSR came under the direction of François Mitterrand.

In the early years of the Fourth Republic, the UDSR's center-left position made it an important party in coalition formation. At the parliamentary level, it was allied with the Radicals in the Rally of the Left Republicans (*see* Radical-Socialist Party). Although socialist in orientation, the UDSR was nonmarxist and had no coherent ideology of its own. Rather, it was basically a grouping of individualists who supported both the political right and left. After its 1945 experience with the Socialist Party, the UDSR maintained a distance from that party and for a time even permitted its parliamentary members to affiliate with General Charles de Gaulle's center-right Rally of the French People (*see* Gaullists).

The UDSR functioned in the National Assembly with an average of 20 deputies throughout most of the Fourth Republic, though only with the support of certain African deputies. Following the 1951 election, the UDSR had dwindled to a mere nine representatives. The inception of the Fifth Republic in 1958 virtually destroyed the party. Former UDSR leader Pleven and his supporters left the party in 1958 in support of the Gaullist movement. In 1959, Pleven's group became the Democratic Union (*Union Démocratique*), which later merged into the Democratic Center (CD)* when that party was formed in 1966. Then, in 1969, Pleven's group became part of the CD splinter, the Center for Democracy and Progress (*see* Democratic Center). With Pleven's departure, Mitterrand was free to reorganize the UDSR as his personal political machine.

In 1965, under Mitterrand's direction, the UDSR merged into the Convention of Republican Institutions (CIR).* The CIR was a progressive association of various political clubs that had been formed in 1964 to promote the unity of the noncommunist left. With Mitterrand elected as the new CIR leader, the Convention supported his candidacy for the presidency in 1965; and in September of that year, the CIR became a constituent element in the Federation of the Democratic and Socialist Left,* which also came under Mitterrand's leadership. The Federation collapsed in 1968, although the CIR, including the old UDSR elements, continued feebly to exist under Mitterrand until 1971, when it merged into the Socialist Party.

DEMOCRATIC CENTER (*Centre Démocratique*: CD). In March 1966, the Democratic Center was formed as a national organization for centrists opposed to Charles de Gaulle (*see* Gaullists). The CD included the bulk of the dwindling Popular Republican Movement (MRP),* the National Center of Independents and Peasants,* as well as other centrist opposition groups. The CD's principal architect was Jean Lecanuet, leader of the MRP, whose unexpectedly strong showing in the 1965 presidential election (16 percent of the first-ballot votes) had given him a national audience. The Democratic Center was a means to perpetuate and extend Lecanuet's national following, particularly since the MRP was losing its viability as an organization (and, in fact, disappeared after the 1967 legislative election).

The Democratic Center lacked the clerical image of the MRP, but the CD enjoyed its greatest support among practicing Catholics. Aiming for support from among anti-Gaullist elements in the Catholic middle class and for the farm vote, the CD lost the working-class support that the MRP had initially enjoyed.

Except for a few areas where traditional MRP ties remained or where popular local leaders had built strong bases, the CD lacked an effective political organization. The CD was strongly pro-European and advocated moderate social and economic reforms. It criticized the Gaullist majority for the latter's lack of respect for traditional French democratic practices.

The CD's political fortune was compromised by its attempt to remain between the center-right Gaullists and the political left at a time of bipolarization in French politics. Since it was neither part of the majority nor a part of the principal opposition forces, the CD was ignored by much of the electorate. In addition, its leaders were constantly subjected to the attraction of the majority and the possibility of participating in the government. In 1967, for example, the CD received only 13.4 percent of the votes in the legislative election. A parliamentary group of 41 was formed, though mostly including centrist-oriented deputies from other tickets. In the 1968 election, this parliamentary group ran as the Center of Progress and Modern Democracy (*Centre du Progrès et de la Démocratie Moderne*), though it was more simply known as Progress and Modern Democracy (*Progrès et Démocratie Moderne*: PDM). On a platform of condemnation for the student and worker unrest of May 1968, the PDM won only 10.3 percent of the vote and 33 seats.

The Democratic Center split in 1969. Alain Poher, as head of the French Senate, was acting president of the country after de Gaulle's resignation. As such, Poher ran as the centrist candidate in the 1969 presidential election. However, a portion of the CD supported Georges Pompidou, a Gaullist (though somewhat more liberal than Charles de Gaulle). These CD defectors were rewarded with several ministerial portfolios when Pompidou won the election. Twenty-five Democratic Center deputies, including René Pleven (earlier of the Democratic and Socialist Union of the Resistance*) and Jacques Duhamel (formerly of the Radical-Socialist Party*), left the CD to form the Center for Democracy and Progress (*Centre pour Démocratie et Progrès*: CDP). The CD continued under Lecanuet's leadership. Both parties remained in the same parliamentary group within the National Assembly.

In 1971 the Democratic Center joined with the moderate Radical-Socialist Party and the Republican Center* (a Radical-Socialist splinter) to form a new grouping known as the Reformers' Movement (*Mouvement Réformateur*). The purpose of this organization was to present a viable alternative to gaullism on the right and socialism on the left. The Reformers' Movement advocated progressive liberal reforms and continued support for European integration. As part of this grouping, the Democratic Center maintained stable parliamentary strength in the 1973 election due to cooperative second-ballot strategies on the part of other centrist and some Gaullist candidates. However, the Reformers' Movement as a whole failed to achieve the anticipated electoral impact, receiving only 13.1 percent of first-ballot votes and 34 seats (29 to CD deputies, four to the Radical-Socialists, and one to a dissident Gaullist). In addition, the organization's unity was tested as the Democratic Center moved toward further collaboration with the Gaullist majority (even though officially the CD stood opposed), while the Radical-Socialists remained firmly in the opposition.

The Reformers' Movement continued to exist, though it did not succeed in becoming a political party and instead was a loose basis for cooperation. The earlier CD splinter, the Center for Democracy and Progress, also continued to exist. In the 1974 presidential election, the Reformers rallied to the candidacy of Valéry Giscard d'Estaing, an Independent Republican (see Republican Party). The CDP supported Jacques Chaban-Delmas, the Gaullist candidate. Both groups, however, supported Giscard d'Estaing on the second ballot, and both were included in the Giscardian governments.

By 1975 the Reformers' Movement was succeeded by two new organizations. In March 1975, the Movement of the Reformist Left (Mouvement de la Gauche Réformatrice: MGR) was established as a grass-roots organization working for centrist unity. The Federation of Reformers (Fédération des Réformateurs) was created in June 1975 as a vehicle for cooperation at the parliamentary level. The CDP allied with this latter formation. Yet the MGR, like the Reformers' Movement before it, was unable to evolve into a unified political party. In the hope of achieving centrist strength, the CD and CDP entered into negotiations and in May 1976 formally merged to create a new political party, the Center of Social Democrats (Centre des Démocrates Sociaux: CDS). Jean Lecanuet was elected CDS president.

With the disintegration of the MGR, the CDS joined with other non-Gaullist center groups in an electoral federation called the Union for French Democracy (UDF)* for the 1978 parliamentary election. The new coalition included some of the MGR constituents but also some new ones. The UDF was designed to provide support for the Giscardian government. As part of this coalition, the CDS returned 36 deputies, and Lecanuet was elected leader of the new formation.

After the 1978 election, however, the Gaullists were still the "majority of the majority," and the centrist groupings realized that their own political survival would require Gaullist cooperation. Therefore, prior to the 1981 parliamentary elections, an agreement between Lecanuet of the UDF and Jacques Chirac of the Rally for the Republic (see Gaullists) led to the formation of the Union for the New Majority (see Gaullists and Union for French Democracy). The UDF as a whole won 62 seats (to the Gaullists' 85). However, the election resulted in Lecanuet's CDS losing almost half of its Assembly representation, being reduced to 19 members.

The CDS continues to be a Christian democratic movement strongly supportive of parliamentary government. It supports both free market conditions and democratic planning as means of achieving social justice. The party is organized into various local and departmental components, and policy is set by a national congress that meets biennially. The CDS also publishes a weekly periodical, Démocratie Moderne (Modern Democracy). CDS membership is estimated to be approximately 30,000.

DEMOCRATIC SOCIALIST FEDERATION. *See* FEDERATION OF THE DEMOCRATIC AND SOCIALIST LEFT.

DEMOCRATIC SOCIALIST MOVEMENT. *See* DEMOCRATIC SOCIALIST MOVEMENT OF FRANCE.

DEMOCRATIC SOCIALIST MOVEMENT OF FRANCE (*Mouvement des Démocrates Socialistes de France*: MDSF). The MDSF is known more simply as the MDS (Democratic Socialist Movement). It was formed in December 1973 by dissidents of the Socialist Party (PS)* who were opposed to the common program agreed upon by the PS and the French Communist Party* in June 1972. The precedent for the MDSF can be traced to 1969 when several Socialist notables bolted the PS over the same issue of common action with the Communists. André Chandernagor, a former Socialist Party deputy, formed Socialist Democracy (*Démocratie Socialiste*) in 1969; and in the same year, Emile Muller, Socialist mayor of Mulhouse, left the PS to form the Independent Democratic Socialist Party (*Parti Démocrate Socialiste Indépendant*). Muller's group was later joined by August Lecoeur's group, Socialism and Freedom (*Socialisme et Liberté*). These various PS splinters came together in 1973 and, with additional PS dissidents, formed the basis of the MDSF.

The MDSF claims to be heir to the liberal socialist traditions of Jean Jaurès and Léon Blum (*see* Socialist Party), and the MDSF has advocated closer ties to the political center. The MDSF cooperated with the various centrist coalitions of the early 1970s, such as the Reformers' Movement in 1973 and the Federation of Reformers in 1975 (*see* Democratic Center). As vice-president of the MDSF, Emile Muller ran for president of France in 1974, but he obtained only 0.7 percent of the first-ballot votes. In the 1978 parliamentary elections, the MDSF was associated with another centrist coalition, the Union for French Democracy.* Although four MDSF deputies were elected in that year, the party failed to elect a single candidate in 1981.

The MDSF's ideology is one of reformist evolutionary socialism with selective state intervention. The party is organized into various federations across France, and membership is estimated to be approximately 4,000. *Le Démocrate Socialiste* (The Socialist Democrat) is the party's publication. The current MDSF leaders are Max Lejeune as president and Charles Bauer as secretary-general.

DEMOCRATIC SOCIALIST PARTY (1946-late 1940s). *See* SOCIALIST PARTY.

DEMOCRATIC SOCIALIST PARTY (1975-   ) (*Parti Socialiste Démocrate*: PSD). The PSD was formed in May 1975 by Eric Hintermann, former secretary of the Socialist Party* parliamentary group in the National Assembly. (This PSD is not to be confused with the Democratic Socialist Party [1946-late 1940s] that had been founded by Paul Faure immediately following World War II. *See* Socialist Party.) Similar to the founders of the Democratic Socialist Movement of France,* Hintermann organized Socialist Party dissidents who were opposed to the formation of a Socialist alliance with the French Communist Party.*

Although the PSD presented over 70 candidates in the March 1978 parliamentary elections, only one deputy was elected. Following plans for the PSD to affiliate with the centrist Union for French Democracy* in May 1978, part of the PSD's left wing seceded to form the Federation of Democratic Socialists (*Fédération des Socialistes Démocrates*: FSD) under the leadership of Christian Chauvel. The PSD executive then decided against joining the centrist Union and contested the 1981 parliamentary elections as an independent group, though with no success.

The PSD promises a "third way" towards social democracy in France. The party claims to have over 100 departmental federations and approximately 15,000 members. Its major publication is *Socialisme 2000* (Socialism 2000).

DEMOCRATIC UNION. *See* DEMOCRATIC AND SOCIALIST UNION OF THE RESISTANCE.

DEMOCRATIC UNION FOR THE FIFTH REPUBLIC. See GAULLISTS.

DEMOCRATIC UNION FOR THE REPUBLIC. *See* GAULLISTS.

DEMOCRATIC UNION OF INDEPENDENTS. *See* MODERATES.

DEMOCRATIC UNION OF LABOR. *See* GAULLISTS AND LEFT-WING GAULLISTS.

DÉMOCRATIE CHRÉTIENNE. *See* POPULAR REPUBLICAN MOVEMENT.

DÉMOCRATIE CHRÉTIENNE FRANÇAISE. *See* POPULAR REPUBLICAN MOVEMENT.

DÉMOCRATIE NOUVELLE. *See* CONVENTION OF REPUBLICAN INSTITUTIONS.

DÉMOCRATIE SOCIALISTE. *See* DEMOCRATIC SOCIALIST MOVEMENT OF FRANCE.

ECOLOGY POLITICAL MOVEMENT (*Mouvement d'Écologie Politique*: MEP). Though not officially established until 1980, the Ecology Political Movement first began to take form with the candidacy of René Dumont, who contested the 1974 presidential election on a "quality of life" platform. Dumont received 1.3

percent of the vote. Various ecology groups had formed an alliance to support Dumont, including *Paris-Écologie*, Network of Friends of the Earth (*Réseau des Amis de la Terre*: RAT), and SOS-Environment. The electoral alliance was continued for the 1977 municipal elections in Paris, an area where the environmental movement was especially strong. In the 1978 national legislative elections, various ecology candidates were presented under the label of Collective Ecology '78, although no representatives were elected to the Assembly. Nor were any French ecologists elected to the European Parliament in June 1979 under their banner of Europe-Ecology (*see* EUROPEAN PARLIAMENT).

Following a congress of environmentalists in 1979, the Ecology Political Movement was officially founded as a political vehicle in February 1980. Bruce Lalonde (Friends of the Earth) was a presidential candidate in 1981 and received 3.09 percent of the vote. In the 1981 parliamentary elections, 82 candidates were presented under the banner of Ecology Today (*Aujourd'hui l'Écologie*). The Ecologists secured over one percent of the vote on the first ballot, but they failed to elect any candidates. Several left-wing ecologists attempted to link various environmental concerns to other socioeconomic issues, especially in the Self-Determination Front (*see* Unified Socialist Party).

The MEP has fared best at the municipal level where the party runs on a variety of "apolitical" quality-of-life platforms. In outlook and structure, the MEP is quite similar to the West German "Green Ones" (*see* WEST GERMANY).

ECOLOGY TODAY. *See* ECOLOGY POLITICAL MOVEMENT.

EUROPEAN LIBERTY RALLY. *See* EXTREME RIGHT.

EUROPEAN NATIONALIST FASCISTS. *See* EXTREME RIGHT.

EXTREME RIGHT. Historically, the extreme political right in France has been represented by a number of diverse small parties and extraparliamentary groups. Ideologically, they have ranged from Monarchists* and fascist leagues in the Third Republic to nationalist, antiparliamentary, and protest groups in the post-World War II period. None of the parties on the extreme right has had any long-term political significance, although they have often engaged in violent activities directed against the extreme left (*see* Maoists and Trotskyites).

The origins of France's extreme right can be found in the various nationalistic, intransigent, conservative groups that appeared toward the close of the 19th century. Prior to World War I, the organizational pattern of the extreme right was to form leagues or direct-action agitation groups, beginning with the League of Patriots (*Ligue des Patriots*) in 1882. The League of Patriots was monarchist in tone, but primarily it sought to foment retaliation against Germany after the Franco-Prussian War. Other groups which followed included the (Orleanist) League of the French Fatherland (*Ligue de la Patrie Française*) in 1898, and the League of French Action (*Ligue de l'Action Français*) in 1905. The avowed purpose of the latter organizations was to defend clerical interests, promote nationalism, and, most of all, to restore the French monarchy (*see also* Monarchists).

After World War I, the older monarchist-nationalist leagues were joined by newer groups of fascist sympathizers. The extreme right was galvanized into further development with the victory of the political left in the *Cartel des Gauches* (*see* France introduction) in 1924. A number of antiparliamentary organizations were formed which sought to increase the powers of the French presidency. Among the more important ones were the National Republican League (*Ligue Républicaine Nationale*); the Propaganda Center of the Nationalist Republicans (*Centre de Propagande des Républicains Nationaux*); and the French Action (*see* Monarchists), which remained monarchist in orientation.

Fascist-type groups began to appear as separate entities in the late 1920s. In 1927, Colonel François de la Rocque organized groups of war veterans who had been awarded the croix de guerre into a group known as the Fiery Cross (*Croix de Feu*). The Fiery Cross stressed nationalism, militarism, and clericalism, and it engaged in several violent demonstrations to promote its goals. Other fascist-type leagues soon followed in the 1930s, such as the King's Henchmen (*Camelots du Roi, see also* Monarchists), French Solidarity (*Solidarité Française*) of Jean Reynaud, *Françisme* of Marcel Bucard, and the Republican Syndicalist Party (*Parti Républicain Syndicaliste*) of Georges Valois. The latter groups were often referred to simply as the Fascists (*Faisceaux*).

The growing threat of fascism prompted the left-dominated government to move against the fascist leagues in 1936. This action led several of the larger groups to form legitimate political parties. La Rocque's Fiery Cross was disbanded and, in combination with other rightist elements, was reconstituted as the French Social Party (*Parti Social Français*: PSF) in 1936. A competing group on the extreme right was the French Popular Party (*Parti Populaire Français*: PPF) of Jacques Doriot, an ex-communist. Doriot's group was anti-British and anti-Semitic. These two parties functioned for a time under the Vichy regime (*see* France introduction).

The extreme right underwent several developments during the Vichy period. La Rocque's PSF was renamed the French Social Progress (*Progrès Social Français*: PSF) in 1941. An attempt was made to coordinate support for Vichy among the various rightist parties through the formation of the Committee of the National Rally (*Comité de Rassemblement National*) under the direction of Jean-Louis Tixier-Vignancour. This effort collapsed in 1942. A rival body had been formed by Doriot and Marcel Deat in Paris and was called the National Popular Rally (*Rassemblement National Populaire*). Instead of support for Vichy, this group urged all-out collaboration with Germany in World War II.

At the time of liberation, the moderate elements of the PSF divided into a number of conservative groupings. Among them were the Patriotic Republican Union (*Unione Patriotique Républicaine*), the Republican Regroupment (*Regroupement Républicain*), the Republican and Social Party of Reconciliation (*Parti Républicain et Social de la Réconciliation*), and the Party of French Republican Renovation (*Parti de Renovation Républicaine Française*). Most of these groups cooperated with the Republican Union for Liberty and Social Progress (*Union Républicain pour la Liberté et le Progrès Social*), an electoral coalition for the constituent assembly in 1945, and later they allied with the Republican Party of Liberty (*see* Moderates). The more radical elements of the French right remained dormant until the emergence of the French Algeria (*Algérie Française*) movement in the late 1950s and the sudden surge of Poujadism (*see* Union for the Defense of Traders and Artisans) in 1956. Some elements of the extreme right were associated with the violence and terrorism of the Secret Army Organization (OAS) in the years after Algerian independence.

The two most important individuals associated with France's contemporary extreme right have been Jean-Marie LePen and Jean-Louis Tixier-Vignancour. Both entered the National Assembly in 1956: LePen as a Poujadist deputy, and Tixier-Vignancour as head of a small right-wing grouping known as the National Rally (*Rassemblement National*), an organization similar to the one Tixier-Vignancour had attempted to found during the Vichy regime. As the Poujadist movement ebbed, Tixier-Vignancour absorbed it into his parliamentary group. The National Rally consisted of nationalists, ex-Vichyites, supporters of the *Algérie Française* movement, and repatriated Algerian settlers in France.

Many elements of the extreme right supported Charles de Gaulle and the Fifth Republic in 1958 in the hopes that he would keep Algeria French. Their disappointment led Tixier-Vignancour to oppose de Gaulle in the 1965 presidential election, where the rightist leader obtained about 1.3 percent of the vote. In January 1966, with Jean-Marie LePen, Tixier-Vignancour organized the Republican Alliance for Liberties and Progress (*Alliance Républicaine pour les Libertés et le Progrès*: ARLP) as a successor to the National Rally. Differences between Tixier-Vignancour and LePen resulted in the latter breaking with the ARLP and forming a new group, the European Liberty Rally (*Rassemblement Européen de la Liberté*: REL) in 1967, though the group was soon renamed as the National Movement of Progress (*Mouvement National du Progrès*). Both the ARLP and LePen's grouping were opposed to supranationalism and the Gaullists, although Tixier-Vignancour rallied to the Gaullist cause in 1969 following an amnesty for certain military and political figures that had been associated with *Algérie Française*.

The crisis events of 1968 led to the formation of new groups on France's extreme right, many exhibiting fascist trends and sympathies. The New Order (*Ordre Nouveau*) was founded in 1970 by Jean Galvaire and attempted to establish ties with the (German) National Democratic Party (*see* WEST GERMANY) and the Italian Social Movement (*see* ITALY). The New Order was ultimately banned by the French government in 1973. Other groups that appeared in 1970 include the French National Popular Party (*Parti National Populaire Français*) and Nationalist Action (*Action Nationaliste*).

Since 1972, LePen and Tixier-Vignancour have attempted to construct viable electoral organizations. In 1972 LePen and his followers formed the National

Front (*Front National*: FN). The FN was joined by elements of the New Order following the ban on that organization in 1973. The merger was short-lived, however, and in the same year the New Order contingent split from the FN to establish a new organization known as *Faire Front* (translated into English, with difficulty, as "To Make a Front"). In 1974, *Faire Front* evolved into the New Forces Party (*Parti des Forces Nouvelles*: PFN) under the direction of Tixier-Vignancour.

LePen's National Front was unsuccessful in the 1973 legislative elections; and LePen himself was a candidate in the 1974 presidential election, receiving a tiny fraction (0.74 percent) of the first-ballot vote. The National Front was similarly unsuccessful in 1978. Tixier-Vignancour's New Forces Party was also unable to elect candidates in 1978, as well as in the 1979 election to the European Parliament.

The National Front (FN) and New Forces Party (PFN) attempted to put forth a single candidate for the 1981 presidential election, but they could not reach an agreement. LePen failed to receive sufficient endorsement. Both groups did agree not to oppose one another in the 1981 legislative elections.

The FN remains primarily a nationalist grouping which has strongly protested immigration policies and the agreements that led to Algerian independence. The FN has advocated greater attention to the problem of internal national subversion and seeks to limit the right to strike. The PFN is somewhat less extreme than the FN. It seeks to build a "new" French right with a commitment to the existing regime. The PFN has attempted to portray itself as fresh and respectable and as the French component of the Euro-Right movement (the label under which the PFN contested the European Parliament elections). Electoral support for both parties is primarily urban and Paris-based, although there has been some support in other French cities.

In the late 1970s, the extraparliamentary elements of France's extreme right displayed an increased propensity for violence. Various autonomous groupings were formed and have taken responsibility for various acts of terrorism, including bombings, against their leftist opponents or other targets of their wrath. In 1966 two militant neonazi groups joined together and formed the violent Federation of National and European Action (*Fédération d'Action Nationale et Européene*: FANE), which claimed responsibility for assorted anti-Semitic acts. The FANE was banned in September 1980, but it was soon revived as the European Nationalist Fascists (*Faisceaux Nationalistes Européens*: FNE) and promises to continue its activity.

FAIRE FRONT. *See* EXTREME RIGHT.

FAISEAUX. *See* EXTREME RIGHT.

FAISEAUX NATIONALISTES EUROPÉENS. *See* EXTREME RIGHT.

FANE. *See* EXTREME RIGHT.

FASAB. *See* REGIONAL AUTONOMIST PARTIES.

FASCISTS. *See* EXTREME RIGHT.

FDS. *See* DEMOCRATIC SOCIALIST PARTY.

FÉDÉRATION ANARCHISTE. *See* ANARCHISTS.

FÉDÉRATION D'ACTION NATIONALE ET EUROPÉENE. *See* EXTREME RIGHT.

FÉDÉRATION DE LA GAUCHE. *See* FEDERATION OF THE DEMOCRATIC AND SOCIALIST LEFT.

FÉDÉRATION DE LA GAUCHE DÉMOCRATE ET SOCIALISTE. *See* FEDERATION OF THE DEMOCRATIC AND SOCIALIST LEFT.

FÉDÉRATION DÉMOCRATE SOCIALISTE. *See* FEDERATION OF THE DEMOCRATIC AND SOCIALIST LEFT.

FÉDÉRATION DES CERCLES MARXISTES-LENINISTES. *See* MAOISTS.

FÉDÉRATION DES RÉFORMATEURS. *See* DEMOCRATIC CENTER.

FÉDÉRATION DES RÉPUBLICAINS DU PROGRÈS. *See* LEFT-WING GAULLISTS.

FÉDÉRATION DES RÉPUBLICAINS INDÉPENDANTS. *See* REPUBLICAN PARTY.

FÉDÉRATION DES SOCIALISTES DÉMOCRATES. *See* DEMOCRATIC SOCIALIST PARTY.

FÉDÉRATION DES TRAVAILLEURS SOCIALISTES. *See* SOCIALIST PARTY.

FÉDÉRATION DES UNIONS ROYALISTES DE FRANCE. *See* MONARCHISTS.

FEDERATION FOR A RADICAL DEMOCRACY. *See* MOVEMENT OF LEFT RADICALS.

FÉDÉRATION NATIONALE DES GAULLISTES DU PROGRÈS. *See* LEFT-WING GAULLISTS.

FEDERATION OF DEMOCRATIC SOCIALISTS. *See* DEMOCRATIC SO-CIALIST PARTY.

FEDERATION OF INDEPENDENT REPUBLICANS. *See* REPUBLICAN PARTY.

FEDERATION OF MARXIST-LENINIST CIRCLES. *See* MAOISTS.

FEDERATION OF NATIONAL AND EUROPEAN ACTION. *See* EXTREME RIGHT.

FEDERATION OF PROGRESSIVE REPUBLICANS. *See* LEFT-WING GAULLISTS.

FEDERATION OF REFORMERS. *See* DEMOCRATIC CENTER.

FEDERATION OF ROYALIST UNIONS OF FRANCE. *See* MONARCHISTS.

FEDERATION OF SOCIALIST WORKERS. *See* SOCIALIST PARTY.

FEDERATION OF THE DEMOCRATIC AND SOCIALIST LEFT (*Fédération de la Gauche Démocrate et Socialiste*: FGDS). The FGDS, also known as the Federation of the Left (*Fédération de la Gauche*), developed out of the 1965 presidential campaign of François Mitterrand. Gaston Defferre, a Socialist Party* notable and mayor of Marseilles, had attempted to construct a political organization in support of his presidential candidacy in Spring 1965. His new organization, the Democratic Socialist Federation (*Fédération Démocrate Socialiste*), was to be composed of the Socialist Party, the Radical-Socialist Party,* the Popular Republican Movement (MRP),* and the Convention of Republican Institutions.* The French Communist Party* would be excluded. Defferre, however, failed to reconcile the differences over clericalism that existed between the Socialists and the MRP, and he withdrew his candidacy.

In September 1965, at the initiative of Guy Mollet, secretary-general of the Socialist Party, the FGDS was formed by the alliance of the Socialists, Radical-Socialists, and the Convention of Republican Institutions (which, by now, included Mitterrand's grouping, the Democratic and Socialist Union of the Resistance*). Shortly thereafter, the FGDS endorsed the presidential candidacy of François Mitterrand. The Federation based its electoral campaign strategy on a coalition with the Communist Party.

Following the 1965 presidential election, Mitterrand assumed the leadership of the FGDS, and in May 1966 he appointed a "shadow cabinet" to reflect the seriousness of the FGDS's quest for political power. In the 1967 parliamentary elections, the Federation negotiated a formal agreement with the Communist Party for mutual withdrawals in favor of their best-placed candidates on the second ballot. While the FGDS succeeded in increasing the representation of the noncommunist left in the Assembly, winning 121 seats, it failed to develop into a full-fledged political party and was destroyed in the industrial and political unrest crisis of 1968 (*see* France introduction). Following the legislative elections of June 1968, the Federation retained only 57 seats. Mitterrand ultimately resigned the leadership of the FGDS in November 1968.

The collapse of the Federation did not quell attempts to construct a new, broader-based organization on the noncommunist left. Remnants of the FGDS were incorporated into a new Socialist Party, founded in July 1969. In June 1971, Mitterrand was elected first secretary of the new Socialist Party.

FEDERATION OF THE LEFT. *See* FEDERATION OF THE DEMOCRATIC AND SOCIALIST LEFT.

FÉDÉRATION POUR UNE DÉMOCRATIE RADICALE. *See* MOVEMENT OF LEFT RADICALS.

FÉDÉRATION RÉPUBLICAINE DE FRANCE. *See* REPUBLICAN FEDERATION OF FRANCE.

FGDS. *See* FEDERATION OF THE DEMOCRATIC AND SOCIALIST LEFT.

FIERY CROSS. *See* EXTREME RIGHT.

FN. *See* EXTREME RIGHT.

FNE. *See* EXTREME RIGHT.

FNGP. *See* LEFT-WING GAULLISTS.

FNRI. *See* REPUBLICAN PARTY.

FRANÇISME. *See* EXTREME RIGHT.

FRENCH ACTION. *See* MONARCHISTS.

FRENCH ALGERIA. *See* EXTREME RIGHT.

FRENCH CHRISTIAN DEMOCRACY. *See* POPULAR REPUBLICAN MOVEMENT.

FRENCH COMMUNIST PARTY (*Parti Communiste Français:* PCF). The PCF is the largest French party in membership, and it is the second-largest communist party in the Western world, having some 670,000 members. The party originated in December 1920 at the Tours congress of the Socialist Party* when pro-Soviet Union delegates sought adherence to the Communist International (Comintern).

The PCF has vacillated between policies of intransigence and cooperation throughout its history. In its early period, between 1921 and 1933, the PCF followed a policy of isolation and noncooperation with the "bourgeois" parties, stressing the theme of class warfare. With the rise of naziism in Germany (*see* HISTORICAL GERMANY), the PCF moderated its stand and engaged in limited cooperative efforts to stem the fascist tide in France after 1934. The PCF supported the Popular Front government in 1936, but the party lapsed back into isolationism following the German-Soviet Non-Aggression Pact of August 1939. The PCF was then ordered dissolved on September 26, 1939.

The French Communists joined the resistance movement in June 1941, following the German invasion of the Soviet Union. In recognition of its contribution to the war effort, the PCF was invited to join the provisional postwar government of General Charles de Gaulle in November 1945. In May 1947, the Communists were excluded from the government, and they remained in opposition until 1981 when they were given four cabinet posts under François Mitterrand's (Socialist Party) presidency.

Under the Fourth Republic, the PCF was isolated from meaningful political roles due to the anticommunist fears engendered by the Cold War and by the PCF's own preference for a policy of total revolutionary opposition to the existing French regime. However, the party continually polled an average of 25 percent of the votes cast in national legislative elections during the Fourth Republic. The high point of PCF support was 28.6 percent, in November 1946.

The electoral base of the French Communist Party is principally among workers, and the PCF styles itself as *the* party of the working class. The PCF is especially strong in the industrial suburbs of Paris and other large cities. Its political power is enhanced by a number of mass-membership auxiliaries, the most important of which is the General Confederation of Labor (*Confédération Générale du Travail*: CGT), the largest trade union in France with an estimated 1.5 million members. The PCF is also the only French party that can still claim to control a mass circulation daily newspaper, *L'Humanité*.

The PCF's electoral support declined to 18.9 percent on the first ballot in 1958. However, in the legislative elections between 1962 and 1978, the PCF polled approximately 20 percent of the first-ballot votes. After 1962, the party gradually began to moderate its policies and to seek allies among the noncommunist leftist parties. By 1965 the PCF had allied with the Socialist Party in endorsing the presidential candidacy of François Mitterrand. From this time onward, the Communists and Socialists gradually increased their cooperation, eventually producing a loose alliance known as the Union of the Left.* Simultaneously, public attitudes toward the PCF's participation in French politics, and even in cabinet responsibilities, also improved.

Until the mid-1960s, the PCF was regarded as the most stalinist and hard-line communist party in the Western world. However, the French Communists then moderated somewhat their marxist-leninist doctrines, abandoning the notion of a dictatorship of the proletariat, accepting the existence of opposition parties in an eventual socialist state, and even agreeing to rotate in and out of power in accord with the results of free elections. The PCF's doctrinal modifications are not as dramatic and sweeping as those in other western European communist parties, and there remain questions about the sincerity of some of the PCF's changes. Nevertheless, the party has moved toward defining a democratic and distinctively French road to domestic socialism.

Also in the past, with regard to foreign policy, the PCF was one of the Soviet Union's most loyal supporters in international communist movement politics. In recent years, the French Communists have alternated between supporting the Soviet Union and charting an independent course. The PCF criticized the Warsaw Pact's invasion of Czechoslovakia in 1968 but endorsed Soviet intervention in Afghanistan in 1981. The party has criticized the state of human rights in the Soviet Union but opposed the Solidarity labor movement in Poland (see POLAND). Also, the PCF has flirted with Eurocommunism, which represents for some observers a schism in the international communist movement of importance equal to the ideological split between the Soviet Union and China (see also Maoists). But the PCF has not moved as far along the road to Eurocommunism as have the Italian and Spanish communist parties (see ITALIAN COMMUNIST PARTY, ITALY; COMMUNIST PARTY OF SPAIN, SPAIN).

The French Communist Party is highly disciplined and hierarchically controlled. Party Secretary Georges Marchais can today count on the loyal and unanimous support of the PCF's Political Bureau and Central Committee in directing the party's affairs. However, the PCF has not been free of schisms and secessionist movements (see Maoists and see Trotskyites) that have fractured internal unity. The PCF experienced unprecedented internal debate and dissension over the party leadership's conduct during and after the 1978 legislative elections. The PCF's break with the Socialist Party during the campaign was sharply criticized by internal elements. More importantly, the 1978 elections confirmed the emergence of a powerful Socialist Party capable of undermining communist electoral bases.

The PCF supported the Socialist Party's François Mitterrand in the second ballot of the 1981 presidential election, which led to a reestablishment of cooperation between the two parties. The Communists and Socialists concluded an agreement of mutual withdrawal in favor of the best-placed candidates in the 1981 legislative elections. The first round showed a dramatic decrease in PCF support, dropping to 16.2 percent. The Communist percentage was approximately the same as Georges Marchais's first-ballot support in the 1981 presidential election, but it was still two percentage points below the 1958 nadir at the beginning of the Fifth Republic.

The second-ballot results in 1981 virtually halved the PCF's representation in the National Assembly, which dropped from 86 to 44 deputies. The Socialist Party obtained an absolute majority with 269 (out of 491) seats. Following an agreement on the text of a joint declaration on government policy, Pierre Mauroy, the Socialist prime minister, was requested to form a new government that would include Communist ministers. Those chosen were Charles Fiterman, minister of state for transport; Anicet Le Pors, minister-delegate for the civil service and administrative reforms; Jack Ralite, minister of health; and Marcel Rigout, minister of professional training.

The PCF is organized into approximately 28,000 cells, which are further grouped into departmental federations. Party congresses are held every three years, at which time the higher party organs (Central Committee, Political Bureau, and Secretariat) are elected. PCF membership is estimated to be about 800,000. In addition to its daily newspaper, *L'Humanité*, the PCF also publishes two weeklies, *France-Nouvelle* (New France) and *La Terre* (The World), and several scholarly-type commentaries dealing with ideological developments and international affairs.

Further Reference. Blackmer, Donald L. M., and Sidney Tarrow, eds., *Communism in Italy and France* (Princeton, N.J.: Princeton University Press, 1975); Kriegel, Annie, *The French Communists: Profile of a People* (Chicago: University of Chicago Press, 1972); Stiefbold, Annette Eisenberg, *The French Communist Party in Transition: PCF-CPSU Relations and the Challenge to Soviet Authority* (New York: Praeger, 1977); Tiersky, Ronald, *French Communism 1920-1972* (New York: Columbia University Press, 1973); Wilson, Frank L., "The French CP's Dilemma," *Problems of Communism* 27 (July-August 1978): 1-14.

FRENCH LABOR PARTY. *See* SOCIALIST PARTY.

FRENCH NATIONAL POPULAR PARTY. *See* EXTREME RIGHT.

FRENCH POPULAR PARTY. *See* EXTREME RIGHT.

FRENCH SOCIALIST PARTY (1901-1905). *See* SOCIALIST PARTY.

FRENCH SOCIALIST PARTY (1919-1926). *See* REPUBLICAN SOCIALIST PARTY.

FRENCH SOCIAL PARTY. *See* EXTREME RIGHT.

FRENCH SOCIAL PROGRESS. *See* EXTREME RIGHT.

FRENCH SOLIDARITY. *See* EXTREME RIGHT.

FRENCH UNION AND FRATERNITY. *See* UNION FOR THE DEFENSE OF TRADERS AND ARTISANS.

FRONT AUTOGESTIONNAIRE. *See* UNIFIED SOCIALIST PARTY.

FRONT AUTONOMISTE ET SOCIALISTE AUTOGESTIONNAIRE BRET-TONE. *See* REGIONAL AUTONOMIST PARTIES.

FRONT DU PROGRÈS. *See* LEFT-WING GAULLISTS.

FRONT LIBÉRATION BRETONNE. *See* REGIONAL AUTONOMIST PARTIES.

FRONT NATIONAL. *See* EXTREME RIGHT.

FRONT OF PROGRESS. *See* LEFT-WING GAULLISTS.

FRONT POPULAIRE. *See* SOCIALIST PARTY.

FRONT PROGRESSISTE. *See* LEFT-WING GAULLISTS.

FRONT RÉPUBLICAIN. *See* RADICAL-SOCIALIST PARTY.

FRONT TRAVAILLISTE. *See* LEFT-WING GAULLISTS.

FRP. *See* LEFT-WING GAULLISTS.

FURF. *See* MONARCHISTS.

GAULLISTES DES GAUCHES. *See* LEFT-WING GAULLISTS.

GAULLISTS (*Gaullistes*). France's party of Gaullists has used a series of names since it was first founded by Charles de Gaulle in April 1947 as the Rally of the French People (*Rassemblement du Peuple Français*: RPF). De Gaulle had been a World War II hero and had served as head of the French provisional government from September 1944 to January 1946 without the benefit of a distinctive political organization of his own, although a short-lived Gaullist Union (*Union Gaulliste*) had been formed by René Capitant for the November 1946 election. The goals of de Gaulle's RPF were vague and idealistic: achievement of stable and effective government, restoration of France's role in world affairs, and hostility to the French party system and constitutional structures of the Fourth Republic.

The RPF was highly successful at the municipal level; and following the legislative elections of 1951, it became the strongest party in the National Assembly. Although de Gaulle had intended that his party become a systematic opposition to the Fourth Republic under his control, divisions within the RPF led about one-third of the party's deputies to support the investiture of Antoine

Pinay (National Center of Independents and Peasants*) as prime minister in 1952, against de Gaulle's wishes. The RPF was officially dissolved by de Gaulle in April 1953 when he judged that the party had failed to achieve its goal of modifying the structures of the Fourth Republic. Following this decision, the RPF, though attempting to stay alive, suffered electoral defeat in the 1953 municipal elections.

Despite de Gaulle's dissolution of the RPF, and the general's ensuing five-year abstention from political activity, a variety of smaller units continued to defend the Gaullist tradition during the life of their hated Fourth Republic. Conservative elements who had been coopted into the Pinay government had formed the Republican and Social Action (*Action Républicaine et Sociale*: ARS) or simply the Social Republicans (*Républicains Sociaux*: RS), even before the RPF had been dissolved as a parliamentary party (and in 1954 the ARS joined the National Center of Independents and Peasants). Following the April 1953 dissolution of the RPF, the loyalist Gaullists were organized as the Union of Republicans of Social Action (*Union des Républicains d'Action Sociale*: URAS), followed by the National Center of Social Republicans (*Centre National des Républicains Sociaux*: CNRS) in February 1954, and finally the Group of Social Republicans (*Groupe des Républicains Sociaux*) in June 1954.

Following de Gaulle's return to French government as premier in June 1958, the Gaullists were divided into left and right elements. Prior to the legislative elections in November 1958, the right wing, under the direction of Jacques Soustelle, formed a new party on October 1, known as the Union for the New Republic (*Union pour la Nouvelle République*: UNR). The UNR included the Social Republicans and Soustelle's own group, the Union for French Renewal (*Union pour le Renouveau Français*), and other groupings that had been active in the World War II resistance. The UNR was the party with which Charles de Gaulle then affiliated. In 1959 the left-wing elements of the Gaullist tendency formed the Democratic Union of Labor (*Union Démocratique du Travail*: UDT, *see also* Left-wing Gaullists) in support of Gaullist-oriented domestic reforms and to provide a vehicle for working-class support.

In an attempt to build a Gaullist majority in the legislative elections of 1962, both wings of Gaullism united as the UNR-UDT, and the mantle of Gaullism was offered to other center-right groups that would accept the discipline of the UNR, by this time headed by Charles de Gaulle. Support for Gaullism split several of France's other parties. Valéry Giscard d'Estaing, for example, left the National Center of Independents and Peasants; and while not wishing to join the UNR, he gathered together other Gaullist supporters in a new party, the Independent Republicans (*see* Republican Party).

Prior to the March 1967 legislative elections, the UNR-UDT was renamed the Democratic Union for the Fifth Republic (*Union Démocratique pour la Cinquième République*: UD-Ve). In November 1967, the UD-Ve was expanded to include former members of the Popular Republican Movement,* a Christian democratic party which had virtually ceased to exist after the elections of that year.

The May 1968 student unrest and industrial turmoil in France resulted in a crisis atmosphere surrounding the legislative elections of June 1968. To illustrate its condemnation for the unrest, the Gaullist party assumed the label of Union for the Defense of the Republic (*Union pour la Défense de la République*: UDR) for the elections, though shortly thereafter the party reverted to a shortened version of its 1967 name, now calling itself the Democratic Union for the Republic (*Union Démocratique pour la République*: UDR). This designation remained until December 1976 when the party was renamed the Rally for the Republic (*Rassemblement pour la République*: RPR). In the 1981 legislative election campaign, the RPR formed an electoral alliance with the centrist Union for French Democracy (UDF),* and the alliance was named the Union for the New Majority (*Union pour la Majorité Nouvelle*: UMN). A common declaration was issued, and second-ballot strategies were devised. On the first ballot, the RPR, as part of the UMN, received 20.8 percent of the vote. Ultimately, the RPR secured 85 seats in the Assembly, compared to 62 for the UDF.

Despite the many changes in the party's label, there has been continuity of leadership, membership, and doctrine among the Gaullists. The Gaullist Party was the dominant political force in France from 1958 through 1974. It provided all prime ministers until 1976 and France's first two presidents until 1974 (following de Gaulle's resignation in 1969, Georges Pompidou was elected president of the republic). At one point, 1968-1973, the Gaullists held an absolute majority of the seats in the National Assembly, the first time a single party had done so in the history of French democracy. Even after 1974, the Gaullists continued to be a strong party, despite the loss of the presidency to the Gaullists' coalition partner, Valéry Giscard d'Estaing of the Republican Party. Yet the Gaullists remained the largest party in terms of votes and Assembly seats through the legislature elected in 1978.

The Gaullist Party has a mass membership, with a claimed body of over 500,000. Unlike most other right-to-center French parties, the Gaullists have a strong and nationwide grass-roots organization, a disciplined parliamentary group, and effective central party control. Its potential for mobilizing supporters, not only for elections but also for other political actions, was demonstrated by its rallying of over one million demonstrators onto the Champs-Elysées to back de Gaulle during the student and industrial unrest of May 1968. Electoral appeal is also broad. The Gaullists attract the votes of an important part of the working class, although this appeal seems to have declined since de Gaulle's resignation from the presidency in 1969. Principal Gaullist support is found among the middle class, women, liberal professions, and white-collar workers.

Proclaiming its continued devotion to the principles of Charles de Gaulle, the Gaullist Party places emphasis on three themes: national independence, institutions, and participation. The party seeks to promote national independence by combatting any surrender of French sovereignty to supranational European institutions, by opposing American influence in Europe, and by insisting on a strong and independent defense capability. The Gaullists defend the institutions of the

Fifth Republic, the strong presidency, and those practices which have replaced the parliamentary games of the Fourth Republic. The party also promotes the vague notion of "participation" in order to reduce the alienation of the individual by prompting citizen involvement in decisions affecting their lives. While the Gaullist Party remains attached to the heritage of de Gaulle, it has demonstrated remarkable flexibility in adapting its doctrine to meet contemporary issues and requirements.

After 1974, when the Gaullists lost the presidency and soon after the prime ministership to the Giscardians (*see* Republican Party), the Gaullist Party experienced internal conflict. Under the leadership of Jacques Chirac, the Gaullists asserted the right to criticize the Giscardian government while at the same time providing it with crucial parliamentary support. Some orthodox Gaullists objected to the alleged foreign policy deviations of Giscard d'Estaing, and in March 1975 these Gaullists formed the Movement of Democrats (*Mouvement des Démocrates*) under the leadership of Michel Jobert. Jobert had served as a confidant to Georges Pompidou during 1969-1973 and as minister of foreign affairs in 1974. The Movement, however, had little political success. Hence, the relationship between the Gaullists and the Giscardians was often strained, but the majority of Gaullists retained their cohesion on critical matters. The problem for the Gaullist Party was to retain its own distinctive personality and identity while serving in a government coalition it could not control.

Growing tensions within the Gaullist Party over party leadership and electoral strategy weakened support in the 1978 legislative elections. This weakness was further highlighted in the 1979 elections to the European Parliament. The Gaullist list, labeled the Defense of the Interests of France in Europe* (*see* EUROPEAN PARLIAMENT), garnered only about 16 percent of the vote. Yet while the overall Gaullist movement today is divided into a number of distinct organizations (*see* Left-wing Gaullists), the Gaullist Party continues to be the movement's majority force.

Further Reference. Anderson, Malcolm, *Conservative Politics in France* (London: Allen & Unwin, 1974); Charlot, Jean, *The Gaullist Phenomenon* (London: Allen & Unwin, 1971); Crisol, P., and J. Y. Lhomeau, *La Machine RPR* (Paris: Editions Intervalle-Fayolle, 1977); McHale, Vincent E., and Sandra Shaber, "From Aggressive to Defensive Gaullism: The Electoral Transformation of a 'Catch-all' Party," *Comparative Politics* 8 (January 1976): 291-306.

GAULLIST UNION. *See* GAULLISTS.

GISCARDIANS. *See* REPUBLICAN PARTY.

GROUPE DES PROGRESSISTES. *See* REPUBLICAN FEDERATION OF FRANCE.

GROUP DES RÉPUBLICAINS SOCIAUX. *See* GAULLISTS.

GROUP OF PROGRESSIVES. *See* REPUBLICAN FEDERATION OF FRANCE.

GROUP OF SOCIAL REPUBLICANS. *See* GAULLISTS.

GUESDEISTS. *See* SOCIALIST PARTY.

INDÉPENDANTS ET PAYSANS D'ACTION SOCIALE. *See* MODERATES.

INDEPENDENT DEMOCRATIC SOCIALIST PARTY. *See* DEMOCRATIC SOCIALIST MOVEMENT OF FRANCE.

INDEPENDENT PEASANTS. *See* FRANCE INTRODUCTION.

INDEPENDENT REPUBLICANS. *See* REPUBLICAN PARTY.

INDEPENDENTS AND PEASANTS OF SOCIAL ACTION. *See* MODERATES.

INDEPENDENT SOCIALISTS. *See* FRANCE INTRODUCTION.

INITIATIVE RÉPUBLICAINE ET SOCIALISTE. *See* LEFT-WING GAULLISTS.

INTERNATIONALIST COMMUNIST ORGANIZATION. *See* TROTSKYITES.

INTERNATIONALIST COMMUNIST PARTY. *See* TROTSKYITES.

IPAS. *See* MODERATES.

JEUNE RÉPUBLIQUE. *See* CONVENTION OF REPUBLICAN INSTITUTIONS.

JEUNESSE COMMUNISTE RÉVOLUTIONNAIRE. *See* TROTSKYITES.

KING'S HENCHMEN. *See* EXTREME RIGHT and MONARCHISTS.

LAMBERTISTS. *See* TROTSKYITES.

LCR. *See* TROTSKYITES.

LEAGUE OF FRENCH ACTION. *See* EXTREME RIGHT and MONARCHISTS.

LEAGUE OF PATRIOTS. *See* EXTREME RIGHT.

LEAGUE OF THE FRENCH FATHERLAND. *See* EXTREME RIGHT and MONARCHISTS.

LEAGUE OF THE RIGHTS OF MAN. *See* CONVENTION OF REPUBLICAN INSTITUTIONS.

LEFT-WING GAULLISTS (*Gaullistes des Gauche*). Charles de Gaulle's commitment to social and economic reforms won him the support of a number of leftist politicians who felt ill at ease in the more conservative major Gaullist party (*see* Gaullists). These leftists therefore tended to form separate parties to promote support of de Gaulle's reformist social ideas. The Gaullists of this tendency, despite the specific groupings to which they belong, are referred to collectively as the *Gaullistes des Gauche*.

Among the earliest of the left-wing Gaullists was the Democratic Union of Labor (*Union Démocratique du Travail*: UDT), which was formed on April 14, 1959, under the direction of René Capitant, Léo Hamon, and Louis Vallon. Though briefly maintaining a separate existence, the UDT was allied with the majority Gaullist party, which at that time was called the Union for the New Republic (UNR) (*see* Gaullists). In December 1962, the Democratic Union of Labor, then claiming a membership of over 5,000, merged with the majority Gaullists to form the UNR-UDT (*see also* Gaullists).

From the beginning, some UDT members resisted this cooperation and soon began to form separate organizations. The Front of Progress (*Front du Progrès*), for example, was established in 1964 under Jacques Dauer because of concerns that the UDT's social goals would be lost in the conservatism of the larger UNR. The Worker's Front (*Front Travailliste*) was formed in 1965 under Yves Morandat and included some moderates of the Radical-Socialist Party* and Socialist Party*; the Workers' Front believed the Gaullist majority to be too greatly influenced by United States interests. Soon, in an attempt to create a federation of left-wing Gaullists, the Convention of the Left Fifth Republic (*Convention de la Gauche Cinquième République*) was formed in 1966. Led by Philippe Dechartre, the Convention included the Front of Progress, the Worker's Front, and several other organizations of similar persuasion. The Convention's program emphasized universal suffrage in presidential elections, reform of the French Senate, European independence from American interests, and better working conditions in industrial establishments. Cooperating with the UDT and running candidates under the UDT label, the Convention even held three ministerial positions in the 1967 government. However, the convention never achieved the unity of a political party, and the various Gaullists of the left dispersed into a variety of very small and ineffective political groups.

This disunity was particularly evident after Charles de Gaulle's resignation from the presidency of the republic in 1969. At that time was formed, for example, the Republican and Socialist Initiative (*Initiative Républicaine et Socialiste*) of Léo Hamon (who had been a UDT founder); the Movement for Participatory

Socialism (*Mouvement pour la Socialisme par la Participation*) of Pierre Billotte and Philippe Dechartre (earlier affiliated with the Convention of the Left Fifth Republic); and the Progress Front (*Front Progrèssiste*) of Dominique Gallet (whose group became the Union of Progressive Gaullists [*Union des Gaullistes de Progrès*: UGP] in May 1977). Some of these groups moved into opposition to the Gaullist coalition with the Giscardian (*see* Republican Party) government and attempted to affiliate with the socialist-communist Union of the Left.*

In November 1976, another attempt was made to consolidate the left-wing Gaullists into an organization known as the Federation of Progressive Republicans (*Fédération des Républicains du Progrès*: FRP) under the leadership of Jean Charbonnel. The Federation was opposed to the policies and leadership of Jacques Chirac in the majority Gaullist party, now called the Rally for the Republic (*see* Gaullists). The FRP absorbed Hamon's Republican and Socialist Initiative in January 1978 and, in the legislative elections of that year, concluded several electoral pacts with various left-wing parties. However, the FRP secured no seats in 1978.

In January 1979, the Democratic Union of Labor (UDT) was revived by elements which had been part of the Union of Progressive Gaullists, and the new UDT became affiliated with the FRP. A small dissident group in the FRP, under the direction of Jacques Blache, formed the National Federation of Progressive Gaullists (*Fédération Nationale des Gaullistes du Progrès*: FNGP) in April 1979 following the refusal of the FRP leadership to support a French Communist Party* candidacy in a local election in the Correze department.

In the 1981 national legislative elections, the leftist Gaullists were associated with various non-Gaullist parties of the political left. The FRP presented 35 candidates and sought support from the Movement of Left Radicals,* while the UGP concluded several electoral agreements with the Communists.

LEGITIMISTS. *See* FRANCE INTRODUCTION.

LIGUE COMMUNISTE. *See* TROTSKYITES.

LIGUE COMMUNISTE RÉVOLUTIONNAIRE. *See* TROTSKYITES.

LIGUE DE L'ACTION FRANÇAISE. *See* EXTREME RIGHT and MONARCHISTS.

LIGUE DES DROITS DE L'HOMME. *See* CONVENTION OF REPUBLICAN INSTITUTIONS.

LIGUE DES PATRIOTS. *See* EXTREME RIGHT.

LIGUE RÉPUBLICAINE NATIONALE. *See* EXTREME RIGHT.

LO. See REGIONAL AUTONOMIST PARTIES and TROTSKYITES.

LUTTE OCCITANE. See REGIONAL AUTONOMIST PARTIES.

LUTTE OUVRIÈRE. See TROTSKYITES.

MAN. See UNIFIED SOCIALIST PARTY.

MAOISTS. The French maoists are composed of a number of disparate political action groups on the extreme left who have drawn inspiration from the writings of Mao-Zedong and who have expressed a sympathetic attitude toward Communist China in its ideological disputes with the Soviet Union. There have been several major maoist movements in France. One of the earliest appeared in 1964 with the formation of the Federation of Marxist-Leninist Circles (*Fédération des Cercles Marxistes-Leninistes*). In 1966 this group evolved into the Communist Movement of France (Marxist-Leninist) (*Mouvement Communiste de France [Marxiste-Leniniste]*) and finally into the Marxist-Leninist Communist Party of France (*Parti Communiste Marxiste-Leniniste de France*: PCMLF) in December 1967.

As a result of the crisis atmosphere generated by the labor and student unrest of Spring 1968, the PCMLF along with 11 other political organizations were ordered dissolved by the French government. The PCMLF continued a clandestine, though not inactive, existence until 1978. In 1974 elements of the PCMLF had formed the Revolutionary Marxist-Leninist Communist Party (*Parti Communiste Révolutionnaire Marxiste-Leniniste*: PCRML) in an attempt to foment labor unrest. Both the PCMLF and PCRML participated in the 1978 legislative elections under the maoist banner of the Peasant and Worker Union for Proletarian Democracy (*Union Ouvrière et Paysanne pour la Démocratie Prolétarienne*: UOPDP).

Two other maoist organizations also participated in the 1978 election. The Communist Organization of France: Marxist-Leninist (*Organisation Communiste de France*: *Marxiste-Leniniste*: OCF-ML) presented six candidates but refused all cooperation with other groups. The OCF-ML's membership is estimated to be less than one thousand. The Marxist-Leninist Union of Communists of France (*Union des Communistes de France Marxiste-Leniniste*: UCFML) was formed in 1971 from dissident elements called the "Current B" in the Unified Socialist Party.* Opposed to the French Communist Party,* the UCFML had initially advocated a policy of electoral abstention. None of these maoist candidates was elected in 1978.

In August 1978, remnants of the PCMLF were reorganized into the Marxist-Leninist Communist Party (*Parti Communiste Marxiste-Leniniste*: PCML); and in October 1979, the PCRML merged with the new party, creating the PCML-PCRML. Both parties claim to represent maoist formations working for a proletarian revolution in France. They advocate a dictatorship of the proletariat and reject revisionism and reformism. They also stand opposed to the French Communist Party. The PCML-PCRML components are each organized on the basis of cells in various industrial enterprises. The parties hold periodic congresses and are directed by a central committee, political bureau, and secretariat. Under the merger, the PCML publishes *Le Quotidien du Peuple* (The People's Daily). Membership is estimated at 3,000 for each party.

Among other maoist groups that have appeared during the Fifth Republic have been the Marxist-Leninist Center of France (*Centre Marxiste-Leniniste de France*), and the Union of Young Marxist-Leninist Communists (*Union des Jeunesses Communistes Marxistes-Leninistes*: UJCML). The former dwindled into insignificance; the latter was banned by the government in 1978.

In the 1981 legislative elections, the PCML and PCRML entered separate lists of candidates—the former 17, the latter one candidate. None was elected. The various maoist groupings continue to direct much of their efforts against each other and against their archenemy, the French Communist Party.

MARXIST-LENINIST CENTER OF FRANCE. *See* MAOISTS.

MARXIST-LENINIST COMMUNIST PARTY. *See* MAOISTS.

MARXIST-LENINIST COMMUNIST PARTY OF FRANCE. *See* MAOISTS.

MARXIST-LENINIST UNION OF COMMUNISTS OF FRANCE. *See* MAOISTS.

MDS. *See* DEMOCRATIC SOCIALIST MOVEMENT OF FRANCE.

MDSF. *See* DEMOCRATIC SOCIALIST MOVEMENT OF FRANCE.

MEP. *See* ECOLOGY POLITICAL MOVEMENT.

MGR. *See* DEMOCRATIC CENTER.

MODERATES (*Modérés*). The designation of "moderates" has been used to classify an assorted array of conservative, right-wing, and independent forces in France. Characteristically, these groups have displayed little electoral or parliamentary cohesion, although in the Third Republic they were more or less organized into the National Republican Bloc (*see* France introduction).

The moderates were largely discredited by collaborationist activities and their support for the Vichy regime during World War II, and so they found little political success in the immediate postwar period. Attempts failed to regroup the moderates, first in the Republican Union for Liberty and Social Progress (*see* Extreme Right) in 1945, and also in the Republican Party of Liberty.* Peasant groups, representing the poor areas of the Massif-Central and heir to the old Agrarian Party (*Parti Agraire*) of the Third Republic, refused to adhere to the

Republican Party of Liberty and instead founded the Peasant and Social Action Party (*Parti Paysan et Action Sociale*), which was known occasionally as the Peasant Party (*Parti Paysan*). Other groups formed the Democratic Union of Independents (*Union Démocratique des Indépendants*: UDI) in 1948. After 1956 these various *Modérés* merged into a large group known as the Independents and Peasants of Social Action (*Indépendants et Paysans d'Action Sociale*: IPAS), which survived until 1962 when it split into various independent groups.

Under the Fourth Republic, the moderates behaved as a "floating" mass of personalities, forces, and organizations, although they did play a role in the formation of various governments. With the inception of the Fifth Republic, the moderates remained scattered into several political formations, the largest of which has been the National Center of Independents and Peasants. *

MODÉRÉS. *See* MODERATES.

MONARCHISTS. Support for the restoration of the monarchy has been a permanent feature of French political life since the revolution of 1789. The monarchists, like other French tendencies, remained loosely organized until the latter part of the 19th century. French monarchists have been divided into Legitimists and Orleanists. The former supported the line of King Charles X, who ruled during the Bourbon restoration period (1814-1830). The Orleanists supported the claims of Louis Philippe, of the Orleanist branch of the Bourbon dynasty, who reigned during the "July Monarchy" (1830-1848). The death of the Count of Chambord in 1883, leaving no legitimate heir, effectively destroyed any Legitimist claims to the French throne.

The first important monarchist organization in France was the League of the French Fatherland (*Ligue de la Patrie Française*), formed in 1898. The League sought to defend interests of the Roman Catholic Church, of nationalism, and a restoration of the Orleanist monarchy. The League of the French Fatherland eventually gave way to the League of French Action (*Ligue d'Action Française*) in 1905 (*see also* Extreme Right), and finally to the French Action (*Action Française*) in the period following World War I. In 1906 a new monarchist organization, the National Restoration (*Restauration Nationale*), had been formed in the French universities (and the name would be readopted by monarchists at a later time, see below).

The French Action group was under the leadership of Charles Maurras and Léon Daudet. It was extremely nationalistic and antirepublican. Arguing in favor of a hereditary monarchy (Orleanist), the French Action managed to coopt a few representatives among independents in the National Assembly, although it did not participate in any electoral campaigns. In the 1930s, the party was aided by a fascist-type youth organization known as the King's Henchmen (*Camelots du Roi, see also* Extreme Right), which engaged in periodic acts of violence.

The French Action was staunchly Catholic and anti-Semitic in orientation.

However, its fascistlike character led to condemnation by the Vatican in 1926, and in 1935 it was dissolved as a party. Even though Maurras was tried and imprisoned, resulting from an attack on Léon Blum, the Socialist Party* prime minister, Maurras was later elected to the prestigious *Académie Française*.

Elements of the French Action engaged in various collaborative acts with the German forces during World War II and constituted an element of support for the Vichy regime of Marshal Philippe Pétain. French royalism was reorganized after the war, and in 1947 the movement readopted the name of the 1906 student group, National Restoration, as its principal political vehicle. The movement was seriously split in 1971 when a majority withdrew from the National Restoration to form the New French Action (*Nouvelle Action Française*: NAF). The new grouping sought to divest French royalism of its fascist image engendered by the pre-World War II French Action party.

Prior to the 1974 presidential election, the NAF changed its name to the New Royalist Action (*Nouvelle Action Royaliste*: NAR). The NAR's leader, Bertrand Renouvin, entered as a presidential candidate and received over 43,000 votes (0.17 percent). The NAR platform called for the restoration of the Count of Paris as king of France under a progressive monarchical system. The party remains opposed both to state capitalism and to marxist socialism. The NAR presented eight candidates in the 1978 legislative elections, though all were unsuccessful.

Other smaller monarchist groupings exist in France, such as the Federation of Royalist Unions of France (*Fédération des Unions Royalistes de France*: FURF), but these groups do not regularly participate in the electoral process. The FURF has instead given its support to the Gaullists.*

MOUVEMENT COMMUNISTE DE FRANCE (MARXISTE-LENINISTE). *See* MAOISTS.

MOUVEMENT D'ÉCOLOGIE POLITIQUE. *See* ECOLOGY POLITICAL MOVEMENT.

MOUVEMENT DE LA GAUCHE RÉFORMATRICE. *See* DEMOCRATIC CENTER.

MOUVEMENT DES DÉMOCRATES. *See* GAULLISTS.

MOUVEMENT DES DÉMOCRATES SOCIALISTES DE FRANCE. *See* DEMOCRATIC SOCIALIST MOVEMENT OF FRANCE.

MOUVEMENT DES RADICAUX DE GAUCHE. *See* MOVEMENT OF LEFT RADICALS.

MOUVEMENT DU 22 MARS. *See* ANARCHISTS.

MOUVEMENT NATIONAL DU PROGRÈS. See EXTREME RIGHT.

MOUVEMENT POUR LA SOCIALISME PAR LA PARTICIPATION. See LEFT-WING GAULLISTS.

MOUVEMENT POUR UNE ALTERNATIVE NON-VIOLENTE. See UNIFIED SOCIALIST PARTY.

MOUVEMENT RÉFORMATEUR. See DEMOCRATIC CENTER.

MOUVEMENT RÉPUBLICAIN POPULAIRE. See POPULAR REPUBLICAN MOVEMENT.

MOUVEMENT SILLON. See POPULAR REPUBLICAN MOVEMENT.

MOUVEMENT SOCIALISTE OCCITAN. See REGIONAL AUTONOMIST PARTIES.

MOVEMENT FOR A NONVIOLENT ALTERNATIVE. See UNIFIED SOCIALIST PARTY.

MOVEMENT FOR PARTICIPATORY SOCIALISM. See LEFT-WING GAULLISTS.

MOVEMENT OF DEMOCRATS. See GAULLISTS.

MOVEMENT OF LEFT RADICALS (Mouvement des Radicaux de Gauche: MRG). The MRG was formed in July 1972 from splinter groups in the Radical-Socialist Party* that broke off after disagreements over the party's general strategy. The left-wing minority that formed the MRG favored continued alliance with the Socialist Party* and accepted the common program issued by the Socialists with the French Communist Party* in June 1972. The majority faction of the Radical-Socialists, under the leadership of Jean-Jacques Servan-Schreiber, had rejected the common program and opted for a centrist federation called the Reformers' Movement (see Democratic Center).

Most Radical deputies, whose reelection depended upon the cooperation of Socialist and Communist voters for second-ballot support, joined in forming the MRG. Under the leadership of Robert Fabre, the MRG allied with the Socialists and Communists in the Union of the Left* and in endorsing the common program of the left in 1972. The MRG collaborated closely with the Socialists in all national and local elections between 1972 and 1978. Advocating a mild form of socialism, the MRG has condemned both collectivism and capitalism. Its proposals for reforms are relatively moderate structural changes, with an emphasis on protecting the civil and economic liberties of the individual.

The MRG was a reluctant supporter of the portions of the common program that called for nationalization. After the failure of the political left to win the 1978 legislative elections, the MRG faced serious internal divisions over continued loyalty to the leftist alliance. Conservative elements within the MRG constituted two distinct factional groupings: the Federation for a Radical Democracy (*Fédération pour une Démocratie Radicale*) and the New Union for Europe (*Union Nouvelle pour Europe*). The former grouping later rejoined the Radical-Socialist Party in October 1979, while some elements, including Fabre, left the MRG to align themselves with various centrist elements.

Michel Crepeau, Fabre's successor as leader of the MRG, has continued the leftist alliance. Crepeau was a candidate in the 1981 presidential election, receiving 1.7 percent of the vote on the first ballot. In the following legislative elections, the MRG reached an electoral agreement with the Socialist Party for mutual withdrawal in favor of the best-placed candidates. The MRG increased its representation by four seats, for a total of 14 deputies.

MOVEMENT OF MARCH 22d. *See* ANARCHISTS.

MOVEMENT OF THE REFORMIST LEFT. *See* DEMOCRATIC CENTER.

MRG. *See* MOVEMENT OF LEFT RADICALS.

MRP. *See* POPULAR REPUBLICAN MOVEMENT.

MSO. *See* REGIONAL AUTONOMIST PARTIES.

NAP. *See* MONARCHISTS.

NAR. *See* MONARCHISTS.

NATIONAL CENTER OF INDEPENDENTS. *See* NATIONAL CENTER OF INDEPENDENTS AND PEASANTS.

NATIONAL CENTER OF INDEPENDENTS AND PEASANTS (*Centre National des Indépendants et Paysans*: CNIP). The CNIP has provided a label and national political office to a variety of local-based conservative political figures. As a party, it has lacked organization, discipline, and a coherent program. The CNIP traces its origins to various independent and peasant groups which were formed in the pre-World War II French Chamber. After the war, efforts to organize the independents took several forms. Rogert Duchet set up a National Center of Independents (*Centre National des Indépendants*: CNI), basically as a documentation center around which Moderates* and republican conservatives might rally. In January 1949, the CNI was joined by the Republican Party of Liberty* and became the National Center of Independents and Peasants (CNIP).

Duchet's efforts were aided by the 1951 electoral law which favored national party labels rather than independent status.

Under the Fourth Republic, the CNIP participated in several governing coalitions. Deputies bearing the CNIP label not only played an important part in the politics of the Fourth Republic but also provided leaders, such as René Coty, president during 1952-1959, and Antoine Pinay, who served briefly as prime minister in 1952. In 1954 the CNIP absorbed those former Gaullist deputies who had formed the Republican and Social Action after bolting the Rally of the French People (see Gaullists).

In 1958 the CNIP strongly supported Charles de Gaulle's return to power, and the party benefitted electorally from the Gaullist landslide. In 1962, however, the CNIP split over continued support of de Gaulle and his Algerian policy. The final breach occurred in October when those supporting de Gaulle (including Valéry Giscard d'Estaing) left the CNIP to become the Independent Republicans (see Republican Party). Most of those national politicians who remained in the CNIP were defeated in the 1962 legislative elections.

Many of the CNIP officials affiliated with the Democratic Center* when that group was founded in 1966. The CNIP leader, Camille Laurens, attempted to unite what remained of the CNIP with the Independent Republicans through support of Giscard d'Estaing's successful presidential bid in 1974, though this attempt failed. The CNIP was represented in the government in 1976. In 1978 the CNIP contested the election as part of the non-Gaullist majority formation outside of the Union for French Democracy,* and the CNIP secured nine seats. Some of these CNIP deputies cooperated with the Union for the New Majority (see Gaullists) in 1981.

CNIP membership is estimated to be approximately 25,000. The party publishes a weekly *Journal of Independents* and has one representative in the European Parliament.

NATIONAL CENTER OF SOCIAL REPUBLICANS. *See* GAULLISTS.

NATIONAL FEDERATION OF PROGRESSIVE GAULLISTS. *See* LEFT-WING GAULLISTS.

NATIONAL FRONT. *See* EXTREME RIGHT.

NATIONALIST ACTION. *See* EXTREME RIGHT.

NATIONAL MOVEMENT OF PROGRESS. *See* EXTREME RIGHT.

NATIONAL POPULAR RALLY. *See* EXTREME RIGHT.

NATIONAL RALLY. *See* EXTREME RIGHT.

NATIONAL REPUBLICAN ASSOCIATION. *See* REPUBLICAN FEDERA-TION OF FRANCE.

NATIONAL REPUBLICAN BLOC. *See* FRANCE INTRODUCTION.

NATIONAL REPUBLICAN LEAGUE. *See* EXTREME RIGHT.

NATIONAL REPUBLICAN PARTY. *See* REPUBLICAN FEDERATION OF FRANCE.

NATIONAL RESTORATION. *See* MONARCHISTS.

NATIONAL SOCIALIST PARTY. *See* REPUBLICAN SOCIALIST PARTY.

NETWORK OF FRIENDS OF THE EARTH. *See* ECOLOGY POLITICAL MOVEMENT.

NEW DEMOCRACY. *See* CONVENTION OF REPUBLICAN INSTITUTIONS.

NEW FORCES PARTY. *See* EXTREME RIGHT.

NEW FRENCH ACTION. *See* MONARCHISTS.

NEW ORDER. *See* EXTREME RIGHT.

NEW ROYALIST ACTION. *See* MONARCHISTS.

NEW UNION FOR EUROPE. *See* MOVEMENT OF LEFT RADICALS.

NOIR ET ROUGE. *See* ANARCHISTS.

NOUVELLE ACTION FRANÇAISE. *See* MONARCHISTS.

NOUVELLE ACTION ROYALISTE. *See* MONARCHISTS.

OCA. *See* ANARCHISTS.

OCC. *See* TROTSKYITES.

OCCITANIAN NATIONAL PARTY. *See* REGIONAL AUTONOMIST PARTIES.

OCCITANIAN SOCIALIST MOVEMENT. *See* REGIONAL AUTONOMIST PARTIES.

OCCITANIAN STRUGGLE. *See* REGIONAL AUTONOMIST PARTIES.

OCF-ML. *See* MAOISTS.

OCI. *See* TROTSKYITES.

ORA. *See* ANARCHISTS.

ORDRE NOUVEAU. *See* EXTREME RIGHT.

ORGANISATION COMBAT ANARCHISTE. *See* ANARCHISTS.

ORGANISATION COMBAT COMMUNISTE. *See* TROTSKYITES.

ORGANISATION COMMUNISTE DE FRANCE: MARXIST-LENINIST. *See* MAOISTS.

ORGANISATION COMMUNISTE INTERNATIONALISTE. *See* TROT-SKYITES.

ORGANISATION RÉVOLUTIONNAIRE ANARCHISTE. *See* ANARCHISTS.

ORLEANISTS. *See* MONARCHISTS.

PARIS-ECOLOGY. *See* ECOLOGY POLITICAL MOVEMENT.

PARTI ACTION LIBÉRALE POPULAIRE. *See* POPULAR REPUBLICAN MOVEMENT.

PARTI AGRAIRE. *See* MODERATES.

PARTI COMMUNISTE FRANÇAIS. *See* FRENCH COMMUNIST PARTY.

PARTI COMMUNISTE INTERNATIONALISTE. *See* TROTSKYITES.

PARTI COMMUNISTE MARXISTE-LENINISTE. *See* MAOISTS.

PARTI COMMUNISTE MARXISTE-LENINISTE DE FRANCE. *See* MAOISTS.

PARTI COMMUNISTE RÉVOLUTIONNAIRE MARXISTE-LENINISTE. *See* MAOISTS.

PARTI DÉMOCRATE POPULAIRE. *See* POPULAR REPUBLICAN MOVE-MENT.

PARTI DÉMOCRATE SOCIALISTE INDÉPENDANT. *See* DEMOCRATIC SOCIALIST MOVEMENT OF FRANCE.

PARTI DE RÉNOVATION RÉPUBLICAIN FRANÇAIS. *See* EXTREME RIGHT.

PARTI DES FORCES NOUVELLES. *See* EXTREME RIGHT.

PARTI NATIONALISTE OCCITAN. *See* REGIONAL AUTONOMIST PARTIES.

PARTI NATIONAL POPULAIRE FRANÇAIS. *See* EXTREME RIGHT.

PARTI OUVRIER FRANÇAIS. *See* SOCIALIST PARTY.

PARTI OUVRIER SOCIALISTE RÉVOLUTIONNAIRE. *See* SOCIALIST PARTY.

PARTI PAYSAN ET ACTION SOCIALE. *See* MODERATES.

PARTI POPULAIRE FRANÇAIS. *See* EXTREME RIGHT.

PARTI RADICAL. *See* RADICAL-SOCIALIST PARTY.

PARTI RADICAL-SOCIALISTE. *See* RADICAL-SOCIALIST PARTY.

PARTI RÉPUBLICAIN. *See* REPUBLICAN PARTY.

PARTI RÉPUBLICAIN DE LA LIBERTÉ. *See* REPUBLICAN PARTY OF LIBERTY.

PARTI RÉPUBLICAIN-DÉMOCRATIQUE ET SOCIAL. *See* DEMOCRATIC ALLIANCE.

PARTI RÉPUBLICAIN ET SOCIAL DE LA RÉCONCILIATION. *See* EXTREME RIGHT.

PARTI RÉPUBLICAIN NATIONAL. *See* REPUBLICAN FEDERATION OF FRANCE.

PARTI RÉPUBLICAIN, RADICAL, ET RADICAL-SOCIALISTE. *See* RADICAL-SOCIALIST PARTY.

PARTI RÉPUBLICAIN SOCIALISTE. *See* REPUBLICAN SOCIALIST PARTY.

PARTI RÉPUBLICAIN SOCIALISTE ET SOCIALISTE FRANÇAISE. *See* REPUBLICAN SOCIALIST PARTY.

PARTY RÉPUBLICAIN SYNDICALISTE. *See* EXTREME RIGHT.

PARTI SOCIAL FRANÇAIS. *See* EXTREME RIGHT.

PARTI SOCIALISTE. *See* SOCIALIST PARTY.

PARTI SOCIALISTE AUTONOME. *See* UNIFIED SOCIALIST PARTY.

PARTI SOCIALISTE DE FRANCE. *See* SOCIALIST PARTY.

PARTI SOCIALISTE DÉMOCRATE. *See* SOCIALIST PARTY and DEMOCRATIC SOCIALIST PARTY (1975-).

PARTI SOCIALISTE FRANÇAIS. *See* SOCIALIST PARTY and REPUBLICAN SOCIALIST PARTY.

PARTI SOCIALISTE NATIONAL. *See* REPUBLICAN SOCIALIST PARTY.

PARTI SOCIALISTE UNIFIÉ. *See* UNIFIED SOCIALIST PARTY.

PARTI SOCIALISTE UNIFIÉ: SECTION FRANÇAISE DE L'INTERNATIONALE OUVRIÈRE. *See* SOCIALIST PARTY.

PARTI SOCIALISTE UNITAIRE. *See* SOCIALIST PARTY.

PARTY OF FRENCH REPUBLICAN RENOVATION. *See* EXTREME RIGHT.

PATRIOTIC REPUBLICAN UNION. *See* EXTREME RIGHT.

PCF. *See* FRENCH COMMUNIST PARTY.

PCI. *See* TROTSKYITES.

PCML. *See* MAOISTS.

PCMLF. *See* MAOISTS.

PCRML. *See* MAOISTS.

PDM. *See* DEMOCRATIC CENTER.

PDP. *See* POPULAR REPUBLICAN MOVEMENT.

PEASANT AND SOCIAL ACTION PARTY. *See* MODERATES.

PEASANT AND WORKER UNION FOR PROLETARIAN DEMOCRACY. *See* MAOISTS.

PEOPLE OF OC. *See* REGIONAL AUTONOMIST PARTIES.

PFN. *See* EXTREME RIGHT.

PNO. *See* REGIONAL AUTONOMIST PARTIES.

POBLE D'OC. *See* REGIONAL AUTONOMIST PARTIES.

POLITICAL CLUBS. *See* CONVENTION OF REPUBLICAN INSTITUTIONS.

POPULAR DEMOCRATIC PARTY. *See* POPULAR REPUBLICAN MOVEMENT.

POPULAR FRONT. *See* SOCIALIST PARTY.

POPULAR LIBERAL ACTION PARTY. *See* POPULAR REPUBLICAN MOVEMENT.

POPULAR REPUBLICAN MOVEMENT (*Mouvement Républicain Populaire*: MRP). The MRP was founded in 1944 by Catholic resistance leaders. It built upon the Christian democratic traditions that had begun to develop in France prior to World War II. The political reconciliation of Catholics to the republican regime first came in the form of the Conservative Rallies (*Conservateurs Ralliés*) in the 1890s. Catholics were urged to differentiate between the regime (which they were encouraged to accept) and particular laws, which, if bad, should be opposed or improved. The Rallies gave way to the formation of the Popular Liberal Action Party (*Parti Action Libérale Populaire*) in 1899. This party was a conservative grouping supported largely by upper-class elements. It formed part of the National Republic Bloc (*see* France introduction) during the interwar period and later became associated with the royalist French Action (*see* Monarchists).

   The strain of Christian democratic traditions that eventually led to the formation of the Popular Republican Movement began with the *Sillon* (furrow) Movement (*Mouvement Sillon*) in 1897. Led by Marc Sangnier, *Sillon*'s purpose was to work for social democracy on the basis of Christian principles. However, conservative tendencies in the Vatican following the death of Pope Leo XIII led to the dissolution of *Sillon* in 1910. It was soon succeeded by another Christian democratic organization, the Young Republic (*Jeune République*), in 1911. Several Young Republic deputies were elected in 1919, including Sangnier; and following the 1924 elections, these Christian democrats established the Popular Democratic Party (*Parti Démocrate Populaire*: PDP) with 14 members in the Chamber. The PDP remained a small party with very little electoral success outside of traditional Catholic and conservative regions. It was led by Paul Simon and Champetier de Ribes.

The PDP deputies were among those who voted against the Pétain regime (*see* France introduction) and later played an active role in the World War II resistance. The PDP, along with elements of the Young Republic, established the Popular Republican Movement (MRP) in 1944. The Young Republic itself continued as a small left-wing party until 1956, after which it dissolved into a "political club" (*see* Convention of Republican Institutions).

The MRP emerged from the war as one of France's three principal political movements, receiving nearly 25 percent of the 1945 vote and being a mass-membership party. The MRP peaked in 1946 with 158 to 160 deputies in the Chamber. However, the emergence of Gaullist movements in 1947 and again in 1958 undermined the MRP's electoral bases. The MRP, unlike the more popular Gaullists, * was strongly in favor of unifying western Europe politically, economically, and militarily. MRP leaders, such as Georges Bidault, played an important role in persuading France to take a leading role in the uniting of Europe. (Bidault, however, later broke with the MRP in 1959 over Charles de Gaulle's policies toward Algeria, and Bidault formed a short-lived dissident group known as the French Christian Democracy [*Démocratie Chrétienne Française*: DCF], which lobbied to keep Algeria French.)

The MRP also supported progressive social and economic legislation; but its voters tended to be more conservative on these issues, and the party gradually retreated from its reformist stance. Eventually, the MRP became identified as a Catholic party interested primarily in defending clerical interests in the debates on state support for the religious schools.

The MRP's parliamentary strength was reduced to 36 seats in 1962, the last election in which the party competed as a separate entity. Most MRP members and leaders defected to the anti-Gaullist and Catholic-supported Democratic Center* in 1966; and the MRP totally disappeared after November 1967 when its few remnants joined the Democratic Union for the Fifth Republic (*see* Gaullists).

Attempting to revive the interests of the old MRP, a small group called Christian Democracy (*Démocratie Chrétienne*) was formed in May 1977 under the leadership of Alfred Coste-Floret. The party entered several candidates in the 1978 elections in association with the Union for French Democracy. *

Further Reference. Irwing, R.E.M., *Christian Democracy in France* (London: Allen & Unwin, 1973).

POSSIBILISTS. *See* SOCIALIST PARTY.

POUJADISTS. *See* UNION FOR THE DEFENSE OF TRADERS AND ARTISANS.

PPF. *See* EXTREME RIGHT.

PR. *See* REPUBLICAN PARTY.

PRL. *See* REPUBLICAN PARTY OF LIBERTY.

PROGRÈS ET DÉMOCRATIE MODERNE. *See* DEMOCRATIC CENTER.

PROGRESS AND MODERN DEMOCRACY. *See* DEMOCRATIC CENTER.

PROGRESS FRONT. *See* LEFT-WING GAULLISTS.

PROGRÈS SOCIAL FRANÇAIS. *See* EXTREME RIGHT.

PROPAGANDA CENTER OF THE NATIONALIST REPUBLICANS. *See* EXTREME RIGHT.

PS. *See* SOCIALIST PARTY.

PSA. *See* UNIFIED SOCIALIST PARTY.

PSD. *See* SOCIALIST PARTY and DEMOCRATIC SOCIALIST PARTY (1946-late 1940s).

PSF. *See* EXTREME RIGHT.

PSU. *See* UNIFIED SOCIALIST PARTY.

RADICAL PARTY. *See* RADICAL-SOCIALIST PARTY.

RADICALS AND RESISTERS OF THE LEFT. *See* RADICAL-SOCIALIST PARTY.

RADICAL-SOCIALIST PARTY (*Parti Radical-Socialiste*; also referred to as the Radical and Radical-Socialist Party, or simply as the Radical Party). The oldest of the current French parties is the Radical-Socialist Party, officially founded in 1901 under the name of the Republican, Radical, and Radical-Socialist Party (*Parti Républicain, Radical, et Radical-Socialiste*). Contrary to connotations that we, today, would associate with radicalism, the Radical Party was—and remains—a centrist coalition whose members range from conservatives to social democrats.

The modern Radical-Socialists trace their ideological roots to the era of the French Revolution. At that time, the grouping was indeed radical, advocating a republican form of government; and by the mid-19th century, the Radicals had developed a set of goals that placed emphasis on individual, democratic rights. In 1869, for example, under the leadership of Léon Gambetta, the Radicals proposed the national adoption of universal manhood suffrage, a variety of individual freedoms (including freedom of assembly and the press), state-supported primary education, dissolution of the Senate and dominance of a popularly elected Chamber of Deputies, and a rigid separation of church and state.

The Radicals were most successful during the Third Republic, when they largely dominated French politics. Early in this period, the Radicals drew most of their support from urban areas. However, with the rise of industrialism, the French socialist movement began to displace the Radicals in the worker cities, and the Radical Party shifted its emphasis to the middle classes of the smaller towns. Developing a watchdog philosophy— government must be watched constantly so that it will not usurp the rights of the average or common man—the Radicals remained staunchly republican and as such became the central pivot to government coalitions that included elements harboring various political ideologies. The Radicals espoused a faith in traditional free enterprise as the economic system best suited to assure the most advantages for the largest proportion of society, and this stand enabled the Radicals to gain cooperation from France's parties on the political right. At the same time, given the historical distrust of the church's power among many Frenchmen, the Radicals' staunch anticlericalism drew to the party cooperation from elements of the political left. This was the program when the Republican, Radical, and Radical-Socialist Party was officially founded in 1901.

By the time of the Fourth Republic, however, the Radicals were unprepared for the type of national politics that permeated post-World War II France. The party, long relying on local notables to obtain votes, could not as efficiently compete with those parties that had developed a national mass base, particularly those that had been more active in the wartime resistance. Also, many of the Radicals' programs were no longer relevant. Their continued support for free enterprise pitted them against the new popular support for nationalization of certain industrial and commercial enterprises. Most French parties were now republican in nature, stripping the Radicals of their previous uniqueness. The Radicals' own legislation of 1905 had successfully separated church and state in France, thus rendering anticlericalism unviable as a political platform. Moreover, the Radicals were opposed to General Charles de Gaulle, who had become a popular, national hero during the war and who then sought to revise many aspects of the Third Republic constitution for which the Radicals had been responsible.

Hence during the Fourth Republic, the Radical electorate fell to half of its prewar size, with many such voters turning to the socialist parties. The Radicals remained important, however, presiding over ten Fourth Republic governments; and the Radicals' centrist position still made the party's participation in cabinets essential for any government's survival.

The October 1945 election for France's constituent assembly brought the Radicals only 35 out of 522 seats (6.7 percent of the representation), compared to 109 out of 608 seats (17.9 percent) held in 1936. Before the 1945 election, the Radicals had attempted to form a Union of Leftists (*Union des Gauches*) with the French Communist Party* and the Socialist Party.* (The Union of Leftists should not be confused with the 1972-1978 coalition called the Union of the Left.*) With the poor poll, however, the Radicals then chose to distance themselves from the Communists. Therefore, in April 1946, the Radicals agreed to join with the Union of Democrats and Socialists of the Resistance (UDSR),* a minor postwar grouping of noncommunist resistance groups that had not earlier been organized into a political party. The Radical-UDSR alliance, joined by several other very minor groupings, was called the Rally of the Left Republicans (*Rassemblement des Gauches Républicaines*: RGR). Shortly thereafter, the Radical Party suffered a split when a small group, under Pierre Cot, formed the Radicals and Resisters of the Left (*Radicaux et Résistants de Gauche*) after being expelled for proposing a continued alliance with the French Communist Party.

Primarily an electoral coalition, the Rally of the Left Republicans was without its own political program, instead merely linking its constituent parties. Yet the RGR enabled the Radicals to secure 55 seats in the election to the first postwar National Assembly in November 1946. Having attempted to appeal to younger voters and members, the Radicals took on a new vitality. But realizing that they were still too weak to compete on a national level, in 1947 the Radicals pragmatically decided to seek various local electoral alliances with de Gaulle's new and popular Rally of the French People (*see* Gaullists). Despite the success of the alliance in local elections, many Radicals remained basically opposed to de Gaulle's ideologies, causing dissent within the Radical Party itself and between the Radicals and their UDSR ally within the RGR.

By the early 1960s, an important Radical personality was Pierre Mendès-France. Serving as minister of national economy in the first de Gaulle government after World War II, Mendès-France had pushed for extreme solutions to France's economic problems, primarily for wage and price freezes and heavy taxation. Vastly opposed, Mendès-France soon resigned his government post, though he continued to lead a grouping of parliamentary Radicals who agreed with his policies. Other influential Radicals included Edgar Faure, with whom Mendès-France often quarreled in parliament; and Édouard Herriot, leader of the Radicals' left wing and an individual who favored cooperation with the Communist Party.

Mendès-France headed the French government from June 19, 1954, to February 5, 1955. His achievements in foreign affairs included conclusions of peace with French colonies in Indochina and initiation of independence negotiations with Morocco and Tunisia. Domestically, however, Mendès-France accomplished very little.

After losing control of the government (ironically to his adversary within the Radical Party, Edgar Faure), Mendès-France logically decided that the solution to France's continuing postwar problems would require a longer-lived government than the nation had so far enjoyed. To achieve such a government, he advocated a leftist bloc; but to promote his policy, he first needed to capture the leadership of the disjointed Radical Party. Supported by the leftist Herriot, Mendès-France proceeded to establish his alliance with the Socialist Party. In the 1956 election, the Republican Front (*Front Républicain*) captured 161 seats, more than any other ticket. But the Socialists under Guy Mollet, taking 88 seats (to the Radicals' 73), received the prime ministership. Mendès-France was named deputy prime minister; but after many intense quarrels, he left the cabinet.

Mendès-France had also proceeded to purge the Radical Party of dissenters to his policies. Jean-Paul David and Bernard Lafay were expelled in late 1955, and by December of that year they revitalized the postwar Rally of the Left Republicans, with David becoming its general secretary. Edgar Faure also joined the RGR, becoming its president, when he was pushed out of the Radical Party in 1956. Two dissidents who left the Radicals voluntarily were André Morice and Henri Queuille, who in October 1956 established the Republican Center. * Mendès-France failed to eliminate all dissenters, however, and his opponents succeeded in ousting him from the Radical Party leadership in 1957. In early 1958, Mendès-France and his few followers themselves broke away from the Radicals and formed the Union of Democratic Forces, which in September of that year joined the Autonomous Socialist Party (*see* Unified Socialist Party), through which Mendès-France continued to be politically active.

By the time of the November 1958 elections, the Radical Party was more severely torn by factions than before Mendès-France's ironically divisive attempts at unification. With 11.5 percent of the vote, the Radicals fell from 73 to only 23 seats.

Under the Fifth Republic, the Radical-Socialists have struggled to maintain a position in French politics. Reviving a move toward the noncommunist left, in 1965, under the leadership of René Billères, the Radicals participated in a coalition with the Socialists called the Federation of the Democratic and Socialist Left (FGDS), * which won a total of 117 seats in the 1967 election. Soon after the election, the FGDS leader, François Mitterrand, entered the Federation into an agreement on goals with the Communist Party. Then, with the massive strikes and student unrest of May 1968, the populace reacted with a shift to conservativism, and the FGDS received only 57 seats in the 1968 election. Attempting to ride the popular wave, Maurice Faure withdrew the Radicals from the FGDS and moved his party toward a centrist position once again.

In 1971 the Radical-Socialists elected to their party presidency the ambitious editor of *L'Express*, Jean-Jacques Servan-Schreiber (a former friend of Mendès-France who did not follow the latter out of the Radical Party in 1958). Servan-Schreiber quickly joined the Radicals with the Democratic Center * in organizing the Reformers' Movement (*see* Democratic Center), a centrist, anti-Gaullist coalition (though the Center tended toward cooperation with the Gaullists). In reaction, a minority of Radicals (but nearly all of the party's Assembly deputies), who favored continued cooperation with the Socialists, left the Radical Party in July 1972 to form the Movement of Left Radicals* (though some of these dissidents rejoined the Radical-Socialist Party starting in 1974). For the 1974 presidential election, the Radicals as part of the Reformers' Movement supported the candidacy of Valéry Giscard d'Estaing (see Republican Party); and after his election, the Radicals joined the government majority. In 1978 the Radical-Socialists joined other majority centrist parties in organizing the Union for French Democracy.*

The Radical-Socialists remain a moderate center-left party supporting gradual economic and social reforms. Party leaders are often drawn from the liberal professions. Electoral support is largely middle class, and the Radicals' traditional strongholds are in the southwest of France. Under the current leadership of Didier Bariani, the Radical-Socialists claim a membership of approximately 20,000.

Further Reference. Servan-Schreiber, Jean-Jacques, *The Radical Alternative* (London: Melvin McCosh, 1971); Tarr, Francis de, *The French Radical Party: From Herriot to Mendès-France* (London: Oxford University Press, 1961).

RADICAUX ET RÉSISTANTS DE GAUCHE. *See* RADICAL-SOCIALIST PARTY.

RALLY FOR THE REPUBLIC. *See* GAULLISTS.

RALLY OF LEFT REPUBLICANS. *See* RADICAL-SOCIALIST PARTY.

RALLY OF THE FRENCH PEOPLE. *See* GAULLISTS.

RASSEMBLEMENT DES GAUCHES RÉPUBLICAINES. *See* RADICAL-SOCIALIST PARTY.

RASSEMBLEMENT DU PEUPLE FRANÇAIS. *See* GAULLISTS.

RASSEMBLEMENT EUROPÉEN DE LA LIBERTÉ. *See* EXTREME RIGHT.

RASSEMBLEMENT NATIONAL. *See* EXTREME RIGHT.

RASSEMBLEMENT NATIONAL POPULAIRE. *See* EXTREME RIGHT.

RASSEMBLEMENT POUR LA RÉPUBLIQUE. *See* GAULLISTS.

RAT. *See* ECOLOGY POLITICAL MOVEMENT.

REFORMERS' MOVEMENT. *See* DEMOCRATIC CENTER.

REGIONAL AUTONOMIST PARTIES. Since 1800, France has been administered in a centralized fashion. Napoleon had devised a hierarchical system in which all territorial units were stripped of local prerogatives and made dependent upon the central authorities for their existence and supervision. Devolution of power and authority in the French politico-administrative system has always been a strongly contested issue, largely because of its perceived potential for somehow damaging a precarious national unity and subverting the will of the French people.

Serious problems of national integration have emerged in Brittany and Corsica with the revival of nationalist sentiment and periodic instances of political violence. In both regions, the problem is compounded by traditional characteristics of independence, individualism, and isolation, and their relatively underdeveloped position when compared to the rest of France.

Until January 1974, when it was banned by the government, a clandestine Breton Liberation Front (*Front Libération Bretonne*) had agitated, sometimes violently, for Breton autonomy. The dominant political group is the Breton Democratic Union (*Union Démocratique Bretonne; Unvaniezh Demokratel Breizh*: UDB), which was formed in 1964. The UDB is electorally oriented and is represented in most of the city councils in Brittany. It maintains close links with the French Communist Party* and claims to be working for self-determination and a socialist Brittany. Condemning violence as a political strategy, the UDB has denied any links with the banned Breton Liberation Front. The UDB is organized into various federations, with a political bureau elected every two years by the party congress. The party maintains an office in Paris.

The second important political group in Brittany is the Breton Autonomist and Socialist Self-Rule Front (*Front Autonomiste et Socialiste Autogestionnaire Bretonne*: FASAB). The FASAB is composed of various local socialist parties in Brittany. While in favor of autonomy for Brittany within France, the Front rejects any linkage of self-determination with marxism and advocates Breton representation in various European organizations. The FASAB remains neutral on the question of political violence but denies any link with the Breton Liberation Front. The FASAB supported François Mitterrand (Socialist Party*) in 1974 and 1981.

The island of Corsica is the least populous region of France. It is also the region that has exhibited the most violent demonstrations for regional autonomy. These actions were undertaken largely by the Corsican National Liberation Front. Prior to 1977, the major autonomist group was the Association of Corsican Patriots (*Associu di Patrioti Corsi*: APC). In July 1977, a new group was formed in an attempt to consolidate autonomist sentiment. This group, the Union of the Corsican People (*Unione di u Populu Corsu*: UPC), has attempted to pursue a nonviolent strategy. It has urged a referendum on internal autonomy and has sought to internationalize the issue of Corsican self-determination. The UPC has also pledged solidarity with imprisoned activists of the Corsican National Liberation Front. UPC membership is estimated to be approximately 10,000.

The emphasis on regionalism and regional problems has sparked the emergence of other latent divisions in French society which have tended to follow the contours of French geography. There has been a renewed interest in the ancient cultural division of the *Pays d'Oil* and *Pays d'Oc* (roughly, northern and southern France respectively). Occitania, which includes the region of Provence-Languedoc in southern France, has produced several small autonomist groups that appear to be directed against the integration of the region into larger economic and political structures.

The Occitanian Nationalist Party (*Parti Nationaliste Occitan*: PNO) was formed in 1959 as a vehicle for Occitania autonomy and as a protest against federalist and European integration. In national elections, the PNO has been supportive of those parties that have opposed European and Atlantic integration. The Occitanian Socialist Movement (*Mouvement Socialiste Occitan*: MSO; *Volem Viure al Pais*: VVAP) has been oriented toward the views of the noncommunist left, in particular the Socialist Party. The VVAP advocates autonomy for Occitania along socialist lines, and the Movement has cooperated with various reformist groups.

The Occitanian extremist groups are represented by Occitanian Struggle (*Lutte Occitane*) and the People of Oc (*Poble d'Oc*). Both are small formations associated with national left-wing extremist groups, especially those Trotskyites* who have stressed worker self-management. Unlike Italy, regional autonomist groups in France have not succeeded in capturing any seats at the level of national representation.

REGROUPEMENT RÉPUBLICAIN. *See* EXTREME RIGHT.

REL. *See* EXTREME RIGHT.

RÉPUBLICANS SOCIAUX. *See* GAULLISTS.

REPUBLICAN ALLIANCE FOR LIBERTIES AND PROGRESS. *See* EXTREME RIGHT.

REPUBLICAN AND SOCIAL ACTION. *See* GAULLISTS.

REPUBLICAN AND SOCIALIST INITIATIVE. *See* LEFT-WING GAULLISTS.

REPUBLICAN AND SOCIAL PARTY OF RECONCILIATION. *See* EXTREME RIGHT.

REPUBLICAN CENTER (*Centre Républicain*). The small centrist Republican Center was established in October 1956 by André Morice and Henri Queuille, who had left the Radical-Socialist Party.* Morice and Queuille dissented against the Radicals' move toward the political left, and they opposed the attempts at personalist rule being perpetrated by the Radical leader, Pierre Mendès-France.

The purpose of the Republican Center was to establish a link among the majority and minor centrist and center-left parties in France.

To further this end, in 1971 the Republican Center joined the Reformers' Movement (*see* Democratic Center). As part of the Reformers' Movement (which also included the newly oriented Radical-Socialist Party), the Republican Center assisted in organizing other centrist and center-left coalitions. In March 1975, the Movement of the Reformist Left (*see* Democratic Center) was established as a grass-roots organization for unity. In June 1975, the Federation of Reformers (*see* Democratic Center) was established as a vehicle for parliamentary cooperation. Then in 1978, Republican Center parliamentary candidates ran on the centrist ticket called the Union for French Democracy,* though the Republican Center had not formally joined the Union.

Since 1974, some Republican Center members have rejoined the larger Radical-Socialist Party.

REPUBLICAN DEMOCRATIC ALLIANCE. *See* DEMOCRATIC ALLIANCE.

REPUBLICAN-DEMOCRATIC AND SOCIAL PARTY. *See* DEMOCRATIC ALLIANCE.

REPUBLICAN FEDERATION OF FRANCE (*Fédération Républicaine de France*). The Republican Federation (occasionally known as the National Republican Party [*Parti Républicain National*]) was formed in November 1903 from a fusion of three smaller conservative groupings: the Liberal Republican Union (*Union Libérale Républicaine*), the Group of Progressives (*Groupe des Progressistes*), and the National Republican Association (*Association Nationale Républicaine*). The Federation was in support of administrative decentralization. It opposed income and business taxes, as well as state intervention in the economy; instead the Federation argued a position of free enterprise. The Federation also opposed the anticlerical Radical-Socialist Party* on various religious issues.

The Federation constituted an important component of the National Republican Bloc (*see* France introduction) during the 1920s and 1930s. The Federation reappeared briefly following World War II under the direction of Louis Marin; but because of its questionable resistance record, it had little popular appeal. Many personalities associated with the Federation had collaborated with the Vichy regime of Marshal Philippe Pétain. A party congress was held in February 1945, but no party lists were presented in the 1946 legislative elections. The Federation ceased to exist by 1946, as most of its former elements had been incorporated into the Republican Party of Liberty* the previous year.

REPUBLICAN FRONT. *See* RADICAL-SOCIALIST PARTY.

REPUBLICAN PARTY (*Parti Républicain*: PR). The Republican Party, originally called the Independent Republicans (*Républicains Indépendants*: RI), was founded in 1962 as the result of the schism in the National Center of Independents and Peasants (CNIP)* over continued support for Charles de Gaulle. Under the leadership of Valéry Giscard d'Estaing, Raymond Marcellin, and Raymond Mondon, those CNIP deputies loyal to de Gaulle, adopted the Independent Republicans label. They remained separate from the Gaullists* but shared governmental power with them from 1962 to 1974, supporting the policies of Presidents de Gaulle and Georges Pompidou and successive Gaullist prime ministers. In 1974, Giscard d'Estaing was elected president of the republic with the support of the Gaullists. His governmental majority depended upon the support of the Gaullist parliamentarians. The Independent Republicans were remarkably loyal during this long period of Gaullist domination. However, some RI members, including Giscard d'Estaing, had opposed the unsuccessful 1969 referendum which brought de Gaulle's resignation. This act of disloyalty won Giscard d'Estaing the enmity of a handful of Gaullist diehards.

The RI remained without much organization from 1962 to 1966. It had no mass following and no national congresses until 1971. In June 1966, however, Giscard d'Estaing and his supporters had begun to build an organization to support his political ambitions, and the Independent Republicans became the Federation of Independent Republicans (*Fédération des Républicains Indépendants*: FNRI). The emergent group quickly became Giscard's personal party and was often labelled the "Giscardian party" or simply the Giscardians. In May 1977, the FNRI was reorganized as the Republican Party (PR), though it was still generally referred to as the Giscardians.

The PR's main sources of electoral support are from middle-class and rural voters, women, and practicing Catholics. Its leaders are drawn from the social elite and traditional local notables. They are unified by their loyal support of Giscard and his political options.

The PR has supported traditional conservative economic and fiscal politics, though also advocating further economic and political unification in Europe. While the party has been known to support moderate social and economic reforms, it has done so without genuine enthusiasm from its rank and file or from its deputies, who are more attuned to the PR electorate. The PR styles itself a liberal party in the European tradition of liberalism: support of free-enterprise economy, centrism, and parliamentary democracy. The imprint of Giscard's own political preferences dominates the party's positions on current issues.

As is the case with most French right-of-center parties, the PR lacks a strong grass-roots membership organization. There were efforts to establish local units and to recruit members in the mid-1960s and again in the mid-1970s. Despite major efforts, these attempts were failures and the PR remained a traditional cadre party without a mass-membership, nationwide organization. The PR achieved its goal of electing Giscard president in 1974, but the party's organizational weakness limited its ability to sustain him while in office. In 1978 the PR joined various centrist parties in creating the Union for French Democracy* as a counterbalance to Gaullist pressure within the governmental coalition. But the

1978 parliamentary elections left the Gaullists as the "majority of the majority." This meant that Giscard's policies depended upon the support of the often-reluctant Gaullists. Giscard lost the presidency to François Mitterrand (of the Socialist Party*) in 1981.

Further Reference. Anderson, Malcolm, Conservative Politics in France (London: Allen & Unwin, 1974); Colliard, Jean-Claude, Les Républicains Indépendants, Valéry Giscard d'Estaing (Paris: Presses Universitaires de France, 1971); Giscard d'Estaing, Valéry, French Democracy, translated by Vincent Cronin (Garden City, N.Y.: Doubleday & Co., 1977).

REPUBLICAN PARTY OF LIBERTY (Parti Républicain de la Liberté: PRL). Founded in December 1945, the PRL was the result of a fusion of various pre-World War II conservative parties. Its principal components were the Republican Federation of France* and the Republican-Democratic and Social Party (see Democratic Alliance). According to PRL leader Joseph Laniel, the party was neither reactionary nor fascist but firmly supportive of parliamentary institutions. It presented a middle-of-the-road program based upon limited government, and it was opposed to state ownership of economic enterprises.

The PRL contested the 1946 legislative elections but failed to develop a popular base. Remaining a party of notables split by various personal rivalries, the PRL disappeared in 1951.

REPUBLICAN, RADICAL, AND RADICAL-SOCIALIST PARTY. See RADICAL-SOCIALIST PARTY.

REPUBLICAN REGROUPMENT. See EXTREME RIGHT.

REPUBLICAN SOCIALIST AND FRENCH SOCIALIST PARTY. See REPUBLICAN SOCIALIST PARTY.

REPUBLICAN SOCIALIST PARTY (Parti Républicain Socialiste). The Republican Socialist Party was founded in July 1911 by dissident socialists who had refused to accept the pact of unification between the French Socialist Party (1901-1905) and the Socialist Party of France (see Socialist Party) in 1905. The Republican Socialist leaders were Aristide Briand and René Viviani. The party was opportunistic in nature, viewing itself as a bridge between the Socialists to its left and the center-left Radicals (see Radical-Socialist Party) to its right. Being mildly anticlerical, the Republican Socialists adhered to the doctrine of evolutionary socialism and accepted state ownership of various economic enterprises.

In 1919, Briand's followers broke away from the party to form a new grouping and readopted the name of one of its grandparent groupings, calling itself the French Socialist Party (1919-1926) (Parti Socialiste Français). This new French Socialist Party was more nationalistic in tone than the Republican Socialists and less supportive of the doctrine of class struggle. Occasionally, it was referred to as the National Socialist Party (Parti Socialiste National).

In May 1926, the small Republican Socialist Party and the smaller French Socialist Party (1919-1926) fused to form the Republican Socialist and French Socialist Party (*Parti Républicain Socialiste et Socialiste Français*). The new grouping became part of the Popular Front (*see* Socialist Party) in 1936, after which the grouping became submerged in the large Socialist Party.

REPUBLICAN SYNDICALIST PARTY. *See* EXTREME RIGHT.

REPUBLICAN UNION FOR LIBERTY AND SOCIAL PROGRESS. *See* EXTREME RIGHT.

RÉSEAU DES AMIS DE LA TERRE. *See* ECOLOGY POLITICAL MOVEMENT.

RESTAURATION NATIONALE. *See* MONARCHISTS.

REVOLUTIONARY ANARCHIST ORGANIZATION. *See* ANARCHISTS.

REVOLUTIONARY COMMUNIST LEAGUE. *See* TROTSKYITES.

REVOLUTIONARY COMMUNIST YOUTH. *See* TROTSKYITES.

REVOLUTIONARY MARXIST-LENINIST COMMUNIST PARTY. *See* MAOISTS.

REVOLUTIONARY SOCIALIST LABOR PARTY. *See* SOCIALIST PARTY.

RGR. *See* RADICAL-SOCIALIST PARTY.

RPF. *See* GAULLISTS.

RPR. *See* GAULLISTS.

RS. *See* GAULLISTS.

SACRED UNION. *See* FRANCE INTRODUCTION.

SELF-DETERMINATION FRONT. *See* UNIFIED SOCIALIST PARTY.

SFIO. *See* SOCIALIST PARTY.

SILLON MOVEMENT. *See* POPULAR REPUBLICAN MOVEMENT.

SOCIALISM AND FREEDOM. *See* DEMOCRATIC SOCIALIST MOVEMENT OF FRANCE.

SOCIALISME ET LIBERTÉ. *See* DEMOCRATIC SOCIALIST MOVEMENT OF FRANCE.

SOCIALIST DEMOCRACY. *See* DEMOCRATIC SOCIALIST MOVEMENT OF FRANCE.

SOCIALIST PARTY (*Parti Socialiste*: PS). The Socialist Party traces its origins to 1879 when Jules Guesde founded the French Labor Party (*Parti Ouvrier Français*) following a congress of labor unions in Marseille. The Laborites, however, represented a diverse collection of ideological types, and after the 1881 elections the party soon split into revolutionary and evolutionary factions. At the extreme left were the "Blanquists," followers of Auguste Blanqui who were basically anarchist in nature and opposed to all governments. The "Guesdeists" were orthodox marxists whose strength was primarily in the industrializing north of France. In 1882 both the Blanquists and Guesdeists were virtually excluded from the main body of the French Labor Party, which remained evolutionist.

The evolutionary Laborites, known as reformists or "possibilists," came under the leadership of Paul Brousse in the Federation of Socialist Workers (*Fédération des Travailleurs Socialistes*) by the late 1880s. Personal rivalries and ideological quarrels soon led to a split, and in 1890, Jean Allemane and his followers left and formed the Revolutionary Socialist Labor Party (*Parti Ouvrier Socialiste Révolutionnaire*). Known as the "Allemanists," these socialists advocated preparation for a general strike rather than for electoral participation. Other groups split off from the Federation in 1896 and formed the Communist Alliance (*Alliance Communiste*).

The main body of the socialist movement became increasingly attuned to electoral competition in the 1890s; and prior to the 1893 elections, several attempts were made to unite the various socialist factions into an effective electoral and parliamentary organization. These efforts led to the formation of two new socialist parties in 1901. Jean Jaurès, an evolutionary socialist close to the Radicals (*see* Radical-Socialist Party), formed the French Socialist Party (1901-1905) (*Parti Socialiste Français*; not to be confused with a later party of the same name, *see* French Socialist Party [1919-1926] under Republican Socialist Party). At the same time, the Guesdists and Blanquists overcame their earlier differences and joined to form the Socialist Party of France (*Parti Socialiste de France*). By 1902 there were over 40 socialist deputies in the Chamber representing these two parties.

To further their parliamentary strength, these two parties merged in 1905 to form the Unified Socialist Party: French Section of the Workers' International (*Parti Socialiste Unifié: Section Française de l'Internationale Ouvrière*: SFIO)—a name it retained until 1969. (This party should not be confused with the Unified Socialist Party [PSU], * founded in 1958.) Socialist unity was only temporary, however. The party was split again by World War I and the Bolshevik Revolution in Russia (*see* SOVIET UNION). The war led to various national socialist groups, such as the Republican Socialist Party, which had long disapproved of the original 1905 merger of the socialist parties. The Bolshevik Revolution resulted in a major SFIO split when a majority of the party's delegates to the 1920 Tours conference voted for adherence to the Comintern and subsequently formed the French Communist Party.*

The SFIO supported various Radical Party governments in the 1920s and 1930s, and in 1936 the SFIO formed the Popular Front government under Léon Blum until 1938. With the outbreak of World War II and the invasion of France in 1940, the major part of the SFIO participated in the resistance and cooperated with General Charles de Gaulle. A small SFIO minority followed Marshal Philippe Pétain (see France introduction) and were later organized after the war by Paul Faure as the Democratic Socialist Party (1946-late 1940s) (Parti Socialiste Démocrate; not to be confused with a 1975 party of the same name, see Democratic Socialist Party [1975-   ]). Faure's group soon dwindled into insignificance. Even after the war, the SFIO experienced splits and divisions. In early 1948, procommunist elements were expelled and formed the Unitary Socialist Party (Parti Socialiste Unitaire), a minor left-wing grouping that soon disappeared.

The SFIO played a major part in French politics during the Fourth Republic, participating in many governments and heading several of them. Major nationalizations in France took place under Socialist auspices. The SFIO also played a constructive role in the development of the European Economic Community (see EUROPEAN PARLIAMENT). The party's fortunes began to decline in the late 1950s, however, largely due to conflicts over the party's foreign policy stance and resulting in a number of defections. In 1958 the SFIO supported de Gaulle's return to power (see Gaullists), but within a few months the Socialists moved into the opposition and remained there for the next 20 years.

Between 1946 and 1969, the SFIO was under the leadership of Guy Mollet and experienced nearly continuous declines in electoral support and membership. From the second-largest party in France with 23.4 percent of the vote in 1945, the SFIO dropped to barely over five percent of the vote in the 1969 presidential election. At this point, the party changed leadership, officially adopted the shortened name of the Socialist Party (PS), and began serious efforts at internal reform. The reform movement gained impetus in 1971 when François Mitterrand joined the PS.

Mitterrand had a long history of leftist political involvement, starting with his World War II activity in the resistance, then as a member and eventual leader (as of 1951) of the Democratic and Socialist Union of the Resistance,* and then as leader (1965-1971) of the Convention of Republican Institutions (CIR).* In this latter position, Mitterrand merged the CIR into the Socialist Party in 1971 and was immediately elected PS leader.

Under Mitterrand's leadership, the PS reversed its long decline and made impressive gains in electoral strength and membership after 1973. Mitterrand used his own popularity to revitalize the old Socialist Party and recruit new members from among intellectual and middle-class circles. By 1978 the PS had regained its 1945 electoral strength, outdistanced the French Communist Party in voting strength for the first time since 1936, and had come very close to equalling the Gaullist Party's vote. Its newly acquired broad electoral base gave the PS a substantial portion of the vote of the working class, the lower-middle class, white-collar workers, and left-wing intellectuals.

Throughout its history, the Socialist Party has struggled to reconcile a relatively radical socialist political doctrine with moderate political behavior when its members are elected to national or local public offices. This continues to be the case with the modern PS. However, since 1971, the party has moved leftward, committing itself to major social and economic reforms once it gains power. It has condemned social democracy, as practiced by other western European socialist parties, as compromises with the bourgeoisie; instead, the PS insists that now that it is in power it will seek the establishment of a genuinely democratic and socialist state. The PS advocates the nationalization of a number of major French enterprises, the establishment of worker self-management (*autogestion*) in French industry, a centrally planned economy, and increased social benefits in order to reduce social inequities. The Socialists favor European unity but see the current European institutions as a means of fighting monopoly capitalism and multinational corporations on an international scale. While many Socialists have a pro-Western bias, the party is officially committed to work for the dissolution of both the Atlantic and Warsaw defense pacts. The intensity with which certain elements of the PS hold these socialist commitments suggests that the PS must indeed pursue these goals or else face the threat of major schisms within its ranks.

To achieve the socialist society that it desires, the PS has sought alliance with other left-wing political groups and especially with the French Communists (PCF). Only with the support of the PCF and its voters can the PS hope to maintain a majority supporting socialist reforms. Mitterrand was the principal architect of the Union of the Left* with the Communists in 1972, though this pact resulted in several PS defections, such as by the Democratic Socialist Movement of France* in 1973 and the Democratic Socialist Party (1975-   ) in 1975. The PS abandoned its former pivotal position where it was able to ally with other parties of the left or with the center in favor of an exclusive alliance with the PCF and other left-wing parties. This strategy was called into question by the PCF's lack of loyalty in the 1978 election campaign. With opinion polls showing a real possibility of a left-wing victory, the PCF sabotaged the prospects of a government of the left by directing most of its campaign against the PS. The Communists' attacks on the Socialists during and after the 1978 election cast doubts on the viability of the Union of the Left and of the PS's strategy for a leftist majority. The Socialists remained firm in their rejection of alliance offers from the center, insisting that the PS would maintain its loyalty to the Union of the Left even if the PCF did not. The PS hoped to pick up additional support from Communist voters who were disillusioned by the PCF's "antiunitary" behavior.

Socialist victory came in May 1981 with the election of François Mitterrand as president of the republic—the first socialist head of state in France since Vincent Auriol (1947-1954). The PS victory was consolidated with the election of a Socialist majority in the subsequent legislative elections. The new Socialist government included four Communist Party ministers.

Further Reference. Bizot, Jean-François, *Au Parti des Socialistes: Plongée Libre dans les Courants d'un Grand Parti* (Paris: Grasset, 1973); Wilson, Frank L., *The French Democratic Left: Toward a Modern Party System* (Palo Alto, Calif.: Stanford University Press, 1971); Wright, Vincent, and Howard Machin, "The French Socialist Party: Success and Politics of Success," *Political Quarterly* 46 (January 1975):36-52.

SOCIALIST PARTY OF FRANCE. *See* SOCIALIST PARTY.

SOCIAL REPUBLICANS. *See* GAULLISTS.

SOLIDARITÉ FRANÇAISE. *See* EXTREME RIGHT.

SOS-ENVIRONMENT. *See* ECOLOGY POLITICAL MOVEMENT.

TOCQUEVILLE CIRCLE. *See* CONVENTION OF REPUBLICAN INSTITUTIONS.

TRIBUNE DU COMMUNISME. *See* UNIFIED SOCIALIST PARTY.

TRIBUNE OF COMMUNISM. *See* UNIFIED SOCIALIST PARTY.

TROTSKYITES. There are several parties in France which have been linked to the views of Leon Trotsky (1879-1940), one of the leaders of the Bolshevik Revolution in Russia (*see* SOVIET UNION). Trostsky argued for permanent revolution as the key to socialist development. Before his assassination in 1940, he had founded the Fourth International as a coordinating body for trotskyite groups.

None of the French trotskyite parties has much political significance except for periodic involvement in political demonstrations. None has any deputies in the National Assembly. Contemporary trotskyites reject the reformism of the Socialist Party,* the state capitalism of the French Communist Party* and the Soviet Union, and the ideological deviations of each other and of other extreme leftist groupings. Instead, France's trotskyites all seek to restore communism to its original pure forms as sought before the advent of stalinism in the Soviet Union. Although the French trotskyite groups share certain common outlooks, efforts at unity have been unsuccessful.

The French trotskyite movement emerged in 1936 with the formation of the Internationalist Communist Party (*Parti Communiste Internationaliste:* PCI) as a movement to the left of the French Communist Party. Following its adherence to the Fourth International, the PCI soon split into various factions. The Workers and Peasants Group joined the left wing of the Socialist Party in 1938. Other members stood as unsuccessful trotskyites in the early postwar elections.

After World War II, the trotskyites were still split over the issue of the Fourth International. In 1952 a dissident group left the PCI under the direction of Pierre Lambert and established the Internationalist Communist Organization (*Organisation Communist Internationaliste*: OCI) or the *Lambertistes*. In recent years, the OCI has been associated with the trotskyite student movement, the Alliance of Youth for Socialism (*Alliance des Jeunes pour le Socialisme*: AJS). The OCI has contested elections and has been supportive of a broad alliance of the left.

The PCI was re-formed in the later 1960s through an association with the Revolutionary Communist Youth (*Jeunesse Communiste Révolutionnaire*), which had been formed in 1966 by trotskyite student expellees from the French Communist Party. Both the PCI and Revolutionary Communist Youth were banned by the French government in 1968, though one year later they were resurrected by Alain Krivine as the Communist League (*Ligue Communiste*). Krivine had been one of the leaders of the student demonstrations in 1968 and had entered the 1969 presidential election; he received a little over one percent of the first-ballot vote. The League was ordered dissolved in 1973 following a violent street clash with elements of the Extreme Right.* Krivine then set up the Revolutionary Communist League (*Ligue Communiste Révolutionnaire*: LCR).

The LCR has cooperated occasionally with another trotskyite group, the Workers' Struggle (*Lutte Ouvriere*: LO), founded in 1968 around a publication of the same name. The LO has been active in various industrial enterprises; and its current leader, Arlette Laguiller, was a candidate in the 1974 presidential election, winning 2.3 percent of the first-ballot vote. In 1978 the LO had entered over 400 candidates in the parliamentary elections, but none was elected. A fusion of the LO and LCR was attempted in 1971 but failed. Both parties cooperated in the 1979 elections to the European Parliament under the joint list called For the Socialist United States of Europe (*see* EUROPEAN PARLIAMENT). Although the list secured 3.1 percent of the vote, no candidates were elected.

Worker control of industrial and commercial establishments (*autogestion*) has been a primary theme of many trotskyite groups. In 1976 a dissident faction of the Revolutionary Communist League merged with Current B (*Courant B*, a trotskyite dissident faction of the Unified Socialist Party*) to form the Communist Committees for Self-Management (Comités Communistes pour l'Autogestion: CCA). The CCA was allied with the Revolutionary Communist League and the Internationalist Communist Organization in the 1978 legislative elections. Other trotskyite elements in favor of self-management broke from the Workers' Struggle in 1974 and formed the Communist Combat Organization (*Organisation Combat Communiste*: OCC). The OCC has spurned electoral participation in favor of organizing activity in the factories.

In the 1981 legislative elections, the Workers' Struggle entered 158 candidates, the CCA sponsored 83, and the Revolutionary Communist League entered 36. The Internationalist Communist Organization submitted none. Trotskyite parties appeared to be united in their support of a broad left-wing alliance and the formation of a Socialist Party government. But no trotskyite candidate was elected to the National Assembly in 1981.

UCFML. *See* MAOISTS.

UCRG. *See* UNIFIED SOCIALIST PARTY.

UDB. *See* REGIONAL AUTONOMIST PARTIES.

UDCA. *See* UNION FOR THE DEFENSE OF TRADERS AND ARTISANS.

UDF. *See* UNIFIED SOCIALIST PARTY and UNION FOR FRENCH DEMOCRACY.

UDI. *See* MODERATES.

UDR. *See* GAULLISTS.

UDSR. *See* DEMOCRATIC AND SOCIALIST UNION OF THE RESISTANCE.

UDT. *See* GAULLISTS and LEFT-WING GAULLISTS.

UD-Ve. *See* GAULLISTS.

UFF. See UNION FOR THE DEFENSE OF TRADERS AND ARTISANS.

UFGB. *See* UNION OF FRENCHMEN OF GOOD SENSE.

UGP. *See* LEFT-WING GAULLISTS.

UJCML. *See* MAOISTS.

UMN. *See* GAULLISTS.

UNIFIED SOCIALIST PARTY (*Parti Socialiste Unifié*: PSU). This PSU is not to be confused with the original name of the Socialist Party (SFIO)* in 1905. The modern PSU was first organized in September 1958 under the label of the Autonomous Socialist Party (*Parti Socialiste Autonome*: PSA). The PSA consisted of SFIO dissidents who were opposed to the relatively conservative policies and personalist rule of SFIO leader Guy Mollet. In the same month as its formation, the PSA absorbed the Union of Democratic Forces (*Union des Forces Démocratiques*: UFD) of Pierre Mendès-France, former leader of the Radical-

Socialist Party* whose leftist policies were often opposed by the centrist Radicals. In early 1960, the PSA was joined by the Tribune of Communism (*Tribune du Communisme*), a small dissident group from the French Communist Party,* and by the Union of the Socialist Left (*Union de la Gauche Socialiste*), a small left-wing faction of the SFIO. The resultant formation in April 1960 was the Unified Socialist Party.

The PSU's principal program is the protection of workers and the establishment of worker self-management (*autogestion*). The PSU has advocated wage increases, larger retirement benefits, better housing, and a steeper progressive tax rate. The party has also called for more local autonomy in government and an end to nuclear armaments. Ideologically, the PSU had hoped to position itself between the Socialist and Communist parties.

The PSU has allowed a variety of viewpoints within its membership, leading to the formation of various factions within the party itself. Its membership includes Catholics of the extreme left, the Current B faction of the Trotskyites,* some anarchists, and other far-leftists. Despite its name, the unity of the PSU has always been precarious, with individuals and factions regularly leaving the party. The PSU is firmly attached to a pure socialist ideology, although its socialism sometimes reflects the technocractic background of its leaders.

In 1965, under Alain Savary, some PSU members left the party to help found the Union of Clubs for the Renovation of the Left (*Union des Clubs pour le Renouveau de la Gauche*: UCRG). Savary had been one of the original Socialist Party dissidents who had helped form the Autonomous Socialist Party in 1958. Savary's new UCRG had wanted the PSU to join the newly formed Federation of the Democratic and Socialist Left (FGDS).* Although remaining outside of the FGDS, the PSU did endorse the presidential candidacy of FGDS leader François Mitterrand in 1965. Also, the PSU cooperated with the Socialists and Communists in the 1967 legislative elections, when the PSU ran 101 candidates and won four seats (including one held by Pierre Mendès-France). Savary himself rejoined the Socialist Party in 1969, serving as that party's first secretary from 1969 to 1971.

Under the leadership of Michel Rocard, the PSU swung sharply to the left. In 1968 it was the only established party to endorse the cause of the student revolt, which led to at least one defection, that of Mendès-France, who then offered his support to the Socialist Party. Also, this PSU stand apparently alienated the general electorate, who moved toward conservatism after the unrest. In the 1968 parliamentary elections, the PSU ran over 300 candidates, won 4.0 percent of the vote, but lost all seats. Nevertheless, the party claimed its membership jumped by some 42 percent, to 15,000, by 1969. Rocard contested the 1969 presidential election, receiving about 3.6 percent of the first-ballot vote. In 1974 the PSU again strongly supported the presidential candidacy of Mitterrand, who had succeeded Savary as leader of the Socialist Party in 1971. This cooperation led Rocard to attempt to merge the PSU with the Socialist Party. Though Rocard took with him some 2,500 to 3,000 PSU members in October

1974, the majority of the PSU refused to follow Rocard into the Socialist Party.

During the 1978 elections, the PSU was allied with the Movement for a Nonviolent Alternative (*Mouvement pour une Alternative Non-Violente*: MAN), led by Jean-Marie Muller, and various ecologist, feminist, and local groups in the Self-Determination Front (*Front Autogestionnaire*), which entered 228 candidates. Following the 1979 elections to the European Parliament, the Self-Determination Front was renamed the Convergence for Self-Determination (*Convergence pour l'Autogestion*); and in 1981 this group was known as Alternative '81, as part of which the PSU ran 182 candidates.

The PSU has continued to remain aloof from efforts to unify the French political left, regarding the Socialists as too reformist, the Communists as too stalinist, and the "common program of the left" as too much in the interests of the bourgeoisie. The political influence of the PSU is limited by its disunity, weak electoral support, lack of parliamentary representation, and an isolated political position. However, its ideas (especially *autogestion*) and former leaders (such as Michel Rocard and Alain Savary) have affected the policies of the Socialist Party.

The PSU organization is similar to those of other established French parties, with the congress as the highest organizational authority. Current PSU membership is estimated to be approximately 7,000. Its current leader is Huguette Bouchardeau.

UNIFIED SOCIALIST PARTY: FRENCH SECTION OF THE WORKERS' INTERNATIONAL. *See* SOCIALIST PARTY.

UNION DE LA GAUCHE. *See* UNION OF THE LEFT.

UNION DE LA GAUCHE SOCIALISTE. *See* UNIFIED SOCIALIST PARTY.

UNION DÉMOCRATIQUE. *See* DEMOCRATIC AND SOCIALIST UNION OF THE RESISTANCE.

UNION DÉMOCRATIQUE BRETONNE. *See* REGIONAL AUTONOMIST PARTIES.

UNION DÉMOCRATIQUE DES INDÉPENDANTS. *See* MODERATES.

UNION DÉMOCRATIQUE DU TRAVAIL. *See* GAULLISTS and LEFT-WING GAULLISTS.

UNION DÉMOCRATIQUE ET SOCIALISTE DE LA RÉSISTANCE. *See* DEMOCRATIC AND SOCIALIST UNION OF THE RESISTANCE.

UNION DÉMOCRATIQUE POUR LA CINQUIÈME RÉPUBLIQUE. *See* GAULLISTS.

UNION DÉMOCRATIQUE POUR LA RÉPUBLIQUE. *See* GAULLISTS.

UNION DES CLUBS POUR LE RENOUVEAU DE LA GAUCHE. *See* UNI-FIED SOCIALIST PARTY.

UNION DES COMMUNISTES DE FRANCE MARXISTES-LENINISTES. *See* MAOISTS.

UNION DES FORCES DÉMOCRATIQUES. *See* UNIFIED SOCIALIST PARTY.

UNION DES FRANÇAIS DE BON SENS. *See* UNION OF FRENCHMEN OF GOOD SENSE.

UNION DES GAUCHES. *See* RADICAL-SOCIALIST PARTY.

UNION DES GAULLISTES DE PROGRÈS. *See* LEFT-WING GAULLISTS.

UNION DES JEUNESSES COMMUNISTES MARXISTES-LENINISTES. *See* MAOISTS.

UNION DES RÉPUBLICAINS D'ACTION SOCIALE. *See* GAULLISTS.

UNION DES TRAVAILLEURS COMMUNISTES LIBERTAIRES. *See* ANARCHISTS.

UNIONE DI U POPULU CORSU. *See* REGIONAL AUTONOMIST PARTIES.

UNIONE PATRIOTIQUE RÉPUBLICAINE. *See* EXTREME RIGHT.

UNION ET FRATERNITÉ FRANÇAISE. *See* UNION FOR THE DEFENSE OF TRADERS AND ARTISANS.

UNION FOR FRENCH DEMOCRACY (*Union pour la Démocratie Française:* UDF). Non-Gaullist elements of the majority coalition organized the UDF in order to coordinate their campaign efforts during the 1978 National Assembly elections. The UDF's constituent parties were the Center of Social Democrats (*see* Democratic Center), the Radical-Socialist Party,* the Republican Party,* and the Democratic Socialist Movement of France.* The National Center of Independents and Peasants* did not adhere to the UDF, although it cooperated with various UDF parties. Likewise, the Republican Center* cooperated with the UDF, though not formally joining the Union. In effect, the UDF was a means of unifying all supporters of Valéry Giscard d'Estaing (from the Republican Party) in order to enable them to come out ahead of the Gaullists* on the first ballot.

After the 1978 elections, these parties formed a single parliamentary group and made efforts to organize the UDF on a national basis under the leadership of Jean Lecanuet (of the Center of Social Democrats). The UDF contested the 1979 European Parliament elections as the Union for France in Europe (see EUROPEAN PARLIAMENT) and polled the highest percentage of the French vote (27.6 percent).

The uncertain status of the UDF and the member parties' desires to retain their own followers and personalities have served to limit the implantation of the UDF across France. In the 1981 legislative elections, the UDF entered an electoral agreement with the Rally for the Republic (see Gaullists) known as the Union for the New Majority (Union pour la Majorité Nouvelle: UMN). A common declaration was issued, and second-ballot strategies were devised. Both UMN constituents were very close on the first ballot, with the UDF receiving 19.2 percent of the vote and the Rally receiving 20.8 percent. Of the UDF constituent parties running under the UMN label in 1981, the Center of Social Democrats received 19 seats in the Assembly, the Radical-Socialists received two seats, the Republicans 32 seats, though the Democratic Socialist Movement obtained no seats. In addition to these 53 deputies, another nine "UDF-Unaffiliated" deputies were elected, raising the UDF representation to a total of 62 seats. This compared to 85 seats won by the Rally for the Republic.

UNION FOR FRENCH RENEWAL. See GAULLISTS.

UNION FOR THE DEFENSE OF THE REPUBLIC. See GAULLISTS.

UNION FOR THE DEFENSE OF TRADERS AND ARTISANS (Union pour la Défense des Commerçants et Artisans: UDCA; most commonly known as the "Poujadists"). In 1953 the French Assembly passed a law which imposed a turnover tax on small shopkeepers and artisans. Pierre Poujade, a stationer from Saint Cere in the Massif-Central, immediately organized a local direct-action group to protest the tax via a tax strike. By 1955 the movement succeeded in expanding to the national level, claiming some 800,000 adherents, where it became a protest vehicle for those who were dissatisfied with socioeconomic conditions under the Fourth Republic. The movement expressed the alienation of the small farmer, merchant, and artisan menaced by the rapid modernization of the French economy.

The Poujadists won some 12 percent of the vote in the 1956 national legislative elections and seated 51 deputies (although 11 were then unseated for alleged violations of the electoral laws). This achievement was unique in the French political system, since the Poujadists reflected an electorally successful pressure group that had not found it necessary to become part of a party with broader interests. Poujadist candidates ran under several labels in addition to the UDCA, the most important of which was the French Union and Fraternity (*Union et Fraternité Française*: UFF). The Poujadist campaign tactics were suspected of occasional violence, including harassment of rival candidates' speeches and the molestation of opponents. Identified as a party of the extreme political right, the UDCA had acquired an anti-Semitic and sometimes fascist flavor. Poujade's father had been a member of the French Action group (*see* Extreme Right and Monarchists), and Poujade himself had fascist affiliations in the 1930s.

Poujadism as a unified movement soon collapsed in the Assembly as members divided over other political issues that they were called upon, as deputies, to face. Following the 1958 legislative elections, in which the Poujadists contested but won no seats, the UDCA disappeared as a political party, although the movement existed into the late 1970s as a pressure group. Believing Charles de Gaulle would obliterate the Fourth Republic—perceived as oppressive—many Poujadists turned their support to the Gaullists.* Other Poujadists transferred their loyalty to groups on the extreme political right, such as the National Rally (*see* Extreme Right), headed by Jean-Louis Tixier-Vignancour. Poujade himself joined the Gaullists in 1966.

Despite the disappearance of poujadism as a political entity, the label continues to be applied to movements that promote the interests of small businessmen. Ironically, one may even hear references in France to a "poujadist communism" at the times that the French communists have addressed themselves to concerns of small farmers and merchants.

UNION FOR THE NEW MAJORITY. *See* GAULLISTS.

UNION FOR THE NEW REPUBLIC. *See* GAULLISTS.

UNION FOR THE NEW REPUBLIC-DEMOCRATIC UNION OF LABOR. *See* GAULLISTS.

UNION GAULLISTE. *See* GAULLISTS.

UNION NOUVELLE POUR EUROPE. *See* MOVEMENT OF LEFT RADICALS.

UNION OF CLUBS FOR THE RENOVATION OF THE LEFT. *See* UNIFIED SOCIALIST PARTY.

UNION OF DEMOCRATIC FORCES. *See* UNIFIED SOCIALIST PARTY.

UNION OF FRENCHMEN OF GOOD SENSE (*Union des Français de Bon Sens*: UFBS). Founded in September 1977, the UFBS was a small personalist movement of Gerard Furnon. Furnon, a manufacturer, dedicated his party to the opposition of political trade unionism following a labor dispute with workers at his factory. The party claims over 10,000 members but was unsuccessful in the 1978 legislative elections.

UNION OF LEFTISTS. *See* RADICAL-SOCIALIST PARTY.

UNION OF LIBERTARIAN COMMUNIST WORKERS. *See* ANARCHISTS.

UNION OF PROGRESSIVE GAULLISTS. *See* LEFT-WING GAULLISTS.

UNION OF REPUBLICANS OF SOCIAL ACTION. *See* GAULLISTS.

UNION OF THE CORSICAN PEOPLE. *See* REGIONAL AUTONOMIST PARTIES.

UNION OF THE LEFT (*Union de la Gauche*). Between 1972 and 1978, the three major parties of France's political left constituted the *Union de la Gauche*: the Socialist Party,* the French Communist Party,* and the Movement of Left Radicals.* (This Union of the Left should not be confused with the 1945 coalition called the Union of Leftists, *see* Radical-Socialist Party.) These Union of the Left parties joined their efforts to offer a left-wing alternative to the Gaullist-Giscardist majority (*see* Gaullists and Republican Party respectively). The three parties cooperated in organizing joint national and local meetings and demonstrations, as well as coordinating parliamentary activities. Most importantly, they signed in 1972 a "common program" which was, in effect, a contract for a governmental coalition of the left. The common program described sweeping social and economic reforms, including a number of proposed nationalizations. It marked a significant convergence of views among these parties on foreign policy and defense issues. In addition, the three constituent parties agreed to reciprocal withdrawals for second-ballot run-off elections in favor of the best-placed candidate of the Union.

Leftist unity contributed to important Socialist and Communist gains in local and national partial elections. But the Union of the Left was defeated in 1978 after the member parties failed to agree on an updated revision of the 1972 common program. During the 1978 campaign, the Communist Party directed its main attacks at the Socialist Party (PS) in an attempt to limit PS gains. The earlier elections had shown that the PS was the major beneficiary of the Union of the Left and that the PS might well cut into the Communists' own potential electorate. The Communist campaign failed to prevent the PS from outpolling it for the first time since 1936, but it did limit the Socialist vote to well below expectations. After the 1978 elections, continued attacks by the Communists and PS recriminations over the Communist election campaign destroyed what remained of the Union of the Left. However, the alliance was patched together in 1981 after serious electoral reverses for the Communists. Despite the alliance, the Socialists managed to obtain a parliamentary majority of their own. They solicited Communist participation in the government in recognition of the support Communist voters gave to Mitterrand's presidential victory.

Further Reference. Machin, Howard, and Vincent Wright, "The French Left under the Fifth Republic: The Search for Identity and Unity," *Comparative Politics* 10 (October 1977): 35-67; Wilson, Frank L., "The Left in French Politics: Prospects for Union," *Contemporary French Civilization* 2 (Winter 1978): 205-229.

UNION OF THE SOCIALIST LEFT. *See* UNIFIED SOCIALIST PARTY.

UNION OF YOUNG MARXIST-LENINIST COMMUNISTS. *See* MAOISTS.

UNION OUVRIÈRE ET PAYSANNE POUR LA DÉMOCRATIE PROLÉ-TARIENNE. *See* MAOISTS.

UNION POUR LA DÉFENSE DE LA RÉPUBLIQUE. *See* GAULLISTS.

UNION POUR LA DÉFENSE DES COMMERÇANTS ET ARTISANS. *See* UNION FOR THE DEFENSE OF TRADERS AND ARTISANS.

UNION POUR LA DÉMOCRATIE FRANÇAISE. *See* UNION FOR FRENCH DEMOCRACY.

UNION POUR LA MAJORITÉ NOUVELLE. *See* GAULLISTS.

UNION POUR LA NOUVELLE RÉPUBLIQUE. *See* GAULLISTS.

UNION POUR LA NOUVELLE RÉPUBLIQUE-UNION DÉMOCRATIQUE DU TRAVAIL. *See* GAULLISTS.

UNION POUR LE RENOUVEAU FRANÇAIS. *See* GAULLISTS.

UNION RÉPUBLICAIN POUR LA LIBERTÉ ET LE PROGRÈS SOCIAL. *See* EXTREME RIGHT.

UNION SACRÉE. *See* FRANCE INTRODUCTION.

UNITARY SOCIALIST PARTY. *See* SOCIALIST PARTY.

UNR. *See* GAULLISTS.

UNR-UDT. *See* GAULLISTS.

UNVANIEZH DEMOKRATEL BREIZH. *See* REGIONAL AUTONOMIST PARTIES.

UOPDP. *See* MAOISTS.

UPC. *See* REGIONAL AUTONOMIST PARTIES.

URAS. See GAULLISTS.

UTCL. *See* ANARCHISTS.

VOLEM VIURE AL PAIS. *See* REGIONAL AUTONOMIST PARTIES.

VVAP. *See* REGIONAL AUTONOMIST PARTIES.

WORKERS AND PEASANTS GROUP. *See* TROTSKYITES.

WORKER'S FRONT. *See* LEFT-WING GAULLISTS.

WORKERS' STRUGGLE. *See* TROTSKYITES.

YOUNG REPUBLIC. *See* CONVENTION OF REPUBLICAN INSTITUTIONS and POPULAR REPUBLICAN MOVEMENT.

Frank L. Wilson

TABLE 23. Distribution of Seats in France's Third Republic Chamber of Deputies, 1902-1936[*]

Party	1902	1906	1910	1914	1919	1924	1928	1932	1936
French Communist Party	—	—	—	—	—	26	14	12	72
Independent Socialists	—	18	24	—	5	—	—	—	—
Socialist Party (SFIO)[a]	46	53	78	103	67	104	99	129	149
Radical-Socialist Party	75	241	121	140	106	162	120	157	109
Republican Socialist Party[b]	—	—	—	27	17		30	37	56
Democratic Alliance[c]	180	52	71	57	79	53	74	72	222[d]
Independent Radicals	120	39	67	96	51		52	62	
Popular Democratic Party	—	—	—	—	—	—	14	16	
Popular Liberal Action Party	18	69	11	0	0	0	0	0	
Republican Federation of France	—	—	103	96	201	204	168	76	
Independents and conservatives	147	109	112	73	88	25	26	33	
Others	3	0	0	0	2	0	5	11	0
Total	589	581	587	592	616	574	602	605	608

[*] All figures in this table represent seat distribution for metropolitan France, including Algerian representatives.

[a] In 1902, figure represents combined seats for the French Socialist Party (1901-1905) and the Socialist Party of France, which merged in 1905 to form the Unified Socialist Party: French Section of the Workers' International (SFIO).

[b] Known as the Republican Socialist and French Socialist Party, 1926-1936.

[c] Known as the Republican Democratic Alliance, 1911-1920; as the Republican Democratic and Social Party, 1920-World War II.

[d] In 1936, represents combined seats for the National Republican Bloc.

312

TABLE 24. Distribution of Seats in France's Fourth Republic National Assembly, 1945-1956*

Party	1945**	June 1946**	Nov. 1946	1951	1956
French Communist Party[a]	148	146	166	97	148
Gaullists[b]	—	—	5	107	16
Moderates[c]	71	62	70	87	96
Popular Republican Movement	137	160	158	82	71
Poujadists[d]	—	—	—	—	52
Radical-Socialist Party[e]	31	39	55	77	73
Socialist Party (SFIO)[f]	135	115	90	94	88
Total	522	522	544	544	544

* All figures in this table represent seat distribution for metropolitan France only.

** The figures for the 1945 and June 1946 elections represent seats to the two constituent assemblies.

[a] French Communist Party seats include various allied groups.

[b] Known as the Gaullist Union, 1946; as the Rally of the French People, 1947-1953; as the Social Republicans, 1954-1956.

[c] The Moderates include various conservative groupings, such as the Republican Party of Liberty, the Peasant and Social Action Party, and the Independent Peasants of Social Action.

[d] Includes candidates who ran under the labels of the Union for the Defense of Traders and Artisans, and as the French Union and Fraternity.

[e] Includes seats won by the Democratic and Socialist Union of the Resistance, which joined with the Radical-Socialists in the Rally of the Left Republicans. In 1956, includes seats won by the Republican Center.

[f] Includes both Independent Socialists and Republican Socialists.

TABLE 25. Ruling Coalitions in France's Fourth Republic, 1947-1958*

Formation Date	Prime Minister	Coalition
Jan. 22, 1947	Paul Ramadier	Socialist Party (SFIO) French Communist Party (until May 1947) Popular Republican Movement Radical-Socialist Party Democratic and Socialist Union of the Resistance Moderates
Nov. 22, 1947	Robert Schuman	Popular Republican Movement Socialist Party (SFIO) Radical-Socialist Party Democratic and Socialist Union of the Resistance Moderates
July 26, 1948	André Marie	Radical-Socialist Party Socialist Party (SFIO) Popular Republican Movement Democratic and Socialist Union of the Resistance Moderates Republican Party of Liberty
Sep. 5, 1948	Robert Schuman	Popular Republican Movement Socialist Party (SFIO) Radical-Socialist Party Democratic and Socialist Union of the Resistance Moderates

Sep. 11, 1948   Henri Queuille   Radical-Socialist Party
                                   Socialist Party (SFIO)
                                   Popular Republican Movement
                                   Democratic and Socialist Union of the Resistance
                                   Republican Party of Liberty
                                   Moderates

Oct. 28, 1949   Georges Bidault   Popular Republican Movement
                                   Socialist Party (SFIO)
                                   Radical-Socialist Party
                                   Democratic and Socialist Union of the Resistance
                                   National Center of Independents and Peasants

July 2, 1950   Henri Queuille   Radical-Socialist Party
                                   Popular Republican Movement
                                   Democratic and Socialist Union of the Resistance
                                   National Center of Independents and Peasants

July 12, 1950   René Pleven   Democratic and Socialist Union of the Resistance
                                   Socialist Party (SFIO)
                                   Popular Republican Movement
                                   Radical-Socialist Party
                                   National Center of Independents and Peasants

Mar. 10, 1951   Henri Queuille   Radical-Socialist Party
                                   Socialist Party (SFIO)
                                   Popular Republican Movement
                                   Democratic and Socialist Union of the Resistance
                                   National Center of Independents and Peasants

315

TABLE 25. (*Continued*)

Formation Date	Prime Minister	Coalition
Aug. 11, 1951	René Pleven	Democratic and Socialist Union of the Resistance Radical-Socialist Party Popular Republican Movement National Center of Independents and Peasants
Jan. 10, 1952	Edgar Faure	Radical-Socialist Party Popular Republican Movement Democratic and Socialist Union of the Resistance National Center of Independents and Peasants
Mar. 8, 1952	Antoine Pinay	National Center of Independents and Peasants Popular Republican Movement Radical-Socialist Party Democratic and Socialist Union of the Resistance
Jan. 8, 1953	René Mayer	Radical-Socialist Party Popular Republican Movement Democratic and Socialist Union of the Resistance National Center of Independents and Peasants Republican and Social Action
June 28, 1953	Joseph Laniel	Moderates Popular Republican Movement Radical-Socialist Party Union of Republicans of Social Action Republican and Social Action
June 19, 1954	Pierre Mendès-France	Radical-Socialist Party Democratic and Socialist Union of the Resistance National Center of Social Republicans

Feb. 23, 1955	Edgar Faure	Radical-Socialist Party Popular Republican Movement Democratic and Socialist Union of the Resistance National Center of Independents and Peasants Group of Social Republicans
Feb. 1, 1956	Guy Mollet	Socialist Party (SFIO) Radical-Socialist Party Group of Social Republicans
June 13, 1957	Maurice Bourgès-Manoury	Radical-Socialist Party Socialist Party (SFIO) Democratic and Socialist Union of the Resistance Rally of the Left Republicans
Nov. 6, 1957	Felix Gaillard	Radical-Socialist Party Socialist Party (SFIO) Popular Republican Movement Group of Social Republicans National Center of Independents and Peasants
May 14, 1958	Pierre Pflimlin	Popular Republican Movement Radical-Socialist Party Socialist Party (SFIO) Group of Social Republicans National Center of Independents and Peasants

Note: First-named party is dominant coalition party.

TABLE 26. Distribution of Seats in France's Fifth Republic National Assembly, 1958-1981

Party	1958	1962	1967	1968	1973	1978	1981
French Communist Party	10	41	73	34	73	86	44
Gaullists[a]	199	232	201	296	183	153	85
Movement of Left Radicals	—	—	—	—		10	14
Socialist Party[b]	44	66	76	42	101	107	269
Popular Republican Movement[c]	57	55	—	—			
Democratic Center[d]	—	—	41	33	60	36	19
National Center of Independents and Peasants[e]	133	13	44	64	55	9	5
Republican Party[f]	—	35	40	15		65	32
Radical-Socialist Party[g]	32	39	4	0	4	8	2
Unified Socialist Party[h]	0	0	8	3	1	0	0
Others[i]	71	0	—	—	13	17	21
Total	546	482	487	487	490	491	491

Note: All figures include results for both metropolitan France and overseas deputies.

a   Known as the Union for the New Republic in 1958; as the Union for the New Republic/Democratic Union of Labor, 1962-1967; as the Democratic Union for the Fifth Republic, 1967-1968; as the Union for the Defense of the Republic (later the Democratic Union for the Republic), 1968-1976; as the Rally for the Republic, 1976-1981. In 1981, the latter joined with the Center of Social Democrats to form an electoral alliance called the Union for the New Majority.

b   Known as the Unified Socialist Party: French Section of the Workers' International (SFIO), prior to 1969. In 1967, the Socialists were part of the Federation of the Democratic and Socialist Left (FGDS), and in 1973 were part of the Union of the Socialist and Democratic Left (UGDS), which also included the Movement of Left Radicals.

c   The Popular Republican Movement (MPR) became part of the Democratic Center in 1966, and the MPR ceased to exist as a separate party in 1967.

d   Formed in 1966 from elements of the Popular Republican Movement and the National Center of Independents and Peasants. The Democratic Center was known as the Center of Progress and Modern Democracy in 1968. The Democratic Center split in 1969: the main body joined with the Radical-Socialist Party and allied groups to form the Reformers' Movement; a dissident group formed the Center for Democracy and Progress. The total of seats won in 1973 includes 30 seats obtained by this latter grouping. Both parties reunited in 1976 to form the Center of Social Democrats (CDS), which in 1981 joined with the gaullist Rally for the Republic to form an electoral alliance called the Union for the New Majority.

e   Formed part of the Democratic Center in 1967-1968; affiliated with the Republican Party in 1973; then contested the elections of 1978 and 1981 separately and under its own label.

f   Known as the Independent Republicans, 1962-1966; as the Federation of Independent Republicans, 1966-1977; as the Republican Party, 1977-present.

g   The Radical-Socialists participated with the Socialist Party and the Convention of Republican Institutions in the Federation of the Democratic and Socialist Left (FGDS) in 1967 and in the Union of the Socialist and Democratic Left (UGDS) in 1968. The totals listed for the Radical-Socialists include 15 and two seats respectively for these elections won by the Convention. In 1968, the Convention merged with the Socialist Party, while the main body of the Socialists became affiliated with the Reformers' Movement (Democratic Center) in 1973.

h   Known as the Autonomous Socialist Party, 1958-1960.

i   Represents minor parties and independents. In 1958, includes 71 deputies from Algeria and the Sahara.

TABLE 27. Ruling Coalitions in France's Fifth Republic since 1958

Formation Date	Prime Minister	Coalition
June 1958	Charles De Gaulle	Union for the New Republic (Gaullists) Popular Republican Movement Radical-Socialist Party Socialist Party (SFIO) Moderates
Jan. 1959	Michel Debre	Union for the New Republic (Gaullists) Popular Republican Movement Radical-Socialist Party Moderates
Apr. 1962	Georges Pompidou	Union for the New Republic (Gaullists) Democratic Union of Labor Popular Republican Movement Radical-Socialist Party Moderates
Dec. 1962	Georges Pompidou	Union for the New Republic (Gaullists) Independent Republicans Radical-Socialist Party
Jan. 1966	Georges Pompidou	Democratic Union for the New Republic (Gaullists) Independent Republicans
Apr. 1967	Georges Pompidou	Democratic Union for the Fifth Republic (Gaullists) Federation of Independent Republicans
May 1968	Georges Pompidou	Democratic Union for the Republic (Gaullists) Federation of Independent Republicans

July 1968	Couve de Murville	Union for the Republic (Gaullists) Federation of Independent Republicans Center of Progress and Modern Democracy
June 1969	Jacques Chaban Delmas	Union for the Republic (Gaullists) Federation of Independent Republicans Center of Progress and Modern Democracy
July 1972	Pierre Messmer	Union for the Republic (Gaullists) Federation of Independent Republicans Center of Progress and Modern Democracy
June 1974	Jacques Chirac	Union for the Republic (Gaullists) Federation of Independent Republicans Center of Progress and Modern Democracy Progress and Modern Democracy Reformers' Movement
Aug. 1976	Raymond Barre (non-party)	Rally for the Republic (Gaullists) Federation of Independent Republicans (renamed as the Republican Party, 1977) Center of Social Democrats Radical-Socialist Party
May 1981	Pierre Mauroy	Socialist Party French Communist Party Movement of Left Radicals

Note: First-named party is dominant coalition party.

GIBRALTAR

GIBRALTAR is a British colonial dependency on the Iberian Peninsula occupying two-and-one-quarter square miles of rocky outcrop overlooking the entrance to the Mediterranean. It was ceded by Spain in 1713 under the terms of the Treaty of Utrecht, which provided that Gibraltar would revert to Spain if ever relinquished by Britain. Political activity in Gibraltar is conditioned by several unique factors. Over 76 percent of the country's land is devoted to British-controlled defense installations, a reflection of Gibraltar's immense strategic importance. In addition, Spain has been conducting an intermittent campaign to regain possession of this last colony on the European mainland and since 1969 has maintained a complete blockade on all land communication with Gibraltar. The dependence of "The Rock" upon Britain is therefore very great, and even the democratization of Spain since Franco's death in 1975 and the prospect of Spain joining Britain as a member of the European Community have not significantly widened the political options open to Gibraltarians.

One party, the Association for the Advancement of Civil Rights (AACR), * has dominated the politics of The Rock since 1945 and (with a break from 1969 to 1972) has controlled the legislature, which was created as a successor to the Gibraltar City Council in 1950. In 1967, by a majority of 12,138 to 44, the electorate rejected a return to Spanish sovereignty, opting instead for democratic local institutions and a continuing link with Britain. Under the 1969 constitution, the Gibraltar House of Assembly consists of a nonvoting speaker; the attorney general and the financial development secretary (both appointed by the governor and not voting on issues of confidence); and 15 elected members. (See table 29.) Control of external relations, defense, and internal security remains in the hands of the British-appointed governor, while other domestic matters are handled by the Council of Ministers, which consists of the chief minister and up to eight elected members of the House of Assembly.

The population of Gibraltar is very small (29,865 in 1977, of which approximately 16,000 are eligible to vote) and is of mixed Spanish, Portuguese, Maltese, and British descent. About three-quarters of the population is Roman Catholic, but religion has not been an important political factor—for example, the leader of the ruling AACR, Sir Joshua Hassan, comes from a Jewish family of Moroccan origin. Each elector may vote for up to eight candidates in the quadrennial elections. (Prior to 1969, proportional representation was used.) In recent elections, voter turnout has been in the 65 to 75 percent range.

Although the AACR can properly be called an organized party, other groups resemble temporary factions. (*See* table 28.) There appears to be no permanent polarization of political views between the parties, and it would be difficult to place them on a left-right spectrum. Perhaps because the British government is the major employer (through its dockyard and other defense installations), there is little room for disagreement among the parties on most domestic matters; and political debate tends to be dormant between elections. During election campaigns, the major issue is the question of Gibraltar's status vis-à-vis Britain and Spain and (given the small-town atmosphere of the colony) the personalities and family ties of the candidates. Gibraltarian politics remain a delicate balance between loyalty to British political traditions versus cultural and family affinities toward Spain.

Bibliography

Daly, Jim. "The Politics of the Rock." *Venture*, vol. 23, no. 2 (February 1971): 6-8.

Dennis, Philip. *Gibraltar*. Newton Abbott: David & Charles, 1977.

Garcia, Joe. *The Gibraltar Who's Who and Year Book*. Gibraltar: Mediterranean Sun Publishing Co., 1974.

Heidenheimer, Arnold J. "Citizenship, Parties and Factions in Gibraltar." *Journal of Commonwealth Political Studies*, vol. 1, no. 4 (1963): 249-265.

Hills, George. *Rock of Contention: A History of Gibraltar*. London: Robert Hale, 1974.

Stewart, John D. *Gibraltar the Keystone*. London: John Murray, 1967.

Political Parties

AACR. *See* ASSOCIATION FOR THE ADVANCEMENT OF CIVIL RIGHTS.

ASSOCIATION FOR THE ADVANCEMENT OF CIVIL RIGHTS (AACR). Founded in 1942 by Joshua Hassan, a lawyer, and Albert Risso, a mechanic, the Association sought to protect the interests of families evacuated during the wartime emergency and to improve the condition of workers remaining in Gibraltar. It emerged as a political party in 1945 with a platform of improving pay and working conditions for Gibraltarians (most of them employed in British defense installations) and promoting a democratic constitution. The AACR has been the ruling party since 1950 (when the Gibraltar City Council was replaced by a legislature), with the exception of the 1969-1972 period when a coalition of opposition parties formed the government.

Under its cofounder and leader, Sir Joshua Hassan, the AACR has adopted a pragmatic, relatively progressive domestic program. In relation to Gibraltar's colonial status, it has sought to strengthen support and assistance from Britain while aiming for as much freedom of action as possible— "With Britain, but not under Britain" is the party's slogan.

Until the 1960s, the AACR was closely allied with a labor union, the Gibraltar Confederation of Labour, which the AACR had founded, and this association provided a major source of electoral support. In recent years, the party's links with organized labor have been less institutionalized, but AACR supporters are still the most disciplined bloc-voters in elections. To mobilize support, the AACR has relied much more on grass-roots organization than family loyalties, unlike many of its rival parties of the past. In 1969 it added "Gibraltar Labour Party" to its title, and in the elections since 1972 the party has maintained eight of the 15 seats in the House of Assembly.

COMMONWEALTH PARTY (CP). Founded in 1953 by Juan Triay, a lawyer of Spanish descent, the Commonwealth Party was intended to promote Catholicism, to replace state welfare programs by voluntary programs, and to protect Gibraltar against extremism and materialism. This attempt to develop a conservative Catholic party was perceived as a threat to the existing consensus, and only Triay himself was elected in the 1953 and 1956 elections. After criticizing the British government for its handling of the border dispute with Spain, Triay resigned his seat in 1957 and the party was dissolved.

Another member of the same family, José Triay, had with others provoked riots in 1968 by proposing an Anglo-Spanish treaty on Gibraltar. In the 1976 elections, José Triay reincarnated the CP in his unsuccessful attempt to be returned on a platform of direct negotiations between Britain and Spain with representation for Gibraltar.

In the 1980 election, a further attempt to field three candidates on a platform of Anglo-Spanish guarantees of Gibraltar's autonomy was rejected by the voters, despite the CP having been renamed the "Party for the Autonomy of Gibraltar."

CP. See COMMONWEALTH PARTY.

DEMOCRATIC PARTY FOR A BRITISH GIBRALTAR. See GIBRALTAR DEMOCRATIC MOVEMENT.

GDM. See GIBRALTAR DEMOCRATIC MOVEMENT.

GIBRALTAR DEMOCRATIC MOVEMENT (GDM). The GDM was founded to contest the 1976 elections, following the dissolution of the Integration With Britain Party (IWBP). * The Movement was initially led by Joe Bossano, a labor union leader and former founder-member of the IWBP. The GDM, despite the leftist sympathies of its first leader, has a broad range of support from associations as diverse as the Chamber of Commerce and the Transport and General Workers' Union.

The Gibraltar Democratic Movement was created after the British government made it clear in 1976 that neither independence nor integration with Britain were viable options. Also, the British government's refusal to include nonelected representatives in future talks on Gibraltar's status stimulated the creation of the GDM to provide a vehicle for concerned groups not represented by the Association for the Advancement of Civil Rights.* Hence the GDM's main aim is to achieve the decolonization of Gibraltar and the creation of a new status that will guarantee Gibraltar's security. The party has not yet developed a distinctive domestic policy platform.

In the 1976 election, the GDM gained four seats in the House of Assembly. Prior to the 1980 election, Peter Isola (formerly of the Isola Group*) became leader of the GDM, which altered its title to the Democratic Party for a British Gibraltar and won six seats in the House of Assembly. Joe Bossano, the original GDM leader, then established a new party, the Gibraltar Socialist Labour Party, on a platform of no negotiations with Spain. Bossano was the only candidate of this new group to be elected in the 1980 contest.

GIBRALTAR LABOUR PARTY. See ASSOCIATION FOR THE ADVANCEMENT OF CIVIL RIGHTS.

GIBRALTAR SOCIALIST LABOUR PARTY. See GIBRALTAR DEMOCRATIC MOVEMENT.

IWBP. See INTEGRATION WITH BRITAIN PARTY.

INTEGRATION WITH BRITAIN PARTY (IWBP). The IWBP was founded in 1967 by R. Peliza, a former member of the Association for the Advancement of Civil Rights (AACR).* Peliza's platform advocated Gibraltar's full integration with Britain (on a pattern analogous to Northern Ireland, with direct parliamentary representation at Westminster). In domestic matters, the IWBP was leftist in orientation, favoring welfare policies which included price controls on imported produce.

Following Spain's imposition of a land blockade in 1969, the IWBP won five seats in the House of Assembly, and Peliza headed a coalition government joined by the three Assembly members of the Isola Group.* In 1972 the defection of one Isola member forced a premature election, and the AACR regained majority control (despite the support the IWBP received from the Transport and General Workers' Union, the largest of the colony's labor unions).

Maurice Xiberras became the IWBP leader in 1972, but the AACR began to preempt IWBP domestic policy proposals (such as wage parity for Gibraltarian and British defense workers). Furthermore, in 1976 the British government ruled out integration as an option for Gibraltar, and these factors caused the dissolution of the party only a month before the 1976 election, although Xiberras himself successfully stood as an independent candidate.

ISOLA GROUP. A right-wing faction led by the two Isola brothers (Peter and William), the Group was identified with the interests of Gibraltar's business community. In 1969 the Isola Group gained three seats in the House of Assembly and joined the Integration With Britain Party* to form a coalition government under R. Peliza. The defection of one Group member in 1972 precipitated a premature election, which led to the return of power of the Association for the Advancement of Civil Rights* and to political oblivion for the Isola Group. However, in 1980 Peter Isola became the leader of the Gibraltar Democratic Movement.*

PARTY FOR THE AUTONOMY OF GIBRALTAR. *See* COMMONWEALTH PARTY.

Michael Hodges

TABLE 28. Ruling Parties in Gibraltar since 1950

Years	Party
1950-1969	Association for the Advancement of Civil Rights
1969-1972	Integration With Britain Party, Isola Group
1972-	Association for the Advancement of Civil Rights

Note: First-named party is dominant coalition party.

TABLE 29. Distribution of Seats in Gibraltar's House of Assembly, 1950-1980

Party	1950	1953	1956	1959	1964	1969	1972	1976	1980
Association for the Advancement of Civil Rights	3	3	4	3	5	7	8	8	8
Commonwealth Party	—	1	1	—	—	—	—	0	0*
Gibraltar Democratic Movement	—	—	—	—	—	—	—	4	6**
Gibraltar Socialist Labour Party	—	—	—	—	—	—	—	—	1
Integration with Britain Party	—	—	—	—	—	5	7	—	—
Isola Group	—	—	—	—	—	3	0	—	—
Independents	2	1	2	4	6	—	—	3	—
Total	5	5	7	7	11	15	15	15	15

* Renamed "Party for the Autonomy of Gibraltar" in this election.
** Renamed "Democratic Party for a British Gibraltar" in this election.

GREECE

GREECE, or the HELLENIC REPUBLIC (*Hellenikia Demokratia*), is situated on the southern portion of the Balkan peninsula and includes numerous islands in the surrounding Ionian and Aegean Seas. Greece is bounded on the north by Albania, Yugoslavia, and Bulgaria. The population of 9.3 million is made up almost entirely of ethnic Greeks and is overwhelmingly Eastern Orthodox in religion. The only significant minorities are Turks and Macedonian Slavs, although they are not so recognized by the Greek state.

Although the political history of Greece started as long ago as 700 B.C., modern political history dates from March 21, 1821, when the Greeks launched their war of independence from the Ottoman Empire. Much earlier, the Greeks had endured 350 years of Roman domination before coming under the Byzantine Empire in A.D. 395. Between 1456 and 1821, Greece was under Turkish rule as part of the Ottoman Empire. A revolution in Greece, assisted by foreign intervention, finally led to the Peace of Adrianople in 1829 and formal Greek independence. Under the terms of the Protocol of London (1830), the independence of the Greek state was placed under the tripartite guarantee of Britain, France, and tsarist Russia.

Local democratic institutions had existed while Greece was still part of the Ottoman Empire, although the principle of representation was weak and somewhat vague. Representation existed at the community (*koinotis*) level with local leaders (*koinotiki archontes*) elected by the people. Electoral systems varied from community to community. Elections were generally held in the spring. In some communities they were held annually, in others twice each year, and in others every two or three years. In most areas the community leaders were elected by universal male suffrage (such as in Peloponnesus), while in special cases (as in Athens) the suffrage was quite restricted.

There were several levels of community representation. In Peloponnesus, every community elected a leader (*dimogerontas*), and the community leaders in turn elected general leaders (*proestoi* or *eparchoi*) who then elected the general leaders or council of the Peloponnesus area (*proestoi* of Morias). This nonpartisan structure characterized the form of Greek politics at the time of independence in 1821. The 59 members of the first national assembly of Epidauros (1821) were already elected leaders of their respective regions (Peloponnesus,

West Greece, and East Greece). The second national assembly of Astros (1823) was a body of 113 representatives elected by a broad popular base. The same held true for the third national assembly of Troizina (1827) when the first Greek republic was established.

The first Greek republic lasted only a few years. In 1832, Greece came under the absolute rule of Otto of Bavaria (1832-1862), a monarch imposed upon Greece by the tripartite powers (England, France, and Russia). Protest and discontent associated with Otto's rule resulted in a bloodless revolution in 1843, after which the monarch accepted, in 1844, a two-chamber national assembly. The upper house was appointed by the king for life. The lower house was elective, based upon an expanded suffrage which included all males 25 years of age (with restrictions on certain occupational classes, such as servants) and a secret ballot. Voting was by list and took place over a four-day period.

A second rebellion and a change in dynasty occurred in 1862 when Otto was forced to abdicate. The chief complaints against Otto included his lack of a male heir, which placed the monarchy in an uncertain position, his system of manipulated elections, and his failures in foreign policy, particularly his inability to liberate those Greeks still living within the Ottoman Empire and his siding with Austria in the Austro-Italian War (1859). The majority of the Greek people had sided with Italy.

Once again the tripartite powers succeeded in imposing a new monarch on Greece. Prince William of Denmark ascended the throne in 1863 as George I (1863-1913). A new constitution was drafted that reduced the powers of the monarch by establishing a system of ministerial government. Parliament was reduced to one chamber, and deputies were chosen to serve for four years as representatives of the nation rather than as regional or local spokesmen. Suffrage was lowered to 21 years and made universal for all males under a list system with proportional representation. This 1864 system established the foundations of modern parliamentary democracy in Greece and set the stage for the development of a competitive system that emerged during the interwar period.

Historically, the Greek party system has been highly unstable, perhaps more so than that of any other European nation. It has been characterized by fragmentation, factionalism, and shifts in allegiance—all of which have denied Greece a stable, majoritarian system of government, except for brief periods. Opportunist deputies have commonly shifted their party labels between elections. Greek parties have also been undisciplined, which has made coalition-building a difficult enterprise. For most of Greece's parliamentary history, parties have been little more than organized personal followings in which individual loyalty to the party leader and not ideology has been the binding force. Over the years, the extensive network of personalist and clientelage relationships in Greek society has worked to inhibit the development of an objective socioeconomic basis for mass political ties and electoral choice.

Three major factors have influenced the development of the Greek party system: (1) the vulnerability of Greek political forces to outside intervention, a situation that dates from the early stages of independence; (2) persistent disagreement over the nature and structure of the regime (republican or monarchical); and (3) the failure of Greek parties to develop into unified, coherent national organizations with distinguishable programmatic bases. The early political groups in Greece were not parties in the modern sense but rather factions (*fatriai*) based upon the personal followings of regional leaders or outgrowths of family rivalries. Two major contending factions had emerged during the final stages of Ottoman rule in the form of the Karytaina-Messenia Party and the Achaikon Party. The latter was named for the region (Achaia) of its leader, M. Solterios. During the latter part of the 1821-1827 Greek war for independence, a Civilian Party had existed that articulated the interests of civilian notables in contrast to the military elements that waged the struggle.

The first generation of political parties (*kommata*) in Greece developed during the struggle for independence—first between the military and civilian elements as noted above, and later between traditional Greek interests and those of the tripartite powers that had engineered Greek independence. Although external in their orientation, these protoparties also reflected loose social divisions brought about by the struggle for autonomy. They took definite form under the authoritarian system of John Capodistrias, a Russian official who had been appointed as the first governor of Greece (1828-1831).

Because of various intrigues surrounding the Greek throne, Britain, France, and Russia became patrons of various Greek political factions, resulting in the formation of distinct foreign parties. The British Party (*Agliko Komma*) was founded by Alexandros Mavrokordatos in 1825. It sought to maintain a strong alliance between Britain and Greece, and it was supported primarily by the merchants, wealthy Peloponnesians, and the shipowners of the islands. The French Party (*Galiko Komma*) was led by John Kolettis after its founding in 1824. Supporting the candidacy of Louis Phillipe, Duke of Orleans, for the Greek throne, the French Party's support was largely derived from intellectuals of the period. The Russian Party (*Rossiko Komma*) emerged in 1824 under the direction of Theodoros Kolokotronis. It provided the bases of support for John Capodistrias between 1828 and 1831.

Despite their foreign affiliations, these groupings were also based internally on various social strata and were dependent upon the clientelage system as well as family and regional rivalries. The foreign parties were also divided into constitutionalists and governmentalists. The former favored a limited monarchy with parliamentary control, and they drew their support from the British and French parties. The governmentalists represented the supporters of the authoritarian system of Capodistrias, and they were drawn almost exclusively from the Russian Party.

Each of the foreign parties had a period of primacy and then declined as domestic issues began to impinge upon the party system. The Russian Party peaked between 1838 and 1839, giving way to the British Party in 1841, and then to the French Party between 1841 and 1842. As hostility to Otto's rule increased, Greek political parties began to move away from foreign interests and patronage, directing themselves toward a new cleavage system based upon internal constitutional issues involving the role of the monarch and the political structure of the regime. The foreign parties completely lost their identity after the Crimean War (1854-1856), and one finds a new generation of political groups based upon the personal followings of leading political figures of the time. Among the important groupings during this period were the Mavrokordatists (old British Party), the Kolettists (old French Party), and the Kolokotronists (old Russian Party).

Between 1855 and 1882, four major partisan groupings dominated Greek political life in the organization of government administrations. They were the personal followings of: Andreas Koumoundouros (ten administrations between 1865 and 1882), Demitrios Voulgaris (eight administrations between 1855 and 1875), Epaminondas Deligiorgis (six administrations between 1865 and 1877), and Benizelos Roufos (four administrations between 1863 and 1866). These were extremely fluid groupings and difficult to distinguish in terms of partisan goals or political orientation. There was little in the way of organization. Deputies often did not reveal their allegiance until after an administration was formed. Disagreements were personal and appeared to be over priorities rather than policy or ideology.

The 1882-1910 period gave the appearance of a bipartisan system involving the rival protagonists Charilaos Trikoupis and Theodoros Deligiannis. Each, with the support of a personal following, alternated in government over the period. In the 11 elections held between January 1882 and August 1910, five were a clear victory for Deligiannis (1885, 1890, 1895, 1902, and 1905), and four for Trikoupis (1882, 1887, 1892, and 1899). The other elections represented an even division. Trikoupis headed a total of seven government administrations between 1875 and 1895, while Deligiannis headed five between 1885 and 1905. Trikoupis died in 1896, and Deligiannis was assassinated in 1905.

The major issues of the period were the same for both Trikoupis and Deligiannis—the liberation and annexation of Greek irredenta and the question of economic development. With the deaths of both leaders, the bipartisan structure began to break down after 1905. After that period, no party appeared dominant until the entry of Eleftherios Venizelos into national politics in 1910.

A new generation of political parties began in Greece in 1910 following several unsuccessful conflicts with Turkey over Greek irredenta, especially the island of Crete (1878, 1886, and 1896-1897). A political crisis ensued in 1909 when the Military League, an organization of young professional officers, formed to protest the mismanagement of domestic and foreign affairs by the politicians. Because the 1910 election failed to provide a clear victory for any of the traditional parties, the king was pressured by the military to invite Eleftherios Venizelos, a representative from Crete, to form a government. Venizelos had made an unsuccessful attempt in 1897 to remove Crete from Turkish rule and had acquired considerable popularity among the Greek people. Shortly after forming a government in 1910, Venizelos established the Liberal Party* and created a political tendency in Greek politics which continues to exist, in current form as the Union of the Greek Democratic Center. *

The coming to power of Venizelos and his Liberal Party sharpened the conflict between royalists and republicans and made it the fundamental cleavage underlying the Greek party system in the period between the world wars. Given the personalist nature of Greek politics at the time, the royalist-republican classification was perhaps the only means of distinguishing among Greek parties in the 1920s and 1930s.

Following the assassination of King George I in 1913, Venizelos was continually at odds with George's son and successor, King Constantine I. This situation served only to widen the gulf between the royalist and republican sympathizers. At the outbreak of World War I, Venizelos was partial to the Allies (Britain, France, and Russia), while Constantine (a relative of the German monarch William II) favored the German cause and urged Greek neutrality. The Allied victory vindicated the Venizelists and resulted in Constantine being deposed in 1917. He was succeeded by his son, King Alexander. Greece entered the war on the Allied side in June 1917, and Greece secured a lavish postwar settlement that nearly doubled the prewar size of the country at the expense of Turkey.

Unfortunately for Greece, fighting erupted with Turkey in 1921-1922, which led to a loss of previous territorial gains. Greece was obliged to sign the Treaty of Lausanne in October 1923, which introduced a new political element into the party system. Under the terms of the treaty, a population exchange occurred that required Greece to absorb about 1.2 million Greek refugees from Asia Minor. The refugee problem would play an important role in Greek politics in the interwar period.

Greece between the wars was a country characterized by much violent strife and government instability, with political feuds, coups, and countercoups. Three monarchs occupied the throne in the span of a few years. King Alexander, who ascended the throne in 1917 after Constantine I departed, died in 1920 of blood poisoning shortly before the electoral defeat of Venizelos. Constantine I was recalled, but he resigned after a few months in favor of his son, George II. Defeat by the Turks fuelled antiroyalist sentiment. A republican coup was staged against George II in 1923, and the ouster was later ratified by a plebiscite in April 1924.

The establishment of the second Greek republic brought little in the way of political stability (see table 30). Governments rose and fell in rapid succession. There was little difference in the programs of the political parties; they still represented the views of their respective leaders, views which often fluctuated between elections. The basic division continued to be between the republicans (Venizelists) and the antirepublicans (anti-Venizelists). The issue of Greek irredenta was replaced by the refugee problem.

The republicans were subdivided into conservative and radical groupings. Among the major conservative parties were the Venizelist Liberals (see Liberal Party) and the Republican Conservatives (see Democratic Coalition), the latter led by Andreas Michalacopoulos and George Kafandaris. The radical republican factions were made up of the Republican Union (*see* Democratic Coalition) of Alexander Papanastassiou and George Papandreou's Democratic Socialist Party (*see* Center Union). In 1936 these major republican groups (with the exception of the Venizelist Liberals) united to form the Democratic Coalition.

The antirepublicans or ex-royalists also contained moderate and extremist wings. Some progressive ex-royalists, such as the Reformist Party* and the Free Opinion Party,* accepted the republic. The more extreme groups, such as the National Radical Party* of General George Kondylis or the Popular Party (*see* Populist Party), showed little sympathy for the republican regime. Kondylis succeeded in uniting several royalist groups in 1936 in an electoral coalition known as the General Union of Populists and Radicals.* A number of minor groupings existed on both sides of the regime issue, but they were so small and personalist they could hardly be classified as political parties.

The Liberals began to decline in electoral strength in the early 1930s and royalist strength increased. In October 1935, a group of army officers under General Kondylis's leadership seized control of the government and abolished the republic. A November plebiscite approved the return of King George II to the throne. George II broke with Kondylis almost immediately, restored the 1911 constitution, and reestablished civilian rule. However, political passions were so high and rivalry so intense that no stable ministry could be formed. New elections were called.

Following elections in January 1936, again no governing coalition appeared possible. A brief caretaker government was formed under the leadership of Constantine Demertzis, but Demertzis died shortly after taking office. General John Metaxas, deputy prime minister and minister of war in the Demertzis cabinet, assumed power with a vote of confidence from the parliament. Under the pretext of an imminent communist coup, Metaxas persuaded King George II in August 1936 to dissolve parliament, ban all political parties, and institute a state of martial law. In 1938, Metaxas was designated prime minister for life.

Metaxas set about to transform Greece into an authoritarian regime along the lines of fascist Italy. He clamped down on political dissent and imprisoned both republicans and communists. However, many Greek politicians, including some communists, found it convenient to cooperate with the Metaxas regime. Metaxas survived the Italian invasion of Greece from Albania in October 1940, but his regime fell in April 1941 under the combined attack of German and Bulgarian forces. Greece was occupied by the Axis powers; and in 1941 an exile government, founded in Britain under Emmanuel Tsouderos, claimed to be the legitimate government of Greece during the war years.

From 1936 to 1944, Greece was without democratic institutions. Following the evacuation of German troops in Fall 1944, Greece came under the control of guerrilla resistance forces under the direction of the National Liberation Front and its military arm, the National Popular Liberation Army (*see* Communist Party of Greece-Exterior). By 1944 both resistance organizations had become communist-dominated and were receiving active support from Albania, Yugo-slavia, and Bulgaria (Greece's neighbors to the north). The royalist and republi-can forces were being aided by Britain and after 1947 by the United States.

In October 1944, George Papandreou, a prewar centrist leader (*see* Center Union), became the head of a national unity cabinet to govern Greece until regular elections could be held. A regency had been established under Arch-bishop Damaskinos. The members of the National Popular Liberation Army (ELAS) soon resigned from Papandreou's government, and civil war broke out between the ELAS and royalist-rightist forces. A partial truce was established in January 1945 under the terms of the Varkiza Accord, wherein the ruling centrist government promised free elections, civil rights, and an end to martial law. The ELAS in turn pledged to cease hostilities and surrender their arms.

A succession of six cabinets in 1945, coupled with low wages and rising prices, led to increasing discontent within Greece. The first postwar election was held in March 1946 (*see* table 31) under Allied supervision and was won by the right-wing Populist Party. A plebiscite was held in September in which Greeks (those who participated) voted by 68 percent to restore the monarchy of King George II. With George's death in 1947, the monarchy passed to his brother Paul, who remained on the throne until his death in 1964 when he was suc-ceeded by his son, Constantine II. The monarchy was abolished by the military junta in June 1973.

Greece was plunged once more into civil war during Fall 1946 when the communists launched a guerrilla campaign, claiming that the government had reneged on its promises made in the Varkiza Accord. The communist party was banned in 1947 as a political force in Greece, and a bitter struggle ensued. With British and American assistance, the communist insurgents were finally defeated in 1949. However, approximately 45,000 people perished in the civil war, leaving a deep scar on the Greek polity.

The first regular elections under peacetime conditions were held in March 1950. The political climate in Greece had changed considerably since the 1930s. Many of the old political leaders had vanished during the war years. New issues and new parties emerged, leading to a confusing collection of acronyms as parties formed, dissolved, or entered coalitions. In addition to the major prewar parties such as the Populist, Liberal, and Center groups, one also finds such minor groupings as the Greek Christian Socialist Party, the Orthodox Christian Party of Adherents to the Old Calendar, the Party of Greek Christians, and the Party of Greek Crusaders. Competition was keen since the parliament had been reduced from 354 to 250 seats.

The Populists held their strength with the most seats (62) in the parliament, but the electorate indicated a swing away from the old parties toward the center-left. The chief beneficiary of this trend was the National Progressive Center Union (EPEK, *see* Liberal Party) of Nicholas Plastiras and Emmanuel Tsouderos, winning 45 seats in 1950 and 74 in September 1951. The EPEK served as a balancing force among the many contending centrist groups.

In 1951 a new political party, known as the Greek Rally,* was formed by a veteran general, Alexander Papagos. The party was modelled in many ways after the Rally of the French People (see GAULLISTS, FRANCE) of General Charles de Gaulle. Although it attracted a variety of center and center-right groups, the Greek Rally's basic foundation was built on the remnants of the old right-wing Populist Party. The rally obtained just under half the seats (114 out of 250) in 1951. After a change in the electoral law to a majoritarian system, the Rally swept the field in November 1952 and secured 247 out of 300 seats. Papagos became prime minister; following his death in October 1955, he was succeeded by Constantine Karamanlis, who headed the Greek government until 1956 under the Greek Rally label.

The disintegration of the Greek Rally after Papagos's death left a political vacuum which was eventually filled by the National Radical Union (ERE)* formed by Karamanlis in 1956. The ERE won the election of February 1956, and Karamanlis was faced with the problem of dealing with the Cyprus issue (see CYPRUS). Karamanlis strengthened his position in the 1958 election, despite a sizable increase in support for the Greek political left. The United Democratic Left,* which served as a communist-front organization, increased its parliamentary strength from 18 in 1956 to 79 in 1958, becoming the second-largest parliamentary group.

The success of the ERE appeared to trigger a process of simplification and coalescence on the part of the center-left. In October 1961, George Papandreou formed the Center Union (EK), which secured 100 seats to the ERE's 176. Charges and countercharges over the propriety of the elections and a dispute with the palace led Karamanlis to resign in June 1963; and in the following election of November, the EK won a slim plurality. Although Papandreou became prime minister, he refused to cooperate with the left and resigned in December, necessitating new elections. In February 1964, the EK was quite successful, and once again Papandreou became prime minister.

Papandreou's identification with the Greek left, his actions in amnestying political prisoners, and his attempts to dissolve various right-wing organizations led to increasing suspiciousness on the part of the Greek right. In May 1965, Papandreou's son, Andreas, was linked to the ASPIDA Affair, in which a number of junior officers were implicated in a plot to take over the Greek military. King Constantine II refused Papandreou's request to dismiss the minister of defense and instead forced Papandreou's resignation.

Defections from the Center Union led to the formation of an EK government without Papandreou. The resulting government of Stephanos Stephanopoulos lasted until December 1966 when the National Radical Union withdrew its support . With tensions mounting among the military over the publicity and the trial of officers accused in the ASPIDA Affair, and with a worsening economic situation, a military coup took place in April 1967 before elections could be held. Parliament was dissolved and the constitution suspended. The new military government was headed by Colonel George Papadopoulos.

Almost at once, all left-wing organizations, including the communist-led United Democratic Left, were banned. An abortive attempt by King Constantine II to move against the junta in December 1967 led to his self-exile and the appointment of a regent. Further attempts to restore the king in May 1973 led the junta to abolish the monarchy and proclaim a republic in June 1973.

Growing economic problems due to Greece's isolation from the Western nations and the abortive coup engineered in Cyprus by the junta, followed by a Turkish invasion of that island (*see* CYPRUS), resulted in the disintegration of the military regime in July 1974. The third Greek republic began when the junta invited Karamanlis to form a transition government. The first elections were held in November 1974. In December, a plebiscite was held in which voters were asked to choose between a constitutional monarchy (with a return of King Constantine II) and a republic. Over 69 percent of the voters rejected the monarchy and opted for a republic.

The party system that emerged in Greece after seven years of military rule contained many of the prejunta parties, as well as a multitude of minor groups seeking to influence political life. Forty-six parties and 1,425 candidates participated in the first postjunta election in November 1974 (*see* table 32). However, the Greek party system also continued the trend toward simplification that had begun as early as 1951 when the Greek Rally had been formed. The result has been the development of a four-party coalition structure (*see* table 33) reflecting the political right (minor conservative and pro-royalist parties), the center-right (New Democracy*), the center (Center Union-New Forces [*see* Center Union]), and the left (Pan-Hellenic Socialist Movement* and United Left Alliance [of the Communist Party of Greece-Exterior]).

The 1974 election was an overwhelming victory for Karamanlis and his New Democracy party. The Center Union placed a distant second, followed by the Pan-Hellenic Socialist Movement (PASOK) and the United Left Alliance. The electoral trend suggests a shift away from militant conservative and pro-royalist parties toward the center and center-left. The center-right tradition has been continued with the formation of New Democracy by Karamanlis, an organization considerably more liberal than its predecessor of the 1960s.

Parliament was dissolved prematurely in October 1977 and new elections were held the next month. A new electoral law lowered the voting age to 20 and modified the system of proportional representation in favor of the smaller parties.

Karamanlis's New Democracy managed to retain its dominant position, followed by the PASOK as the chief opposition party. The Union of the Greek Democratic Center dropped to third place, followed by the Communist Party-Exterior. In May 1980, Karamanlis was elected president of the republic by the new parliament, and he resigned as leader of New Democracy. The new government was formed under his successor in the party, George Rallis, who pledged to follow a liberal, democratic program. The New Democracy government appeared to have achieved some success in moving Greece forward. It successfully consummated Greece's entry into the European Common Market (*see* EURO-

PEAN PARLIAMENT), returned Greece to the military wing of NATO, and engaged in discussions with Turkey over the future of Cyprus. However, the party was defeated by PASOK the following year.

The general elections held on October 18, 1981, resulted in the establishment of Greece's first socialist government. PASOK managed to control 174 seats in the new parliament compared to 113 for New Democracy, while the Communist Party-Exterior won 13 seats. The election was conducted under a complex system of proportional representation in which 288 seats were filled on the basis of 56 electoral districts and 12 from national party lists. Elections were also held simultaneously to fill Greece's 24 seats in the European Parliament. The results for this body were PASOK (10), New Democracy (8), Communist Party-Exterior (3), Communist Party-Interior (1), Progressive Party (1), and Democratic Unity (1). The latter grouping was an electoral alliance between the Agrarian Party* and the Party for Democratic Socialism.*

Under the constitution of 1975, the president is elected by parliament for a five-year term, and he shares both executive and legislative powers with the government and parliament respectively. The Greek parliament (*Vouli*) is composed of 300 members who serve for four years. Voting has been made compulsory and has been consistently high (over 80 percent). The current size of the Greek electorate is approximately 7.3 million.

Bibliography*

Campbell, J. S., and P. Sherrard. *Modern Greece.* New York: Praeger, 1968.

Dakin, Douglas. *The Unification of Greece, 1870-1923.* London: Ernest Benn, 1972.

Daphnes, Gregory. *He Hellas metaxy Dyo Polemon, 1923-1940.* 2 vols. Athens, Greece: Ikaros, 1955.

Forster, Edward S. *A Short History of Modern Greece, 1821-1940.* London: Methuen, 1941.

Kaltchas, Nicholas. *Introduction to the Constitutional History of Modern Greece.* New York: Columbia University Press, 1941.

Kitsikis, Dimitri. "Greece." In *International Guide to Electoral Statistics,* edited by Stein Rokkan and Jean Meyriat, pp. 163-182. The Hague: Mouton, 1969.

Korisis, Hariton. *Die politischen Partein Griechenlands.* Nuremburg: Karl Pfeiffer, 1966.

Kousoulos, D. G. *Modern Greece: Profile of a Nation.* New York: Scribners, 1974.

Legg, Keith. *Politics in Modern Greece.* Stanford, Calif.: Stanford University Press, 1969.

Penniman, Howard R., ed. *Greece at the Polls: 1974 and 1977.* Washington, D.C.: American Enterprise Institute, 1981.

Petropoulos, John Anthony. *Politics and Statecraft in the Kingdom of Greece, 1933 to 1943.* Princeton, N.J.: Princeton University Press, 1968.

Vatikiotis, P. S. *Greece: A Political Essay.* Beverly Hills, Calif.: Sage Publications, 1974.

Political Parties

ACHAIKON PARTY. *See* GREECE INTRODUCTION.

AGLIKO KOMMA. *See* GREECE INTRODUCTION.

---

*I wish to thank Professors D. George Kousoulas and Nikolaos A. Stavarou for their advice and assistance in the writing of this chapter.

AGRARIAN PARTY (*Agrotikon Komma*: AGROT). The designation "agrarian" has been used by several Greek parties, both leftist and rightist, since 1926. A loosely organized Agrarian Party, which had united various agrarian elements, functioned during the pre-World War II period. It reached its high point in representation in 1932 with 11 seats. In 1936 the Agrarians split into left and right factions. The left wing allied itself with various communist elements (*see* Communist Party of Greece-Exterior), while the right continued under the old designation. The latter's strength was in the rural areas of northern Greece, especially in Epirus, Thessaly, and Thrace.

The Agrarian Party reappeared in 1946 under the leadership of Alexander Baltadzis. The party contested several postwar elections either independently or in alliance with other groups before disappearing as an electoral force in the early 1960s. A short-lived New Agrarian Party was established in February 1957 by Parsanias Katsotas. Forming part of the Democratic Union (*see* Center Union) in 1958, the New Agrarians disappeared after the 1958 election. Most of the old Agrarian Party elements were also absorbed by the Center Union in 1961. A small Agrarian Party appeared in 1974 and became part of Democratic Unity (*see also* Party for Democratic Socialism) in 1981.

AGROT. *See* AGRARIAN PARTY.

AGROTIKON KOMMA. *See* AGRARIAN PARTY.

ALLIANCE OF PROGRESSIVE AND LEFT-WING FORCES (APLF). The APLF was an electoral coalition of various leftist elements formed in November 1977 to contest the parliamentary elections of that year. It was composed of the Communist Party of Greece-Interior,* Christian Democracy,* Socialist Course,* Socialist Initiative,* and United Democratic Left.* The coalition secured two seats, won by the Communists and the United Democratic Left.

The APLF ceased to exist by mid-1978, although it was not formally dissolved. The coalition was not reconstructed for the 1981 election.

APLF. *See* ALLIANCE OF PROGRESSIVE AND LEFT-WING FORCES.

ASPIDA. *See* GREECE INTRODUCTION and CENTER UNION.

BRITISH PARTY. *See* GREECE INTRODUCTION.

CENTER UNION (*Enosis Kendrou*: EK). The Center Union was established by George Papandreou in September 1961 following the collapse of the Liberal Party* after the 1958 election. Papandreou had had a long history of political activity, having founded the Democratic Socialist Party (*Demokratikon Sosialistikon Komma*: DSK) in 1935. One year later, he entered the DSK into an electoral alliance called the Democratic Coalition.* Following World War II, Papandreou's

Democratic Socialists joined with dissidents of the Liberal Party and others to form the National Political Union (see Liberal Party) in 1946. When that Union dissolved in 1947, the DSK resumed an independent existence. Papandreou renamed his group as the Party of George Papandreou (*Komma Georgiou Papandreou*: KGP) in 1950, and in 1952 he allied with the Greek Rally* of Alexander Papagos. Though Papandreou formally merged his KGP into the Liberal Party in 1953, he retained his own followers within the larger grouping. Hence, in 1956 the KGP elements allied with the United Democratic Left* to form a new coalition, one joined by the New Agrarian Party (see Agrarian Party) in 1958. This coalition was the Democratic Union (*Demokratiki Enosis*: DE), elements of which, under the leadership of Elias Tsirimokos, later joined Papandreou's Center Union in 1961. After intense conflicts with the Liberal Party leadership, Papandreou left that party in 1959 and formed the Liberal Democratic Party (*Phileleftheron Demokratikon Komma*: PDK), which in 1961 was renamed the Center Union.

The EK was designed to build a large centrist bloc around the personalist following of Papandreou. While the Center Union advocated a variety of educational, governmental, and economic reforms, its programs were vague and lacking in specificity, stressing only the general need to apply democracy to economic, political, and social problems. The party was supposed to have an elaborate, formal, organizational structure, including a congress to set policy and deal with organizational matters, and an executive committee presided over by the party leader. Neither functioned in reality, and the EK remained under the personal control of Papandreou.

The Center Union was the governing party of Greece from November 1963 to March 1965, when Papandreou was forced by the king to resign. Papandreou won the 1963 election largely through an ambitious campaign to attract the alienated voter: rural elements and the urban youth. Dissatisfaction had been growing in military and conservative circles with Papandreou's administration and his style of politics. The points in contention were Papandreou's previous association with the Greek political left, his attempts to reduce defense spending in favor of economic development programs, and the alleged involvement of his son, Andreas, in the ASPIDA Affair in 1965. The ASPIDA was alleged to be a secret military cabal under Andreas Papandreou's leadership that was plotting the installation of a military dictatorship similar to Nasser's Egypt. (Andreas Papandreou later established the Pan-Hellenic Socialist Movement.*)

George Papandreou declared his forced resignation to be unconstitutional, and he frustrated attempts by the king to form a Center Union government under different leadership. Many dissidents left the EK at this time, including those who later established the New Liberal Party (see Liberal Party) and the National Democratic Union.* A serious split in the EK occurred in Summer 1965 when Stephanos Stephanopoulos and others broke with the Center Union to form the Liberal Democratic Union (PDK) (see National Front). The PDK was composed of Center Union members who opposed Papandreou's leadership and who agreed to join Stephanopoulos in forming a new government. This PDK government lasted until late 1966. However, before new elections could take place in Spring 1967, a military coup occurred and all parties were suppressed.

The Center Union continued to function clandestinely under the military dictatorship, although many of its leaders, including George Papandreou, were either imprisoned or under house arrest. Following the restoration of civilian rule, the Center Union was reorganized in 1974 by George Mavros as the Center Union-New Forces (*Enosis Kendrou-Nees Dynameis*: EKND). The EKND joined with the New Political Forces (*Nees Politikes Dynameis*: NPD), which had formed earlier in 1974 to advocate a continuation of republican government, an independent foreign policy, and progress toward social democracy. The enlarged EKND received about 20 percent of the vote in the November 1974 election. In 1977, under the leadership of John G. Zighdis, the party was reorganized once again and renamed the Union of the Greek Democratic Center. *

CENTER UNION-NEW FORCES. *See* CENTER UNION.

CHRISTIAN DEMOCRACY. A small left-wing party, the Christian Democracy was formed in 1977 by Nikolaos Psaroudakis, editor of the newspaper *Christianiki*. The party had been highly critical of the military dictatorship. Its goal is to forge a basic left program with other elements in Greek society; as a result, the party was associated with the Alliance of Progressive and Left-Wing Forces* in 1977 but won no seats.

CIVILIAN PARTY. *See* GREECE INTRODUCTION.

COALITION OF NATIONALISTS. *See* UNITED FRONT OF NATIONALISTS.

COMMUNIST PARTY OF GREECE-EXTERIOR (*Kommunistiko Komma Ellados-Exoterikou*: KKEex). The KKEex was formed from elements of the Socialist Party of Greece (*Sosialistikon Komma Ellados*: SKE) in November 1918. The Socialists at that time were an extremely small group in Greek politics. The Communists first organized as the Socialist Workers' Party of Greece (*Sosialistikon Ergatikon Komma Ellados*: SEKE). The SEKE was recognized by the Comintern in 1920 and then changed its name to the Communist Party of Greece in 1924. The "Exterior" suffix was applied in the late 1960s (see below).

The KKE was of little significance in the 1920s. It was composed of about 2,500 members, mostly drawn from the middle classes. The party gradually became the spokesman for all the discontented elements in Greek society, and by the 1930s it had penetrated the industrial sectors. As a result, the Greek Communists played a role in pre-World War I elections until they were banned by the Metaxas government in 1936. The party's electoral behavior at that time was to form coalitions with other left groups and to operate without the Communist label (such as the United Front of Workers, Peasants, and Refugees in 1926; or the Popular Front in 1936).

The Greek Communist Party was an active force in organizing the resistance to the Axis invading forces in World War II. The KKE came to dominate the National Liberation Front (*Ethnikon Apelephtherotikon Metopon*: EAM) and its military arm, the National Popular Liberation Army (*Ethnikos Laikos Apelephtherikos Stratos*: ELAS), and eventually the party embarked on a civil war and was outlawed in 1947. The Communists continued their insurgency until they were defeated again in August 1949. At this time, some 100,000 KKE members fled the country, many of whom remained active in Greek Communist activities from abroad throughout the period of military rule. The KKE continued to promote its political interests during the 1951-1967 period through the United Democratic Left.*

After the advent of the military regime in 1967, a split developed over the issue of how to deal with the junta. Another point of conflict within the KKE was its unflagging support for the Soviet Union's foreign policy. A highly significant break occurred in 1968 when the Communist Party of Greece-Interior* was formed from KKE breakaway elements who rejected Soviet leadership of the world communist movement. The KKE-Interior called the other faction the KKE-Exterior. However, this latter group considers itself as the only communist party in Greece and keeps its title as simply the KKE. In 1980, following the Soviet invasion of Afghanistan, over 400 members left the KKEex in protest, although they did not immediately form a new political group.

Following legalization in 1974, the KKEex joined with the United Democratic Left and the Communist Party-Interior to form the United Left Alliance in the 1974 election, securing five seats. The KKEex contested the 1977 election independently of other leftist groups and increased its representation to 11 seats, and then to 13 in 1981.

The KKEex continues to be an ardent supporter of the Soviet Union. Also, the party's avowed goal is to establish a popular government in Greece free of United States imperialistic control. The KKEex publishes two daily papers, *Nea Ellada* and *Rizospastis*, and a monthly theoretical journal, *Kommunistiki Epitheorisi*.

Further Reference. Kousoulas, D. George, *Revolution and Defeat* (London: Oxford University Press, 1965).

COMMUNIST PARTY OF GREECE-INTERIOR (*Kommunistiko Komma Ellados-Esoterikou*: KKEes). The KKEes was formed in 1968 following the Soviet Union's invasion of Czechoslovakia. The party represents a dissident element from the Communist Party of Greece-Exterior* which refuses to recognize the Soviet Union as the leader of the world communist movement. In 1974, however, the KKEes joined its parent party and the United Democratic Left* to form the United Left Alliance, and the KKEes won two parliamentary seats. In 1977 the KKEes ran as part of the Alliance of Progressive and Left-Wing Forces* and obtained one of the two seats won by the coalition. The KKEes won no seats in 1981, however.

The first congress of the KKEes was held in June 1976. The party's basic orientation is Eurocommunism and a peaceful transition to Greek socialism, including a willingness to cooperate with all democratic forces in Greek society. The KKEes policy platform calls for nationalization of key industries, energy supplies, financial institutions, and public transportation, although not without reasonable compensation. The party also supported Greece's entry into the European Common Market (*see* EUROPEAN PARLIAMENT).

The present leader of the KKEes is Haralambos Drakopoulos. The party publishes a daily newspaper, *Avgi*, with a circulation of approximately 10,000.

COTZAMANIS KOMMA. *See* REFORMIST PARTY.

COTZAMANIS PARTY. *See* REFORMIST PARTY.

DE. *See* CENTER UNION and UNITED DEMOCRATIC LEFT.

DELIGIORGIS PARTY. *See* GREECE INTRODUCTION.

DELIGIANNIS PARTY. *See* GREECE INTRODUCTION.

DEMOCRATIC COALITION (*Demokratikos Sinaspismos*: DS). The Democratic Coalition was formed to contest the January 1936 parliamentary election. It merged together three republican parties: the Republican Union (of Alexander Papanastassiou), the Republican Conservatives or Moderate Republican Party (of George Kafandaris), and the Democratic Socialist Party (of George Papandreou, *see* Center Union). The DS won seven seats in 1936 but was dissolved with the Metaxas ban on parties in August 1936 (*see* Greece introduction).

DEMOCRATIC FRONT. *See* UNITED DEMOCRATIC LEFT.

DEMOCRATIC PARTY OF WORKING PEOPLE. *See* UNITED DEMOCRATIC LEFT.

DEMOCRATIC SOCIALIST PARTY. *See* CENTER UNION.

DEMOCRATIC UNION. *See* CENTER UNION and UNITED DEMOCRATIC LEFT.

DEMOCRATIC UNITY. *See* PARTY FOR DEMOCRATIC SOCIALISM.

DEMOKRATIKI ENOSIS. *See* CENTER UNION and UNITED DEMOCRATIC LEFT.

DEMOKRATIKI PARATAKSIS. *See* UNITED DEMOCRATIC LEFT.

DEMOKRATIKON KOMMA ERGAZOMENOU LAOU. *See* UNITED DEM-
OCRATIC LEFT.

DEMOKRATIKON SOSIALISTIKON KOMMA. *See* CENTER UNION.

DEMOKRATIKOS SINASPISMOS. *See* DEMOCRATIC COALITION.

DKEL. *See* UNITED DEMOCRATIC LEFT.

DP. *See* UNITED DEMOCRATIC LEFT.

DS. *See* DEMOCRATIC COALITION.

DSK. *See* CENTER UNION.

EAK. *See* UNITED DEMOCRATIC LEFT.

EAM. *See* COMMUNIST PARTY OF GREECE-EXTERIOR.

EDA. *See* UNITED DEMOCRATIC LEFT.

EDE. *See* NATIONAL DEMOCRATIC UNION.

EDES. *See* NATIONAL PARTY OF GREECE.

EDHK. *See* UNION OF THE GREEK DEMOCRATIC CENTER.

EE. *See* NATIONAL UNITY PARTY.

EEE. *See* GREEK FASCISM.

EF. *See* FREE OPINION PARTY.

EK. *See* CENTER UNION.

EKE. *See* NATIONAL PARTY OF GREECE.

EKKE. *See* REVOLUTIONARY COMMUNIST PARTY OF GREECE.

EKND. *See* CENTER UNION.

ELAS. *See* COMMUNIST PARTY OF GREECE-EXTERIOR.

ELD. *See* UNITED DEMOCRATIC PARTY.

ELEFTHEROFRONON. *See* FREE OPINION PARTY.

ELK. *See* POPULIST PARTY.

ELLINIKOS SYNAGERMOS. *See* GREEK RALLY.

EM. *See* NATIONAL FRONT.

ENIAIA DEMOKRATIKI ARISTERA. *See* UNITED DEMOCRATIC LEFT.

ENOSE DEMOKRATIKOU HELLINIKOU KENDROU. *See* UNION OF THE GREEK DEMOCRATIC CENTER.

ENOSIS KENDROU. *See* CENTER UNION.

ENOSIS KENDROU-NEES DYNAMEIS. *See* CENTER UNION.

ENOSIS LAIKOU KOMMATOS. *See* NATIONAL FRONT and POPULIST PARTY.

EPANASTATIKO KOMMUNISTIKO KOMMA ELLADOS. *See* REVOLUTIONARY COMMUNIST PARTY OF GREECE.

EPE. *See* LIBERAL PARTY.

EPEK. *See* LIBERAL PARTY.

EPEL. *See* FREE OPINION PARTY.

EPK. *See* LIBERAL PARTY.

ERE. *See* NATIONAL RADICAL UNION.

ERK. *See* NATIONAL RADICAL PARTY.

ES. *See* GREEK RALLY.

ETHNIKI DEMOKRATIKI ENOSIS. *See* NATIONAL DEMOCRATIC UNION.

ETHNIKI ENOSIS. *See* NATIONAL UNITY PARTY.

ETHNIKI PARATAKSIS ERGAZOMENOU LAOU. *See* FREE OPINION PARTY.

ETHNIKI POLITIKI ENOSIS. *See* LIBERAL PARTY.

ETHNIKI PROODEFTIKI ENOSIS KENDROU. *See* LIBERAL PARTY.

ETHNIKI RIZOSPASTIKI ENOSIS. *See* NATIONAL RADICAL UNION.

ETHNIKO LAIKO KOMMA. *See* POPULIST PARTY.

ETHNIKON AGROTIKON KOMMA. *See* UNITED DEMOCRATIC LEFT.

ETHNIKON AGROTIKON KOMMA XITON. *See* "X" NATIONAL RESISTANCE PARTY.

ETHNIKON APELEPHTHEROTIKON METOPON. *See* COMMUNIST PARTY OF GREECE-EXTERIOR.

ETHNIKON KOMMA ELLADOS. *See* NATIONAL PARTY OF GREECE.

ETHNIKON METOPON. *See* NATIONAL FRONT.

ETHNIKON PHILELEFTHERON KOMMA. *See* LIBERAL PARTY.

ETHNIKO RIZOSPASTIKO KOMMA. *See* NATIONAL RADICAL PARTY.

ETHNIKOS DEMOKRATIKOS ELLINIKOS STRATOS. *See* NATIONAL PARTY OF GREECE.

ETHNIKOS LAIKOS APELEPHTHEROTIKOS STRATOS. *See* COMMUNIST PARTY OF GREECE-EXTERIOR.

FREE OPINION PARTY (*Eleftherofronon:* EF). The Free Opinion Party or Free Thinkers' Party was established by General John Metaxas in the 1920s. It developed into a right-wing personalist following by 1936 when Metaxas formed the government. The party's orientation was moderate royalist and anti-Venizelist (*see* Greece introduction). Elements of the EF reappeared in 1950 as a coalition of small personalist parties of the political right known as the National Front of Working People (*Ethniki Parataksis Ergazomenou Laou:* EPEL), which unsuccessfully contested the 1950 election.

FREE THINKERS' PARTY. *See* FREE OPINION PARTY.

FRENCH PARTY. *See* GREECE INTRODUCTION.

GALIKO KOMMA. *See* GREECE INTRODUCTION.

GENERAL UNION OF POPULISTS AND RADICALS (*Geniki Laiki Rizospastiki Enosis*: GLRE). Formed in 1936, the GLRE was an electoral coalition composed of the National Radical Party* of George Kondylis and elements of the Populist Party* led by John Theotokis. A number of independents such as John Rallis also adhered to the coalition. The GLRE secured 60 seats in the 1936 parliament and was royalist in orientation, but it was dissolved under the Metaxas ban on parties in August 1936.

GENIKI LAIKI RIZOSPASTIKI ENOSIS. *See* GENERAL UNION OF POPULISTS AND RADICALS.

GLRE. *See* GENERAL UNION OF POPULISTS AND RADICALS.

GOUNARIS KOMMA. *See* POPULIST PARTY.

GOUNARIST PARTY. *See* POPULIST PARTY.

GREEK CHRISTIAN SOCIALIST PARTY. *See* GREECE INTRODUCTION.

GREEK FASCISM. The fascist movement, as manifested by mass political movements, did not appear in Greece until after World War II. Political life in Greece in the 1920s and 1930s was dominated by the cleavage between republicans and monarchists, and also by the refugee problem. Four fascist organizations of the interwar period, however, are worth noting. The Nationalist Union of Greece (EEE) was a paramilitary organization with a base in Salonika. It was anticommunist and anti-Semitic in orientation. The EEE attempted to transform itself into a political party in 1933 but eventually disintegrated through numerous splits.

A Greek National Socialist Party was formed in 1932 in Athens by George Merkouris, composed of ex-servicemen and largely royalist in orientation. It had little influence on Greek politics. Other organizations, such as the National Socialist Party of Macedonia and the Pan-Hellenic National Front, were extremely minor groupings with little organizational structure and of no political importance.

GREEK NATIONAL SOCIALIST PARTY. *See* GREEK FASCISM.

GREEK RALLY (*Ellinikos Synagermos*: ES). The Greek Rally was created in August 1951 by Field Marshall Alexander Papagos following his resignation from the Greek army. The ES, formed by remnants of the old Populist Party,* was joined by the New Party (*see* Progressive Party) of Spyros Markezinis and the Populist Union Party (*see* National Front) of Stephanos Stephanopoulos. The Greek Rally won the election in 1951 with 114 seats and in 1952 with 247 seats. It dissolved in 1955 following the death of Papagos, and the ES's parliamentary delegation under the leadership of Constantine Karamanlis formed part of the National Radical Union* in 1956.

HPE. *See* UNITED FRONT OF NATIONALISTS.

INDEPENDENT POLITICAL FRONT (*Politiki Aneksartitos Parataksis*: PAP). Formed in 1950, the PAP was an electoral alliance of various right-wing personalist elements. The PAP was headed by Theodore Tourkovassiles, Constantine Kotzias, and Constantine Maniadakis. Maniadakis had been an official in the Metaxas regime (*see* Greece introduction). The PAP won 16 seats in the 1950 election.

INOMENI ETHNIKI PARATAKSI. *See* UNITED FRONT OF NATIONALISTS.

KOMMA XITON ETHNIKIS ANTISTASSEOS. *See* "X" NATIONAL RESISTANCE PARTY.

KOMMUNISTIKO KOMMA ELLADOS-ESOTERIKOU. *See* COMMUNIST PARTY OF GREECE-INTERIOR.

KOMMUNISTIKO KOMMA ELLADOS-EXOTERIKOU. *See* COMMUNIST PARTY OF GREECE-EXTERIOR.

KOUMOUNDOUROS PARTY. *See* GREECE INTRODUCTION.

KP. *See* PROGRESSIVE PARTY.

LAIKO ENOTIKO KOMMA. *See* NATIONAL FRONT.

LAIKO KOMMA. *See* POPULIST PARTY.

LEFT LIBERALS. *See* UNITED DEMOCRATIC LEFT.

LEK. *See* NATIONAL FRONT.

LIBERAL DEMOCRATIC PARTY. *See* CENTER UNION.

LIBERAL DEMOCRATIC UNION. *See* NATIONAL FRONT.

LIBERAL PARTY (*Phileleftheron Komma*: PK). The Liberal Party was founded by Eleftherios Venizelos on November 26, 1910. The PK was originally designed to be a modern political party representing the first centrist coalition in Greek politics. However, it soon became a personalist vehicle for Venizelos. The party's mass base was on the island of Crete, home of Venizelos. The PK represented the emergent middle-class elements in Greek society and in the 1920s also received substantial support from the refugee community.

Conflict over Greek foreign policy during World War I, particularly the issue of Greek neutrality, led the Liberals (*Phileleftheri*) to oppose the monarchy and created an issue which was to be the major cleavage in Greek politics during the 1920s and 1930s. Although the Liberals remained the dominant political group in the pre-World War II period, their base of support began to shift in the 1930s as the refugee groups transferred their allegiance to the parties of the political left. Also, Venizelos died in exile in Paris in 1936. Ultimately, the PK was subjected to a number of splits in the period before 1940—a tendency that eventually led to the party's decline after 1945.

In 1946 two major splits occurred in the Liberal Party. Sophocles Venizelos (son of Eleftherios Venizelos) broke away from the main party to form the Venizelist Liberal Party (*Venizelikon Phileleftheron Komma*: VenPK). It constituted part of the National Political Union (*Ethniki Politiki Enosis*: EPE) with the Democratic Socialist Party (*see* Center Union) of George Papandreou, the National Unity Party* of Panayotis Kanellopoulos, the National Party of Greece* of Napoleon Zervas, and several other smaller groups. The VenPK returned to the parent Liberal Party in 1947. Also in 1946, another Liberal fragment, under the leadership of Stulianos Gonatas, left the PK to form the National Liberal Party (*Ethnikon Phileleftheron Komma*: EPK). The EPK then joined the United Front of Nationalists,* which won 206 seats in the 1946 election. When the United Front broke up, Gonatas returned the EPK to the Liberal Party in 1950.

A Liberal coalition was created in 1949 to contest the 1950 and 1951 elections. Under the direction of General Nicholas Plastiras and Emmanuel Tsouderos, this coalition was known as the National Progressive Center Union (*Ethniki Proodeftiki Enosis Kendrou*: EPEK), winning 45 seats in 1950 and 74 seats in 1951. The EPEK, along with other Liberal Party elements, allied with the Greek Rally* in 1951. An independent EPEK movement was founded in 1953 by John Zighdis and Demetrios Papaspyrou. Ultimately, the original EPEK became part of the Center Union* in 1961.

By 1958 the Liberals were losing coherency. Leadership conflicts between Sophocles Venizelos, George Papandreou, and others who sought to control the Liberal organizations ultimately fragmented the PK. Papandreou, who had merged his Party of George Papandreou (*see* Center Union) with the Liberals in 1953, left the PK to form the Liberal Democratic Party (*see* Center Union) in 1959. In November 1960, several Liberal Party deputies joined the National Rejuvenation Movement (*see* "X" National Resistance Party) of General George Grivas, although the latter grouping disintegrated the following year.

In September 1961, the remnants of the Liberal Party were amalgamated by Papandreou into a new political organization called the Center Union. This group eventually won the elections of 1963 and 1964 before being suppressed by the military junta. Papandreou's party reappeared as the Center Union-New Forces (see Center Union) in 1974, and later as the Union of the Greek Democratic Center* in 1977.

A New Liberal Party (Neophileleftheroi) was formed in September 1977 by Konstantinos Mitsotakis, a former conservative Center Union minister who had rejected the leadership of George Papandreou in 1965. Mitsotakis had stood as an independent Liberal in 1974 but failed to be elected. The New Liberal Party was dissolved in May 1978 when Mitsotakis accepted a cabinet post as minister of coordination and planning. The dissolved party merged into New Democracy.*

LK. See POPULIST PARTY.

MAVROKORDATISTS. See GREECE INTRODUCTION.

MEA. See NATIONAL UNITY PARTY.

METARRITHMISTIKON KOMMA. See REFORMIST PARTY.

METOPON ETHNIKIS ANADIMIOURGIAS. See NATIONAL UNITY PARTY.

MILITARY LEAGUE. See GREECE INTRODUCTION.

MK. See REFORMIST PARTY.

MODERATE REPUBLICAN PARTY. See DEMOCRATIC COALITION.

NAK. See UNITED DEMOCRATIC LEFT.

NATIONAL AGRARIAN PARTY. See UNITED DEMOCRATIC LEFT.

NATIONAL AGRARIAN PARTY "X". See "X" NATIONAL RESISTANCE PARTY.

NATIONAL DEMOCRATIC GREEK ARMY. See NATIONAL PARTY OF GREECE.

NATIONAL DEMOCRATIC UNION (Ethniki Demokratiki Enosis: EDE). The EDE was formed in October 1974 by Petros Garofilias, a Center Union* notable who had served as minister of defense in George Papandreou's cabinet in 1965. Garofilias supported King Constantine's demand for an investigation of Papandreou's son, Andreas, as to his involvement in the ASPIDA Affair (see Center Union), a scandal that eventually led to the downfall of the Papandreou government.

Garofilias stayed outside of the New Democracy* government of Constantine Karamanlis. The EDE failed to secure any seats in parliament in 1974 and 1977. The EDE presented itself as a right-wing party, royalist in orientation, and advocating a renewal of Greece's military position within the NATO alliance.

NATIONAL FRONT (Ethnikon Metopon: EM). The National Front was organized in October 1977 by Stephanos Stephanopoulos, who had been prime minister of Greece during 1965-1966. Stephanopoulos had a long political history prior to 1977. Originally a member of the Populist Party,* in January 1951 Stephanopoulos led 26 other Populist dissidents in merging with the small National Regeneration Front (see National Unity Party) to form the Populist Union Party (Laiko Enotiko Komma: LEK), which became part of the Greek Rally* later that same year. When the Greek Rally dissolved in 1955, Stephanopoulos was temporarily reunited with the old Populist Party when those elements reorganized the Greek Rally as the National Radical Union* in 1956. To contest the 1958 parliamentary election, however, Stephanopoulos and other Populist elements split from the National Radical Union and established the small and conservative Union of Populist Parties (Enosis Laikou Kommatos: ELK), which won only two seats. As the ELK began to disintegrate, Stephanopoulos joined the Center Union* in 1961. In a December 1965 dispute with Center Union leader George Papandreou, Stephanopoulos left that grouping and formed the Liberal Democratic Union (Phileleftheron Demokratikon Kendron: PDK). The PDK, composed of Center Union elements opposed to Papandreou's 1963-1965 leadership of the Greek government, presided over the country from the end of 1965 to December 1966, with Stephanopoulos as prime minister. Initially assisted by both the National Radical Union and the Progressive Party,* the PDK government ended with the loss of National Radical support. Before new elections could take place in Spring 1967, a military coup occurred and all parties were suppressed.

Stephanopoulos formed the National Front in order to contest the 1977 elections after Greece's return to civilian rule. He portrayed his new party as a conservative alternative to New Democracy* (the reorganized National Radical Union) of Constantine Karamanlis. Stephanopoulos advocated a renewed military role for Greece in NATO, as well as the release of certain political leaders imprisoned during the period of military rule. He also advocated a restoration of the monarchy. The National Front secured five seats in 1977 but won no seats in 1981.

NATIONAL FRONT OF WORKING PEOPLE. See FREE OPINION PARTY.

NATIONALIST UNION OF GREECE. See GREEK FASCISM.

NATIONAL LIBERAL PARTY. See LIBERAL PARTY.

NATIONAL LIBERATION FRONT. *See* COMMUNIST PARTY OF GREECE-EXTERIOR.

NATIONAL PARTY OF GREECE (*Ethnikon Komma Ellados*: EKE). Established in 1946 as a regional political movement in Epirus, the EKE was formed by General Napoleon Zervas based on his guerrilla resistance organization during World War II, the National Democratic Greek Army (*Ethnikos Demokratikos Ellinikos Stratos*: EDES). The EKE, royalist in orientation, participated in the 1946 parliamentary election as part of the National Political Union (*see* Liberal Party*). The EKE was dissolved after the 1950 election, with the majority of its supporters moving to various centrist groups.

NATIONAL POLITICAL UNION. *See* LIBERAL PARTY.

NATIONAL POPULAR LIBERATION ARMY. *See* COMMUNIST PARTY OF GREECE-EXTERIOR.

NATIONAL POPULIST PARTY. *See* POPULIST PARTY.

NATIONAL PROGRESSIVE CENTER UNION. *See* LIBERAL PARTY.

NATIONAL RADICAL PARTY (*Ethniko Rizospastiko Komma*: ERK). Under the leadership of George Kondylis, the National Radical Party emerged in 1932 as a royalist party. The ERK won six parliamentary seats in 1932, 11 in 1933, and 33 in 1935. In 1936 the ERK merged with a faction of the Populist Party to form the General Union of Populists and Radicals,* which won 60 seats to the January 1936 parliament but was then dissolved with the Metaxas ban on political parties.

NATIONAL RADICAL UNION (*Ethniki Rizospastiki Enosis*: ERE). The ERE was founded in January 1956 from conservative elements that had been part of the dissolved Greek Rally* and the old Populist Party.* Similar to the Center Union,* the ERE contained several formal party organs, including a general assembly and a general council to formulate party policy; the party, however, remained under the personal direction of its leader, Constantine Karamanlis, who had been a notable in the Greek Rally and had headed the Greek government from October 1955 to February 1956 under the Greek Rally label.

The ERE won the 1956 election and functioned as the ruling party in Greece for seven years. The Union attracted many centrist elements, even though it was basically a conservative organization that supported free enterprise, wage controls, and restrictions on the organized labor movement.

In 1963 the ERE was narrowly defeated, and Karamanlis announced his retirement from politics. Panayotis Kanellopoulos of the old National Unity Party* was appointed successor as the ERE leader. Karamanlis emerged from retirement, however, and reorganized the ERE in September 1974 as a new political party, the New Democracy.* Under his new party label, Karamanlis was elected president of the republic in May 1980.

NATIONAL REGENERATION FRONT. See NATIONAL UNITY PARTY.

NATIONAL SOCIALIST PARTY OF MACEDONIA. See GREEK FASCISM.

NATIONAL UNION PARTY. See NATIONAL UNITY PARTY.

NATIONAL UNITY PARTY (*Ethniki Enosis*: EE). The National Unity Party (also known as the National Union Party) was a small personalist grouping founded by Panayotis Kanellopoulos in 1936. It was based on his following at the University of Athens. The party reappeared in 1946 and contested the election as part of the National Political Union (*see* Liberal Party). In 1950 the EE became the National Regeneration Front (*Metopon Ethnikis Adadimiourgias*: MEA) and secured seven seats in the election of that year. Kanellopoulos joined the short-lived Populist Union Party (*see* National Front) in January 1951 with 27 dissident Populist Party* members led by Stephanos Stephanopoulos. The Populist Union Party dissolved in Summer 1951 to join the Greek Rally.*

In 1956, Kanellopoulos supported the National Radical Union* of Constantine Karamanlis (newly formed from remnants of the Greek Rally), but in 1958 Kanellopoulos constituted part of another Stephanopoulos grouping, the Union of Populist Parties (*see* National Front). Kanellopoulos then continued to adhere to the National Radical Union, and following the 1963 election he became its leader. Kanellopoulos held this post until Karamanlis reorganized the party in 1974 as the New Democracy.*

ND. See NEW DEMOCRACY.

NEA DEMOKRATIA. See NEW DEMOCRACY.

NEES POLITIKES DYNAMEIS. See CENTER UNION.

NEOKOSMOS GRIGORIADES. See UNITED DEMOCRATIC LEFT.

NEON KOMMA. See PROGRESSIVE PARTY.

NEOPHILELEFTHEROI. See LIBERAL PARTY.

NEW AGRARIAN MOVEMENT. See UNITED DEMOCRATIC LEFT.

NEW AGRARIAN PARTY. See AGRARIAN PARTY.

NEW DEMOCRACY (*Nea Demokratia*: ND). New Democracy was founded in September 1974 by Constantine Karamanlis as a successor organization to his National Radical Union* of the 1960s. The new party appeared to be more liberal than the old grouping, largely because it had absorbed many centrist elements. The ND defined its ideological stance as radical liberalism—a position between traditional liberalism and democratic socialism.

New Democracy succeeded in becoming the governing party of Greece following the end of military rule. The ND won 220 out of 300 seats in 1974, though its representation dropped to 172 seats in the election of 1977 and to 113 in 1981. The party had declared its adherence to six basic principles: (1) belief in the concept of nation that supersedes political notions of the left, center, and right; (2) a commitment to parliamentary democracy; (3) social justice; (4) free-market economy with state regulation where appropriate; (5) international alignment with the Western nations; and (6) strong support of education and the development of youth.

Karamanlis was elected president of the republic in May 1980. His successor as party leader was George Rallis, who had served as foreign minister in the Karamanlis cabinet.

NEW LIBERAL PARTY. *See* LIBERAL PARTY.

NEW PARTY. *See* PROGRESSIVE PARTY.

NEW POLITICAL FORCES. *See* CENTER UNION.

NK. *See* PROGRESSIVE PARTY.

NPD. *See* CENTER UNION.

ORTHODOX CHRISTIAN PARTY OF ADHERENTS TO THE OLD CAL-ENDAR. *See* GREECE INTRODUCTION.

PAME. *See* UNITED DEMOCRATIC LEFT.

PAN-DEMOCRATIC AGRARIAN FRONT OF GREECE. *See* UNITED DEM-OCRATIC LEFT.

PANDEMOKRATIKI AGROTIKON METOPON ELLADOS. *See* UNITED DEMOCRATIC LEFT.

PANELLINION SOSIALISTIKON KINEMA. *See* PAN-HELLENIC SOCIAL-IST MOVEMENT.

PAN-HELLENIC NATIONAL FRONT. *See* GREEK FASCISM.

PAN-HELLENIC NATIONAL PARTY. *See* UNITED FRONT OF NATION-ALISTS.

PAN-HELLENIC SOCIALIST MOVEMENT (*Panellinion Sosialistikon Kinema*: PASOK). The PASOK was founded in 1974 by Andreas Papandreou, son of former premier George Papandreou (*see* Center Union). Although it secured only 12 seats in the 1974 parliamentary election, the PASOK increased its representation to 93 seats in 1977, becoming the chief opposition party to Constantine Karamanlis's New Democracy.* In 1981 the PASOK won an absolute majority (174 out of 300 seats) and formed the new government, with Andreas Papandreou as prime minister.

In foreign policy, the PASOK strongly supports Greek independence and has opposed Greece's entry into the European Common Market (*see* EUROPEAN PARLIAMENT). The party desires a socialist transformation of Greek society under a system of decentralization and self-management. It has refused to join any electoral alliances in order to maintain its independence of action, a stand that resulted in a PASOK splinter that formed the Socialist Course* grouping in 1975.

The PASOK has an elaborate organizational structure with local secretariats, a central coordinating committee, and various specialized commissions. The party publishes a weekly newspaper, *Exormisi*, and its membership is estimated to be approximately 40,000.

PAP. *See* INDEPENDENT POLITICAL FRONT.

PARTY FOR DEMOCRATIC SOCIALISM (*Komma Demokratikou Sosialismou*: KDS). The KDS was founded in March 1979 by Ioannis Pesmazoglou, a dissident from the Union of the Greek Democratic Center (EDHK).* Pesmazoglou had been elected in 1974 as part of the Center Union-New Forces (*see* Center Union) and in 1977 as a member of the EDHK. He was expelled from the latter grouping in March 1978 for advocating socialist policies in conflict with the EDHK leadership.

The KDS had four seats in the parliament after its founding, based on defections from other parties. The KDS's policies were similar to those of the social-democratic movement in western Europe. The KDS supported Greece's entry into the European Common Market (*see* EUROPEAN PARLIAMENT) and continued political participation in NATO, although the party was opposed to the continuation of a United States military presence in Greece. In 1981, the KDS formed an electoral alliance with the small Agrarian Party.* This alliance, Democratic Unity, won no seats in the Greek parliament but did win one seat in the European Parliament.

PARTY OF GEORGE PAPANDREOU. *See* CENTER UNION.

PARTY OF GREEK CHRISTIANS. See GREECE INTRODUCTION.

PARTY OF GREEK CRUSADERS. See GREECE INTRODUCTION.

PASOK. See PAN-HELLENIC SOCIALIST MOVEMENT.

PDK. See CENTER UNION and NATIONAL FRONT.

PHILELEFTHERON DEMOKRATIKON KENDRON. See NATIONAL FRONT.

PHILELEFTHERON DEMOKRATIKON KOMMA. See CENTER UNION.

PHILELEFTHERON KOMMA. See LIBERAL PARTY.

PK. See LIBERAL PARTY.

POLITIKI ANEKSARTITOS PARATAKSIS. See INDEPENDENT POLITICAL FRONT.

POPULAR FRONT. See COMMUNIST PARTY OF GREECE-EXTERIOR.

POPULAR PARTY. See POPULIST PARTY.

POPULIST PARTY (*Laiko Komma*: LK). The Populist Party or Popular Party developed out of various right-wing personalist groups that were active in the latter part of the 19th century. The grouping was formerly known as the Gounarist Party (*Gounaris Komma*), having developed out of the personal following of Demetrios Gounaris (1866-1922), leader of a royalist faction in Greek politics. The Populists began to coalesce into a cohesive political organization in the 1920s and eventually became a major political force in pre-World War II Greece. The Populists were extreme antirepublicans and anti-Venizelist Liberals (*see* Liberal Party and Greece introduction). The LK reached its peak in 1935 with 254 (out of 300) seats in parliament, and then the party began to split apart over personal and policy differences.

One group of Populists under P. Tsaldaris joined with the National Radical Party* and others to form the General Union of Populists and Radicals* in 1936. In the 1946 election, the main body of Populists under Constantine Tsaldaris joined the United Front of Nationalists.* In January 1951, dissident Populists under Stephanos Stephanopoulos merged with the National Regeneration Front (*see* National Unity Party) of Panayotis Kanellopoulos to form the Populist Union Party (*see* National Front). In August of that same year, this grouping, along with the remnants of the parent Populist Party, formed the main body of the Greek Rally*; and with the disintegration of this group in 1955, the

loosely reunited Populists became the foundation of the National Radical Union*
in 1956. A splinter group of Populist elements led by C. Tsaldaris, Stephanopoulos,
and Kanellopoulos split from the National Radical Union and formed the Union
of Populist Parties (*Enosis Laikou Kommatos*: ELK) in 1958, but this alliance
soon broke apart after winning only two seats to parliament in the election of
that year. Tsaldaris and Kanellopoulos rejoined the National Radical Union,
while Stephanopoulos joined the Center Union* in 1961. Both of these latter
parties would become ruling forces in Greece during the late 1950s and early
1960s.

The old Populist Party had thus dispersed by the late 1950s, though some
remnants emerged in the National Radical Union's 1974 successor, the New
Democracy.* In November 1976, a new group called the National Populist Party
(*Ethniko Laiko Komma*: ELK) was formed under the direction of General George
Kouroukeis. It was an extreme right-wing party, calling for a return of the
monarchy and continued restrictions on the activities of the Greek political left.
This ELK failed to achieve representation in the 1977 election and died out
shortly thereafter.

POPULIST UNION PARTY. *See* NATIONAL FRONT.

PROGRESSIVE PARTY (*Komma Proodeftikon*: KP). The Progressive Party was
founded in 1955 by Spyros Markezinis following his departure from the dissolved
Greek Rally.* The KP constituted a right-wing personalist group of Markezinis's
supporters who had been active in his previous organization, the New Party
(*Neon Komma*: NK), which had been formed in 1950. The KP's initial existence
was rather short, and Markezinis was allied with the Center Union* in 1961 and
the National Radical Union* in 1964.

Markezinis revived the Progressive Party in November 1979. He had served as
prime minister in 1973 during the last year of the military junta. The first
postjunta election of November 1974 brought victory for Constantine Karamanlis
and his New Democracy* party. Markezinis opposed Karamanlis's government
for its position on NATO and for allegedly pursuing a variety of quasi-socialist
measures domestically.

The Progressive Party advocates a free-market system with a minimum of state
interference in the economy. It does not, however, support a return of the
monarchy. In 1981, it won one seat in the European Parliament.

REFORMIST PARTY (*Metarrithmistikon Komma*: MK). As a splinter from the
Populist Party,* the Reformist Party was created in Macedonia in 1936 by
Soltiros Cotzamanis. The MK was also sometimes known as the old Stratos Party
(*Stratos Komma*) or the Cotzamanis Party (*Cotzamanis Komma*). The Reformists
were ex-royalists who indicated some support for the republic. The MK reappeared briefly after World War II to join the United Front of Nationalists* in
1946, after which the MK disappeared.

REPUBLICAN CONSERVATIVES. *See* DEMOCRATIC COALITION.

REPUBLICAN UNION. *See* DEMOCRATIC COALITION.

REVOLUTIONARY COMMUNIST PARTY OF GREECE (*Epanastatiko Kommunistiko Komma Ellados*: EKKE). The EKKE was a pro-maoist grouping that emerged in 1974 following the collapse of the military junta and the legalization of the political left. The party contested the 1974 and 1977 elections with little success, receiving approximately .02 percent of the vote each time.

ROSSIKO KOMMA. *See* GREECE INTRODUCTION.

ROUFOS PARTY. *See* GREECE INTRODUCTION.

RUSSIAN PARTY. *See* GREECE INTRODUCTION.

SEKE. *See* COMMUNIST PARTY OF GREECE-EXTERIOR.

SKE. *See* COMMUNIST PARTY OF GREECE-EXTERIOR.

SOCIALIST COURSE (*Sosialistiki Poria*). The Socialist Course, also known as the Socialist Way or the Social Progress Party, was formed in 1975 by marxist-oriented dissidents from the Pan-Hellenic Socialist Movement (PASOK).* These dissidents were opposed to the PASOK's policy of no electoral alliances, and instead they favored a broad electoral coalition of the noncommunist left. The Socialist Course formed part of the Alliance of Progressive and Left-Wing Forces* in 1977.

SOCIALIST INITIATIVE (*Sosialistiki Protovoulia*). Hoping to become the nucleus of a new Greek social-democratic party, the founders of the Socialist Initiative were leftist dissidents of the Union of the Greek Democratic Center* who left that party in 1976 and urged a more radical stance on economic policy. Two of the Socialist Initiative leaders, George-Alexander Mangakis and Haralambos Protopapas, had been part of the government of Constantine Karamanlis (*see* New Democracy) which had been appointed in July 1974 as a transition between military and civilian rule. The Socialist Initiative formed part of the Alliance of Progressive and Left-Wing Forces* in 1977.

SOCIALIST PARTY. *See* UNITED DEMOCRATIC LEFT.

SOCIALIST PARTY OF GREECE. *See* COMMUNIST PARTY OF GREECE-EXTERIOR.

SOCIALIST WAY. *See* SOCIALIST COURSE.

SOCIALIST WORKERS' PARTY OF GREECE. *See* COMMUNIST PARTY OF GREECE-EXTERIOR.

SOCIAL PROGRESS PARTY. *See* SOCIALIST COURSE.

SOSIALISTIKI PORIA. *See* SOCIALIST COURSE.

SOSIALISTIKI PROTOVOULIA. *See* SOCIALIST INITIATIVE.

SOSIALISTIKON ERGATIKON KOMMA ELLADOS. *See* COMMUNIST PARTY OF GREECE-EXTERIOR.

SOSIALISTIKON KOMMA ELLADOS. *See* COMMUNIST PARTY OF GREECE-EXTERIOR.

STRATOS KOMMA. *See* REFORMIST PARTY.

STRATOS PARTY. *See* REFORMIST PARTY.

TRIKOUPIS PARTY. *See* GREECE INTRODUCTION.

UNION OF DEMOCRATIC LEFTISTS. *See* UNITED DEMOCRATIC LEFT.

UNION OF POPULIST PARTIES. *See* NATIONAL FRONT and POPULIST PARTY.

UNION OF THE GREEK DEMOCRATIC CENTER (*Enose Demokratikou Hellinikou Kendrou*: EDHK). Under the leadership of Dr. John G. Zighdis, the EDHK was formed in 1977 as a reorganization of the pre-military junta Center Union.* The EDHK platform calls for a gradual transformation of Greek society through the introduction of economic democracy. The instruments of change are viewed as labor, cooperatives, and local government organizations, though the party is clearly antisocialist. Decentralization, designed to further democratic development, is strongly supported by the EDHK, and the party favored Greece's entry into the European Common Market (*see* EUROPEAN PARLIAMENT).

The EDHK remains opposed to the formation of electoral alliances with other opposition parties. Two splinters have occurred in the EDHK's short life, both by socialist dissidents: one in 1976, producing the Socialist Initiative* grouping; and one in 1979, resulting in the formation of the Party for Democratic Socialism.*

UNITED DEMOCRATIC LEFT (*Eniaia Demokratiki Aristera*: EDA). The United Democratic Left was created in 1951 as a political-front organization for the banned Communist Party (*see* Communist Party of Greece-Exterior). The EDA's basis was the Democratic Front (*Demokratiki Parataksis:* DP), formed in 1950. The DP electoral coalition had joined together remnants of the Communist Party and several other minor leftist groupings, including the Socialist Party (ELD) of Alexander Svolos (founded in 1945), the Union of Democratic Leftists of John Sofianopoulos, and the Left Liberals (*Neokosmos Grigoriades*). Svolos left the EDA in 1953, dissolved his Socialist Party, and merged with a faction of the National Progressive Center Union (*see* Liberal Party)under George Kartalis to form the Democratic Party of Working People (*Demokratikon Komma Ergazomenou Laou:* DKEL).

The United Democratic Left has contested all post-World War II elections, either alone or in coalition with other leftist-oriented political groups. In 1956 the EDA cooperated with George Papandreou (*see* Center Union) in forming the Democratic Union (*Demokratiki Enosis:* DE). In 1958 the EDA secured 79 seats by running in conjunction with its own New Agrarian Movement (NAK). In 1961, along with its own National Agrarian Party (*Ethnikon Agrotikon Komma:* EAK), the EDA formed the basis of the Pan-Democratic Agrarian Front of Greece (*Pandemokratiki Agrotikon Metapon Ellados:* PAME), which obtained only 24 seats. The EDA representation increased slightly to 28 seats in 1963, then dropped to 21 in 1964. The party's chief platform was opposition to the United States military presence in Greece and to the slow pace of economic and social progresss within the country.

The EDA was dissolved, along with all other left-wing groupings, in April 1967 by the military junta. Upon return of civilian rule, the EDA reappeared in 1974, independent of and despite the legalization of the grouping's creators, the Greek Communist Party. However, the EDA secured only one seat in the 1974 parliamentary election.

Since the end of military rule, the EDA has attempted to distinguish itself from the communist movement in Greece. Rejecting the concept of the dictatorship of the proletariat and ideological dogmatism, instead the EDA argues for socialism with a more human face. In conjunction with the EDA's acceptance of a multiparty system, the party supported Greece's entry into the European Common Market (*see* EUROPEAN PARLIAMENT).

With its electoral fortunes in decline, however, the EDA has attempted to forge broad unity among the Greek left-wing parties as an alternative to the center-right New Democracy* government. Therefore, in the 1977 elections, the EDA joined with the Communist Party of Greece-Interior,* Christian Democracy,* Socialist Course,* and Socialist Initiative* in forming the Alliance of Progressive and Left-Wing Forces (APLF),* and the EDA won one of the two seats obtained by the APLF in that year's election. Furthermore, the EDA has even announced its intention to attempt cooperation with its parent grouping, the Communist Party of Greece-Exterior. However, the EDA lost all parliamentary representation in the 1981 elections.

The EDA has developed formal organizations throughout Greece, but the party is especially strong in the trade unions and universities. EDA membership is estimated to be about 30,000.

UNITED FRONT OF NATIONALISTS (*Inomeni Parataksis Ethnikofronon*: HPE). The HPE, also known as the Coalition of Nationalists or the United National Front (*Inomeni Ethniki Parataksi*), was an electoral alliance of several center-right parties formed in 1946. The HPE was composed of the Populist Party* of Constantine Tsaldaris, the Reformist Party* of Apostolos Alexandris, the National Liberal Party (*see* Liberal Party) of Stulianos Gonatas, and the small Pan-Hellenic National Party of Alexandros Sakelariou. The HPE secured 206 out of 300 seats in the first postwar parliament.

UNITED FRONT OF WORKERS, PEASANTS, AND REFUGEES. *See* COMMUNIST PARTY OF GREECE-EXTERIOR.

UNITED LEFT ALLIANCE. *See* COMMUNIST PARTY OF GREECE-EXTERIOR and COMMUNIST PARTY OF GREECE-INTERIOR.

UNITED NATIONAL FRONT. *See* UNITED FRONT OF NATIONALISTS.

VENIZELIKON PHILELEFTHERON KOMMA. *See* LIBERAL PARTY.

VENIZELIST LIBERAL PARTY. *See* LIBERAL PARTY.

VenPK. *See* LIBERAL PARTY.

VOULGARIS PARTY. *See* GREECE INTRODUCTION.

X. *See* "X" NATIONAL RESISTANCE PARTY.

"X" NATIONAL RESISTANCE PARTY (*Komma Xiton Ethnikis Antistasseos*: X). An extreme-right political movement, the "X" National Resistance Party was founded by General George Grivas in 1946. Grivas drew his support from the paramilitary National Defense Units. After 1946, the party changed its name to the National Agrarian Party "X" (*Ethnikon Agrotikon Komma Xiton*: X), which disappeared after the 1950 election. Grivas later formed the National Rejuvenation Movement in 1960, which attracted many liberals, but this party dissolved in 1961. Prior to the military coup of 1967 in Greece, Grivas had been in charge of the Greek army contingent in Cyprus and also headed the Cypriot National Guard (*see* CYPRUS INTRODUCTION).

Vincent E. McHale

TABLE 30. Distribution of Seats in Greece's *Vouli*, 1926-1936

Party	1926	1928	1932	1933	1935	1936
Agrarian Party	4	0	11	8	•	5
Communist Party of Greece[a]	10	0	10	0	0	15
Free Opinion Party	51	1	3	6	7	7
General Union of Populists and Radicals[b]	—	—	—	—	—	60
Liberal Party	102	203	98	80	•	126
National Radical Party	—	—	6	11	33	—
National Unity Party	—	—	—	—	0	0
Populist Party[c]	60	19	95	118	254	72
Reformist Party	—	—	—	—	—	4
Republican Conservatives	—	3	17	12	•	7**
Republican Union	17	20	8	13	•	—
Independents and others	35	4	2	0	6	4
Total	279	250	250	248	300	300

• The 1935 election was boycotted by the Agrarian Party, the Liberal Party, the Republican Conservatives, and the Republican Union.

•• Represents seats won by the Democratic Coalition, which included the Republican Conservatives, the Republican Union, and the newly formed (in 1935) Democratic Socialist Party.

a Known as the United Front of Workers, Peasants, and Refugees in 1926; as the United Front of Workers and Peasants, 1928-1933; as the Popular Front in 1936; Communist Party was outlawed during 1947-1974, during which time the party functioned through the United Democratic Left (see table 31).

b An electoral coalition composed of the National Radical Party and elements of the Theotokis wing of the Populist Party.

c In 1935, part of the Populist Party joined with the Free Opinion Party to form the Union of Royalists, and the other Populists joined with the National Radical Party to form the government coalition.

TABLE 31. Distribution of Seats in Greece's *Vouli*, 1946-1964

Party	1946	1950	1951	1952	1956	1958	1961	1963	1964
Party of George Papandreou[a]	27*	35	0	0	114	10	—	—	—
Center Union[b]	—	—	—	—	—	—	100	138	171
United Front of Nationalists[c]	206	—	—	—	—	—	—	—	—
Populist Party	—	62	2	—	—	—	—	—	—
Greek Rally[d]	—	—	114	247	—	—	—	—	—
National Radical Union	—	—	—	—	165	173	176	132	108
Independent Political Front	—	16	—	—	—	—	—	—	—
Liberal Party	48	56	57	0	0	36	—	—	—
National Party of Greece	20*	7	—	—	—	—	—	—	—
National Progressive Center Union	—	45	74	51	—	—	—	—	—
National Unity Party[e]	9*	7	—	—	—	—	—	—	—
New Party[f]	—	1	—	—	0	—	—	2	—
United Democratic Left[g]	—	18	10	2	18	79	24	28	21
Union of Populist Parties	—	—	—	—	—	2	—	—	—
Venizelist Liberal Party	31*	—	—	—	—	—	—	—	—
Independents and others	13	3	1	0	3	0	0	0	0
Total	354	250	258	300	300	300	300	300	300

* These four parties ran as the National Political Union coalition in the 1946 election.

a Known as the Democratic Socialist Party, 1935-1946; as the Liberal Democratic Party, 1959-1961; became the Center Union (see separate listing, this table), 1961-1974.

b New name of the former Party of George Papandreou; see also Union of the Greek Democratic Center, table 32.

c An electoral coalition composed of the Populist Party (156 seats), the Reformist Party, the National Liberal Party, and the Pan-Hellenic National Party.

d Formed largely as a reorganization of the Populist Party, became the National Radical Union, 1956-1974 (see separate listing, this table); see also New Democracy, table 32.

e Known as the National Regeneration Front in 1950.

f Known as the Progressive Party in 1956 and 1963.

g Known as the Democratic Front in 1950; as the Pan-Democratic Agrarian Front of Greece in 1961; these were front organizations for the

TABLE 32. Distribution of Seats in Greece's Postjunta *Vouli*, 1974-1981

Party	1974	1977	1981
Communist Party of Greece-Exterior	5[*]	11	13
Communist Party of Greece-Interior	2[*]	1[**]	0
National Front	—	5	0
New Democracy[a]	220	172	113
New Liberal Party	—	2	—
Pan-Hellenic Socialist Movement	12	93	174
Union of the Greek Democratic Center[b]	60	15	0
United Democratic Left	1[*]	1[**]	0
Total	300	300	300

[*] These three parties formed the United Left Alliance electoral coalition in the 1974 election.

[**] These two parties formed part of the Alliance of Progressive and Left-Wing Forces electoral coalition in 1977; the Alliance also included Christian Democracy, Socialist Course, and Socialist Initiative, though these latter parties won no seats.

[a] Formerly the National Radical Union, *see* table 31.

[b] Formerly known as the Center Union, *see* table 31; contested as the Center Union-New Forces in 1974.

TABLE 33. Ruling Parties or Coalitions in Greece since 1926

Years	Party or Coalition
1926 - 1928	All-party coalition
1928 - 1932	Liberal Party
1932 - Sep. 1932	All-party coalition
Sep. 1932 - Jan. 1933	Populist Party
Jan. 1933 - Mar. 1933	Liberal Party
Mar. 1933 - 1935	Populist Party (Tsaldaris wing)
1936 - 1941	Regime of John Metaxas (parties banned)
1941 - 1944	German military occupation
1944 - 1946	All-party National Unity cabinet
1946 - 1949	Populist Party Liberal Party Independents
1949 - 1950	Populist Party Liberal Party New Party National Unity Party
Jan. 1950 - Nov. 1950	Nonpartisan government
Nov. 1950 - 1951	Liberal Party Democratic Socialist Party
1951 - 1956	Greek Rally
1956 - 1963	National Radical Union
1963 - 1965	Center Union
1965 - 1966	Liberal Democratic Union
1967 - 1974	Military dictatorship
1974 - 1981	New Democracy
1981 -	Pan-Hellenic Socialist Movement

Note: First-named party is dominant coalition party.

HISTORICAL ESTONIA, 1917-1940

The REPUBLIC OF ESTONIA is today an integral part of the Soviet Union and is known officially as the Estonian Soviet Socialist Republic. After domination at various times by the Danes, Germans, Poles, and Swedes, Estonia then came under tsarist Russian rule as a result of the Great Northern War (1700-1721). Sovereignty was reestablished in 1917-1918 when the Russian empire crumbled under the force of the Bolshevik Revolution (see SOVIET UNION). Although Estonia was not the first of the western border regions to proclaim independence from Russia, it was the first successor state whose sovereignty was recognized de jure by Soviet Russia, which occurred through the Peace of Tartu (*Dorpat*), signed on February 2, 1920. From 1919 to 1940, when Estonia was occupied by Soviet forces and incorporated into the USSR, the country enjoyed a brief period of parliamentary life.

At the time of independence, Estonia (*Eesti*) occupied about 23,160 square miles of territory representing the former Russian gubernia of Estonia (*Estland*, *Eestimaa*), the northern areas of Livonia (*Livland*, *Liivimaa*), small western sections of the Russian guberniia of Petrograd and Pskov, and several nearby islands (Moon Sound). The country was bounded by the Baltic Sea to the west, the Gulf of Finland to the north, Russia and Lake Peipus to the east, and Latvia to the south. The population (about 1,126,400 in 1934) was quite homogeneous in terms of religion and ethnicity. About 88 percent of the inhabitants were the eponymous Esths, an ethnic group similar to the Finns, and 78 percent were Lutheran. The other important ethnic groups were the Russians (8.2 percent), Germans (1.5 percent), Swedes (0.7 percent), Latvians (0.5 percent), and Jews (0.4 percent); and about 19 percent of the people were Russian Orthodox in religious affiliation.

Political activism in Estonia grew out of reforms pursued by Russia's Tsar Alexander II, especially the introduction of a system of local councils (*zemstvos*) in the late 19th century. While Estonia was formally under the Russian crown, local political power was in the hands of a small group of Baltic Germans, who also were the local upper class. Therefore, while issues of political autonomy were addressed toward the Russian state, early questions of social justice were directed toward the Baltic Germans. By the turn of the century, the emerging Estonian political elites began to work for electoral success at the municipal level. In 1904 the Estonians secured a majority in the Tallinn city council, having built an alliance with the city's Russians against the dominant Baltic Germans. By 1913 the Estonians had also secured the mayoralty.

Beginning with the activism encouraged by the *zemstvos*, Estonian political thought developed generally along two simultaneously overlapping and parallel paths: one stream focused on national rights, the other on social justice and class. The national path was championed foremost by Jaan Tônisson and the individuals gathered around his newspaper, *Postimees*, which was centered in the university city of Tartu. The centrality of class was emphasized by various socialist currents, which were strongest in the largest industrial center, Tallinn. Developments on the political left were somewhat more complex because of three separate activist groups, namely those that would become affiliated with the Communist Party of Estonia, * the Social Revolutionary Party, * and the Social Democratic Party. * The general political situation was made more complicated because the two key cities, Tallinn and Tartu, were located in different administrative areas. Tallinn was the capital of the gubernia of Estonia, while Tartu was in the gubernia of Livonia, the capital of which was Riga.

Politically between Tônisson's followers and the socialists was a third important element, those gathered around Konstantin Päts's newspaper, *Teataja*, in Tallinn. While placing stronger emphasis on economic issues than the followers of Tônisson, Päts's activists brought forth the question of national rights more forcefully than the socialists. Päts's group was, indeed, very mixed, giving subsequent leaders to political parties of all hues (Farmers' Party, * National Democratic Party, * Labor Party, * and the Social Democratic Party).

Formal partisan organization in Estonia developed almost simultaneously with the emergence of political parties in the first Russian *Duma* (1905; *see* SOVIET UNION). The replacement of tsarist autocracy with a constitutional monarchy permitted representatives from the Baltic provinces to take part in the various legislative matters before the *Duma*. Initially, at the first and second *Dumas*, Estonia was authorized five representatives. Following the Russian electoral revisions of 1907, this number was reduced to two seats for the third and fourth *Dumas*. The three original Estonian parties represented in the Russian *Duma* were the Radicals of Konstantin Päts (*see* Radical Democratic Party), the Progressive National Democrats of Jaan Tônisson (*see* National Democratic Party), and the Social Democrats of Peeter Speek. Although all three parties were moderate in political outlook, their respective programs called for full internal political autonomy for Estonia.

It is important to note that between 1905 and Estonia's declaration of independence in 1917-1918, all of the Estonian parties were closely affiliated with their Russian counterparts. In the end, however, all except the Estonian Communists split from the Russian parties over the issue of national rights. Yet the Estonian parties had never been mere subbranches of the Russian parties; all of the main Estonian groups had strong, direct contacts with developments in northern, central, and eastern Europe.

The movement for Estonian independence found an opportunity for realization between the two Russian revolutions of 1917. Meeting in Tartu on March 4, 1917, a group of prominent Estonian politicians, under the leadership of Jaan Tônisson, pressed for a separate Estonian administration responsible to the home community. On March 12, 1917, a decree by the Russian provisional government finally provided for the joining of all the Baltic lands inhabited by Estonians into a single, autonomous administration within the Russian confederation. Estonia was placed under the jurisdiction of a High Commissioner (appointed by the Russian government), who was to be assisted by a locally elected Estonian Diet (Maapäev or Maanoûkogu).

The Diet was to be composed of one representative for every 20,000 inhabitants. It was mandated indirectly by an electoral college composed of the various urban and rural local assemblies, with a ratio of one elector for every 1,000 inhabitants. The election process was cumbersome and extended over several months since Estonian parties were still in the process of developing and were thus ill-prepared to conduct election campaigns at the local level. The political parties did not run electoral lists but simply allowed the voters to choose among slates which represented landed peasants, landless peasants, or a compromise list made up of both groups.

The election to the Diet was held on July 7-8, 1917. Voter participation, especially in the rural areas, was low, with a turnout of about 30 percent of the eligible electorate. When the selection process finally reached its completion in October 1917, the Diet totalled 62 members, 30 of whom had socialist viewpoints. Among the parties represented in the Diet were the Rural League (see Farmers' Party), with 14 seats; the National Democrats, six seats; and the Radicals, six seats; and together these three parties constituted the Democratic Bloc. Also represented were the Laborites (the Social Travaillist Party* and the Radical Socialist Party*), with a combined representation of nine; the Social Democrats, six seats; the Social Revolutionary Party, ten seats; the Communists, five seats; and nonaffiliated individuals, six seats (of whom two represented the national minorities [see National Minority Parties]).

With the collapse of the provisional government in Russia under the weight of the autumn Bolshevik Revolution, the Estonian Diet on November 28, 1917, declared itself the highest authority in Estonia. The country immediately saw a competition for power between the Bolsheviks and the other parties. By January 1918, the non-Bolshevik groupings had all come to support the goal of full sovereignty, while the Communists favored Estonia's inclusion in a revolutionary Soviet Russia. The Estonian Diet, however, insisted that Estonia's final political form should be decided by an Estonian constituent assembly. The Bolsheviks, nominally ruling Estonia during the winter of 1917-1918, also voiced support for self-determination, and in January 1918 they called for a national election to such a body. However, with about two-thirds of the vote in, the Communists found they had received only about one-third of the ballots counted thus far, and they abruptly cancelled the elections.

In the turmoil of these events, the Estonian *Diet* had delegated its powers to a smaller leadership called the Council of Elders. In turn, this body had appointed a three-man Emergency Committee. This latter committee, on February 24, 1918, formally proclaimed Estonia's independence and established a provisional government. Political developments, however, were almost immediately interrupted by the arrival of German forces in Tallinn, beginning an occupation that lasted until the November 11, 1918, armistice ending World War I. The Baltic Germans and the occupying Germans hoped to make Estonia an integral crown land of Germany. While most Bolsheviks had withdrawn to Russia with the German invasion, the Estonian provisional government remained underground at home. Upon the German withdrawal, the provisional government reasserted its political authority.

The Communists attempted to regain power by the force of arms, and in late November 1918 they declared a competing governmental authority in Narva. Russian Bolshevik forces by the end of the year had moved west, about half-way through Estonia, but were forced to retreat again in early January 1919.

Estonia's provisional government held elections for a constituent assembly on April 5-7, 1919. These elections were based on proportional representation and universal, direct, equal, and secret suffrage. Some 458,000 people cast ballots (out of approximately 700,000 eligible voters, who were all those of at least 20 years of age who had been Estonian citizens for at least one year). On April 23, 1919, the constituent assembly reaffirmed the proclamation of independence made by the Emergency Committee. The assembly was dominated by the democratic left, with the Social Democratic Party having 34.1 percent of the delegates and providing the assembly's president and the newly formed Labor Party having another 25 percent of the seats. The only other large grouping in the assembly was the National Democrats with 20.8 percent of the delegates.

The constituent assembly almost immediately began to institute a series of constitutional and economic reforms. Under the premiership of Otto Strandmann (Labor Party), a substantial agrarian reform program was enacted, involving the liquidation of the large estates and the elimination of all feudal tenure rights. A land reserve was set up under state ownership, and the issue of compensation was postponed for future consideration. The land issue was the single most important political, economic, and social issue for the bulk of the Estonian population, which was rural and landless, and the reform was the primary instrument in mobilizing the Estonians to the cause of the republic during the war for independence against the Soviet Russians. In addition, the land reform displaced the Baltic Germans from their centuries-long position of political and social dominance, and it laid the groundwork for far-reaching political realignments among the citizenry. In 1919 most Estonians voted for the two leftist parties favoring land reform; but after the landless masses had been transformed into propertied farmers, their votes would shift rightward to agrarian groupings.

The constituent government concluded the peace treaty (of Tartu) with the new Soviet Union government on February 2, 1920. A few months later, on June 15, 1920, the Estonian constitution came into being. It established a parliamentary system with a unicameral State Assembly (*Riigikogu*) composed of 100 seats filled every three years by an electoral system identical to the one used for the constituent assembly. The constitution also provided for legislative initiative, requiring the signatures of 25,000 qualified voters, and the holding of plebiscites. Executive leadership was vested in the prime minister or "elder statesman" (*Riigivanem*). The cabinet itself was responsible to the State Assembly.

The six elections (1919, 1920, 1923, 1926, 1929, 1932) held during Estonia's democratic period witnessed a gradual shift to the right (*see* table 34). In 1919 the main leftist parties (the Social Democrats and the Independent Socialist Workers' Party*) had been elected to 40 percent of the constituent assembly's seats, but by 1932 the parties of the left (by then also including the Communists) had fallen to 27 percent of the mandates in the *Riigikogu*. The main centrist parties (Labor, National Democrats, Christian Democratic Party,* and Landlords' Party*) experienced a similar decline, from 50 percent of the seats in 1919 to 23 percent in 1932. The conservative Farmers' Party, however, and later in its brief merger with the Homesteaders' Party,* enjoyed a dramatic increase in electoral support, rising from 6.6 percent to 42 percent of the delegates during the same time period.

This shift to the political right did not cure Estonia's chronic cabinet instability. Between April 1919 and the bloodless coup of March 12, 1934, 21 separate cabinets had been formed, producing an average cabinet life of about eight months. Often the same parties of the dissolving cabinet would attempt to form the new government, and so only 15 of these 21 cabinets reflected any changes in party composition (*see* table 35). The result was widespread popular dissatisfaction with the style of party politics and the operation of the Estonian parliamentary system.

The Social Democrats received a high degree of blame for Estonia's governmental instability. The Social Democrats consistently ranked among the top three, most-represented parties in the State Assemblies and therefore would have been a likely partner in government coalitions. Furthermore, being a moderate rather than a radical leftist grouping, the Social Democrats might have succeeded in cooperating with the centrist parties, many of whom shared various political or social interests with the Social Democrats. However, the Social Democrats were disinclined to participate in cabinets; they were even more reluctant to head any governing coalition and did so only once (in 1928-1929). Eventually on the extreme right, various protofascist groups, such as the Front Soldiers' League (*see* Veterans' League), emerged to threaten the moderate parties. Highly vocal and supported by various industrial elements, these radical-right groups were composed mainly of veterans who were dissatisfied with party strife and the undisciplined and ineffective parliamentary system.

Attempts to reform the Estonian party system by curbing fragmentation were only partially successful. Twenty-five parties competed in the 1923 *Riigikogu* elections, with 14 achieving representation. By 1926 parties fielding candidates had to post a deposit which they would forfeit if they secured less than two seats. Also at about this time, the Estonian parties attempted to gain strength and stability through mergers. The democratic left was consolidated through the merger of the Social Democrats and Independent Socialists in 1925. The two agrarian parties, the Farmers Party and the newer Homesteaders' Party, merged in early 1932. The winter of 1931-1932 also saw the merger of various centrist groups (the National Democrats, Labor, Christian Democrats, and the Land-lords' Party) into the National Center Party. * Nevertheless, these mergers did not provide the required cabinet stability. Although the three new, merged parties held 87 percent of the seats in the State Assembly that was elected in 1932, four cabinets were formed between mid-1932 and October 1933.

As the international economic crisis worsened in the early 1930s, the citizenry increased its demands for cabinet stability and for constitutional reforms which would strengthen the executive. Two referenda (August 1932 and June 1933) were proposed by the United Agrarians (*see* Farmers' Party) and the National Center Party respectively to accomplish this goal. Both were defeated, due largely to opposition from the Social Democrats. However, a third referendum (October 14-16, 1933), sponsored by the Veterans' League, was successful by a wide margin (73 percent of those voting), with an unusually heavy voter turnout of about 56 percent. The constitutional revision consolidated power in a president, to be elected by popular vote for a five-year term. The premiership remained as a separate office but with little executive authority. The president could dissolve parliament, issue decrees, appoint and dismiss cabinets, and was authorized to declare the existence of a state of emergency. The State Assembly's composition was to be reduced from 100 to 50 members who would serve four-year terms.

Konstantin Päts formed a new government on October 21, 1933, and became acting president as well as premier following the resignation of Jaan Tônisson's National Center cabinet. Meanwhile, the Veterans' League had continued its antigovernmental agitation and achieved unexpected popularity with victories in local elections in January 1934. The general political situation in Estonia was becoming tense, with the major parties having formed paramilitary elements. In this climate, Päts moved to restore public order with the consent of the major democratic parties and the State Assembly. He declared a state of emergency, dissolved the Veterans' League, and arrested several of its leaders. But Päts apparently had more extensive doctoring in mind for Estonia because soon after he banned all political meetings, rallies, and speeches. He also postponed indefinitely the scheduled presidential elections. In October 1934, when the State

Assembly refused to endorse his moves, Päts suspended that body. Finally, on March 6, 1935, all parties were "dissolved," and on March 9, a one-party system was established under the Fatherland League, * a new mass organization based on Päts's following in the Farmers' Party.

In order to legalize the new authoritarian regime, Päts ordered a referendum to be held on February 24, 1936, to propose a new assembly and the drafting of a new constitution. The proposal was approved by about 63 percent of the electorate, albeit under the conditions of censorship and the ban on political party activity. The new constitution, however, did little to curtail the powers of the president, except to change the method of selection. After 1938, the president was to be elected for a six-year term by an electoral college composed of assembly members of local government representatives. The new assembly was bicameral: an upper house, the Council of State (Riiginõukogu), consisted of 40 members appointed either by the president or various professional bodies; and the lower house, the State Representative Assembly (Riigivolikogu), had 80 members elected by the people on a simple majority, single-list system. Members in both houses would serve five-year terms. National minorities, such as the Germans and Jews, were permitted to nominate a joint delegate to serve in the Council of State; only the Russians could fill one seat in the elected lower house. Candidate nominations could not come from any political parties but only from various professional and community associations.

The general election for the new State Representative Assembly was held on Estonia's 20th anniversary of independence, February 24, 1938. This election resulted in 63 seats for the Fatherland League and 17 for the opposition, the latter composed mainly of members of liberal and centrist parties who ran as independent candidates since the 1935 ban on political parties had not yet been officially lifted. In 26 of 80 electoral districts, independent opposition candidates won against the government's candidates. Päts was elected president, and he appointed Kaarel Einbund (Farmers' Party) as premier.

However, in the longer run, Päts failed to legitimize his rule. In November 1936, for example, four former premiers published a letter in the main Finnish daily newspaper, protesting Päts's dictatorial regime and the curtailment of political rights. Jaan Tônisson, Päts's most severe critic during these years, then proceeded to win more votes than any other single candidate in the 1938 elections, and the total national vote was split approximately in half between the government and the opposition. In retaliation against Tônisson's persevering criticism, the government sequestered his newspaper, Postimees, which had championed Estonian national rights since the late 19th century.

Tônisson's National Centrists continued to be the most active opposition. The Social Democrats, finding Päts a lesser evil than the Veterans' League, remained, so to speak, neutral. Päts continued to rule basically by decree, censorship remained in force, and political parties continued to be banned. Indeed, the government began to advocate a notion of "guided democracy," which implied a long-range intent to maintain an authoritarian system. Although there had been hope that the crisis atmosphere would soon end, the state of emergency was extended indefinitely as threats on the Baltic states from the Soviet Union and Germany grew in intensity.

The outbreak of war in 1939 signalled the beginning of the end to Estonian independence. Attempts were made in June 1939 to enlist the support of fascist elements by restoring pension rights to several of the veterans' leaders convicted in 1935. But on September 29, 1939, Estonia was forced to sign a mutual assistance pact with the Soviet Union, which resulted in some 35,000 Red Army troops being stationed on Estonian territory. In October, under the leadership of Jüri Uluots (Farmers' Party), an effort was made to fashion a Cabinet of National Unity composed of all major political groups (except the national minorities). Uluots resigned on June 21, 1940, following a Soviet ultimatum on June 16 for greater free passage of troops across Estonian territory and for the formation of an Estonian government friendly to the Soviet Union. Under the direction of a Soviet foreign ministry representative, Andrei Zhdanov, a puppet cabinet was established in Estonia with Johannis Vares as premier. In quick fashion, on July 4, this cabinet legalized the Estonian Communist Party, which proceeded to establish a front group, the Working People's League (see Communist Party of Estonia), with various noncommunist, left-wing elements. Parliament was dissolved, and new elections were held on July 14-15, 1940, with only candidates of the Working People's League allowed to participate. The new assembly met on July 21, proclaimed the establishment of an Estonian Soviet Socialist Republic, and immediately requested Estonia's incorporation into the Soviet Union. On August 24-25, 1940, Estonia became the 16th constituent republic of the USSR.

Although the Soviet government was displaced when Germany again invaded the Baltic republics in June 1941, and remained in occupation until 1944, Estonian independence was never restored. A provisional government under Jüri Uluots appeared briefly in Fall 1944. But with the return of Soviet troops in November of that year, Estonia was reclaimed by the Soviets, and the Estonian provisional government members either fled or were captured by the Soviet authorities. Since 1944, the major Estonian parties, such as the Social Democrats and the Farmers, have remained active outside of the Soviet sphere.

Bibliography*

Baltic State Handbook. London: Chatham House, 1938.

Davis, Malcolm W., ed. A Political Handbook of Europe: Parliaments, Parties and Press. New York: Council on Foreign Relations, 1927-1940.

Graham, Malbone W. New Governments of Eastern Europe. New York: Henry Holt & Co., 1927, pp. 246-315.

---

*The author wishes to thank Professor Tönu Parming for his assistance in providing information and advice in the writing of this chapter.

Parming, Tönu. *The Collapse of Liberal Democracy and the Rise of Authoritarianism in Estonia.* London: Sage Publications, 1975.

————. "The Pattern of Participation of the Estonian Communist Party in National Politics, 1918-1940." *The Slavonic and East European Review*, vol. 59, no. 3 (July 1981): 397-412.

Pulleritis, Albert. *Estonia.* Tallinn: KUT, 1937.

Rothschild, Joseph. *East Central Europe between the Two World Wars.* Seattle: University of Washington Press, 1974.

Roucek, Joseph, ed. *Central Eastern Europe.* New York: Prentice-Hall, 1946.

Vardys, V. Stanley, and Romuald J. Misiunas, eds. *The Baltic States in Peace and War, 1917-1945.* University Park: Pennsylvania State University Press, 1978.

Von Rauch, Georg, translated by Gerald Onn. *The Baltic States: The Years of Independence, 1917-1940.* Berkeley and Los Angeles: University of California Press, 1974.

Political Parties

Note: In the English translations of the party names which follow, the adjective "Estonian" (noted by *Eesti* in the vernacular) has been omitted since most Estonian parties included this adjective as the first word of their respective labels.

AGRARIAN UNION. *See* FARMERS' PARTY.

ASSOCIATION OF ESTONIAN FREEDOM FIGHTERS. *See* VETERANS' LEAGUE.

ASUNIKKUDE KOONDIS. *See* HOMESTEADERS' PARTY.

ASUNIKKUDE PARTEI. *See* HOMESTEADERS' PARTY.

ASUNIKKUDE, RIIGIRENTNIKKUDE, JA VÄIKEPÕLLUPIDAJATE KOONDIS. *See* HOMESTEADERS' PARTY.

BALTIC GERMAN PARTY. *See* NATIONAL MINORITY PARTIES.

CENTRAL LEAGUE OF TALLINN LABOR UNIONS. *See* COMMUNIST PARTY OF ESTONIA.

CHRISTIAN DEMOCRATIC PARTY (*Kristlik demokraatlik partei*). The Christian Democratic Party (also known in some sources as the Christian Party or Christian People's Party) originated in January 1918 during the first, incompleted elections for an Estonian constituent assembly, when a group of "Independent

Christians" appeared on the ballot. These Independent Christians had been organized to represent the interests of Lutheran conservatives, especially in the area of education, and to stress moderate social reforms and democratic government. Before the successful 1919 constituent assembly elections, these individuals were joined by some defectors from the National Democratic Party* to form the Christian Democratic Party. The principal leaders of the new party included F. Akel, H. Bauer, and J. Lattik.

In the 1919 elections, the Christian Democrats received four percent of the national vote. In the 1920 elections to the first State Assembly, the Christian Democrats polled seven percent of the vote. After agreeing to join the government of Konstantin Päts (Farmers' Party*), on January 5, 1921, the Christian Democrats received the post of ministry of education and participated in almost every coalition after 1921. The party ruptured the Päts coalition in 1922 by introducing a measure to provide religious instruction in the public schools at state expense. Unsuccessful in parliament, the Christian Democrats forced a referendum on this issue on February 17-19, 1923, which resulted in popular approval of the measure. Considered to be a vote of no confidence in the government, this referendum poll led to the dissolution of the first State Assembly.

The Christian Democrats received eight percent of the national vote in the 1923 elections. They formed a minority ministry under the Tallinn doctor, Friedrich Akel, between March 6 and December 1, 1924, during which they enacted numerous economic and financial reforms. This government resigned after the abortive communist coup of December 1, 1924. The party underwent a name change prior to the 1926 elections and became the Christian Nationalist Party (*Kristlik rahvaerakond*). Suffering electoral losses in both 1926 and 1929 (down to five and four percent of the vote, respectively), the Christian Nationalists joined with the National Democratic Party in October 1931 to form the United Nationalists Party (*Ühinenud rahvaerakond*). In January 1932, the new United Nationalists joined with the Labor Party* to form the National Center Party,* which one month later was also joined by the Landlords' Party.* Friedrich Akel served briefly as foreign minister under the Päts dictatorship of the late 1930s.

CHRISTIAN NATIONALIST PARTY. *See* CHRISTIAN DEMOCRATIC PARTY.

CHRISTIAN PARTY. *See* CHRISTIAN DEMOCRATIC PARTY.

CHRISTIAN PEOPLE'S PARTY. *See* CHRISTIAN DEMOCRATIC PARTY.

COMMUNIST PARTY OF ESTONIA (*Eestimaa kommunistlik partei*). The Estonian communist movement began in the early 20th century as an extension of the Bolshevik wing of the Russian Social Democratic Workers' Party (*see* SOVIET UNION). The primary strength of the Estonian movement was in the two major industrial centers, Tallinn and Narva. In July 1917, under the name of the Northern Baltic Committee of the Russian Social Democratic Workers' Party, the communists won representation in the Estonian *Diet* with eight percent of the vote. In August 1917, a Bolshevik conference in Tallinn changed the name of the local party group to Province of Estonia Committee of the Russian Social Democratic Workers' Party. As such, the Estonian communists became the dominant group in the Tallinn Soviet of 1917-1918.

What in the end distinguished the communists from all of the other Estonian parties was the communists' opposition to Estonian sovereignty. The communist goal was that Estonia should be a part of Soviet Russia and later the Soviet Union. Believing this goal would receive popular support, the communists initially supported the *Diet*'s call for the formation of a constituent assembly to determine Estonia's future form of government. However, in these elections of January 1918, occurring under the nominal rule of the Russian Bolsheviks, the communists found that when about two-thirds of the poll had been counted, they had received only about one-third of those tallied votes. The elections were then promptly aborted. In the struggle for Estonian statehood, the communists from late 1918 to mid-1919 operated a competing governmental authority, the Estonian Working People's Commune (*Eesti töörahva kommuun*), located in Narva. Because of this separate stance, the Estonian communists did not participate when the constituent assembly elections were finally reheld in April 1919. At this time, much of the direction of the communist movement inside Estonia actually lay in the Estonian section of the Soviet Russian communist party. The main leaders of the Estonian grouping were J. Anvelt, H. Pöögelmann, and V. Kingissepp.

The communists attracted like-minded factions of Estonia's other leftist parties, such as the left wing of the Social Revolutionary Party. * After the Soviet Union recognized Estonian sovereignty with the Peace of Tartu (February 1920), and in part conforming to the directives of the Communist International, a separate Communist Party of Estonia was founded inside Estonia in November 1920. The party operated as an underground entity and chose to participate in national politics through front organizations, most of which were to be officially banned by the sovereign Estonian government. In the early 1920s, for example, the main fronts were the Central League of Tallinn Labor Unions (*Tallinna ametiühisuste keskühisus*) and the Working People's Party of Estonia (*Eestimaa töörahva partei*). The latter was the remnant of the Independent Socialist Workers' Party, * which had been infiltrated by the Communist Party in 1922. The Central League, which had secured five seats in the 1920 Estonian State Assembly, was prohibited by the authorities in 1921; and the Working People's Party met a similar fate in 1924. For the elections to the second State Assembly in 1923, another Communist label was the Working People's United Front (*Eesti töörahva ühine väerind*), which secured ten seats.

Despite the Estonian Communists' claim to autonomy from the Communist Party of the Soviet Union (*see* SOVIET UNION), the Estonian Communists became suspected of being under control of the Comintern, particularly after the December 1, 1924, attempted Communist coup engineered from Moscow. The coup was vigorously suppressed; in opposition, a grand coalition of all the major parties, including for the first time the Social Democratic Party,* was formed under the leadership of Jüri Jaakson (of the National Democratic Party*); and both the Communist Party of Estonia and its United Front were outlawed in early 1925. This experience severely reduced the appeal of communism in Estonia, although the Communists continued to be active in municipal elections in Tallinn and Tartu. Some of the more radical members of the banned Communist Party formed a new group called the Workers' Party (*Eesti tööliste partei*) and sought the support of urban workers in the major towns, particularly the dock workers in Tallinn. This group secured six seats in the State Assemblies of 1926 and 1929. It dissolved in 1930, however, and its seats were distributed among the other parties in the Assembly (four representatives declared themselves nonparty, and two others left the country). For the last parliamentary elections in 1932, the new Communist front was the Leftist Workers' and Poorer Peasants' Party (*Pahempoolsed töölised ja kehvikud*). This group was banned along with all other political parties by the Päts regime in 1934-1935 (*see* Historical Estonia introduction).

After Soviet Union forces had entered Estonia in large numbers in June 1940, the Communist Party of Estonia was legalized by the occupying power while all of the other parties were still banned. In the Soviet-sponsored elections held that month for the reorganized State Representative Assembly, the Communists nevertheless preferred to hide once more behind a front, this time the Working People's League (*Eesti töölahva rahva liit*). The ballots contained only one name in each electoral district, in every case the representative of the Working People's League. The election was a step toward Estonia's incorporation into the Soviet Union on August 25, 1940.

It is difficult to assess the degree of popular support that had been offered to the Communist Party of Estonia. In the elections of 1917 and 1918, the Communists received a large share of the vote, up to 40 percent. But this may be deceiving because a sizable share of this vote was from Russian military garrisons and Russian workers living in Estonia temporarily. Also, voter participation in rural areas, where the Communists had very little support, had been low in these elections. During State Assembly elections, the Communist fronts received five percent of the national vote in 1920, ten percent in 1923, six percent in 1926 and 1929, and five percent in 1932. Almost all of this support came from the industrial workers; the Communists had virtually no support in the rural areas or among intellectuals.

When the Communist Party of Estonia was founded in 1920, it had about 700 members; this figure grew to 2,000 by 1924 but declined sharply after the failed revolt that December. Many party members then fled to the Soviet Union. In 1929 the party had 300 members and in June 1940 a mere 150. The central organs of the party operated from abroad in the early 1930s (from Denmark and

Sweden), and its 1934 Congress was held in Moscow. Since June 1940, the Communist Party of Estonia, again a part of the larger, parent Soviet party, has been the only legal party in Estonia. In 1970, only 52 percent of its membership was ethnic Estonian; most of the remainder was Russian.

DEMOCRATIC BLOC. *See* FARMERS' PARTY, NATIONAL DEMOCRATIC PARTY, and RADICAL DEMOCRATIC PARTY.

DEMOCRATIC PARTY. *See* NATIONAL DEMOCRATIC PARTY.

EESTI DEMOKRAATLIK ERAKOND. *See* NATIONAL DEMOCRATIC PARTY.

EESTIMAA KOMMUNISTLIK PARTEI. *See* COMMUNIST PARTY OF ESTONIA.

EESTI MAARAHVA LIIT. *See* FARMERS' PARTY.

EESTIMA TÖÖRAHVA PARTEI. *See* COMMUNIST PARTY OF ESTONIA.

EESTI RADIKAAL-DEMOKRAATLIK ERAKOND. *See* RADICAL DEMO-CRATIC PARTY.

EESTI RAHVAERAKOND. *See* NATIONAL DEMOCRATIC PARTY.

EESTI RAHVAMEELNE EDUERAKOND. *See* NATIONAL DEMOCRATIC PARTY.

EESTI SOTSIAALDEMOKRAATLIK PARTEI. *See* SOCIAL DEMOCRATIC PARTY.

EESTI SOTSIAALDEMOKRAATLIK TÖÖLISTE PARTEI. *See* SOCIAL DEM-OCRATIC PARTY.

EESTI SOTSIAALDEMKRAATLIK ÜHENDUS. *See* SOCIAL DEMOCRATIC PARTY.

EESTI SOTSIALISTIDE-REVOLUTSIONÄÄRIDE PARTEI. *See* SOCIAL REVOLUTIONARY PARTY.

EESTI SOTSIALISTLIK TÖÖLISTE PARTEI. *See* SOCIAL DEMOCRATIC PARTY.

EESTI TÖÖERAKOND. *See* LABOR PARTY.

EESTI TÖÖLAHVA RAHVA LIIT. *See* COMMUNIST PARTY OF ESTONIA.

EESTI TÖÖLISTE PARTEI. *See* COMMUNIST PARTY OF ESTONIA.

EESTI TÖÖRAHVA ÜHINE VÄERIND. *See* COMMUNIST PARTY OF ESTONIA.

ESTONIAN FASCISTI. *See* NATIONAL LIBERAL PARTY.

EX-SERVICEMEN'S FEDERATION. *See* VETERANS' LEAGUE.

EX-SERVICEMEN'S PARTY. *See* VETERANS' LEAGUE.

FARMERS', HOMESTEADERS', AND SMALLHOLDERS' GROUP. *See* HOMESTEADERS' PARTY.

FARMERS' PARTY (*Põllumeestekogud*). The Farmers' Party (also known in some sources as the Agrarian Union) was formed in 1921. Its roots went back into the 19th-century farmers' societies (*põllumeeste seltsid*) founded by southern Estonian agrarians who succeeded in breaking away from the yoke of the Baltic German manor owners and in acquiring their own farms. The creation of such societies reflects general developments in western European countries. It was especially advocated in Estonia by C. R. Jakobson in the second half of the 19th century and then by Jaan Tônisson afterwards. In Spring 1917, C. Arro, J. Grünberg, J. Hünerson, H. Johani, A. Jürman, and J. Kalm of the Southern Estonian Farmers' Central Society (*Lôuna-Eesti põllumeeste keskselts*) called upon the rural population, in a piece in Tônisson's influential newspaper, *Postimees*, to form political associations to represent their interests in the rapidly changing political arena. The result was the Rural League (*Eesti maarahva liit*).

Initially, the Rural League opposed radical land reform, a position which reflected the interests of the party's main constituency, the wealthier native Estonian farmers in the north. The Rural League received 22 percent of the vote in the elections for the 1917 Estonian *Diet* and was the largest single grouping in that body. Together with Tônisson's Democratic Party (*see* National Democratic Party) and the Radical Democratic Party,* the Rural League helped form the Democratic Bloc. In early 1918, the League was seriously considering "inviting" the German Army (in Latvia at the time and planning a move north in any case) to occupy Estonia to counter Russian (and Estonian) Bolshevik influences. To combat this development, Konstantin Päts, a prominent political activist formerly associated with the Tallinn Radicals (*see* Radical Democratic Party), formally joined the Rural League and became its best-known leader. The League's main newspaper was *Maaliit*.

With the social changes wrought by the conclusion of World War I, the Rural

League did very poorly in the constituent assembly elections of 1919, receiving only seven percent of the vote. The Labor Party* formed the 1919 government and proceeded to introduce radical measures of land nationalization and redistribution to the landless masses. The Rural League opposed these efforts. Yet in the 1920 elections to the first State Assembly, the League significantly increased its support to 21 percent of the vote, which reflected the rightward trend of the now propertied, formerly landless population. In 1921 the Rural League was reorganized as the Farmers' Party. Besides Päts, the new party's most influential leaders were J. Teemant, K. Eenpalu, and J. Uluots. Its main newspaper became *Kaja*.

Increasing its share of the vote to 23 percent in 1923 and to 24 percent in 1929, the Farmers' Party was either the largest or second-largest group in the State Assemblies and therefore played a key role in cabinet formation. Päts, of course, was an influential political activist in northern Estonia even before the Rural League had been founded. As a League member in the *Diet*, he headed the home front at the most critical juncture of Estonia's struggle for independence in 1918-1919. Of the 21 cabinets formed during the period of the constituent assembly and the five State Assemblies, the Farmers' Party supplied the prime minister in ten instances (Päts five times, Teemant four times, and Eenpalu once). The Farmers' Party participated in other cabinets as well.

The Rural League and the successor Farmers' Party was the most conservative democratic party in Estonia. Although the Farmers were foremost an agrarian grouping, this was not the full scope of their support. The wealthiest segment of urban ethnic Estonians also supported the Farmers. Indeed, many of the Farmers' leaders were actually urban professionals, even though the roots of these individuals were on farms. In summary, the Farmers' Party was the most important conservative grouping, and it represented the political interests of the wealthiest Estonians, both rural and urban.

With the land reform measures of the Otto Strandmann (Labor Party) government, granting land to new farmers and demobilized soldiers, the Farmers' Party split into liberal and conservative groups. The conservative elements continued to support the Farmers' Party, while in 1923 the new liberal elements formed the Homesteaders' Group, which in 1925 became the Homesteaders' Party.* Another dissident faction, the Smallholders' Group, was able to elect one representative to the 1923 legislature; but this party disappeared within one year, and its membership was reabsorbed by the Farmers' Party.

The two wings were briefly reunited in 1932 to form the United Agrarian Party (officially titled the United Agrarians', Homesteaders', and Smallholders' Group, *Põllumeeste kogud ja põllumeeste, asunikkude, ning väikemaapidajate koondus*). The new United Agrarians received 42 percent of the national vote in 1932 and stood at the head of the coalition in three of the four cabinets preceding the last Päts cabinet of 1933 in the fifth State Assembly. These were headed by the old Farmers' leaders J. Teemant, K. Eenpalu, and Päts. The merger, however, was ultimately unsuccessful due to differences of both class interests of the separate constituencies and their general ideologies. The middle segment of Estonia's farmers supported the Homesteaders' Party, and the poorest segment of the rural population voted for the Social Democratic Party.* In turn, the rural intelligentsia of teachers and clergy most often voted for the National Democratic Party. As a result, the merger shattered in Spring 1933 when a large share of the original Farmers' Party—its most conservative faction—withdrew from the United Agrarians to oppose the centrist Tônisson cabinet.

When Päts seized power in 1934, some Farmers' leaders played important roles in the Päts regime, while the remaining United Agrarians were an active opposition. Kaarel Eenpalu of the Farmers' Party headed the Päts cabinet, and Jüri Uluots became head of the Fatherland League,* the government's own front during the dictatorship. Päts became Estonia's first and last president under the 1938 constitution, and Uluots headed the last cabinet of the republic—the Cabinet of National Unity—before displacement by a puppet cabinet under Soviet pressure in 1940. Uluots proclaimed a new government in 1944 when the Germans were retreating and before the Soviet Army again conquered Estonia. This cabinet, which never formally took office because of the war, had broad support from the old political parties that were otherwise banned during Päts's rule. Uluots and most of this cabinet fled to Sweden in late 1944. This "government in exile" continues to this date, even though Uluots died soon after arriving in Sweden. The Farmers' Party, also headquartered in Sweden, has continued its political activity in exile.

FATHERLAND FRONT. See FATHERLAND LEAGUE.

FATHERLAND LEAGUE (*Isamaa liit*). The Fatherland League (also known as the Fatherland Front or Patriotic League) was formed by the Konstantin Päts authoritarian government on March 9, 1935, as a means of political mobilization after political parties had been banned in 1934-1935 (*see* Historical Estonia introduction). As the government's own front, the Fatherland League was the only legal party in Estonia until June 1940, when a Soviet-installed cabinet legalized the Communist Party of Estonia.* The League's leadership, as in the Päts government of 1934-1940, came from the political right, foremost from the radical conservative leaders of the old Farmers' Party.* The League was highly centralized and functioned similarly to the extraparliamentary Veterans' League,* which the Päts government had banned because it was too authoritarian.

The Fatherland League did not directly participate in the 1938 election to the lower chamber of the reconstituted State Assembly. For this purpose, the government created the National Front for the Implementation of the Constitution (*Pôhiseaduse elluviimise rahvarinne*), which, however, was indistinguishable from the League in a practical sense. Although other parties were still banned in 1938, individual opposition candidates were on the ballot in 72 of 80 electoral districts. The Front's candidates won in 54 of the 80 districts, but the national vote was approximately split in half. The most popular centrist leader, Jaan

Tônisson (*see* National Center Party), contested as an opposition independent and won more votes than any other candidate in the country.

The Fatherland League's chief leader, second only to Päts, was Jüri Uluots, and he was the last prime minister of the Republic of Estonia in 1939-1940 (*see also* Farmers' Party). Other key leaders of the League were A. Jürima and A. Oidermaa.

FREEDOM FIGHTERS. *See* VETERANS' LEAGUE.

FRONT SOLDIERS' LEAGUE. *See* VETERANS' LEAGUE.

GERMAN-SWEDISH ELECTORAL BLOC. *See* NATIONAL MINORITY PARTIES.

HOMESTEADERS' GROUP. *See* HOMESTEADERS' PARTY.

HOMESTEADERS' PARTY (*Asunikkude partei*). The Estonian land reforms promulgated in 1919 and implemented in the early 1920s transformed the rural population both socially and politically. The most important direct consequence was the more than doubling of the number of family farms. In the 1919 constituent assembly elections, the bulk of the rural vote went to parties championing land reform: the Social Democratic Party,* the Labor Party,* and the National Democratic Party.* But afterwards, the newly propertied farmers began to support the older, conservative Farmers' Party,* although that group represented primarily the interests of the wealthier agrarians.

The Homesteaders' Party was founded in 1923 as a splinter from the Farmers' Party and was initially titled the Homesteaders' Group (*Asunikkude koondis*). The party was registered under its official name—the State Leaseholders', Homesteaders' and Smallholders' Group (*Asunikkude, riigirentnikkude, ja väikepôllupidajate koondis*)—in December 1925, though it was popularly known as simply the Homesteaders' Party. Its main leaders were R. Penno and O. Köster.

Striving to represent the interests of Estonia's less wealthy farmers, particularly those newer agrarians who had benefitted from the Labor Party's land reform, in the 1923 parliamentary elections the Homesteaders received about four percent of the national vote. In 1926 and 1929, this figure rose to 14 percent. The party was renamed again in 1931, this time as the Farmers', Homesteaders' and Smallholders' Group (*Pôllumeeste, asunikkude, ja väikemaapidajate koondis*), though it continued to be known as the Homesteaders' Party. (In some sources, this name change is referred to as the New Farmers' and Settlers' Party.)

Overall, the Homesteaders were a centrist party, but their agrarian interests led to a merger in January 1932 with their conservative parent grouping, the Farmers' Party. The resulting United Agrarian Party (*see also* Farmers' Party) was not particularly stable. The merger split apart in 1933, though the United Agrarian name was retained by the remaining members, most of whom were from the old Homesteaders' Party. The latter supported the Jaan Tônisson cabinet (headed by the National Center Party*) from May to October 1933 but not the succeeding Päts cabinet which led to dictatorial rule. The old Homesteaders were among the staunchest opponents of the Päts regime, and they tried with the centrists to elect individual opposition candidates for the "party-less" 1938 parliamentary elections and the 1940 Soviet-controlled elections. The Homesteaders remain active in postwar exile in Sweden.

HOUSE-OWNERS' PARTY. See LANDLORDS' PARTY.

INDEPENDENT CHRISTIANS. See CHRISTIAN DEMOCRATIC PARTY.

INDEPENDENT SOCIALIST WORKERS' PARTY (*Iseseisev sotsialistlik tööliste partei*). Resulting from a 1919 split in the Social Revolutionary Party* and joined by defectors from the Social Democratic Party,* the Independent Socialist Workers' Party attempted to form a middle group between the Communist Party of Estonia* on their left and the Social Democrats on their right. The major leaders of the Independent Socialists were M. Bleimann, E. Joonas, and H. Kruus.

In the 1919 constituent assembly elections, the Independent Socialists received six percent of the vote. In the elections to the first State Assemblies, elected in 1920 and 1923, the Independent Socialists secured 11 percent and five percent of the vote respectively. The party did not participate in any cabinets.

In 1922 the Independent Socialists were penetrated by members of the Communist Party, and a struggle for control of the party ensued. By mid-1923, the Communist faction had won, and the group was officially redesignated as the Working People's Party of Estonia (*Eestimaa töörahva partei; see also* Communist Party of Estonia), which became an electoral front organization for the underground Communists. The Working People's Party was officially banned by the authorities in mid-1924, after which, in 1925, the bulk of the old Independent Socialists joined the Social Democratic Party.

ISAMAA LIIT. See FATHERLAND LEAGUE.

ISESEISEV SOTSIALISTLIK TÖÖLISTE PARTEI. See INDEPENDENT SOCIALIST WORKERS' PARTY.

KRISTLIK DEMORAATLIK PARTEI. See CHRISTIAN DEMOCRATIC PARTY.

KRISTLIK RAHVAERAKOND. See CHRISTIAN DEMOCRATIC PARTY.

LABOR PARTY (*Eesti tööerakond*). The Labor Party was formed in 1919 as a formal amalgamation of the Radical Socialist Party,* which had been founded by Jüri Wilms and Otto Strandmann, and the Social Travaillist Party,* led by Ants Piip and J. Seljamaa. These two parties had cooperated closely since their respective foundings in 1917 and were known collectively as the Laborites in the 1917 Estonian *Diet*. The Labor Party advocated a nonrevolutionary program of social and agrarian reform, and it should not be confused with the Workers' Party (*see* Communist Party of Estonia), which existed between 1926 and 1930. The Labor Party was supported by small landowners, artisans, commercial and government employees, intellectual groups, and nonsocialist elements of the working class. The roots of the Labor Party went back to the activism of radical socialists in Tallinn in 1905 and to the same city's "autonomists' clubs" before the Bolshevik Revolution of February 1917 (*see* Historical Estonia introduction). The Labor Party's main newspaper was *Vaba Maa*.

From 1917 to 1923, the Laborites played the pivotal role in Estonian politics, forming a bridge between the socialists and the national centrists. The allied Radical Socialists and Social Travaillists constituted the second-largest grouping in the 1917 Estonian *Diet*. The amalgamated Labor Party won the same ranking in the 1919 constituent assembly (with about 25 percent of the vote). Labor's Otto Strandmann headed the first cabinet of May 8, 1919, and Ants Piip headed the assembly's last cabinet before the first *Riigikogu* convened.

In the first State Assembly (*Riigikogu*), elected in 1920, Labor won 22 percent of the vote and rose to the position of largest parliamentary party, with 22 of 100 seats, though Konstantin Päts of the Farmers' Party* formed the government in January 1921. Afterwards, Labor's popularity declined—to 12 percent of the vote in 1923, 13 percent in 1926, and to ten percent in 1932—as its original goals were achieved and as it shifted from left to center. Nevertheless, Labor continued to participate in most cabinets of the parliamentary period, and Labor headed cabinets in 1922-1923 (under Juhan Kulek) and 1929-1931 (under Strandmann). The latter was the longest-lived cabinet in Estonia's parliamentary history.

Although socialist in its early years, the Labor Party was evolutionary rather than revolutionary in its orientation toward social change. The party's early appeal cut across class lines, covering intellectuals, the emerging urban middle class, elements of the working class, and segments of the rural population. In general, it was the party of the left for those who did not wish to join the various socialist groupings. The Labor Party was a champion of the separation of church and state and of land reform, as indicated by Strandmann's radical land redistribution of the early 1920s (*see* Historical Estonia introduction).

Amid the moves to counter Estonia's high degree of party fragmentation and instability (*see* Historical Estonia introduction), in 1932 the Labor Party merged with the centrist United Nationalists Party (*see* Christian Democratic Party) to form the National Center Party.* The National Centrists, however, were banned along with all other Estonian parties by the Päts regime in 1934-1935.

LANDLORDS' PARTY (*Majaomanikkude seltside liit*). The Landlords' Party (also known as the House-Owners' Party or Landowners' Party) first appeared in the elections to the second State Assembly in May 1923. The party was composed of a small number of private property advocates who represented a type of classical capitalist ideology. The party had minor electoral popularity; and although it represented the interests of urban property owners, it cooperated very closely with the Farmers' Party* and was a part of several cabinets. The leader of the Landlords' Party was J. Sepp, who also served for a time as minister of justice.

In February 1932, in an attempt to oppose the increasingly powerful United Agrarian (*see* Farmers' Party) government and to stem the tide of party fragmentation, the Landlords joined with the Labor Party* and the United Nationalists Party (*see* Christian Democratic Party) in the National Center Party,* which had been founded one month earlier.

LANDOWNERS' PARTY. *See* LANDLORDS' PARTY.

LEFTIST WORKERS' AND POORER PEASANTS' PARTY. *See* COMMU-NIST PARTY OF ESTONIA.

LIBERATORS. *See* VETERANS' LEAGUE.

MAJAOMANIKKUDE SELTSIDE LIIT. *See* LANDLORDS' PARTY.

NATIONAL CENTER PARTY (*Rahvuslik keskerakond*). There was widespread popular opinion in Estonia that a major weakness of the nation's political system was the large number of parties in the State Assembly (*see* Historical Estonia introduction). As a result, and also in an attempt to counter the dominant government of Konstantin Päts (Farmers' Party*), there were major mergers of the left, right, and center, especially during 1931-1932. In the political center, the National Democratic Party* and the Christian Nationalist Party (*see* Christian Democratic Party) joined forces to form the United Nationalists Party in October 1931. They were joined in January 1932 by the Labor Party* to form the National Center Party; in February 1932, the latter was joined by the Landlords' Party.*

The new National Center Party won 23 percent of the vote in the parliamentary elections of 1932. The National Centrists supported all of the cabinets formed in the fifth State Assembly except the last one, which was Päts's transitional cabinet to dictatorial rule. The Centrists' Jaan Tônisson (formerly of the National Democratic Party contingent) was prime minister during May-October 1933. This cabinet made several important economic decisions that helped pull Estonia out of the Great Depression. The Tônisson cabinet resigned because the electorate had rejected the State Assembly's proposals for a new constitution but had approved instead the proposal of the extraparliamentary Veterans' League.*

The National Center Party, along with all other Estonian parties, was banned by the Päts regime in 1935. The National Centrists' Tônisson contingent, in particular, was among Päts's most persistent critics. As a result, the government sequestered Tônisson's newspaper, *Postimees*, in 1936. The party contested the 1938 election to Päts's reconstituted State Assembly, though the candidates ran as independents since the 1935 ban on political parties was still in effect. Tônisson contested as an opposition independent, and he secured more votes than any other single candidate. In the Assembly, Tônisson's severely critical speeches were often banned from print or even summarization in the newspapers by the government censors during 1938-1939. Finally, Tônisson was very active in getting individual opposition candidates on the ballot in the communist-controlled and Soviet-supervised elections of June 1940. However, at the last minute these candidates were removed from the ballot by the supervising forces.

NATIONAL DEMOCRATIC PARTY (*Eesti rahvaerakond*). The National Democratic Party (also known in some sources as the Populist Party or the National Party) was the main centrist grouping during Estonia's parliamentary period. The party's roots went back to the mainstream of the Estonian national movement in the late 19th century. Its direct lineage extended to the Progressive National Democratic Party (*Eesti rahvameelne eduerakond*) founded by the "grand old man" of Estonia's political center, Jaan Tônisson, in the university city of Tartu in 1905. Tônisson, among others, represented southern Estonia in the 1905 Russian *Duma* as a member of this party. In 1917, Tônisson changed the party's name to Democratic Party (*Eesti demokraatlik erakond*, and this grouping was part of the Democratic Bloc in the 1917 Estonian *Diet*. The National Democratic Party itself came into existence in March 1919 through the merger of the Democratic Party with the Radical Democratic Party.* The main newspaper of the Estonian political center from the late 19th century through 1940 was Tônisson's *Postimees*, published in Tartu.

In the first Russian *Duma*, the Estonian representatives of the Progressive National Democratic Party were closely affiliated with the Kadets (*see* PARTY OF PEOPLE'S FREEDOM, SOVIET UNION). However, the Progressive Nationalists had split from the Russian party by 1917, largely over the question of Estonia's national rights. The Estonian Democrats, and later the National Democrats, emphasized the nation rather than social class in their ideologies. Both groups fought for Estonian cultural as well as economic and political rights already in the early 1900s. Improved educational opportunities and the state's development of natural resources were prominent goals in the parties' programs. As such, Tônisson's Democrats drew their support from southern Estonia's emerging urban middle class and two parts of the rural population: propertied farmers and the rural intelligentsia (namely, teachers and pastors). The Radical Democrats, with whom Tônisson merged, were strongest among the emerging middle class in Tallinn and northern Estonia's propertied farmers. Overall, from 1920 onward, the National Democrats represented foremost the urban middle class.

The Democrats and Radical Democrats each had ten percent of the representatives in the Estonian *Diet* of 1917-1919, and together as the National Democrats they had 20.8 percent of the delegates to the constituent assembly elected in 1919. However, in the State Assemblies elected from 1920 through 1929, the National Democrats lost ground, falling to ten percent in 1920, eight percent in 1923 and 1926, and nine percent in 1929.

In 1919 some rightist dissidents had opposed the Democrats' merger with the more leftist Radical Democrats, and these dissidents split off to join the conservative center-right Christian Democratic Party.* With the ensuing dominance of the Farmers' Party,* and in an attempt to curtail Estonia's party fragmentation, in 1931 the remaining National Democrats under Tônisson merged with the Christian Democrats (by then renamed the Christian Nationalist Party) to form the United Nationalists Party. Then, in 1932, the new grouping merged with the center-left Labor Party* to form the National Center Party.*

Tônisson, in addition to his central role in forging a sense of Estonian national identity, played a crucial role for the republic by heading the foreign delegation of 1917-1919 which sought diplomatic recognition for Estonia. He then headed two successive cabinets in 1919-1920, including the government which in February 1920 concluded the Peace of Tartu with Soviet Russia. Tônisson also headed cabinets during the parliamentary period in 1927-1928 and in 1933. The National Democrats' Jüri Jaakson headed the coalition government after the abortive coup by the Communist Party of Estonia* in December 1924. As a party, the National Democrats participated in almost all governments. (*See also* National Center Party.)

NATIONAL FRONT FOR THE IMPLEMENTATION OF THE CONSTITUTION. *See* FATHERLAND LEAGUE.

NATIONAL LIBERAL PARTY (*Rahvuslik vabameelne partei*). The National Liberals (also known as the Estonian Fascisti) were one of several protofascist groups that emerged in Estonia's early period of parliamentary democracy. The party's development in Estonia was similar to that of the Hitler Movement in Germany (*see* HISTORICAL GERMANY). Electing four representatives to the State Assembly of 1923, the success of the National Liberals appeared to be related to the workings of proportional representation, which allowed splinter parties to thrive. However, the National Liberal electoral base eroded completely in the 1926 election, and the party's main support is thought to have shifted to the Veterans' League* in the early 1930s.

NATIONAL MINORITY PARTIES. Estonia's cultural pluralism laws enabled parliamentary participation of the major non-Estonian ethnic groups: the Russians (8.2 percent of the population in 1934), the Germans (1.5 percent), Swedes (0.7 percent), and Jews (0.4 percent). These four groups had their own political parties, all of which were organized at the time of Estonia's proclamation of independence (1917-1918).

The primary goal of all Estonian minority groups was that of cultural autonomy, especially in the area of education where each wished to employ its own language. The role of the minority parties was to represent the cultural and economic interests of its group and to secure a voice on those parliamentary committees that dealt with such matters. Occasionally, the minority parties cooperated with one another; but there was some resistance, especially within the Baltic German Party (see below), which insisted upon a special status.

The various, small Jewish parties contested the 1923 parliamentary elections, but they received only 395 votes of 471,228 nationally and did not achieve representation. There is no record of any subsequent Jewish parties.

The Swedish Party (Rootsi erakond) represented the tiny but articulate Swedish minority in Estonia but, like the Jewish parties, had too small a constituency to have any national impact alone. Prior to the 1929 elections, a coalition was formed between the Baltic German and Swedish parties. Known as the German-Swedish Electoral Bloc (Saksa-rootsi valimisblokk), the coalition was quite successful and increased the two parties' combined support by over 20 percent. The Swedish Party's most prominent leader was Hans Pöhle, who originally had been a candidate of the Christian Democratic Party* in 1926. After Pöhle's death in 1930, the Swedish Party was led by Mathias Westerblom.

The Russian minority in Estonia was fragmented into a number of small groups which cooperated only infrequently. The primary political vehicle was the Russian United Party (Vene ühendatut partei), which was later renamed as the Russian National Union (Vene rahvuslik liit). Led by P. Iacobi, this party received its support from the Russian welfare and teachers' organizations. The Russians placed one delegate in the constituent assembly of 1919 and one to five delegates in the State Assemblies of 1920 to 1932. Their share of the national vote was one percent in 1920, four percent in 1923, three percent in 1926, two percent in 1929, and five percent in 1932. In 1929 the Union had lost support to the Social Democratic Party,* which had fielded two Russian candidates in the predominantly Russian areas. The Russians never participated in a cabinet, although they did cooperate closely with other minority parties in the State Assembly in order to secure appointments to various parliamentary committees.

The most politically effective ethnic group was the Baltic German Party (Saksa-Balti erakond). In 1917-1919, the Baltic Germans had wanted to make Estonia a German province through personal union with the German royal family. When this proved futile, some of these individuals formed the Baltic German Party in 1919 to work for national and cultural interests of the German minority within the independent Estonian republic. Among the party's leadership was A. de Vries, who also edited Revaler Bote, the German minority newspaper. Although numerically the second-largest Estonian minority in population, the Germans sometimes formed the largest minority group in terms of parliamentary representation. The Baltic German Party secured two seats to the constituent assembly of 1919. It increased its representation to four in the State Assembly of 1920 and dropped to three in 1923 and to two in 1929, prior to which it had allied with the Swedish Party in the German-Swedish Electoral Bloc.

Taken together, these ethnic minority parties obtained about 3.3 to 6.7 percent of the Estonian legislature's membership from 1919 to 1932; none of these parties served in cabinets. In the 1919 constituent assembly, neither the Russian nor the Baltic German delegates voted in support of the otherwise unanimous declaration of independence (reaffirming the provisional government's proclamation of February 1918). The Russians abstained and the Baltic Germans walked out for the vote; the latter, however, reportedly signed the declaration post facto. In late 1933, a minority of Baltic Germans, led by Viktor von zur Mühlen and others, attempted to forge ties both to the Estonian extraparliamentary and right-wing movement, the Veterans' League,* and to Germany's national socialist (nazi) movement (see NATIONAL SOCIALIST GERMAN WORKER'S PARTY, HISTORICAL GERMANY). The Estonian government reacted with arrests and the banishment of a number of Baltic German Party members from Tallinn. From 1933 to 1938, the majority of the Baltic German Party attempted to steer a neutral course with respect to the Third Reich (see HISTORICAL GERMANY), even though the community was dependent upon the German government for financial support of its cultural and educational programs.

All political and parliamentary activities of the minority parties ended with the Päts ban on all parties in March 1935. Although minority representatives were appointed to the body that drew up the third Estonian constitution in 1938, a new voting law permitted only the Russian group to have representation in the elected lower-house State Representative Assembly. The others were allowed one combined seat in the appointed upper-house Council of State, and this seat was filled by Baron Wilhelm Wrangell. The new constitution also limited the scope of self-administration and educational rights for minority groups.

NATIONAL PARTY. *See* NATIONAL DEMOCRATIC PARTY.

NEW FARMERS' AND SETTLERS' PARTY. *See* HOMESTEADERS' PARTY.

NORTHERN BALTIC COMMITTEE OF THE RUSSIAN SOCIAL DEMO-CRATIC WORKERS' PARTY. *See* COMMUNIST PARTY OF ESTONIA.

PAHEMPOOLSED TÖÖLISED JA KEHVIKUD. *See* COMMUNIST PARTY OF ESTONIA.

PATRIOTIC LEAGUE. *See* FATHERLAND LEAGUE.

PÕHISEADUSE ELLUVIIMISE RAHVARINNE. *See* FATHERLAND LEAGUE.

PÕLLUMEESTE, ASUNIKKUDE, JA VÄIKEMAAPIDAJATE KOONDIS. *See* HOMESTEADERS' PARTY.

PÔLLUMEESTEKOGUD. See FARMERS' PARTY.

PÔLLUMEESTE KOGUD JA PÔLLUMEESTE, ASUNIKKUDE, NING VÄIKEMAAPIDAJATE KOONDIS. See FARMERS' PARTY.

POPULIST PARTY. See NATIONAL DEMOCRATIC PARTY.

PROGRESSIVE NATIONAL DEMOCRATIC PARTY. See NATIONAL DEMOCRATIC PARTY.

PROVINCE OF ESTONIA COMMITTEE OF THE RUSSIAN SOCIAL DEMOCRATIC WORKERS' PARTY. See COMMUNIST PARTY OF ESTONIA.

RADICAL DEMOCRATIC PARTY (*Eesti radikaal-demokraatlik erakond*). The roots of the Radical Democratic Party were in the "Tallinn Radicals" of the early 1900s who had gathered around Konstantin Päts and his newspaper, *Teataja*. Päts's Radicals had won representation to the first Russian *Duma* in 1905 while strongly advocating national rights for Estonia rather than questions of social class. By 1917 these nationalists organized themselves into a formal political party, the Radical Democratic Party, which won ten percent of the representatives to the Estonian *Diet* of 1917-1919, elected after Estonia's declaration of independence from Russia. Within the *Diet*, the Radical Democrats formed part of the Democratic Bloc, along with the Democratic Party (*see* National Democratic Party) and the Rural League (*see* Farmers' Party). Later in 1917, however, Päts shifted rightward toward the economic and social policies of the center-right Rural League (and formally joined that party in 1918). Upon Päts's departure, the Radical Democrats' most prominent leader was Aadu Birk.

Under Birk, the Radical Democrats gained support from the emerging Estonian middle class in Tallinn and from northern Estonia's propertied farmers. In preparation for the constituent assembly elections of 1919, the Radical Democrats sought to increase their base of electoral support and merged with their ideological counterparts in Tartu, the Democratic Party, whose support lay in southern Estonia's emerging middle class and propertied farmers, as well as in the rural intelligentsia. The grouping that resulted from this merger was the National Democratic Party.

RADICAL SOCIALIST PARTY. In July 1917, the Radical Socialist Party was founded by Jüri Wilms and Otto Strandmann to contest elections to the Estonian *Diet*. The Radical Socialist program was similar to that of the Russian *Trudoviki* (*see* LABORITE GROUP, SOVIET UNION) in the Imperial *Duma*. However, the Radical Socialists soon shed their revolutionary demands and moved toward the political center and the bourgeois parties. Two years after its founding, the Radical Socialist Party fused with the Social Travaillist Party* to form the Labor Party,* under which Otto Strandmann formed the first cabinet after the constituent assembly elections of 1919 and instituted substantial agrarian and economic reforms.

RAHVUSLIK KESKEROND. See NATIONAL CENTER PARTY.

RAHVUSLIK VABAMEELNE PARTEI. See NATIONAL LIBERAL PARTY.

ROOTSI ERAKOND. See NATIONAL MINORITY PARTIES.

RURAL LEAGUE. See FARMERS' PARTY.

RUSSIAN NATIONAL UNION. See NATIONAL MINORITY PARTIES.

RUSSIAN UNITED PARTY. See NATIONAL MINORITY PARTIES.

SAKSA-BALTI ERAKOND. See NATIONAL MINORITY PARTIES.

SAKSA-ROOTSI VALIMISBLOKK. See NATIONAL MINORITY PARTIES.

SMALLHOLDERS' GROUP. See FARMERS' PARTY.

SOCIAL DEMOCRATIC PARTY (Eesti sotsialdemokraatlik partei). Social democracy had a complex history in Estonia. One component of the movement's roots went back to Tartu, where Peeter Speek, Eduard Vilde, and K. Ast founded the Social Democratic Unity (Eesti sotsiaaldemokraatlik ühendus) immediately after the issuance of the Russian October Manifesto (October 30, 1905; see SOVIET UNION). This promised reform provided for the development of constitutional government in Russia and resulted in the formation of an elective assembly, the Russian Duma, in which the Baltic provinces were granted representation. The Social Democratic Unity achieved representation in that body. This component of the Estonian social-democratic movement attracted intellectuals and was distinguished by its emphasis of both class struggle and national rights. The party supported the idea of an ethnically federated, social-democratic political structure in Russia. The party also demanded autonomy for Estonia. Ühendus was the party's newspaper in Tartu.

The other component of Estonia's social-democratic roots was among Tallinn's industrial workers, where socialist leaders such as Mihkel Martna, August Rei, Karl Ast, Hans Pöögelmann, and Aleksander Kesküla were very much a part of the Estonian section of the Russian Social Democratic Workers' Party (see SOVIET UNION). With the failure of the 1905 revolution in Russia, many Estonian socialist leaders fled abroad. Some of the activism continued in exile: both Speek and Pöögelmann came to the United States, where they were affiliated with the Estonian workers' movement and its newspaper, Uus Ilm; Speek remained in the United States, while Pöögelmann returned to Russia in

1917. Between 1905 and 1917, the strongest socialist elements in Estonia were the Social Revolutionary Party* and the Communist Party of Estonia.*

In May 1917, the Social Democratic Workers' Party (*Eesti sotsiaaldemokraatlik tööliste partei*) was founded in Tallinn by Estonian Mensheviks (of the Russian Social Democratic Workers' Party). Its most prominent members were Mihkel Martna, August Rei, Karl Ast, and V. Masik; its main newspapers were *Sotsiaaldemokraat* (1917-1921), *Tulevik* (1921-1923), *Ühendus* (1923-1927), and *Rahva Sôna* (1927-1935).

The Social Democratic Workers' Party participated in the Estonian *Diet* elected in 1917, receiving about ten percent of the national vote. At about this time, the Social Democrats split both with the Estonian Communists and with their own Russian counterparts, primarily over the nationality issue. The group played an especially important role in the emergence of Estonian sovereignty. Mihkel Martna was one of the members of the foreign delegation of 1917-1919 which secured diplomatic recognition for Estonia.

With the 1919 election to the constituent assembly, the Social Democrats with their 34.1 percent share of the total vote became the largest political group in Estonia and provided the president, August Rei, of that assembly. However, in 1919-1920 some of the left wing of the party broke away and joined the right wing of the collapsed Social Revolutionary Party to form the new Independent Socialist Workers' Party.* This split weakened the Social Democrats electorally. In the next two elections, their level of support dropped sharply—to 18 percent in 1920 and to 15 percent in 1923—while the new Independent Socialists received 11 percent and five percent in these respective elections. Then, with the attempt to consolidate the political left, and after the Independent Socialists had been infiltrated by the Estonian Communists, the remnants of the Independent Socialists merged into the Social Democratic Workers' Party in April 1925. The new group underwent a final name change, this time to the Socialist Workers' Party (*Eesti sotsialistlik tööliste partei*). The merger strengthened the Social Democrats at the polls, and the new Socialist Workers secured 24 percent of the vote in 1926, 25 percent in 1929, and 22 percent in 1932.

Throughout their history, beginning with their representation in the Russian *Duma*, the Estonian Social Democrats were not very different in their overall policies and goals from other western European social-democratic parties. The Estonians split from the Russian Social Democrats mainly over the question of national rights. Of the three main currents of socialism in revolutionary Estonia in 1917, the Social Democrats were the most moderate in their demands; and after Estonia's independence, they became evolutionary rather than revolutionary. Although the Social Democrats in 1917 opposed small-unit agriculture, by 1919 they and the Labor Party* became the champions of a radical land reform which broke up the old Baltic German manors into tens of thousands of family farms. The land reform advocated by these two parties and promulgated by the constituent assembly was the key factor in mobilizing the rural population to the cause of the Estonian republic and in winning the war of independence against Soviet Russia in 1918-1920.

However, the Social Democrats generally refused to head governments and did so only once, when August Rei briefly became prime minister from December 1928 to July 1929. Given their relatively significant share of the votes, the Social Democrats' failure in this regard is often blamed for Estonia's high degree of cabinet instability. Still, the Social Democrats offered their support to cabinets both in the constituent assembly and the State Assemblies, and the party often directed the ministries which dealt with the social and economic concerns of the Social Democrats' constituency.

Unfortunately, the Social Democrats were also supportive of the last Päts cabinet of 1933-1934, which led to a period of dictatorial rule (see Historical Estonia introduction). A prime reason for this was Päts's crackdown on the extraparliamentary and right-wing movement, the Veterans' League,* which, if it had come to power, would have probably dealt very harshly with all leftists. As it was, Päts in his younger days with the Tallinn Radicals (see Radical Democratic Party) of the early 20th century was well known to the Social Democrats. Päts's newspaper, *Teataja*, almost became the main voice of Estonia's social-democratic movement at that time. The Social Democratic Party, therefore, did not play a vocal role in the democratic opposition to the Päts dictatorship.

The Estonian Social Democrats have remained very active in exile, since 1940 headquartered in Sweden. The party's current news organ is the quarterly, *Side*.

SOCIAL DEMOCRATIC UNITY. *See* SOCIAL DEMOCRATIC PARTY.

SOCIAL DEMOCRATIC WORKERS' PARTY. *See* SOCIAL DEMOCRATIC PARTY.

SOCIALIST WORKERS' PARTY. *See* SOCIAL DEMOCRATIC PARTY.

SOCIAL REVOLUTIONARY PARTY (*Eesti sotsialistide-revolutsionääride partei*). In 1905 the Social Revolutionary Party was founded in Estonia as an extension of the larger Russian party (*see* SOCIALIST REVOLUTIONARY PARTY, SOVIET UNION). The Estonian party was officially founded as a separate entity in September 1917. Its important early leaders included H. Kruus, K. Freiberg, E. Joonas, E. Meister, and J. Püskar; its main newspapers were *Töölipp* (1917), *Vôitlus* (1918-1919), and *Töörahva vôitlus* (1919).

Of the three main currents of socialism in Estonia in 1917 (the other two being the bolshevism of the Communist Party of Estonia* and the more moderate Social Democratic Party*), the Social Revolutionaries were the strongest in terms of parliamentary representation. Though both the Social Democrats and the Social Revolutionaries had received about ten percent of the vote to the 1917 *Diet*, the Social Democrats obtained six seats while the Social Revolutionaries held ten seats. Borrowing from their Russian counterpart, the Estonian Social Revolutionaries stood for the nationalization of land and the organization of various agricultural cooperatives. They also favored governmental decentralization and greater popular control of governmental institutions. The party's following was mostly among intellectuals and some industrial workers.

However, another segment of the party's ideology resulted in a substantial loss of popular support after 1917 and also created internal disunity. Although some Social Revolutionaries during 1917-1919 were staunch supporters of a sovereign Estonian state, many others in the party favored Estonia's continued affiliation with Russia. The party was also divided over the question of to what degree nationality rights should be a part of revolutionary change. Therefore, in 1919 the Social Revolutionary Party split. The left wing joined the Communist Party of Estonia, while the right wing, together with some defectors from the Social Democratic Party, founded a new Independent Socialist Workers' Party.*

A few old Social Revolutionaries, such as H. Kruus, who had joined neither the Communists nor the Independent Socialists in 1919, served as ministers in the cabinet created under Soviet pressure in 1940. It was this puppet cabinet, controlled by the Soviet and Estonian Communists, that directed Estonia's incorporation into the USSR, and the Social Revolutionaries concerned later joined the Communist Party of Estonia.

SOCIAL TRAVAILLIST PARTY. In July 1917, the Social Travaillist Party was formed by Ants Piip and J. Seljamaa to contest elections to the Estonian *Diet*. The party was patterned after a French model (*see* RADICAL SOCIALIST PARTY, FRANCE), and hence the use of the French word *travail* (work) in the Estonian party name. The Social Travaillists sought to play a mediating role between the conservative agrarian parties on the political right and the revolutionary-marxist parties on the left. As such, the Social Travaillists cooperated in the *Diet* with the centrist-tending Radical Socialist Party,* and together these two parties were known as the Laborites. The Social Travaillists were supported by various commercial and government employees.

Two years after its formation, the Social Travaillist Party fused with the Radical Socialist Party to form the Labor Party.* Under the new party name, Ants Piip would form a brief cabinet (October 26-November 26, 1920) to direct Estonia's constituent assembly. He would also serve as minister of foreign affairs and ambassador to the United States.

SWEDISH PARTY. *See* NATIONAL MINORITY PARTIES.

TALLINNA AMETIÜHISUSTE KESKÜHISUS. *See* COMMUNIST PARTY OF ESTONIA.

TALLINN RADICALS. *See* RADICAL DEMOCRATIC PARTY.

ÜHINENUD RAHVAERAKOND. *See* CHRISTIAN DEMOCRATIC PARTY.

UNITED AGRARIANS', HOMESTEADERS', AND SMALLHOLDERS' GROUP. *See* FARMERS' PARTY.

UNITED AGRARIAN PARTY. *See* FARMERS' PARTY and HOMESTEADERS' PARTY.

UNITED NATIONALISTS PARTY. *See* CHRISTIAN DEMOCRATIC PARTY.

VABADUSSÔJALASTE KESKLIIT. *See* VETERANS' LEAGUE.

VABADUSSÔJALASTE LIIT. *See* VETERANS' LEAGUE.

VAPS. *See* VETERANS' LEAGUE.

VENE RAHVUSLIK LIIT. *See* NATIONAL MINORITY PARTIES.

VENE ÜHENDATUT PARTEI. *See* NATIONAL MINORITY PARTIES.

VETERANS' LEAGUE (*Vabadussôjalaste keskliit* or *Vabadussôjalaste liit*). Several protofascist parties grew out of the disenchantment of various middle-class elements and demobilized soldiers (*demobiliseeritud sôdurid*) in the early 1920s, soon after the signing of the Peace of Tartu (February 1920), which ended the war of independence against Russia. Veterans' groups were especially strong and in 1923 formed an Ex-Servicemen's Party, which succeeded in electing one representative to the State Assembly that year and then promptly disappeared. Remnants of this group were later reorganized into the Ex-Servicemen's Federation or Front Soldiers' League, a loose organization of veterans' societies. The veterans were extremely hostile to democratic parties, to communism and other socialisms, and to what they perceived to be the "leaderless" parliamentary system of Estonian government, which was characterized by great cabinet instability (*see* Historical Estonia introduction). The veterans continually pressed for constitutional changes that would strengthen the power of the executive.

In 1929 the Veterans' League was established in Tallinn through an amalgamation of various local societies, including the Front Soldiers' League. Billing itself as a patriotic, nationalistic association, the Veterans' League held its First Congress in 1930 and began to publish its own magazine, *Vôitlus* (Struggle). The League modeled itself after the peasant-based Lapua Movement in Finland (*see* PATRIOTIC PEOPLE'S MOVEMENT, FINLAND).

The Veterans' League was known by several additional names and acronyms, such as the Liberators, the Association of Estonian Freedom Fighters or simply Freedom Fighters, VAPS, and WABSE. At first, the League claimed to be nonpolitical. However, the consolidation of the Nazi Party in Germany (*see* NATIONAL SOCIALIST GERMAN WORKER'S PARTY, HISTORICAL GERMANY) after 1932 incited the VAPS to step up its attack on the Estonian government. From its Second Congress in that year, the League quickly shed its veterans' association character and took on all the trappings of a full-fledged fascist movement. Under the guidance of Artur Sirk, the VAPS was organized along military lines, with uniforms of grey-green shirts, black-and-white arm bands, and the insignia of a hand grasping a sword with the dates 1918-1920 (war of independence). The group claimed to support land reform and workers' rights and pledged to struggle against partisan politics and marxism. However, the League pursued its work outside of parliament.

The VAPS pitted itself against the major parties and forced a referendum on October 14-16, 1933, to consolidate executive power in a new presidential office. Two earlier referenda aimed at curtailing Estonia's cabinet instability—in August 1932 and June 1933, proposed respectively by the United Agrarian Party (*see* Farmers' Party) and the National Center Party—had been soundly defeated. The VAPS referendum, however, was extremely successful, supported by 73 percent of those voting and with a relatively high voter turnout of 56 percent. As a result, the Tônisson (National Center Party) government resigned.

Ironically, the VAPS's success in passing their October 1933 referendum resulted in Konstantin Päts (United Agrarians) filling the new presidential chair on October 21, 1933. Under his direction, in early 1934, the Estonian parliament affirmed Päts's ban on extremist organizations and threatened the leaders of the banned groupings with arrest. VAPS leader Sirk was soon arrested, although he escaped to Finland in November 1934. Sirk remained in exile until his death in Luxembourg in 1937.

Functioning under various guises, the Veterans' League won an overwhelming victory in the January 1934 municipal elections; however, these mandates were subsequently annulled after President Päts dissolved parliament in October 1934. The VAPS continued to operate clandestinely; and in 1935, suspected of planning a coup, over 500 VAPS members were arrested and tried for their role in the abortive coup to overthrow the government.

The threat of war loomed over Estonia as pressures increased from both the Soviet Union and Germany in the late 1930s. In an attempt to enlist support for his government, Päts was forced to restore military decorations and pension rights to 14 VAPS members in June 1939. But in July 1940, the Veterans' League disappeared with the other Estonian parties under the advent of Soviet rule.

WABSE. *See* VETERANS' LEAGUE.

WORKERS' PARTY. *See* COMMUNIST PARTY OF ESTONIA.

WORKING PEOPLE'S LEAGUE. *See* COMMUNIST PARTY OF ESTONIA.

WORKING PEOPLE'S PARTY OF ESTONIA. *See* COMMUNIST PARTY OF ESTONIA.

WORKING PEOPLE'S UNITED FRONT. *See* COMMUNIST PARTY OF ESTONIA.

Vincent E. McHale

Party	1919[a]	1920	1923	1926	1929	1932	1938
Christian Democratic Party[b]	5	7	8	5	4		—
Labor Party	30	22	12	13	10	23*	—
Landlords' Party	—	1	2	2	3		
National Democratic Party	25	10	8	8	9		—
Communist Party[c]	—	5	10	6	6	5	
Farmers' Party[d]	8	21	23	23	24	42	—
Homesteaders' Party	—	—	4	14	14		—
Fatherland League[e]	—	—	—	—	—	—	63
Independent Socialist Workers' Party[f]	7	11	5	—	—	—	—
Social Democratic Party[g]	41	18	15	24	25	22	—
Baltic German Party	2	4	3	2	3**	3**	—
Swedish Party	1	0	0	0	2	5	
Russian National Union	1	1	4	3	0	0	—
Independents and others[h]	0	0	6	0	0	0	17
Total	120	100	100	100	100	100	80

a The 1919 election was for a constituent assembly.

b Known as the Christian Nationalist Party, 1926-1931.

c Did not participate in constituent assembly elections; known as the Central League of Tallinn Labor Unions, 1920-1921; as the Working People's United Front, 1923-1925; as the Workers' Party, 1926-1930; as the Leftist Workers' and Poorer Peasants' Party, 1932-1935; as the Working People's League in the Soviet-controlled election of 1940 (not shown in table).

d Known as the Rural League before 1921; formed part of the United Agrarian Party, 1932-1933; resumed Farmers' Party identity, 1933-1935; became basis of the Fatherland League, 1935-1940.

e Contested the 1938 election as the National Front for the Implementation of the Constitution.

f A party formed by splinters from the Social Revolutionary Party and the Social Democratic Party; merged into the Social Democratic Party in 1925.

g Officially titled as the Social Democratic Workers' Party, 1917-1925; as the Socialist Workers' Party, 1925-1935.

h In 1923, represents seats won by the National Liberal Party (4), the Ex-Servicemen's Party (1), and the Smallholders' Group (1); in 1938, represents primarily centrists who ran as independents since the 1935 ban on political party activity had not yet been officially lifted.

*

**

TABLE 35. Ruling Coalitions in Historical Estonia, 1921-1940

Dates	Coalition
Jan. 1921 - Oct. 1922	Farmers' Party Labor Party National Democratic Party Christian Democratic Party
Nov. 1922 - June 1923	Labor Party Farmers' Party National Democratic Party
Aug. 1923 - Mar. 1924	Farmers' Party Labor Party National Democratic Party Christian Democratic Party
Mar. 1924 - Dec. 1924	Christian Democratic Party National Democratic Party Labor Party
Dec. 1924 - Nov. 1925	National Democratic Party Christian Democratic Party Labor Party Farmers' Party Social Democratic Party
Dec. 1925 - June 1926	Farmers' Party Christian Democratic Party Homesteaders' Party National Liberal Party
July 1926 - Nov. 1927	Farmers' Party Homesteaders' Party National Democratic Party Christian Democratic Party Landlords' Party
Dec. 1927 - Nov. 1928	National Democratic Party Farmers' Party Labor Party Homesteaders' Party
Dec. 1928 - July 1929	Social Democratic Party Labor Party Homesteaders' Party Christian Democratic Party
July 1929 - Feb. 1931	Labor Party Farmers' Party Homesteaders' Party National Democratic Party Christian Democratic Party

TABLE 35. (*Continued*)

Dates	Coalition
Feb. 1931 - Jan. 1932	Farmers' Party National Democratic Party Landlords' Party Social Democratic Party
Feb. 1932 - Oct. 1932	United Agrarian Party National Center Party
Nov. 1932 - Apr. 1933	United Agrarian Party National Center Party Social Democratic Party
May 1933 - Oct. 1933	National Center Party United Agrarian Party
Oct. 1933 - Mar. 1935	Farmers' Party Social Democratic Party
Mar. 1935 - Sep. 1939	Fatherland League
Oct. 1939 - June 1940	"Cabinet of National Unity"—all-party coalition, headed by Farmers' Party

Note: First-named party is dominant coalition party.

HISTORICAL GERMANY, PRE-1945

Relative to the rest of Europe, the Germans were rather late to form a unified nation-state. When they finally accomplished unification in 1871, the Germans had still not resolved the many regional, religious, and ethnic loyalties which had divided their people for centuries. Nonetheless, the new German nation's large and rapidly expanding population (growing from approximately 41 million in 1871 to more than 65 million before World War I) and its vast resources soon made Germany one of the world's most powerful nations. But economic and military power came more easily than political consensus, sophistication, and restraint. Germany's extreme heterogeneity and its citizens' extreme consciousness of lack of national unity made stable, democratic government nearly impossible and too often led the Germans to resign themselves to authoritarian rulers.

Warfare and industrialization were instrumental in Germany's unification. For many centuries, the various German peoples had been spread over central Europe, bounded by the Rhine River area to the west, the Alps to the south, the Russian plains to the east, and by the North and Baltic Seas to the north. These German peoples lived peacefully and individually under the Holy Roman Empire (dating from A.D. 800). However, Napoleon abolished this archaic First Reich in 1806, and the Napoleonic Wars greatly stirred a pan-German, nationalist sentiment. Upon Napoleon's defeat, the major European powers met at the Congress of Vienna (1815) to establish political and geographic obstacles to Napoleon's France; and the German peoples, realizing that new forms of political organization were needed to protect themselves from hostile and warring neighbors, were thus given further impetus to form the German Confederation (*Deutscher Bund*, 1815-1866). The only serious protest to the Confederation came from the dispossessed dukes, knights, and other feudal satraps who had been leaders in the over 300 independent states and kingdoms of the pre-Napoleon empire.

A *Diet* (congress) was established to preside over the Confederation. Although designed to be an assembly of 39 sovereign states, the *Diet* was little more than a body that registered and promulgated decrees of the presiding Austrian government. Content with this new state of affairs in central Europe, Austria hoped to prevent any further efforts to reform or unify the German states. Prussia, second only to Austria in power, was also, at first, uninterested in greater changes; but gradually Prussia emerged as the champion of the unification movement and as Austria's competitor.

Without the dramatic social and economic changes occasioned by the Industrial Revolution, however, unification still might have been impossible. Liberal and nationalist interest spread rapidly through Germany with the rise of middle-class wealth and influence. The obvious advantages of economic unification (greatly facilitated by the Customs Union of 1834, which established free trade throughout most of Germany) helped the cause of greater political unity. During the revolutionary years of 1848-1849 in Europe, many well-respected Germans attempted to forge this unity through constitutional and democratic means, most vividly through the activities of the Frankfort Assembly, which proposed a draft constitution for all of Germany.

That their idealism did not succeed is one of Germany's greatest tragedies. Unification, in the famous words of the Prussian leader, Otto von Bismarck, came ultimately through blood and iron. In 1866, Prussia defeated Austria in a brief but decisive war. Shortly afterward, Austria reached a compromise with Hungary, establishing the Austro-Hungarian Empire. Nearly all German states north of the Main River united with the victor to form the North German Confederation (1867-1870). The remaining German states, mostly of southern Germany, came on board quickly when the North German Confederation went to war with France in 1870. Owing to its military successes, Germany became a unified empire on January 18, 1871, with the coronation of Wilhelm I of Prussia as German emperor.

Rapidly this Imperial Germany (or the Second Reich) became an awesome economic and military power. By 1914 only Russia had a larger population in Europe, and only England possessed a larger industrial base. However, this speedy maturation process did not apply in internal political matters. Though the powerful Bismarck had endowed the new German nation with many of the formal trappings of a democratic state—such as a popularly elected lower house of parliament (*Reichstag*) and political parties representing various interests—the federalized, constitutional monarchy of Imperial Germany was far from being an authentic democracy. Its constitution did not guarantee individual liberties; the emperor held considerable authority; ministers were not responsible to parliament, only to the monarch; the *Reichstag* was rent with too many ideological, religious, and political divisions to be effective; and the state of Prussia was too dominant. Nearly two-thirds the size of the Reich itself and in control of Germany's only real army, Prussia exercised almost complete dominance over the other German states: its king was the German emperor, its prime minister (Otto von Bismarck) was the German chancellor, and its delegates controlled the parliament.

Another problem with Imperial democracy was representation in the *Reichstag*. The system of voting in *Reichstag* elections, shaped by Bismarck, greatly favored the countryside over the city. Thus conservative interests were favored over liberal and socialist, because delegates were chosen from single-member districts which were never modified after 1871 to keep them in line with population shifts—mostly from rural to urban areas in these years. Furthermore, proportional representation in the *Reichstag* was nonexistent. In Prussia, the average number of voters per district was 121,000; in Berlin and other large non-Prussian cities, the average was 345,000. Yet despite these population distributions, Prussia held 236 out of the total 397 seats in the *Reichstag*.

In the upper house, or Federal Council (*Bundesrat*), where delegates were appointed by leaders of the 25 individual German states for an indefinite term, Prussia held a smaller share of the membership (17 of 58 members). However, by contract and other devices with the South German kingdoms, Bismarck's Prussia controlled an additional three votes. Because of Prussia's size and special, self-awarded privileges within the empire, its authoritarian traditions often held sway over all of Germany. Only defeat in World War I and massive external pressure was able to change this state of affairs.

Despite the democratic deficiencies of Imperial Germany, national-level political life flourished for the first time in German history. Many of the emergent political parties made valiant efforts to represent their supporters; some also attempted to expand the base of democracy. *Reichstag* deputies were elected from single-member districts under a two-ballot system. To be elected, an absolute majority was required on the first ballot. If no candidate reached this amount, a second ballot was held two weeks later between the two candidates who had received the largest share of the first-ballot vote. Because of the multiplicity of political groups, second balloting occurred in over half the districts throughout the Imperial era.

All males over 25 years of age usually exercised their right to vote. Voter turnout climbed steadily throughout the period to nearly 85 percent in the last elections before World War I. Elections were held every three years until 1888, after which the term of office was extended to five years. Although some parties had real success in individual elections, no single party ever garnered a majority of the votes cast. Elections during the 19th century turned largely on the personalities of the candidates rather than abstract party programs. Nor did any single party ever achieve a majority in parliament, such "majorities" reflecting only shifting coalitions, often manipulated by the emperor and chancellor to achieve support for government policies.

As table 36 shows, more than ten major parties managed to elect *Reichstag* representatives at one time or another in the 13 elections of the Imperial period, but only six parties consistently received sizable support from the electorate: two of these parties represented primarily conservative interests (the German Conservative Party* and the German Reich Party*), two represented liberal interests (the National Liberal Party* and the Progressive Party*), one represented the interests of German Catholics (the Center Party*), and one represented working-class interests (the Social Democratic Party of Germany*). Minor parties tended to represent various ethnic and regional interests (Alsace-Lorraine Party,* Danish Party,* German Hanover Party,* and Polish Party*); specific class and economic interests (Farmers League* and Economic Union*); or extremist ideologies (Anti-Semites*).

The National Liberals were the largest party at the beginning of the Imperial period, and they strongly backed the policies of Chancellor Bismarck. But by the 1880s this alliance broke down, and the National Liberals never regained their earlier status. The Social Democrats made great strides shortly before World War I, causing some to believe that socialism could be voted into power. The Center Party, however, was the most consistent. Its stable share of about 25 percent of the vote ensured the strong representation of Germany's more than 20 million Catholics. The Progressives were probably the most democratic of all the major parties, but they suffered from many splits within their ranks. The Conservatives and the Free Conservatives (see German Reich Party) formed the strongest right-wing opposition to further democratization efforts, and their influence often exceeded their voter strength.

Upon Kaiser Wilhelm I's death in 1886, his son, Frederick III, ascended the German throne; but dying less than four months later, Frederick was in turn succeeded by his son, Wilhelm II. Unlike his grandfather, who had submitted to the direction of "Iron Chancellor" Bismarck, Wilhelm II took strategic advantage of deficiencies in Bismarck's Imperial constitution to institute a rule of authoritarianism. Empowered to appoint the Reich chancellor, young Wilhelm dismissed Bismarck in 1890 and thereupon initiated a period of decline in Germany's stability. Now unchecked by the earlier control of an Iron Chancellor, the Reichstag parties were free to establish their own coalitions and party platforms, even if not totally in support of government policies, and the parties began to seek influence over parliament's constitutional authority to help shape budgetary and legislative matters. However, the kaiser still maintained primary political power, and he sought to obstruct the parliament in any way possible.

With the onset of World War I, Germany's parties were united in patriotism and willingly agreed to the constitution's provision for the declaration of a state of seige, knowing that such a provision meant transfer of executive power from civil to military authorities throughout the Reich. Thus between 1914 and 1918, Germany functioned under the military dictatorship known as the War Government. In each state or kingdom, local governments and monarchs were eclipsed by appointed military administrators, all of whom were responsible only to the recentralized Reich government, which in turn was responsible to the army's Supreme Command. Even Wilhelm II was overpowered by the military authorities, who merely ignored the kaiser's pretensions as continuing head of state. The *Reichstag* was permitted continued existence for reasons of national unity and morale, though it, too, was stripped of meaningful power.

However, facing military defeat at the hands of the Allied Powers, by late 1918 the military authorities sought an armistice and gave way to a new parliamentary government that might be recognized to achieve such a political end to the war. Formed in September 1918 under the direction of Prince Max of Baden, members of the majority parties constituted the new cabinet, and an appeal was made for an armistice on October 3, 1918. The growing revolutionary fervor on the part of the war-weary German masses led Kaiser Wilhelm II to abdicate and flee to Holland on November 8, 1918; and following a one-day mass demonstration on November 9, a second government was formed with the collaboration of various elements of the Social Democratic Party, who immediately proclaimed the birth of Germany's first republic.

Against the hopes of many revolutionaries, Friedrich Ebert (the Social Democratic leader and new Reich chancellor, appointed by Prince Max), acted quickly to restore order and defend democracy. He called for elections to a constituent national assembly, which would determine the future political structure of Germany. This body convened in Weimar on February 6, 1919, and its delegates created a government that became known as the Weimar Republic.

In constitutional terms, Weimar was a model democracy. With all monarchs of the former German kingdoms having abdicated at war's end, the new republic could act as a truly centralized nation. The new constitution, adopted on August 14, 1919, gave sovereignty to the people and guaranteed fundamental rights such as freedom of the person, of association and assembly, of the press, of selecting one's occupation, and of academic teaching. Real governmental authority now resided in the *Reichstag*, whose members were elected every four years (by all men and women over age 20) by means of proportional representation in 35 multimember constituencies.

The Weimar Republic, in relation to Imperial Germany, had an even greater range of political parties representing different shades of political opinion. *Reichstag* members were elected according to party lists in each constituency, using the Baden system of proportional representation. The total membership of the *Reichstag* was left indeterminate, with party seats allocated on the basis of one seat for every 60,000 votes obtained in that district. (A party received an additional seat if its remainder vote in that district exceeded 30,000.) The party's remaining votes from throughout the republic were pooled into a *Reichlist* of that particular party: 60,000 additional votes, even if scattered among many electoral districts, sufficed to elect one additional candidate, and 90,000 or more votes allowed the party to seat two additional candidates. New and small parties found it easy to achieve the required quota, while the details of the electoral system seemed to work against the formation of large national blocs. The term of office was four years, unless the *Reichstag* was dissolved sooner by the president of the republic.

Although most of the old Imperial parties reappeared with only cosmetic name changes (*see* table 37), Weimar witnessed the dramatic rise of two new extremist parties hostile to democracy in any form: the Communist Party of Germany* on the left and the Nazis (or National Socialist German Worker's Party*) on the right. These parties' revolutionary goals and behavior, combined with growing memberships and voter support, posed a dire challenge to each other, to the other parties, and to the Weimar Republic itself. The Nazi Party finally won the ideological battle and acted as Weimar's executioner.

The other significant Weimar parties were: the German National People's Party,* which replaced the old Conservative and Reich parties; the German People's Party,* which took over for the National Liberals; the German Democratic Party,* replacing the Progressives; the German Business Party,* a new grouping representing bourgeois interests; the Center Party, under its old name but now competing with the Bavarian People's Party* for the Catholic vote; the Social Democratic Party of Germany, which had split apart during World War I and during the Weimar period faced competition for the workingman's vote from the Communist Party and from the Independent Social Democratic Party of Germany*; and finally the tiny German Hanover Party, which carried over from Imperial Germany to protest the severing of Hanover's ties to England.

There were numerous small parties of special interest which appeared in the Weimar's *Reichstag* at various times. Many were too small and unstable to be properly called parties. Most prominent among them were: the German Agriculturalists (*Deutsche Landvolk*), German Farmers Party (*Deutsche Bauernpartei*), Rural Union (*Landbund*), Saxony Agriculturalists (*Sächsisches Landvolk*), Christian Social People's Service (*Christlich-Sozialer Volksdienst*), Conservative People's Party (*Konservative Volkspartei*), and the People's Rights Party (*Volksrecht Partei*).

The boundaries of the old German states (or *Länder*) remained much the same, with some minor exceptions owing to the territorial losses mandated by World War I's Versailles Peace Treaty (such as the loss of Alsace-Lorraine to France) and to the merger of the eight individual states of Thuringia into one. Germany had hoped to reclaim Austria, because of Austria's Germanic population and its historic ties to the other German states, but the Allied Powers refused approval of this reunion. The Federal Council, now named the *Reichrat*, no longer possessed an absolute veto over legislation. The central government now took over many powers previously held by the individual states, such as control over transportation and communications and the right to levy direct taxes. Finally, the new constitution gave executive authority to the new office of the Reich president. Elected by all citizens for a seven-year term, the president's prime task in normal times was to appoint a chancellor and cabinet, and then step aside to let the government function by itself. But in times of crisis, the president's powers were extensive. He could dissolve the *Reichstag* and call for new elections, and he could invoke the notorious Article 48 of the constitution which, in effect, allowed him to rule by decree as long as the crisis continued and the *Reichstag* did not act to rescind his orders.

Unfortunately, crisis was too often the normal state of affairs in the Weimar period. The popularly elected Reich president retained a power (reminiscent of the Imperial days) to appoint the chancellor and cabinet, but the stable functioning of these influential latter positions also required support of the popularly elected *Reichstag*. Such mutual support among all of these positions and bodies was difficult to achieve, resulting in frequent deadlocks, resignations, and dissolutionments. Hence in its brief lifespan of slightly more than 14 years, Weimar had eight *Reichstag* elections and 21 different cabinets. Furthermore, Weimar was constantly plagued by economic insecurity, military revanchism, and attempted revolutionary overthrows from both the left and right; it had no party representing democratic interests that could ever secure a parliamentary majority; and even in the best of times, it had to rely on an unstable governmental coalition of socialists, centrists, and democrats (*see* table 38).

Apologists argue that the Weimar system could not survive because of its deficiencies (such as proportional representation allowing too many parties, the failure to replace the conservative administrative machinery and personnel of Imperial Germany, the concentration of too much power in the president's hands in times of crisis). A better argument might be that the German people had too little experience with and too little faith in democratic government to permit Weimar more than a fleeting tenure. Ultimately, Weimar succumbed in 1933 to Adolf Hitler, who exploited the insecurity of the German people and used loopholes in the constitution, especially Article 48, to stage a "legal" revolution.

The Third Reich (1933-1945) was the creation of Adolf Hitler and his National Socialist movement. At first, the National Socialist German Worker's Party (NSDAP) was only one of many small fringe groups which had sprung up in Germany in the immediate post-World War I years. Hitler, a former soldier, joined the group in 1919 as its seventh member. The party was antimarxist, antidemocratic, and violently ultranationalistic in outlook. It was centered in Bavaria, the site of the short-lived Soviet Republic in 1919.

On November 8-9, 1923, the NSDAP staged an abortive revolt in a Munich beer hall, known as the "Beer Hall *putsch.*" Easily quelled, this action led to the banning of the party and a short jail term for its members, during which time Hitler composed the future NSDAP program—*Mein Kampf* (My Struggle). Six years after the Munich *putsch*, Hitler became the undisputed NSDAP leader. He had come to realize that the road to political power could not be revolutionary if the army and security forces remained loyal to the presiding government, and that political power was initiated in the ballot box. Playing on the German people's emotionalism in the throes of the world depression, Hitler staged mass assemblies in which he employed his showmanship and oratory powers to attack Germany's treatment by the Allies in the World War I peace settlements and to use anti-Semitism to establish a scapegoat for Germany's ills. These tactics unified the emotionally and economically depressed German people in a way never before experienced. The NSDAP contested the *Reichstag* elections of 1928 and 1930, and Hitler's tactics were so successful that the party increased its representation from 12 to 107 deputies respectively.

Between 1930 and 1933, the NSDAP consolidated its electoral strength as the world depression spread economic misery across Weimar Germany. During this time, Hitler and his movement made several unsuccessful attempts to obtain control of the government by legal means. Hitler failed by a wide margin to win the Reich presidency in 1932 against Hindenburg. Also, the NSDAP failed to capture the government seats of the key *Länder*.

Finally, after a series of political intrigues, on January 30, 1933, Hitler was appointed to the chancellorship as the head of an 11-member cabinet of National Socialists (three members) and of the German National People's Party (eight members). This cabinet was known as the National Concentration. Hitler's close colleague, Hermann Göring, was appointed to this cabinet as minister without portfolio, as well as to the powerful position as head of the Prussian police. Although Hitler's government was instituted in conformity with existing constitutional and parliamentary practice, he immediately began to dismantle the institutions of the Weimar government. With *Reichstag* elections scheduled for March 5, 1933, Hitler arranged for the Reich president's signature on an emergency ordinance restricting the freedom of press and assembly. On February 26, supposedly outraged at these restrictions on campaigning activities, communists and socialists had set fire to the *Reichstag* building. Göring immediately arrested all Communist Party *Reichstag* deputies, as well as numerous additional Communist, Social Democrat, and other opposition party functionaries. Though later revealed that men under Göring's and Hitler's direction had set this fire, the intrigue had succeeded in moving President Hindenburg to sign yet another emergency ordinance, this one revoking all civil liberties and introducing the death penalty for any "attacks" on government officials.

Through such means of terror and oppression, the Nazis won 43.9 percent of the March 5 vote and emerged as the largest *Reichstag* party. Hitler's appointment as chancellor still stood, and he continued to direct further acts of political terror. None of the Communist Party's 81 elected deputies appeared at the first *Reichstag* session after the election, all having been assassinated, jailed, or having fled into hiding. Mob violence ruled the streets, and armed Brownshirts of the NSDAP filled the *Reichstag* building. In this atmosphere of terror and pressure, Hitler's famous "Enabling Act" was passed on March 24, 1933, carried by 441 votes and opposed by only 94 Social Democrat votes.

The Enabling Act, though not formally suspending the Weimar constitution, allowed the government to rule by decree. Almost at once, the political parties were either abolished or eliminated by voluntary self-dissolution, including the NSDAP's coalition partner, the German National People's Party. By the end of 1933, Germany was a one-party state, and any attempt at reconstructing old parties or founding new ones was declared to be a treasonable act.

Following the death of President Hindenburg on August 1, 1934, Hitler added the final touch to his consolidation of power, and the offices of Reich president and chancellor were fused into a single office—that of *Fuehrer* (Supreme Leader) held by Hitler. The *Reichstag* was transformed into a rubber-stamp body, made up of an assemblage of government appointees. Nominally, the electoral provisions of the Weimar Republic still operated under the Third Reich, although elections ceased to have any meaning. Voting was restricted to those of German or "racially similar blood." New electoral districts were added to the original 35 after the annexation of Austria and the Sudetenland to Germany in 1938. Virtually all members of the *Reichstag* were NSDAP candidates, with a few special nonpartisans as official "guests." The *Reichstag* met only 20 times between 1933 and 1939.

Between 1938 and 1941, German military adventures in Europe vastly increased Germany's territorial control. This military expansion resulted from Hitler's and the Nazis' philosophy either to unite all Aryan/Nordic (denoting Greek, Roman, Germanic) races to a homeland or to secure the territories of "inferior races" to provide additional living area for the "master race." Germany's decision to attack the Soviet Union in June 1941, and the entry of the United States into the war, greatly taxed Germany's military power and placed a tremendous strain on the civilian population. In 1943, Hitler withdrew as active commander of the German military and recalled the traditional aristocracy to take his place. By 1944, Germany's defeat seemed a foregone conclusion. Friction increased between various elements in the military and the Nazi Party, and in July 1944 an unsuccessful attempt was made on Hitler's life. Later revealed to be a military plot, a purge of the army followed which seriously weakened what was left of Germany's war effort.

In June 1944, the Allied forces had invaded Europe from the west and east. On April 30, 1945, with Russian troops converging on Berlin from all sides, Hitler committed suicide in his bunker below the Reich chancellery. On May 7-8, the German command surrendered to the Allied military authorities, and the Third Reich was at an end. Under the terms of the Yalta Agreement (1945) and the Berlin Declaration (1945), Germany was divided into three major zones of occupation, with control to be shared among the United States, the Soviet Union, and Britain and France. Between 1945 and 1948, Germany was governed by the Allied Control Council, which operated in lieu of a central government. A similar agency was designated for Berlin (*see* WEST GERMANY). Allied control ended in 1948; and after local and state governments had been constituted, the (West) German Federal Republic came into being in September 1949 (*see* WEST GERMANY), followed shortly thereafter by the formation of the (East) German Democratic Republic (*see* EAST GERMANY).

Bibliography

Bergstraesser, Ludwig. *Geschichte der politischen Parteien in Deutschland.* Munich: Günter Olzug Verlag, 1960.

Booms, Hans. *Die Konservative Partei, Preussischer Charakter, Reichsauffassung, Nationalbegriff.* Düsseldorf: Droste Verlag, 1954.

Craig, Gordon. *Germany 1866-1945.* New York: Oxford Univeristy Press, 1978.

Flechtheim, Ossip K. *Die Kommunistische Partei Deutschlands in der Weimarer Republik.* Offenbach a.M.: Bollwerk Verlag, 1948.

Halperin, S. William. *Germany Tried Democracy: A Political History of the Reich from 1918-1933.* New York: Thomas Y. Crowell Co., 1946.

Hartenstein, W. *Die Anfänge der Deutschen Volkspartei.* Düsseldorf: Droste Verlag, 1963.

Heberle, Rudolf. *From Democracy to Nazism: A Regional Case Study on Political Parties in Germany.* New York: H. Fertig, 1970.

Hertzmann, Lewis. *DNVP: Right-wing Opposition in the Weimar Republic.* Lincoln: University of Nebraska Press, 1963.

Holborn, Hajo. *A History of Modern Germany, 1840-1945.* New York: Alfred A. Knopf, 1959.

Lidtke, Vernon L. *The Outlawed Party: Social Democracy in Germany, 1878-1890.* Princeton, N.J.: Princeton University Press, 1966.

Liebe, Werner. *Die Deutschnationale Volkspartei, 1918-1924.* Düsseldorf: Droste Verlag, 1956.

Loewenstein, Karl. "Germany and Central Europe." In *Governments of Continental Europe,* edited by James T. Shotwell. New York: Macmillan Co., 1940.

Maser, Werner. *Die Frühgeschichte der NSDAP.* Frankfurt: Athenäum, 1965.

Milatz, Alfred. *Wähler und Wahlen in der Weimarer Republik.* Bonn: Bundeszentrale für politische Bildung, 1965.

Mommsen, Wilhelm. *Deutsche Parteiprogramme.* Munich: Isar Verlag, 1960.

Morgan, David W. *The Socialist Left and the German Revolution: A History of the German Independent Social Democratic Party, 1917-1922.* Ithaca, N.Y.: Cornell University Press, 1975.

Morsey, Rudolf. *Die deutsche Zentrumspartei 1917-1923.* Düsseldorf: Droste Verlag, 1966.

Neumann, Sigmund. *Die deutschen Parteien: Wesen und Wandel nach dem Kriege.* Berlin: Junker und Dünnhaupt Verlag, 1932.

Nicholls, A. J. *Weimar and the Rise of Hitler.* New York: St. Martin's Press, 1968.

Nipperdey, Thomas. *Die Organization der deutschen Parteien vor 1918.* Düsseldorf: Droste Verlag, 1961.

Orlow, Dietrich. *History of the Nazi Party, 1919-1933.* Pittsburgh: University of Pittsburgh Press, 1969.

Ritter, Gerhard. *Die Arbeiterbewegung im Wilhelminischen Reich: Die Sozialdemokratische Partei und die Freien Gewerkschaften, 1890-1900.* Berlin-Dahlem: Colloquium Verlag, 1963.

————, ed. *Deutschen Parteien vor 1918.* Cologne: Kiepenheuer und Witsch, 1973.

Roth, Gunther. *The Social Democrats in Imperial Germany: A Study in Working Class Isolation and National Integration.* Totowa, N.J.: Bedminster Press, 1963.

Schauff, Johannes. *Die deutschen Katholiken und die Zentrumspartei: Eine politisch-statistische Untersuchung der Reichstagswahlen seit 1871.* Berlin: Weltgeist-Bücher Verlag, 1928.

Schönhoven, Klaus. *Die bayerische Volkspartei, 1924-1932.* Düsseldorf: Droste Verlag, 1972.

Schorske, Carl W. *German Social Democracy, 1905-1917.* Cambridge, Mass.: Harvard University Press, 1955.

Sheehan, James J. *German Liberalism in the Nineteenth Century.* Chicago: University of Chicago Press, 1978.

Stegmann, Dirk. *Die Erben Bismarcks. Parteien und Verbände in der Spätphase des Wilhelminischen Deutschlands: Sammlungspolitik, 1897-1918.* Cologne: Kiepenheuer und Witsch, 1970.

Stehlin, Stewart A. *Bismarck and the Guelph Problem, 1866-1890: A Study in Particularist Opposition to National Unity.* The Hague: Martinus Nijhoff, 1973.

Stephan, Werner. *Aufstieg und Verfall des Linksliberalismus, 1918-1933: Geschichte der Deutschen Demokratischen Partei.* Göttingen: Vandenhoeck und Ruprecht, 1973.

Stürmer, Michael. *Koalition und Opposition in der Weimarer Republik, 1924-1928.* Düsseldorf: Droste Verlag, 1967.

Tormin, Walter. *Geschichte der deutschen Parteien seit 1848.* Stuttgart: Kohlhammer, 1966.

Westarp, Count Kuno von. *Konservative Politik im letzten Jahrzehnt des Kaiserreiches.* Berlin: Deutsche Verlagsgesellschaft, 1935.

Zeender, John K. *The German Center Party, 1890-1906.* Philadelphia: American Philosophical Society, 1976.

Political Parties

ALSACE-LORRAINE PARTY (*Elsäss-Lothringen Partei:* ELSÄSSER). The Alsace-Lorraine Party represented autonomist sentiments of the largely French-speaking population of the Alsace-Lorraine area. These former French territories, west of the upper Rhine River, had been ceded by France to Germany in 1871 after France's defeat in the Franco-Prussian War. First campaigning in the 1874 elections, the ELSÄSSER elected an average of 15 representatives to the German *Reichstag.* Between 1871 and 1914, however, over 400,000 out of a population of 1.2 million emigrated from Alsace-Lorraine to France; and by 1890, the ELSÄSSER's representation in parliament dwindled to ten and never regained its former size. Despite its smaller representation, the party continued throughout the period to protest the "colonialist" policies of the German government toward the people of Alsace-Lorraine and toward other Roman Catholics and minorities in the Reich (such as those represented by the ELSÄSSER's frequent allies, the German Hanover Party,* the Danish Party,* and the Polish Party*). The ELSÄSSER disappeared after Germany's defeat in World War I and the reversion of the Alsace-Lorraine territory back to control of France.

ANTI-SEMITEN. *See* ANTI-SEMITES.

ANTI-SEMITES (*Anti-Semiten*). In the Imperial *Reichstag,* the Anti-Semites was an electoral alliance of two small parties, the Christian Social Party* and the German Reform Party.* The Anti-Semites' principal policy was resistance to Jewish influence in German society. This group elected its first *Reichstag* member in 1887 and was represented in parliament until the collapse of the Imperial system (1914). From a high of 16 members in 1893 and 1907, the party declined to three members in 1912. In 1918 the Anti-Semites disappeared as a separate political grouping when most of its members helped to found the German National People's Party.*

BAVARIAN CATHOLIC PARTY. *See* BAVARIAN PEOPLE'S PARTY.

BAVARIAN PEOPLE'S PARTY (*Bayerische Volkspartei*: BVP). In November 1918, Bavarian Catholics formed their own grouping under the leadership of Georg Heim and Heinrich Held. At first, the Bavarians remained united within the parent Center Party* and were represented by one member in the national cabinet. But severe differences over the issues of centralization versus federalism, taxation, and cooperation with the Social Democratic Party of Germany* soon proved too great, and the Bavarians defected in January 1920 under the BVP label. At that time, the BVP (also known as the Bavarian Catholic Party) constituted about one-fourth of the total membership of the Center Party. After this formal split, the two parties often acted in alliance on matters pertaining to foreign policy, the church, schooling, and cultural affairs, but diverged on many other important issues. Proclaiming the policy of "Bavaria for the Bavarians," the BVP bitterly resented the loss of many of Bavaria's special rights in the new, more centralized Weimar Republic. In general, the BVP was more conservative, less enamoured of the Weimar system, and less democratic than the Center Party—many BVP leaders were preferably monarchist and even lamented the loss of the Wittelsbach dynasty on the Bavarian throne.

The Bavarian People's Party also differed from the Centrists in that most BVP support came from rural and small-town people, owing to Bavaria's less industrialized nature. Although the party did very well among Bavaria's Catholic majority, this support was not enough to provide the BVP with more than a small fraction of the voter turnout—usually three or four percent. But this was many times enough to gain representation in the fleeting cabinets of the fragmented Weimar Republic. One of the BVP's members was included in each of the nine separate cabinets governing Germany between 1924 and 1932.

After World War II and the breakup of "historical" Germany, the concerns of the BVP were carried on primarily by the Bavarian Party (*see* WEST GERMANY). Other BVP elements eventually found their way into the postwar Christian Democratic Union/Christian Social Union (*see* WEST GERMANY).

BAYERISCHE VOLKSPARTEI. *See* BAVARIAN PEOPLE'S PARTY.

BVP. *See* BAVARIAN PEOPLE'S PARTY.

CATHOLIC PARTY. *See* CENTER PARTY.

CENTER PARTY (*Zentrumspartei*: Z). From the time of its founding in December 1870 to the present, the Center Party has remained a major force in German politics. In Imperial Germany, the Centrists always had a strong parliamentary representation—in the years between 1890 and 1907 they had more *Reichstag* members than any other party. The Center Party (also known as the Catholic Party) emerged after each of the world wars to play an often leading role in both the Weimar and the Federal (*see* WEST GERMANY) Republic. Today the Christian Democratic Union (*see* CHRISTIAN DEMOCRATIC UNION/CHRISTIAN SOCIAL UNION, WEST GERMANY) represents many of the Center Party's concerns.

The Centrists' prime task has always been to represent the interests of the large Catholic minority, which numbered about one out of every three persons in Imperial Germany. Matters of religion and morality were of primary concern, but the party also strongly expressed views on all political, social, and economic questions. The Center Party was antisecular and antistatist; thus it usually opposed measures which would increase the Imperial government's power over individual German citizens and states. The party fervently struggled to uphold the autonomy of the church from the state and the Christian character of its schools. Although opposed to the laissez-faire economic principles of the liberal parties, the Centrists shared their interest in greater constitutional development, reasoning that this would provide legal protection against Germany's Protestant majority. The Centrists also shared the liberals' disdain for socialism.

Ludwig Windthorst was the Center Party's early spokesman. Along with Eugen Richter of the Progressive Party, * Windthorst was often considered Chancellor Bismarck's fiercest and most skilled parliamentary opponent. Between 1871 and 1878, a battle known as the *Kulturkampf* raged between the chancellor and the Center Party. Bismarck, in his belief that Catholicism was his greatest enemy in both domestic and foreign matters, carried out a discriminatory policy against the German Catholics. However, with the 1878 ascendency of a new and more liberal pope (Pope Leo XIII), with the rise of a new and more dangerous enemy in the form of the Social Democratic Party of Germany, * and with a desire for an alliance with Catholic Austria, Bismarck opted to promptly end the *Kulturkampf*. In the 1880s, perhaps because of their common fear of socialism, both the chancellor and the Center Party displayed a new interest in improving the economic and social existence of the masses. Together they devised and passed through parliament a broad series of social welfare measures. Further evidence of the Catholics' new temporal concerns was the founding of Catholic trade unions.

The Center Party became more conservative in the years before 1914 under the leadership of people like Count Georg von Hertling, who served a brief term near the end of World War I as Reich chancellor. But, under Matthias Erzberger, the party's left wing also remained well represented. Desiring to make the party more than a religious organization, Erzberger attempted to move the Centrists closer to other progressive political groups. Thus Erzberger laid the foundation for the coalition governments of the Weimar years. Nevertheless, the Center Party's support continued to follow religious rather than class or ethnic lines. This accounted for the Centrists' huge following in Westphalia and the Rhineland, Bavaria, and the Polish provinces of eastern Prussia.

At first critical of the November 1918 revolution to establish the Weimar Republic, the Center Party emerged as one of Weimar's leading supporters. The party was renamed the Christian People's Party (*Christliche Volkspartei*: CVP) in 1919 (not to be confused with a later party of the same name, *see* WEST GERMANY). But the group reverted to its Center Party designation for succeeding Weimar elections. As the only party to serve in every cabinet until 1932, the Centrists' crucial role in the Weimar Republic was further evidenced in its production of nine of Weimar's 22 chancellors, far more than any other party. Led at first by its left wing, headed by Matthias Erzberger and later by Dr. Joseph Wirth, the party often cooperated with the German Democratic Party* and the Social Democrats. The Centrists' party program was flexible in all matters outside of religious issues, where it strongly defended the rights of Germany's Catholics. Often the party leaders would criticize liberal capitalism and support social legislation in concert with its Democratic and Social Democratic colleagues, but the Centrists also defended the right to hold private property. Toward the end of the Weimar years, the party's policies became more conservative and nationalistic, keeping in step with the changing mood of Germany's citizens in general, and leadership devolved into the hands of the party's right wing under Monsignor Ludwig Kaas and Heinrich Brüning.

The Center Party differed from most of the other Weimar parties in that it was not a class-based grouping, and its share of the electorate remained relatively stable. The party was open to non-Catholics and actively sought the female vote. Usually the Centrists could count on about 60 percent of the Catholic voters, irrespective of their social or economic standing, thereby netting about 13 percent of the total national vote. Centrist strength would have been even greater had the Bavarian Catholics not decided to form their own Bavarian People's Party,* which defected from the Center Party in 1920, taking with them about one-fourth of the Center Party's membership. This, however, did not jeopardize the interests of Germany's Catholics because the two parties almost always supported each other on religious questions.

Outlawed by the Third Reich with all other political parties, the Center Party reemerged in post-World War II Germany under its same label (*see* CENTER PARTY, WEST GERMANY), though some Center Party elements found their way into the Christian Democratic Union groupings that appeared both in West Germany and East Germany.

CHRISTIAN PEOPLE'S PARTY. *See* CENTER PARTY.

CHRISTIAN SOCIAL PARTY (*Christlich-Soziale Partei*). The Christian Social Party was formed in 1868 by three Catholic societies of Crefeld in the Prussian

Rhineland. Toward the reconstruction of the German social order, the party advocated a socioeconomic ideology which combined socialism and medieval corporatism. However, according to their ideology, reform would come through the church, not through the working classes.

The Christian Socialists never achieved electoral significance. The party's importance, however, came from its introduction of anti-Semitism into German politics and from its strong intellectual influence on the politics of German Catholicism. After 1871, the majority of the Christian Socialists was absorbed into the Catholic-oriented Center Party.* The remnants of the Christian Social Party joined with the German Reform Party* to form an electoral alliance known as the Anti-Semites.*

CHRISTIAN SOCIAL PEOPLE'S SERVICE. *See* HISTORICAL GERMANY INTRODUCTION.

CHRISTLICHE VOLKSPARTEI. *See* CENTER PARTY.

CHRISTLICH-SOZIALE PARTEI. *See* CHRISTIAN SOCIAL PARTY.

CHRISTLICHA-SOZIALER VOLKSDIENST. *See* HISTORICAL GERMANY INTRODUCTION.

COMMUNIST PARTY OF GERMANY (*Kommunistische Partei Deutschlands*: KPD). The Communist Party of Germany was formed on January 1, 1919. Previously, the group was known as the Spartacus League, a left-wing faction of the Independent Social Democratic Party of Germany.* The original Communist program called for a revolutionary overthrow of German society, followed by the establishment of a proletarian dictatorship. Any and all means, such as strikes, demonstrations, and street-fighting, would be employed to achieve these ends. But the early deaths of the party's best-known revolutionaries, Rosa Luxemburg and Karl Liebknecht, during the Sparticist Uprising in Berlin in January 1919, deprived the Communists of their greatest potential leaders and dashed most members' hopes for a quick triumph.

Acting on the belief that revolution was imminent, the KPD had initially decided not to participate in elections to the National Assembly. But the Communists soon recognized that they could gain propagandistic advantages by running candidates for the *Reichstag*, and thereafter they took part in all Weimar elections. The KPD had only scant success at first, winning 2.6 percent of the vote and seating four members in the first Weimar election of June 1920. But their fortunes rapidly improved in following elections, largely as a result of the dissolution of the Independent Social Democratic Party. The Communists thus gained millions of new supporters, making the KPD the largest communist party outside of the Soviet Union, and KPD representation in the *Reichstag* increased to 62 members in 1924. By 1925, Ernst Thälmann had assumed party leadership, and under his guidance the Communists remained committed to revolutionary ends but followed dutifully the dictates of the Bolshevik regime in Moscow.

In accord with Moscow's wishes, the KPD came to view the Social Democratic Party of Germany* as its greatest enemy and thus refused to cooperate in that party's program of effecting change through parliamentary action. Of course, the Communists also detested the bourgeois and right-wing parties, especially the Nazis (see National Socialist German Worker's Party) with whom they often waged bloody street battles. The economic depression after 1929 swelled the KPD's ranks, and by the November 1932 election the Communist Party, with 100 members in the *Reichstag*, almost equalled the size of the Social Democratic representation (121 seats). But the KPD's growth reflected only a small fraction of the millions of Germans who sought a radical solution for Weimar's economic and political ills. The Nazis, who capitalized on the middle and upper classes' fear of bolshevism and on the disunity of the political left, were the real beneficiaries. The Communists continually refused to make common cause with the Social Democrats and hardly lamented Hitler's destruction of the hated Weimar Republic. Many Communists rationalized that the Nazi regime's triumph merely represented capitalism's most authoritarian, final stage. Such ideological blindness prevented them from recognizing that the Nazis would more certainly put an end to their dream of proletarian revolution. In fact, the Communists served as one of Adolf Hitler's first political scapegoats in his rise to power through terror and oppression (see Historical Germany introduction), and the KPD was outlawed by the Third Reich in 1933.

After World War II, the KPD's genealogical line was perpetuated by the German Communist Party (see WEST GERMANY). (See also SOCIALIST UNITY PARTY, EAST GERMANY.)

CONSERVATIVE PEOPLE'S PARTY. See HISTORICAL GERMANY INTRODUCTION.

CVP. See CENTER PARTY.

DÄNISCHE PARTEI. See DANISH PARTY.

DANISH PARTY (*Dänische Partei*). The smallest party to gain continuous representation in the Imperial *Reichstag*, the Danish Party usually elected only one member, except in 1881 when it elected two. The party, organized in 1871, represented the Danes of North Schleswig (approximately 50,000) who protested their severence from Denmark as a result of the Danish war of 1864. In its struggle against German dominance, the Danish Party often allied with other small ethnically or regionally based groups, such as with the Alsace-Lorraine Party,* the German Hanover Party,* and the Polish Party.* The Danish Party disappeared with the collapse of the Imperial system after World War I. (*See also*

SCHLESWIG PARTY, DENMARK; and SOUTH SCHLESWIG VOTER'S LEAGUE, WEST GERMANY.)

DDP. *See* GERMAN DEMOCRATIC PARTY.

DEUTSCHE ARBEITERPARTEI. *See* NATIONAL SOCIALIST GERMAN WORKER'S PARTY.

DEUTSCHE BAUERNPARTEI. *See* HISTORICAL GERMANY INTRO-DUCTION.

DEUTSCHE DEMOKRATISCHE PARTEI. *See* GERMAN DEMOCRATIC PARTY.

DEUTSCHE HANNOVER PARTEI. *See* GERMAN HANOVER PARTY.

DEUTSCHE LANDVOLK. *See* HISTORICAL GERMANY INTRODUCTION.

DEUTSCHE REFORMPARTEI. *See* GERMAN REFORM PARTY.

DEUTSCHE REICHSPARTEI. *See* HISTORICAL GERMANY INTRO-DUCTION.

DEUTSCHE STAATSPARTEI. *See* GERMAN DEMOCRATIC PARTY.

DEUTSCHE VOLKSPARTEI. *See* GERMAN PEOPLE'S PARTY (1868-1907) and (1919-1933).

DEUTSCHE WIRTSCHAFTSPARTEI. *See* GERMAN BUSINESS PARTY.

DEUTSCHKONSERVATIVE PARTEI. *See* GERMAN CONSERVATIVE PARTY.

DEUTSCHNATIONALE VOLKSPARTEI. *See* GERMAN NATIONAL PEO-PLE'S PARTY.

DHP. *See* GERMAN HANOVER PARTY.

DNVP. *See* GERMAN NATIONAL PEOPLE'S PARTY.

DR. *See* GERMAN REICH PARTY.

DVP. *See* GERMAN PEOPLE'S PARTY.

ECONOMIC UNION (*Wirtschafts Vereinigung*). The Economic Union was a right-wing group with representation in the last two *Reichstags* of the Imperial period (1907, 1912) with five and ten deputies respectively. Although the Union favored both agrarian and social legislation, the party reflected the views of conservative middle-class elements seeking to maintain their position in German society. The Economic Union became part of the German People's Party (1919-1933)* in the Weimar Republic.

ELSÄSSER. *See* ALSACE-LORRAINE PARTY.

ELSÄSS-LOTHRINGEN PARTEI. *See* ALSACE-LORRAINE PARTY.

FARMERS LEAGUE (*Bund der Landwirte*). More of a demagogic pressure group than a full-fledged political party, the Farmers League was founded in 1893 to agitate for a reversal of the prevailing trade policy which had sacrificed agrarian interests to industrial profit-making. The Farmers League appealed to those favoring the private ownership of property and, therefore, successfully played on the antisocialist and anti-Semitic fears of the lower-middle class.

The Farmers League closely associated itself with the German Conservative Party.* In 1894, after just one year of existence, the League claimed about 200,000 members, thus helping to revitalize the then-declining Conservatives by providing a base of mass support. After the turn of the century, however, the League ran its own candidates in parliamentary elections and won four seats in 1903, eight in 1907, and two seats in 1912. By 1914 the League's membership had risen to about 300,000; but after the upheaval of World War I, the Farmers League disappeared from German politics.

FREE CONSERVATIVES. *See* GERMAN REICH PARTY.

FREE THINKING PARTY. *See* PROGRESSIVE PARTY.

FREE THINKING PEOPLE'S PARTY. *See* PROGRESSIVE PARTY.

FREE THINKING UNION. *See* PROGRESSIVE PARTY.

FREI CONSERVATIVEN. *See* GERMAN REICH PARTY.

FREISINNIGE PARTEI. *See* PROGRESSIVE PARTY.

FREISINNIGE VEREINIGUNG. *See* PROGRESSIVE PARTY.

FREISINNIGE VOLKSPARTEI. *See* PROGRESSIVE PARTY.

FORTSCHRITTLICHE VOLKSPARTEI. *See* PROGRESSIVE PARTY.

FORTSCHRITTSPARTEI. *See* PROGRESSIVE PARTY.

GERMAN AGRICULTURISTS. *See* HISTORICAL GERMANY INTRO-
DUCTION.

GERMAN BUSINESS PARTY. (*Deutsche Wirtschaftspartei*; also known as the
German Middle Class Business Party: *Reichspartei des Deutschen Mittelstands-
Wirtschaftspartei*). The German Business Party was one of the more sizable of
Weimar's splinter parties that owed its existence to the system of proportional
representation. Clearly a party of special interests, the Business Party attracted
the many predominantly apolitical small businessmen—craftsmen, shopkeepers,
landlords, innkeepers—who were primarily concerned with their precarious economic position. The party was represented only in the Brüning cabinet of
1931-1932, but its normal share of the electorate (about three percent) helped
to keep the middle classes divided until, of course, Hitler was able to unite them
in the throes of the worldwide economic depression.

GERMAN CONSERVATIVE PARTY (*Deutschkonservative Partei*). Always the
greatest defenders of the Prussian monarchy, the German Conservative Party
first appeared in the Prussian Assembly during the 1850s as one of the two
original Assembly groups (the other being the Progressive Party*). The leaders
of the Conservative Party in its early period were Ernst von Gerlach, Leopold
von Gerlach, and Count von Voss. The *Kreuzzeitung* newspaper was the party's
official mouthpiece.

In 1876 the Conservatives split into two groups over Chancellor Bismarck's
policies following the Austrian War of 1866. The ultra-Conservatives, who
opposed Bismarck at this time, retained the party name, while those who supported Bismarck called themselves the Free Conservatives (*Frei Conservativen*).
The latter group also came to be known as the German Reich Party.*

The Conservatives' prime task was to represent the goals and interests of the
Prussian landowning classes and the orthodox Lutheran church. Although they
desired a slow, evolutionary growth of the state, the Conservatives advocated a
strong military for its defense. In their view, the individual should be a "subject"
rather than a "citizen" of the state, and thus the emperor should retain a wide
range of powers. In their strong belief in the virtues of organized inequality and
Christian morality, the Conservatives were adamantly opposed to any leveling
or anti-Christian influences, such as those posed by liberals, socialists, and Jews.
Perhaps because of their extreme hostility to laissez-faire economic liberalism,
they eventually supported Bismarck's social reform policies during the 1880s.
Earlier, the Conservatives had been at odds with the chancellor because they
thought the organizational structure he helped impose on the Reich was too
liberal. During the *Kulturkampf* (1871-1878) they often sided with the Center

Party* in its struggle to protect the sanctity of religious marriage and religious control over education.

The Conservatives' electoral fortunes varied. When they were in opposition to Bismarck in the 1870s, they suffered from the competition of other conservative groups such as the German Reich Party which supported Bismarck. Although the chancellor never became a member of any party, he aligned himself closely with the Conservatives in the 1880s, and this greatly benefited the party at the polls. After Bismarck's departure from government power, the party suffered a modest decline, but it still remained the leading conservative party in the country. Typical supporters of the party were large landowners, army officers, high administration officials, and also many peasants—especially those residing in the old Prussian provinces of East and West Prussia, Pomerania, Mecklenburg, and Brandenburg.

After the fall of the Imperial system, elements of the German Conservative Party appeared during the Weimar Republic, joining with the Anti-Semites* and rejoining with the Free Conservatives (or German Reich Party) to form the German National People's Party.*

GERMAN DEMOCRATIC PARTY (*Deutsche Demokratische Partei*: DDP). As the liberal representative of what has been called the "Weimar Coalition" of the Social Democratic Party of Germany,* the Center Party,* and the German Democratic Party, the DDP served in a majority of Weimar cabinets. Consisting mainly of old Progressive Party* members, but also including some left-wing members of the National Liberal Party* (which itself was a splinter from the Progressives), the DDP organized in November 1918 under the leadership of Professor Alfred Weber (the brother of Max Weber) and Theodor Wolff, the chief editor of the *Berliner Tageblatt*. In the *Reichstag* elections which soon followed, the party had its greatest electoral success, garnering almost 19 percent of the vote and 75 deputies.

The most progressive and nonreligious of the bourgeois parties, the DDP leadership enthusiastically embraced the Weimar system and helped sponsor programs aiming at greater democratization and justice through social legislation. It was truly unfortunate for the fate of German parliamentary democracy that the party was not able to attract a broader base of support (its strongest competitor was the Social Democratic Party). After its fine start in the National Assembly elections, the DDP tapered off quickly. Its support was more than halved in the 1920 elections, and thereafter it managed only about four to eight percent of the popular vote.

In 1928 the DDP was renamed the German State Party (*Deutsche Staatspartei*), which in 1948 became a founder of the Free Democratic Party (*see* WEST GERMANY). In the postwar eastern zone, DDP elements emerged as part of the Liberal Democratic Party (*see* EAST GERMANY). The German Democrats' most ardent supporters were always the intellectuals, some of whom were very famous: Max Weber, Albert Einstein, Freidrich Naumann, and Hugo Preuss, among others.

GERMAN FARMERS PARTY. *See* HISTORICAL GERMANY INTRO-DUCTION.

GERMAN HANOVER PARTY (*Deutsche Hannover Partei*: DHP; also known as the Guelph Party or *Welfen*). The German Hanover Party, or Guelph Party, formed in 1867 for the purpose of protesting the severing of Hanover's ties to England and its inclusion in the German Empire. The Guelphs were an old German ruling family who served as kings of Hanover between 1814 and 1866. Party supporters were anti-Prussian, and they refused to recognize the extinction of the Hanoverian dynasty resulting from the deposing of George V in 1866.

The Hanover Party's strongest support came from the rural districts surrounding Hanover, and the party had varied electoral fortunes. In 1907 the party elected only one *Reichstag* deputy, but in other years (such as 1884) it managed as many as eleven. The party reappeared under the Weimar Republic and secured between one and five *Reichstag* seats in those elections. After World War II and the breakup of "historical" Germany, the concerns of the Hanover Party were carried on by the German Party (*see* WEST GERMANY).

GERMAN MIDDLE CLASS BUSINESS PARTY. *See* GERMAN BUSINESS PARTY.

GERMAN NATIONAL PEOPLE'S PARTY (*Deutschnationale Volkspartei*: DNVP). The DNVP was formed in late 1918 when supporters of the old German Conservative Party,* the German Reich Party,* and the Anti-Semites* joined forces. In the following years, the DNVP became the leader of the right-wing opposition to Weimar's republican form of government. The party program denounced the terms of World War I's Versailles peace settlement and demanded equality for Germany in foreign affairs. Also, the party denounced the German revolution of 1918-1919 which had produced the Weimar Republic, proclaimed the inviolability of private property, advocated Christian teaching in the schools, and promoted racialist ideas and policies.

The Nationalists added to the German Conservative Party's old strongholds among the peasants of agricultural Prussia east of the Elbe River by expanding the DNVP base into southern and western Germany where new support was found in industrial and academic circles. The Nationalists were extremely influential in Weimar politics, despite the fact that the party never gained more than about 20 percent of the *Reichstag* electorate and that only a few DNVP members served sporadically in the fleeting Weimar cabinets.

Alfred Hugenberg, a director of a huge newspaper combine which controlled most of the movie industry, became the party's leader in 1928. At that time, the Nationalists cemented their close association with the bosses of industry. At the street level, they also had formidable strength and influence, especially because of their close association with the leading ex-serviceman's organization, the *Stahlhelm*. For proof of their often crucial role in Weimar affairs, one can look to their successful backing of the archconservative von Hindenburg's candidacy for president in 1925 and 1932; to their eventual inglorious alliance with the Nazis (*see* National Socialist Germany Worker's Party) in 1931, known as the Harzburg Front; and to their participation in Hitler's National Cabinet in 1933.

After World War II and the breakup of "historical" Germany, remnants of the DNVP made their way into the Christian Democratic Union/Christian Social Union (*see* WEST GERMANY) and into the eastern zone's Christian Democratic Union (*see* EAST GERMANY).

GERMAN PEOPLE'S PARTY (1868-1907) (*Deutsche Volkspartei*). The first German People's Party was founded in 1868 in the southern German area of Württemburg. The chief spokesman for this small, regionally based party was Friedrich von Payer. Also referring to themselves as Southern Democrats, this party claimed to stand for the radical democracy promulgated in the 1848 revolution. Upon electing von Payer and a few other representatives, the German People's Party temporarily disappeared from the *Reichstag* in 1887 after heavy attack by Chancellor Otto von Bismarck. After Bismarck's departure from government power in 1890, the party reappeared and reached its parliamentary strength in 1893 with 11 *Reichstag* seats. Thereafter, suffering declining electoral support, the German People's Party finally disappeared after the 1907 elections.

GERMAN PEOPLE'S PARTY (1919-1933) (*Deutsche Volkspartei*: DVP). The second German People's Party (not connected to an earlier party of the same name, *see* German People's Party [1868-1907]) was formed from elements of the Free Conservatives (*see* German Reich Party) and the Economic Union* prior to the elections for the National Assembly in 1919. The establishment of the DVP made certain that the supporters of the old National Liberal Party* would retain a separate voice in Weimar politics and that German liberalism would remain divided. Although most DVP members probably preferred a constitutional monarchy, the party came to play an important role in the republic through its able and influential leader, Gustav Stresemann. Many argue that Stresemann's untimely death in 1929 precipitated the downfall of the German democracy. From 1923 to 1929, he was Weimar's most important leader and served in every Weimar cabinet, at first as chancellor and later as foreign minister. His skillful diplomatic dealings helped reduce tensions between Germany and its neighbors and eased the reparation payments problems left by defeat in World War I. A man with strong nationalist credentials, he also believed in cultural freedom and political rights for the individual. But the DVP's support for the republic evidently depended greatly upon Stresemann, for after his death the party moved quickly toward the nationalists and the political right.

Despite Stresemann's importance, the German People's Party never achieved success at the polls. The DVP's voter support came mostly from the nationalistically minded middle class, which usually amounted to about a 10 percent share of the electorate. (After 1930, however, these middle-class elements apparently flocked to the Nazi Party [National Socialist German Worker's Party*] in hopes that Hitler could cure Germany's economic and political woes.) The DVP's platform placed stress on a vigorous foreign policy. Also, it represented the strong desire of the propertied classes to combat socialist legislation and to safeguard economic individualism and free trade.

After World War II, remnants of the DVP in the western zone joined with a variety of other parties to help form both the Free Democratic Party and the Christian Democratic Union/Christian Social Union (*see* WEST GERMANY), while DVP remnants in the eastern zone appeared as part of that Germany's Christian Democratic Union (see EAST GERMANY).

GERMAN REFORM PARTY (*Deutsche Reformpartei*). Originating in the late 1860s, the German Reform Party capitalized on the feelings of German nationalism which were growing at that time. The party's strength resided in the industrial city of Dresden and among the rural districts of Hesse. The Reformists primarily served in electoral alliances with other very small parties. The Reformists did not achieve success, however, until they joined with the Christian Social Party* to form the Anti-Semites* electoral alliance, which succeeded in electing *Reichstag* representatives throughout the late 1800s and early 1900s.

GERMAN REICH PARTY (*Deutsche Reichspartei*: DR). (This German Reich Party should not be confused with a later party of the same name found in West Germany.) The German Reich Party, known in Prussia as the Free Conservatives (*Frei Conservativen*), was the second-most prominent party representing conservative interests in Imperial Germany, with the most prominent being the German Conservative Party.* The DR formed in 1867 under the leadership of Eduard Count von Bethusy-Huc after the German Conservative Party split over Bismarck's unification policy. Unlike the Conservatives, the Reich Party supported Bismarck's form of constitutional government and his unification policy. During the early years of Imperial Germany, the DR must be counted along with the National Liberal Party* as Bismarck's strongest allies. Moreover, the DR benefited from this alliance by having its greatest success at the polls and having many of its members placed in Bismarck's ministries. But the party suffered in the 1880s when the chancellor and the Conservatives mended their disagreements. From that time on, the DR never gained more than a fraction of the Conservatives' vote and parliamentary representation.

The German Reich Party held views similar to those of the Conservatives in political, economic, religious, and most other matters. Backed by the usual bastions of conservatism—the aristocracy, military, bureaucracy, and diplomatic corps—the DR also gained the favor of many wealthy industrialists and capital-ists. The Reichists did best among the largest landowners outside of the old Prussian provinces, particularly in Silesia and the Rhineland.

During the Weimar period, elements of the German Reich Party reestablished themselves in other parties. In 1918 some DR members joined with the Anti-Semites* and the DR's former parent party, the German Conservatives, to form the German National People's Party.* Then in 1919 the remainder of the DR merged with the Economic Union* to form the German People's Party (1919-1933).*

GERMAN SOCIAL PARTY. *See* NATIONAL SOCIALIST GERMAN WORKER'S PARTY.

GERMAN STATE PARTY. *See* GERMAN DEMOCRATIC PARTY.

GERMAN WORKER'S PARTY. *See* NATIONAL SOCIALIST GERMAN WORKER'S PARTY.

GUELPH PARTY. *See* GERMAN HANOVER PARTY.

INDEPENDENT SOCIAL DEMOCRATIC PARTY OF GERMANY (*Unabhängige Sozialdemokratische Partei Deutschlands*: USPD). The USPD was formed in April 1917 under the leadership of Hugo Haase, Karl Kautsky, Wilhelm Dittmann, and George Ledebour. The prime reason for the party's existence, and the only major issue on which there was real internal party agreement, was the USPD's hostility to the war effort (World War I). Although the majority of Independent Social Democrats were more truly marxist than their former colleagues in the Social Democratic Party of Germany,* the USPD members ranged widely on ideological grounds from the revisionism of Eduard Bernstein to the orthodox marxism of Karl Kautsky. Thus when World War I ended, there was little reason for the USPD's continued existence, and the party did not survive through two more years.

In 1919 a radical revolutionary faction split from the USPD. This group, calling themselves the Spartacists, immediately formed the Communist Party of Germany.* Within the USPD, disagreement over the question of joining the Moscow-dominated Third International led, at the party congress in Halle in October 1920, to the USPD's final dissolution. The left-wing majority under Ernst Däuming decided to join, and soon merged with the Communists. The smaller right-wing faction under Rudolf Hilferding and Wilhelm Dittmann finally opted in 1922 to reunite with the Social Democrats.

KOMMUNISTISCHE PARTEI DEUTSCHLANDS. *See* COMMUNIST PARTY OF GERMANY.

KONSERVATIVE VOLKSPARTEI. *See* HISTORICAL GERMANY INTRODUCTION.

KPD. *See* COMMUNIST PARTY OF GERMANY.

LANDBUND. *See* HISTORICAL GERMANY INTRODUCTION.

LIBERALE REICHSPARTEI. *See* NATIONAL LIBERAL PARTY.

LIBERALE VEREINIGUNG. *See* NATIONAL LIBERAL PARTY and PROGRESSIVE PARTY.

LIBERAL REICH PARTY. *See* NATIONAL LIBERAL PARTY.

LIBERAL UNION. *See* NATIONAL LIBERAL PARTY and PROGRESSIVE PARTY.

NATIONAL LIBERALE PARTEI. *See* NATIONAL LIBERAL PARTY.

NATIONAL LIBERAL PARTY (*Nationalliberale Partei*). The National Liberal Party formed in 1867 as a result of a split in the Progressive Party* over the issue of supporting Chancellor Otto von Bismarck's constitution for the North German Confederation. The National Liberals represented the larger portion of the split and strongly backed Bismarck's policies. After the parliamentary elections of 1871, the National Liberals were joined by a small grouping of nationalists from the southern German states, known as the Liberal Reich Party (*Liberale Reichspartei*), and thus became the preponderant, most highly represented party in the Imperial *Reichstag* until they lost control in 1878.

The National Liberal party leaders were unified in their desire for greater governmental centralization, laissez-faire economics, and a vigorous foreign policy; but they were divided over how much they should push for further constitutional development. Rudolf von Bennigsen headed the party's right wing, and Eduard Lasher headed the party's left wing. Strains began to develop between these two wings before the *Reichstag* elections of 1877, and in the debates that raged over the prolongation of the antisocialist laws, tariffs, and the *Kulturkampf* (between Chancellor Bismarck and the Center Party*), disaffected elements broke away from the main body of the National Liberals and formed a new grouping called the Liberal Union (*Liberale Vereinigung*). The new party included many of the former leftist members of the National Liberals and represented elements that had grown disenchanted with Bismarck's policies, so much so that in 1884 the Liberal Union remerged with its grandparent party, the Progressives, to form a new anti-Bismarck grouping called the Free Thinking Party (*see* Progressive Party). The remainder of the National Liberals continued under the leadership of right-winger Bennigsen. However, the National Liberals' alliance with Bismarck finally ended in 1878 when he refused to admit National Liberal members other than Bennigsen into his ministries.

Ernst Basserman assumed the party leadership in 1898; thereafter, the National Liberals became more nationalistic and less liberal. The party's influence never reached the same level that it had enjoyed during the years of alignment with Bismarck. With the exception of the 1887 *Reichstag* elections, National Liberal voter support dropped to about half of its earlier strength, and the party seated 45 deputies in the last *Reichstag* (1912) before World War I.

The party's adherents came especially from the Protestant bourgeois and professional ranks, including many famous people such as the historian Heinrich von Treitschke and the eminent jurist Rudolf von Gneist, as well as many important bankers and industrialists. The National Liberals truly had a national base, for the party did extremely well outside of Prussia, especially in Saxony, Hanover, Baden, and the industrial areas of the Rhineland. After World War I, elements of the National Liberals reappeared during the Weimar Republic within the German Democratic Party.*

NATIONAL SOCIALIST GERMAN WORKER'S PARTY (*Nationalsozialistische Deutsche Arbeiterpartei*: NSDAP). The NSDAP was more commonly known as the Nazi Party, the name "nazi" coming from the vernacular pronunciation of *National*. The party developed out of a tiny, right-wing party called the German Worker's Party (*Deutsche Arbeiterpartei*), founded in 1919 by the Munich locksmith, Anton Drexler. The NSDAP was one of many small splinter groupings that sprang up in the turbulent days following the World War I armistice. Adolf Hitler joined the party sometime in 1919, becoming its seventh member.

At the German Worker's Party's first mass demonstration, attended by some 2,000 people meeting in a Munich beer hall, Adolf Hitler made a bid for party leadership by proclaiming the party's new name (the NSDAP) and presenting a 25-point party program. Under the firm-willed guidance of this erstwhile, would-be artist and common soldier, the NSDAP eventually grew into the largest of all of Weimar's political parties. In 1933 it overthrew the republic itself and soon created perhaps the most infamous, ruthless, and powerful totalitarian state the world has known.

The party's original supporters came mainly from the ranks of the lower-middle classes: shopkeepers, artisans, tradesmen. Later it was particularly successful in attracting people from the upper-middle classes as well. But Hitler did not intend for the NSDAP to be strictly a bourgeois party. Brilliant orator and propagandist that he was, Hitler was never committed to any particular aspect of the party program; and, depending upon his needs at the moment, he laid stress on varying points of the program or sometimes reinterpreted it so much that it was nearly unrecognizable from the original content.

The Nazi program as enunciated in 1920 was a somewhat curious mixture of nationalist, racist, and socialist demands. It called for a greater Germany uniting all German peoples, thus for the remerger of Austria with Germany; it demanded abrogation of the Versailles and Saint Germain peace treaties of World War I; it asserted the primacy of the German Aryan race; and it promised to exclude Jews from public office and citizenship. Hitler cared more for the nationalist and racist aspects of the program than for its socialist assertions because he hated communism and social democracy nearly as much as he hated Jews. His feelings no doubt were influenced by the experience of the short-lived Bavarian Soviet Republic of 1919 and the antidemocratic, antimarxian, and extreme nationalistic tendencies swirling throughout southern Germany at that time.

Despite the catchall nature and flexibility of the NSDAP program, the Nazis had very little success in attracting a large-scale following until the economic depression set in after 1929. First, they sought to secure the allegiance of the lower-middle classes by incorporating into the party program various economic demands, such as the abolishment of all unearned income, a sharing in the profits of large industries, and the breakup of department stores. At the polls, the NSDAP had performed abysmally, never gaining more than 6.5 percent of the voters in any election. Nevertheless, the party did gain some notoriety, and it expanded its organizational base and membership.

In 1920 the Nazis began publishing a weekly paper, the *Völkischer Beobachter*, and the party formed a paramilitary organization of brown-shirted assault guards, known as the SA (*Sturmabteilung*). This organization was led by Captain Ernst Röhm, who provided the NSDAP with the needed muscle of many ex-servicemen. In 1925, Hitler created the black-garbed elite guard, or SS (*Schutzstaffel*), which in 1929 came under the leadership of Heinrich Himmler. The SS was a kind of personal bodyguard and additional paramilitary organization to the SA. These and other militaristic and secret-police-type organizations—such as the later Gestapo (German Secret Police)—were used to harass opponents, to give the impression of the movement's invulnerability, and to instill fear in the German citizenry. But without a mass base of support from the German population, Hitler, preferring to administer violence in measured, though often brutal doses, was convinced that events would soon play into his hands and provide him with the large popular base he deemed necessary.

On November 8-9, 1923, in a Munich beer hall, Hitler staged an unsuccessful attempt at revolution (a *putsch*) in which he greatly miscalculated his support from governmental leaders in Bavaria. While serving only nine months of the five-year term to which he was sentenced in the relatively comfortable Landsberg Fortress, Hitler dictated the first volume of *Mein Kampf* (My Struggle) and reevaluated his tactics. The result was a firm decision to renounce revolution by violent overthrow and henceforth to pursue revolution through legal means. The NSDAP was officially banned after the Munich *putsch*; it registered instead as an "association," joining with a number of small "folkish" parties, such as the Racial Freedom Party, to contest the elections of May 4, 1924. This collection of parties ran as the German Social Party (*Völkisch-sozialer*), or Racial Social Bloc, and secured 25 seats in the *Reichstag*. The NSDAP won seven of these seats. In the elections of December 7, 1924, the NSDAP managed to run alone legally and secured 14 seats. Almost four years later, in the elections of May 5, 1928, Nazi representation was reduced to 12 members.

The worldwide economic depression in 1929 provided the political catalyst for the Nazi Party. Staging mass demonstrations, Hitler employed his oratory powers to stir up the passions of the already emotionally and economically depressed German people. Blaming the Jews and the Versailles Peace Treaty (which, among other things, had strained Germany's finances through its war reparation payments demands) for all of Germany's ills, Hitler led the NSDAP to its first great electoral triumph in the elections of September 14, 1930. Overnight, the NSDAP became the second-largest party in the *Reichstag*, having 107 representatives. As economic conditions worsened, the party continued to grow in size and popularity. It succeeded in absorbing all of its competitors on the extreme political right. Although Hitler failed to win the Reich presidency against Paul von Hindenburg in March-April 1932, in the parliamentary elections of July 31, 1932, the Nazis made huge gains. After a series of staged political intrigues (*see* Historical Germany introduction), almost 14 million Germans voted for the NSDAP, enough to give it 230 seats and twice the *Reichstag* delegation of any other party. The Nazis suffered a mild setback in the next elections of November 6, 1932, reducing their share of the electorate from 37.4 to 33.1 percent and to 196 *Reichstag* seats. Nevertheless, the German government could no longer operate without Nazi cooperation. This, Hitler would not allow unless he were in the government itself.

On January 30, 1933, President Hindenburg appointed Adolf Hitler to the post of Reich chancellor. Within two months, Hitler used this position, along with a number of defects in the Weimar constitutional apparatus, to realize his revolution through "legal" means. On March 23, 1933, by a vote of 441 to 94, the *Reichstag* passed the Enabling Act which allowed Hitler's government to rule by decree and effectively ended democracy in Germany. By June 1933, the Nazi Party was the only political grouping allowed to operate legally in Germany.

On June 30, 1934, Hitler directed a purge of the NSDAP, resulting in a bloody massacre of high-ranking party officials, including Captain Röhm. The purge was linked to a conspiracy against Hitler's life. The results of the purge broke the power of the SA and left Hitler in supreme command. On August 1, 1934, Hindenburg died, allowing Hitler to merge the offices of the Reich president and Reich chancellor into one—*Der Fuehrer*, or Supreme Leader, a post of course held by Hitler.

Special regulations issued by Hitler in March 1935 detailed the organization, structure, and powers of the NSDAP and integrated the party into the state. The party was composed of two distinct parts: structural units (*Gliederung*) and affiliated organizations (*angeschlossene Verbaende*). The *Gliederung*, six in all, comprised the controlling machinery of the party: the SA, SS, National Socialist Motor Corps, Hitler Youth, National Socialist Students Association, and National Socialist Women's Association. The latter was made up of nine occupational or professional groups: physicians, lawyers, technicians, teachers, university professors, public officials, and the German Labor Front. Individual party membership in the early years was approximately four million (exact figures were never published), though membership was severely tightened in the later years.

Party congresses, originally scheduled to meet each year at Nuremburg, were suspended after 1938.

The Central Directorate of the Party (*Oberste Reichsleitung*) was the controlling organ of the NSDAP. It closely resembled the structure of the Third Reich government itself, although only a few Directorate members actually held official state positions. Flowing from this apex was a vast bureaucracy of party officials organized into offices, sections, and departments, all filled by patronage from the top.

Territorially, the organization of the NSDAP resembled the lines of traditional military authority in Germany. There were many resemblances to the organization of the National Fascist Party of Italy (*see* ITALY). The Reich was divided into 32 party districts called *Gau*, in addition to the newly annexed areas of Austria, Sudentenland, Bohemia, and Moravia. Party district leaders were known as *Gauleiter* and were second in influence only to those in the Central Directorate. Below the *Gau*, regional divisions were known as *Kreis*, with each *Kreis* subdivided into local party groupings called *Ortsgruppe*. The *Gauleiter* were appointed directly by Hitler, and the *Kreisleiter* were appointed by Hitler upon suggestions of the *Gauleiter*. Below the *Kreis* level, towns and cities were split into numerous cells and blocs.

The NSDAP and the Third Reich under Hitler ruled Germany through the World War II years. By June 1944, the Allied forces had invaded Europe from the east and west, and Germany's defeat seemed imminent. In July of that year, the German military made an unsuccessful attempt on Hitler's life, and the resulting purge of the army seriously drained the remainder of Germany's war effort. While attempting to defend Berlin from Allied attack, Hitler committed suicide on April 30, 1945, and on May 7-8 the German command surrendered to the Allies. On those dates, the Third Reich and the NSDAP ended.

NATIONALSOZIALISTISCHE DEUTSCHE ARBEITERPARTEI. *See* NATIONAL SOCIALIST GERMAN WORKER'S PARTY.

NAZI PARTY. *See* NATIONAL SOCIALIST GERMAN WORKER'S PARTY.

NSDAP. *See* NATIONAL SOCIALIST GERMAN WORKER'S PARTY.

PEOPLE'S RIGHTS PARTY. *See* HISTORICAL GERMANY INTRODUCTION.

PÖLEN. *See* POLISH PARTY.

POLISH PARTY (*Polnische Partei* or *Pölen*). With its roots in the national associations that formed during the German revolution of 1848, the Polish Party formally appeared with the establishment of the *Reichstag* (1871) and became the largest of the antinational, minority parties of Imperial Germany. With its comparatively stable *Reichstag* delegation of between 13 and 20 members, the Polish Party continuously protested the incorporation of the Polish provinces into the German empire and sought to protect the rights and interests of Polish citizens. Struggling against the government's Germanizing and secularizing policies, the party often allied itself with the Center Party* and other ethnically based minority groupings, such as with the German Hanover Party,* the Danish Party,* and the Alsace-Lorraine Party.* Electoral support for the Polish Party came from wherever Polish citizens resided, particularly in the eastern Prussian districts of Posen, Silesia, and West Prussia. With the territorial settlements after World War I, the Polish Party disappeared.

POLNISCHE PARTEI. *See* POLISH PARTY.

PROGRESSIVE PARTY (*Fortschrittspartei*). The Progressive Party was founded in 1861 in Prussia under the leadership of Max von Forckenbeck, Freiherr von Hoverbeck, Hermann Schulze-Delitzsch, Hans Victor von Unruh, Rudolf Virchow, and Theodor Mommsen. Always the party of liberal interests, the Progressives' strength suffered from numerous splits, and they came under different names at various times during the Imperial era. In 1867 the Progressive Party split over various aspects of Chancellor Otto von Bismarck's government program. Those who supported Bismarck formed a separate grouping, the National Liberal Party,* while the more radical faction retained the name and policies of the original Progressive Party. The latter grouping opposed Bismarck's 1867 constitution as being too illiberal, and they withheld support from Bismarck's government.

As liberal fortunes declined at the polls, the Progressives continued to divide and reorganize. After 1884 the party joined with the Liberal Union (a splinter from the National Liberals) to form the Free Thinking Party (*Freisinnige Partei*). In 1889 that party's left and right wings split off to form the Free Thinking People's Party (*Freisinnige Volkspartei*) and the Free Thinking Union (*Freisinnige Vereinigung*) respectively. Then in 1910 these two factions merged again to form the Progressive People's Party (*Fortschrittliche Volkspartei*).

Throughout its history of name changes, the Progressives had shared most of the liberal economic views of the National Liberals, but the Progressives were much more in favor of the extension of parliamentary rights and much more critical of government policy in general. The Progressive Party's parliamentary representatives—led by Eugen Richter for much of the Imperial period, and later by Friedrich Naumann after Richter's death in 1906—continually protested against the military and monarchical elements in the German nation. The Progressives' continuous fractionalization, in addition to some of their less popular stands (such as their opposition to social welfare), prevented them from gaining a powerful enough following to have much real influence. The weakness of this most democratically minded of all German political parties certainly manifested and contributed to the overall weakness of democracy in Imperial Germany.

The Progressive Party's adherents resided mainly in urban areas, particularly in Berlin and the towns of East Prussia. Typically, Progressive Party supporters were intellectuals, artisans, small merchants, or other members of the commercial middle class. After World War I, the party reappeared in the Weimar Republic as the German Democratic Party.*

PROGRESSIVE PEOPLE'S PARTY. *See* PROGRESSIVE PARTY.

RACIAL FREEDOM PARTY. *See* NATIONAL SOCIALIST GERMAN WORKER'S PARTY.

RACIAL SOCIAL BLOC. *See* NATIONAL SOCIALIST GERMAN WORKER'S PARTY.

REICHSPARTEI DES DEUTSCHEN MITTELSTANDS-WIRTSCHAFTS-PARTEI. *See* GERMAN BUSINESS PARTY.

RURAL UNION. *See* HISTORICAL GERMANY INTRODUCTION.

SÄCHSISCHES LANDVOLK. *See* HISTORICAL GERMANY INTRODUCTION.

SAXONY AGRICULTURALISTS. *See* HISTORICAL GERMANY INTRODUCTION.

SOCIAL DEMOCRATIC LABOR PARTY. *See* SOCIAL DEMOCRATIC PARTY OF GERMANY.

SOCIAL DEMOCRATIC PARTY OF GERMANY (*Sozialdemokratische Partei Deutschlands*: SPD). Socialism in Germany first appeared in organized form in 1863 with the formation of the Universal German Worker's Association (*Allgemeinen Deutschen Arbeiterverein*). In 1869 the more radical wing of this socialist grouping gained political organizational expression with the formation of the Social Democratic Labor Party (*Sozialdemokratische Arbeiterpartei*), under the leadership of August Bebel and Wilhelm Liebknecht. Although both groups were in competition for a time, a congress was held at Gotha in May 1875 at which both organizations, along with several other socialist societies, merged to form the Social Democratic Party of Germany. Bebel became the party's parliamentary leader, a position he did not relinquish until his death in 1913.

Although the SPD eventually became orthodox marxist in its theoretical position and voted as a bloc on the *Reichstag* floor, the party often acted more in a reformist than in a revolutionary manner. This contradiction reflected a severe division between radical revolutionaries and moderate reformists, which long plagued the German socialist movement and led to its formal split into the opposed Independent Social Democratic Party of Germany* and the Communist Party of Germany* during the early Weimar years. Nonetheless, the SPD had tremendous success in attracting voters and members in Imperial Germany, making it a formidable enemy of the Imperial government and of most other political parties.

In 1891 the SPD had become avowedly marxist. However, the party program (Erfurt Program) contained both theoretical and practical parts. The theoretical part, largely the work of the orthodox marxist Karl Kautsky, represented rather standard marxist revolutionary principles. In this vein, the program advocated the abolition of classes and class government, the end of labor exploitation and oppression of workers, the destruction of capitalism, and an equitable system of distributing goods in society. In contrast, the practical part of the party program read more like that of a normal opposition party, interested more in attracting voter support than in attaining revolutionary ends. The moderate position was given a theoretical base in 1899 when Eduard Bernstein published his *Evolutionary Socialism*, calling for the eventual establishment of socialism through democratic parliamentary action. By this time, the SPD was highly dependent on the votes and funds provided by labor union members, who desired concrete improvements in their wages and living conditions more than they understood or cared for marxist formulae; therefore, revolution for the SPD became increasingly more of a slogan than a real possibility.

The Social Democrats had great obstacles to overcome in developing their huge electoral and parliamentary base. First was the opposition of the government. In 1878, Chancellor Otto von Bismarck (with the support of the National Liberal Party,* the German Conservative Party,* and the German Reich Party*) passed his famous Anti-Socialist Laws. These laws made it illegal for the SPD to hold organizational and public meetings, and they outlawed the party's publications, though they did not prohibit the party's participation in elections and in parliament. Undaunted, the SPD moved its meetings to foreign soil, and the party suffered only mildly at the polls. After Bismarck's departure from government power in 1890, the Anti-Socialist Laws were allowed to lapse. The Social Democrats immediately demonstrated their strength by gaining almost 1.5 million votes in the *Reichstag* election of 1890, more than any other party. But because of the electoral system which greatly discriminated against the urban populace in favor of the countryside (*see* Historical Germany introduction), this poll netted the SPD only 35 seats in the *Reichstag*, which was less than half that of the Conservatives, who had received less than one million votes. Not until the 1912 election did the SPD *Reichstag* membership outstrip that of any other party, and it took the SPD over twice the voter support of their next closest rival, the Center Party,* to do this.

The Social Democrats always did best in large urban centers, attracting their large following mostly from artisans and industrial workers. Also, the party enjoyed the support of many professionals and intellectuals. In addition to its revolutionary aspirations, the SPD advocated the separation of church and state, freedom of organization and expression, free and compulsory secular education, universal suffrage for all legislative bodies, equal rights for women, and progressive taxation. With the exception of only a minor fraction of its members, the party had initially opposed all forms of militarism and nationalism. But the SPD gradually dispensed with its revolutionary and antimilitarism mission by the end of the Imperial period, and in August 1914 the party's *Reichstag* delegation voted with the other parties for war credits. After the initial war hysteria subsided, however, the long-lasting division between reformists and revolutionaries reappeared. During the later World War I years, the always tenuous unity of the German socialist movement finally broke down completely, leading to the formation of the separate and often hostile leftist parties of Weimar Germany. The radical revolutionaries left the SPD and formed the Independent Social Democratic Party of Germany in 1917. The split became threefold on January 1, 1919, when the most revolutionary elements founded the Communist Party of Germany.

The cause of socialism in post-World War I Germany was further compounded by the unfortunate role in which the Social Democratic leaders found themselves at the war's end. Under the leadership of Friedrich Ebert, the last chancellor of the Imperial government (appointed November 9, 1918) and later Weimar president (1919-1925), the Social Democratic Party assumed the enormous task of liquidating the old Reich, ending the revolutionary chaos, preparing the way for the new Weimar Republic, feeding the population, and seeking a reasonable peace settlement. Sadly, the SPD had little cooperation from other political groupings in these endeavors, except when the SPD was compelled to rely on assistance from the German rightist parties to quash the revolutionary activities of its own former colleagues, the Independent Social Democrats and the Communists. In many ways, the nearly impossible plight of the SPD reflected that of the Weimar Republic they founded. In the face of hatred from the political left, bitter resentment and scorn from the political right, confusion and indifference from the center, and enormous economic and social difficulties, there could be but scant hope for the future of German democracy.

The Social Democrats, nevertheless, made a noble attempt. They presided over the establishment of a democratic, constitutional republic; they were that republic's largest political party until the 1932 rise of the Nazis (*see* National Socialist German Worker's Party); they gave the republic its first president and first four governments; in 1924 they founded a paramilitary organization, the *Reichsbanner*, to serve in the government's defense; and they helped secure the passage of important social legislation.

Final proof of their occasionally heroic and oftentimes unaided commitment to a democratic Germany came on March 23, 1933, when the Social Democrats stood alone against the Nazis in voting against Hitler's Enabling Act. (*See also* SOCIAL DEMOCRATIC PARTY OF GERMANY, WEST GERMANY.)

SOUTHERN DEMOCRATS. *See* GERMAN PEOPLE'S PARTY (1868-1907).

SOZIALDEMOKRATISCHE ARBEITERPARTEI. *See* SOCIAL DEMOCRATIC PARTY OF GERMANY.

SOZIALDEMOKRATISCHE PARTEI DEUTSCHLANDS. *See* SOCIAL DEMOCRATIC PARTY OF GERMANY.

SPARTACUS LEAGUE. *See* COMMUNIST PARTY OF GERMANY.

SPD. *See* SOCIAL DEMOCRATIC PARTY OF GERMANY.

UNABHÄNGIGE SOZIALDEMOKRATISCHE PARTEI DEUTSCH-LANDS. *See* INDEPENDENT SOCIAL DEMOCRATIC PARTY OF GERMANY.

USPD. *See* INDEPENDENT SOCIAL DEMOCRATIC PARTY OF GERMANY.

VÖLKISCH-SOZIALER. *See* NATIONAL SOCIALIST GERMAN WORKER'S PARTY.

VOLKSPARTEI. *See* PEOPLE'S PARTY.

VOLKSRECHT PARTEI. *See* HISTORICAL GERMANY INTRODUCTION.

WELFEN. *See* GERMAN HANOVER PARTY.

WIRTSCHAFTS VEREINIGUNG. *See* ECONOMIC UNION.

Z. *See* CENTER PARTY.

ZENTRUMSPARTEI. *See* CENTER PARTY.

Eric A. Johnson

TABLE 36. Distribution of Seats in Historical Germany's Imperial _Reichstag_, 1871-1912

Party	1871	1874	1877	1878	1881	1884	1887	1890	1893	1898	1903	1907	1912
Alsace-Lorraine Party	—	15	15	15	15	15	15	10	8	10	9	7	9
Anti-Semites*	—	—	—	—	—	—	1	5	16	13	11	16	3
Center Party	62	91	93	94	100	99	98	106	96	102	100	105	91
Danish Party	1	1	1	1	2	1	1	1	1	1	1	1	1
German Conservative Party*	57	22	40	59	50	78	80	73	72	56	54	60	43
German Hanover Party	7	4	4	10	10	11	4	11	7	9	6	1	5
German People's Party (1868-1907)	1	1	4	3	9	7	0	10	11	8	6	7	—
German Reich Party*	67	35	38	57	28	28	41	20	28	23	21	21	14
National Liberal Party	125	155	128	99	47	51	99	42	53	46	51	54	45
Polish Party	13	14	14	14	18	16	13	16	19	14	16	20	18
Progressive Party[a]	47	50	48	36	106	67	32	66	37	41	30	42	42
Social Democratic Party[b]	2	9	12	9	12	24	11	35	44	56	81	43	110
Independents and others	0	0	0	0	0	0	2	2	5	18	11	17	16
Total	382	397	397	397	397	397	397	397	397	397	397	397	397

* These three parties became the German National People's Party in the Weimar Republic (see table 37).

[a] Split into the Free Thinking Union and the Free Thinking People's Party, 1889-1910; remerged in 1910 to form the Progressive People's Party. Reappeared in the Weimar Republic as the German Democratic Party (see table 37).

[b] Known as the Social Democratic Labor Party until 1875.

TABLE 37. Distribution of Seats in Historical Germany's Weimar Republic *Reichstag*, 1919-1933

Party	1919*	1920	May 1924	Dec. 1924	1928	1930	July 1932	Nov. 1932	1933
Bavarian People's Party	—	21	16	19	16	19	22	20	18
Center Party[a]	91	64	65	69	62	68	75	70	74
Christian Social People's Service	—	—	—	—	—	14	3	5	4
Communist Party of Germany	—	4	62	45	54	77	89	100	81
German Agriculturalists	—	—	—	—	10	19	1	0	—
German Business Party	4	4	10	17	23	23	2	1	—
German Democratic Party[b]	75	39	28	32	25	20	4	2	5
German Farmers Party	—	—	—	—	8	6	2	3	2
German Hanover Party	1	5	5	4	3	3	0	1	0
German National People's Party	44	71	95	103	75	41	37	52	52
German People's Party (1919-1933)	19	65	45	51	45	30	7	11	2
Independent Social Democratic Party	22	84	—	—	—	—	—	—	—
National Socialist German Worker's Party (Nazi Party)	—	—	7	14	12	107	230	196	288
Social Democratic Party	163	102	100	131	153	143	133	121	120
Independents and others[c]	2	0	39	8	5	7	3	2	1
Total	421	459	472	493	491	577	608	584	647

* Election to national constituent assembly.

[a] Known as the Christian People's Party for the 1919 election.

[b] Known as the German State Party, 1928-1933.

[c] In May 1924, this figure includes 25 seats won by various extremist groupings contesting jointly as the Racial Social Bloc. The Nazi Party cooperated electorally with the Racial Social Bloc.

435

TABLE 38. Ruling Coalitions in Historical Germany's Weimar Republic, 1919-1933

Years	Coalition
Feb. 13, 1919 - June 19, 1919	Social Democratic Party Center Party German Democratic Party
June 19, 1919 - Oct. 3, 1919	Social Democratic Party Center Party
Oct. 3, 1919 - Mar. 26, 1920	Social Democratic Party German Democratic Party
Mar. 27, 1920 - June 8, 1920	Social Democratic Party Center Party
June 20, 1920 - May 4, 1921	Center Party German Democratic Party
May 9, 1921 - Oct. 22, 1921	Center Party German Democratic Party Social Democratic Party
Oct. 26, 1921 - Nov. 14, 1922	Center Party German Democratic Party Social Democratic Party
Nov. 22, 1922 - Aug. 12, 1923	Center Party German Democratic Party German People's Party (1919-1933) National German People's Party
Aug. 13, 1923 - Oct. 3, 1923	German People's Party (1919-1933) Social Democratic Party Center Party German Democratic Party
Oct. 6, 1923 - Nov. 23, 1923	German People's Party (1919-1933) Social Democratic Party Center Party German Democratic Party
Nov. 30, 1923 - May 26, 1924	Center Party German Democratic Party German People's Party (1919-1933) Bavarian People's Party
June 3, 1924 - Dec. 15, 1924	Center Party German Democratic Party German People's Party (1919-1933) Bavarian People's Party

TABLE 38. *(Continued)*

Years	Coalition
Jan. 16, 1925 - Oct. 29, 1925	Center Party German National People's Party German People's Party (1919-1933) Bavarian People's Party
Jan. 20, 1926 - May 18, 1926	Center Party German Democratic Party German People's Party (1919-1933) Bavarian People's Party
May 18, 1926 - Feb. 1, 1927	Center Party German Democratic Party German People's Party (1919-1933) Bavarian People's Party
Feb. 1, 1927 - June 28, 1928	Center Party German People's Party (1919-1933) Bavarian People's Party German National People's Party
June 28, 1928 - Mar. 29, 1930	Social Democratic Party German Democratic Party German People's Party (1919-1933) Bavarian People's Party
Mar. 29, 1930 - Oct. 7, 1931	Center Party German Democratic Party German People's Party (1919-1933) Bavarian People's Party German National People's Party German Business Party
Oct. 9, 1931 - May 30, 1932	Center Party Bavarian People's Party German National People's Party
May 31, 1932 - Nov. 17, 1932	Nonpartisan government
Dec. 2, 1932 - Jan. 28, 1933	Nonpartisan government
Jan. 30, 1933 - Mar. 24, 1933	National Socialist German Worker's Party German National People's Party
Mar. 24, 1933 - end of World War II	National Socialist German Worker's Party

Note: First-named party is dominant coalition party.

HISTORICAL LATVIA, 1918-1940

The REPUBLIC OF LATVIA (now an integral part of the Soviet Union and known officially as the Latvian Soviet Socialist Republic) existed as a fully independent state from November 18, 1918, to August 5, 1940, when it was annexed by the Soviet Union. Prior to independence, the regions of Latvia—Livonia, Latgale, Courland—were part of the Russian Empire, since 1721, 1772, and 1795 respectively, although dominated in large part by the culture and authority of the Germanic Baltic barons. The Germans, in fact, formally occupied Latvia from 1915 to the end of World War I and vied with the Russians for total control of many Latvian regions. Independence from Russia was formally established with the Treaty of Riga on August 11, 1920.

Latvia was the largest of the Baltic republics, consisting of 24,400 square miles with a population of approximately two million. At the time of independence, Latvia included the former Russian province of Courland, four southern districts of Livonia, and three western districts of Vitebsk. The country was bounded on the north by Estonia, on the east by Russia, on the south by Lithuania and Poland, and on the west by the Baltic Sea. The Latvian population contained a sizable proportion of ethnic minorities: in the majority were the Latvians (75.6 percent), followed by Russians (12.6 percent), Jews (5.2 percent), Germans (3.8 percent), and Poles (2.8 percent). Most of the ethnic minorities were concentrated in the eastern region of Latgale, which was largely Roman Catholic (rather than Lutheran), spoke a distinctive dialect, and exhibited a strong sense of regional identity. Latgale was relatively underdeveloped economically when compared to the rest of Latvia. Prior to independence, Latgale had been under separate Russian administration after many years of Polish rule.

Embryonic political parties in Latvia began with the emergence of strong nationalist feelings in the late 19th century and evolved with the struggle for political independence in the early 20th century. By the end of the 1800s, the older nationalist cultural associations, such as the Latvian Society of Riga, founded in 1868, and a conservative Nation's Party (*Tautas partija*), founded in 1883 by Frīdrichs Veinbergs, faced a Young Latvian Movement known as the New Current (*Jauna strāva*). This latter group was greatly influenced by socialist ideas and was Latvia's first (though illegal) organized political party. As in the other Baltic nations, Latvian nationalism found political expression as Russia's Tsar Alexander II introduced a system of local councils (*zemstvos*), and the emergent Latvian political elites began to direct their attention toward capturing control of various municipal councils. After 1897, Latvian representatives managed to gain control of the towns of Valmiera, Tukums, Kandava, and Cēsis, although the capital of Riga remained under German influence until after 1914.

Also at the turn of the century, the emergence in Russia of a constitutional monarchy provided for representation of the·Russian-held Baltic provinces in the Russian legislative assembly, the *Duma* (*see* SOVIET UNION). In 1905 two new bourgeois democratic parties—the Latvian Constitutional Democratic Party (*Latviešu konstitucionāli demokratiskā partija*) and the Latvian Democratic Association (*Latviešu demokratiskā apvienība*)—were founded, but they only lasted until 1906. The Latvians were permitted five seats in the first (1905) and second *Dumas*; following a suffrage reform in 1907, this number was reduced to four seats in the third *Duma* and finally to two seats in the fourth and last *Duma*. This participation, of course, allowed even greater means of expression for Latvian nationalism.

Harassed by tsarist officials, the more militant leaders of the Latvian nationalist movement sought refuge abroad in the United States, England, Germany, and Switzerland. Although leftist in orientation, these nationalists were far from united on tactics and ideology, or on the nature of Latvian independence. In 1903, under the direction of Dr. Mikelis Valers, one Zurich group formed an independence movement from elements of the Latvian Social Democratic Association, which had been founded in 1892, and proceeded to organize an armed militia. This group was social democratic in outlook, although it was opposed to dogmatic marxism. Latvian groups in Germany formed other social-democratic organizations and came under the influence of German socialism. The social democrats finally emerged as a united force in 1904 with the formation of the Latvian Social Democratic Workers' Party. *

The democratic revolution of 1917 in Russia, followed by the Bolshevik Revolution (*see* RUSSIAN SOCIAL DEMOCRATIC WORKERS' PARTY, SOVIET UNION), led to a series of rapid developments culminating in the emergence of Latvia as an independent state in 1918. Shortly before the collapse of the tsarist regime, Latvian deputies in the Russian *Duma*, along with representatives of various Latvian social and political groups, had formed in Petrograd the Central Committee of Latvian Refugee Welfare (*Latviešu bēglu apgādāšanas centrālā komiteja*), under the leadership of Vilis Olaus. This group sought the establishment of an autonomous administrative district. Immediately after the

Russian Bolshevik Revolution, on November 17, 1917, representatives of virtually all Latvian political groups (except for Bolsheviks and minorities) met at Walk (Livonia) to form a Latvian National Council. The Council declared Latvia's autonomy, pledged opposition to the Russians' Brest-Litovsk Treaty which had relegated Latvia to German authority, and called for the convening of a constituent assembly to determine the nation's political future. In December, operating clandestinely in Riga, which was under German occupation, Kārlis Ulmanis of the Peasants' Union* led the formation of a secret Latvian Democratic Bloc and issued declarations similar to those of the National Council. Also at this time, a socialist Association for Self-Determination of Latvia (*Latvijas pašnolemšanas savienība*) made its appearance in Russia and Switzerland.

Prior to the World War I armistice of November 11, 1918, the Russian Bolsheviks, despite an earlier decree on national self-determination, had invaded Latvia in resistance to independence for the Baltic nations. With the conclusion of the armistice, the members of the Latvian Refugee Welfare Committee, the National Council, and the Democratic Bloc formed an All-Latvian Council of State. This state council was composed at first of 100 members (later up to 183) representing all political parties except the right-wing Germans, Bolsheviks, and the Bolshevik-supporting Latvian Socialist Revolutionary Party.* Meeting at Riga on November 18, 1918, the Council of State declared Latvia's independence from all nations, formed a provisional government under Kārlis Ulmanis, and again called for the convening of a constituent assembly whose members would be elected by universal suffrage.

Unfortunately, after Russian Bolshevik troops occupied half of Latvia in December 1918, the new provisional government was forced to move to Liepaja in January 1919. Also, the Germans still occupied parts of Latvia, continuing to pursue control of Latvian land which could later be awarded to German soldiers. Although the Bolshevik advance was halted, a coup by the reinvading German elements was launched against the provisional government on April 16, 1919, and a new figurehead government was soon set up under the direction of Pastor Andrieos Niedra. German armies continued to drive out the Bolsheviks and recaptured Riga on May 22, 1919. Alarmed by German advances contrary to the armistice agreement, Allied intervention forced the Germans to evacuate Riga, and the Latvian provisional government was reestablished on July 3, 1919. The liberation of Latgale and the rest of Latvia continued for several more months (until January 1920) before the constituent assembly could be elected (in April 1920). After four years of being a battlefield, compounded by Bolshevik and German occupation, Latvia had to address the problems of rebuilding its shattered economy, commerce, and agriculture. Thus the constituent assembly met on May 20, 1920, for the purpose of beginning the process of state construction.

The constituent assembly was made up of 150 representatives drawn in almost equal numbers from the peasant, socialist, and moderate parties, including ethnic minorities. A provisional constitution was adopted on June 1, 1920. Ulmanis, who had served as provisional premier, established the first government. As in the fellow-Baltic state of Estonia, the Latvian constituent assembly under agrarian leadership succeeded in passing a land reform bill. Under this legislation, passed on September 16, 1920, 1,300 estate owners were deprived of their land and 3.7 million hectares were to be redistributed among the peasants. The government would subsidize the purchase by new farmers of seeds, machinery, and other farming implements. The issue of compensation to the estate owners was put off until a later time, an issue that aroused political feelings among most of the Latvian parties. Later, in 1925, the parliament decided that no payment was to be made for the expropriated land.

The Latvian constitution was officially adopted on February 15, 1922. The new governmental structure vested power in a legislative assembly (*Saeima*) whose 100 members were elected for three-year terms by universal suffrage beginning at age 21 (except for soldiers 18 years and older). Elections were based on proportional representation with the country divided into five separate electoral districts: Riga, Vidzeme, Latgale, Kurzeme, and Zemgale. The *Saeima* was charged with the selection of the president of the republic, who was responsible to the legislature and served for a three-year term (not to exceed six consecutive years in office). The president had the right of initiative in dissolving the parliament, but not the right of dissolution itself. Dissolution could come about only through a popular referendum; and should the electorate vote against the dissolution of parliament, the president was required to resign. The 1922 constitution also provided for plebiscites.

In terms of basic organization, the party system that emerged in Latvia following independence was similar to that of Estonia, with parties falling into five major groupings: agrarian, right, center, left, and ethnic minority. In contrast to Estonia, however, Latvian political life was characterized by a large number of parties with fissiparous tendencies. Six hundred candidates representing 44 parties took part in the elections to the first (1922) *Saeima*, with 25 parties successful in their bid for representation (*see* table 40). In 1928, over 2,000 candidates were on the ballot representing 59 political groups. Party fragmentation appeared to be the result of an initially loose electoral law and the fact that many political interests had little time to organize themselves into coherent groups until after independence was firmly established. After 1928, modifications in the electoral law required parties presenting a list to pay a deposit, which was forfeited if no candidate was elected from that list. However, this law was only partially successful: 27 parties managed to secure seats in the 1931 *Saeima*, with only two parties having more than ten seats each.

Despite the system's extreme multiplicity, Latvian parties did exhibit a tendency to coalesce into blocs in the *Saeima*. Five major groupings emerged, as stated above. Since no bloc commanded a majority, governments could be formed only on the basis of party coalitions, a tendency that came to highly characterize Latvian politics.

The agrarian parties, principally the Peasants' Union of Kārlis Ulmanis, dominated political life in Latvia. Despite holding fewer *Saeima* seats than the social democratic-socialist parties, the agrarians led 14 out of the 18 governments formed between 1918 and 1934. The only two governments in which the agrarians did not participate in some form were those of V. Zāmuelis (1924) and M. Skujenieks (1926-1928), the latter being a government headed by the Reform Social Democratic Party* (see table 39).

Conservative elements in Latvian society were divided among several partisan groupings. The oldest Latvian conservative party—Nation's Party—was in existence from 1883 to 1918, when it became discredited because of its cooperation with German conservative and imperialist circles. Other conservative groupings were the Christian National Union (see National Union), the short-lived National Workers' Party of Latvia (Latvijas nacionālā strādnieku partija), the National Peasants' Association (Nacionālā zemnieku savienība), and the Christian Working Men's Association (Kristīgo darba ļaužu savienība). The latter grouping was the political arm of Latvian Baptists. The most important conservative party was the National Union.

The political center in Latvia was represented by three major parties (Democratic Party, Radical Democratic Party, People's Party) known collectively after 1922 as the Democratic Center.* The center parties held the strategic balance in the Saeima since the right and left forces were too evenly divided to form separate respective governments. The center was reinforced in 1925 with the founding of the Labor Union of Latvia (Latvijas darba savienība) by Professors K. Balodis and P. Zalite, and in 1929 by the formation of the Progressive Union (see Reform Social Democratic Party), a leftist, social-democratic grouping that allied itself with the centrist parties, thus making the center groupings in Latvia more powerful than their counterparts in Estonia. Other centrist groups were the Latvian Independence Association (Latvju neatkarības apvienība) and the Republican Party of Latvia (Latvijas republikāņu partija).

The left constituted the largest political grouping in the Saeima, represented principally by the Latvian Social Democratic Party. Originally, the left was fairly united in the period of Latvian participation in the Russian Dumas and had formed a single group. However, splits began to occur even prior to election to the 1920 constituent assembly and resulted in the formation of several socialist groupings, including the small underground Latvian Communist Party.* The Social Democrats participated in only three governments: J. Pauļuks (1923, a nonpartisan coalition) and the governments of V. Zāmuelis (1924) and M. Skujenieks (1926). Social Democratic electoral support declined steadily in Latvia, especially in the rural areas where agrarian reforms undermined the party's appeal among the once landless peasants. The left concentrated its attention on an opposition role and relinquished early any intentions of governmental responsibility.

Latvia differed considerably from Estonia in its treatment of regional and ethnic minorities. While no regional political groups existed in Estonia, the province of Latgale in Latvia supported a number of parties. In 1916, the Latgalian Working People's Party, later known as the Socialist Working People's

Party of Latgale (*Latgales sociālistisko darba ļaužu partija*), was founded by Francis Kemps in order to unite Latgalian separatists.

Latgale had existed for a long time under Polish rule, resulting in a bitter hatred of the Poles among the Latgalian regional parties. Once under Russian influence, for many years the Latgalians were administered separately from the other Latvian provinces. Conscious of its special regional and religious needs (being Roman Catholic versus the rest of Latvia's Lutheran orientation), the Latgalians maintained their own distinct parties and put up their own electoral lists. Among the important Latgalian parties were the Latgalian Social Democrats (*see* Latvian Social Democratic Party), the Latgalian Farmer-Labor Party, * the Latgalian Progressive Party, * and the Latgalian Christian Peasant and Catholic Party. * Although these parties cooperated with their corresponding Latvian parties, they did interject a religious cleavage into Latvian political life which had not existed before independence.

The ethnic minorities in Latvia (Russians, Jews, Germans, Poles) formed a large proportion of the Latvian population and were more important politically than the minorities in either Estonia or Lithuania. The 1922 Latvian constitution made no reference to the position of the minorities in the nation's society or politics, although they were allowed to seek political representation through the electoral process. Early laws permitted some autonomy in educational matters, with state subsidies for certain educational activities. However, strong Lettish nationalist feelings, coupled with the emergence of fascism in Latvia, led to a number of attacks on minority privileges and culminated in the 1930s with the closing of ethnic schools and the dissolution of various minority political organizations. Electorally, the minorities were split into a number of small groups. The various Jewish minority parties* and Russian minority parties* remained as small and separate groupings, irreconcilable with other parties of the same ethnicity on religious, political, and economic issues; only the Germans (through the Baltic German Democratic Party*) and the Poles (through the Polish Catholic Party*) were able to fashion respective united ethnic lists. Throughout the period 1922-1931, total ethnic minority representation in the *Saeima* ranged from 16 to 19 members.

The emergence of fascism and other ultranational, antiparliamentarian forces in 1926-1927 placed a severe strain on the Latvian political system. Encouraged by Benito Mussolini's success in Italy (*see* ITALY) and the parliamentary crisis in Germany (*see* HISTORICAL GERMANY), the Latvian antiparliamentarians criticized the multitude of parties and the protracted negotiations necessary for cabinet formations. Fearful of a revolt by the Latvian fascist groups, armed and unarmed security units were organized by several democratic parties and splinter groups to protect themselves and the parliamentary system.

By 1933 the struggle between the fascists and the government "defenders" had become open and virulent. In a special session of the *Saeima* in August 1933, the Social Democrats introduced legislation which would dissolve all fascist organizations, dismiss fascist officials from government employment, and expel all

German nazis from the country. This particular bill was rejected, although shortly thereafter the Latvian government took steps to ban the wearing of uniforms by political associations. The agrarians attempted to undercut the fascist demands in October 1933 by proposing a series of constitutional revisions that would strengthen the presidency, including an extension of the term of office from three to six years; also, the *Saeima* was to be reduced to half its membership, accompanied by a curtailment of powers. This bill, too, was defeated.

Kārlis Ulmanis formed a new government on March 17, 1934, and discharged all government employees who were associated with fascist organizations. On May 15, Ulmanis effectively staged a personal coup d'état by proclaiming a state of emergency and dissolving the *Saeima*. All party activities were banned, and martial law was imposed for six months. A new, nonparty government was formed on May 17 with Ulmanis as premier. As a result of government action, several political leaders from the Social Democrats, fascist, and minority party organizations were arrested and given short prison terms.

The Ulmanis government set about to enact constitutional reforms based upon corporatist principles and the formation of a State Economic Council. Ulmanis merged the offices of president and premier. On December 21, 1934, a Chamber of Commerce and Industry (90 members) was founded. This grouping was followed by the founding of a Chamber of Agriculture (100 members) on March 29, 1935; the Chamber of Crafts (90 members) on December 30, 1935; the Chamber of Labor (100 members) on May 7, 1936; the Chamber of Arts and Letters (100 members) on May 5, 1938, and the Chamber of Professions (150 members) also on May 5, 1938. The latter two were united in the State Council of Culture. The first session of the State Economic Council took place on January 11, 1938. The State Council of Culture met for the first time on February 1, 1939.

On October 5, 1939, under pressure from the Soviet Union government, Ulmanis signed a mutual assistance pact with the Soviets identical to the Soviet-Estonian pact of September 28, allowing the Soviets access to Latvian territory for military bases and troop movement. On June 16, 1940, the Soviet government demanded the formation of a pro-Soviet government in Latvia. In the hopes of avoiding further encroachment of the world war into Latvia, Ulmanis assented. Nevertheless, Soviet troops entered Latvia the following day (June 17). A pro-Soviet "peoples' government" was installed by Soviet plenipotentiary Andrej Vishiňsky on June 20 with Augusts Kirchenšteins as premier. Controlled parliamentary elections were held July 14-15 under restricted electoral arrangements, with only candidates of the Working People's Bloc (*see* Latvian Communist Party) allowed to participate. The Bloc received 97.6 percent of the vote.

Meeting on July 21, 1940, the new pro-Soviet parliament officially removed Ulmanis from office without the required plebiscite and petitioned the Soviet Union for annexation. On August 5, 1940, Latvia became a constituent republic of the USSR. Ulmanis was deported to southern Russia where he died in imprisonment in 1942.

Germany invaded Latvia in June 1941 and occupied the country until 1944. Surviving Latvian political groups futilely demanded the restoration of an independent government. A Latvian resistance movement was organized in 1943, and during February 1944 it issued a proclamation calling for the reestablishment of an independent Latvian republic. Soviet troops reoccupied Latvia during May 1945, and Latvia was effectively brought back into the Soviet system.

Bibliography*

Anderson, Edgar. *Cross-Road Country Latvia*. Waverly, Iowa: Latvju Gramata, 1953.
———. "Latvia." In *World Communism: A Handbook, 1918-1965*, edited by Witold Sworakowski. Stanford, Calif.: Hoover Institution Press, 1973.
———. *Latvia: Past and Present*. Waverly, Iowa: Latvju Gramata, 1969.
Bilmanis, Alfred. *A History of Latvia*. Princeton, N.J.: Princeton University Press, 1951.
———. *Latvia as an Independent State*. Washington, D.C.: Latvian Legation, 1947.
———. *Latvia in the Making, 1918-1928*. Riga, Latvia: Riga Times, 1928.
Bļodnieks, Adolfs. *The Undefeated Nation*. New York: Robert Speller & Sons, 1960.
Davis, Malcolm W., ed. *A Political Handbook of Europe: Parliaments, Parties and Press*. New York: Council on Foreign Relations, 1927-1940.
Ezergailis, Andrew. *The 1917 Revolution in Latvia*. New York: Columbia University Press, 1974.
Freivalds, Osvalds. *Latviešu politiskās partijas 60 gados*. Copenhagen: Imanta, 1961.
Graham, Malbone W. *New Governments of Eastern Europe*. New York: Henry Holt & Co., 1927.
Manning, Charles A. *The Forgotten Republics*. Westport, Conn.: Greenwood Press, 1952.
Salts, Albert. *Die politischen Partein Lettlands*. Riga, Latvia: ZD, 1926.
Vardys, V. Stanley, and Romuald J. Misionas, eds. *The Baltic States in Peace and War, 1917-1945*. University Park: Pennsylvania State University Press, 1978.
von Rauch, Georg. *The Baltic States*. Berkeley: University of California Press, 1974.

Political Parties

AGRARIAN PARTY. *See* PEASANTS' UNION.

AGRARIAN PARTY OF THE LANDLESS. *See* NEW FARMERS AND SMALL LANDOWNERS.

AGRARIAN SETTLERS' PARTY. *See* NEW FARMERS AND SMALL LANDOWNERS.

---

*The author wishes to thank Professor Edgar Anderson for his assistance in providing information and advice in the writing of this chapter.

AGUDAS ISROEL. *See* JEWISH MINORITY PARTIES.

AIZSARGI. *See* PEASANTS' UNION.

ASSOCIATION FOR SELF-DETERMINATION OF LATVIA. *See* HISTOR-ICAL LATVIA INTRODUCTION.

ASSOCIATION OF LEGIONNAIRES. *See* LATVIAN FASCISTS.

BALTIC GERMAN DEMOCRATIC PARTY. Although the Baltic German minority comprised only 3.8 percent of the Latvian population, the Germans were historically the most important national minority grouping of Latvia. At the time of independence, the Baltic Germans represented the bulk of the expropriated landlords and merchants, and thus they were more homogenous in class terms than the other ethnic minorities. Heavily concentrated in and around the capital city of Riga, as early as 1920 the Baltic German Democratic Party succeeded in uniting all of the German political groups in Latvia under the leadership of Paul Schiemann. This move, not achieved by most of Latvia's other ethnic minorities, enabled the Baltic Germans to secure and maintain a sizable bloc of five to six deputies in the *Saeima*.

Prior to the elections for the 1920 constituent assembly, Schiemann took the lead and sought the formation of a united electoral list composed of all Latvian national minorities. While he was only partially successful, the Baltic Germans played an important role in various *Saeima* coalitions. Similar to the other ethnic groups, the Baltic Germans sought cultural autonomy in the areas of education and religion. They also pressed for compensation of landlords and a revision of the 1920 agrarian reforms in favor of these "Baltic Barons."

After Kārlis Ulmanis's (Peasants' Union*) coup of May 15, 1934, all parliamentary and political party activities of the Baltic Germans were terminated. Following the ban, various attempts were made by German fascist elements to seize control of the party, an effort which was finally accomplished in 1938.

CENTRAL COMMITTEE OF LATVIAN REFUGEE WELFARE. *See* HIS-TORICAL LATVIA INTRODUCTION.

CHRISTIAN NATIONALISTS. *See* NATIONAL UNION.

CHRISTIAN NATIONAL UNION. *See* NATIONAL UNION.

CHRISTIAN UNION. *See* NATIONAL UNION.

CHRISTIAN UNION OF LATVIAN ORTHODOX. *See* RUSSIAN MINOR-ITY PARTIES.

CHRISTIAN WORKING MEN'S ASSOCIATION. *See* HISTORICAL LATVIA INTRODUCTION.

DEMOCRATIC CENTER (*Demokrātiskais centrs*). Formed prior to the first *Saeima* elections of 1922, the Democratic Center was the result of a merger among three small centrist parties: the Democratic Party, the People's Party, and the Radical Democratic Party. The new party hoped to strengthen the position of urban liberals (professionals and intellectuals) and middle-class elements by combining their previously scattered votes into a single political grouping. Ideologically, the Democratic Center was pledged to the eradication of class conflict in Latvian society. However, in the early 1930s the party gradually moved toward a narrow nationalist program with antiminority overtones.

Although small in terms of parliamentary representation (three to six seats), the Democratic Center exerted a strong influence on public opinion through its support by *Jaunākās ziņas*, the largest daily newspaper in Latvia. Led by Janis Chakste, the Democratic Center played a crucial balancing role in the *Saeima* due to the almost even division between the rightist (agrarian) and leftist (socialist) Latvian parties.

DEMOCRATIC PARTY. *See* DEMOCRATIC CENTER.

DEMOKRĀTISKAIS CENTRS. *See* DEMOCRATIC CENTER.

DEVASTATED AREAS. *See* PEASANTS' UNION.

ECONOMIC CENTER. *See* LATVIAN FASCISTS.

ETHNIC SOCIALIST PARTY. *See* JEWISH MINORITY PARTIES.

FIRE CROSS. *See* LATVIAN FASCISTS.

INDEPENDENT SOCIAL DEMOCRATS. *See* LATVIAN SOCIAL DEMOCRATIC PARTY.

JAUNA STRĀVA. *See* HISTORICAL LATVIA INTRODUCTION.

JAUNA ZEMNIEKU APVIENĪBA. *See* NEW FARMERS AND SMALL LANDOWNERS.

JAUNSAIMNIEKU. *See* NEW FARMERS AND SMALL LANDOWNERS.

JEWISH BUND. *See* JEWISH MINORITY PARTIES.

JEWISH LEAGUE. *See* JEWISH MINORITY PARTIES.

JEWISH MINORITY PARTIES. The Jewish minority made up about 5.2 percent of the Latvian population during the nation's period of independence. The Jewish population was subdivided into several groupings according to political outlooks and partisan organization. First, Latvian Jews were divided into Zionist and non-Zionist factions. The second cleavage separated those oriented toward the German culture from those who associated themselves with the Russian culture. The third division was between those Hebrew-speaking Jews who were influenced by Zionism versus those who spoke Yiddish. These divisions caused considerable disunity for the Latvian Jewish community in terms of political articulation. Six Latvian Jewish parties contested seats in the *Saeima*, although only four (United Jews, *Mizrochi, Zeire-Zion,* and the Jewish League) managed to obtain representation.

The most conservative Jewish party was the United Jews (*Agudas Isroel*), a party of orthodox Jews headed by Morduch Dubins. The United Jews were national in scope and sought to limit the power of state monopolies. They elected two members to the first, second, and fourth *Saeimas* and filled one seat in the third *Saeima*.

Mizrochi was a Zionist organization led by Markus Nurok. Its major program called for the free readmission of Jews to Latvian citizenship, and its representation fluctuated between one and two deputies in the *Saeima* between 1922 and 1934.

Zeire-Zion was a left-center group under the leadership of Professor Max Lazerson. The party secured one representative for the first three *Saeimas* and then disappeared as an electoral force. The party was also known occasionally as the Ethnic Socialist Party.

The Jewish League (or Jewish *Bund*) was also known in some areas of Latvia as the Jewish Socialist Workers' Party. It managed to elect one representative to each of the first three *Saeimas*. As the most leftist of the Latvian Jewish parties, the *Bund* in 1923 affiliated itself with the Latvian Social Democratic Party* as an autonomous faction.

Two other Jewish groups—the bourgeois *Zeire agudas Isroel* (led by J. Baranchik) and the Marxist Socialist Party of the Zionists (led by J. Kron and J. Meierson) —failed to secure any representation in the *Saeima*.

JEWISH SOCIALIST WORKERS' PARTY. *See* JEWISH MINORITY PARTIES.

KRISTĪGĀ APVIENĪBA. *See* NATIONAL UNION.

KRISTĪGO DARBA ĻAŬZA SAVIENĪBA. *See* HISTORICAL LATVIA INTRODUCTION.

LABOR UNION OF LATVIA. *See* HISTORICAL LATVIA INTRODUCTION.

LATGALES KRISTIGIE ZEMNIEKI UN KATOLI. *See* LATGALIAN CHRISTIAN PEASANT AND CATHOLIC PARTY.

LATGALES PROGRESIVO ZEMNIEKU APVIENĪBA. *See* LATGALIAN PROGRESSIVE PARTY.

LATGALIAN CHRISTIAN FARMERS PARTY. *See* LATGALIAN CHRISTIAN PEASANT AND CATHOLIC PARTY.

LATGALES SOCIĀLISTISKO DARBA ĻAUŽU PARTIJA. *See* HISTORICAL LATVIA INTRODUCTION.

LATGALIAN CHRISTIAN PEASANT AND CATHOLIC PARTY (*Latgales kristigie zemnieki un katoli*). The Latgalian Christian Peasant and Catholic Party (also known as the Latgalian Christian Farmers Party) was the largest Latgalian party in terms of *Saeima* representation. The party secured an average of 20 percent of the popular vote in Latgale between 1920 and 1931.

The economic and political programs of the Latgalian Christians were virtually identical with those of the Peasants' Union* and the Christian National Union (*see* National Union). The Latgalian party, however, claimed to represent the special clerical interests of the region's Catholic population. Domestically, the party favored compensation for expropriated landlords. In foreign affairs, the party supported the idea of a Baltic union but, in contrast to the Peasants' Union, maintained a stance against the Poles, who had long ruled the Latgalian people before administration by Russia. Throughout the period of Latvian independence, the Latgalian Christians were led by Bishop J. Rancans.

LATGALIAN DEMOCRATIC PARTY. *See* LATGALIAN PROGRESSIVE PARTY.

LATGALIAN FARMER-LABOR PARTY. The Latgalian Farmer-Labor Party (also known as the Latgalian Progressive Farmers) was formed to represent the interests of nonsocialist workers and farmers in Latgale. The party consistently advocated radical political reforms and supported land redistribution without compensation to the original estate owners. Like the other Latgalian parties, the Farmer-Labor Party was anti-Polish in rejection of the region's once long-time rulers. The Farmer-Labor Party was under the leadership of J. Trasuns and secured an average of three deputies in the *Saeima*.

LATGALIAN POPULISTS. *See* LATGALIAN PROGRESSIVE PARTY.

LATGALIAN PROGRESSIVE FARMERS. *See* LATGALIAN FARMER-LABOR PARTY.

LATGALIAN PROGRESSIVE PARTY. Known first as the Latgalian Populists in the 1920 constituent assembly, the Latgalian Progressive Party became the second-largest regional grouping in the Latvian *Saeima*. Also known as the Latgalian Democratic Party, because of its often close alignment with the Democratic Center,* the Latgalian Progressives shared its coalition partner's ideology and sought to mobilize the same centrist elements in Latgale. Although clerics were found among its leadership, the Latgalian Progressives were nonclerical in outlook. The party, however, worked very closely with the Latgalian Christian Peasant and Catholic Party* on virtually all matters affecting Latgale.

Latgalian Progressive representation in the *Saeima* ranged from four (1922) to two (1931) seats. One party leader, M. W. Rubuls, served as the Latvian minister of social welfare during the first *Saeima* (1922-1925). After 1933 the party was known as the Latgalian Progressive Peasants Association (*Latgales progresivo zemnieku apvienība*).

LATGALIAN PROGRESSIVE PEASANTS ASSOCIATION. *See* LATGALIAN PROGRESSIVE PARTY.

LATGALIAN WORKING PEOPLE'S PARTY. *See* HISTORICAL LATVIA INTRODUCTION.

LATVIAN COMMUNIST PARTY. The Latvian Communist Party was seeded in 1917 by elements who broke away from the Latvian Social Democratic Workers' Party (*see* Latvian Social Democratic Party) in support of the Russian Bolshevik's revolutionary path to socialism (*see* RUSSIAN SOCIAL DEMOCRATIC WORKERS' PARTY, SOVIET UNION). However, these Latvian dissidents lacked an open, formal political organization, and rather they pressed their political demands through sympathetic groups drawn from extreme radical elements among the Independent and Latgalian Social Democrats (*see* Latvian Social Democratic Party) in the *Saeima*. The Communists were opposed to a coalition with the nonsocialist parties and adhered to the Third International.

The Latvian Communists became more open in 1928 and entered a separate electoral list known as the Left Trade Unions, which succeeded in electing six deputies to the *Saeima*. However, the Communists were declared illegal in 1930. Reemerging in 1931 as the Trade Union Workers and Peasants Group, the Communists elected seven deputies to that year's parliament. By that time, Latvian popular and governmental sentiment was running high against extremist groups; the Latvian Communist Party was dissolved by the nation's supreme court in Fall 1933, and the party's *Saeima* deputies were arrested on charges of treason.

Following the arrival of Soviet Union troops in June 1940 and the installation of a pro-Soviet government in Latvia, the Communist Party was again legalized and became the Working People's Bloc for the July elections. As the only party permitted to put up candidates, the Bloc secured 97.6 percent of the vote, removed Kārlis Ulmanis of the Peasants' Union* from the presidency, and obtained annexation of Latvia to the USSR on August 5, 1940.

LATVIAN CONSTITUTIONAL DEMOCRATIC PARTY. *See* HISTORICAL LATVIA INTRODUCTION.

LATVIAN DEMOCRATIC ASSOCIATION. *See* HISTORICAL LATVIA INTRODUCTION.

LATVIAN FASCISTS. Fascist elements first appeared in Latvia in 1923 with the organization of the Latvian National Club, also known as the Nationalist Association of Latvian Fascists. As a small right-wing group, it argued for constitutional revision which would strengthen the position of the president as a means of frustrating a possible communist takeover and as a means of introducing direction into the development of Latvian society. Supporters were strongly influenced by the example set by Fascist Italy (*see* NATIONAL FASCIST PARTY, ITALY). The Latvian National Club was dissolved in 1928.

Many of the early fascist groups in Latvia differed in their outlooks on how to increase the power of the executive and in their motives behind these outlooks. Some, like the National Revolutionary Work Force, advocated a planned economy but coupled this demand with a call for the persecution of leftist elements and Jews. The small Economic Center expressed admiration for Hitler and dressed its youthful members in brown shirts, while the Association of Legionnaires was made up of former military officers.

The Latvian fascist groups shared many important characteristics. First, they were violently anti-Soviet. Second, they showed great admiration for Benito Mussolini (*see* ITALY) as a model to be emulated in Latvia and hence their call for a strengthening of executive power. Third, the Latvian fascists seemed to be composed of disenchanted veterans, alienated intellectuals, and marginal elements who were moved by jingoistic appeals to violence, romantic primitivism, and blind obedience. By the 1930s, many such groups chose names that connoted violence and strength. The major democratic Latvian parties responded to the fascist threat by forming paramilitary organizations such as the *Aizsargi* (*see* Peasants' Union) for their own and Latvia's protection.

Fascism in Latvia exhibited a variety of political manifestations. The Latvian National Socialist Party was formed in 1932 and bore a striking similarity in program and organization to its German Nazi Party counterpart (*see* NATIONAL SOCIALIST GERMAN WORKER'S PARTY, HISTORICAL GERMANY). Strongly anti-Semitic, the Lativian National Socialists found sympathetic support among the German ethnic minority community and by the late 1930s had infiltrated and gained control of the Baltic German Democratic Party.*

Another native fascist organization emerged in 1930 and, under the direction of Gustav Celmiņš (a veteran of the War of Liberation), designated itself as the Fire Cross (*Ugunkrusts*). Almost immediately, the Fire Cross was outlawed by the Latvian government, after which the grouping appeared as the Thunder Cross (*Perkonkrusts*) in 1933. Although the Thunder Cross members imitated the Italian Fascists with distinctive uniforms and salute, the Latvian group was extremely nationalistic, anti-Semitic, but also strongly anti-German. Their slogan was "Latvia for the Latvians," and they were supported largely by urban elements, especially students. Membership estimates vary, but the Thunder Cross at its peak in 1934 had approximately 6,000 adherents. The group was proscribed following the Kārlis Ulmanis (Peasants' Union) coup of May 1934.

LATVIAN INDEPENDENCE ASSOCIATION. *See* HISTORICAL LATVIA INTRODUCTION.

LATVIAN LABOR PARTY. *See* LATVIAN SOCIAL DEMOCRATIC PARTY.

LATVIAN NATIONAL SOCIALIST PARTY. *See* LATVIAN FASCISTS.

LATVIAN PEASANTS' LEAGUE. *See* PEASANTS' UNION.

LATVIAN PROGRESSIVE ASSOCIATION. *See* REFORM SOCIAL DEMOCRATIC PARTY.

LATVIAN SOCIAL DEMOCRATIC ASSOCIATION. *See* HISTORICAL LATVIA INTRODUCTION.

LATVIAN SOCIAL DEMOCRATIC PARTY (*Latvijas social-demokrātija*). The socialist movement in Latvia traced its ancestry to the formation of various students' clubs and discussion groups in the 1890s. Many of the early socialist and social-democratic groups were based on the strong feelings of nationalism that began to emerge in Latvia at the end of the 19th century. Falling prey to the harassment of the Latvian governmental authority—at that time administered by the Russian tsarist regimes—most of these Latvian nationalist social-democratic groups fled to England, Germany, and Switzerland from where they attempted to organize formal political parties.

This effort at formal, structured organization did not succeed until 1904 when the Latvian Social Democratic Workers' Party (*Latvijas sociāldemokratiskā stradnieku partija*) was established, uniting several social-democratic labor organizations, including the old Latvian Labor Party. Following the first Russian *Duma* (*see* SOVIET UNION)—in which Latvia and the other Baltic provinces were permitted representation—the Latvian Social Democrats joined the Russian Social Democratic Workers' Party* (*see* SOVIET UNION) as an autonomous section. Prior to the outbreak of World War I, the Latvian Social Democrats played an active role in the conflict within the Russian party between the revolutionary Bolsheviks and evolutionary Mensheviks. Though the bulk of the Latvian party supported the Mensheviks, in 1917 a radical Bolshevik-supporting faction split from the Latvian Social Democrats and formed the basis of a group that would eventually become the Latvian Communist Party. *

In 1918, less than one year after the Russian Bolsheviks had succeeded in overthrowing the tsarist system of their homeland, the issue of adherence to the Russian party arose again. A small, remaining, Bolshevik-supporting element broke from the Latvian party and assumed the name of the Independent Social Democrats. This grouping adhered to the Third Socialist International and continued to function closely with the Russian party. The Independent Social Democrats succeeded in electing only one deputy to the Latvian *Saeima* in 1928 and 1931. The majority of the Latvian Social Democratic Workers' Party disassociated itself from its Russian counterpart and renamed itself the Latvian Social Democratic Party, dropping the word "Workers" from its title so as to underscore its separation from the Russian Social Democratic Workers' Party.

The new Latvian Social Democrats continued to adhere to the principles of the Second Socialist International and claimed to represent the interests of the Latvian working classes and trade unions. The party opposed many policies of the agrarian parties who dominated the Latvian government, and thus the Latvian Social Democrats took a stance against agrarian protectionism and compensation for expropriated land of the former estate owners. Antagonistic to both Germany and Poland, the party favored closer ties to the Soviet Union, which at that time was promising national self-determination to the Baltic republics within the protection of a Soviet federation. Although supported by the leftist Jewish *Bund* (*see* Jewish Minority Parties), the Latvian Social Democrats were generally antagonistic to the Latvian ethnic minority groupings, whom the Social Democrats viewed as simply religious and/or rightist organizations hostile to the principles of socialism.

By 1920, the year of Latvia's constituent assembly elections, the Latvian Social Democratic Party had become less nationalistic than before, creating a schism within its ranks. Prior to the elections, M. Skujenieks led a less ideologically radical and more nationalistic faction in leaving the organization and establishing the Reform Social Democratic Party. * Though securing representation in the constituent assembly, the Reform Social Democrats proved no real threat to the Latvian Social Democrats, who entered their first electoral campaign with relatively strong popular support (38.7 percent of the total vote).

However, with the elections to the first *Saeima* in 1922, the Latvian Social Democrats began to lose their popular appeal, and they secured only 19 percent of the 1922 vote. A portion of their electoral base was lost as a result of land reforms passed by the agrarian parties in 1920. The previously landless peasants, who had earlier supported the Social Democrats, abandoned their radicalism after being awarded land allocations by the government. Soon the endowed peasants drifted to other parties more geared to their newfound interests, such as to the Peasants' Union* and later to the New Farmers and Small Landowners. * Class warfare slogans also declined in appeal among the urban industrial workers, who shifted their allegiance to the newer nationalist groupings, such as the National Union. *

The Latvian Social Democrats appeared to be unwilling to offer a constructive alternative to the existing governmental system, and they were reluctant to participate in governance, preferring to play an opposition role. The party took part in only three governments: J. Pauluks (1923), V. Zāmuelis (1924), and M. Skujenieks (1926-1928).

In addition to support from the Jewish *Bund*, the Latvian Social Democrats were also supported by its regional branch, the Latgalian Social Democratic Party. Remaining disciplined throughout the period of Latvian independence, the Latvian Social Democrat leaders included Felix Cielens (a former minister of foreign affairs), Janis Ranis (a former minister of education), A. Rudevics (former minister of health), and Paul Kalnin (speaker of the *Saeima*).

LATVIAN SOCIAL DEMOCRATIC WORKERS' PARTY. *See* LATVIAN SOCIAL DEMOCRATIC PARTY.

LATVIAN SOCIALIST REVOLUTIONARY PARTY. Formed in 1913, the Latvian Socialist Revolutionary Party adopted the same policies and programs as its Russian counterpart (*see* SOCIALIST REVOLUTIONARY PARTY, SOVIET UNION). The Latvian Socialist Revolutionaries advocated the establishment of agricultural cooperatives and the nationalization of land. Also supporting greater popular control of political and administrative institutions, the party proclaimed the social benefits of governmental decentralization.

At the end of World War I, as Latvia attempted to reconstruct itself, the Russian Bolsheviks (*see* RUSSIAN SOCIAL DEMOCRATIC WORKERS' PARTY, SOVIET UNION) occupied the republic contrary to their earlier promises of self-determination for the Baltic provinces. Because of their support for the Bolsheviks, the Latvian Socialist Revolutionaries were one of the few parties denied participation in the 1918 All-Latvian Council of State (*see* Historical Latvia introduction). Never obtaining much popular appeal, the party declined even further after the agrarian reforms instituted by the Latvian government in 1920 in which the once landless peasants were awarded farming allocations, thus displacing an earlier Socialist Revolutionary program.

LATVIAN SOCIETY OF RIGA. *See* HISTORICAL LATVIA INTRODUCTION.

LATVIEŠU DEMOKRATISKĀ APVIENĪBA. *See* HISTORICAL LATVIA INTRODUCTION.

LATVIEŠU KONSTITUCIONĀLI DEMOKRATISKĀ PARTIJA. *See* HISTORICAL LATVIA INTRODUCTION.

LATVIJAS DARBA SAVIENĪBA. See HISTORICAL LATVIA INTRO-DUCTION.

LATVIJAS NACIONĀLĀ STRĀDNIEKU PARTIJA. See HISTORICAL LAT-VIA INTRODUCTION.

LATVIJAS REPUBLIKĀŅU PARTIJA. See HISTORICAL LATVIA INTRODUCTION.

LATVIJAS SOCIAL-DEMOKRĀTIJA. See LATVIAN SOCIAL DEMOCRATIC PARTY.

LATVIJAS SOCIĀLDEMOKRATISKĀ STRADNIEKU PARTIJA. See LATVIAN SOCIAL DEMOCRATIC PARTY.

LATVJU NEATKARĪBAS APVIENĪBA. See HISTORICAL LATVIA INTRO-DUCTION.

LEFT TRADE UNIONS. See LATVIAN COMMUNIST PARTY.

MARXIST SOCIALIST PARTY OF THE ZIONISTS. See JEWISH MINOR-ITY PARTIES.

MIZROCHI. See JEWISH MINORITY PARTIES.

NACIONĀLĀ APVIENĪBA. See NATIONAL UNION.

NACIONĀLĀ ZEMNIEKU SAVIENĪBA. See HISTORICAL LATVIA INTRODUCTION.

NATIONAL ASSOCIATION OF LATVIAN FASCISTS. See LATVIAN FASCISTS.

NATIONAL PEASANTS' ASSOCIATION. See HISTORICAL LATVIA INTRODUCTION.

NATIONAL REVOLUTIONARY WORK FORCE. See LATVIAN FAS-CISTS.

NATIONAL UNION (Nacionālā apvienība). The National Union, led by law-yer Arved Bergs, was formed in 1919 as a political spokesman for conservative elements in the Latvian commercial, professional, and industrial classes. The party favored a strong nationalistic policy in foreign relations and opposed radical domestic measures. The party supported compensation to landlords for property seized under the agrarian reform program.

The National Union worked very closely with the Christian National Union (also called the Christian Nationalists), which was founded in 1920. Both parties advocated the same general policies, except that the Christian Nationalists stressed the role of the Lutheran religion as a basis and guideline to government action. The Christian Nationalists also advocated prohibition of alcohol. The National Union and the Christian Nationalists joined forces in 1931 to form the Christian Union (*Kristīgā apvienība*).

NATIONAL WORKERS' PARTY OF LATVIA. *See* HISTORICAL LATVIA INTRODUCTION.

NATION'S PARTY. *See* HISTORICAL LATVIA INTRODUCTION.

NEW CURRENT. *See* HISTORICAL LATVIA INTRODUCTION.

NEW FARMERS AND SMALL LANDOWNERS (*Jaunsaimnieku*). The New Farmers and Small Landowners was formed in 1925 as a major splinter group that broke away from the Peasants' Union. * The new party's origins could be traced back to the Agrarian Party of the Landless (or Agrarian Settlers' Party) which had achieved representation in the 1920 constituent assembly and was later absorbed in large measure into the Peasants' Union though continuing to exist as a separate entity. The New Farmers and Small Landowners was organized by Adolfs Bļodnieks (Landowners wing) and M. Gailītis (Farmers wing) in an attempt to represent the interests of newly endowed farmers and smallholders who had been provided with land under the agrarian reforms of 1920 (*see* Historical Latvia introduction). The party also supported the idea of a Baltic union but opposed closer ties with Poland.

Elements of the Agrarian Settlers' Party within the Peasants' Union articulated a more radical position than that of the New Farmers and Small Landowners, demanding additional government credits to aid agriculture. However, with the dwindling electoral appeal of the Peasants' Union, which more strongly represented the interests of older and well-to-do farmers, the Agrarian Settlers ended their association with the Peasants' Union and were fully absorbed by the New Farmers in 1928. The merger soon broke down, and radical elements of the Agrarian Settlers separated from the New Farmers in 1931 to form the New Peasants' Union (*Jauna zemnieku apvienība*). The latter group succeeded in electing only one representative to the *Saeima* (in 1931).

NEW PEASANTS' UNION. *See* NEW FARMERS AND SMALL LANDOWNERS.

PARTY FOR COMMUNAL ACTIVITIES. *See* RUSSIAN MINORITY PARTIES.

PARTY FOR PEACE AND ORDER. A small, conservative, urban-based group, the Party for Peace and Order sought to defend the interests of house owners. The party first appeared in 1925 and secured one seat in the second, third, and fourth *Saeimas*. In structure and outlook, the party was similar to the House-Owners Party of Estonia (*see* HISTORICAL ESTONIA). In the *Saeima*, the Party for Peace and Order joined with the National Union, * the Christian Nationalists (*see* National Union), and elements of the Latgalian community to form a legislative grouping known as the "national bloc."

PARTY OF THE ORTHODOX. *See* RUSSIAN MINORITY PARTIES.

PEASANTS' LEAGUE. *See* PEASANTS' UNION.

PEASANTS' UNION (*Zemnieku apvienība*). The Peasants' Union (also known as the Latvian Peasants' League or simply the Peasants' League) was founded in 1917 as a continuation of Latvia's old Agrarian Party. The Agrarian Party had been a nationalist opposition group to the German Baltic landowners prior to Latvian independence (*see also* Baltic German Democratic Party). The newer Peasants' Union, under the leadership of Kārlis Ulmanis, advocated strong national government but disavowed nationalization and state monopolies in the economy. With respect to religious questions, the Peasants' Union was supportive of Lutheran interests. In foreign policy, the party advocated closer ties with the other Baltic states but, unlike most other Latvian parties, maintained a friendly attitude toward Poland.

The Peasants' Union supported various agrarian reform measures. Indeed, the party had been greatly helpful in passing the land reform measures of 1920, which gave allocations of property to the once landless peasants (*see* Historical Latvia introduction). However, as the party represented more strongly the interests of the older and relatively well-to-do farmers, the Peasants' Union avidly supported the idea of compensation to the former estate owners whose land had been expropriated for redistribution to the peasants. This issue of compensation, not settled by the Latvian government until 1925, in combination with the party's socially conservative outlook, resulted in cleavages within the party ranks. Unable to accommodate the interests of many smallholders and new farmers, the Peasants' Union experienced a split in 1925 when Adolfs Bļodnieks left the party and formed the New Farmers and Small Landowners. *

Unlike the appeal of its Estonian counterpart (*see* AGRARIAN UNION, HISTORICAL ESTONIA), the popularity of the Latvian Peasants' Union declined dramatically over the period of independence. Nevertheless, the Peasants' Union continued to exercise considerable political influence and was represented in virtually every cabinet between 1920 and 1934. Ten of the 14 prime ministers over the same period were members of the Peasants' Union.

In the *Saeima*, the Peasants' Union allied itself with a number of smaller agrarian parties, including the New Farmers and Small Landowners, the various Latgalian parties, and a group representing the "Devastated Areas." This latter group secured one seat in the 1922 and 1925 *Saeimas* and pressed claims for government compensation in those regions heavily damaged during the World War I years. In terms of economic policies and political beliefs, the agrarian parties represented a fairly cohesive bloc. The only significant difference was with the Latgalians who, because of their Roman Catholic constituency, differed from the Peasants' Union on religious questions; the Latgalians also opposed closer relations with Poland, the former ruler of Latgale.

In the early 1930s, in opposition to the many fascist groups that were forming in Latvia (*see* Latvian Fascists), the Peasants' Union established a paramilitary arm, the *Aizsargi*. The agrarian leader, Kārlis Ulmanis, soon employed the *Aizsargi* for his own ends, including facilitation of his personal coup d'état of May 15, 1934 (*see* Historical Latvia introduction). Following the coup, Ulmanis banned all political parties, including the Peasants' Union. Unlike Konstantin Päts, the agrarian leader who seized governmental control in Estonia, Ulmanis did not organize a mass party to support his rule; instead he transformed Latvia into a corporate state and governed through the army and bureaucracy.

PEOPLE'S PARTY. *See* DEMOCRATIC CENTER.

PERKONKRUSTS. *See* LATVIAN FASCISTS.

POLISH CATHOLIC PARTY. The Polish Catholic Party had been organized in 1917 to represent the cultural and economic interests of the Polish ethnic minority in Latvia. The Poles tended to belong to the small-landowner and middle-class sectors of Latvian society, and they were concentrated primarily in the nation's border areas. Although the Poles constituted only about 2.8 percent of the Latvian population, they were represented in every *Saeima* during the republic's period of independence.

The Polish Catholic Party provided strong support for the agrarian-dominated governments, although the party favored revision of the agrarian reform laws to provide compensation for expropriated landlords (*see* Historical Latvia introduction). This support, however, did not protect the Poles from attacks on the privileges of ethnic minorities which broke out in 1931. Polish schools were closed, news media suppressed, and various Polish cultural and political associations were ordered dissolved. After a vigorous protest in the *Saeima*, and after a gradual decline in strong Latvian nationalist sentiment following the 1931 elections, the Poles were permitted full cultural autonomy in March 1932. The Polish Catholic Party was led by J. Wierzbicki.

PROGRESIVA APVIENĪBA. *See* REFORM SOCIAL DEMOCRATIC PARTY.

PROGRESSIVE UNION. *See* REFORM SOCIAL DEMOCRATIC PARTY.

RADICAL DEMOCRATIC PARTY. *See* DEMOCRATIC CENTER.

REFORM SOCIAL DEMOCRATIC PARTY. The Reform Social Democratic Party (also known as the Right Socialist Party) was formed in 1920 as a result of a split in the Latvian Social Democratic Party.* The Reform Social Democrats were led by M. Skujenieks, who within the Latvian Social Democratic Party had been a leader of the wing that supported the gradual, evolutionary path to socialism as espoused by the Russian Mensheviks (*see* RUSSIAN SOCIAL DEMOCRATIC WORKERS' PARTY, SOVIET UNION). The new Reform Social Democrats began with 17 delegates to the 1920 constituent assembly, though they secured only seven seats in the first *Saeima* in 1922. Retaining the same social bases as the Latvian Social Democrats, the Reform party, however, represented a less radical and more nationalistic ideology. Furthermore, the Reform Social Democrats advocated cooperation, not conflict, with other class parties in the interests of national welfare, a stance not accepted by the Latvian Social Democrats. Skujenieks served as premier between 1926 and 1928 and again from 1931 to 1933.

The Reform Social Democratic Party gradually drifted toward the political center and in 1929 changed its name to the Latvian Progressive Association (also known as the Progressive Union: *Progresiva apvienība*). Skujenieks later rejoined the Ulmanis government as deputy premier, but he resigned in 1938 over policy differences regarding Ulmanis's newly instituted "corporate state" in Latvian government.

Throughout the period of Latvian independence, the Reform Social Democrats experienced declining electoral fortunes, dropping from a high of seven deputies in 1922 to three seats in the fourth *Saeima* of 1931.

REPUBLICAN PARTY OF LATVIA. *See* HISTORICAL LATVIA INTRODUCTION.

RIGHT SOCIALIST PARTY. *See* REFORM SOCIAL DEMOCRATIC PARTY.

RUSSIAN COMMUNES. *See* RUSSIAN MINORITY PARTIES.

RUSSIAN MINORITY PARTIES. The Russian ethnic group constituted the largest national minority in Latvia, comprising approximately 12.6 percent of the total population. Deep divisions within the Russian community, resulting from divergent class and economic interests, inhibited the formation of a single, unified, Russian political party in Latvia. Similar to their counterparts in Estonia, the Latvian Russians were unable to translate their numerical population base into political strength.

Three major Russian parties in Latvia represented, respectively, the interests of Russian peasants in Latgale, the Russian merchants, and Russian officialdom. The Russian Orthodox peasants of Latgale were organized into the Party of the

Orthodox, led by Archibishop Janis Pommers; their principal political interests involved the revision of the agrarian reform laws in their favor, extending the reform measures to allow the Russian peasants yet further credits. The Christian Union of Latvian Orthodox, also known as the Old Believers, was headed by M. Kalistratov; this party strongly opposed compensation of landlords in the agrarian reform program (see Historical Latvia Introduction). The Union of Russian Officials, also known as the Party for Communal Activities, or the Russian Communes, was made up chiefly of Russian municipal workers who wished to articulate their interests in the Latvian government; the Russian Communes were led by Leontin Spolianski and changed their party name to the Russian Public Workers in 1928.

Beginning with the first *Saeima* in 1922, the Russian ethnic minority parties taken together were represented by three to six deputies.

RUSSIAN PUBLIC WORKERS. *See* RUSSIAN MINORITY PARTIES.

SOCIALIST WORKING PEOPLE'S PARTY OF LATGALE. *See* HISTORICAL LATVIA INTRODUCTION.

TAUTAS PARTIJA. *See* HISTORICAL LATVIA INTRODUCTION.

THUNDER CROSS. *See* LATVIAN FASCISTS.

TRADE UNION WORKERS AND PEASANTS GROUP. *See* LATVIAN COMMUNIST PARTY.

UGUNKRUSTS. *See* LATVIAN FASCISTS.

UNION OF RUSSIAN OFFICIALS. *See* RUSSIAN MINORITY PARTIES.

UNITED JEWS. *See* JEWISH MINORITY PARTIES.

WORKING PEOPLE'S BLOC . *See* LATVIAN COMMUNIST PARTY.

YOUNG LATVIAN MOVEMENT. *See* HISTORICAL LATVIA INTRODUCTION.

ZEIRE AGUDAS ISROEL. *See* JEWISH MINORITY PARTIES.

ZEIRE-ZION. *See* JEWISH MINORITY PARTIES.

ZEMNIEKU APVIENĪBA. *See* PEASANTS' UNION.

Vincent E. McHale

TABLE 39. Heads of Government in Historical Latvia, 1918-1940

Date	Prime Minister	Party of the Prime Minister
Nov. 18, 1918 - June 18, 1921	K. Ulmanis	Peasants' Union
June 19, 1921 - Jan. 26, 1923	S. Meierovics	Peasants' Union
Jan. 27, 1923 - June 27, 1923	J. Pauļuks	Nonpartisan
June 28, 1923 - Jan. 26, 1924	S. Meierovics	Peasants' Union
Jan. 27, 1924 - Dec. 18, 1924	V. Zāmuelis	Democratic Center
Dec. 19, 1924 - Dec. 23, 1925	H. Celmiņš	Peasants' Union
Dec. 25, 1925 - May 6, 1926	K. Ulmanis	Peasants' Union
May 7, 1926 - Dec. 18, 1926	A. Alberings	Peasants' Union
Dec. 19, 1926 - Jan. 23, 1928	M. Skujenieks	Reform Social Democratic Party
Jan. 24, 1928 - Nov. 30, 1928	P. Juraševskis	Peasants' Union
Dec. 1, 1928 - Mar. 26, 1931	H. Celmiņš	Peasants' Union
Mar. 27, 1931 - Dec. 5, 1931	K. Ulmanis	Peasants' Union
Dec. 6, 1931 - Mar. 23, 1933	M. Skujenieks	Reform Social Democratic Party
Mar. 24, 1933 - Mar. 16, 1934	A. Bļodnieks	New Farmers and Small Landowners
Mar. 17, 1934 - June 19, 1940	K. Ulmanis	Peasants' Union
June 20, 1940 - Aug. 5, 1940		Pro-Soviet government
Aug. 5, 1940 -		Annexed by Soviet Union

461

TABLE 40. Distribution of Seats in Historical Latvia's *Saeima*, 1922-1931

Party	1922	1925	1928	1931*
Christian National Union	4	2	4	6**
National Union	4	3	2	6
Democratic Center[a]	6	4	3	6
Devastated Areas	1	1	—	—
Latgalian Christian Peasant and Catholic Party	4	5	6	9
Latgalian Farmer-Labor Party	4	2	3	3
Latgalian Progressive Party	4	2	3	2
Latvian Communist Party[b]	—	—	6	7
Latvian Independent Social Democratic Party	—	—	1	1
Latvian Social Democratic Party[c]	30	32	26	20
New Farmers and Small Landowners	—	3	4	9
New Peasants' Union	—	—	—	1
Party for Peace and Order	—	1	1	1
Peasants' Union	16	16	16	14
Reform Social Democratic Party[d]	7	4	2	3
Ethnic minority parties:				
Germans	6	5	6	6
Jews[e]	6	5	5	3
Polish Catholic Party	1	2	2	2
Russians	3	5	6	6
Independents and others	4	9	4	1
Total	100	100	100	100

* Elections were also held in July 1940, but only candidates of the Working People's Bloc (Latvian Communist Party) were permitted to participate.

** A merger of the Christian National Union and the National Union in 1931 to form the Christian Union.

a An electoral alliance consisting of the Democratic Party, People's Party, and the Radical Democratic Party.

b Founded in 1917 but did not contest *Saeima* elections under own label until 1928. Known as the Left Trade Unions in 1928; as the Trade Union Workers and Peasants Group in 1931.

c Also includes the affiliated Latgalian Social Democrats.

d Starting in 1929, known as the Latvian Progressive Association or the Progressive Union.

e The election results for the Jewish minority parties were as follows for each respective election, 1922-1931: Jewish League - 1, 1, 1, 0; *Mizrochi* - 2, 1, 2, 1; United Jews - 2, 2, 1, 2; and *Zeire-Zion* - 1, 1, 1,—.

463

HISTORICAL LITHUANIA, 1918-1940

The REPUBLIC OF LITHUANIA existed as an independent state from February 16, 1918, when the Lithuanians declared their independence (on July 12, 1920, by the Treaty of Moscow, Russia accorded de jure recognition to the new republic), until August 1, 1940, when the country was annexed to the USSR. Lithuania is now an integral part of the Soviet Union and is known officially as the Lithuanian Soviet Socialist Republic. Although it had been an autonomous power between the 13th and 16th centuries, Lithuania concluded the Union of Lublin with Poland in 1569, and both countries became a dual monarchy—two states under one sovereign, similar to Austria-Hungary. Polish influence was strong and inhibited the development of a national political consciousness in Lithuania. Then in 1772, 1792, and 1795, the Polish-Lithuanian Kingdom was partitioned among Russia, Prussia, and Austria (*see also* POLAND INTRO-DUCTION). All of Lithuania fell under Russian control and remained part of the tsarist empire until 1918.

At the time of independence, the Lithuanian population numbered 2,028,971 (1923 census), spread over approximately 22,000 square miles. Lithuania included the former Russian province of Kovno (Kaunas), virtually all of the province of Vilnius with the exception of two districts, the province of Suvalki, and parts of Courland and Grodno. In 1920, Poland occupied the city of Vilnius. The addition to Lithuania of the Memel Territory in 1924 raised the republic's population by 140,000, added 700 square miles of land, and gave Lithuania a seaport. Lithuania was bounded on the west by the Baltic Sea, to the north by Latvia, to the east by Poland, and on the south by Germany and Poland.

Although predominantly a Roman Catholic culture, Lithuanian society was also ethnically diverse. National minorities made up 16.1 percent of the total population. The Jews were the largest group (7.6 percent), followed by the Poles (3.2 percent), Russians (2.7 percent), and Germans (1.4 percent). While the

1922 Lithuanian constitution (Articles 73 and 74) accorded minorities the right of cultural autonomy, this tolerance declined in the latter 1930s in the wake of the Vilnius dispute with Poland and problems with the anti-Lithuanian German population in the Memel Territory.

The development of political parties in Lithuania grew out of the 19th-century national movement, which was generally associated with the university town of Vilnius and the 1879 founding of the Lithuanian Literary Society in Tilsit. The Roman Catholic Church also played an important role in the fostering of national sentiment through its maintenance of schools and seminaries and its instruction in the Lithuanian language. Nationalist feelings were directed first toward resistance to Russian and Orthodox dominance and later toward ending the cultural and social dominance of Poland.

The nationalist trend was also evident in Lithuanian journalism, beginning in 1883 with the publication of *Aušra* (Dawn) by Jonas Basanavičius, *Varpas* (The Bell) by Vincas Kudirka, and the magazine *Viltis* (Hope) by Antanas Smetona. Basanavičius and Smetona, with others, formed the cadre of the Nationalist Union.* The Roman Catholic Church also contributed with its own publication, the *Samogitian and Lithuanian Review*, in 1890, although this journal was less responsive to secular nationalism; nevertheless, the *Review* became the organizing catalyst for the Lithuanian Christian Democratic Party* in 1904.

Marxist groups appeared in the late 1890s with the creation of a Social Democratic Party of Lithuania,* which soon became independent of its Polish mentors. By the time of the 1905 revolution in Russia, resulting among other things in provincial representation in the Russian *Duma* (*see* SOVIET UNION), Lithuania already possessed the skeletal outlines of an emergent multiparty system reflecting a tripartite division of nationalists, agrarians, and social democrats (similar to that of Estonia and Latvia). However, in Lithuania the agrarian economy, coupled with a devout Catholic population, led to an imbalance in which the Christian Democratic Party emerged as the predominant force in political life.

Although partisan tendencies had existed in embryonic form since the late 19th century, partisan organization began to solidify in the Vilnius Provincial *Diet* of 1905. The *Diet* was convened on December 4, during the peak of revolutionary activity, as a meeting of over 2,000 representatives from all Lithuanian associations. While efforts to endorse an independent state were rejected, the *Diet* did call for the national autonomy of Lithuania within the structure of a Russian federation. The work of the *Diet* was continued with the formation of a Lithuanian Center in 1914.

By September 1915, following the outbreak of World War I, all of Lithuania was occupied by German forces, and Lithuania was administered by the German military government for the next three and one-half years. At that point, the quest for Lithuanian independence depended less on Russia than on Germany. In the aftermath of the February Revolution in Russia in 1917 (*see* SOVIET UNION), concessions were made to Lithuanian nationalists, who were authorized by the German government to form a Lithuanian Council. On September 17, 1917, the second *Diet* was called in Vilnius and was composed of two representatives from each district and every political party. This second Vilnius *Diet* called for the complete independence of Lithuania, and it elected a Lithuanian National Council (*Taryba*) of 20 members under the leadership of Antanas Smetona. Although a rival group of *Duma* deputies had set up a Lithuanian National Council in Saint Petersburg on March 26, this Russian-based council was overshadowed by Smetona and other nationalist leaders. Independence from Germany was declared by the *Taryba* on February 16, 1918, and was formally acknowledged by the German government on March 23, 1918. The last work of the *Taryba* in October 1919 was to call for elections to a constituent assembly and the establishment of a democratic government for Lithuania.

The conclusion of the World War I armistice on November 11, 1918, and the withdrawal of the German Army from the Baltic area allowed Bolshevik forces (*see* RUSSIAN SOCIAL DEMOCRATIC WORKERS' PARTY, SOVIET UNION) to overrun virtually all of Lithuania and Poland by January 1919. A Bolshevik government was set up under the leadership of V. Mickevičius-Kapsukas (communist), and plans were made for a federation of Lithuania within the Russian Republic. The Bolshevik forces were expelled by late Summer 1919 by the Lithuanian Army, which had been created by the *Taryba* on November 23, 1918. The Treaty of Moscow of July 12, 1920, ended hostilities between Lithuania and Soviet Russia and recognized Lithuanian independence, with the city of Vilnius as the capital of Lithuania.

Elections to the 112-seat constituent assembly (*Steigiamasis Seimas*) were held April 14-15, 1920. Suffrage was universal, equal, secret, and direct, with one representative for every 15,000 inhabitants. While the joint electoral lists of the Socialist Populists Democratic Party of Lithuania and the Peasant Union (*see* Peasant Populist Union) won the most number of per-ticket seats (29), the Christian Democrats (with 25 seats) formed an assembly bloc with the peasant-based Farmers' Union* (18 seats) and the Christian, nonsocialist Federation of Labor* (16 seats) to give the Catholic-oriented Christian Democratic Bloc an absolute assembly majority of 59 seats. Other groups represented in the constituent assembly were the Social Democratic Party of Lithuania (14 seats); and the Jews, Poles, and Germans (*see* National Minority Parties) with six, three, and one seat respectively.

The constituent assembly met on May 15, 1920, in Kaunas. Aleksandras Stulginskis (Farmers' Union) was elected by the assembly as temporary president of Lithuania, and Kazys Grinius (Peasant Union) formed the first cabinet. The resulting Peasant-Christian Democratic coalition governed with 88 delegates.

The constituent assembly passed the Lithuanian constitution on August 1, 1922. The constitution provided for a unicameral parliamentary body known as the *Seimas* (Assembly) whose members would be elected by universal suffrage starting at 21 years of age. Officeholders were required to be 24 years of age or older and were elected for three-year terms under the d'Hondt system of proportional representation. The size of the *Seimas*, although initially set at 78, was variable, with one deputy elected for every 25,000 votes cast. The *Seimas*, in turn, elected the president of the republic for a corresponding three-year term. The president could dissolve the *Seimas* and had the responsibility of appointing and dismissing the premier (or prime minister). Constitutional revision could be proposed by the *Seimas* or by petition of 50,000 citizens. Revisions could be submitted to a referendum or passed by a three-fourths majority in the *Seimas*.

Between November 9, 1922, and May 10, 1926, political life in Lithuania was dominated by the Christian Democratic Bloc (*see* table 41). Six cabinets were formed under this coalition, with Aleksandras Stulginskis serving as president. The first *Seimas*, with the Christian Democratic Bloc missing a majority by four seats, was prematurely dissolved with the resignation of Ernestas Galvanauskas (nonparty) as cabinet head in March 1923. Galvanauskas failed to receive a majority vote of confidence on his proposed cabinet (38 to 38, with two no votes). The *Seimas* was also divided over the question of Lithuanian independence from Russia: the Communist Party of Lithuania* (with five seats) opposed independence, while the national minorities (five seats combined) adopted a neutral line, and hence 10.3 percent of the *Seimas* remained ununited on this issue.

The second *Seimas*, elected on May 7-9, 1923, was almost identical in composition to the first, though the Christian Democratic Bloc increased its representation from 37 to 40 seats, giving them the majority of the then 78-seat Assembly. Stulginskis was reelected president and was followed by the cabinets of Galvanauskas, 1923-1924; A. Tumenas (Christian Democratic), 1924-1925; V. Petrulis (Christian Democratic), February 4, 1925-September 19, 1925; and L. Bistras (Christian Democratic), September 25, 1925-May 31, 1926. The second *Seimas* ran its normal term. Land reform was a major point of attention, as well as public education at the primary and secondary levels.

Elections to the third *Seimas* on May 8-9, 1926, witnessed a fundamental realignment in Lithuanian politics. The Christian Democratic Bloc met electoral defeat, securing a combined total of only 30 of 85 seats. Power shifted to a coalition of Peasant Populists and Social Democrats, with support from the national minority groupings and the newly reformed Farmers Party* (*see* table 42). Kazys Grinius was elected president, and Mykolas Sleževičius (also a Peasant Populist) formed the cabinet. The reasons for the Christian Democratic loss were tied to general economic difficulties, corrupt practices within the Christian Democratic Party, and to the Bloc's failure to prevent Vatican recognition of the city of Vilnius as a Polish, not Lithuanian, diocese.

Vilnius posed one of two special territorial problems in Lithuanian politics during the interwar period. Prior to 1569, Vilnius had been the historical capital of the Lithuanian kingdom. However, through various partitions and annexations, Vilnius had developed as a center of Polish influence rather than Lithuanian culture. Both Poland and Lithuania claimed the city and its environs after World War I. The German retreat from Lithuania in 1918 allowed the Lithuanian forces to occupy the district and make it the capital of the new state. In January 1919, the Bolshevik Army forced the Lithuanian government to give up Vilnius and withdraw to Kaunas. The Poles, who were also fighting against the Bolshevik Army, reentered Vilnius in April 1919 and held the city until July 1920 when the Bolsheviks drove out the Poles and returned the area to Lithuania. Vilnius was ceded by Russia to Lithuania in the July 1920 Treaty of Moscow; but in early October 1920, Polish Army units occupied Vilnius. The resulting tension between Lithuania and Poland led to mutual ill feelings, and the League of Nations intervened to partition the area. An armistice was concluded on October 7, 1920, but diplomatic relations between Poland and Lithuania ceased. The Vatican's recognition of Vilnius as a Polish diocese in 1925 was met with hostility by the Lithuanian population and was a factor in eroding support for the Catholic-oriented Christian Democratic Bloc.

The Memel Territory was another trouble spot in Lithuanian interwar politics. Memel, also known as Klaipēda, was a strip of land about 70 miles long and 10 to 20 miles wide between Lithuania and East Prussia. It had certain strategic importance in controlling the Nieman (Nemunas) waterway and served as Lithuania's outlet to the Baltic Sea. The area had been under German control since the 16th century. Although Lithuanian immigration had been encouraged until the 18th century when German colonization began, the Memel population by 1918 was virtually all German-Protestant stock. Under the Treaty of Versailles (Article 99), Germany had renounced all rights to Memel in favor of the Allied Powers, and the French had kept the area under military protection until January 11, 1923. A Lithuanian uprising seized Memel City, forcing the French garrison to give up control on January 15. Following the summoning of a local council, which promptly voted for uniting the territory with Lithuania, a provisional government was put in place. The Memel Convention, which took effect on August 25, 1925, formally recognized Lithuania's sovereignty over the territory and provided for local autonomous institutions, as well as representation in the national Lithuanian *Seimas*.

Throughout the interwar period, the German population in Memel continued to articulate anti-Lithuanian sentiments. With the rise of naziism in Germany (*see* NATIONAL SOCIALIST GERMAN WORKER'S PARTY, HISTORICAL GERMANY), similar types of parties also appeared in Memel in anticipation of support from the Hitler government. These parties (Christian Social-Workers' Community* and Socialist National Community*) were suppressed and their leaders imprisoned. However, in the mid-1930s, the Lithuanian government set about to curtail German nazi activity. This action led to an increase in civil disturbances and further fuelled an anti-Lithuanian sentiment.

In December 1938, elections to the local Memel *Diet* resulted in overwhelming support (87.2 percent) for Dr. Ernst Neumann and his United Front of German Parties (*see* Memel Territory Party). German friction culminated in an ultimatum from the Hitler government that Memel be ceded to Germany or else it would be taken by force. With few options, the Lithuanian *Seimas* acceded to this demand, and the transfer took place on March 22, 1939.

On the national Lithuanian level, the Populist-Social Democratic government that had come into office in May 1926 lasted only six months. On December 16-17, 1926, a military coup by elements of the Lithuanian Army brought the small conservative Nationalist Union to power. The political reforms of the third *Seimas*—repeal of martial law and press censorships; freedom of activity for all political groups, including the Communists; support for the national minorities, including establishment of Polish schools at a time when Poland was closing its Lithuanian school in Vilnius—all came to an abrupt end. The Nationalists redeclared martial law under the pretext of a planned Communist uprising for January 1927. Political opponents were arrested, some minorities were ousted from political office, various leftist groups were dissolved by decree, and four Communists were executed.

A new government was formed under the leadership of Augustine Voldemaras (Nationalist), and Antanas Smetona (also Nationalist) was declared president until new elections could be held. Although the Christian Democratic Bloc initially supported the regime—since Smetona had served as president from 1917 to 1922—the Populists and Social Democrats boycotted the *Seimas*, resulting in the Assembly's dissolution on April 12, 1927. Populist and Social Democratic leaders were imprisoned, and by May 1928 the Christian Democrats also withdrew their support from the Smetona regime. The Nationalist Union ruled alone.

A new constitution was promulgated on May 15, 1928, which provided for a president elected for a seven-year term by an electoral college. The president had the power to dissolve the *Seimas* and rule by decree when he deemed necessary. The voting age was raised to 24 years, and the term of the *Seimas* was extended to five years, although its membership was cut to 49 seats. However, elections to the fourth and last *Seimas* did not occur until June 9-10, 1936. With only Nationalist Union-approved candidates permitted to contest, the Nationalists took 46 seats, the German minority party took three seats, and Smetona continued as president.

Opposition to Smetona's government steadily increased throughout the 1930s, despite attempts to return to normal political life. The trade unions were dissolved in 1932, and in November 1935 the Christian Democratic Party and Peasant Populist Union were dissolved by decree. The Social Democrats had already been suppressed in April 1929. By February 1936, all parties or political groups opposed to the regime were banned.

The Smetona government became increasingly authoritarian in the late 1930s. By Summer 1938, church and state were separated, civil liberties were curbed, various political organizations were merged into government-controlled front organizations, and Smetona himself took on the title of *Tautos Vadas* (The Nation's Leader).

As World War II approached, Lithuania was subject to pressure from many sides. In 1938, Poland demanded the renewal of diplomatic relations, which had ceased with the 1919-1920 Polish occupation of Vilnius. Germany, in 1939, seized the Memel Territory. Further faced by increasing popular discontent at home, the Nationalist Union government attempted to broaden its base of support by coopting elements of the banned Christian Democratic and Populist parties into the cabinet.

The outbreak of World War II in September 1939, however, set off a chain of events that doomed Lithuanian independence. The secret protocol attached to the Soviet-German Non-Aggression Pact of August 23, 1939, divided eastern Europe into Soviet and German spheres of influence. Lithuania was originally designated a German sphere, although in the additional secret protocol of September 28, 1939, the Soviet government renounced certain Polish claims in exchange for all of Lithuania. Soviet pressure on Lithuania grew in intensity. Soviet armies marched into Poland on September 17 and Vilnius was occupied. On October 10 a military pact was concluded, allowing the establishment of Soviet military bases on Lithuanian territory. On June 7, 1940, the Soviet government accused the Lithuanian government of provoking various incidents involving the Soviet troops garrisoned in Lithuania and of concluding a secret military alliance with the other Baltic states. The Soviet government issued an ultimatum demanding the formation of a new government friendly to the Soviet Union, which was followed by a military occupation of Lithuania. President Smetona and other leading Lithuanian public figures fled the country on June 15, at which time a Communist-Soviet sympathizer, M. Paleckis, formed a new government and became president.

All noncommunist groupings were forcibly dissolved, and many Lithuanian political leaders, particularly the Peasant Populists, Christian Democrats, and Nationalists, were executed or deported to Siberia. On July 14, 1940, new elections were held for a national assembly. In Lithuania, as in the fellow Baltic states of Estonia and Latvia, the electoral procedure was like that of the Soviet Union, with no opposition candidates permitted to run. In Lithuania, 80 percent of the elected deputies were Communist Party members; and the new government policy was Soviet in every detail. Hence in August 1940, Lithuania was incorporated into the Soviet Union and became the Lithuanian Soviet Socialist Republic of the USSR.

Bibliography*

Baltic States Handbook. London: Chatham House, 1938.

Davis, Malcolm W., ed. *A Political Handbook of Europe: Parliaments, Parties and Press.* New York: Council on Foreign Relations, 1927-1940.

---

*The author wishes to thank Professor Bronis Kaslas for his assistance in providing information and advice in the writing of this chapter.

Graham, Malbone W. *New Governments of Eastern Europe.* New York: Henry Holt & Co., 1927.

Kaslas, Bronis J. *The Baltic Nations.* Pittston, Penna.: Euramerica Press, 1976.

Rothschild, Joseph. *East Central Europe Between the Two World Wars.* Seattle: University of Washington Press, 1974.

Roucek, Joseph, ed. *Central Eastern Europe.* New York: Prentice-Hall, 1946.

Sužiedeis, Simas, and Antanas Vasaitis, eds. *Encyclopedia Lituanica.* 6 vols. Boston: Juozas Kapočius, 1978.

von Rauch, Georg. *The Baltic States: The Years of Independence.* Translated by Gerald Onn. Berkeley and Los Angeles: University of California Press, 1974.

Political Parties

AGRARIAN UNION. *See* NATIONALIST UNION.

ASSOCIATION OF CHRISTIAN WORKERS OF LITHUANIA. *See* FEDERATION OF LABOR.

BELLITES. *See* PEASANT POPULIST UNION.

CATHOLIC DEMOCRATIC PARTY. *See* LITHUANIAN CHRISTIAN DEMOCRATIC PARTY.

CHRISTIAN DEMOCRATIC BLOC. *See* LITHUANIAN CHRISTIAN DEMOCRATIC PARTY.

CHRISTIAN LABOR PARTY. *See* FEDERATION OF LABOR.

CHRISTIAN SOCIAL-WORKERS' COMMUNITY (*Christliche-Sozialistiche Arbeitsgemeinschaft*: CSA). The CSA was founded in Spring 1933 in the Memel Territory by the German cleric, Pastor Theodor Freiherr von Sass. Although the party presented a left-wing social program, it was sympathetic to and modelled after the nazi movement in Germany (*see* NATIONAL SOCIALIST GERMAN WORKER'S PARTY, HISTORICAL GERMANY). With the accession of Adolf Hitler to German power in January 1933, the CSA sought to mobilize the German population in Memel against attempts to "Lithuanize" the territory by the government of Antanas Smetona (Nationalist Union*).

The CSA directed its political attention to the local *Diet* in Memel and, along with the Socialist National Community,* won a sweeping victory. In June 1934, the CSA was dissolved and Pastor von Sass arrested for conspiracy against the state in plotting to detach Memel from Lithuania. He was imprisoned in 1935 and released in 1938.

CHRISTLICHE-SOZIALISTICHE ARBEITSGEMEINSCHAFT. *See* CHRISTIAN SOCIAL-WORKERS' COMMUNITY.

COMMUNIST PARTY OF LITHUANIA (*Lietuvos Komunistų Partija*: LKP). The LKP remained an insignificant political organization in Lithuanian politics until 1941. The origins of the party could be traced to a meeting of radical elements in the international labor movement that took place in Vilnius on May 1, 1893. This small clandestine group of about 40 members claimed to represent the interests of the Kaunas and Vilnius working classes. The group became affiliated with the Social Democratic Party of Lithuania, * which was established in 1895.

By 1904 the communist wing of the Social Democrats was under the leadership of Zigmas Angarietas and Vincas Mickevičius-Kapsukas. The latter man established close ties to Russia's Lenin and in 1907 succeeded in passing a resolution to join the Lithuanian Social Democratic Party with its Russian Bolshevik counterpart (*see* RUSSIAN SOCIAL DEMOCRATIC WORKERS' PARTY, SOVIET UNION). This merger was never carried out, and in 1916 the pro-Bolshevik faction of Mickevičius-Kapsukas's followers broke from the Lithuanian Social Democrats and joined the Russian Bolshevik party.

On August 14, 1918, a separate Lithuanian-Byelorussian Communist Party was established in Russia. In September 1918, approximately 34 delegates of the Lithuanian-Byelorussian party met in Vilnius at its first congress and claimed to represent 800 members, most of them Byelorussians. With the retreat of the German forces following the World War I armistice of November 1918, the Bolshevik Army occupied eastern Lithuania. On December 22, a Lithuanian-Byelorussian Soviet Republic was proclaimed; and on January 6, 1919, a Bolshevik-type government was established in the occupied area under the leadership of Mickevičius-Kapsukas and the Lithuanian-Byelorussian Communist Party. This government lasted only a few months, and by Summer 1919 the Bolshevik government was routed by the Lithuanian Army. The federation of Lithuania and Byelorussia was never consumated, and the Lithuanian-Byelorussian Communist Party promptly disappeared.

The Communist Party of Lithuania was declared illegal in 1919 by the new Lithuanian government. A reorganization of the LKP occurred in Königsberg, East Prussia, in 1920, and the party joined the Comintern as a constituent unit. Mickevičius-Kapsukas continued his role as party leader.

The LKP reappeared in 1922 to contest elections to the first *Seimas*. The party was known under a variety of assumed names, such as the Labor Group, the Workers' League, and the Work Companies. The Communists succeeded in electing five deputies, who in reality represented a bloc of radical Poles and Germans. After 1922 the Communists failed to elect a single *Seimas* deputy and disappeared from Lituanian political participation until 1941.

A second congress of the LKP was held in Moscow on July 17-20, 1924. At that time, the party claimed to represent 700-900 members, most of whom were non-Lithuanians in nationality. No other congresses were held until 1941. During the Soviet Union-sponsored elections of July 14, 1940, the LKP was declared legal and represented the guiding force in the Working People's Bloc, a front organization that promptly disappeared following Lithuania's annexation by the Soviet Union.

CSA. *See* CHRISTIAN SOCIAL-WORKERS' COMMUNITY.

DARBININKŲ FEDERACIJA. *See* FEDERATION OF LABOR.

DEMOCRATIC NATIONAL FREEDOM LEAGUE. *See* FARMERS' PARTY.

DEMOCRATIC PARTY OF LITHUANIA. *See* PEASANT POPULIST UNION.

DEMOKRATINE TAUTOS LAISOES SANTARA. *See* FARMERS' PARTY.

EINHEITLISTE. *See* MEMEL TERRITORY PARTY.

FARMERS' PARTY (*Ūkininkų Partija*). The Farmers' Party grew out of the Democratic National Freedom League (*Demokratine Tautos Laisoes Santara* or *Santara*), which was formed during March 1917 in Saint Petersburg, Russia, by Lithuanian World War I evacuees. The *Santara* was a small secular group with a liberal political outlook, seeking to bring together the interests of agriculture and industry. In contrast to other agrarian parties, the *Santara* favored religious tolerance. The League also strongly supported measures designed to develop and foster Lithuanian culture.

In 1925 the *Santara* became the Farmers' Party. The grouping's only electoral success came in 1926 when it managed to elect two representatives to the *Seimas*. After the 1926 military coup, the party entered the Smetona regime briefly as a coalition partner to the Nationalist Union.* The Farmers' Party withdrew in 1928 and was banned the same year. Elements of the Farmers' Party were revived during World War II and played a small role in Lithuanian resistance. The most important party leaders were M. Sidzikauskas (minister to Germany) and M. Žalkauskas (minister of the interior).

FARMERS' UNION (*Ūkininkų Sąjungą*). The Farmers' Union traced its origins to the 1905 formation of the Lithuanian Peasant League around the newspaper *Ūkininkus* (The Farmer). After Lithuania's independence, the Peasant League changed its name to the Farmers' Union in 1920 and became closely associated with the Lithuanian Christian Democratic Party* in the constituent assembly. The two parties, along with the Federation of Labor,* formed the Christian Democratic Bloc (*see* Lithuanian Christian Democratic Party), a coalition that would dominate Lithuanian politics until 1926.

The Farmers' Union represented the interests and perspectives of the Catholic peasantry. The party called for the improvement of agricultural land and stressed the need for agricultural credits. The Union also functioned as a business organization in managing a number of farm and dairy cooperatives.

In the *Seimas* the strength of the Farmers' Union varied from 11 to 18 deputies. The Union declined sharply in 1926 with the electoral rise of the Peasant Populist Union* and the decline of the Christian Democratic Bloc generally. Prior to the 1926 military coup against the Lithuanian government, the Farmers' Union leaders (A. Stulginskis, V. Petrulis, and K. Jokantas) were among the most influential personalities in Lithuanian politics. Aleksandras Stulginskis served as speaker of the *Seimas* and as president of the republic (1922-1926), Petrulis served as premier (part of 1925), and Jokantas was a minister of education. After the party moved into opposition of the Smetona (Nationalist Union*) regime, the political activities of the Farmers' Union were suspended in 1928 by decree.

FEDERATION OF LABOR (*Darbininkų Federacija*). The Federation of Labor (also known as the Workers' Federation or the Christian Labor Party) was established on September 28, 1919, at the Kaunas convention of the Lithuanian Christian Workers' Association. The latter organization, consisting of various professional and cultural organizations of nonsocialist workers, was opposed to the marxist theory of class conflict. The Federation, in aiming to provide unified political expression for the Christian Workers' Association, also sought to link the support of small landholders and new settlers to the interests of labor under a program of Christian principles. The Federation supported land reform, a revision of work rules, and higher wages.

Domestically, the Federation was closely allied with the Lithuanian Christian Democratic Party* in the Christian Democratic Bloc. Although fielding candidates for elections, the Federation did not participate directly in governing and preferred to act as a pressure group in the *Seimas*. Internationally, the Federation was an affiliate of the Utrecht Christian International Labor Movement.

Federation strength declined from 12 to five members in the third *Seimas* of 1926, along with the decline of the Christian Democratic Bloc generally. The Federation soon joined the opposition to the Smetona (Nationalist Union*) regime in the late 1920s; and as a result, the Federation of Labor was dissolved by decree in 1932. Reorganized as a nonpartisan group on April 15, 1934, the Federation assumed the name of the Association of Christian Workers of Lithuania (*Lietuvos Krikščionių Darbininkų Sąjungą*). The Association had 42 chapters and claimed 6,000 members in 1938. Among the Federation's principal leaders had been K. Ambrozaitis, P. Radzevičius, and V. Kasakaitis.

GELEZINAS VILKAS. *See* IRON WOLF.

IRON WOLF (*Gelezinas Vilkas*). Founded in 1926, the Iron Wolf was a semiclandestine, radical, national society. It was formed under the direction of Augustine Voldemaras, who in 1918 had been premier and minister of foreign affairs under the *Taryba* presidency of Antanas Smetona. Following its inception, the Iron Wolf was quickly transformed by Voldemaras into a fascist militia, designed to challenge the political influence of the officers' clubs of the Lithuanian Army.

Unlike the fascist organizations in the other Baltic states (see ASSOCIATION OF ESTONIAN FREEDOM FIGHTERS, HISTORICAL ESTONIA; LATVIAN FASCISTS, HISTORICAL LATVIA), Lithuania's Iron Wolf did not function as an electoral organization. It was a political auxiliary group composed of young to middle-aged men drawn from the ranks of the military and civil service. Its motto was "Honor of the nation; welfare of the state."

Serving again as premier in 1926, Voldemaras was forced to resign from the Smetona (Nationalist Union*) government in September 1929 after a series of intrigues designed to seize power from Smetona with the aid of the Iron Wolf. In July 1930, Voldemaras was banished to a rural area. The Iron Wolf began to disintegrate into various factions by 1930 and was officially dissolved in August 1931, although it continued to function as a loosely organized "sports association."

Supporters of Voldemaras in the Iron Wolf regrouped and formed the Voldemarites (*Voldemarininkai*), which continued to criticize the Smetona regime. Joined by a radical faction of Smetona's party, the Nationalist Union, the Voldemarites soon transformed themselves into the Lithuanian Nationalist Party (*Lietuvių Tautininkų Partija*) and established a periodical, *Tautos Balsa* (Nation's Voice). Voldemaras failed in a second coup attempt on June 6, 1934. He was sentenced to 12 years imprisonment, though he was granted amnesty in February 1938 and was allowed to leave the country. He returned to Lithuania in 1940 during the Soviet occupation, at which time he was deported to the Soviet Union where it is thought that he died in 1944. The Lithuanian Nationalist Party had dissolved in 1935, with most of its supporters being absorbed by the Nationalist Union.

JAUNOJI LIETWA. See NATIONALIST UNION.

KLAIPĖDA PARTIJA. See MEMEL TERRITORY PARTY.

LABOR GROUP. See COMMUNIST PARTY OF LITHUANIA.

LDP. See PEASANT POPULIST UNION.

LIETUVIŲ DEMOKRATŲ PARTIJA. See PEASANT POPULIST UNION.

LIETUVIŲ KRIKŠČIONIŲ DEMOKRATŲ PARTIJA. See LITHUANIAN CHRISTIAN DEMOCRATIC PARTY.

LIETUVIŲ TAUTININKŲ PARTIJA. See IRON WOLF.

LIETUVOS DEMOKRATŲ PARTIJA. See PEASANT POPULIST UNION.

LIETUVOS KOMUNISTŲ PARTIJA. See COMMUNIST PARTY OF LITHUANIA.

LIETUVOS KRIKŠČIONIŲ DARBININKŲ SAJUNGĄ. See FEDERATION OF LABOR.

LIETUVOS REVOLIUCINIŲ SOCIALISTŲ LIAUDININKAI PARTIJA. See PEASANT POPULIST UNION.

LIETUVOS SOCIALDEMOKRATŲ PARTIJA. See SOCIAL DEMOCRATIC PARTY OF LITHUANIA.

LIETUVOS SOCIALISTŲ LIAUDININKAI DEMOKRATŲ PARTIJA. See PEASANT POPULIST UNION.

LIETUVOS SOCIALISTŲ LIAUDININKAI PARTIJA. See PEASANT POP-ULIST UNION.

LIGHT INFANTRY ASSOCIATION. See NATIONALIST UNION.

LITHUANIAN-BYELORUSSIAN COMMUNIST PARTY. See COMMUNIST PARTY OF LITHUANIA.

LITHUANIAN CHRISTIAN DEMOCRATIC PARTY (*Lietuvių Krikščionių Demokratų Partija*: LKDP). The Christian democratic movement in Lithuania was founded in 1890 as a political grouping of Catholic intellectuals and Roman Catholic clergy. The first statement of the movement's objectives was presented in the publication *Apzvalga* (Review) and constituted an attack on the Russian administration of Lithuania, a call for Lithuanian patriotism, a defense of the Roman Catholic faith in the encroachment of the Russian Orthodox Church, and a vague hope for eventual national independence. Social objectives were added to the movement in 1904 through the efforts of priests teaching at the Roman Catholic Theological Academy in Saint Petersburg, Russia, who were influenced by the encyclicals of Pope Leo XIII. Their political program was presented and promulgated in the *Samogitian and Lithuanian Review* and contributed to the rising Lithuanian nationalist trend.

The Christian democratic movement in Lithuania became increasingly nationalistic and anti-Polish after 1904. A small dissident Catholic Democratic Party was founded in 1905, which opposed national autonomy for Lithuania and argued instead for the development of a united community of Lithuanians, Poles, and Byelorussians. This Catholic Democratic Party had little influence and soon disappeared after the attainment of Lithuanian independence.

The LKDP was organized as a formal party in 1917 and held its first congress on November 20, 1918, in Vilnius. The Lithuanian Christian Democrats were primarily peasant-oriented but sought to incorporate voters of all classes. Supporting moderate democratic principles, the LKDP advocated reforms along the lines of Catholic social doctrine, especially in the area of education. The party was a strong advocate of free, but compulsory, religious education, as well as of ecclesiastical rights that would make Catholicism a state religion. The Christian Democrats were also in favor of the rights of labor, including the right to strike and the eight-hour workday. Although they expressed support for agrarian land reforms, they also defended the rights of private property and the obligation of payment for any land expropriations.

With its rather broad though conservative program, the LKDP played an important role in the Vilnius Council (1905), the *Taryba* (1917), and was heavily represented in the 1920 constituent assembly (25 seats). Acting in concert with the nonsocialist Federation of Labor* (16 seats) and the Catholic-oriented Farmers' Union* (18 seats), the LKDP formed the basis of an electoral and parliamentary group known as the Christian Democratic Bloc. Holding a majority of 59 out of 112 constituent assembly seats (53 percent), the Bloc soon fashioned the constitutional and state structures of Lithuania in accordance with its own nationalist-religious ideology.

The Christian Democratic Bloc's share of parliamentary seats declined somewhat with the first two *Seimases* (48 percent in 1922, 51 percent in 1923). But still enjoying a powerful base of mass support, the Bloc functioned as Lithuania's governing coalition for the first four years of *Seimas* authority. However, the Bloc met electoral defeat in 1926, winning only 30 out of 85 seats (35 percent). Humiliation and resentment over the loss of Vilnius to Poland (*see* Historical Lithuania introduction), charges of corruption, and economic difficulties all contributed to the Bloc's decline.

The LKDP initially supported the Smetona (Nationalist Union*) government, formed in the aftermath of the December 1926 military coup. However, in June 1927 the party joined the opposition led by the Peasant Populist Union* and the Social Democratic Party of Lithuania,* following the dissolution of the *Seimas* in April and the resignation of Christian Democratic cabinet members in May. Several LKDP leaders were imprisoned briefly in 1928, and the party was dissolved in November 1935. As Smetona's dictatorial government met with increasing popular discontent in the late 1930s, some LKDP members were coopted into the Smetona cabinet in March 1939 in the attempt to broaden the government's base of mass support, especially after the loss of the Memel Territory to Germany (*see* Historical Lithuania introduction).

Among the important Christian Democratic leaders were L. Bistras (premier, late 1925-early 1926) and P. Karvelis (a former minister of finance). Lithuanian exiles have attempted to keep alive the traditions of the LKDP in western Europe and the United States.

LITHUANIAN CHRISTIAN WORKERS' ASSOCIATION. *See* FEDERATION OF LABOR.

LITHUANIAN DEMOCRATIC PARTY. *See* PEASANT POPULIST UNION.

LITHUANIAN NATIONALIST PARTY. *See* IRON WOLF.

LITHUANIAN PEASANT LEAGUE. *See* FARMERS' UNION.

LKDP. *See* LITHUANIAN CHRISTIAN DEMOCRATIC PARTY.

LKP. *See* COMMUNIST PARTY OF LITHUANIA.

LRSLP. *See* PEASANT POPULIST UNION.

LSDP. *See* SOCIAL DEMOCRATIC PARTY OF LITHUANIA.

LSLDP. *See* PEASANT POPULIST UNION.

LSLP. *See* PEASANT POPULIST UNION.

MEMEL TERRITORY PARTY (*Klaipēda Partija*). On August 25, 1925, the Memel Territory Convention transferred the predominantly German city of Memel from Allied control (United Kingdom, France, Italy, Japan) to Lithuanian sovereignty (*see* Historical Lithuania introduction). The Convention provided for the establishment of a local *Diet* (or chamber of representatives) consisting of 29 seats to be filled every three years by universal direct suffrage. The Memel Territory (also known as *Klaipēda*) was also entitled to send delegates to the Lithuanian national *Seimas* under the terms of Lithuanian electoral law.

The Memel Territory Party constituted a group of five deputies elected to the third *Seimas* in 1926. The group had a broad base of support in the region and acted to safeguard the interests of the local, predominantly German population. Among the important party leaders were R. Grabovas, A. Milbrechtas, J. Jakstaitis, and J. Suiselis.

Within the Memel Territory itself, elections to the local *Diet* revealed a strong anti-Lithuanian sentiment, manifested in the formation of an ethnic bloc known as the United Front of German Parties (*Einheitliste*). The *Einheitliste* included all the German political groupings in the territory except social democrats. Extremely popular, the *Einheitliste* captured over three-fourths of the *Diet* seats.

With the advent of naziism in Germany (*see* NATIONAL SOCIALIST GERMAN WORKER'S PARTY, HISTORICAL GERMANY), two Lithuanian pronazi parties were formed to protest Lithuanian rule in Memel and to seek assistance from the German government. Both parties (the Christian Social-Workers' Community* and the Socialist National Community*) were dissolved in June 1934 and their leaders imprisoned. In 1935 the Lithuanian government changed the electoral law in Memel to dilute German strength by disenfranchising those voters not having a knowledge of the Lithuanian language. Pressure from Germany led the Lithuanian government to rescind most of its anti-German measures. The Memel *Diet* election of 1935 therefore resulted in the mandates of 24 *Einheitliste* candidates and only four Lithuanians. The *Diet* election of 1938 resulted in 87.2 percent of the vote for the *Einheitliste*, by that time led by Dr. Ernst Neumann, former leader of the naziist Socialist National Community.

Although there was some improvement in German-Lithuanian relations after 1936, the political calm was only temporary. German friction increased in the late 1930s, and Lithuania was forced to cede the Memel Territory to Germany on March 22, 1939.

NATIONALIST PARTY. *See* NATIONALIST UNION.

NATIONALIST UNION (*Tautininkų Sajungą*). The Nationalist Union (also known as the Nationalist Party, *Tautininkų Partija*) traced its origins to the Lithuanian national movement that emerged during the latter part of the 19th century. The dominant personalities in the quest for Lithuanian independence formed a small political party around the newspaper *Viltis* (Hope), which was edited by Antanas Smetona in Vilnius. Smetona and his followers sought to occupy a middle ground between the radical left and the conservative right, and they acquired the name *Tautininkai* or Nationalists.

For a brief period, two separate nationalist parties existed. The first such grouping was the National Progress (*Tautos Pažanga*), formed in 1916 in Saint Petersburg, Russia, by Lithuanian refugees led by Juozas Kubilius and Liudas Noreika. The second party, the *Tautininkai*, was organized by Smetona, who had been elected to head the Lithuanian Provincial Council (*Taryba*) in Vilnius in September 1917. After Lithuanian independence, the National Progress changed its name to the Agrarian Union (*Žemdirbių Sajungą*), which by then had evolved into a political grouping of well-to-do farmers who considered many of the proposed land reform measures too radical or economically unsound. Both the Agrarian Union and the *Tautininkai* were unsuccessful in their electoral bids for representation in the 1920 constituent assembly and the first two *Seimases* of 1922 and 1923. In 1924 the two groupings merged as the Nationalist Union.

At first, the Nationalist Union was hardly a significant force in Lithuanian politics, given the electoral supremacy of the Lithuanian Christian Democratic Party* and its agrarian and labor allies. The Nationalist Union's role was limited to opposition criticism of agrarian reform and the inefficiency of the parliamentary system. The Nationalists made their first electoral breakthrough in 1926, winning three seats to the third *Seimas*. Following the military coup of December 16-17, 1926, a minority government was formed by the Nationalist Union and elements of the Christian Democratic Party. The Christian Democrats soon withdrew from the coalition; and with the dissolution of the *Seimas* in April 1927, the Nationalist Union remained as the dominant political group.

Beginning in 1931, certain fascist tendencies had become evident in the Nationalist Union. A tighter organizational link was forged between the party and government, similar to the experience of fascist Italy. Although Smetona stressed his desire to follow a middle course between a multiparty system and a fascist-type dictatorship, the Nationalist Union specifically adopted fascism as a governing principle at its congress on December 16, 1933.

A major split occurred in the party in 1934 when a radical Nationalist Union faction of Augustine Voldemaras's supporters formed the Lithuanian Nationalist Party (see Iron Wolf). Voldemaras, who had earlier served as premier under Smetona (1918 and 1926-1929), failed in two coup attempts in 1929 and on June 6, 1934. Voldemaras was imprisoned until 1938; and the Lithuanian Nationalist Party had disintegrated in 1935, with most of its supporters being reabsorbed into the Nationalist Union.

Smetona, as president, ruled dictatorially for ten years before new Seimas elections were called in 1936. Smetona had suspended many civil liberties earlier promulgated by the Seimas, and by February 1936 all political groupings opposed to the regime were banned. Hence when the Nationalists finally permitted new Seimas elections, the Union won 46 of 49 seats. Smetona continued as president, a position he held until fleeing the country in 1940 upon Soviet occupation.

The Nationalist Union stressed the need for a cooperative governmental system, with political representation through corporate bodies. The party also developed two auxiliary organizations to consolidate its political power. The Light Infantry Association (Šaulių Sajunga) was made up of veterans and older male members of the party who constituted a paramilitary force similar to the fascist militia of Benito Mussolini in Italy. Young Lithuania (Jaunoji Lietwa) was as association that endoctrinated party youth with a heavy dose of Lithuanian nationalism and also provided them with military training. The most important party leaders were Smetona, Voldemaras (premier and minister of foreign affairs), I. Tomašaitis, and L. Noreika.

NATIONAL MINORITY PARTIES. Taken together, the national minorities in Lithuania during the period of independence constituted approximately 16.1 percent of the nation's total population. The Jews were the largest group (7.6 percent) and the most active politically, followed by the Poles (3.2 percent), Russians (2.7 percent), and Germans (1.4 percent). Each national minority attempted to organize its own political representation in the Seimas in order to protect the cultural and economic interests of its respective community.

The Jewish group in the Seimas was under the leadership of O. Finkelšteinas and J. Robinsonas, and it fluctuated from three to seven deputies. The Polish group ranged from two deputies in 1922 to four in 1923 and 1926; the Poles were led by V. Budzinkis and B. Liutykas. The Russian minority was the least successful and elected only one deputy to the 1923 Seimas.

The position of the German minority in Lithuania was more complex. Although the Germans were represented by one or two deputies in the *Seimas*, the addition to Lithuania of the Memel Territory in 1925 and the formation of the Memel Territory Party* significantly increased the German presence in Lithuanian politics. The German minority outside of Memel was led by V. Rogalis and R. Kinderis.

NATIONAL PROGRESS. *See* NATIONALIST UNION.

NAUJOLI LIETUVA. *See* SOCIAL DEMOCRATIC PARTY OF LITHUANIA.

NEW LITHUANIA. *See* SOCIAL DEMOCRATIC PARTY OF LITHUANIA.

PEASANT POPULIST UNION (*Valstiecių Liaudininkų Sajungą*: VLS). The ideological and political heritage of the Peasant Populist Union extended back to 1889 and the publication of *Varpas* (The Bell) in East Prussia. *The Bell* was a clandestine paper edited by Vincas Kudirka, which attracted the attention of various liberal intellectuals who came to be known as the Bellites (*Varpininkai*). As the group began to coalesce politically, it was organized in 1902 as the Lithuanian Democratic Party (*Lietuvių Demokratų Partija*: LDP).

Since at that time political organizations were prohibited by the Russian administration, the LDP worked clandestinely in the rural areas of northwestern Lithuania. Party leaders were influenced by the ideas of the Russian *Narodniki* (*see* POPULISTS, SOVIET UNION) and the Constitutional Democrats (*see* PARTY OF PEOPLE'S FREEDOM, SOVIET UNION). Hence the LDP was largely concerned with agrarian issues, especially reforms that would distribute land to new settlers.

The Democrats grew more radical after the 1905 revolution in Russia. Younger members of the party formed a new group called the Peasant Union (*Valstiecių Sajungą*), advocating direct action among the peasantry. Although formally independent, the Peasant Union retained close ties to the Lithuanian Democratic Party. In 1906 the LDP included in its program a call for the creation of an independent democratic Lithuanian republic and the relaxation of restraints against cultural expression. In 1914 the party adopted a detailed social welfare program and changed its name to the Democratic Party of Lithuania (*Lietuvos Demokratų Partija*: LDP). The name change, though slight, was designed to broaden the party's base of support.

The membership of the Democratic Party was divided by the events of World War I. One party grouping remained in German-occupied Lithuania, while the other represented evacuees to Russia. The latter came under the influence of the marxist socialist-populist movement; and following the Russian February revolution of 1917, this group broke away from the LDP and established a new party in Petrograd called the Socialist Populists Party of Lithuania (*Lietuvos Socialistų Liaudininkai Partija*: LSLP). After the Russian October revolution of 1917, this group became the Revolutionary Socialist Populists Party of Lithuania (*Lietuvos*

Revoliuciniŭ Socialistŭ Liaudininkai Partija: LRSLP), but it soon disappeared in 1920 due to lack of electoral success.

Conservative elements of the Democratic Party formed their own political organization in 1917. To distinguish themselves from the marxist LSLP, the conservatives took the name of the Socialist Populists Democratic Party of Lithuania (*Lietuvos Socialistŭ Liaudininkai Demokratŭ Partija*: LSLDP). In 1920 the remainder of the Democratic Party of Lithuania dissolved, with its membership being absorbed by the LSLDP and Peasant Union offshoots.

The LSLDP and the Peasant Union ran a joint electoral slate for the 1920 constituent assembly elections and together obtained 29 seats. The parties competed separately in the November 9, 1922, elections to the first *Seimas*, winning six and 14 seats respectively. Very shortly after these elections, on November 24, 1922, the LSLDP and Peasant Union merged to form the Peasant Populist Union. The new VLS secured 16 seats in the second *Seimas* (1923) and participated until June 1924 in the cabinet of Ernestas Galvannauskas.

In elections to the third *Seimas* (May 8-9, 1926), the VLS won 22 seats, making it the largest single Assembly grouping and ousting from power the previously dominant Christian Democratic Bloc (*see* Lithuanian Christian Democratic Party). VLS leader Kazys Grinius was elected president of the republic, and Mykolas Sleževičius was elected premier. The Peasant Populists formed a coalition government with the Social Democratic Party of Lithuania.* However, this government was deposed on December 16-17, 1926, by a military coup, and a minority government under Nationalist Union* leadership was established. Several Populist leaders were imprisoned by the new regime in 1927; and after a period of opposition activity, including a peasants' strike in southwestern Lithuania, the party was dissolved by decree in November 1935.

The political program of the Peasant Populist Union stressed the role of secularism in political life, nationalization of large estates (more than 50 hectares), and the development of cooperatives in industry, agriculture, and banking. The party published two influential organs: *Lietuvos Ūkininkas* (Farmers of Lithuania) and *Varpas* (The Bell). The VLS leaders were Kazys Grinius (elected premier in 1920 and president in 1926), Mykolas Sleževičius (three terms as premier), Justinas Staugaitis, and F. Bortkeviciene.

PEASANT UNION. *See* PEASANT POPULIST UNION.

REVOLUTIONARY SOCIALIST POPULISTS PARTY OF LITHUANIA. *See* PEASANT POPULIST UNION.

ŠAULIŲ SAJUNGĄ. *See* NATIONALIST UNION.

SOCIAL DEMOCRATIC PARTY OF LITHUANIA (*Lietuvos Socialdemokratŭ Partija*: LSDP). The LSDP represented one of the oldest political parties in Lithuania, having been founded in 1895 in Vilnius under the influence of the

Polish socialist movement (see POLISH SOCIALIST PARTY, POLAND). The LSDP's original program was to defend the workers, fight against Russian oppression, and strive for an autonomous Lithuania within a loose Russian confederation. The party broke with the Polish movement in 1896 over the issue of Lithuanian independence, and a distinct Lithuanian national party was formed under the leadership of A. Moravsk and Andrius Domaševičius.

Before and after Lithuanian independence, the Social Democrats had little influence on the course of national politics, which was virtually dominated by the Lithuanian Christian Democratic Party* and that grouping's agrarian and labor allies. The Social Democrats were also weakened by a number of splits in their party organization. In 1902 liberal LSDP members, concerned with agrarian issues, broke away to join the newly formed Lithuanian Democratic Party (see Peasant Populist Union). Then, when Lithuania was granted representation to the Russian assembly, the Social Democrats boycotted the first Russian *Duma* in 1905, though the party succeeded in electing five of the seven Lithuanian delegates to the second *Duma*. The Lithuanian representatives were eventually imprisoned for advocating an expansion of civil rights. Also, in 1916, an internationalist LSDP faction that supported the Russian Bolsheviks (see RUSSIAN SOCIAL DEMOCRATIC WORKERS' PARTY, SOVIET UNION) left the LSDP under the leadership of Vincas Mickevičius-Kapsukas officially to form the Communist Party of Lithuania.* The main body of the LSDP then evolved into a more purely nationalist group in support of constitutional government, with an economic program calling for the nationalization of banking, industry, and natural resources.

The LSDP published several organs, such as *Lietuvos Darbininkas* (Worker of Lithuania) and *Socialdemokratas* (Social Democrat). The latter was edited by M. Kairys. The LSDP at its peak in the mid-1920s had about 3,000 members. They also had about 1,500 individuals in their youth group, Spark (*Žiezirba*), which served as an auxiliary to the LSDP organization.

Following the electoral defeat of the previously dominant Christian Democratic Bloc (see Lithuanian Christian Democratic Party), the Social Democrats formed a brief coalition government with the Peasant Populist Union in June 1926 under the Peasant Populist leadership of M. Sleževičius (premier) and Kazys Grinius (president). The coalition, however, was terminated six months later in a military coup and the subsequent establishment of the Antanas Smetona (Nationalist Union*) regime. The Social Democrats were subjected to immediate persecution by the Smetona government, and several LSDP leaders were imprisoned. The party was officially dissolved by decree in April 1929.

The most important LSDP leaders during the period of Lithuanian independence were M. Kairys, K. Bielinis, and M. Čepinskis. The party formed an underground organization in 1941 known as New Lithuania (*Naujoli Lietuva*), which disappeared at the end of World War II.

SOCIALIST NATIONAL COMMUNITY (*Sozialistiche Volksorganisation*: SOVOG). The Socialist National Community (also known as the Socialist

People's Community) was formed in Summer 1933 in the Memel Territory by Dr. Ernst Neumann. The SOVOG was established as a conservative alternative to the left-oriented Christian Social-Workers' Community (CSA)* founded earlier by Pastor von Sass. The SOVOG took on all the characteristics of an indigenous pronazi movement (see NATIONAL SOCIALIST GERMAN WORKER'S PARTY, HISTORICAL GERMANY) and was favored by Lithuanian German political elements over the CSA. An attempt by German Nazi leaders to unify the two movements under Dr. Neumann failed in July 1933.

Both the CSA and SOVOG sought to mobilize the German population against attempts to "Lithuanize" the Memel Territory by the government of Antanas Smetona (Nationalist Union*). Because of these efforts, in June 1934 the SOVOG was dissolved by decree. Neumann was arrested for conspiracy against the state, imprisoned in 1935, and released in 1938. Upon his release, Neumann assumed leadership of the United Front of German Parties (see Memel Territory Party), which opposed Lithuanian rule over Memel and sought assistance from the German Nazi government. In the 1938 elections to the local Memel *Diet*, Neumann's United Front secured 87.2 percent of the vote. Neumann's political activities declined after Lithuania ceded Memel to Germany in March 1939.

SOCIALIST PEOPLE'S COMMUNITY. *See* SOCIALIST NATIONAL COMMUNITY.

SOCIALIST POPULISTS DEMOCRATIC PARTY OF LITHUANIA. *See* PEASANT POPULIST UNION.

SOCIALIST POPULISTS PARTY OF LITHUANIA. *See* PEASANT POPULIST UNION.

SOVOG. *See* SOCIALIST NATIONAL COMMUNITY.

SOZIALISTICHE VOLKSORGANISATION. *See* SOCIALIST NATIONAL COMMUNITY.

SPARK. *See* SOCIAL DEMOCRATIC PARTY OF LITHUANIA.

TAUTININKŲ PARTIJA. *See* NATIONALIST UNION.

TAUTININKŲ SAJUNGĄ. *See* NATIONALIST UNION.

TAUTOS PAŽANGA. *See* NATIONALIST UNION.

UKININKŲ PARTIJA. *See* FARMERS' PARTY.

UKININKŲ SAJUNGĄ. *See* FARMERS' UNION.

UNITED FRONT OF GERMAN PARTIES. *See* MEMEL TERRITORY PARTY.

VALSTIECIŲ LIAUDINKŲ SAJUNGĄ. *See* PEASANT POPULIST UNION.

VALSTIECIŲ SAJUNGĄ. *See* PEASANT POPULIST UNION.

VARPININKAI. *See* PEASANT POPULIST UNION.

VLS. *See* PEASANT POPULIST UNION.

VOLDEMARININKAI. *See* IRON WOLF.

VOLDEMARITES. *See* IRON WOLF.

WORK COMPANIES. *See* COMMUNIST PARTY OF LITHUANIA.

WORKERS' FEDERATION. *See* FEDERATION OF LABOR.

WORKERS' LEAGUE. *See* COMMUNIST PARTY OF LITHUANIA.

WORKING PEOPLE'S BLOC. *See* COMMUNIST PARTY OF LITHUANIA.

YOUNG LITHUANIA. *See* NATIONALIST UNION.

ŽEMDIRBIŲ SAJUNGĄ. *See* NATIONALIST UNION.

ŽIEZIRBA. *See* SOCIAL DEMOCRATIC PARTY OF LITHUANIA.

Vincent E. McHale

TABLE 41. Distribution of Seats in Historical Lithuania's _Seimas_, 1920-1936

Party	1920[a]	1922	1923	1926	1936
Farmers' Party	—	—	—	2	—
Farmers' Union[b]	18	12	14	11	—
Federation of Labor[b]	16	11	12	5	—
Lithuanian Christian Democratic Party[b]	25	15	14	14	—
Lithuanian Communist Party	—	5	0	0	—
Nationalist Union	0	0	0	3	46
Peasant Union[c]	29	14	16	22	—
Socialist Populists Democratic Party[c]		6			
Social Democratic Party	14	10	8	15	—
National Minority Parties:					
Germans	1	0	2	1	3
Jews	6	3	7	3	0
Memel Territory Party (German)	—	—	—	5	—
Poles	3	2	4	4	0
Russians	0	0	1	0	0
Total	112	78	78	85	49

[a] Constituent assembly elections.

[b] In 1922, these three parties (Christian Democrats, Farmers' Union, and Federation of Labor) became known as the Christian Democratic Bloc.

[c] The Peasant Union and Socialist Populists formed a joint electoral list in 1920. They ran separately for 1922 election, but shortly thereafter merged to become the Peasant Populist Union.

TABLE 42.   Ruling Coalitions in Historical Lithuania, 1920-1940

Years	Coalition
May 1920 - Nov. 1922	Peasant Union Christian Democratic Bloc*
Nov. 1922 - May 1923	Nonpartisan Christian Democratic Bloc*
May 1923 - May 1926	Christian Democratic Bloc*
May 1926 - Dec. 1926	Peasant Populist Union Social Democratic Party of Lithuania Farmers' Party
Dec. 1926 - May 1928	Nationalist Union Christian Democratic Bloc* Farmers' Party
May 1928 - June 1940	Nationalist Union

Note: First-named party is dominant coalition party.
*   The Federation of Labor formed part of the Christian Democratic Bloc in the legislature and in electoral campaigns but did not participate directly in governance.

HUNGARY

The HUNGARIAN PEOPLE'S REPUBLIC (*Magyar Népköztársaság*) was created on August 20, 1949, following a communist takeover of the nation's brief post-World War II republic, which had been originally declared on February 1, 1946. Hungary is a central European country of 35,918 square miles (approximately the size of Indiana), situated in the midst of Czechoslovakia, the USSR, Romania, Yugoslavia, and Austria. The Hungarian population of almost 10.7 million (1981 estimate) is about two-thirds Roman Catholic and the rest Calvinist, Jewish, and Eastern Orthodox in religious makeup. Ethnic heritage is predominantly Magyar (Hungarian, 97 percent), with traces of other ethnicities reminiscent of Hungary's earlier inhabitants.

The Kingdom of Hungary, also known as the Crownlands of Saint Stephen, had existed as a political entity until World War I, dating its founding back to A.D. 1000. In that year, King Stephen I was crowned by Pope Sylvester II to rule over a territory originally settled by Slavs and Germanics and later invaded by eastern Huns and Magyars. Constitutional development stemmed from the provisions of a Golden Bull (*Arany bulla*), promulgated by Andrew II in A.D. 1222 and confirming national liberties in a fashion similar to that of the Great Charter of England (*Magna Carta*). By the 15th century, all of central Europe was subject to repeated Turkish invasions, fought mostly by the expanding Austrian Habsburg dynasty (*see also* AUSTRIA INTRODUCTION). In the early 16th century, in an attempt to expand even farther and to protect its claims against the Turks, Austria brought Hungary under its rule. And when the Turks were finally defeated in the late 17th century, Austria emerged as the dominant power. The Habsburgs repeatedly pledged to uphold the customary and established laws of Hungary, even though these laws were largely ignored in practice.

Political party development in Hungary began during the 1840s, with the efforts of Lajos Kossuth and Ferenc Deák in uniting a liberal grouping in the subservient Hungarian legislature. Their goal was to reestablish Hungarian autonomy with a series of governmental reforms. However, their efforts were preempted by the 1848 revolt of the Hungarians against Habsburg rule. Although unsuccessful, the revolt forced a series of changes in the Hungarian political system. The ancient parliament was revised, suffrage was broadened, and cabinet responsibility was instituted. In 1867, after some seven years of negotiation by Deák and his followers, the ruling elite of Hungary and the Habsburg emperor, Francis Joseph I, concluded a compromise known as the *Kiegyezés* or, in German, as the *Ausgleich*. The compromise created a Dual Monarchy which allowed Hungary independence in internal affairs but which placed foreign relations, defense matters, and finance under joint ministers. There were separate prime ministers and parliaments for both Hungary and Austria. Thus, the Austro-Hungarian Empire emerged under Francis Joseph, who was titled Emperor of Austria and Apostolic King of Hungary.

Until the collapse of the Dual Monarchy in 1918, Hungarian political parties focused on whether the compromise with Austria was to be accepted, altered, or dissolved. The Deák Party* supported the compromise that had been negotiated by the party's founder, and after an electoral success in 1869, the Deákists formed the early ministries. The Left Center (*see* Liberal Party), which was the chief rival of the Deákists, favored no union whatsoever between Austria and Hungary except through the personality of the crown.

The Deák Party began to disintegrate in the early 1870s, amid charges of corruption coupled with commercial and financial crises. In 1875 the Left Center, under the leadership of Kálmán Tisza, abandoned its opposition to the *Ausgleich* and joined with the remnants of the Deákists to form the Liberal Party. Hence the Deák Party and then its successor, the Liberal Party, were the dominant ruling groups in Hungary until 1918.

Opposed to the Deákists-Liberals in the early period were the Kossuth Party (or the Party of Independence and 1848*), which continued to press for complete economic separation from Austria; a dissident Kossuth Party faction led by Count Albert Apponyi, which strongly advocated Magyarization; and a group of clerical interests embodied in the small Clerical People's Party and in the Christian Party (*see* Wolff and Zichy Party). In 1910, after several years of intense political struggle and parliamentary obstructionism, Count István Tisza (son of Kálmán Tisza) reorganized the ruling Liberal Party as the National Party of Work (*see* Liberal Party). As World War I approached, the Kossuth Party split into two factions over German policy: one group joined Count Apponyi and supported an alliance with Germany in the hopes that a German war victory would result in Hungary's freedom from Austria; the other faction was reorganized by Count Mihály Károlyi in July 1916 as the Károlyi Party (*see* Party of Independence and 1848) and opposed support for Germany. Hungary, as part of the Austro-Hungarian Empire, did ally with Germany and fought on the German side throughout World War I, 1914-1918.

The Austro-Hungarian Empire began to disintegrate in the last months of World War I. Austria-Hungary came under pressure from the Allied forces to settle on peace agreements, including recognition of independence for Czechs, Yugoslavs, and Poles. Therefore, on October 16, 1918, King Karl proclaimed the Federalization Manifesto, establishing Austria as a federal state in which each nationality would become a commonwealth. Viewing this as a breakup of Hungary's power, Hungarian Prime Minister Sándor Wekerle of the National Party of Work, successor to István Tisza, declared Hungary's independence from Austria in all matters except recognition of the throne. Thus the Kingdom of Hungary reemerged, but without its previous lands in Czechoslovakia, Romania, and Yugoslavia.

During this period, Count Károlyi had become an important figure in Hungarian politics, particularly in his advocacy of pacifism and acceptance of the Allied peace settlements. Also, Károlyi saw the success of his political future as resting on his ability in gaining broad-based support from all of Hungary's political elements. This attempt to appeal to all was a view not held by most Hungarian parliamentarians at that time, a view rising from their fear of losing their elitist power. Károlyi therefore undertook the formation of the Hungarian National Council, a body that was illegal since it was formed outside of parliament. Nevertheless, by the time of its formal proclamation on October 25, 1918, the National Council contained supporting elements from most of the Hungarian political parties, both within and outside of parliament. And as the only truly organized and cohesive political body in the midst of wartime confusion, the National Council (and Károlyi) were granted administrative power by the king on October 31. On November 2, Károlyi requested to be released from loyalty to King Karl, a request granted by a monarch who knew his authority was already broken. Finally, on November 16, Károlyi proclaimed the establishment of the Republic of Hungary.

Efforts at peace-seeking, the postwar chaos of defeat, foreign military intervention, and the impossibility of implementing his proposed land reforms, all caused Károlyi's resignation on March 20, 1919. In the midst of military defeat, economic disorder, and "Bolshevik" (see RUSSIAN SOCIAL DEMOCRATIC WORKERS' PARTY, SOVIET UNION) enthusiasm, Béla Kun emerged as the leader of a socialist-communist coalition in which the Communist Party of Hungary* clearly dominated; and for 133 days (March 21-July 31, 1919), Kun headed the communist regime of the Hungarian Soviet Republic. Romanian military intervention and the lack of popular support saw the demise of Kun's government by August 1, 1919. However, during Kun's regime, assorted anti-Bolshevik forces had formed and produced a small army commanded by Admiral Miklós Horthy. Kun's "Red Terror" of revolution was now followed by the "White Terror" of reaction.

After the collapse of the Hungarian Soviet, virtually all of the pre-World War I parties disappeared, as the war had eliminated most of the issues upon which they were based. New foci of conflict emerged, largely based upon economic issues caused by the war and upon Hungary's brief communist interlude. The period between the two world wars was characterized by four major partisan divisions: clerical parties, liberal-bourgeois groups, social democrats, and various agrarian interests.

Hungary saw a very short-lived (six-day) Social Democratic government under Gyula Peidl (see Hungarian Social Democratic Party) in August, and there followed several cabinets under István Friedrich (between August and November 1919) lacking support of the political parties. A government of members of various political groupings formed on November 24 under Károly Huszár, who was succeeded as prime minister by Sándor Simonyi-Semadam, succeeded in turn by Count Pál Teleki (all members of the diverse Christian National Union Party [see Wolff and Zichy Party]). Amid the chaos of rapidly shifting governments, a vote of March 1, 1920, called for the dissolution of the Hungarian republic and reinstitution of a monarchy. As a result, Admiral Horthy (who had led the 1919 anticommunist army) was elected Regent of the Kingdom of Hungary, and his name has become associated with the Hungary of the interwar years—the authoritarian, right-wing Horthy regime.

Teleki was succeeded as prime minister on April 14, 1921, by Count István Bethlen. Bethlen's coming to power reestablished a ruling political party in Hungary. On February 2, 1922, Bethlen had succeeded in gaining the support of the Agrarian Party (see Independent Smallholders' Party) to join him in forming the Unitary Party (see Government Party). Also known as the Christian and Bourgeois Party of Small Landowners and Agrarians, Bethlen's party was strongly anti-Habsburg and only partially democratic. Through various changes of name, leadership, political tendencies, coalitions, mergers, and affiliations, Bethlen's group became known as the Government Party, for indeed it was the government of Hungary until the developments wrought by World War II.

Hungarian politics in the decade before World War II was consumed by conflicts summed up in five words: legitimism, Trianon, communism, Jews, and Germany. Existing in a kingdom without a king, most Hungarian parties contained both legitimists (that is, royalists supporting a Habsburg restoration) and antilegitimists. All parties wanted a revision of the Treaty of Trianon, which was signed by Hungary in 1920 as a result of her defeat in World War I and which decreed the loss of territory and population to surrounding countries (Transylvania had been lost to Romania, Croatia to Yugoslavia, Slovakia and Carpatho-Ruthenia to Czechoslovakia). For some, a hatred and fear of communism instilled a counterrevolutionary and basic antileft attitude, which in turn helped give rise to an anti-Semitism stemming, in part, from the Jewish composition of Béla Kun's never-forgotten communist regime. Last was the issue of Nazi Germany (see NATIONAL SOCIALIST GERMAN WORKER'S PARTY, HISTORICAL GERMANY). Here the issue was whether the ruling Government Party was resisting sufficiently, or yielding sufficiently, to Nazi pressures for Hungarian support. The pro-Nazi factions were responding to Germany's 1938 role in securing the return to Hungary of territory (about one-fifth) previously lost to Czechoslovakia after World War I. Also, on August 30, 1940, under the terms of the Second Vienna Award, Hungary regained approximately two-fifths of its World War I territorial losses to Romania. Representatives from these territories were allocated seats in an expanded National Assembly, where they formed several ethnic groupings (Transylvanian Party, Ruthenian or Sub-Carparthian Party, and the Upper Hungarian

Union). For the most part, these ethnic groupings supported Hungary's Government Party.

Hungary joined Germany in World War II and was occupied by German troops in 1944. As a result, Horthy was removed from the regency on October 16, 1944, and replaced by Ferenc Szálasi of the naziist Arrow Cross* party, who served as acting regent and prime minister. During the Szálasi nazi regime, the Communists formed the Peace Party (see Communist Party of Hungary), which was joined by the Independent Smallholders' Party, the Social Democrats, and agrarian elements in establishing the National Independence Front (see Communist Party of Hungary).

With the arrival of the Russian Army, a provisional government was set up under Russian auspices in December 1944, the Szálasi government eventually collapsed, and Hungry was considered "liberated" in early April 1945. The provisional government was composed of members drawn from the prewar political groupings who had agreed to form a government of national unity. Elections were held on November 4, 1945, resulting in a majority of seats (245 out of 409) going to the Independent Smallholders' Party. The remainder of seats were allocated to the Communists (70), the Social Democrats (69), the National Peasant Party* (23), and the Democratic People's Party (2, see Wolff and Zichy Party). Zoltán Tildy of the Independent Smallholders was elected president, and the new National Assembly voted on January 31, 1946, to declare Hungary a republic.

Although the Communists had received only 17 percent of the vote in 1945, they managed to obtain key governmental posts with the help of the Soviet military authorities. As a result of electoral irregularities and various political maneuverings designed to discredit the anticommunist elements, the Communist Party-dominated bloc secured a majority vote (271 out of 411 seats) in the August 1947 elections and succeeded in forcing Tildy from the presidency. The Independent Smallholders' Party had dropped to third place in the popular vote.

The Communist-dominated regime continued to allow several small political groupings to function in an attempt to fragment the anticommunist opposition forces. Among the opposition were the Democratic People's Party; the Hungarian Independence Party led by Zoltán Pfeiffer, a right-wing successor to the Freedom Party (see Independent Smallholders' Party); a group of Independent Democrats led by Father István Balogh (see Independent Smallholders' Party); a group known as the Hungarian Radical Party, which emerged in 1945 to represent white-collar classes in Budapest; and the Christian Women's League, a Catholic women's organization. Following a forced merger of the Communist and Social Democratic parties in June 1948, the government announced in February 1949 that all parties would be subsumed within the Hungarian Independent People's Front. On August 20, 1949, a Soviet-type constitution was instituted, and only Communist or Communist-selected candidates could stand for office.

The early Communist rule was headed in Hungary by Mátyás Rákosi, who governed dictatorially in stalinist fashion. Following Stalin's death on March 5,

1953, and the ensuing relaxation of stalinism in eastern Europe, Rákosi was deposed in July 1953 and replaced by Imre Nagy. By Spring 1955, Nagy was out, and Rákosi returned to power until July 1956, when he was again removed and this time replaced by Ernő Gerő.

Nagy's "new course" and de-stalinization had helped to set a new mood, however. On October 23, 1956, students and others in Budapest demonstrated in sympathy with Poland's anti-Soviet revolutionary movement. Events moved swiftly as the demonstrators went on to call for an independent national policy and urged the return of Nagy. When Gerő accused them of slandering the Soviet Union, the demonstrators reacted by smashing the huge statue of Stalin and demanding that their grievances against Gerő be broadcast. As the police fired into the crowds, the Hungarian revolution of 1956 erupted. The people continued to demand Nagy. Gerő conceded, asking Nagy to reassume the premiership.

Nagy's cabinet finally comprised a majority of non-Communist ministers drawn from the Smallholder, Social Democrat, and National Peasant parties. While "negotiating" for the withdrawal of their troops from Hungarian soil, the Russians began moving yet more troops into Hungary; and on November 4 they commenced an attack, terminating the revolt by the end of the year. Approximately 200,000 Soviet troops were involved, casualties were in the thousands, and an estimated 150,000 to 200,000 Hungarians fled the country under fear of deportation or execution.

Nagy was removed, eventually executed, and replaced by János Kádár. Kádár has continued as the leader of Hungary, having obtained over the years an amount of internal liberalization while steadfastly rendering support to the Soviet Union in foreign affairs. Thus, since the close of World War II, Hungary has been relegated to a one-party state under the leadership of the Communist Party, known since 1956 as the Hungarian Socialist Workers' Party. *

Throughout its modern history, Hungary had evolved with considerable variation in patterns of representation and franchise arrangements. (For the effect on the distribution of seats in Parliament during the 1920-1947 period, and on Hungary's governing coalitions, see tables 43 and 44 respectively.) Prior to independence in 1918, most governmental institutions were designed to insure Magyar dominance in Hungarian political life. For example, the pre-World War I Hungarian parliament consisted of two houses, the Chamber of Magnates and Chamber of Deputies. The former was an aristocratic body with a variable membership, similar to the British House of Lords (see UNITED KINGDOM INTRODUCTION). The Chamber of Deputies was the lower house, containing 453 members, with 413 representing Hungary proper and 40 delegates from Croatia-Slavonia (areas politically linked to Hungary at that time). Deputies were first elected for three-year terms, but this was lengthened to five years in 1885. The suffrage was extremely limited, extending only to males of at least 20 years of age. A law in 1848 provided for suffrage based on a low property qualification. It was altered in 1879 and 1881 by a complex qualification based on a combination of property, taxation, profession or official position, and ancestry, continuing a system where the non-Magyar nationalities and the workers and peasants were practically unrepresented. To provide for electoral reform, a suffrage bill was introduced in 1908, but it was not passed. In 1848 only 6.7 percent of the population was enfranchised; in 1874 it was 5.0 percent, and in 1910 it was 8.0 percent.

The brief interlude of the Hungarian Soviet (1919) ushered in sweeping electoral reforms. All workers of at least 18 years of age, regardless of sex, were given the right to vote, while those not contributing to the society by their labor or those living off unearned income were disenfranchised. The latter provision automatically eliminated the nobility, large sections of the middle class, and others who had been influential in the old regime.

The overthrow of the Hungarian Soviet saw a return to a more limited franchise in the election of 1920. With only 164 districts (out of 453) left from the old parliament as a result of territorial changes after World War I, suffrage via secret ballot was made universal and compulsory for men and women, the latter voting for the first time in Hungarian history; as a result, 39.2 percent of the population had the franchise. In 1922 a decree abolished the relatively wide and secret suffrage enjoyed in 1920. Suffrage was once again restricted, this time primarily to males at least 24 years of age who had been citizens for a minimum of ten years and who had at least a primary education. Female suffrage began at age 30, and special provisions were made for the military. Secret voting remained in the cities, but open voting was reinstituted in the rural areas. By 1925 the franchise stood at 29.5 percent of the population against the 39.2 of 1920.

In 1926 the unicameral parliament was reorganized with the reconstitution of an upper chamber (Felső Ház), which would give representation to the aristocracy. The lower house (Képviselő Ház) continued with 245 seats, elected for five-year terms from single-member constituencies. Law XXVII of 1937 made the upper house equal in power with the lower except in matters of finance. Law XIX of 1938 raised the lower-house membership to 260 and increased the voting age requirement of males to 26 (women remaining at 30) in an intricate arrangement whereby 135 members were elected in straight contests and 125 elected on the list system. In 1939 the lower house was increased again, to 296, and in 1940 to 359, thereby accommodating representatives from the territories acquired from Czechoslovakia and Romania.

Following World War II, the size of the National Assembly was gradually reduced, and electoral laws were tightened to screen out anticommunist opposition elements. By early 1949, all remaining political parties were merged into a single list under the Hungarian Independent People's Front (Magyar Független Népfront: MFN). This front was succeeded in 1954 by the People's Patriotic Front (Hazafias Népfront), without the former noncommunist political parties. The new Front encompasses all political organizations within the country, and it operates to select candidates for election to the National Assembly.

Hungary's current governmental structure, instituted by the Communist Party since their takeover after World War II, has a constitution of 1949, amended in 1971, which assigns supreme power to a unicameral National Assembly (*Országgyűlés*). This Assembly is composed of 352 members elected for five-year terms by direct and secret universal suffrage starting at age 18 (since 1971). Candidates are nominated by the People's Patriotic Front to run in single-member constituencies (though about ten percent of the constituencies ran more than one candidate in 1975, and about four percent did in 1980). The Assembly, however, meets infrequently and in reality is a pro-forma organization that gives rubber-stamp approval to government policy. The National Assembly, in turn, elects the 21-member Presidential Council, which serves as an interim legislative body, and the Assembly also elects an executive Council of Ministers, whose chairman serves as prime minister. The current size of the Hungarian electorate is approximately 7.8 million.

Bibliography

Deák, István. "Hungary." In *The European Right*, edited by Hans Rogger and Eugen Weber. Berkeley: University of California Press, 1965.

Graham, Malbone W. *New Governments of Central Europe*. New York: Henry Holt & Co., 1924.

Helmreich, Ernst C. *Hungary*. New York: Praeger, 1957.

Kállay, Nicholas. *Hungarian Premier*. New York: Columbia University Press, 1954.

Lackó, M. *Arrow-Cross Men, National Socialists, 1935-1944*. Budapest: Akadémiai Kiadó, 1969.

Macartney, C. A. *The Habsburg Empire, 1790-1918*. New York: Macmillan Co., 1969.

———. *October Fifteenth: A History of Modern Hungary, 1929-1945*. 2 vols. Edinburgh: Edinburgh University Press, 1957.

Nagy-Talavera, Nicholas M. *The Green Shirts and the Others: A History of Fascism in Hungary and Rumania*. Stanford, Calif.: Hoover Institution Press, 1970.

Rothschild, Joseph. *East Central Europe Between the Two World Wars*. Seattle: University of Washington Press, 1974.

Tőkés, Rudolf L. *Béla Kun and the Hungarian Soviet Republic*. New York: Praeger, 1967.

———. "Hungary." In *World Communism: A Handbook, 1919-1965*, edited by Witold S. Sworakowski. Stanford, Calif.: Hoover Institution Press, 1973.

Váli, Ferenc A. *Rift and Revolt in Hungary*. Cambridge, Mass.: Harvard University Press, 1961.

Völgyes, Iván, ed. *Hungary in Revolution, 1918-19*. Lincoln: University of Nebraska Press, 1971.

Political Parties

AGRARIAN PARTY. *See* INDEPENDENT SMALLHOLDERS' PARTY.

ARROW CROSS (*Nyilaskereszt*). Hungary had various parties of the radical right and parties of the nazi strain (*see* NATIONAL SOCIALIST GERMAN

WORKER'S PARTY, HISTORICAL GERMANY). All such Hungarian parties utilized some form of a cross as their symbols: the Dual or Double Cross (*Kettőskereszt*), the Scythe Cross (*Kaszáskereszt*), the Swastika (*Horogkereszt*), and what evolved as the most prominent of these symbols, to become the covering term for the Hungarian nazi movement, the Arrow Cross (*Nyilaskereszt*).

The first Hungarian party to use the Arrow Cross symbol began in June 1932 when Zoltan Meskó (a former member of the Independent Smallholders' Party*) founded the Hungarian National Socialist Agricultural Laborers' and Workers' Party. This party fused with a rival grouping in 1933, becoming the Hungarian National Socialist People's Party, and adopted the wearing of green shirts and the crossed arrows as a symbol. Similar "National Socialist"-type parties followed, such as those founded by Counts Sándor Festetics and Fidel Pálffy. There were various fusions and separations, and there were variations in the utilization of the term *Arrow Cross*. All of these right-wing radical parties became known as *Nyilas* (Arrow) parties. Membership in these groupings was diverse, including pro-Germans, anti-Semites, adventurers, assorted political extremists, criminals, those who saw opportunity in these parties for political and social reforms, and members of the neglected social classes who had supported Béla Kun in 1919 (*see* Communist Party of Hungary).

No name is more associated with the Arrow Cross than that of Ferenc Szálasi, a fanatic. Szálasi resigned his army commission in March 1935 and formed the Party of National Will (*Nemzeti Akarat Pártja*), which was dissolved in 1937. Szálasi, however, soon became the leader of the foremost *Nyilas* party, named the Arrow Cross, which contested elections for the first time in 1939 and became the strongest opposition party in the National Assembly. The Arrow Cross pursued an anti-Semitic policy, called for cooperation with nazi Germany, and received financial support from Germany. It would be incorrect, however, to label Szálasi as just another imitator of naziism or other fascisms. He fostered the Hungarist Movement, simply described as a reorganization of the Danubian basin in federal form, under Hungarian leadership, and with the adaptation of German nazi ideas to Hungarian conditions.

Szálasi was imprisoned more than once. Others associated with him were Kálmán Hubay and Jenő Szöllösi. Prime Minister Pál Teleki of the Government Party* dissolved the Arrow Cross in February 1939, but the party reconstituted itself within a few days. When Regent Miklós Horthy abdicated on October 16, 1944, under pressure from the Germans, they secured Szálasi's appointment as minister president and acting regent. Szálasi ruled what was left of Hungary until the end of World War II in April 1945. He was tried and executed by the Communist regime in March 1946.

BÉKE PÁRT. *See* COMMUNIST PARTY OF HUNGARY.

CHRISTIAN AND BOURGEOIS PARTY OF SMALL LANDOWNERS AND AGRARIANS. *See* GOVERNMENT PARTY.

CHRISTIAN ECONOMIC PARTY. *See* WOLFF AND ZICHY PARTY.

CHRISTIAN NATIONAL ECONOMIC PARTY. *See* WOLFF AND ZICHY PARTY.

CHRISTIAN NATIONAL LEAGUE. *See* WOLFF AND ZICHY PARTY.

CHRISTIAN NATIONAL UNION PARTY. *See* WOLFF AND ZICHY PARTY.

CHRISTIAN PARTY. *See* WOLFF and ZICHY PARTY.

CHRISTIAN SOCIAL ECONOMIC PARTY. *See* WOLFF AND ZICHY PARTY.

CHRISTIAN SOCIAL PARTY. *See* WOLFF AND ZICHY PARTY.

CHRISTIAN WOMEN'S LEAGUE. *See* HUNGARY INTRODUCTION.

CITIZEN'S LIBERTY PARTY. *See* NATIONAL LIBERAL PARTY.

CLERICAL PEOPLE'S PARTY. *See* HUNGARY INTRODUCTION.

COMMUNIST PARTY OF HUNGARY (*Kommunisták Magyarországi Pártja*: KMP). Hungary's communist party began in Moscow on March 24, 1918, as a section of the Communist Party of the Soviet Union (*see* SOVIET UNION). The founders of the Hungarian wing were Béla Kun and Tibor Szamuély. The founding of the party on Hungarian soil occurred on November 24, 1918, under Kun's leadership and took the name of the Communist Party of Hungary. On March 21, 1919, the KMP merged with the Hungarian Social Democratic Party* to form the Socialist Party of Hungary, also known as the Hungarian Socialist Party (*Magyar Szocialista Párt*: MSZP), and later as the Socialist-Communist Workers' Party of Hungary.

The MSZP, under Kun's rule, governed the Hungarian Soviet Republic (*see* Hungary introduction) for 133 days (March 21-July 31, 1919). Lacking popular support and suffering foreign military intervention, the Hungarian Soviet collapsed— Social Democratic elements left the Socialist Party, whose leaders fled abroad, and the establishment of the Horthy regime (*see* Hungary introduction) saw the suppression of all Communist Party activity. The Comintern dissolved the KMP in 1922 but allowed its reorganization in 1925. That year also saw the First Congress of the KMP, held clandestinely in Vienna, and the formulation of a communist-front organization in Hungary, the Hungarian Socialist Workers' Party, led by István Vági. Vági's arrest in 1927 temporarily ended that grouping's activities.

The interwar years brought little success for the Hungarian Communists. There was not much to cheer at the party's Second Congress, held in 1930 in the Soviet Union. However, there were some underground cadres in Hungary, where the party was still illegal, and the movement's revolutionary aspects and its opposition to fascism, irredentism, and Magyar chauvinism did appeal to numbers of intellectuals, artists, writers, and university students. Members of the KMP in the Soviet Union lost their lives or were deported to Siberia during Stalin's purges, Béla Kun among them. He was executed on November 30, 1939.

During World War II, the underground and illegal KMP repeatedly attempted to unite various Hungarian elements against nazi Germany (see HISTORICAL GERMANY) and against the nazis' influence in Hungary. But the Communists saw their efforts interrupted by the dissolution of the Comintern in May 1943. When the Germans invaded Hungary in March 1944, the Communists organized as the Peace Party (*Béke Párt*) which, along with the Independent Smallholders' Party,* the Social Democrats, and a Communist-sponsored National Peasant Party,* became the National Independence Front (*Nemzeti Függetlenségi Front:* NFF). In September 1944, the KMP abandoned its Peace Party designation and took the name of Hungarian Communist Party (*Magyar Kommunista Párt:* MKP). The postwar resuscitation of the party was led by Mátyás Rákosi and Hungarian comrades who had been in exile with him in Moscow, such as Ernő Gerő, Imre Nagy, Mihály Farkas, and József Révai. Assistance was also rendered by a group who had remained in Hungary during the war, among them János Kádár and László Rajk. Rákosi began a drive to secure power in Hungary. Although the MKP garnered only 17 percent of the vote in the elections of November 1945, compared to the Independent Smallholders' 57 percent, Rákosi's famous "salami tactics" (divide and discredit the opposition) and the Soviet military presence produced the eventual establishment of a communist regime in Hungary.

In June 1948, the Social Democratic Party, a captive of its own left wing under Arpád Szakasits, united with the MKP to form the new communist party in Hungary, the Hungarian Workers' Party (*Magyar Dolgozók Pártja:* MDP), led by Rákosi. By 1949 the Hungarian People's Republic was well established, but not without problems: party luminary Rajk was executed on charges of titoist deviation (see YUGOSLAVIA) in the same year, and Rákosi's stalinist economic policies were a failure. After Stalin's death in 1953, Moscow ordered the premiership to be taken from Rákosi and given to Imre Nagy, leaving the former as general secretary of the party. In that position, Rákosi and his adherents impeded what had become known as Nagy's "new course," essentially an attempt at de-Rákosi-ization and de-Stalinzation. By July 1956, the Russians forced Rákosi out as general secretary, and Ernő Gerő became the party leader.

Unsolved economic and political grievances, coupled with support for Poland's anti-Russian stand, helped to produce the Hungarian revolt of 1956 (see Hungary introduction). The Russians crushed the revolt, the MDP was dissolved, and a new communist party, the Hungarian Socialist Workers' Party (MSZMP),* assumed control of the country. Under attempts to further de-

Stalinize, the MSZMP took a page from Nikita Khrushchev's 22d Party Congress of the Communist Party of the Soviet Union (see SOVIET UNION), and the new MSZMP addressed itself to "violations of socialist legality" during the years of the "cult of personality." As a result, many former MDP leaders were expelled from the new MSZMP, including Rákosi and Gerő. Executions and arrests also followed, including the announcement on June 17, 1958, that former Prime Minister Imre Nagy had been secretly tried and executed. (See also Hungarian Socialist Workers' Party.)

DEÁK PÁRT. See DEÁK PARTY.

DEÁK PARTY (Deák Párt). The Deák Party was named after Ferenc Deák, a representative in the Hungarian legislature who began in the 1840s to attempt to unite fellow representatives to work for Hungarian independence from Austria (see Hungary introduction). It was Deák who had negotiated the 1867 compromise (Ausgleich) which gave Hungary limited independence from Austria. The Deák Party organized the first ministry under the new arrangements and obtained a substantial majority in the election of 1869. Deák withdrew from political life in 1873 and thereafter the party began to decline, not able to cope with problems of ministerial instability and financial and commercial crises. In February 1875, the Deák Party merged with the so-called Left Center and formed the Liberal Party,* which continued to govern Hungary until the end of World War I.

DEMOCRATIC PEOPLE'S PARTY. See WOLFF AND ZICHY PARTY.

EGYSÉG PÁRTJA. See GOVERNMENT PARTY.

EGYSÉGES PÁRT. See GOVERNMENT PARTY.

EP. See GOVERNMENT PARTY.

EXTREME LEFT. See PARTY OF INDEPENDENCE AND 1848.

FAJVÉDŐ PÁRT. See GOVERNMENT PARTY.

FKP. See INDEPENDENT SMALLHOLDERS' PARTY.

FREEDOM PARTY. See INDEPENDENT SMALLHOLDERS' PARTY.

FÜGGETLEN KISGAZDA PÁRT. See INDEPENDENT SMALLHOLDERS' PARTY.

FÜGGETLENSÉGI PÁRT. See PARTY OF INDEPENDENCE AND 1848.

GOVERNMENT PARTY (*Kormánypárt*). Count István Bethlen founded the Unitary Party (*Egységes Párt*), shortly changed to the Party of Unity (*Egység Pártja*: EP), and became prime minister on April 14, 1921. This party, under yet other changes of name (such as the Christian and Bourgeois Party of Small Landowners and Agrarians), ruled Hungary until the World War II years. Despite the existence of other parties, Bethlen's grouping had such complete control that it became known as the Government Party, for it was the government of Hungary.

Bethlen was in office for a decade (1921-1931), rightly called the Bethlen era, after which he was succeeded as prime minister by Count Gyula Károlyi (half brother of Mihály Károlyi, *see* Party of Independence and 1848). Big landowning and financial interests were represented in the party, and it was deserving of appellations such as restoration, reaction, and conservatism. General Gyula Gömbös became prime minister on October 1, 1932, and changed the name of the Party of Unity to the Party of National Unity (*Nemzeti Egység Pártja*: NEP), titled officially as the Party of National Unity, Christian, Smallholders', Farmers', and Bourgeois Party, but still popularly known as the Government Party. Gömbös had left the Government Party in 1923 and had formed the Hungarian National Independence Party (*Magyar Nemzeti Függetlenségi Párt*: MNFP). This grouping was also known as the Race-Defenders Party or Race-Protecting Party (*Fajvédö Párt*) and was characterized by fascist and anti-Semitic tendencies. Gömbös returned to the Government Party in 1928, thereby dissolving the MNFP. Under Gömbös, an anti-Semite who advocated closer relations with Germany and Italy (the term "Axis" is attributed to him), the Government Party became much more middle-class and right-radical.

The only theme common to all elements of the Government Party was their counterrevolutionary position and push for a revision of the Treaty of Trianon, which Hungary had signed upon defeat in World War I and which resulted in large losses of Hungarian lands to other nations (*see* Hungary introduction). For politicians, the idea was to join this ruling party, work to control it, and then hope to mold it to one's particular politics, essentially right-wing/conservative or traditional. Professor C. A. Macartney (*see* Hungary Bibliography) has summed it up by writing that the party was "the permanent vehicle of the parliamentary majority."

Gömbös died on October 6, 1936, and was succeeded as prime minister on October 12 by Kálmán Darányi, under whom the first anti-Jewish law was passed. He was succeeded by Béla Imrédy on May 13, 1939. It was expected that Imrédy would follow a more conservative line, but there was surprise that his fascist and anti-Semitic policies outdid those of any of his predecessors. Imrédy attempted to found a movement to supercede the party, the Movement of Hungarian Life (*Magyar Élet Mozgalma*: MÉM). Ironically, he resigned the prime ministership after a bizarre allegation that one of his great-grandmothers may have been Jewish. He also left the Government Party and established the Party of Hungarian Renewal. *

Imrédy was succeeded by Count Pál Teleki on February 17, 1939. Teleki eliminated Imrédy's Movement of Hungarian Life by placing it under the Government Party, which then became known as the Party of Hungarian Life (*Magyar Élet Pártja*: MÉP). Teleki committed suicide on April 4, 1941, rather than allow German troops to cross Hungary in order to attack Yugoslavia. László Bárdossy became prime minister on the same day. Thus Teleki's successors, Bárdossy and later Miklós Kállay, carried on amid a welter of German pressure and influence. Hungary's role in World War II caused many of the nation's political elements to submerge their differences and accept the MÉP, acceptance given according to whether it was felt there was sufficient resistance, or sufficient yielding, to Germany. Of course, the war ended the party.

HAZAFIAS NÉPFRONT. See HUNGARY INTRODUCTION.

HUNGARIAN COMMUNIST PARTY. See COMMUNIST PARTY OF HUNGARY.

HUNGARIAN INDEPENDENCE PARTY. See INDEPENDENT SMALL-HOLDERS' PARTY.

HUNGARIAN NATIONAL INDEPENDENCE PARTY. See GOVERN-MENT PARTY.

HUNGARIAN NATIONAL SOCIALIST AGRICULTURAL LABORERS' AND WORKERS' PARTY. See ARROW CROSS.

HUNGARIAN NATIONAL SOCIALIST PEOPLE'S PARTY. See ARROW CROSS.

HUNGARIAN RADICAL PARTY. See HUNGARY INTRODUCTION.

HUNGARIAN SOCIAL DEMOCRATIC PARTY (*Magyar Szociál Demokrata Párt*: MSZDP). Founded as the Labor Party in 1880, the name of the Hungarian Social Democratic Party was adopted in 1890, with a marxist program copied from that of the Austrian equivalent grouping (*see* SOCIAL-DEMOCRATIC PARTY, AUSTRIA). The Hungarian Social Democrats had no one in parliament before 1918. The party served in the coalition government of Count Károlyi (Party of Independence and 1848*) in 1918-1919 and then temporarily merged with the Communist Party of Hungary (KMP)* on March 21, 1919, to form the Socialist Party of Hungary (*see* Communist Party of Hungary). It was this latter Communist-dominated party, produced by the KMP-MSZDP merger, which was in power during the 133-day regime of Béla Kun from March 21 to July 31, 1919. When Kun's Hungarian Soviet Republic collapsed and a conservative backlash began, many Social Democrats escaped abroad. Thus they did not participate in the elections of January 1920, although Gyula Peidl was prime minister of a Social Democratic government for the period of August 1-6, 1919.

The Social Democrats made a deal with the Bethlen government (*see* Government Party) on December 22, 1921: for the return of trade-union funds and liberties, and secret suffrage in the towns, the Social Democrats would not engage in socialist agitation in the rural districts nor foment political strikes, and would present a definite Magyar attitude on political questions. Hence by 1922, the Social Democrats controlled nearly all of organized labor. The MSZDP was an organized and disciplined party, though it came to be regarded with suspicion by many as a rootless and unpatriotic group. It was also a target of the anti-Semites because of its Jewish intellectual leadership and because of its association with the Jews of the Kun regime.

The ensuing years saw the Social Democrats engage in what amounted to a tacit alliance with Hungary's conservative rulers—for example, the MSZDP never elected Jews to prominent positions. But by 1932 the party felt its arrangement with Bethlen had been broken. It began to allow Communists a few posts in trade unions and on the staff of its newspaper, the *Népszava* (Voice of the People). The MSZDP pushed for a conciliatory foreign policy and for compromise agreements with the neighboring states who had benefitted from the World War I Treaty of Trianon—Czechoslovakia, Romania, and Yugoslavia—in gaining lands previously belonging to Hungary. The Social Democrats supported the idea of a separate peace without Germany during World War II, leading the party into difficulties that caused its dissolution in March 1944. Later that summer, the government offered to rescind the dissolution. By October, however, the Social Democrats made an agreement with the Communists, who had formed the Peace Party (*see* Communist Party of Hungary). The agreement was to seek peace, independence, and the realization of socialism, and the MSZDP joined the Communists' National Independence Front along with other parties.

The Social Democrats did well in the elections of the 1945-1947 period, much better than the Communists. The Communists' poor showing was not to be tolerated by the Soviet Union, however; and in June 1948, by which time Hungary was under Soviet control, the MSZDP, under the pro-communist Arpád Szakasits, was forced to unite with the Communists in forming the Hungarian Workers' Party (MDP). Following the Hungarian revolt of 1956, the MDP became and remains the ruling party, now under the designation of the Hungarian Socialist Workers' Party. * Along with other parties, the MSZDP was briefly revived as a result of the 1956 revolt, and the party's secretary-general, Gyula Kelemen, along with József Fischer and Anna Kéthly, served in a short-lived coalition government.

HUNGARIAN SOCIALIST PARTY *See* COMMUNIST PARTY OF HUNGARY.

HUNGARIAN SOCIALIST WORKERS' PARTY (*Magyar Szocialista Munkáspárt*: MSZMP). After the Hungarian revolt of October 1956 (*see* Hungary introduction), the Communist Party of the Soviet Union (CPSU, *see* SOVIET UNION) interceded in the inability of the Hungarian communists to keep their own peace and to maintain adherence to CPSU directives. The Hungarian Communist Party (at that time named the Hungarian Workers' Party [MDP], *see* Communist Party of Hungary) was dissolved, many of the MDP's leaders were arrested and executed, and a new Hungarian communist grouping was established. Hence on November 4, 1956, the Hungarian Socialist Workers' Party came into being, readopting the name of a 1927 Communist-front organization in Hungary. The MSZMP was established under Soviet direction, and Soviet leader Nikita Khrushchev appointed János Kádár as head of the MSZMP and leader of the new pro-Soviet Hungarian government.

Kádár's regime was rigidly authoritarian in its attempt to reconcile by force the Hungarian people to pro-Soviet policy. The MSZMP's Eighth Congress in 1962 instituted a somewhat new direction in seeking pragmatism in Hungary's domestic affairs, although still rigidly subservient to the Soviet Union in foreign matters. Kádár resigned the premiership in 1965 but continued as head of the MSZMP. The 1962 policy was sustained under Hungary's next premiers, Gyula Kállai and Jenő Fock, and Hungary took part in the Soviet 1968 invasion of Czechoslovakia. Under Fock, Hungary launched its New Economic Model in January 1968, an attempt to better the nation's domestic economic situation by manufacturing goods that would earn better prices on the export market. Since the New Economic Model proved unworkable by the early 1970s, Fock was replaced as premier by an economist, György Lázár, in May 1975, although the Model still receives approval and support from the MSZMP. (*See also* Communist Party of Hungary.)

HUNGARIAN WORKERS' PARTY. *See* COMMUNIST PARTY OF HUNGARY.

IMRÉDY PÁRT. *See* PARTY OF HUNGARIAN RENEWAL.

IMRÉDY PARTY. *See* PARTY OF HUNGARIAN RENEWAL.

INDEPENDENT DEMOCRATS. *See* INDEPENDENT SMALLHOLDERS' PARTY.

INDEPENDENT SMALLHOLDERS' PARTY (*Független Kisgazda Párt*: FKP). A Smallholders' Party (*Kisgazda Párt*) or Agrarian Party had been founded by István Szabó of Nagyatád shortly following World War I. As a coalition of agrarian elements, the party presented the largest political grouping in the 1920 National Assembly. Szabó served in the post-World War I cabinet of Count

Károlyi and in some succeeding cabinets, eventually supporting the Government Party. * When Szabó died in 1924, the Agrarians merged into the Government Party.

In October 1930, Gaston Gaál seceded from the Government Party and founded the Independent Smallholders' Party. Tibor Eckhardt joined the FKP in 1931 and assumed party leadership upon Gaál's death in 1932. Eckhardt adhered to the "legitimist" cause (the monarchical restoration, see Hungary introduction) in 1937. By the time of World War II, the FKP was the only party representing peasant interests. Standing as an opposition party, it suffered from dissension and the fact that Eckhardt had gone to the United States in 1941 as a "Free Hungarian" leader. The FKP had pursued political democracy and land reform, and it drew its strength chiefly from small and medium farmers, tending to neglect the landless agricultural proletariat. The party participated in the National Independence Front organized by the Communist Party of Hungary * in 1944. Hence, along with the Hungarian Social Democratic Party, * the Independent Smallholders were dissolved by the Horthy government (see Hungary introduction) on March 28, 1944.

In the postwar elections of November 1945, the FKP won overwhelmingly with 57 percent of the vote, and the FKP's Zoltán Tildy became prime minister. Tildy assumed the presidency on January 31, 1946, and party colleague Ferenc Nagy became prime minister on February 6, 1946. Even though the Communists had secured only 17 percent of the 1945 vote, with Soviet assistance the Communists held key cabinet posts and controlled the police. With such Communist permeance, coupled with the presence of the Soviet Army, Nagy's government could not maintain power. Indeed, in July 1946 the Communists pressured 22 Smallholders to leave the FKP and to form the Freedom Party (*Szabadság Párt*), headed by Dezső Sulyok. The Freedom Party was dissolved in July 1947 on charges of fascist tendencies, and it was briefly succeeded by an extreme right-wing grouping called the Hungarian Independence Party, led by Zoltán Pfeiffer. An anticommunist Smallholder group broke from the FKP and formed the Independent Democrats under the leadership of Father István Balogh, former secretary of the FKP. The Independent Democrats survived as an opposition group until early 1949.

In early May 1947, while visiting Switzerland, Prime Minister Nagy was informed of the undesirability of his return to Hungary; and, in exchange for his son joining him abroad, Nagy resigned on May 29. Lajos Dinnyés, an Independent Smallholder sympathetic to the Communists, replaced him. In the August 1947 elections, a Communist-led leftist bloc, including the FKP, secured the majority of the vote. Dinnyés continued as premier until December, when he was replaced by Smallholder István Dobi, also easily controlled by Communist leader Mátyás Rákosi. On February 1, 1949, Rákosi announced that all political parties would be subsumed within the Hungarian Independent People's Front (see Hungary introduction). Along with other parties, the FKP was briefly revived as a result of the 1956 Hungarian revolt; and the party's secretary-general, Béla Kovács, along with Tildy, served in a short-lived coalition government.

KÁROLYI PÁRT. *See* PARTY OF INDEPENDENCE AND 1848.

KÁROLYI PARTY. *See* PARTY OF INDEPENDENCE AND 1848.

KISGAZDA PÁRT. *See* INDEPENDENT SMALLHOLDERS' PARTY.

KMP. *See* COMMUNIST PARTY OF HUNGARY.

KOMMUNISTÁK MAGYARORSZÁGI PÁRTJA. *See* COMMUNIST PARTY OF HUNGARY.

KORMÁNYPÁRT. *See* GOVERNMENT PARTY.

KOSSUTH PÁRT. *See* PARTY OF INDEPENDENCE AND 1848.

KOSSUTH PARTY. *See* PARTY OF INDEPENDENCE AND 1848.

LEFT CENTER. *See* LIBERAL PARTY.

LIBERAL PARTY (*Szabadelvű Párt*). The Liberal Party was formed in February 1875 out of the merger of the Deák Party* and a rival grouping called the Left Center. The Deák grouping was the party of Ferenc Deák, who had negotiated the 1867 compromise (*Ausgleich*) that gave Hungary limited independence from Austria (*see also* Hungary introduction). The Left Center was led by Kálmán Tisza and Kálmán Ghyczy and had also been formed in the initial *Ausgleich* period. However, the Left Center completely rejected the 1867 compromise and instead demanded an independent Hungarian Army. The fusion with the Deák Party in 1875 saw the Left Center change its views and pledge maintenance of the agreement. Elements of the Left Center briefly and unsuccessfully reemerged in 1877 as some followers did not like the results of the change of view on the compromise, nor Tisza's economic policies.

Although known as the Liberal Party, there was little that was "liberal" about the grouping. Serving as prime minister between 1875 and 1890, Tisza's policy was to convert Hungary into a centralized and homogenous Magyar state, but within the *Ausgleich*. The Liberals, therefore, supported the government in Vienna, Austria. Although it possessed no absolute majority in Hungary, the Liberal Party did enjoy a majority in the lower chamber, gained by violence at elections.

Tisza retired in 1890 and the Liberals continued in power through a succession of ministries. There was no real opposition to challenge their dominant position. However, after scoring an electoral success in 1896, a period of parliamentary obstructionism set in, and the party was forced into a coalition between 1905 and 1909. In an attempt to rally additional support, Count István Tisza (Kálmán Tisza's son) renamed the Liberals in 1910 as the National Party of Work (*Nemzeti Dolgozók Pártja*). This was to emphasize the party's goal of practical achievement in government policy. The National Party tended to defend the interests of large agrarian enterprises. Except for the brief coalition period, it was this pro-*Ausgleich* grouping—the Deák-Liberal-National Party of Work—that governed Hungary from 1867 to the end of World War I in 1918.

MAGYAR ÉLET MOZGALMA. *See* GOVERNMENT PARTY.

MAGYAR ÉLET PÁRTJA. *See* GOVERNMENT PARTY.

MAGYAR DOLGOZÓK PÁRTJA. *See* COMMUNIST PARTY OF HUNGARY.

MAGYAR FÜGGETLEN NÉPFRONT. *See* HUNGARY INTRODUCTION.

MAGYAR KOMMUNISTA PÁRT. *See* COMMUNIST PARTY OF HUNGARY.

MAGYAR MEGÚJULÁS PÁRTJA. *See* PARTY OF HUNGARIAN RENEWAL.

MAGYAR NEMZETI FÜGGETLENSÉGI PÁRT. *See* GOVERNMENT PARTY.

MAGYAR SZOCIÁL DEMOKRATA PÁRT. *See* HUNGARIAN SOCIAL DEMOCRATIC PARTY.

MAGYAR SZOCIALISTA MUNKÁSPÁRT. *See* HUNGARIAN SOCIALIST WORKERS' PARTY.

MAGYAR SZOCIALISTA PÁRT. *See* COMMUNIST PARTY OF HUNGARY.

MDP. *See* COMMUNIST PARTY OF HUNGARY.

MÉM *See* GOVERNMENT PARTY.

MÉP. *See* GOVERNMENT PARTY.

MFN. *See* HUNGARY INTRODUCTION.

MKP. *See* COMMUNIST PARTY OF HUNGARY.

MMP. *See* PARTY OF HUNGARIAN RENEWAL.

MNFP. See GOVERNMENT PARTY.

MOVEMENT OF HUNGARIAN LIFE. See GOVERNMENT PARTY.

MSZDP. See HUNGARIAN SOCIAL DEMOCRATIC PARTY.

MSZMP. See HUNGARIAN SOCIALIST WORKERS' PARTY.

MSZP. See COMMUNIST PARTY OF HUNGARY.

NATIONAL INDEPENDENCE FRONT. See COMMUNIST PARTY OF HUNGARY.

NATIONAL LIBERAL PARTY (Nemzeti Szabadelvű Párt: NSZP). In February 1930, Károly Rassay formed the National Liberal Party. Although Rassay was an active and accomplished politician, the party never had much influence. It represented Jewish urban business and intellectual interests, supported a French orientation as a bulwark against fascism, and it was anti-Nazi (see NATIONAL SOCIALIST GERMAN WORKER'S PARTY, HISTORICAL GERMANY). Rassay had taken an active stand against Hungary's anti-Jewish legislation. In October 1937, he expressed his adherence to the "legitimist" cause (the monarchy's restoration, see Hungary introduction).

The National Liberal Party was dissolved in 1944 by the Communist Party of Hungary.* Also dissolved were the Hungarian Social Democratic Party* and the Independent Smallholders' Party.* Rassay was arrested and imprisoned. The NSZP reappeared briefly as the Citizen's Liberty Party in 1945 and, as an anticommunist opposition grouping, obtained three seats in the 1947 election. It was banned by the Communist regime prior to the 1948 election and never reappeared.

NATIONAL PARTY OF WORK. See LIBERAL PARTY.

NATIONAL PEASANT PARTY (Nemzeti Paraszt Párt: NPP). The NPP was organized by Imre Kovács, Ferenc Erdei, and others in July 1939, but it did not officially come into being until September 19, 1944, when Kovács announced its formation. The National Peasants represented the interests of agricultural laborers and supported land reform. Moreover, the National Peasants were sponsored by the Communist Party of Hungary,* who used the NPP to push Communist programs since many landless peasants, had they known of the Communist origin of those programs, would not have supported them. The NPP formed part of the governing coalition until 1949 when the party was absorbed into the Communist-led Hungarian Independent People's Front (see Hungary introduction).

In 1956 the NPP attempted to expunge the stalinist taint derived from its

Communist affiliation. At that time, the NPP became the Petőfi Party (*Petőfi Párt*), named after Sándor Petőfi, the great Hungarian poet of the 1848 anti-Habsburg revolt (*see* Hungary introduction). Ferenc Farkas became the secretary-general of that party and, along with István Bibó, served in the short-lived coalition government established when the Hungarian revolt of 1956 (*see* Hungary introduction) interrupted the hegemonic Communist rule and caused a temporary restoration of a multiparty system.

NEMZETI AKARAT PÁRTJA. *See* ARROW CROSS.

NEMZETI DOLGOZÓK PÁRTJA. *See* LIBERAL PARTY.

NEMZETI EGYSÉG PÁRTJA. *See* GOVERNMENT PARTY.

NEMZETI FÜGGETLENSÉGI FRONT. *See* COMMUNIST PARTY OF HUNGARY.

NEMZETI PARASZT PÁRT. *See* NATIONAL PEASANT PARTY.

NEMZETI SZABADELVŰ PÁRT. *See* NATIONAL LIBERAL PARTY.

NEP. *See* GOVERNMENT PARTY.

NFF. *See* COMMUNIST PARTY OF HUNGARY.

NPP. *See* NATIONAL PEASANT PARTY.

NSZP. *See* NATIONAL LIBERAL PARTY.

NYILASKERESZT. *See* ARROW CROSS.

PARTY OF 1848. *See* PARTY OF INDEPENDENCE AND 1848.

PARTY OF HUNGARIAN LIFE. *See* GOVERNMENT PARTY.

PARTY OF HUNGARIAN RENEWAL (*Magyar Megújulás Pártja*: MMP). While leader of the Government Party* and while prime minister from May 1938 to February 1939, Béla Imrédy founded the Movement of Hungarian Life (*see* Government Party) with András Jaross. In February 1939, Imrédy's successor as prime minister and leader of the Government Party, Count Pál Teleki, placed the Movement under the Party of National Unity and renamed the latter the Party of Hungarian Life (MÉP) (*see* Government Party). Imrédy left the MÉP after charges of his having had a Jewish ancestry, and he formed the Party of Hungarian Renewal (also known as the Rejuvenation Party) in October 1940.

Imrédy drew with him dissident naziist elements from the Party of Hungarian Life and from the Upper Hungarian Union (see Hungary introduction).

The MMP, which also became known as the Imrédy Party (Imrédy Párt), formed one-half of the radical-right opposition to the ruling Government Party, and the nazi Arrow Cross* party and its affiliates formed the more extreme other half. Genuinely more fascist than any other party, the MMP was anti-Semitic, dictatorial, middle-class, but also somewhat more moderate and erudite in its policies. Imrédy's well-known abilities as a financier gave the MMP a certain status not enjoyed by the Arrow Cross and other nazi groupings. The MMP sometimes cooperated with the Arrow Cross and also urged close collaboration with Germany and Italy. The MMP, of course, disappeared in the ashes of World War II; and with the advent of Hungary's rule by the Communist Party of Hungary,* Imrédy was executed in 1946, as was the leader of the Arrow Cross.

PARTY OF INDEPENDENCE. See PARTY OF INDEPENDENCE AND 1848.

PARTY OF INDEPENDENCE AND 1848. The significant opposition to the ruling Liberal Party* in the pre-World War I period was a group known as the Extreme Left. This group consisted of the Party of 1848 and the Party of Independence (Függetlenségi Párt), the latter established in 1875. By 1881, these two parties merged to form the Party of Independence and 1848, 1848 being the year of the unsuccessful Hungarian revolt against Habsburg rule. The revolt had been crushed with the aid of Russia.

Lajos Kossuth, the hero of the revolt, was the spiritual leader of the party until his death in 1894, and hence the party is sometimes referred to as the Kossuth Party. The party regularly attacked the 1867 Ausgliech (compromise), which had established the Dual Monarchy (see Hungary introduction) and also opposed Austria-Hungary's foreign policy. The Kossuth Party recognized only a personal union with Austria through the monarch, advocated complete economic separation from Austria, and supported the establishment of a national Hungarian Army. It always had a majority in Hungary's elections, especially in the Magyar (Hungarian) districts of the multinational country.

The Party of Independence and 1848 developed factions in 1909 over various policies of magyarization. One faction was led by Kossuth's son, Ferenc, along with Count Albert Apponyi; and the other faction was led by Gyula Justh, succeeded later by Count Mihály Károlyi. By 1914 there was a right wing led by Apponyi that supported an alliance with Germany, and a left wing led by Károlyi that opposed binding Hungary's future to Germany. In July 1916, the party split when Károlyi left and founded the United Party of Independence and 1848 (also known as the Károlyi Party, Károlyi Párt). The original party eventually dwindled to insignificance.

Károlyi headed the government for a brief time after the dissolution of the Dual Monarchy in 1918-1919 (see Hungary introduction). His government was overthrown by Béla Kun's regime (*see* Communist Party of Hungary). Károlyi's party disappeared, failing to elect any candidates in the 1920 election.

PARTY OF NATIONAL UNITY. *See* GOVERNMENT PARTY.

PARTY OF NATIONAL UNITY, CHRISTIAN, SMALLHOLDERS', FARMERS', AND BOURGEOIS PARTY. *See* GOVERNMENT PARTY.

PARTY OF NATIONAL WILL. *See* ARROW CROSS.

PARTY OF UNITY. *See* GOVERNMENT PARTY.

PEACE PARTY. *See* COMMUNIST PARTY OF HUNGARY.

PEOPLE'S PATRIOTIC FRONT. *See* HUNGARY INTRODUCTION.

PETŐFI PÁRT. *See* NATIONAL PEASANT PARTY.

PETŐFI PARTY. *See* NATIONAL PEASANT PARTY.

RACE-DEFENDERS PARTY. *See* GOVERNMENT PARTY.

RACE-PROTECTING PARTY. *See* GOVERNMENT PARTY.

REJUVENATION PARTY. *See* PARTY OF HUNGARIAN RENEWAL.

RUTHENIAN PARTY. *See* HUNGARY INTRODUCTION.

SMALLHOLDERS' PARTY. *See* INDEPENDENT SMALLHOLDERS' PARTY.

SOCIALIST-COMMUNIST WORKERS' PARTY OF HUNGARY. *See* COMMUNIST PARTY OF HUNGARY.

SOCIALIST PARTY OF HUNGARY. *See* COMMUNIST PARTY OF HUNGARY.

SUBCARPATHIAN PARTY. *See* HUNGARY INTRODUCTION.

SZABADELVŰ PÁRT. *See* LIBERAL PARTY.

SZABADSÁG PÁRT. *See* INDEPENDENT SMALLHOLDERS' PARTY.

TRANSYLVANIAN PARTY. *See* HUNGARY INTRODUCTION.

UNITARY PARTY. *See* GOVERNMENT PARTY.

UNITED CHRISTIAN PARTY. *See* WOLFF AND ZICHY PARTY.

UNITED PARTY OF INDEPENDENCE AND 1848. *See* PARTY OF INDEPENDENCE AND 1848.

UPPER HUNGARIAN UNION. *See* HUNGARY INTRODUCTION and PARTY OF HUNGARIAN RENEWAL.

WOLFF AND ZICHY PARTY. Dr. Károly Wolff founded an association in 1919 known as the Christian National League. It was based on the pre-World War I Christian Party, which had been opposed to the largely Calvinist-based National Party of Work (*see* Liberal Party). By January 1920, Wolff's association became known as the Christian National Union Party. Its program was Catholic, feudal, reactionary, anti-Semitic, pro-Habsburg, and somewhat pro-German. The membership of such strong political personalities as István Friedrich, Count Pál Teleki, Dr. Sándor Ernszt, and Károly Huszár (most of whom were later to become leaders in the Government Party*) produced an individualism and heterogeneity which caused the Union's disintegration by Spring 1921. The Christian National Union that survived under Wolff became known as the Wolff Party. It continued as pro-Habsburg, reactionary, anti-Semitic, and later as anti-Horthy (*see* Hungary introduction).

In 1925, Count János Zichy founded the Christian Economic Party, largely composed of former civil servants and based on "legitimism" (the return to Austrian Habsburg rule). It emerged as the Christian National Economic Party or the Zichy Party. Amalgamation around the turn of the decade of the Wolff Party, the Zichy Party, and a small grouping called the Christian Social Party produced the Christian Social Economic Party. In 1937 this grouping changed its name to the United Christian Party, although it was still popularly known as the Wolff and Zichy Party.

In the 1940s, under the leadership of István Barankovics, the Wolff and Zichy Party was officially titled the Democratic People's Party. It attracted large numbers of Catholics and clergy. The Democratic People's Party won 60 seats in the 1947 parliamentary elections. As a result, it soon became the target of opposition by the ruling Communist Party of Hungary,* and it was dissolved in 1948.

WOLFF PÁRT. *See* WOLFF AND ZICHY PARTY.

WOLFF PARTY. *See* WOLFF AND ZICHY PARTY.

ZICHY PÁRT. *See* WOLFF AND ZICHY PARTY.

ZICHY PARTY. *See* WOLFF AND ZICHY PARTY.

James S. Pacy

TABLE 43. Distribution of Seats in Hungary's *Képviselő Ház*, 1920-1947

Party	1920*	1922	1926	1931	1935	1939	1945	1947
Arrow Cross parties[a]	—	—	—	—	2	45	—	—
Government Party	—	143	171	152	170	179	—	—
Hungarian Communist Party[b]	—	—	—	—	—	—	70	100[e]
Hungarian Social Democratic Party	—	25	14	14	11	5	69	67
Independent Democrats	—	—	—	—	—	—	—	18
Independent Smallholders' Party[c]	71	—	—	14	24	14	245	68
National Liberal Party	—	—	—	5	7	5	0	3
National Peasant Party	—	—	—	—	—	—	23	36
Radicals	—	—	—	—	—	—	0	6
Wolff and Zichy Party[d]	68	20	35	30	14	8	2	60
Czechoslovak representatives	—	—	—	—	—	36	—	—
Independents	3	35	7	25	11	1	0	0
Others	22	22	18	5	6	3	0	53[f]
Total	164	245	245	245	245	296	409	411

Note: During 1949-1951, all parties subsumed under communist-controlled Hungarian Independent People's Front, which was then called People's Patriotic Front from 1954 to the present.

- Only 164 seats remained of the old parliament's 453 seats after Hungary's territorial losses due to World War I. Between 1922 and 1938, the total number was 245. Membership was raised to 260 in 1938, and to 296 in 1939 to allow for 36 representatives from the returned Czechoslovak territories.

a   In 1939, this grouping included: the Arrow Cross (29 seats), the National Front (3), the National Socialist Front (5), the Christian National Socialist Front (3), the Party of the People's Will (1), and the Racialists (4).

b   Banned from 1919-1945. In June 1948, with the absorption of the Social Democratic Party, the communists became the Hungarian Workers' Party, until subsumed by the Hungarian Socialist Workers' Party in 1956.

c   A Smallholders' Party joined the Government Party after 1922. The former was revived as the Independent Smallholders' Party in 1920.

d   K:own under various formal names: in 1920, the Christian National Union Party; in 1922, the Wolff Party; in 1926, the Christian National Economic Party; in 1931 and 1935, the Christian Social Economic Party; in 1939, the United Christian Party; in 1945 and 1947, the Democratic People's Party.

e   Allied with the Communists in the government bloc were the Independent Smallholders' Party, the Hungarian Social Democratic Party, and the National Peasant Party.

f   This figure includes 49 seats for the Hungarian Independence Party (a splinter group of the Independent Smallholders' Party) and 4 seats for the Christian Women's League.

TABLE 44. Ruling Coalitions in Hungary since Collapse of Dual Monarchy, 1918

Years	Coalition
Oct. 1918-Mar. 1919	"National Council"—all-party government headed by United Party of Independence and 1848
Mar. 1919-July 1919	"Hungarian Soviet Republic"—headed by Socialist Party of Hungary
Aug. 1-Aug. 6, 1919	Hungarian Social Democratic Party
Aug. 1919-Mar. 1921	Wolff Party
Apr. 1921-1935	Government Party Wolff and Zichy Party Independents
1935-1939	Government Party Wolff and Zichy Party Independent Smallholders' Party
1939-Oct. 1944	Party of Hungarian Life (new name of Government Party)
Oct. 1944-Dec. 1944	Arrow Cross
Dec. 1944-Nov. 1945	Provisional all-party government under Russian auspices
Nov. 1945-1947	Independent Smallholders' Party Hungarian Social Democratic Party National Peasant Party
1947-1949	Independent Smallholders' Party Hungarian Social Democratic Party National Peasant Party Hungarian Communist Party
1949-1951	"Hungarian Independent People's Front"—headed by Hungarian Communist Party
1951-Oct. 1956	"Patriotic People's Front"—headed by Hungarian Communist Party
Oct. 1956-Nov. 1956	Hungarian Workers' Party Independent Smallholders' Party National Peasant Party Hungarian Social Democratic Party
Nov. 1956-	Hungarian Socialist Workers' Party

Note: First-named party is dominant coalition party.

ICELAND

The REPUBLIC OF ICELAND (*Lýdveldid Ísland*), a North Atlantic volcanic island with a 1979 population of approximately 227,000, is the smallest nation in the world with a full panoply of modern institutions, excepting only the military. Iceland was formally established as an independent republic on June 17, 1944. The country has its own language and literature, a strong national consciousness, a full-fledged university, a foreign service, and a developed party system similar to those of the other Nordic countries. Half of the Icelandic population is concentrated in the capital of Reykjavík and adjacent towns, and most of the other half is in towns and villages around the country's perimeter. Fewer than ten percent of the labor force is engaged in agriculture.

The principal political institutions of Iceland include a president, elected by direct universal suffrage for a four-year term, and a 60-member bicameral parliament (*Althing*), whose members also serve for four years, subject to early dissolution. Suffrage eligibility begins at age 20, and the 1979 electorate numbered approximately 142,100. Election to parliament is based upon both direct and proportional representation. A total of 49 members are elected by proportional representation in eight constituencies of mixed single and multimember representation; 11 additional seats are allotted to parties for equalization in achieving a more precise proportional representation of electoral sentiment. One-third of the membership is chosen to sit in the upper house (*Efri deild*), while the remaining two-thirds constitute the lower house (*Nedri deild*). A prime minister and cabinet representing the majority coalition functions as the working executive.

Modern Icelandic political history can be conveniently divided into three periods: prior to 1845 when Iceland was a colony under Danish absolutism; 1845-1918 when the central issue in Icelandic politics was home rule; and the period since 1918 after Iceland achieved self-government and developed a modern political party system.

Iceland was settled in the years 870-930 and had a more or less independent existence until 1262, when the country fell under the hegemony of the king of Norway and later of Denmark (from 1380). These early centuries, called the Commonwealth Period, have been celebrated throughout subsequent Icelandic history, especially during the first half of the 19th century when national romanticism came as a flood over the country. The roots of the modern independence movement can be found in a number of national poets who came to the fore in the 1830s. In 1845 the old Icelandic parliament was reconstituted (it had been dissolved in 1801 after it became clear that the body had no function), but the parliament had only a consultative basis. In 1848 the king of Denmark renounced his absolutism; and during the next 70 years, Iceland gained increasing autonomy, culminating in the 1918 Act of Union whereby Denmark recognized the full independence of Iceland. Foreign affairs, however, continued to be handled by Denmark until 1944 when the Icelanders voted overwhelmingly in a plebiscite to discontinue the union with Denmark. This transformation from complete colonial status to a position of sovereign independence, excepting matters of foreign affairs and defense, occurred peacefully and without a single incident of violence.

While the independence movement was central to Icelandic politics of the 1845-1918 period, it was never carried out with popular passion. The first political organization in Iceland that can be considered a protoparty was the Patriots' Society,* which existed between 1871 and 1874. However, until the election of 1902 only a small minority of the eligible electorate even bothered to vote. In the *Althing* election of 1874, for example, a mere 19.6 percent of the eligible electorate voted, and this was a population in which literacy was universal, at least insofar as the ability to read. The eligible electorate was expanded in 1903 and suffrage was made universal for all men and women over age 25 in 1915, excluding only those who received community assistance. The secret ballot was introduced in 1903 and was first put into practice in the 1904 by-elections.

The political parties and other associations of interest aggregation were primitively developed until home rule was achieved in 1918. The eight or ten parties that existed were mostly parliamentary groupings. The Social Democratic Party,* belatedly founded in 1916, was the first political party in Iceland (as in the other Scandinavian countries) to be organized outside of parliament for the express purpose of electing members to that body. During the pre-World War II period, only five parties managed to elect representatives to the *Althing* (see table 45); since 1946, this number has increased only to seven parties (see table 46). Cabinets have consisted of only one to three parties (see table 47). A number of minor parties exist, but they capture only a tiny proportion of the vote. There are several cases of two Icelandic parties with the same name (the Progressive Party,* Farmers' Party,* Independence Party*) but which are totally unrelated.

Three factors stand out as having shaped the political culture of Iceland: size, the homogeneity of the population, and isolation. First, as a result of geographic and demographic smallness, Icelandic politics have been strongly personalistic. Traditionally, there has been a tendency for leading political figures to come from a few high-status families and for a few individuals to be politically dominant for long periods. Also, women are almost totally absent from leading political positions.

Second, there is a pervasive social and political homogeneity among Ice-landers. There have never been religious or ethnic differences to complicate the nation's politics. In fact, of the more than 20 groupings that might be called political parties in both 19th- and 20th-century Iceland, none has developed along religious or ethnic lines. A pervasive belief in freedom, individualism, and tolerance, combined with consensus on the legitimacy of the nation's political institutions, has balanced highly personalistic and partisan politics. This is noted by an absence of serious violence in Iceland since the Protestant Reforma-tion. Furthermore, the modern population is homogenous in its high level of literacy and political awareness. In all national elections since 1956, at least 90 percent of the electorate has voted, a level achieved elsewhere in the north only by Sweden.

Finally, Iceland is isolated in the North Atlantic; the shortest distance to neighboring Norway is just over 600 miles and to Scotland just under 500 miles. A consequence of this isolation has been to focus Icelandic politics on domestic issues, and domestic issues often shape foreign policy positions. Major excep-tions since World War II have been NATO membership with U.S. military presence, together with the issue of extending the country's fisheries limits, both of which have declined as central issues in Icelandic politics in the late 1970s. Isolation has also had cultural effects, resulting in "primordial sentiments" and provincialism growing out of an isolated and misery-filled history. Icelanders disproportionately read their own literature (unique with its historical continu-ity of language and the common descent of its readers), they are highly ethno-centric, and they often have little awareness of Iceland's insignificance in the world.

In the 1978 and 1979 elections, however, Icelanders demonstrated that they have become as volatile and changeable in their voting behavior as the voters of any modern society—traditional party affiliations appear to have become less salient, and specific policy issues and the state of the economy have become more important electorally. The 1978 elections demonstrated the largest shifts in party voting in Icelandic history. The two parties in power (the Independence Party [1929-   ]* and the Progressive Party [1916-   ]*) fell in seats held, while the two major opposition parties (the Social Democratic Party* and the People's Alliance*) by contrast reached new highs in electoral support. In the December 1979 elections, the opposite pattern occurred, though less extreme.

The preeminent issue of the 1974-1979 period was the precarious state of the economy, with inflation galloping at an annual rate of between 40 and 60 percent—an intolerable level even for the most persistently inflationary econ-omy of all Organization for Economic Cooperation and Development (OECD) nations. The 1978-1979 leftist government took strong steps to control inflation—freezing wages after some adjustments, increasing income taxes, and abolishing the sales tax on food. Also, the government continued to devalue the *Krona* (Icelandic monetary unit).

Of importance in bonding the three government coalition parties of 1978-1979

(Progressive Party, Social Democratic Party, People's Alliance) were the perennial issues of continued Icelandic membership in NATO and the presence of United States military forces at the NATO base in Keflavík, 40 kilometers east of the capital. The People's Alliance opposed both, and agreement was reached among the coalition partners that new major constructions on the military base would not be allowed.

Nevertheless, the center-left governing coalition collapsed in October 1979, resulting in new *Althing* elections being held on December 2-3 of that year. Following the inability of the four elected parties to agree on a new governing coalition, President Kristján Eldjárn announced on January 29, 1980, that if the deadlock was not broken within two weeks he would then appoint a nonpartisan cabinet. Hence in early February, an agreement was successfully negotiated by Gunnar Thoroddsen to enter his Independence Party into a coalition with the Progressives and the People's Alliance. Thoroddsen, who had served as minister of industry and social affairs during 1974-1978, stated that the primary goal of his administration would be the continuing fight against inflation and the restabilization of Iceland's economy.

For the present, there will be no change in Iceland's relationship with NATO; and the U.S. military presence will continue to be tolerated, even by the People's Alliance, as a result of certain underlying economic realities. It would be quite impossible for Iceland to withdraw from NATO and force out the American military without doing enormous damage to Iceland's fragile economy. It is doubtful that Icelandic Airlines (*Loftleider*), the country's largest wholly owned industry and its chief means of communication with the outside world, could profitably survive without American personnel and support at the Keflavík airfield. The base also employs a large number of Icelanders and is a diverse source of revenue for the country.

Bibliography

There are no systematic treatments of Icelandic political parties in English or other major languages, other than a few theses and dissertations. Two journals which sometimes publish articles on Icelandic politics are the *Scandinavian Review* (previously *American-Scandinavian Review*), published in New York; and *Atlantica and Iceland Review* (previously *Icelandic Review*), published in Reykjavík. An annual, *Scandinavian Political Studies*, published in various places in Scandinavia, occasionally includes articles dealing with Iceland.

Asgeirsson, Thorhallur. "Development of the Progressive Party in Iceland." Master's thesis, University of Minnesota, 1942.

Davis, Morris. *Iceland Extends Its Fisheries Limits*. Oslo: Universitetsforlaget, 1963.

Grimsson, Olafur R. "Iceland." In *International Guide to Electoral Statistics*, edited by Stein Rokkan and Jean Meyriat, vol 1. The Hague: Mouton, 1969.

———. "Political Power in Iceland prior to the Period of Class Politics, 1845-1918." Ph.D. dissertation, University of Manchester, England, 1970.

Gröndal, Benedikt. *Iceland from Neutrality to NATO Membership*. Oslo: Universitetsforlaget, 1971.

Magnússon, Sigurdur A. *Northern Sphinx: Iceland and the Icelanders from the Settlement to the Present*. Montreal: McGill-Queens University Press, 1977.

Nordal, Jóhannes, and Valdimar Kristinsson, eds. *Iceland, 874-1974*. Reykjavík: Central Bank of Iceland, 1975. (See particularly Sigurdur Lindal, "Political Parties," pp. 150-159, and "Bibliography," pp. 397-407.)

Nordic Council. *Yearbook of Nordic Statistics*. Copenhagen: Nordic Statistical Secretariat, annually.

Nuechterlein, Donald E. *Iceland: Reluctant Ally*. Ithaca, N.Y.: Cornell University Press, 1961.

—————. "Small States in Alliances: Iceland, Thailand, Australia," *Orbis*, vol. 13, no. 2 (1966): 600-623.

Olmstead, Mary. "Communism in Iceland," *Foreign Affairs*, vol. 36, no. 2 (1958): 340-347.

Sallé, M. Michel. "La vie economique et politique en Íslands." Ph.D. dissertation, Paris, Foundation Nationale des Sciences Politiques, Cycle Supérieur d'Études Politiques, 1968.

Statistical Bureau of Iceland. *Statistical Abstract of Iceland 1974*. Reykjavík: Hagstofa Íslands, 1976.

Tomasson, Richard F. "Iceland's Survival and the Law of the Sea," *Current History*, vol, 70, no. 415 (1976): 155-158, 181-182.

—————. *Iceland: The First New Society*. Minneapolis: University of Minnesota Press, 1980.

Political Parties

ALTHÝDUBANDALAG. *See* PEOPLE'S ALLIANCE.

ALTHÝDUFLOKKUR. *See* SOCIAL DEMOCRATIC PARTY.

ASSOCIATION FOR NATIONAL FREEDOM (*Hid Íslenzka Thjódfrelsisfélag*). The Association, like the Icelandic Nationalists,* was founded in 1884 to promote parliamentary democracy similar to that achieved in Norway in 1884. While the Nationalists was a farmers' group, the Association consisted of Reykjavík citizens. The Association was antibureaucratic and survived only a short time.

BAENDAFLOKKUR. *See* FARMERS' PARTY (1912-1916) and (1933-1942).

BORGARAFLOKKUR. *See* CITIZENS' PARTY.

CITIZENS' PARTY (*Borgaraflokkur*). The Citizens' Party was a 1923 electoral alliance formed from the unification of the disbanded Home Rule Party* and Independence Party (1907-1927).* The Citizens' platform was hostility to both the Social Democratic Party* and to the anti-home rule Progressive Party

(1916-   ).* As it was only a loose electoral alliance, the Citizens' Party was dissolved in 1924 in an attempt to form a more close-knit party. Thus was formed the Conservative Party* in that same year. A small number of Citizens' Party members who did not join their colleagues in the Conservative Party retained the name of the Independence Party until they formed their own grouping in 1927, the Liberal Party.*

COMMONWEALTH PARTY (Thjódveldisflokkur). The Commonwealth Party was founded in 1941 by right-wing members of the Independence Party (1929-   )* who believed that party had moved too far to the left in its support of economic planning and regulation. Contesting two 1942 elections, the Commonwealth Party never succeeded in electing a member to the Althing, but it received 2.2 percent of the vote in the second 1942 election.

COMMUNIST PARTY (Kommunistaflokkur). The Communist Party was founded in 1930 by radicals of the Social Democratic Party.* In 1938 the Communists invited additional leftist Social Democrats to help form another new grouping, the Socialist Party.* Since 1970, Iceland's Communists have existed under the label of the People's Alliance.*

CONSERVATIVE PARTY (Íhaldsflokkur). Founded in 1924, the Conservative Party was the result of an attempt to shape a more formal party out of the 1923 electoral alliance known as the Citizens' Party.* After contesting one election, the Conservatives in 1929 merged with the Liberal Party* to form the contemporary Independence Party (1929-   ).*

DEMOCRATIC PARTY (Thjódraedisflokkur). The title Democratic Party was the result of a name change in 1905 of the former Progressive Party (1900-1905).* The Democratic Party joined with the National Defense Party* in 1907 to form the Independence Party (1907-1927).*

FARMERS' PARTY (1912-1916) (Baendaflokkur). The first Farmers' Party was founded in 1912 by several members of the Althing to promote the interests of farmers. The Independent Farmers' Party* broke away from the parent party in 1916. After the 1916 elections, the two parties came together again as the new Progressive Party (1916-   ),* which for six decades was the second-largest party in Iceland.

FARMERS' PARTY (1933-1942) (Baendaflokkur). The second Farmers' Party was founded in 1933 by dissidents from the Progressive Party (1916-   )* who wanted a party dedicated to the interests of farmers, not a party that made a broad appeal to the electorate. These dissidents readopted the goals and name of one of their grandparent parties, the Farmers Party, (1912-1916).* The second

Farmers' Party dissolved in 1942, after having elected three members to the *Althing* in 1934 and two in 1937.

FLOKKUR THJÓDERNISSINNA. *See* NATIONAL SOCIALIST PARTY.

FRAMSÓKNARFLOKKUR. *See* PROGRESSIVE PARTY (1900-1905) and 1916-   ).

FRJÁLSLYNDIFLOKKUR. *See* LIBERAL PARTY.

HEIMASTJÓRNARFLOKKUR. *See* HOME RULE PARTY.

HID ÍSLENZKA THJÓDFRELSISFÉLAG. *See* ASSOCIATION FOR NATIONAL FREEDOM.

HID ÍSLENZKA THJÓDVINAFÉLAG. *See* PATRIOTS' SOCIETY.

HOME RULE PARTY (*Heimastjórnarflokkur*). Founded in 1900 in opposition to the Progressive Party (1900-1905),* the main issue promoted by the Home Rule Party was to make the Danish minister for Iceland reside in Reykjavík, not Copenhagen. The Home Rule Party believed that if Iceland must be governed by foreigners, at least that government official should reside locally to observe firsthand the needs and actions of the governed. This position contrasted with the more conservative stance of the Progressives (1900-1905), who accepted a nonresident minister. The Home Rule Party won its point. It, along with the Independence Party (1907-1927),* were the dominant parties until 1923 when both dissolved themselves to form the Citizens' Party,* a loose electoral alliance which opposed the Progressive Party (1916-   )* and the Social Democratic Party.*

ICELANDIC NATIONALISTS (*Thjódlid Íslendinga*). The party of the Icelandic Nationalists was formed in 1884, the same year as the Association for National Freedom,* by farmers in the north of Iceland. Like the Reykjavík-based Association, the Icelandic Nationalists promoted parliamentary democracy. This party also favored the whole governmental administration being in Iceland, not Denmark. The Icelandic Nationalists was a short-lived grouping.

ICELANDIC NAZI PARTY. *See* NATIONAL SOCIALIST PARTY.

ÍHALDSFLOKKUR. *See* CONSERVATIVE PARTY.

INDEPENDENCE PARTY (1907-1927) (*Sjálfstaedisflokkur*). The first Independence Party was founded in 1907 by the joining of the Democratic Party* and the National Defense Party.* The Independents and the Home Rule Party* were the two dominant parties until 1923 when both dissolved themselves to form the Citizens' Party,* a loose electoral alliance which opposed the Progressive Party (1916-   )* and the Social Democratic Party.* When the Citizens' Party became the Conservative Party* in 1924, some Citizens' members remained outside the new grouping and continued under the name of the old Independence Party (1907-1927) until they formed their own organization, the Liberal Party,* in 1927.

INDEPENDENCE PARTY (1929-   ) (*Sjálfstaedisflokkur*). The second Independence Party came into being in 1929 as a result of the merger of the Conservative Party* and the Liberal Party.* The new group readopted the name of one of its grandparent parties, the Independence Party (1907-1927),* which had initially provided the founders for the short-lived Liberals. Since the election of 1931, this second Independence Party has, without exception, been the largest party in Iceland, with generally around 40 percent of the popular vote and of the mandates. Also, it has participated in the government for more than two-thirds of the years between 1932 and 1980; and in 23 of 36 years (1945-1980), Iceland's prime minister has been from the Independence Party (1929-   ).

The Independents were originally committed to an ideology of laissez-faire individualism, low taxes, and minimal governmental interference in the economy. However, since the 1930s the party has increasingly come to discard its laissez-faire ideology and to accept economic planning, regulation, and the essentials of the modern welfare state. As a result of these changes, right-wing dissidents have left the party on two occasions: in 1941 to form the Commonwealth Party* and in 1953 to form the Republican Party.* Both offshoot parties were unsuccessful in electing members to the *Althing* and consequently were short-lived.

The Independence Party has been the most positive, and at times the least hostile, of the Icelandic parties toward the U.S. military presence and to international cultural influences. The party is particularly strong in Reykjavík and the larger towns, weaker in the rural and outlying areas of the nation. The party is supported by *Morgunbladid* (Morning News), by far the most important of the six national daily papers (all of which are published in the capital city). *Vísir*, the sole afternoon daily in Iceland, also supports the Independence Party, giving it the support of two-thirds of the daily newspaper circulation (which on a per capital basis is among the highest in the world).

The Independence Party occupies a far more important position in the political life of Iceland than do the conservatives, or perhaps even the conservatives plus the liberals, of the other Scandinavian countries. Iceland's Independents are also probably a little less conservative on economic and social issues than their Scandinavian counterparts. More than any other party, leadership of the Independence Party tends to come from the ranks of distinguished families. The Independence Party is highly pragmatic, as are all the Icelandic parties, and has entered into coalitions with the Progressive Party,* Social Democratic Party,* Socialist Party,* and the People's Alliance.*

INDEPENDENT FARMERS' PARTY (Óhádir Baendur). The Independent Farmers' Party was formed in 1916 by dissidents from the Farmers' Party (1912-1916).* The Independent Farmers regrouped with the parent party that same year to form the Progressive Party (1916-   ).

KOMMÚNISTAFLOKKUR. See COMMUNIST PARTY.

LANDVARNARFLOKKUR. See NATIONAL DEFENSE PARTY.

LIBERAL PARTY (Frjálslyndiflokkur). The Liberal Party was founded in 1927 by a few Althing members who had belonged to the Citizens' Party* (1923) but did not join their colleagues in forming the Conservative Party* in 1924. Until they formed their own party, these individuals continued under the name of the old Independence Party (1907-1927),* which had been one of the founders of the Citizens' Party. The Liberals, however, did join with the Conservatives in 1929 to form the new Independence Party (1929-   ).*

LÝDVELDISFLOKKUR. See REPUBLICAN PARTY.

NATIONAL DEFENSE PARTY (Landvarnarflokkur). Founded in 1902, the National Defense Party had a radical independence program, advocating complete separation from Denmark. It joined with the unsuccessful Democratic Party* (previously the anti-home rule Progressive Party [1900-1905]*) to form the Independence Party (1907-1927)* in 1907.

NATIONAL PRESERVATION PARTY (Thjódvarnarflokkur). The National Preservation Party was founded in 1953 by wings of the Progressive Party (1916-   ),* the Social Democratic Party,* and the Socialist Party.* National Preservation's central theme was for Iceland to follow a policy of strict neutrality in foreign affairs, a policy followed between 1918 and 1940 when such was generally considered to be an everlasting policy (like that of Switzerland). The National Preservationists advocated pacifism, national cultural values against international culture, and vigorously opposed Iceland's membership in NATO and the U.S. military presence in the country. In domestic affairs, the party held to a liberal social-democratic policy.

The National Preservation Party contested four elections between 1953 and 1959, winning two Althing seats in 1953 and two in the first election of 1959. The party was part of the electoral coalition, the People's Alliance,* which had formed in 1956. By 1967, however, some National Preservationists rebelled against the communist-dominated Alliance; and in 1970, these dissidents reconstituted themselves as the Union of Liberals and Leftists.*

NATIONAL SOCIALIST PARTY (*Flokkur Thjódernissinna*). The official name of the Icelandic nazi party, the National Socialists organized in 1933, demonstrated actively in Reykjavík, but received only 0.7 percent of the vote in 1934 and 0.2 percent in 1937. Never electing a member to the *Althing*, the National Socialist Party survived only until 1940.

ÓHÁDIR BAENDUR. *See* INDEPENDENT FARMERS' PARTY.

PATRIOTS' SOCIETY (*Hid Íslenzka Thjódvinafélag*). Founded in 1871 by elected members of the *Althing*, the Patriots' Society sought to promote independence and public enlightenment. It existed as a protoparty until 1874.

PEOPLE'S ALLIANCE (*Althýdubandalag*). The People's Alliance began as an electoral alliance formed prior to the 1956 national elections by the communist-dominated Socialist Party* and some members of both the Social Democratic Party* and the National Preservation Party.* The People's Alliance did not become a full-fledged party until 1970 when the Socialist Party disappeared. Like many other communist parties in western Europe, the Alliance has moved to a position of independence from the Soviet Union and adheres to a democratic philosophy while also proclaiming a socialist program. The Alliance's opposition to the U.S. military presence is less salient than previously. It continues to be Iceland's third-largest party, as was its predecessor (the Socialists); and the Alliance has served in government coalitions during 1956-1958, 1971-1974, and 1978-present.

PEOPLE'S UNIFICATION PARTY. *See* SOCIALIST PARTY.

PROGRESSIVE PARTY (1900-1905) (*Framsóknarflokkur*). The first Progressive Party was founded in 1900 by supporters of Valtýr Gudmundsson, a university teacher of Icelandic in Copenhagen, in opposition to the Home Rule Party.* The Progressives' central plank was that the Danish minister for Iceland reside in Copenhagen, not Reykjavík. It lost its point, changed its name to the Democratic Party* in 1905, and finally combined with the National Defense Party* in 1907 to become the Independence Party (1907-1927).* (Note that this Progressive Party had no ties with a later party of the same name.).

PROGRESSIVE PARTY (1916-) (*Framsóknarflokkur*). This second Progressive Party (with no ties to the earlier Progressive Party [1900-1905]*) was formed in 1916 as a farmers' party, reuniting the old Farmers' Party (1912-1916)* and the Independent Farmers' Party* (which had previously split from the former). Effective political organization among farmers has been a general characteristic of Nordic party systems, and Iceland is typical in this regard. Through the years, as the proportion of farmers had declined, the Progressive Party expanded its appeal to include more nonfarmers, who now make up a majority of its supporters. The closest counterpart to the present Icelandic Progressive Party is the Center Party of Sweden (see SWEDEN), which has also greatly expanded its support beyond farmers with an antibureaucratic appeal.

The Progressive Party, for six decades the second-largest party in Iceland, has always been relatively weak in Reykjavík and its environs, and the party has obtained most of its support in the rest of the country where it is generally the strongest party. The Progressives have a close relationship with the cooperative movement, which has been particularly strong in Iceland. As a result of the party's attempts to broaden its appeal, in 1933 a dissident faction formed the new Farmers' Party (1933-1942)* to appeal to all farmers of the country. This dissident party collapsed in 1942, but it did succeed in electing three members to the Althing in 1934 and two in 1937. A few more dissidents again left the Progressives in 1953 to help establish the National Preservation Party.*

The Progressive Party is supported by the fourth-largest newspaper in the country, Tíminn (The Times), with most of its circulation outside of the Reykjavík area. The party has been enormously successful in forming coalitions, enabling it to have been in the government most of the time since 1927, except for the 1942 and 1958-1971 periods.

REPUBLICAN PARTY (Lýdveldisflokkur). The Republican Party was founded in 1953 by right-wing Independence Party (1929-   )* members who believed that party had become too socialistic. The Republicans received 3.3 percent of the vote in the 1953 election but could not elect a member to the Althing. The party did not participate in elections thereafter.

SAMTÖK FRJÁLSLYNDRA OG VINSTRI MANNA. See UNION OF LIBERALS AND LEFTISTS.

SJÁLFSTAEDISFLOKKUR. See INDEPENDENCE PARTY (1907-1927) and (1929-   ).

SOCIAL DEMOCRATIC PARTY (Althýduflokkur). The Social Democratic Party of Iceland is far and away weaker than its sister parties elsewhere in the north (not excluding the Faroe Islands [see DENMARK]) and in western Europe in general. The party's place has declined drastically since 1956 and 1967 peaks when it received 18 and 16 percent of the popular vote respectively, dropping to a nine percent nadir in 1974. The party had performed better in the 1930s when it had averaged 20 percent of the vote.

The Social Democrats came into being in 1916 along with the Icelandic Federation of Labor, of which the party was to be the political arm. This was the first Icelandic political organization to elect members to the Althing but which was formed outside of that representative body. The party adopted the principles of socialism similar to all European social-democratic and labor parties of an earlier time. Differences between the moderates and radicals became immediately apparent. However, the radicals did not break away to form the Communist Party* until 1930, a decade later than in most other countries. Nevertheless, a high level of internal conflict has continually characterized the Social Democrats. In 1938 a radical faction broke away and joined the Communists to establish the Socialist Party.* In 1953 a nationalist faction left the Social Democrats and joined with nationalists from the Progressive Party (1916-   )* and the Socialist Party to form the National Preservation Party.* And in 1956 still another faction broke away and joined with dissidents from the Socialists and National Preservationists to form the People's Alliance.* After these last major eruptions to the nationalist and more radical left, the Social Democrats became more moderate, giving up ideas of nationalizing industry; and they have gone the way of the other Scandinavian social-democratic parties.

The Social Democrats have been less anti-NATO than the Progressive Party (1916-   ) or the more leftist parties. On foreign policy issues in general, they have been closest to the Independence Party (1929-   ).* Most of the support for the Social Democrats is in the towns, with little from rural areas, least of all in the eastern part of the country where support is less than five percent.

SOCIALIST PARTY (Sósíalistaflokkur). The Socialist Party was founded under the name People's Unification Party-Socialist Party by leftist members of the Social Democratic Party* who aligned with the Communist Party* in 1938. This was accomplished at the invitation of the latter, who soon came to dominate the new grouping. Hence the Socialists, led by the Communists, continued to support the policies of the Soviet Union (though the Socialists' successor, the People's Alliance,* has eased on this position). Due in part to Socialist support of Soviet policy, some dissidents left the party in 1953 and, by joining with nationalist dissidents of the Progressive Party (1916-   )* and the Social Democratic Party, helped to establish the National Preservation Party.*

Both the Socialists and the People's Alliance always received somewhat more support than the Social Democrats. Iceland, Finland, France, and Italy are the only western countries with large communist parties. However, Iceland and Finland are the only ones in which the communists have been included in coalition governments (in Iceland, under either the Socialist or People's Alliance label, during 1944-1947, 1956-1958, 1971-1974, 1978-1979, and 1980-   ). Between the elections of 1942 and 1953, the Socialist Party's support—most of which was in the towns—fell to between 16 and 20 percent of the popular vote, although this was still more than twice what the old Communist Party had received in the elections between 1931 and 1937. In 1970, however, the Socialist Party disappeared when the People's Alliance, initially formed as an electoral alliance, became a formal political party.

SÓSÍALISTAFLOKKUR. See SOCIALIST PARTY.

THJÓDLID ÍSLENDINGA. See ICELANDIC NATIONALISTS.

THJÓDRAEDISFLOKKUR. See DEMOCRATIC PARTY.

THJÓDVARNARFLOKKUR. See NATIONAL PRESERVATION PARTY.

THJÓDVELDISFLOKKUR. See COMMONWEALTH PARTY.

UNION OF LIBERALS AND LEFTISTS (Samtök Frjálslyndra og Vinstri Manna). In the 1967 Althing elections, some dissidents of the communist-dominated People's Alliance* ran on an independent ticket. These dissidents had previously been grouped around the social-democratic National Preservation Party* (one of the founders of the People's Alliance). In 1970, when the People's Alliance became a full-fledged party, these dissidents reformed themselves into the Union of Liberals and Leftists. After an initial note of success in the 1971 Althing election, winning five seats, the Union dropped to two seats in 1974 and then lost all mandates in the election of 1978. Though the Union did not contest the 1979 election, it continues to advocate the same policies as its predecessor (the National Preservation Party), except in a more moderate form. Most of the party's support comes from townspeople.

Richard F. Tomasson

TABLE 45. Distribution of Seats in Iceland's Althing, 1927-1942

Party	1927	1931	1933	1934	1937	July 1942	Oct. 1942
Communist Party*	—	0	0	0	3	6	10
Farmers' Party (1933-1942)	—	—	—	3	2	—	—
Independence Party (1929-)**	14	12	17	20	17	17	20
Progressive Party (1916-)	17	21	14	15	19	20	15
Social Democratic Party	4	3	4	10	8	6	7
Independents	1	0	1	1	—	—	—
Total	36	36	36	49	49	49	52

* Known as the Socialist Party, 1938-1970. (See also People's Alliance, table 46.)
** In 1927, includes 1 Liberal and 13 Conservatives; these parties merged in 1929 to form the Independence Party (1929-   ).

TABLE 46. Distribution of Seats in Iceland's *Althing*, 1946-1979

Party	1946	1949	1953	1956	July 1959	Oct. 1959	1963	1967	1971	1974	1978	1979
Independence Party (1929-)	20	19	21	19	20	24	24	23	22	25	20	21
National Preservation Party	—	—	2	0	—	—	—	—	—	—	—	—
People's Alliance*	—	—	—	8	7	10	9	10	10	11	14	11
Progressive Party (1916-)	13	17	16	17	19	17	19	18	17	17	12	17
Social Democratic Party	9	7	6	8	6	9	8	9	6	5	14	10
Socialist Party**	10	9	7	—	—	—	—	—	—	—	—	—
Union of Liberals and Leftists	—	—	—	—	—	—	—	—	5	2	0	—
Independents	—	—	—	—	—	—	—	—	—	—	—	1
Total	52	52	52	52	52	60	60	60	60	60	60	60

* During 1956-1970, an electoral alliance among the communist-dominated Socialist Party and elements of both the Social Democratic Party and National Preservation party; became formal political party in 1970.

** Known as the Communist Party prior to 1938 (see table 45).

528

TABLE 47. Ruling Parties or Coalitions in Iceland since 1918 Independence

Year	Party or Coalition
1918 - 1920	Home Rule Progressive (1916-) Independence (1907-1927)
1920 - 1922	Home Rule
1922 - 1924	Home Rule Independence (1907-1927)
1924 - 1927	Conservative
1927 - 1932	Progressive (1916-)
1932 - 1934	Progressive (1916-) Independence (1929-)
1934 - 1938	Progressive (1916-) Social Democratic
1938 - 1939	Progressive (1916-)
1939 - 1942	Progressive (1916-) Independence (1929-) Social Democratic
1942	Independence (1929-)
1942 - 1944	Nonpartisan cabinet (no ministers in *Althing*)
1944 - 1947	Independence (1929-) Social Democratic Socialist
1947 - 1949	Social Democratic Independence (1929-) Progressive (1916-)

TABLE 47. (*Continued*)

Year	Party or Coalition
1949 - 1950	Independence (1929-)
1950 - 1953	Progressive (1916-) Independence (1929-)
1953 - 1956	Independence (1929-) Progressive (1916-)
1956 - 1958	Progressive (1916-) Social Democratic People's Alliance
1958 - 1959	Social Democratic
1959 - 1971	Independence (1929-) Social Democratic
1971 - 1974	Progressive (1916-) People's Alliance Union of Liberals and Leftists
1974 - 1978	Independence (1929-) Progressive (1916-)
1978 - 1979	Progressive (1916-) Social Democratic People's Alliance
1980 -	Independence (1929-) Progressive (1916-) People's Alliance

Note: First-named party is dominant coalition party.

IRELAND

The REPUBLIC OF IRELAND (*Éire*) is located on a large island in the Atlantic, lying between 50 and 100 miles west of Great Britain. Formerly, Ireland had been an integral part of the United Kingdom of Great Britain and Ireland. In 1921, however, following the Irish revolution, 26 of the island's 32 counties became known officially as the Irish Free State. (The remaining six counties, located in northern Ireland, continue to be linked to Britain. For information on Northern Ireland, *see* UNITED KINGDOM.) The Free State broke its external ties with Great Britain with the adoption of the present Irish constitution on December 29, 1937. Commonwealth status with Britain was terminated on April 18, 1949, and Ireland became a member of the European Economic Community (*see* EUROPEAN PARLIAMENT) in 1973.

The major governmental institutions of Ireland consist of a popularly elected president and a bicameral legislature (*Oireachtas*). The lower house (*Dáil*) is currently composed of 166 members elected for five-year terms (though no *Dáil* has sat that long because of early dissolutions, generally necessitating elections every four years). *Dáil* members are elected by direct adult suffrage (beginning at age 21) under a system of proportional representation with a single transferable vote. Constituencies are multimember with three or more seats each. The prime minister (*Taoiseach*) is elected by a majority in the *Dáil*.

The Irish electoral system affords the voter an opportunity to rank each candidate in order of preference. Votes are counted by first preferences until a given quota is reached, after which the candidates are declared elected. If the number of candidates elected at first count falls short of the number of seats to be filled, surplus votes are transferred to the second preference or next available choice indicated by the voters. The transfer process continues until all seats are filled. The current size of the eligible electorate is approximately 1,735,000. Turnout in Irish elections has averaged around 73 percent of the eligible electorate.

The membership of the 60-seat upper house (*Seanad*) is chosen indirectly by an electoral college made up of the prime minister, local government councillors, members of the *Dáil*, and outgoing senators. Six seats are elected by graduates of Dublin University and the National University of Ireland. Selection has usually been made along partisan lines.

Politics in the Republic of Ireland are defined by five factors. First, and perhaps most important with regard to political parties, is the revolutionary/civil war heritage. While more than 50 years have elapsed since the conclusion of the civil war, any understanding of political parties must be based upon knowledge of the war's events. Indeed, the civil war cleavage is responsible for the existence of the two largest parties in the state, the United Ireland Party* (*Fine Gael*) and the Republican Party* (*Fianna Fáil*). The second factor in Irish political life is the overwhelming adherence to the Roman Catholic Church. At least 96 percent of the population is Catholic, with most being active communicants. A third factor is the influence of the British parliamentary tradition. Despite the formal act of separation from Britain, the Irish have retained most of the features found at Westminster with relatively few modifications. Fourth, Ireland has a strong rural tradition. While the economic sector, devoted to primary production, has grown smaller as a percentage of the entire work force, much industry and most exports are based on agriculture. And fifth, Ireland has lost population consistently since 1845, despite a fairly high birth rate which has only recently declined. After the initial starvation of the famine years, this population loss has occurred through emigration.

All of these five factors contribute to the conservative nature of Irish politics. Rather than having a stable political environment, Ireland has been notable for its stagnation. Unlike other western European countries, no significant socialist parties have emerged. Even those political parties that could conceivably be defined as radical are such by virtue of their interest in unification of Northern and Southern Ireland, rather than by their devotion to major questions of social welfare policy.

The history of Ireland is inextricably linked to the actions of the British and, more particularly, the English. From the 12th century until the present, the British have had a great interest in Ireland, generally neither courted nor welcomed by the majority of the Irish. Today, of course, the interest has changed. In political terms, only part of the island of Ireland—six of the nine counties of Ulster—is still part of the United Kingdom. While the United Kingdom is still Ireland's main trading partner, their political connection is increasingly related to their joint membership in the European Economic Community. But the continued British presence in Northern Ireland has deeply affected the Republic's political system. In many respects, politics in the Republic have been frozen around the issue of the North; and as troubles in the North continue, it is difficult for politicians in the Republic to focus on other issues.

Ireland's political conflict with the English started in 1495, when the Irish assembly was placed under control of the English parliament, and all acts passed in England were binding upon the Irish. In 1542 the Irish island was labeled a kingdom, though the appellation was meaningless as the crowns of England and Ireland were held by the same person. Among the earliest of Ireland's major revolts against the English was that of 1597-1601, led by Hugh O'Neill, Earl of Tyrone. A later uprising was in 1690 at Boyne, where the Irish Catholics supported the efforts of England's exiled King James II (*see* UNITED KING-

DOM) to reestablish his kingdom in Ireland. The Catholics were suppressed by the Protestant "Orangemen" forces of England's King William III (Prince of Orange; hence the association of the color orange with Irish Protestants). As a result of this uprising against the Catholic-hating Protestants of England, the Irish were subjected to various discriminations, including a prohibition of Catholic schools, Irish trade restrictions, and denial of Catholics to serve in many Irish public offices. Only a century later did the British hope to help solve the "Irish problem" by permitting the Irish to send representatives to the British parliament; and on January 1, 1801, the "United Kingdom of Great Britain and Ireland" was proclaimed.

Once having this degree of influence in British politics, the Irish made a few gains, though hardly at the speed and to the extent necessary to quell the Anglo-Irish conflict. By the Catholic Emancipation Act of 1829, the British finally allowed the Irish to elect Catholic individuals to public office. In 1869 the Anglican Church was finally disestablished in Ireland, thereby no longer requiring that church to be state-supported through taxation of both members and nonmembers. In the 1880s, the Nationalist Parliamentary Party* was organized into Ireland's first forceful political party by Charles Parnell, a Protestant but an adamant nationalist; and this grouping soon became one that could swing parliamentary power between Britain's two major parties, the Conservative Party and Liberal Party (see UNITED KINGDOM).

In 1885, Britain's William Gladstone (Liberal Party, United Kingdom) attempted to pass through parliament a home-rule bill for Ireland, though this first effort failed and, in fact, split Gladstone's party. A second home-rule bill in 1892 was passed through the British House of Commons (with support of 81 Irish nationalists) but was defeated in the Conservative-dominated House of Lords. Another home-rule bill was not attempted until the Liberals were back in power after 1905. By that time, the British parliamentarians realized they needed the Irish MPs' support to enact the Liberal-sponsored Parliament Act, which would strip the House of Lords of their centuries-long veto power. In return for Irish support of this act of 1911, the Liberals proposed in 1912 the third home-rule bill for Ireland. The Ulster (Northern Ireland) Protestants, however, were so agitated about this proposed severance from Britain that it was decided to postpone enactment of the 1912 bill until after the Ulster question was settled. World War I intervened, however, and home rule was again tabled.

At the roots of the Irish revolution that started in 1916 had been the failure of the English to penetrate fully the Irish hinterlands. Catholicism survived the Protestant Reformation throughout most of Ireland. Only the Ulster settlement remained a small Protestant beachhead in the northeast part of the island. After the Great Famine of 1845-1851, a combination of land agitation and cultural nationalism created a separatist movement. The British were able to satisfy the land hunger; but by the time they did, cultural nationalism touched enough of the Irish population to create a situation fraught with danger for the British. By 1912 the British had fallen into a trap largely of their own making. Their

home-rule plan did not go far enough to satisfy the most devoted Irish nationalists but went too far for the Ulster Protestants. Thus the revolution which
followed the 1916 Easter Rising in Dublin was violently opposed by the Protestants of the North; and the eventual Anglo-Irish Treaty of 1921, establishing
the Irish Free State, applied to only 26 of Ireland's 32 counties. The remaining
six counties of the North remained with Britain. Although this was only one of
the issues that had precipitated the civil war, since the early 1930s it has
complicated all other issues in Ireland's relations with the British government.

Irish political parties, with the exception of the Labour Party,* developed
into their present form after independence. In the War for Independence,
virtually all nationalist elements came together under the mantle of Ourselves
Alone* (Sinn Féin), which had been founded in 1905 by Arthur Griffith. It was
an organization devoted to securing limited independence for Ireland. The
concept of limited independence was vital because if ties to Britain were maintained, it was hoped that the Protestants in Ulster particularly could be mollified. As things turned out, however, once the Rising of 1916 occurred, Sinn
Féin became the core of the nationalist movement that followed the executions
of the Rising leaders, although the party bore no real responsibility for the
insurrection. But from the outset, the new role was not a comfortable one. The
movement was composed of at least two major elements. The first represented
the more moderate groups who would be willing to accept continued connection
with Britain. The second represented the irreconcilables, people who were
firmly committed to the concept of an Irish Republic with no links to Britain, at
any cost.

When the revolutionary era ended with the 1921 treaty, which was substantially less than the irreconcilables wished, Sinn Féin split and the civil war
followed. The moderate elements won, and out of that group emerged the
United Ireland Party (Fine Gael), now the second-largest political grouping in
the state. The losers in the civil war, or at least the more moderate losers,
eventually founded Fianna Fáil (the Republican Party), which since the election
of 1932 has been the largest party in the state. Thus during most of the period
since the late 1920s, the two parties which grew out of the Sinn Féin split and
the civil war have received 70 to 80 percent of first-preference votes cast and the
most seats in the Dáil (see tables 48 and 49). The Labour Party has generally
received upwards of 15 percent of the vote.

Governments in Ireland are generally formed by Fianna Fáil when it has the
majority of representation (or as a minority with support from independents) or
by a coalition of Fine Gael, Labour, and perhaps other minor parties (see table
50). The Republicans have not been coalition-minded. Especially interesting is
the fact that Fianna Fáil tends to occupy a center position on socioeconomic
matters, although the issue range in Irish politics is not very great, and such a
coalition formation pattern is, therefore, reasonable. These are the only government options that currently exist.

While minor parties and independents have occasionally played a reasonably
significant role (such as the National Labour Party* in the 1948-1951 govern-

ment coalition), these groups have generally had little impact on Irish politics. Most of the minor parties either were splinters from the more important groupings or later merged with those larger parties. Some parties bearing the same name in different time periods are basically unrelated except in outlooks.

Bibliography

Chubb, Basil. *Cabinet Government in Ireland*. Dublin: Institute of Public Administration, 1974.

——. *The Government and Politics of Ireland*. London: Oxford University Press, 1970.

Cohan, A. S., R. D. McKinlay, and Anthony Mughan. "The Used Vote and Electoral Outcomes: The Irish General Election of 1973." *British Journal of Political Science* 5 (July 1975): 363-383.

Farrell, Brian. *The Founding of Dáil Éireann*. Dublin: Gill and Macmillan, 1971.

Garvin, Tom. "Nationalist Elites, Irish Voters and Irish Political Development: A Comparative Perspective." *Economic and Social Review* (Dublin), vol. 8, no. 3 (July 1977): 161-186.

——. "Political Cleavages, Party Politics and Urbanisation in Ireland: The Case of the Periphery-Dominated Centre." *European Journal of Political Research* 2 (1974): 303-327.

——. "Political Parties in a Dublin Constituency." Ph.D. dissertation, University of Georgia, 1974.

Mair, Peter, "The Autonomy of the Political: The Development of the Irish Party System." *Comparative Politics*. vol. 11, no. 4 (July 1979): 445-465.

——. "Labour and the Irish Party System Revisited: Party Competition in the 1920s." *Economic and Social Review* (Dublin), vol. 9, no. 1 (October 1977): 59-70.

Manning, Maurice. *Irish Political Parties: An Introduction*. Dublin: Gill and Macmillan, 1972.

Moss, Warner. *Political Parties in the Irish Free State*. New York: Columbia University Press, 1933.

Penniman, Howard R. *Ireland at the Polls: The Dáil Elections of 1977*. Washington, D.C.: American Enterprise Institute, 1978.

Sacks, Paul. "Bailiwicks, Locality and Religion: Three Elements in an Irish Dáil Constituency Election." *Economic and Social Review* (Dublin), vol., 1, no. 4 (July 1970): 531-554.

Starr, Richard F., ed. *Yearbook of International Communist Affairs 1973*. Stanford, Calif.: Hoover Institution Press, 1973.

Whyte, J. H. "Ireland: Politics Without Social Bases." In *Electoral Behavior: A Comparative Handbook*, edited by Richard Rose. New York: Free Press, 1974.

Political Parties

AONTACHT ÉIREANN. Formed by a former Republican Party* (*Fianna Fáil*) minister, Kevin Boland, *Aontacht Éireann* followed the 1970 split in the Republican Party over the issue of reunification with the North (and the Republicans' somewhat eased position on that issue). *Aontacht Éireann* is a militantly republican group but has enjoyed no electoral success.

BLUESHIRTS. *See* UNITED IRELAND PARTY.

CLANN ÉIREANN. *See* IRISH PARTY.

CLANN NA POBLACHTA. *See* PARTY OF THE REPUBLIC.

CLANN NA TALMHAN. *See* PARTY OF THE SOIL.

COMMUNIST PARTY OF IRELAND. Ireland's original Communist Party was founded in 1921 but dissolved soon after. The party was reestablished in 1933, which is the date currently given by the party for its founding. In 1948 the Irish Communists established the Communist Party of Northern Ireland, and in the south formed the Irish Workers' Party. These two groups were reunited under the label of the Communist Party of Ireland at a March 1970 congress, though in the Republic the Communists still sometimes use the name of Irish Workers' Party for electoral purposes. Also, the Communist Party maintains two branches, one each to deal with the particular interests of the North and South.

The Irish Communist Party is affiliated with the "Official" Irish Republican Army (IRA) and rejects the violence used by the "Provisional" IRA. As such, the Communists advocate a reunification of North and South through nonsectarian, common interests of economics, employment, and opposition to the Common Market. The Communist Party of Ireland is very small (only a few hundred members), and it has had ideological competition from other small but more radical left-wing groups, such as the violent People's Democracy (*Saor Éire*), the Trotskyist Revolutionary Marxist Group, and the maoist Communist Party of Ireland (Marxist-Leninist). As the only one of these groupings attempting to participate in electoral politics, the Irish Communists contested two seats to the 1977 *Dáil*, running a joint electoral list with Ourselves Alone* (*Sinn Féin*). As with all previous bids, however, the Communists were unsuccessful. However, the electoral alliance, known as *Sinn Féin*, The Workers' Party, then won one seat in 1981 and three in 1982. It supported the formation of the Republican Party* government in 1982.

COMMUNIST PARTY OF IRELAND (MARXIST-LENINIST). *See* COMMUNIST PARTY OF IRELAND.

CUMANN NA nGAEDHEAL. *See* LEAGUE OF GAELS.

DEMOCRATIC LABOUR PARTY. The Democratic Labour Party was a personal grouping formed by Michael Lipper, a dissident Labour Party* member, to contest the 1977 election. Lipper won his seat from Dublin and was admitted to the Labour parliamentary delegation in that same year.

FARMERS' PARTY. The Farmers' Party was created in 1922 as the political arm of the Irish Farmers' Union. The party tended to represent the more affluent farmers and advocated free trade and expanded agricultural exports. The party's electoral success gradually weakened, and the Farmers' Party merged with the League of Gaels* in 1932. A new farm party, the Party of the Soil,* was founded in 1938.

FIANNA FÁIL. See REPUBLICAN PARTY.

FINE GAEL. See UNITED IRELAND PARTY.

IRISH PARTY (*Clann Éireann*). Organized in 1925 by Professor William Magennis, a *Dáil* deputy from the National University, the Irish Party broke away from the League of Gaels* over the Northern boundary settlement and the republican issue. The Irish Party contested seven seats in the 1927 election but died out shortly thereafter.

IRISH REPUBLIC SOCIALIST PARTY. The Irish Republic Socialist Party unsuccessfully contested one seat to the 1977 *Dáil*.

IRISH WORKERS' PARTY. See COMMUNIST PARTY OF IRELAND.

LABOUR PARTY (*Páirti Lucht Oibre*). Among western European democracies, only Ireland has failed to develop a major socialist party or group of parties. Since the end of World War II, Labour (and whatever other socialist parties existed, usually as breakaway groups) has managed to attain between ten and 15 percent of the vote in *Dáil* elections.

The Labour Party has its origins in Ireland's pre-World War I industrial turmoil; the party was founded in 1912 but lost its most important leader, James Connolly, in the Easter Rising of 1916. While it enjoyed some electoral success in the 1920s, the Labour Party never really took off; and by the time that the Republican Party* (*Fianna Fáil*) came to power in the early 1930s, Labour, the party of the working class, found itself to be second in popularity with working-class voters. That is still the case. Labour tends to be the party of the unionized workers, while *Fianna Fáil* is the party of the nonunionized. Labour also has a rural following among agricultural workers, especially in the east of the country.

While not an especially radical socialist-oriented party, after the 1954-1957 experience in government coalition Labour followed a more independent course, with little interest in coalition with the United Ireland Party* (*Fine Gael*), and Labour developed a somewhat left-leaning program. The election of 1969, in which Labour made no gains, propelled the party leadership into a coalition direction once again, and in 1973 Labour joined with United Ireland. Following the electoral defeat of 1977, the party changed its leadership, with Frank Cluskey taking the head post, and Labour became a more pronounced Dublin-based party, Dublin being the major working-class city in the Republic.

In the elections of June 11, 1981, the Labour Party won only 15 seats to the expanded 166-seat *Dáil*, giving the party the lowest percentage of total *Dáil* seats since 1957. Party leader Cluskey was not reelected to parliament by his constituency, and he was therefore replaced as party leader soon after the elections. In an effort to topple *Fianna Fáil* from government power, the new Labour leader, Michael O'Leary, brought the Labour Party into a proposed coalition with United Ireland. In the *Dáil* vote of June 30, 1981, the proposed coalition succeeded, as Garret FitzGerald of United Ireland was elected prime minister.

Labour retained 15 seats in the election of February 18, 1982, but remained outside of the governing coalition.

Further Reference. Orridge, Andrew, "The Irish Labour Party," in *Social Democratic Parties in Western Europe,* edited by William E. Patterson and Alastair H. Thomas (New York: St. Martin's Press, 1977).

LEAGUE OF GAELS (*Cumann na nGaedheal*). Originally the name of a turn-of-the-century cultural society, the League of Gaels was formed into a political party by William T. Cosgrave, whose purpose was to contest the election of 1923 in support of the 1921 Anglo-Irish Treaty. The League governed the country from 1922 to 1932, not a particularly happy time in Irish history given the conflict rising out of the separation of Northern Ireland from the Irish Free State. The League suffered splits, such as those leading to the formation of the Irish Party* and the National Party.*

Despite a shaky hold on government due to its own internal problems and its dependence upon other groups, the League of Gaels held power and managed to legitimize the new Irish governmental institutions. Therefore, when the Republican Party* (*Fianna Fáil*) came to power in 1932, transition was reasonably peaceful and the future of the established parliamentary democracy was assured. In 1933 the League joined with the National Centre Party* and other groups to form the United Ireland Party* (*Fine Gael*).

MULTICHANNEL TV PARTY. The Multichannel TV Party unsuccessfully contested one seat to the 1977 *Dáil*.

NATIONAL CENTRE PARTY. The National Centre Party was formed in 1932 as a result of a merger between the National Farmers' and Ratepayers' League* and elements from the old Nationalist Parliamentary Party.* The National Centre Party lasted only a very brief period, hardly one year. Its leadership brought it into the new United Ireland Party* (*Fine Gael*) when that group was founded in 1933. That same National Centre leadership became central to *Fine Gael* in the 1950s.

NATIONAL FARMERS' AND RATEPAYERS' LEAGUE. Formed in 1932 by Frank McDermot, an independent from Roscommon, the National Farmers' and Ratepayers' League sought to strengthen the position of agriculture and to point out the detrimental effects to be suffered by agriculture as a result of continued violence and economic warfare with Britain. Later in 1932, after merging with other groups drawn from the remains of the old Nationalist Parliamentary Party,* the National Farmers' and Ratepayers' League changed its name to the National Centre Party.*

NATIONAL H-BLOCK/ARMAGH COMMITTEE. *See* OURSELVES ALONE.

NATIONALIST PARLIAMENTARY PARTY. During the time when Ireland constituted an integral part of the United Kingdom of Great Britain and Ireland, Irish MPs (Members of Parliament) sat on equal footing with other members of the kingdom in the House of Commons. The Irish delegation solidified under the strong leadership of Charles Parnell in the late 1880s by advocating home rule for Ireland. Following the 1885 election, the Nationalists controlled approximately four-fifths of the Irish delegation, placing them in a strong bargaining position with William Gladstone's Liberal Party (*see* UNITED KINGDOM) in the British parliament.

Parnell's implication in a divorce scandal and the final defeat of a second home-rule bill in 1900 weakened the Nationalists beyond repair. John Redmond assumed the party leadership in that same year. However, by the time of the general election of 1918, the party had all but disappeared electorally. The Nationalists failed to achieve their objective and were replaced by the more militant Ourselves Alone* (*Sinn Féin*) in the voters' preferences. With the creation of the Irish Free State in 1921-1922, elements of the Nationalist Parliamentary Party found their way into various other groups, such as the National League* in 1926 and the National Centre Party* in 1932.

NATIONAL LABOUR PARTY. Breaking away from the Labour Party* in 1944, the National Labour Party charged Labour with being communist-dominated. After participation with Labour in the government coalition of 1948-1951, the National Labour Party rejoined the Labour Party.

NATIONAL LEAGUE. In 1926 some remnants of the old Nationalist Parliamentary Party* were reorganized by Captain William Redmond into the National League, which captured eight seats in the general election of 1927. The National League, which was basically a center group, merged with the League of Gaels* in 1931.

NATIONAL PARTY. The National Party was a breakaway group from the League of Gaels,* splitting with the more moderate League over the republican issue. The National Party died out in 1925.

NATIONAL PROGRESSIVE DEMOCRATIC PARTY. The National Progressive Democratic Party was formed in 1958 by Dr. Noel Browne, a former minister of health and member of the Party of the Republic. * Dr. Browne formed his new party as a result of a dispute over certain welfare policies. The National Progressive Democrats elected two candidates in 1961 and subsequently became part of the Labour Party. *

OURSELVES ALONE (*Sinn Féin*). Ourselves Alone was founded in 1905 by Arthur Griffith, growing out of a moderate, middle-class cultural movement known as the League of Gaels. (*See also* League of Gaels.) *Sinn Féin* became the embodiment of Irish nationalism by the close of World War I. However, the party's post-revolution leadership was willing to consider only limited independence for a united Ireland, hoping that if some ties to Britain were maintained, the Ulster Protestants could be mollified. Hence, subsequent splits over the 1921 Anglo-Irish Treaty, the Irish civil war, and the founding of the total-independence-oriented Republican Party* (*Fianna Fáil*) by a former *Sinn Féin* leader (Éamon De Valera) reduced *Sinn Féin* to a hard-core nationalist grouping. The party was abstentionist republican (that is, it did not recognize the Irish Free State) and began to die away after electoral defeat in 1927.

The contemporary *Sinn Féin* had been the political arm of the "Official" Irish Republican Army (IRA) until the mid-1970s. During that time, the party had no success at the polls in terms of electing candidates, but its voting total in some constituencies had been such that its lower preferences helped to elect candidates from other parties. By the late 1970s, two separate *Sinn Féin* groupings existed. The more radical and violence-prone elements of the party broke away to form the Provisional *Sinn Féin*, which represented the political wing of the Provisional IRA. They advocated complete British withdrawal from Northern Ireland.

Moderate elements of *Sinn Féin* attempted to recast the party as "*Sinn Féin*, The Workers' Party" (SFWP) in the 1977 *Dáil* election by joining with the Irish Workers' Party (*see* Communist Party of Ireland) in a united, but unsuccessful, electoral list. *Sinn Féin* electoral fortunes improved in 1981 with the Provisional *Sinn Féin* winning two seats running as the National H-Block/Armagh Committee, and the SFWP winning one.

In the 1982 *Dáil* election, the Provisional *Sinn Féin* vowed to abstain from the *Dáil* if any of its candidates were elected. The SFWP increased its representation to three seats and supported the formation of the Republican Party* government in 1982.

(The party has also existed in Northern Ireland. See OURSELVES ALONE, UNITED KINGDOM.)

PÁIRTI LUCHT OIBRE. See LABOUR PARTY.

PARTY OF THE REPUBLIC (*Clann na Poblachta*). The Party of the Republic was a fairly radical republican party with a strong interest in improving social welfare. Its founders were from the Irish Republican Army (IRA) of the 1930s who, like the leaders of the Republican Party* (*Fianna Fáil*) in the 1920s, decided that electoral politics were probably more productive than continued violence. The *Clann* leader was Sean MacBride, later a winner of the Nobel Peace Prize for his work with the United Nations.

The Party of the Republic enjoyed considerable early success, and in 1948 it elected ten members to the *Dáil*. As a result of this strength the *Clann* participated in a coalition government of 1948-1951. However, during this time the party split over a social welfare program, and the resulting furor led indirectly to the dissolution of the government. Weakened in the next two elections, the *Clann* did not participate in the 1954-1957 government when its earlier coalition partners were returned to power, though the *Clann* voted with that government. However, withdrawal of *Clann* support of the Republic-North border issue led to the dissolution of that government.

The *Clann's* party leadership had been instrumental in the 1949 decision to remove Ireland from the Commonwealth and to make Ireland a republic—a controversial decision, then and now, because of the failure to achieve unification. The Party of the Republic ceased operation after the 1965 election.

PARTY OF THE SOIL (*Clann na Talmhan*). Essentially a farmers' party, the Party of the Soil had a maximum *Dáil* membership of fourteen. Founded in 1938, the party first elected TDs (*Teachta Dala*, Member of the *Dáil*) in 1943. During 1948-1951, the party participated in the coalition government and did so once again during 1954-1957. After the election of 1957, the party began to decline; and after the 1965 election, it ceased to exist. Never a national party, the Party of the Soil represented disgruntled farmers during what was generally a difficult period in Irish politics. The party's decline coincided with the improving economic conditions that characterized the 1960s.

PEOPLE'S DEMOCRACY. *See* COMMUNIST PARTY OF IRELAND.

PROVISIONAL SINN FÉIN. *See* OURSELVES ALONE.

REPUBLICAN PARTY (*Fianna Fáil*). *Fianna Fáil* (literally, "Soldiers of Destiny") was founded in 1926 by Éamon De Valera, who drew with him a wing of the republican-oriented Ourselves Alone* (*Sinn Féin*). Both of these parties sought unification of Northern and Southern Ireland; but Ourselves Alone was willing to consider continued links to Britain, while the Republican Party supported the concept of a totally independent, unified Ireland.

Fianna Fáil was established once it was clear that the Irish Free State, as it was then called, would not be brought down by force. Thus the Republicans perceived that only through electoral success could they hope to influence the direction of the new state, particularly with regard to what they considered to be the primary remaining questions that had been left unresolved by the Anglo-Irish Treaty of 1921. *Fianna Fáil* was dedicated to the founding of an Irish republic that would include all 32 counties, without continued links to Britain; and the party was heavily committed to the restoration of a Gaelic Ireland, with strong emphasis on the use of the native Irish language rather than English.

From 1927 the party grew steadily. By 1932 it won enough seats to gain control of the government. From 1932 to 1981, *Fianna Fáil* has held power for 39 of 49 years, including two unbroken 16-year periods. Being the largest party in the republic, *Fianna Fáil* has received between 40 and 50 percent of the first-preference votes cast. The party draws its voting strength from all segments of Irish society, and it has come to be both the largest working-class and largest middle-class party at the same time. In terms of the political spectrum, the Republicans tend to be the center party on questions of social and economic policy, but they are somewhat more radical on the national question (that is, unification of the 26 southern countries with the six counties of the north), though they are opposed to violent means to achieve that end. *Fianna Fáil*, for example, was responsible for the virtual dismantling of the provisions of the Anglo-Irish Treaty, as well as gaining control of British naval bases in Ireland shortly before World War II broke out.

Under De Valera's leadership, Ireland remained neutral during World War II. After leading the party for some 33 years, De Valera relinquished the posts of prime minister and party leader to become president. He died August 29, 1975. The succeeding leaderships have continued to be troubled by the national question (as evidenced by the party split in 1970-1971, resulting in breakaway parties such as *Aontacht Éireann* *). Nevertheless, in 1977 the Republicans won the general election by the largest majority in Irish history, despite a constituency arrangement thought to be disadvantageous to the party. Among the political parties of the state, only *Fianna Fáil* is able to form a government on its own, eschewing coalitions. The Irish prime minister of 1977-1979 was the Republican Party leader, Jack Lynch, who in the 1977 election also won the most first-preference votes (20,077) of any candidate in the history of the republic. Lynch's personal position as leader of the party was weakened by his apparent moderation on the national question, and he resigned as prime minister and party leader on December 5, 1979. These posts passed to Charles Haughey, former minister of health and social welfare, who was seen to represent a harder line on the northern issue.

In the June 11, 1981, elections, *Fianna Fáil* won 78 out of 166 seats (47 percent) in the expanded *Dáil*. The party's failure to gain a parliamentary majority was attributed to the Republicans' inability to deal with Ireland's severe economic problems, including an 11 percent unemployment rate and an escalating national debt. Furthermore, though winning more seats than any other single party, *Fianna Fáil's* Charles Haughey lost the *Dáil's* prime ministership vote on June 30, 1981, when the United Ireland Party* (*Fine Gael*, with 65 seats) formed a coalition with the Labour Party* (15 seats). United Ireland's Garret FitzGerald became prime minister by the *Dáil* vote of 81 to 78.

During the referendum on the European Communities (*see* EUROPEAN

PARLIAMENT), the Republican Party leadership strongly supported entry into the Common Market. This policy could reflect both a desire to expand the Irish economy, as well as a way to reduce trade dependency on the United Kingdom. *Fianna Fáil* is known for its strong constituency organizations and its generally pragmatic approach to policy matters. Following the general election on February 18, 1982, it organized the government with the support of *Sinn Féin*, The Workers' Party (*see* Ourselves Alone). Charles Haughey again became prime minister.

SAOR ÉIRE. *See* COMMUNIST PARTY OF IRELAND.

SFWP. *See* OURSELVES ALONE.

SINN FÉIN. *See* OURSLEVES ALONE.

SINN FÉIN, THE WORKERS' PARTY. *See* OURSELVES ALONE.

SOLDIERS OF DESTINY. *See* REPUBLICAN PARTY.

TRIBE OF GAELS. *See* UNITED IRELAND PARTY.

TROTSKYIST REVOLUTIONARY MARXIST GROUP. *See* COMMUNIST PARTY OF IRELAND.

UNITED IRELAND PARTY (*Fine Gael*). *Fine Gael* (literally, "Tribe of Gaels") was formed in 1933 as an amalgam of the League of Gaels*; the National Centre Party* (basically an agricultural party); and the Blueshirts, a fascist-type organization that formed after Éamon De Valera came to power with the Republican Party* (*Fianna Fáil*) in 1932. With the emphasis of the Blueshirt element, *Fine Gael* performed badly in the early and mid-1930s elections. But during the latter part of that decade, the party's original leader, William T. Cosgrave (earlier the founder of the League of Gaels), reassumed the leadership; the party at that time again became a respectable, conservative grouping. *Fine Gael* entered government leadership in 1948 when, along with four other parties, it formed the government and the *Taoiseach* (prime minister) came from United Ireland. That coalition held power until 1951. A similar coalition came to power in 1954; and in 1973, *Fine Gael* joined with the Labour Party* to form a coalition government that lasted until 1977. *Fine Gael's* leader, Liam Cosgrave, son of William T. Cosgrave, was *Taoiseach*.

The United Ireland Party tends to draw the greater proportion of its support from larger farmers and the middle class. The party is conservative on socioeconomic issues, although in recent years it has been becoming more liberal, largely through the work of a younger generation of members and supporters who have been influenced by factors such as Vatican II. Indeed, *Fine Gael's* post-1977 leadership has been from the liberal wing of the party. Of Irish parties, United Ireland probably has the strongest commitment to Catholic social policy. The party can rely upon 30 to 35 percent of first-preference votes and, as a result, would play the leading role in any coalition government, as did occur in 1981.

In the June 11, 1981, election, under the leadership of Garret FitzGerald, the United Ireland Party won 65 out of 166 seats in the expanded *Dáil* (39 percent), an increase of ten percent over its share of seats in 1977. This gain corresponds to a 10 percent loss of seats experienced by the long-ruling Republican Party. By forming a coalition with the Labour Party, which obtained 15 seats, *Fine Gael* again headed the government, with party leader FitzGerald securing the prime ministership in a *Dáil* vote of 81 to 78 on June 30, 1981. Upon his election, FitzGerald announced his goals of working to solve Ireland's deteriorating economy and the nationalist question with regard to Northern Ireland.

Fine Gael is a moderate party with regard to the North, not insisting upon a British timetable for withdrawal. Also, it is a strongly pro-European party, largely because of the economic benefits that can be derived from Ireland's association with the European Communities (*see* EUROPEAN PARLIAMENT), especially in the agricultural sector. *Fine Gael* lost control of the government after the general election on February 18, 1982, when the Republican Party again gained the lead.

WOMEN'S POLITICAL ASSOCIATION. The Women's Political Association unsuccessfully contested one seat to the 1977 *Dáil*.

WORKERS' PARTY. *See* OURSELVES ALONE.

A. S. Cohan

TABLE 48. Distribution of Seats in Ireland's *Dáil* under the Irish Free State, 1921-1949

Party	1922	1923	June 1927	Oct. 1927	1932	1933	1937	1938	1943	1944	1948
Farmers' Party	7	15	11	6	4	—	—	—	—	—	—
Labour Party	17	16	23	13	9	9	15	9	17	8	14
National Centre Party	—	—	—	—	—	11	—	—	—	—	—
National Labour Party	—	—	—	—	—	—	—	—	—	4	5
Party of the Republic	—	—	—	—	—	—	—	—	—	—	10
Party of the Soil	—	—	—	—	—	—	—	—	14	11	7
Republican Party (*Fianna Fáil*)	35	44	44	57	72	76	68	76	66	76	68
United Ireland Party (*Fine Gael*)*	58	63	46	61	56	48	48	45	32	30	31
Independents and others	11	15	21**	14	12	9	7	8	9	9	12
Total	128	153	153	153	153	153	138	138	138	138	147

* Known as the League of Gaels prior to 1933.

** Includes five seats for Ourselves Alone (*Sinn Féin*).

545

TABLE 49. Distribution of Seats in Ireland's *Dáil* under the Republic of Ireland, 1949-1982

Party	1951	1954	1957	1961	1965	1969	1973	1977	1981	1982
Democratic Labour Party	—	—	—	—	—	—	—	1	—	—
Labour Party	16	19	12	16	22	18	19	17	15	15
National Progressive Democratic Party	—	—	—	2	—	—	—	—	—	—
Party of the Republic	2	3	1	1	1	—	—	—	—	—
Party of the Soil	6	5	3	2	0	—	—	—	—	—
Republican Party (*Fianna Fáil*)	69	65	78	70	72	75	69	84	78	81
United Ireland Party (*Fine Gael*)	40	50	40	47	47	50	54	43	65	63
Independents and others*	14	5	9	4	2	1	2	3	8	7
Total	147	147	143	142	144	144	144	148	166	166

* Includes one seat for *Sinn Féin*, The Workers' Party in 1981 and three in 1982.

TABLE 50.   Ruling Parties or Coalitions in Ireland since 1922

Years	Party or Coalition
1922-1932	League of Gaels
1932-1948	Republican Party
1948-1951	United Ireland Party Labour Party Party of the Republic Party of the Soil National Labour Party
1951-1954	Republican Party
1954-1957	United Ireland Party Labour Party Party of the Soil
1957-1973	Republican Party
1973-1977	United Ireland Party Labour Party
1977-1981	Republican Party
1981-1982	United Ireland Party Labour Party
1982-	Republican Party

Note: First-named party is dominant coalition party.

ITALY

The REPUBLIC OF ITALY (*Repubblica Italiana*) is situated on a peninsula which extends from the base of the Alps over 700 miles southward into the Mediterranean Sea. Italy's northern borders touch on France, Switzerland, Austria, and Yugoslavia. Also included within the Italian republic are the two large islands of Sardinia and Sicily, as well as numerous smaller islands in the surrounding waters of the Adriatic and Tyrrhenian Seas. The republic's current population is approximately 57 million (1980 estimate), which is relatively homogenous ethnically. Small pockets of ethnic minorities exist in the regions of Bolzano (Germans) and Val d'Aosta (French), and also near the Yugoslav border around the city of Trieste (Slovenes). In religious terms, Italy is overwhelmingly Roman Catholic, with Catholicism being the official state religion since 1929. Protestants and Jews make up only about one percent of the total population.

Italy continues to be hampered by sharp regional disparities in economic development, which have exacerbated long-standing sociopolitical differences between the industrialized north and the underdeveloped south. Geographical differences have resulted in contrasting patterns of political culture, with a strong impact on the structure and functioning of the Italian party system.

With its southernmost areas originally settled by the ancient Greeks, what is now the Republic of Italy became, of course, the home of the great Roman Empire. As the empire disintegrated in the 5th century A.D. and with the ensuing Middle Ages of European history, the Italian territory retained importance in that it continued as the base of Christianity through the presence of the Roman Catholic Church. Administratively, most of the Italian lands fell to control of the Franks under Charlemagne and then, by the late 10th century A.D., to the Holy Roman Emperors of the Germanic people. Locally, however, Italy by the later part of the medieval period had become controlled by powerful regional despots, many with allegiances to the monarchs of France or Spain, or to the sometimes politically ambitious popes of the Roman Catholic Church. The popes themselves were political authorities of a territorial band through central Italy known as the Papal States. Even by the 16th century, when most of Europe was ruled by either the Ottoman Empire or the Spanish and Austrian Habsburgs, the Papal States were permitted to continue under the popes' administration in deference to the importance of the church. The only other Italian area able to maintain autonomy during this period was the Republic of Saint Mark (Venice), long a European center of trade and finance.

In the first years of the 19th century, Italy, too, fell to France's Napoleon. The Congress of Vienna (1815), which attempted to reshape Europe's political and geographic boundaries after Napoleon's defeat, resurrected the Papal States and a few other Italian kingdoms, though these latter areas were in reality linked to the Austrian Habsburgs or to Spain (by now under the Bourbons). By 1848, the year of revolution throughout Europe, the Italians sought to remove themselves from foreign control. Three broad groups of Italian liberal elements emerged to rally for unification of the various Italian kingdoms, though there was lack of agreement as to the exact form the hoped-for nation should take. One moderate group advocated the supremacy of Piedmont, under the influence of Count Camillo di Cavour. Another grouping saw unification best achieved through the domination of the pope. A third group called Young Italy, created by Giuseppe Mazzini, advocated a democratic and constitutional form of government once unification was achieved. Mazzini (1805-1872) aimed his impassioned concepts particularly at the youth of Italy, instilling in them an ardent sense of Italian nationalism and liberalism. Mazzini's Young Italy movement inspired similar revolutionary movements in other European states. Throughout 1848, local revolutions succeeded in seizing control of many Italian kingdoms, including Mazzini's seizure of the Papal States, which briefly became the Roman Republic. By late 1849, however, the Bourbons and Habsburgs successfully reestablished their control over all of Italy.

Count Cavour (1810-1861) became the architect of Italian unification. In 1852 he rose to the post of chief minister of the Kingdom of Piedmont. While introducing modern agricultural and business techniques learned in western Europe, Cavour also brought the kingdom into various alliances with England and France in the hope of winning their support in an ultimate war for Piedmont's release from Austrian rule. In 1859, France did join Piedmont in battle against Austria, though the French negotiation of the settlement was less than Cavour had wanted—Piedmont secured Lombardy, but the area of Venice would remain with Austria. Yet many of the smaller, northern Italian states (Moderna, Parma, Tuscany, and the Emilia) requested annexation to Cavour's Piedmont. Then in May 1860, a radical nationalist, Giuseppe Garibaldi, pledged his loyalty to Piedmont's King Victor Emmanuel II and organized an army to conquer Italian lands still under foreign domination. Cavour, however, feared Garibaldi's republican sentiments and intended the unified Italian lands to exist under Piedmont's control. Cavour, therefore, sent his own army to secure the Papal States before Garibaldi could arrive. Taking all but Rome itself, Cavour's troops were joined by King Victor Emmanuel. As additional Italian states, particularly Naples and Sicily, sought union with Piedmont, it appeared that unification had been sufficiently achieved. On March 17, 1861, the creation of the Kingdom of Italy was announced. Victor Emmanuel II (of Piedmont's House of Savoy) would rule as king of Italy, the city of Turin would be the capital (moved to Florence in 1865), and Cavour would serve as prime minister.

By October 1870, most of the Italian peninsula was under a single regime. Venice was added to the kingdom in 1866 as war spoils, following an alliance with Prussia against Austria. In 1870, after the withdrawal of French forces from Rome, that city was seized by force and proclaimed the new capital of the Italian Kingdom. Only certain territories on the eastern border (Trentino, Trieste, Gorizia, and Venezia-Giulia) were still under Austrian control, and these Italian *irredenta* (unredeemed lands) would remain as a significant factor in Italy's politics until the end of World War I. Other factors, however, weakened the fledgling Italian state in the late 19th century: poverty, regressive taxation, and overcentralization produced peasant uprisings and even separatist movements in the south; while more generally, Italian politics were hampered by the Roman Question—the church-state conflict over the incorporation into the kingdom of the pope's former territories.

Italy's governing document in 1861 was based upon the 1848 constitution of Piedmont (*statuto fondamentale del regno*), which had been granted under Victor Emmanuel's father, King Charles Albert, and was therefore often referred to as the *Statuto Albertino*. This constitution provided for monarchical rule with a bicameral national assembly and a cabinet system. The assembly's upper house, the Senate, was based upon royal appointment for life, with eligibles drawn from among 31 various categories in Italian society. The lower house, the Chamber of Deputies, contained a variable membership elected by a narrow suffrage. The original Chamber was of 204 seats, but following successive territorial additions in 1866 (Venice) and 1870 (Rome), the membership rose to 508. Delegates served five-year terms. Prior to 1882, the suffrage began at 25 years of age and was limited to tax-paying male property-owners. It has been estimated that only 600,000 people (about 2.5 percent of the total population) made up the electorate at this time.

Italy has passed through several distinct stages of party development. Political parties were not sharply defined in the early postunification period. Illiteracy, economic backwardness (due to lack of capital and industrial resources), and restrictive suffrage requirements prevented the development of elaborate national party organizations. Local issues remained dominant at the national level, a result of Italy's disparities between north and south. The north, led by Piedmont, had attempted to mold itself to the cultural, commercial, and political forms of western Europe. The people of southern Italy, however, had always experienced oppressive despotism and economic servitude. Also, memories of the past great Italian kingdoms still overshadowed much of the nationalist sentiment, especially where unification had not improved the conditions of existence. Hence, political groupings in the postunification Chamber were largely ministerial divisions formed around leading notables.

Cavour's followers in the old Piedmont assembly had been called liberals, and these elements continued to serve in the new Italian parliament. After Cavour's untimely death on June 6, 1861, his "liberal" government bloc soon began to develop partisan cleavages. History, in retrospect, has named Cavour's heirs the "Historical Right" (*destra storica, see also* Italian Liberal Party), for they represented the industrial Italian north and in actuality stood for the conservative values of centralization, restricted suffrage, and regressive taxation. Those opposed to these policies, finding their strength primarily in the backward agrarian south, have been referred to as the "Historical Left" (*sinistra storica*). The Right remained dominant until 1876 when, after being weakened by internal dissension and unpopular policies, the political balance shifted to the Left.

The two principal figures of the Historical or Liberal Left were Agostino De Pretis (ruling 1876-1887) and Francesco Crispi (1887-1896). During these years, they succeeded in increasing national unity and made an attempt to address various social and political problems. From 1876 to 1887, under De Pretis, the Liberal Left extended the franchise, reaffirmed a policy of secularism, engaged in fiscal reforms, and pursued a strong military and naval policy. One of the most important political reforms was the broadening of the suffrage in 1882. It reduced the property and tax qualifications and lowered the voting age to 21 for those with a primary education or who could pass a literacy test. This change increased the eligible electorate from 600,000 to over two million. Italy also experimented with multimember electoral districts but reverted to single-member districts in 1891.

Although the suffrage requirements were substantially relaxed, electoral abstention was high. One factor was the continuing hostility of the papacy to the Italian regime and the Liberal Party policy of secularism. The papal encyclical of *Non Expedit*, issued by Pius IX in 1874, had ordered Roman Catholics to abstain from active political life—*ne életti ne élettori* (neither elected nor electors). The papal edict, however, was only partially successful. Only in the ultra-Catholic province of Bergamo was the ban fully effective. Over time, Catholics gradually ignored the ban and by 1905 were taking part in elections as voters and political candidates. The ban itself was not lifted until January 1919, by Pope Benedict XV, and led immediately to the creation of the Catholic-based Italian Popular Party. *

The Liberal Left majority began to break apart after 1882, forcing the De Pretis governing coalition to seek an alliance with moderates on the political right. This action led to a blurring of party differences, and parliamentary life degenerated into a system known as *transformismo*—a permanent governing majority based upon shifting centrist coalitions, held together by patronage-wielding parliamentary notables adept at manipulating elections, especially in the backward south. Crispi followed De Pretis as Liberal leader in 1887 after the latter's death. However, bank scandals, social unrest, and defeats of the Italian Army brought an end to Crispi's government with the general election of 1895. In 1900, King Humbert I (who had ascended the throne upon the 1878 death of Victor Emmanuel II) was assassinated by an anarchist. King Humbert was followed by Victor Emmanuel III (1900-1947), who was somewhat more liberal in outlook than his predecessor.

During the last decades of the 19th century, the large ministerial Liberal Party bloc broke up into a multitude of factions. Some, such as the Radical Party (1878-1921)* and the Italian Republican Party,* had grown out of splits in the Liberal ranks. Others, such as the Italian Socialist Party,* emerged as entirely new partisan elements. Explanations for partisan fragmentation at this time have been linked to such factors as the papal ban on participation, the preponderance of local and regional issues defining partisanship, and the basic inability of the parties to form compact, disciplined majorities to deal with important governmental issues.

The period between 1901 and 1914 is often referred to as the Giolittian period because of the dominance of Italian political life by Giovanni Giolitti and his Liberal Party (*see* table 51). Giolitti's four Liberal Party ministries were associated with civil progress and social welfare legislation, as well as financial and political reforms. The latter in 1912 provided for universal male suffrage at age 30, younger if certain educational requirements were met. Giolitti's reforms raised the total electorate from three million to approximately eight million and provided a strong incentive for partisan mobilization. Even with these reforms, however, the percentage of nonvoters in 1913 was approximately 40 percent.

Several important changes in party evolution occurred during the Giolittian era. Italy's involvement in colonial ventures culminated in war with Turkey (1911-1912) and gave Italy the Dodecanese Islands in the Aegean Sea, as well as areas in North Africa which formed Italian Libya. These actions, coupled with demands for the Italian *irredenta* from Austria, were spurred on by nationalists (such as those in the Italian Nationalist Association*), who advocated a policy of imperialism and catered to the expansionist sentiment in Italian society.

Some of the old political groups on the left, such as the Radicals and Republicans, began to decline at this time. The political left was now being mobilized by an expanding Socialist Party. The first Socialist congress had been held in 1891, and by 1894 attempts were being made by the Liberals to disband the Socialist Party and purge it from the electoral lists. Despite strong hostility, the Italian Socialist Party persisted as an important political grouping, although they failed to build a strong united organization due to divisive internal quarrels over ideology and strategy.

Another feature of party life during the Giolittian era was the reentry of Catholics into the political arena. At first they appeared as independents (in 1904) without a partisan label. This experience was to provide the foundation for a large Catholic party—the Italian Popular Party—which was to emerge after World War I with the introduction of proportional representation.

With weak political institutions, a fragmented party system, and an underdeveloped economy, Italy fought World War I at a cost of 600,000 lives. Ostensibly, Italy entered the war in 1915 against Austria and Germany to obtain the Italian *irredenta*. With the issue of irredentism solved by the war, the Republican Party and its allies lost an important partisan appeal.

The post-1918 period was chaotic: proportional representation and universal manhood suffrage overwhelmed the old political arrangements under an influx of alienated Socialist and Catholic voters who pressed for social reforms. The old Liberal Party was seriously weakened; and in the face of powerful new political machines, it was unable to maintain its dominant position. It broke apart into a series of fragments known collectively as Constitutionalists or simply Giolittian Liberals. The old political leadership could not cope with economic readjustment, disappointments at the peace conference, the frustrations of veterans, nor revolutionary and counterrevolutionary violence.

Proportional representation was introduced in 1919 and operated in conjunction with a party list system. Italy was reorganized into 34 electoral districts, with an average of 15 deputies per party list. The size of the Chamber of Deputies was increased to 535 to accommodate representation from the redeemed territories. The new electoral arrangements greatly benefitted the disciplined parties, the Socialists and Populists; after the 1919 election, the Socialists emerged as one of the largest cohesive groups in the Chamber with 156 seats, along with the Liberals (now reduced to a loose collection of assorted "democrats" and "constitutionalists") with 197 seats, and the newly-formed Populists with 100 seats. Electoral abstentionism remained exceedingly high at about 48 percent.

Disillusionment following World War I led to the formation of several small protest parties that sought special favors for sacrifices made during the war years (see Ex-Servicemen's Party). Among these groups were the Fascists. Beginning as a collection of small armed bands (fascio di combattimento), the Fascists had been organized by Benito Mussolini in 1919 as the vanguard of a revolutionary, patriotic, anti-Bolshevik movement (for a discussion of bolshevism, see RUSSIAN SOCIAL DEMOCRATIC WORKERS' PARTY, SOVIET UNION). At first, the Fascist movement attracted little support beyond the ranks of idle youth and disenchanted veterans. Only 35 Fascist deputies (including Mussolini) were elected in May 1921, for the most part on a ticket called the National Bloc (Fascist) (see National Fascist Party); Mussolini did not form an official party until November 1921. With its moderate leadership, Italy did little to stem the rising Fascist tide. Many Liberals viewed Mussolini's group as a potent counterweight to the militant left, and the Liberals sought to profit politically from Socialist-Fascist confrontations. Other elements, such as the Populists (who actually held the balance of power in the Chamber), were opposed to Giolitti personally and refused to support a strong Liberal government, even for the purpose of restoring civil order and combatting the increasingly strong National Fascist Party.

By October 1922, the Fascist momentum was too powerful to be stopped. Fascist sympathizers had sprung up within the bureaucracy, the military, among leading industrialists, and even among the royal family. In the wake of Mussolini's famous March on Rome (see National Fascist Party), he was invited by the king to form a coalition government. Armed with dictatorial powers that might be lost in the upcoming elections, Mussolini took over the administration and pressured parliament into passing a new electoral law (Acerbo Law) to insure future Fascist victories at the polls. Henceforth, Italy was divided into 15 large electoral districts. The party that received the largest number of votes (if not less than 25 percent) in the general election automatically received two-thirds of the Chamber seats. The remaining seats would be divided among the remaining parties on a basis proportional to their shares of the vote. Taking effect in 1924, this law resulted in the formation of an all-Fascist Party government.

The June 1924 murder of Giacomo Matteoti, an outspoken Socialist Party critic of the Mussolini regime, led to the boycotting of parliament by 124 opposition deputies. These representatives were deprived of their seats; and with the suppression of all parties except the Fascists by November 1926, Italy became a one-party state.

The development of Italy as a corporative state led to further changes in the nation's parliamentary system in 1928. The Chamber of Deputies was reduced to 400 members, nominated by various syndicates, cultural, and charitable organizations. The Grand Council of Fascism exercised a veto over all nominees, and voters were simply to vote yes or no on the final list. Universal suffrage was abolished, and citizens were required to pay syndicate dues or a minimum tax in order to be permitted to vote. Other changes were made in the structure of government so that by 1938 little remained of the old Liberal parliamentary constitution.

On February 11, 1929, Mussolini concluded the Lateran Accords with the Vatican, an agreement that officially settled the long-standing Roman Question. The Vatican was recognized as an independent state, given an indemnity, and granted a number of privileges in Italian society, including the designation of Roman Catholicism as the official religion of the state. Although the agreements initially raised Mussolini's prestige among devout Italian Catholics, friction soon developed over Fascist youth and educational policies and over Mussolini's fatal alliance with Germany's Adolf Hitler. The latter culminated in Italy's defeat in World War II and brought an end to the Fascist regime.

Mussolini fell from power in July 1943 following the Allied invasion of Italy. He was replaced by Marshal Pietro Badoglio, who promptly dissolved the National Fascist Party and began to dismantle the Fascist regime. After the capture of Rome by the Allies, King Victor Emmanuel III retired in favor of his son, Crown Prince Humbert II, and an armistice was concluded on September 29, 1943. Mussolini was rescued from imprisonment by German forces and set up as head of a German puppet state, known as the Salò Republic. As the Allied forces advanced across Italy, however, Mussolini was ultimately captured by Italian communist partisans in April 1945 and executed.

The post-World War II period was one of difficult attempts at renewal for the Italian party system. The economy was in shambles due to wartime destruction, and a political vacuum existed after 20 years of dictatorship under the dominance of the National Fascist Party. At first, political parties were banned by the Badoglio government, but in 1944 they began to reappear in the local Committees of National Liberation. Although about 20 parties emerged in early 1944, only six were of importance: the radical-democratic Action Party,* the Christian Democratic Party,* the Italian Communist Party,* the moderate-socialist Democratic Labor Party,* the Liberals, and the Socialist Party. With the exception of the Action and Socialist parties, all were represented in the coalition government of Ivanoe Bonomi, appointed December 12, 1944; and except for the Action Party, all had existed prior to the inception of the Fascist dictatorship (with the Christian Democrats being a postwar continuation of the old Italian Populists).

A constituent assembly was elected in 1946 and Italy opted, by a narrow margin, for a new constitution and a republican form of government. The constitution, which came into force in 1948, ended the monarchy and reestablished a bicameral legislative system with legal equality between the two houses. The republican form of government was not subject to change by amendment, and the constitution also forbade the reorganization of the Fascist Party in any form whatsoever. The Lateran Accords were incorporated into the new constitution under Article 7.

Italy's contemporary Senate of the Republic (*Senato della Repubblica*) is composed of variable membership. At the present, 315 senators are elected for five-year terms on the basis of regional constituencies. Five additional senators may be designated by the president of the republic, and all former presidents are automatically life members unless they specifically decline.

The Chamber of Deputies (*Camera dei Deputati*) had fluctuated between 556 and 596 members prior to 1963. After 1963, the size of the Chamber was fixed at 630 members, elected for five-year terms on the basis of direct universal suffrage beginning at age 21 (later lowered to 18). With the exception of the Val d'Aosta region, where a single-member majority system continues, Italian elections are now conducted under proportional representation on the basis of party lists. Constituencies are multimember, ranging from four to 40 deputies. Party representation is determined by the percentage of the total vote received in each constituency, with one deputy for every 80,000 votes. Surplus votes are accumulated into a national pool from which the parties may receive additional seats. Although this system (*imperiali*) tends to favor the larger parties, it does result in a more equitable distribution between votes and seats. Referenda are permitted for certain classes of legislation.

The president of the republic is chosen by an electoral college consisting of a joint session of parliament and an additional body of electors made up of three delegates from each of Italy's 19 regions. Presidents are elected for seven-year terms with no ban on reelection.

The post-World War II political scene in Italy was soon dominated by the rivalry between Catholics and marxists. The former were organized into the new Christian Democratic Party, which carried on the traditions of the pre-Fascist Italian Popular Party. Italy's marxists were composed of the Socialist and Communist left, who had built their political bases on a distinguished record of wartime anti-Fascist resistance and who sought to capitalize on the desire for social and political change. Proportional representation and regionalism, however, perpetuated a divisive multiparty structure, and difficulties in coalition-building led to frequent cabinet changes.

Italy's contemporary party system took shape following the 1948 election (see table 52). The Christian Democrats had succeeded in becoming the largest grouping; and until 1981, when the party leadership was rocked by a major scandal, the Christian Democrats constituted the core element of all postwar Italian governments (see table 53). The wartime unity of the left was shattered after a brief Popular Front experience (see Italian Communist Party and Italian Socialist Party), which ultimately broke down in 1948. The Socialists have remained divided since 1947 into several small parties disagreeing over strategies of cooperation with either the Christian Democrats or the Communists. Attempts at unity have had little success.

The Italian Communist Party has grown to become a powerful force in Italian society. It has competed with the Christian Democrats for control of local and regional governments and, in actuality, represents the principal opposition. The Italian Communists constitute the largest communist party in western Europe.

The Liberal and Republican parties continued in the postwar period with declining electoral fortunes. Their importance has been magnified by a willingness to serve as coalition partners with the Christian Democrats. Monarchism enjoyed a brief period of support in the immediate postwar period, but soon declined as an anachronistic political force (see Monarchist Party). Neofascism also emerged in the form of the Italian Social Movement,* despite the constitutional ban on the revival of the defunct Fascist Party. Both the Monarchists and other elements of the Italian political right have cooperated electorally on an intermittent basis.

Italy experienced a remarkable period of growth in the early 1960s, often referred to as the "Italian miracle." However, as the nation's economic pace slowed toward the end of the decade, rising discontent among students, workers, and other disadvantaged elements led to a disenchantment with the traditional Italian parties. This growing dissatisfaction fostered the emergence of various extremist groups, on both the right and left, who frequently pressed their political demands through violent means (for discussion of such groups on the right, see Italian Social Movement; and on the left, see groups included under Italian Socialist Party of Proletarian Unity [1964-1972]). Party fragmentation, cabinet instability, and rising levels of violence have placed considerable strain on the Italian political system.

The Italian government has been under the control of the Christian Democratic Party for over 30 years. Between 1948 and 1962, the Christian Democrats ruled alone or as leader of a center-right coalition with various combinations of Liberals, Republicans, or the Italian Democratic Socialist Party.* In 1962 the Christian Democrats embarked on a strategy known as the "opening to the left," which was designed to build a center-left coalition with the Italian Socialist Party.

Several center-left coalitions were constructed, although not without a considerable degree of friction and opposition within each party. The Christian Democrats attempted to expand this strategy in 1977 by negotiating a "historic compromise" with the Italian Communist Party (the principal opposition). Under an agreement concluded in 1978, the Communists agreed to support but not participate in the Christian Democratic government. The agreement broke down in 1979, after which the Christian Democrats returned to their former centrist coalition partners.

The Christian Democrats continued as the largest party after the 1979 election with 262 seats and a 38 percent share of the vote. They failed, however, to achieve majoritarian party status. The Communist electorate appeared to be in flux and dropped from 34 percent in 1976 to a little over 30 percent in 1979; Communist representation dropped from 228 seats to 201 between those years. By 1979 gains in seats were registered by the Radical Party (1955-)* (a dissident grouping from the Liberal Party) and by the Party of Proletarian Unity for Communism (see Italian Socialist Party of Proletarian Unity [1964-1972]) on the left; the Republicans and Liberals made gains in the center-right; and electoral support also increased for certain regional autonomist groups in Trieste and Val d' Aosta (see Regional Autonomist Parties), with the latter groups each securing one seat. The size of the 1979 electorate was approximately 42 million, and electoral abstention was about ten percent.

Criticism against Christian Democratic dominance of the Italian government has mounted in recent years. In May 1981, three government ministers were linked to a secret Masonic lodge known simply as P-2. This lodge had been under investigation for financial misconduct and possible acts of conspiracy against the state. The resulting furor led to a reorganization of the government under the premiership of Giovanni Spaldolini, a Republican Party senator, an event which has broken the 36-year-long monopoly of government by the Christian Democrats. Spaldolini's coalition includes the Liberals, Republicans, Christian Democrats, Socialists, and Democratic Socialists, and it represents Italy's forty-first postwar government.

Bibliography

Allum, P. A. Italy: Republic without Government. New York: W. W. Norton and Co., 1973.

Barnes, S. H. "Italy: Oppositions on Left, Right, and Center." In Political Oppositions in Western Democracies, edited by Robert A. Dahl. New Haven, Conn.: Yale University Press, 1966.

Blackmer, D. L. M., and Sidney Tarrow, eds. Communism in Italy and France. Princeton, N. J.: Princeton University Press, 1975.

Galli, Giorgio, and Alfonso Prandi. Patterns of Political Participation in Italy. New Haven, Conn.: Yale University Press, 1970.

Germino, Dante, and Stefano Passigli. The Government and Politics of Contemporary Italy. New York: Harper & Row, 1968.

Kogan, Norman. *A Political History of Postwar Europe*. New York: Praeger, 1966.

Lowell, A. Lawrence. *Government and Politics in Continental Europe*. Vol. 1. Boston: Houghton Mifflin, Co. 1896, pp. 189-231.

Penniman, Howard R., ed. *Italy at the Polls: 1976*. Washington, D.C.: American Enterprise Institute, 1977.

————.*Italy at the Polls: 1979*. Washington, D.C.: American Enterprise Institute, 1981.

Salomone, A. William. *Italy in the Giolittian Era: Italian Democracy in the Making*. Philadelphia: University of Pennsylvania Press, 1960.

Schepis, Giovanni. "Italy." In *International Guide to Electoral Statistics: 1*, edited by Stein Rokkan and Jean Meyriat. The Hague: Mouton, 1969.

Smith, Denis Mack. *Italy: A Modern History*. Ann Arbor: University of Michigan Press, 1969.

Spencer, H. R. *Government and Politics of Italy*. Yonkers-on-Hudson: World Book Co., 1932.

Vinciguerra, Mario. *I Partiti Italiani, 1848 al 1955*. Rome: Centro Editoriale dell'Osservatore, 1955.

Young, W. Hilton. *The Italian Left*. London: Longmans, Green & Co., 1949.

Zariski, Raphael. *Italy: The Politics of Uneven Development*. Hinsdale, Ill.: Dryden Press, 1972.

Political Parties

ACTION PARTY (*Partito d'Azione*: Pd'A). The Action Party (or the Party of Action) was formed by Italian antifascist exiles in Paris during the early 1930s. The Pd'A grew out of a loose radical-democratic movement known as Justice and Liberty (*Giustizia e Libertà*), which was organized and led by theoretician Carlo Rosselli. Rosselli and his followers sought to define a new theory of liberal socialism devoid of marxist determinism, the class struggle, and ultimate revolution. They laid greater emphasis on Italy's liberal revolution and the tradition of Giuseppe Mazzini (*see* Italy introduction) as a historical base. Although Rosselli's group acknowledged the need for structural reform of Italian society, they argued for carrying out these reforms within a system of individual freedom and political democracy rather than revolution and dictatorship.

The Action Party adopted the ideological tenets of the Justice and Liberty group and expanded upon these philosophies during the Action Party's clandestine period in Italy (1943-1945). The Pd'A newspaper, *L'Italia Libertà* (Free Italy), which was published and circulated secretly, advocated a new constitution with a republican form of government. It also called for the establishment of regional governments and economic development for the Italian south. In the area of social and economic policies, the Action Party called for elimination of Catholic Church privileges, for improved educational levels and facilities, and for land reform and selected nationalization.

The Pd'A was a small elitist party with little popular following. Unidentified with any important political group, the Pd'A was composed mainly of various intellectual elements such as teachers, writers, artists, and other professionals. It was predominantly anticlerical in outlook. As a party of ideas with strong personalities, the Pd'A was prone to many divisive forces that prevented development of a large mass base. The party also failed to distinguish itself politically as its program was similar to many others in the immediate postwar period, such as that of the Italian Liberal Party* and the Italian Republican Party.*

As a result of its organizational and ideological problems, the Action Party suffered a disastrous defeat in the 1946 parliamentary election (receiving only 1.5 percent of the vote and seven seats), after which the Pd'A disappeared as a separate political party. Prior to the election, the Action Party had already been seriously weakened by a split over cooperation with the Italian Communist Party,* as a result of which, in February 1946, Ferruccio Parri left the Pd'A to join the Democratic Labor Party* and the Italian Liberals in the National Democratic Union (see Italian Liberal Party). Also, Ugo La Malfa eventually allied his followers with the Italian Republicans. After the 1946 election, what was left of the Action Party merged with the Italian Socialist Party (PSI)* in October 1947 and became affiliated with the Nenni wing of the PSI.

ALLEANZA DEMOCRATICA DEL LAVORO. See MONARCHIST PARTY.

ANI. See ITALIAN NATIONALIST ASSOCIATION.

AO. See ITALIAN SOCIALIST PARTY OF PROLETARIAN UNITY (1964-1972).

ARMED PROLETARIAN NUCLEI. See ITALIAN SOCIALIST PARTY OF PROLETARIAN UNITY (1964-1972).

ASSOCIAZIONE NAZIONALISTA ITALIANA. See ITALIAN NATION-ALIST ASSOCIATION.

AVANGUARDIA NAZIONALE. See ITALIAN SOCIAL MOVEMENT.

AVANGUARDIA OPERAIA. See ITALIAN SOCIALIST PARTY OF PRO-LETARIAN UNITY (1964-1972).

BLOCCO NAZIONALE. See ITALIAN LIBERAL PARTY and NATIONAL FASCIST PARTY.

BLOCCO NAZIONALE DELLA LIBERTÀ. See MONARCHIST PARTY.

BRIGATE ROSSE. See ITALIAN SOCIALIST PARTY OF PROLETARIAN UNITY (1964-1972).

CATHOLIC COMMUNIST PARTY. *See* CHRISTIAN DEMOCRATIC PARTY.

CATHOLICS. *See* ITALIAN POPULAR PARTY.

CATTOLICI. *See* ITALIAN POPULAR PARTY.

CHRISTIAN DEMOCRACY. *See* CHRISTIAN DEMOCRATIC PARTY.

CHRISTIAN DEMOCRATIC PARTY (*Democrazia Cristiana*: DC). The DC is the heir to the pre-World War II Italian Popular Party,* which had been founded in 1919 by the Sicilian priest Don Luigi Sturzo. The Italian Popular Party was subsequently suppressed by the National Fascist Party* government in 1926.

The present-day Christian Democratic Party took shape during 1942-1943 when a number of former Popular Party leaders laid the foundations for a new political movement called Christian Democracy. The leader of the movement was Alcide De Gasperi, a prewar politician who had been imprisoned by the Fascist Party government but who later escaped to asylum in the Vatican. De Gasperi was joined by Stefano Jacini, Giovanni Gronchi, and Achille Grandi, who together constituted the DC directorate.

The Christian Democratic Party was officially organized in September 1943, with considerable assistance from various agencies of the Catholic Church, including a network of parishes, cooperatives, banks, and labor unions across Italy. The Christian Democrats benefitted from (1) the vast wartime prestige of Pope Pius XII, (2) the enfranchisement of women, (3) fear of the Popular Front (*see* Italian Communist Party and Italian Socialist Party), which drove large segments of the electorate into the DC ranks, (4) the fact that the most important leaders of the Italian political left, after some 20 years of exile in France and Russia, were simply out of touch with Italian postwar conditions, and (5) the decision of Pius XII to mobilize Italian Catholics for the electoral contest of 1948.

The original political program of the DC was similar to that of the old Italian Popular Party. The Christian Democrats accepted the division of church and state, although the DC emphasized the defense of Christian values and the positive contribution of the Catholic Church in Italian society, especially Catholic views on education and matrimony. In conjunction with this, the DC considered the Lateran Accords (*see* Italy introduction) to be valid. Strongly supporting the idea of constitutionalism, the DC urged the creation of regional governments and the strengthening of communal organizations. The DC also acknowledged the rights of labor to organize into unions and to participate in the management of their enterprises. Social programs of the DC stressed the need for social welfare, progressive taxation, and land reform. In foreign affairs, the DC was (and remains) a strong supporter of European integration and the NATO alliance.

As an interclass party attracting elements across the Italian socioeconomic spectrum, the DC has been prone to factionalism. Dissatisfied with the DC's antagonism toward communism, a group of intellectuals broke off from the DC to form the Catholic Communist Party in September 1944. Because of Vatican hostility, the Catholic Communists changed their name to the Christian Party of the Left (also known as the Christian Social Party). The grouping's avowed goal was to work for cooperation between the Christian Democrats and the Italian Communist Party.* The Catholic Communists, however, had little popular following outside of a small group of intellectuals, and the group soon disappeared after the 1946 election.

Other factions have become institutionalized within the DC itself, and segments of the party are found on all sides of any economic issue. Factionalism, however, is largely a matter of personalities involving prominent party leaders or notables. DC leaders are expected to provide patronage and a sense of identity; the followers provide a base of electoral strength. The result has been keen inner-party competition over control of party organizations and resources.

The DC scored electoral successes from the very beginning of the post-World War II Italian republic. The DC emerged as the strongest party in 1946, and after the 1948 election it became the principal element in all Italian governments until 1981. From 1947 to 1953, the DC followed a centrist policy by forming coalitions with the Italian Democratic Socialist Party,* the Italian Republican Party,* and the Italian Liberal Party.* However, after 1954 sharp differences arose among the three center parties and ultimately doomed the DC centrist approach to governing. Between 1954 and 1962, the DC occasionally governed alone as a minority government.

In 1962 the DC embarked on a program of reconciliation with the Italian Socialist Party.* Known as the "opening to the left" (*apertura a sinistra*), this cooperation resulted in the formation of DC coalition governments that included Socialists during December 1963-June 1968, December 1968-March 1970, August 1970-February 1972, July 1973-November 1974, and April 1980-June 1981. Attempting to expand the opening to the left, in March 1977 the DC took steps to conclude a "historic compromise" with the Italian Communist Party (PCI). The compromise led to an agreement in March 1978 in which the Communists would support but not participate in the DC government. The agreement lasted until January 1979 when the PCI withdrew, at which time the DC returned to its former center coalition partners. This event cost the DC some leftist support; in the June 1979 election, the DC vote declined slightly, though the party remained the largest political formation in Italy.

Support for the Christian Democrats had begun to erode in the late 1970s amid criticism and scandals. As the governing party, the DC had long been accused of government corruption and favoritism. Such "favoritism," however, was widespread, as the DC tried to be everything for everybody—a "catch-all" party seeking to retain power at all costs. In May 1981, with criticism reaching an apex, the Christian Democratic Party was displaced by a Republican Party coalition after three ministers of Arnaldo Forlani's DC government (as well as other government members) were linked to a secret Masonic lodge known as P-2. The lodge had been under investigation for financial misdeeds and possible acts of conspiracy against the state. Although the DC retained most of the cabinet seats, the party no longer holds either the premiership or the presidency (the latter had been relinquished to Sandro Pertini, a Socialist, in 1978).

The current membership of the DC is about 1.5 million, composed primarily of civil servants, small farmers, teachers, and homemakers. There is also an important working-class element. The DC is organized into approximately 13,000 local centers, 94 federations, and over 55,000 precinct committees. Members elect delegates to a National Congress, which meets periodically, usually every two years. This body chooses a National Council, which in turn elects the party Directorate and Secretariat. The DC is also allied with a number of economic organizations, such as the Italian Confederation of Free Trade Unions (CISL) and the National Federation of Small Farmers (*Coldiretti*). The Christian Democrats support numerous publications, of which the most important is the daily *Il Popolo* (The People).

Further Reference. Webster, R., *Christian Democracy in Italy, 1860-1960* (London: Hollis and Carter, 1961); Zuckerman, Alan S., *The Politics of Faction: Christian Democratic Rule in Italy* (New Haven, Conn.: Yale University Press, 1979).

CHRISTIAN PARTY OF THE LEFT. *See* CHRISTIAN DEMOCRATIC PARTY.

CHRISTIAN SOCIAL PARTY. *See* CHRISTIAN DEMOCRATIC PARTY.

CLN. *See* DEMOCRATIC LABOR PARTY.

COMBATTENTI. *See* EX-SERVICEMEN'S PARTY.

COMMON MAN FRONT (*Fronte dell'Uomo Qualunque; Uomo Qualunque*: UQ). The Common Man Front was first organized as a loose political movement in 1944 by Guglielmo Giannini, editor of the satirical weekly, *L'Uomo Qualunque* (The Common Man). An extremely popular periodical in the immediate post-war period, *L'Uomo Qualunque* claimed to have a circulation of over 700,000. The publication criticized Italian political parties and politicians, and it continually highlighted the weaknesses of parliamentary democracy. It was opposed to technicians and specialists in government, instead lauding the virtues of the average or common man. Accused of fascist leanings, the movement's offices in Milan were subjected to a police raid in 1945.

The first congress of the Common Man Front was held in February 1946; and following the parliamentary election in June, the UQ emerged unexpectedly as the fourth-largest party in the Italian parliament with about 5.3 percent of the vote and 30 deputies. In December 1946, the party changed its name to the

Liberal Democratic Front of the Common Man (*Fronte Democratica Liberale dell'Uomo Qualunque*: FDLUQ) in an attempt to shed its neofascist image. The FDLUQ claimed to espouse liberal democratic principles and advocated an orderly reform of Italian society. It directed its appeals to middle-class voters in an opposition to both communism and socialism.

The FDLUQ offered to merge with the Italian Liberal Party* in early 1947, but the Liberals refused. Dissension within the FDLUQ peaked in November 1947 when Giannini attempted to align the party with elements of the political left who were attempting to bring down the centrist government coalition. The FDLUQ split into various progovernment and antigovernment factions. In January 1948, prior to the election in April of that year, Giannini and Francesco Nitti led a breakaway group into joining with the Liberals to form an electoral alliance known as the National Bloc (Liberal) (*see* Italian Liberal Party). The Bloc lost heavily to both the Christian Democratic Party* and the Italian Communist Party.* At about the same time, an ultranationalist group was formed under the leadership of Emilio Patrissi. Known as the National Movement for Social Democratic Action (*Movimento Nazionalista per la Democratizzazione Sociale*), Patrissi's grouping failed to elect a single deputy despite considerable financial support.

What remained of the FDLUQ continued under the old name of the Common Man Front for a very brief period after the 1948 election. The remnants of the Front were eventually absorbed into the Italian Social Movement.*

COMMUNIST PARTY OF ITALY (MARXIST-LENINIST). *See* ITALIAN COMMUNIST PARTY.

COMMUNITÀ. *See* COMMUNITY OF CULTURE OF THE WORKERS AND PEASANTS OF ITALY.

COMMUNITY FRONT. *See* COMMUNITY OF CULTURE OF THE WORKERS AND PEASANTS OF ITALY.

COMMUNITY OF CULTURE OF THE WORKERS AND PEASANTS OF ITALY (*Concentrazione della Cultura, degli Operaii et dei Contadini d'Italia*; also known simply as the Community Front: *Communità*). The Community of Culture was founded by Adriano Olivetti to contest the 1958 parliamentary election. The grouping was composed mainly of left-center elements who advocated a type of nonmarxist Christian socialism stressing cooperation instead of class conflict. Waging a strong campaign against poverty and unemployment in southern Italy, the *Communità* succeeded in electing one deputy in 1958, after which it disappeared as a political group.

COMPASS CARD. *See* ITALIAN SOCIAL MOVEMENT.

CONCENTRAZIONE DELLA CULTURA, DEGLI OPERAII ET DEI CONTADINI D'ITALIA. *See* COMMUNITY OF CULTURE OF THE WORKERS AND PEASANTS OF ITALY.

CONSERVATIVE CATHOLICS. *See* ITALIAN POPULAR PARTY.

CONSERVATORI CATTOLICI. *See* ITALIAN POPULAR PARTY.

CONSTITUTIONALISTS. *See* ITALY INTRODUCTION.

CONTINUOUS STRUGGLE. *See* ITALIAN SOCIALIST PARTY OF PRO-LETARIAN UNITY (1964-1972).

DC. *See* CHRISTIAN DEMOCRATIC PARTY.

DEMOCRATIC ALLIANCE OF LABOR. *See* MONARCHIST PARTY.

DEMOCRATIC LABOR PARTY (*Partito Democratico del Lavoro*). The Democratic Labor Party (or Labor Democrats) traced its ancestry to the Reformist Socialist Party, which was separated from the Italian Socialist Party* in 1912. In contrast to the revolutionary policies of the majority, the Reformist Socialists emphasized a program of gradual social change within the framework of the Italian parliamentary system. The Reformists attempted to cooperate with the Italian Socialist Party until 1922, at which time the Reformists changed their name to the Unitary Socialist Party (1922-1926), which was banned with all other political parties by the National Fascist Party* regime in 1926.

The leaders of the Reformist or Unitary Socialists, Ivanoe Bonomi and Meuccio Ruini, reorganized their grouping as the Democratic Labor Party in 1943, and the new group became one of the constituent parties in the antifascist National Liberation Committee (CLN). The Labor Democrats, however, were able to maintain only a small electoral base in central and southern Italy; the party was virtually nonexistent in the north. Prior to the 1946 election, the Democratic Labor Party merged with elements of the Action Party* and the Italian Liberal Party* to form the National Democratic Union (*see* Italian Liberal Party), after which the Labor Democrats disappeared as a separate political grouping.

DEMOCRATIC PARTY OF PROLETARIAN UNITY FOR COMMUNISM. *See* ITALIAN SOCIALIST PARTY OF PROLETARIAN UNITY (1964-1972).

DEMOCRAZIA CRISTIANA. *See* CHRISTIAN DEMOCRATIC PARTY.

DEMOCRAZIA NAZIONALE-COSTITUENTE DI DESTRA. *See* ITALIAN SOCIAL MOVEMENT and MONARCHIST PARTY.

DEMOCRAZIA PROLETARIA. *See* ITALIAN SOCIALIST PARTY OF PRO-
LETARIAN UNITY (1964-1972).

DESTRA NAZIONALE. *See* ITALIAN SOCIAL MOVEMENT and MON-
ARCHIST PARTY.

DN. *See* ITALIAN SOCIAL MOVEMENT and MONARCHIST PARTY.

DP. *See* ITALIAN SOCIALIST PARTY OF PROLETARIAN UNITY
(1964-1972).

ECONOMIC PARTY (*Partito Economico*). Appearing after World War I, the
Economic Party was a small liberal grouping. The party formed part of a broad
group of centrist parties known as the Constitutionalists or Giolittian Liberals
(*see* Italy introduction). There was little programmatic difference among these
various parties; they differed only in the personalities of their leaders. The
Economic Party secured seven seats in the 1919 parliamentary election and only
five seats in 1921, after which the party disappeared.

EX-SERVICEMEN'S PARTY (*Combattenti*). Formed after World War I, the
Ex-Servicemen's party was to serve as a vehicle for the protection of interests of
military veterans and to commemorate their wartime sufferings and sacrifices.
The *Combattenti* grew out of the national Ex-Servicemen's Organization, founded
by Francesco Nitti, which had lobbied for settling veterans on small plots of farm
land. The Ex-Servicemen's Party was strongly opposed to socialism and pacifism, and it remained bitter over the lack of patriotism demonstrated by many
Italian workers during the war years.
    The *Combattenti* succeeded in electing 20 deputies in 1919, but representation
declined to ten in 1921 with the rise of the National Fascist Party.* Benito
Mussolini's emphasis on veterans' self-defense caused many elements in the
Ex-Servicemen's Party to join Mussolini's Fascists, thereby eroding the *Combattenti*
electoral base. Although some elements of the *Combattenti* later broke with the
Fascists and joined the opposition, the Ex-Servicemen's Party ceased to exist
after 1922.

FASCI D'AZIONE RIVOLUZIONARIA. *See* NATIONAL FASCIST PARTY.

FASCIO DI COMBATTIMENTO. *See* NATIONAL FASCIST PARTY.

FDLUQ. *See* COMMON MAN FRONT.

FIGHTING BANDS. *See* NATIONAL FASCIST PARTY.

FRIULI MOVEMENT. *See* REGIONAL AUTONOMIST PARTIES.

FRONTE DELLA GIOVENTU. *See* ITALIAN SOCIAL MOVEMENT.

FRONTE DELL'UOMO QUALUNQUE. *See* COMMON MAN FRONT.

FRONTE DEMOCRATICA LIBERALE DELL'UOMO QUALUNQUE. *See* COMMON MAN FRONT.

GAP. *See* ITALIAN SOCIALIST PARTY OF PROLETARIAN UNITY (1964-1972).

GIOLITTIAN LIBERALS. *See* ITALY INTRODUCTION.

GIOVANE ITALIA. *See* ITALIAN SOCIAL MOVEMENT.

GIOVANI FASCISTI. *See* NATIONAL FASCIST PARTY.

GIUSTIZIA E LIBERTÀ. *See* ACTION PARTY.

GRUPPI AZIONE PARTIAGIANA. *See* ITALIAN SOCIALIST PARTY OF PROLETARIAN UNITY (1964-1972).

HISTORICAL LEFT. *See* ITALY INTRODUCTION.

HISTORICAL RIGHT. *See* ITALY INTRODUCTION.

INIZIATIVA SOCIALISTA. *See* ITALIAN DEMOCRATIC SOCIALIST PARTY.

INTERNATIONAL COMMUNIST PARTY. *See* ITALIAN COMMUNIST PARTY.

ITALIAN COMMUNIST PARTY (*Partito Comunista Italiano*: PCI). The Italian Communist Party was founded at Leghorn, on January 21, 1921, by secessionists from the Italian Socialist Party* who were opposed to the inclusion of right-wing elements in that party and who sought adherence to the Comintern. The antecedents of the Communist faction can be found in the intransigent "maximalist" wing of the Socialist Party. The PCI's principal early leaders were Antonio Gramsci, founder, theoretician, and later party secretary; Amadeo Bordiga; and Palmiro Togliatti. Gramsci, who died in 1937 after 11 years internment in an Italian prison, has been recognized as an original marxist thinker.

At the outset, the PCI was closely tied to the Comintern and the Communist Party of the Soviet Union (*see* SOVIET UNION). Most of the ideological conflicts and leadership struggles affecting the Soviet party during the interwar years also spilled over into the PCI. A trotskyite International Communist Party

(*Partito Comunista Internazionale*) was formed during this time; it reappeared after World War II but had no electoral success. The PCI also experienced an important factional quarrel over cooperation with noncommunist forces. Amadeo Bordiga, a doctrinaire marxist-leninist, was opposed to any form of collaboration, while Antonio Gramsci advocated collaboration in an antifascist front. Bordiga's faction was defeated in January 1926 with the adoption of the PCI's Lyons Theses, which paved the way for "partial action" with noncommunist political groups to further the aims of the working class.

The Communists first appeared in the Italian parliament with 15 deputies elected in May 1921, followed by 19 elected in April 1924. Initially the Communists were unmolested. However, following the ban on political parties in November 1926, the Communist deputies were unseated and persecuted in a series of conspiracy trials conducted by the Fascist Special Tribunal for the Defense of the State. Many of the important PCI leaders were arrested and imprisoned, including Gramsci; others, such as Palmiro Togliatti, escaped into exile in the Soviet Union. Togliatti served as a member of the Comintern's Presidium during 1934-1943, and he engineered the antifascist Unity of Action Pact between the PCI and the Italian Socialist Party, signed in Paris in 1934.

The PCI was the only political group in Italy with the organizational skills required to launch a successful resistance operation against the National Fascist Party* regime. Although small in numbers, the party apparatus was disciplined and familiar with clandestine activities. In addition, many of the Communist leaders (such as Luigi Longo) had taken part in the Spanish Civil War (*see* SPAIN) where they had gained valuable military experience.

Returning to Italy in 1943 as party secretary, Togliatti built on PCI strengths, which included popular prestige from the party's anti-Fascist record; a base in the historic strongholds of the alienated left; the prestige of the victorious Soviets; Russian financing; and the tactic of emphasizing constitutionalism while downplaying anticlericalism and revolution in favor of recovery. After World War II, the Communist delegates to the Italian constituent assembly voted for the inclusion of the Lateran Accords (*see* Italy introduction) in the new Italian constitution.

In another postwar move, the Communists succeeded in defeating both the Socialists and the Christian Democratic Party* over control of the giant National Confederation of Italian Labor (CGIL). Factionalism and schisms within the Socialist and Christian Democratic organizations contrasted sharply with the apparent monolithic "democratic centrism" of the PCI.

The Italian Communists also benefitted from widespread control of local administrations and a good record of efficiency in such places as Bologna. The PCI was, especially after 1960, the only serious opposition to the entrenched Christian Democrats. A network of newspapers, credit unions, and sports clubs helped the Communists to insulate their growing clientele. Yet the main strength of communism in Italy is the PCI itself. The party's very size has made impossible the creation of a stable, reformist majority to attack structural obstacles to social and economic advantage. Hence, Italy's problems of late industrialization linger, compounded by labor militancy and a lack of natural resources.

The PCI participated in the cabinet from 1944 to 1947, with Togliatti often serving as minister of justice. Abruptly dismissed in May 1947, Togliatti forged the Italian Communist-Socialist "Popular Front," whose unexpectedly decisive defeat in the April 1948 election called for a new strategy. Togliatti, convinced that the PCI would be a minority grouping for his lifetime, embarked on a long-term, bridge-building program toward key groups, like Catholics and small farmers. The popular front tactic gave way to a call for a "historic compromise" between the PCI and the Christian Democrats, who were also seeking to expand their electoral support across the political spectrum. For Togliatti, polarization of the frontist type was rejected as having caused the triumph of fascism a generation earlier. The Allende experience in Chile reinforced PCI determination not to divide Italy into two camps. Thus, although the party continued to view the Soviet Union as a model society, the Italian Communists claimed to accept pluralism and free elections.

This strategy benefitted the PCI electorally. With an initial strength of 19 percent of the electorate in 1946, the PCI grew to 25.3 percent in 1963. Togliatti, pioneer of this Italian road to socialism, died in 1964 and was succeeded as the party's secretary-general by Luigi Longo and then in 1972 by Enrico Berlinguer, both of whom continued to cultivate an image of the PCI as parliamentary and respectable. This effort has involved a dilemma: cooperation in the solution of national problems undercuts PCI appeal to the alienated political left, while a policy of intransigence would appear irresponsible.

Despite its outward appearance of monolithic unity, the PCI has not been immune to factional strife, although early factions generally remained latent to the outsider and confined to the highest levels of party leadership. As with the internal conflicts of the 1920s, dissent has generally crystallized around ideological or policy disputes rather than around personalities. Later disputes involved the popular front strategy and the PCI's independence from the Soviet Union.

During the 1960s, however, factional strife became more overt. Pro-Chinese and pro-Castro factions emerged among the younger PCI members, in addition to disputes between those who continued to oppose or support cooperation with the left or the right. Dissent within the PCI was alluded to as early as 1963; the situation was then exacerbated with the outburst of student unrest in 1968-1969 and with Italy's "hot autumn" of general strikes in 1969.

The PCI's centrist position was firmly established by Longo at the party's congress in February 1969. This action precipitated a number of pending defections and expulsions from the party. Some led to the formation of new left-wing groups, such as the Manifesto Movement (*see* Italian Socialist Party of Proletarian Unity [1964-1972]) in 1971. Other factions formed new dissident communist parties, such as the Communist Party of Italy (Marxist-Leninist) (*Partito Comunista [Marxista-Leninista] de Italia*: PC[ML]I) and the pro-Chinese Unified Communist Party of Italy (*Partito Comunista Unificado de Italia*: PCUI). The latter two parties have few followers and no parliamentary representation.

The current line of the Italian Communist Party is supportive of polycentrism within the international communist movement and advocates a peaceful, democratic path to socialism. The PCI has sought to be included in the government, but these overtures have been rebuffed by the dominant Christian Democrats and their coalition allies. The only PCI inroad was after the 1976 election when, with 228 out of 630 seats, PCI notable Pietro Ingrao was elected as president of the lower house of parliament.

The PCI organization is based upon democratic centralism and cooptation of leaders. Local cells are united into federations, and a national congress is held every four years to decide party policy and elect higher party organs. The major PCI publication is the daily newspaper *L'Unità* (The Unity). With roughly 1.7 million party members, the PCI attracts nearly half of the working-class vote. The party has also been "southernized" owing to an expansion in the south of Italy (its main source of new voters) and the conversion of southern immigrants in northern cities. Working-class persons are rare in higher leadership posts, however, especially in the south.

The PCI's electoral history shows impressive gains: 19 percent of the vote in 1946 to 30.4 percent in 1979, with close to a majority in certain provinces in the "red belt" regions of Tuscany, Emilia-Romagna, and Umbria. Yet while the Italian Communists have demonstrated a substantial electoral increase in the past three decades, the entire Italian political left has grown more slowly. Southerners aside, the Italian Communist Party appears to have grown at the expense of the nation's other leftist parties.

Further Reference. Cammett, J., *Antonio Gramsci and the Origins of Italian Communism* (Stanford, Calif.: Stanford University Press, 1967); Grant, Amyot, *The Italian Communist Party* (New York: St. Martin's Press, 1981).

ITALIAN DEMOCRATIC PARTY. *See* MONARCHIST PARTY.

ITALIAN DEMOCRATIC PARTY OF MONARCHICAL UNITY. *See* MONARCHIST PARTY.

ITALIAN DEMOCRATIC SOCIALIST PARTY (*Partito Socialista Democratico Italiano*: PSDI). The PSDI traces its origins to January 1947 when Guiseppe Saragat and his followers seceded from the Italian Socialist Party (PSI).* Saragat was opposed to PSI cooperation with the Italian Communist Party* in the Popular Front (*see* Italian Communist Party and Italian Socialist Party)—a policy pursued by PSI leader Pietro Nenni. Saragat was joined by other Socialist Party dissidents, such as those following Matteo Matteotti in the grouping called the Socialist Initiative (*Iniziativa Socialista*), and the secessionists were originally known as the Socialist Party of Italian Workers (*Partito Socialista dei Lavoratori*

Italiani: PSLI), also known simply as the Saragat Socialists. In the 1949 parliamentary election, the PSLI joined with other leftist factions in an electoral alliance called Socialist Unity (*Unità Socialista*). This election remains as the high point of electoral strength (seven percent) for the Saragat Socialists.

In May 1951, the PSLI merged with the Unitary Socialist Party (1949-1951) (*Partito Socialista Unitario*: PSU). The PSU had been formed in December 1949 by Socialist Party dissidents Giuseppe Romita and Ignazio Silone as an attempted bridge between the Saragat and Nenni Socialist parties. (This PSU should not be confused with an earlier Unitary Socialist Party that had formed in 1922. *See* Italian Socialist Party.) The grouping resulting from the PSU-PSLI merger was called the Unitary Socialist Party of Italian Workers (*Partito Socialista Unitario de Lavoratori Italiani*: PSULI). The new PSULI name was short-lived, however, as the party name was changed later in the summer of 1951 to the Socialist Party: Italian Section of International Socialism (*Partito Socialista: Sezione Italiana del Internazionale Socialista*: PS,SIIS). In January 1952, with the addition of other leftist factions, the party's designation was altered once again, this time to the Italian Democratic Socialist Party (PSDI).

Verbally marxist, the PSDI has stood for gradual economic reform and the construction of a welfare state, rather than for a socialist society in Italy. The party has been firmly supportive of NATO and European integration. Although opposing state aid to parochial schools, the party's anticlericalism has been muted, and the PSDI has provided important backing for a number of cabinets formed by the Catholic-oriented Christian Democratic Party.* The PSDI remains steadfast in its opposition to any collaboration with the Italian Communist Party, either electorally or as part of any governing coalition.

When the Italian Socialist Party (PSI) reconsidered its political position in the 1960s, that party began to move away from the Communists and toward cooperation with the Christian Democrats. Approving of this action, the Italian Democratic Socialists reunited with the PSI in October 1966, forming the Unified Socialist Party (PSU) (*see* Italian Socialist Party). However, a poor poll for the new PSU in the 1968 election led the PSI to a renewed interest in its former ally; and the PSU merger broke apart in July 1969, once again over the question of collaboration with the Italian Communist Party. Both the Socialists and the Democratic Socialists reverted to their premerger designations, though a small, right-wing faction led by Mario Tanassi and Mauro Ferri continued under the label of the Unitary Socialist Party for a brief period.

The Italian Democratic Socialist Party has played an important role in the Italian labor scene, though the party's base of electoral support is largely composed of skilled and white-collar workers from the Milan-Genoa-Turin geographical triangle. The PSDI is organized into approximately 3,000 local groups, which in turn are linked to provincial and regional committees. The party is governed by a central committee and a smaller executive body, both elected by the national party congress. Estimates of party membership vary from 50,000 to

100,000. In recent years, the PSDI's electoral support has stabilized at about 3.5 percent in any national election.

ITALIAN FARMERS' PARTY. See PEASANT PARTY.

ITALIAN LIBERAL PARTY (*Partito Liberale Italiano*: PLI). From the time of national unification until the end of World War I, the Italian Liberal Party was the dominant political party in Italy. Founded as a parliamentary group in 1848, the Liberals enjoyed vast prestige as the party of Count Camillo di Cavour, the architect of modern Italy (*see* Italy introduction). The power of the Liberal Party was rooted in severe suffrage restrictions and the refusal of qualified Catholics to participate in the politics of an illegitimate state (*non-expedit, see* Italian Popular Party for further discussion). The Liberals, in retrospect, acquired the title of the "Historical Right" (*destra storica, see also* Italy introduction), for the party actually stood for the conservative values of retrenchment, free trade, regressive taxation, centralization, coexistence with the Vatican, and peace abroad (despite entry under Liberal rule into the Austro-Prussian War to obtain Venetia).

After Cavour's death in 1861, the Liberals began to develop leftist factions, referred to as the Left Liberals. In 1876 the main Liberal Party relinquished power to the leader of the Left Liberals, Agostino De Pretis, and then began a period of party decline. Raising electoral manipulation to an art form in the backward south of Italy, De Pretis also devised the practice of forming centrist governing coalitions based on patronage (*transformismo*) and cooptation of real or potential opposition elements. Any possibility of principled alternation in office was thereby effectively undermined. In response to De Pretis's style of rule, more radical leftist factions soon split away from the Liberal Party. Progressive democratic elements dissented in 1878 and formed the Radical Party (1878-1921),* which was a grouping willing to accept the monarchical form of Italian government. An antimonarchical and anticlerical Left Liberal faction split from the main party in 1895 and formed the Italian Republican Party.*

With De Pretis, Italy entered a period of "parliamentary dictators," and this period culminated with Giovanni Giolitti (1903-1914), the most important figure between Cavour and Benito Mussolini. Italy's industrial revolution began under Giolitti's administration, and he attempted to stabilize Italian politics by integrating the socialist and Catholic masses into the system, though Giolitti would be sure to do so in a manner still favorable to the Liberal Party. World War I, however, interrupted these plans.

After the war, political integration was accomplished through the introduction of proportional representation in 1919, thus wrecking the old Liberal elitist system. Still the largest party (really a collection of personal followings with only a plurality of the vote), the Liberals continued to represent the ideas of the old conservative right. They failed to construct a stable governing coalition to deal with Italy's severe problems after World War I, and thus they helped set the stage for the development of fascism from a small sect in 1919 to the country's chief political force in 1922 (*see* National Fascist Party). Some members of the Liberal Party openly supported fascism; most maintained a critical attitude toward the Fascist Party regime but without open resistance. Benedetto Croce, an internationally known philosopher and Liberal, continued to publish his work unmolested by the Fascist Party censors. Croce later reorganized the Liberal Party in 1943.

The Liberals appeared after World War II with a mixed electoral image. In some ways, the party was discredited by its failure to prevent the growth of fascism. On the other hand, the postwar Liberal Party was invested with a good deal of prestige since many of the important political personalities of the pre-Fascist period of Liberal dominance were still alive and had assumed prominent positions within the Liberal Party. Although the Liberals attempted to recast their ideology toward a modern reformist stance, the party was split between newer reformist elements and older conservative forces. The newer professional circle in the Liberal Party was imbued with progressive ideas. The older elements, particularly southern landowners and northern businessmen, comprised the conservative wing and sought a return to the party's pre-Fascist governmental system. The result was a conservative party opposed to radical changes in Italian society and whose political ideas were defensive rather than innovative.

The Italian Liberal Party continued in the post-World War II period as a party of notables. With the Democratic Labor Party* and part of the Action Party,* the Liberals formed part of Ferruccio Parri's National Democratic Union (*Unione Democratica Nazionale*) in 1946. The Union, however, obtained only 6.8 percent of the vote and 41 seats in that year's election. In 1948 the Liberals formed the National Bloc (Liberal) (*Blocco Nazionale*), set up by Francesco Nitti with remnants of the Common Man Front,* but obtained only 3.8 percent of the votes. (This National Bloc should not be confused with an earlier fascist grouping of the same name. *See* National Bloc [Fascist] under National Fascist Party.) By 1948 most of the Liberal Party electorate had gone over to the Christian Democratic Party,* leaving the Liberals with only 19 seats. Ferruccio Parri's attempt to form a third force of left-wing Liberals, Republicans, and independent socialists to oppose the extremist parties had been unsuccessful.

Although never regaining major party status, the Liberals nonetheless participated in many cabinets. Today, the Liberals are strongly pro-NATO, pro-European integration, and supportive of the United States. The Italian Liberal Party advocates a free market economy with limited government planning. Also, the party long ago abandoned its traditional anticlericalism but still calls for legislation opposed by the Catholic Church, such as the liberalization of Italy's divorce laws. The party has still not been liberal enough for some members, however, as evidenced by the 1955 splinter group that formed the Radical Party (1955-   ).*

The Liberal Party electoral base continues to be the upper and upper-middle class, especially in Lombardy where the party obtained 22 percent of the vote in 1968. The Liberals' national high point came in 1963 when they vigorously opposed the "opening to the left" by the Christian Democrats (meaning, that party's cooperation with the Italian Socialist Party*) and the Liberals received seven percent of the vote and 40 seats. In 1972, however, after return of a Christian Democrat-only government, the Liberal poll dropped to 3.9 percent, and to only 1.3 percent (nine seats) in 1979.

ITALIAN NATIONALIST ASSOCIATION (*Associazione Nazionalista Italiana*: ANI). A small but extremely vocal group, the Italian Nationalist Association functioned primarily in early 20th-century Italian politics. The ANI had its origins as a pressure group within the Italian Liberal Party,* following the revival of nationalist sentiment in 1896. The Association remained loosely associated with the Liberals until the ANI merger with the National Fascist Party* in February 1923.

Nationalist sentiment in Italy grew in intensity during the early decades of the 20th century, spurred on by Italy's humiliating defeat in Abyssinia and the rise of a pacifist leftist political force. Expressions of nationalism were found in the influential periodical *Il Regno* (The Kingdom), founded by Enrico Corradini in 1904, and in Luigi Federzoni's 1910 publication, *Idea Nazionale* (National Idea). The radical nationalist sentiment that led to the formation of the ANI despised democracy and stressed the values of discipline, inequality, and hierarchy. Such individuals also argued vociferously against the abandonment of Italy's imperialistic ambitions.

The ANI was formally organized following a congress in Florence in December 1910. The party advocated a flexible program devoid of mysticism, racism, and unsound economic ideas. In attempting to provide a modern, authoritarian alternative to liberal democracy, the ANI sought to align itself with other parties on the political right sharing similar economic and ideological concerns. Despite the attempt to find a mass base in the various veterans' organizations following World War I (for example, in the Ex-Servicemen's Party*), the Nationalist Association remained essentially an elitist grouping supported mainly by business interests who were attracted to the promise of expanded trade. It must also be noted that the Nationalists were not opposed to the occasional use of political violence.

In November 1922, shortly after the Fascist Party's seizure of power, the leaders of the Fascist and Nationalist parties agreed to joint political action; and on February 26, 1923, the ANI was absorbed in the National Fascist Party. Nationalist leaders Luigi Federzoni and Alfredo Rocco were appointed ministers of interior and justice respectively in 1924, and for the next two years these men played an important role in shaping the institutions of the Italian Fascist state. However, with Mussolini's abolition of political parties in 1926, even the ANI's influence declined, and the Association disintegrated as a political force in the wake of the Fascist Party's omnipotence.

Further Reference. DeGrand, Alexander J., *The Italian Nationalist Association and the Rise of Fascism in Italy* (Lincoln: University of Nebraska Press, 1978).

ITALIAN POPULAR PARTY (*Partito Popolare Italiano*: PPI). In its drive for completing the unification of Italy, the Italian government forcibly occupied Rome in September 1870, proclaimed it the capital of the Italian nation, and ended the temporal sovereignty of the pope. As a result of papal humiliation, the Catholic Church at once assumed an openly hostile attitude toward the new Italian regime. Although attempts were made to heal the breech caused by the "Roman Question," the papacy remained adamant in its stand. In 1874, Pope Pius IX issued a papal directive (*Non-Expedit*) which forbade Roman Catholics from active participation in Italian politics. They were to be neither the elected nor electors. Attempts by the clergy to mobilize rural elements against the regime prompted the Italian government to enact a series of strong anticlerical measures (*see* Italy introduction).

The papal ban did not prevent the majority of Italians from participating in political life, and Catholics gradually abandoned their passive attitude, beginning with the 1904 parliamentary election. At first, Catholics were persuaded to support candidates of the dominant Italian Liberal Party,* and in 1909 several Catholics were elected by running as independents, though not hiding their religious orientation. Since no formal Catholic party organization yet existed, these individuals functioned as a tendency and were divided into two groups known as the Catholics (*Cattolici*) and Conservative Catholics (*Conservatori Cattolici*).

After 1908, the Italian government under Liberal Party leader Giovanni Giolitti engaged in a "silent reconciliation" with the Catholic Church. In 1913, Giolitti's party formed an electoral alliance (Gentiloni Pact) with the Italian Catholic Union, a sociopolitical group that pledged Catholic support for Liberal Party candidates in return for the Liberals' agreement to church policy in the areas of education and divorce. Giolitti's aim was to frustrate the development of an official Catholic political party.

The period following World War I brought a new set of attitudes toward church-state relations in Italy. The Vatican's ban on Catholic participation in Italian politics was lifted by Pope Benedict XV in January 1919 (revoked officially on November 10, 1919); and in the same year, Don Luigi Sturzo, a Sicilian priest, founded the Italian Popular Party (PPI). The party rose like a meteor, winning 100 seats in the 1919 election. The PPI's electoral success was due largely to good organization and skilled leadership, with a network of branch organizations, publications, and financial resources.

The goal of the Popular Party was to Christianize and democratize the Italian social order. Opposed to imperialism and class warfare, the PPI urged electoral reforms, including proportional representation and female suffrage. The party also called for land reform and an increase in local autonomy, especially on behalf of the cities and provinces. Finally, the PPI advocated a rejuvenation of Italian political life and a complete separation of church and state. In terms of the latter platform, the party attempted to free itself from church domination and to function as a national political party.

Between 1919 and 1922, the Italian Popular Party held the pivotal role in the nation's parliament, and no government could remain in power without its support. However, the party was far from being a united entity—only the Catholic faith provided a common denominator of cohesion. In an attempt to fashion rules of behavior designed to curb factional conflict, the party secretary was given broad policy responsibilities and the deputies were bound to support policies formulated by the party executive.

Despite its impressive electoral showing and novel organizational methods, the Popular Party was short-lived. The rise of the National Fascist Party* split the PPI's ranks. Many of the conservative PPI elements openly approved of Fascist Party attacks on leftist political groups and were reluctant to join the Liberal Party in an anti-Fascist coalition. PPI founder Sturzo opposed the return to power of Giolitti's Liberal Party shortly before the Fascist seizure of the government in February 1923, and Sturzo even collaborated briefly with the Mussolini Fascist regime until April of the same year when Popular Party ministers were dismissed from the cabinet.

Gradually, the Roman Catholic Church withdrew its support from Sturzo and the Popular Party and adopted a more favorable attitude toward the Fascist regime. Sturzo proclaimed his opposition to fascism, and between 1925 and 1946 he lived in voluntary exile in the United States. With Sturzo's departure in 1925, the Popular Party began to disintegrate. Those elements who were favorable to the Fascist regime were reorganized into the National Catholic Party under the leadership of Paolo Mattei-Gentile and others. The anti-Fascist elements continued under the PPI designation and were led by Alcide De Gasperi, who was elected as Sturzo's successor in 1925. Both factions were outlawed in 1926 and were ultimately disbanded in 1927. De Gasperi sought refuge in the Vatican, and he reemerged during 1942-1943 to found the grouping that has been dominant in Italian politics since the end of World War II, the Christian Democratic Party.

ITALIAN REPUBLICAN PARTY (*Partito Repubblicano Italiano:* PRI). Established in April 1895, the Italian Republican Party was based on a faction of the old parliamentary Left Liberals (*see* Italian Liberal Party). The Republicans drew on the radical and republican traditions of Giuseppe Mazzini (*see* Italy introduction) and the Young Italy Movement of the Italian National Awakening (*Movimento Giovane Italia di Risorgimento Italiano*).

The Republicans remained small and somewhat poorly organized. They never counted more than 29 seats (achieved in the 1900 election) in the Chamber of Deputies. The party was strongly antimonarchical and anticlerical, and it was heavily influenced by the freemasonry movement. In foreign policy, the Republicans were pro-French and championed the cause of Italian irredentism, seeking the return of territories (Trentino and Trieste) then in Austrian possession. Following World War I, the issue of irredentism had been solved, and the Republicans had little to offer in concrete reforms. Similar to the Radical Party

(1878-1921),* another Liberal Party splinter, the Republicans' middle-class electoral base was being eroded by the Italian Socialist Party.* In the 1924 election, the small group of Republicans securing seats joined the forces opposing the regime of the National Fascist Party,* and the Republican Party was dissolved with Mussolini's 1926 ban on political organizations.

The Italian Republican Party (PRI) was reorganized in 1943 and enjoyed considerable respect because of its previous opposition to the Fascist Party regime. The PRI program espoused after World War II was quite similar to the one proposed by the liberal-socialist Action Party.* It called for a constitutional system based on federal principles in which the Italian regions would have broad autonomous powers—a position which ultimately found partial realization in the Italian constitution of 1948. The PRI also advocated gradual social and economic reforms, and the party strongly supported NATO and European integration.

The Republicans secured 23 seats in the 1946 parliamentary election, after which the party began to decline electorally. The PRI's base of support lies in the regions of Romagna, Tuscany, and in certain Sicilian districts where the party draws heavily from intellectuals. Although the Republicans have dwindled in parliamentary terms, they have played a very important role in government coalition-building because of their position on the left. Republican leaders have held many important posts in governments led by the Christian Democratic Party.*

The PRI reached a low electoral point in 1953, winning only five seats, but subsequent elections have shown some increase in support, although not reaching the high of the immediate post-World War II period. The party surpassed the Italian Liberal Party* in popular votes in 1976, and the PRI obtained 16 seats (against nine for the Liberals) in 1979. The Republican Party's official organ, *La Voce Repubblicana* (The Republican Voice), has approximately 25,000 subscribers. The high point of PRI governmental influence came in July 1981 following the end of the 36-year-long monopoly held by the Christian Democrats. When that government fell amid criticism and scandal, Giovanni Spaldolini, a Republican Party senator, formed Italy's forty-first postwar government.

ITALIAN SOCIALIST PARTY (*Partito Socialista Italiano*: PSI). The PSI was founded in 1892, drawing its intellectual heritage from the humanitarian socialism of Giuseppe Mazzini (*see* Italy introduction) and the ideas of Karl Marx. Socialism came late to Italy, largely because of the slow pace of the country's industrial development in the 19th century. The Socialists participated in parliamentary life; and through their support of various governments, they obtained modest social and political reforms.

Similar to socialist parties in other European systems, the Italian Socialists were divided from the beginning by various ideological currents. Prior to World War I, the two main PSI schools were the maximalists (*massimalismo*) and the reformists (*riformista*). The maximalists, with their base in the industrial north, were orthodox marxists who opposed both the parliamentary system and gradual reform. They were ardent supporters of revolutionary action. The reformists, who drew strength from various agricultural sectors, were evolutionary socialists who supported gradual reforms within the structure of a parliamentary system.

The first major split in the PSI came in 1912 when militant left-wing elements (one of whom was Benito Mussolini) seized the party leadership and expelled the reformist group of Leonida Bissolati, Ivanoe Bonomi, and Filippo Turati. The reformists promptly formed their own Reformist Socialist Party (*Socialisti Riformisti*), a grouping that continued to cooperate with the PSI until 1922 (*see* below).

Following the expulsion of the reformists, the PSI policy was one of militant opposition to the government. Although its electoral support increased after 1912 with the expansion of Italian suffrage, the PSI steadfastly refused to participate in any cabinet. In particular, the Socialists stressed pacifism and uncompromising opposition to World War I. By 1912, Benito Mussolini was one of the leading figures in the Italian Socialist Party. His position changed after 1914 when he supported Italy's intervention against Austria in order to obtain Italian irredenta (*see* Italy introduction). Mussolini was subsequently expelled from the party in 1914, and in 1919 he founded a movement that would soon lead to the formation of the National Fascist Party.*

The PSI remained officially neutralist during World War I, although many Socialist rank and file responded to the draft under promises of major postwar social reforms. When these were not forthcoming, the Socialists drifted toward a policy of revolutionary action. The post-1918 period also witnessed violent street confrontations between Socialists and veterans.

Despite the 1919 departure of the Reformist Socialists, the PSI was the largest party in the Italian parliament in November 1919 (with 156 out of 508 seats). Yet the badly divided PSI, continuing its prewar stance, refused to make a cabinet. Instead, the party pursued a policy of revolutionary rhetoric, exhausting strikes, and factory seizures during 1920 and 1921. The Socialists' sectarian ineptness during this period has been widely blamed by scholars for the triumph of Italy's Fascist Party.

The second major split in the PSI occurred in January 1921 when the extreme left wing of the maximalists broke away to form the Italian Communist Party.* Hence on the eve of the Fascist takeover of Italy, there were three socialist-type parties: the Communists, led by Antonio Gramsci; the Reformist Socialists, led by Filippo Turati; and the remaining PSI maximalists, led by Costatino Lazzari, who then actually formed the middle or centrist socialist group. The Reformists, though separately contesting the parliamentary elections of 1919 and 1922, had engaged in uneasy cooperation with the PSI until October 1922, at which time the Reformist Socialist Party renamed itself as the Unitary Socialist Party (1922-1926) (*Partito Socialista Unitario*: PSU), while the maximalists retained the PSI label. After this time, the PSU cooperated with the PSI only in terms of anti-Fascist efforts. Following World War II, the PSU reemerged as the Democratic Labor Party.*

After the Fascist seizure of power, conflicts between Socialists and Fascists intensified and moved from the streets to the parliamentary arena. In 1924, Giacomo Matteoti, a Socialist deputy, gave a scathing criticism of Mussolini in the Chamber of Deputies. He was later kidnapped and executed by Fascist squads. In 1926 the PSI deputies were unseated, with some being tried and imprisoned. Many who were able to escape reassembled in Paris, where in 1934 they concluded the Unity of Action Pact against Fascism with the Communists (*see also* Italian Communist Party).

Between 1945 and 1947, the Socialists were known as the Italian Socialist Party of Proletarian Unity (1945-1947) (*Partito Socialista Italiano di Unità Proletaria*: PSIUP; this designation is not to be confused with a dissident faction that broke away from the PSI in January 1964, *see* Italian Socialist Party of Proletarian Unity [1964-1972]*). Under the PSIUP label, the Socialists reaffirmed the Unity of Action Pact after World War II, and the Pact culminated in the Popular Front, a policy of close collaboration between the Socialists and Communists (*see also* Italian Communist Party). The Popular Front was dissolved in August 1948. Before its dissolution, however, the Front caused the third serious schism within the Socialist Party when an anti-Communist right wing, under Giuseppe Saragat, broke away in January 1947 to form the Socialist Party of Italian Workers (*see* Italian Democratic Socialist Party). After the Saragat Socialists left the party in 1947, the main body of the PSIUP reverted to the designation of the Italian Socialist Party under the leadership of Pietro Nenni. At this time, the PSI became occasionally known as the Nenni Socialists.

Debate over cooperation with the Communists and the desirability of forging a united left led to the formation of several other, though short-lived, PSI splinter groups in the immediate postwar period. For example, the Union of Socialists, formed in December 1947 by Ivan Matteo Lombardo, advocated complete unity of action with the Communists. In December 1949, the name of an earlier splinter was readopted when the Unitary Socialist Party (1949-1951) was formed by Giuseppe Romita and Ignazio Silone as a bridge between the Saragat and Nenni Socialists. However, when the "bridge" proved unworkable, this group merged in May 1951 with the Saragat Socialists (*see* Italian Democratic Socialist Party). Most of these post-World War II splinter groups existed for only a brief period and were then reabsorbed into one of the major socialist parties.

In 1953, Prime Minister De Gasperi, of the Christian Democratic Party,* offered PSI leader Nenni seats in the cabinet if the Socialists would cut their ties with the Italian Communist Party and accept Italy's participation in NATO. Nenni refused, and Italy plunged into almost a decade of weak cabinets. By the 1960s, however, the better-disciplined Communist Party was making electoral gains, and the PSI experienced corresponding losses. The new Christian Democratic leader, Amintore Fanfani, continued his predecessor's offer to the PSI. As a result of this situation, Nenni reconsidered the PSI's political role, finally accepted the De Gasperi/Fanfani formula, and the long-awaited "opening to the left" in Italy's long-time center-right government (that is, a coalition of the Christian Democrats and Socialists) was consumated in 1963. The PSI action prompted another Socialist secession in January 1964 by a group wanting renewed and even closer ties between the Socialists and Communists (see Italian Socialist Party of Proletarian Unity [1964-1972]*).

The PSI's rightward trend also led to a reunion with the anti-Communists of the Italian Democratic Socialist Party (or Saragat Socialists) in October 1966, forming the Unified Socialist Party (*Partito Socialista Unificato*: PSU). However, enough animosities and suspicions remained to doom the venture. Furthermore, the outcome of the 1968 election resulted in great PSI dissatisfaction, with the new PSU polling only 14.5 percent of the vote and 91 seats, compared to the PSI's previous total of 19.9 percent and 119 seats in 1963. Losing so many leftist votes, the PSI turned from its Christian Democratic partners to rethink its relations with its former Communist allies. This policy change led to a breakup of the PSU in 1969, with both the Italian Democratic Socialists and the PSI reverting to their premerger designations. In 1976, the PSI announced that it would join no cabinet without the Communists.

The PSI considers itself to be a marxist-leninist party, yet it has displayed on occasion a willingness to engage in pragmatic compromise. The party now accepts Italy's participation in NATO and has expressed weak support for European integration. Also, it has stressed the need for planning and governmental intervention in order to achieve socialist goals. The PSI has been traditionally anticlerical, despite its 1960s alliance with the Christian Democrats.

Factionalism and splits have continuously weakened the PSI's credibility as a leftist alternative to the Italian Communist Party. Once the largest party in Italy (during the post-World War I era), currently the PSI is only the largest of the nation's minor parties. With a membership of about 300,000, of which about 30 percent are working class, the PSI polls about 9.5 percent of the total vote in parliamentary elections. The party's strength remains in the northern and central regions of Italy. The PSI continues to publish a daily newspaper, *Avanti* (Forward), and a monthly paper, *Mondo Operaio* (Workers' World).

Further Reference. Barnes, Samuel H., *Party Democracy: Politics in an Italian Socialist Federation* (New Haven, Conn.: Yale University Press, 1967); Hostetler, R., *The Italian Socialist Party: Origins* (Princeton, N.J.: Princeton University Press, 1958).

ITALIAN SOCIALIST PARTY OF PROLETARIAN UNITY (1945-1947). *See* ITALIAN SOCIALIST PARTY.

ITALIAN SOCIALIST PARTY OF PROLETARIAN UNITY (1964-1972) (*Partito Socialista Italiano di Unità Proletaria*: PSIUP). The PSIUP (not to be confused with the name of the Italian Socialist Party* between 1945 and 1947) was formed in January 1964 by a dissident faction in the Italian Socialist Party (PSI). The PSIUP element had refused to vote for the Christian Democratic Party*-Socialist coalition government in December 1963. Composed of extreme left-wing members of the Socialist Party, the PSIUP viewed itself as a bridge between the PSI and the Italian Communist Party,* with whom the PSI had severed ties in 1962 in order to enter the government. Among the leaders of the PSIUP was Tullio Vecchetti, editor of the publication *Mondo Nuovo* (New World). Although overtly pro-Soviet Union in its ideological orientation, the party in 1968 opened its leadership to representatives from various pro-Castro and pro-Chinese elements.

The PSIUP ran a common slate of candidates with the Italian Communist Party in both 1968 and 1972. The PSIUP won 23 seats in 1968. But despite claiming over 200,000 adherents, in 1972 the PSIUP polled only 4.5 percent of the vote (with the Communists obtaining 1.9 percent), and thus the PSIUP failed to secure any seats in the Chamber of Deputies. As a result of its poor electoral outcome by running under its own name, the PSIUP merged into the Communist Party in July 1972.

However, angered at the possibility of a "historic compromise" between the Communists and the Christian Democrats (*see* Italian Communist Party and Christian Democratic Party), the more extreme elements of the former PSIUP split from the Communists and joined the Manifesto Movement (*Movimento Manifesto*), which had been formed by five deputies who had seceded from the Communist Party in November 1971. The Manifesto Movement was also joined by the small Workers' Political Movement (*Movimento Politica dei Lavoratori*: MPL), which had been organized by a dissident Christian Democratic deputy and several left-wing independents. The MPL was based on the daily newspaper *Il Manifesto* (The Manifesto) and was opposed to any cooperation between the Communists and the Christian Democratic Party. Viewing such tactics as an illusion and a betrayal of the ideals of the political left, the MPL urged a return to more radical leftist policies.

The Manifesto Movement (now including the Workers' Political Movement and the extremists of the old PSIUP) dissolved in Summer 1972 and in December reconstituted itself as the Democratic Party of Proletarian Unity for Communism (*Partito di Unità Proletaria per il Comunismo*: PdUP), under the leadership of Lucio Magri. The avowed goal of the new party was to build a united left around the workers' movement and to end Christian Democratic domination of Italian political life.

In 1976 the PdUP formed an electoral alliance known as Proletarian Democracy (*Democrazia Proletaria*: DP), which included two small extremist organizations: the Worker's Vanguard (*Avanguardia Operaia*: AO) and the Continuous Struggle (*Lotta Continua*: LC). The latter group, taking its name from an underground daily, *Continuous Struggle*, was a maoist organization under the direction of Guido Vale. Both the Worker's Vanguard and the Continuous Struggle had been involved in a number of violent incidents. Nevertheless, the Proletarian Democracy alliance managed to secure six seats in the 1976 election.

However, in 1979 the PdUP broke away from Proletarian Democracy, ran a separate list of candidates, and retained its six-seat membership in the Italian

Chamber. The Worker's Vanguard and Continuous Struggle had joined with other extremist elements in a coalition called the New United Left (*Nuova Sinistra Unità*: NSU), which failed in its bid to secure representation in the Italian assembly. The New United Left did secure one seat in the European Parliament in 1979 under the label of Proletarian Democracy, and the PdUP also secured one seat (*see* TECHNICAL COORDINATION GROUP, EUROPEAN PARLIAMENT).

Though not necessarily linked directly, the former Italian Socialist Party of Proletarian Unity had become associated, as the leftist parliamentary pivot, with several extraparliamentary extremist groups in the late 1960s, a few of which bear mention here. Many of these violent groupings had their origins in the university agitations of the maoist Student Movement (*Movimento Studentesco*) organization in 1968-1969. As the Student Movement declined (now representing only about five percent of the student body at the university level), other violent groups began to surface on the extreme left. Although they appear to be extremely fluid organizations, there does appear to be evidence of cooperation among them in selected instances.

Among the important extraparliamentary groups on the extreme left in Italy are the Red Brigades (*Brigate Rosse*), which has operated as an urban guerrilla unit engaging in kidnapping and assassinations; the Partisan Action Groups (*Gruppi Azione Partiagiana*: GAP), which has directed violence primarily against NATO targets; the Armed Proletarian Nuclei (*Nuclei Armati Proletari*), a criminal terrorist organization linked to the now-defunct Baader-Meinhof group in West Germany; and Workers' Power (*Potere Operaio*), a movement of intellectuals whose members have been allegedly involved in various terrorist acts. Action against these various left-wing extremist groups has been attempted not only by the Italian government but also by comparable terrorist groups on the Italian extreme right, such as those that have become affiliated, at least in the public's eyes, with the Italian Social Movement. *

ITALIAN SOCIAL MOVEMENT (*Movimento Sociale Italiano*: MSI). The Italian Social Movement first made its appearance in the general election of 1948. The MSI managed to attract most of the supporters of the old Common Man Front, * a grouping that had acquired a neofascist image and had suffered severe electoral losses. The MSI sought to represent the interests and political positions of the conservative political right, and the Movement included many elements who still harbored nostalgic sympathies for the defeated regime of the National Fascist Party. * Among the MSI's ranks were many individuals who had held minor posts in the Mussolini government or, after 1943, in the Salò Republic (*see* Italy introduction).

Neofascist groups were slow to emerge in post-World War II Italian politics. The strong antifascist mood which pervaded Italy in the immediate post-liberation period worked against any sudden revival of the Fascist Party. In addition, Clause XII of the postwar Italian constitution prohibited (and still forbids) the

scist Party in any form whatsoever. However, antifascism de-
ld War heated up, and the struggle between communism and
intensified in Italian society.

cial Movement initially suffered a series of internal conflicts
intransigent elements who were associated with the Salò
moderate elements of southern origin who were in favor of
collaboration with other rightist elements, particularly with the Monarchist
Party.* Eventually, the southern elements became dominant, and the MSI
acquired the character of a conservative party appealing to both low-income and
lower-middle-class individuals, to southern landowners, and to student groups.
Lacking a clear-cut program, however, the MSI also appealed to general discontent and electoral volatility by stressing the themes of nationalism and
anticommunism.

Winning six seats in the 1948 parliamentary election, the MSI representation
grew with each succeeding election. Between 1953 and 1972, the Movement
ranged from 24 to 29 deputies in the Chamber. At first, the party was viewed as
a threat to the Italian political system. However, the Movement's mass base now
appears limited to certain areas of strength in the south, particularly in the
Naples area where the MSI has polled close to 20 percent of the regional vote.

The MSI peaked in the 1972 election after it joined forces with the Italian
Democratic Party of Monarchical Unity (*see* Monarchist Party) in an electoral
alliance called the National Right (*Destra Nazionale*: DN). The DN alliance
resulted in a combined parliamentary representation of 56 seats. Both constituent parties formally merged in January 1973, retaining the name of the electoral
coalition.

The MSI-dominated National Right experienced a serious schism in late 1976
over the question of fascist tendencies within the party and over the use of
violence. Several of the MSI members of the National Right had been charged
with acts of terror (and the MSI itself had been the subject of a government
inquiry in 1971). The conflict came to a head in December 1976 when nearly
half of the DN parliamentary delegation (nine senators and 17 deputies) broke
away from the party to form a new, rightist group known as the National
Democracy-Right Constituent (*Democrazia Nazionale-Costituente di Destra*: DN;
see also Monarchist Party). The new group included a portion of the Monarchist
element, under the leadership of Alfredo Covelli, that rejected neofascism and
political violence. In the 1979 election, the National Democracy splinter secured no representation, while the Italian Social Movement, readopting its old
appellation, won 30 seats.

Membership in the MSI has been estimated to be about 400,000. The party is
organized into approximately 7,500 sections with over 100 federations. It is
represented in the Italian Senate and in many of the regional, provincial, and
municipal councils across Italy. The MSI claims to be a confessional party, more
Catholic than the Christian Democratic Party.* The Movement advocates a
corporativist doctrine similar to the one practiced by the Fascist regime, but the

MSI denies being a revival of the Fascist Party. Instead, the MSI sees itself as a bulwark against any attempt by the political left to seize the Italian government.

In the 1950s and early 1960s, acts of violence between the Italian Social Movement and its political adversaries were rare and limited to general rowdiness of the Movement's younger members. MSI leaders such as Augusto De Marsanich and Filippo Anfuso viewed such behavior as counterproductive to the party's quest for respectability, and so they stressed the need to stay within the bounds of legality. However, with the rise of a militant and violent leftist force in Italian politics, beginning with the 1970s, some within the MSI have urged direct, forceful action against the Italian Communist Party* and other left-wing groups. While the MSI has officially denied any association with the violence-prone, extremist groups of Italy's political right (such as those discussed below), the party itself has claimed as legitimate the exercise of physical self-defense against violent attacks from its opponents. Scores of MSI members and supporters have been charged with the commission of terrorist acts.

Parallel to the Italian Socialist Party of Proletarian Unity (1964-1972)* on the extreme left, the MSI has become the rightist parliamentary pivot of several extraparliamentary extremist groups. The largest organization to the right of the MSI is the New Order (Nuovo Ordine), founded by the journalist Pino Rauti. Claiming to have over 500 active members and organizations in every major Italian city, the New Order professes a doctrine of national socialism. This grouping was declared illegal in November 1973, and several of its members received prison sentences for attempting to revive the National Fascist Party.

Other extremist groups on the right include the National Vanguard (Avanguardia Nazionale); Young Italy (Giovane Italia); the Youth Front (Fronte della Gioventu); the Compass Card (Rosa dei Venti); and the Mussolini Action Squad (Squadre Azione Mussolini: SAM), which has admitted to several bombings of left-wing organizational headquarters.

JUSTICE AND LIBERTY. See ACTION PARTY.

LABOR DEMOCRATS. See DEMOCRATIC LABOR PARTY.

LC. See ITALIAN SOCIALIST PARTY OF PROLETARIAN UNITY (1964-1972).

LEFT LIBERALS. See ITALIAN LIBERAL PARTY.

LIBERAL DEMOCRATIC FRONT OF THE COMMON MAN. See COMMON MAN FRONT.

LOTTA CONTINUA. See ITALIAN SOCIALIST PARTY OF PROLETARIAN UNITY (1964-1972).

MANIFESTO MOVEMENT. See ITALIAN SOCIALIST PARTY OF PRO-
LETARIAN UNITY (1964-1972).

MAXIMALIST SOCIALISTS. See ITALIAN SOCIALIST PARTY.

MONARCHIST PARTY (*Partito Monarchico*: PM). The Monarchist Party was
formed by Alfredo Covelli and Achille Lauro following the institutional referendum of June 2, 1946, which abolished the monarchical form of Italian government and established a republican regime. The PM's purpose was to organize
a political movement among those who still harbored pro-monarchy sentiment
and to press for a restoration of the House of Savoy to the Italian throne. In
realistic terms, the possibility of restoration was excluded by Article 139 of the
Italian constitution, which specifically guaranteed against any changes in the
form of government by amendment.

The Monarchist Party was based in the south of Italy (especially the Naples
area), and it capitalized on long-standing southern resentments against the
Italian north. The party appealed to both the conservative nobility and many of
the underprivileged classes who respected the institution of the monarchy. Italian monarchism, like the areas in which it flourished, was traditionalist, legitimist, and superficially Catholic.

In the 1946 parliamentary election, the Monarchist Party joined with other
rightist elements in forming an electoral coalition called the National Freedom
Bloc (*Blocco Nazionale della Libertà*). In 1948 the PM changed its name to the
National Monarchist Party (*Partito Nazionale Monarchico*: PNM) and contested
that year's election with another small rightist group called the Democratic
Alliance of Labor (*Alleanza Democratica del Lavoro*). The new PNM reached its
electoral peak in 1953 when it contested alone and polled about 6.8 percent of
the vote, placing 40 deputies in the Chamber.

The Monarchists declined electorally after 1953 due to a series of schisms and
quarrels between Covelli and Lauro. Personal differences over the issue of European defense led to a party split in June 1954, with Covelli remaining as head of
the National Monarchist Party and Lauro breaking away to form the new Popular Monarchist Party (*Partito Monarchico Popolare*: PMP). The 1958 elections
resulted in the seating of 25 monarchist deputies—11 from the National Monarchists and 14 from the Popular Monarchists.

Hoping for renewed strength, in April 1959 the two monarchist parties were
reunited into a new grouping called the Italian Democratic Party (*Partito Democratica
Italiana*: PDI), dropping the "monarchist" label but retaining the crown as a
political symbol. Prior to the 1963 election, the party once again changed its
name to include the monarchist connotation and referred to itself as the Italian
Democratic Party of Monarchical Unity (*Partito Democratico Italiano di Unità
Monarchica*: PDIUM). The PDIUM suffered severe losses in 1963 and 1968,
declining to a mere 1.3 percent of the vote and six deputies in the Chamber.

By 1970 the monarchist appeal had faded drastically, especially since the former king refused to press any restoration claims. The PDIUM had gradually given tacit acceptance to the republican system and sought to support conservative government coalitions. The PDIUM's economic policies were confusing and contradictory, espousing both free enterprise and government protectionism. In foreign policy, the party had been especially pro-Western, with little support for European integration.

In the 1972 election, the PDIUM formed an electoral alliance with the extreme right-wing Italian Social Movement,* and the coalition was known as the National Right (*Destra Nazionale*: DN). The DN alliance captured 56 seats, which led to a formal merger of the PDIUM and the Italian Social Movement in January 1973. The new party, continuing to use the National Right designation, obtained only 35 seats in the 1976 election.

Sharp disagreements over the use of political violence and over accusations of the Italian Social Movement's neofascist tendencies led to a major schism in the National Right party. In December 1976, almost half of the National Right parliamentary delegation (17 deputies and nine senators) left the party to form a new group called National Democracy-Right Constituent (*Democrazia Nazionale-Costituente di Destra*: DN; *see also* Italian Social Movement). The new DN was led by Ernesto De Marzio and included Covelli in the party executive. The National Democracy repudiated fascism and the use of violence, and the group indicated that in the future it would align itself with the Christian Democratic Party.* The National Democracy failed to secure representation in the 1979 election, while the monarchists' former coalition partner, the Italian Social Movement, managed to retain 30 seats.

MOVEMENT FOR TRIESTE. *See* REGIONAL AUTONOMIST PARTIES.

MOVIMENTO GIOVANE ITALIA DE RISORGIMENTO ITALIANO. *See* ITALIAN REPUBLICAN PARTY.

MOVIMENTO MANIFESTO. *See* ITALIAN SOCIALIST PARTY OF PROLETARIAN UNITY (1964-1972).

MOVIMENTO NAZIONALISTA PER LA DEMOCRATIZZAZIONE SOCIALE. *See* COMMON MAN FRONT.

MOVIMENTO PER L'INDEPENDENZA DELLA SICILIA. *See* REGIONAL AUTONOMIST PARTIES.

MOVIMENTO PER TRIESTE. *See* REGIONAL AUTONOMIST PARTIES.

MOVIMENTO POLITICA DEI LAVORATORI. *See* ITALIAN SOCIALIST PARTY OF PROLETARIAN UNITY (1964-1972).

MOVIMENTO SOCIALE ITALIANO. *See* ITALIAN SOCIAL MOVEMENT.

MOVIMENTO STUDENTESCO. *See* ITALIAN SOCIALIST PARTY OF PRO-
LETARIAN UNITY (1964-1972).

MPL. *See* ITALIAN SOCIALIST PARTY OF PROLETARIAN UNITY
(1964-1972).

MSI. *See* ITALIAN SOCIAL MOVEMENT.

MUSSOLINI ACTION SQUAD. *See* ITALIAN SOCIAL MOVEMENT.

NATIONAL BLOC (Fascist). *See* NATIONAL FASCIST PARTY.

NATIONAL BLOC (Liberal). *See* ITALIAN LIBERAL PARTY.

NATIONAL CATHOLIC PARTY. *See* ITALIAN POPULAR PARTY.

NATIONAL DEMOCRACY-RIGHT CONSTITUENT. *See* ITALIAN SOCIAL
MOVEMENT and MONARCHIST PARTY.

NATIONAL DEMOCRATIC UNION. *See* ITALIAN LIBERAL PARTY.

NATIONAL FASCIST PARTY (*Partito Nazionale Fascista:* PNF). The foundations of the National Fascist Party were laid on March 23, 1919, in Milan, when
Benito Mussolini first organized his Fighting Bands (*Fascio di Combattimento*)
with a core of 145 ex-servicemen. Their program was a simple one of nationalism and veterans' self-defense. The Fighting Bands were modelled after the
earlier Revolutionary Action Bands (*Fasci d'Azione Rivoluzionaria*) that had sprung
up in 1915 in support of Italy's participation in World War I. The Italian word
fasces represented the emblem of the Roman state. The term *fascio* implies a
union, generally of individually weak elements that find strength in unity.

Mussolini was born in 1883 in Romagna province, near the town of Forli. He
was familiar with the circumstances of poverty in Italian society. Mussolini
became influenced by the combative notions of direct action and intelligent
violence, and he was soon attracted to the cause of socialism. He spent his
late teens and early twenties travelling through neighboring countries, supporting himself through manual labor and occasionally contributing to socialist
publications.

Upon his return to Italy, Mussolini achieved national prominence as a dominant figure in the Italian Socialist Party,* and in 1912 he was made editor of
Avanti (Forward), the leading Socialist Party newspaper. He soon dissented
against the party over the issue of intervention in World War I, with Mussolini
supporting Italian military action against Austria in order to obtain Italian

irredenta (see Italy introduction). When the Socialists refused to allow these views to appear in their publications, Mussolini resigned as editor of *Avanti* and in November 1914 founded his own newspaper, *Il Popolo d'Italia* (The People of Italy). Upon using this paper to advocate an immediate Italian declaration of war on the Allies, Mussolini was expelled from the Socialist Party, along with his followers. Once Italy did enter World War I in 1915, Mussolini was drafted. After serving at the front, he was wounded in 1917 during an Italian artillery practice. Upon recovery, Mussolini resumed his extremely nationalistic rhetoric in *Il Popolo d'Italia.*

After the war, Mussolini's new Fighting Bands attracted support from veterans, students, farmers, businessmen, and dissatisfied elements in the Socialist Party. Fascism also enjoyed sympathy within military and ecclesiastical circles. The movement spread rapidly across Italy in the form of local lodges, which were coordinated nationally under Mussolini's direction. Prior to the parliamentary election of November 1919, the fascist movement produced a basic, socialist-type manifesto that called for radical changes in the franchise and for social insurance programs, labor reforms, and worker's participation in management at their places of employment. Although not yet the leader of a party, Mussolini entered fascist lists for the Chamber of Deputies, but he failed to elect a single candidate.

After 1919, fascist ideology gradually shifted away from socialism and toward extreme nationalism and antisocialism. The ranks of the movement were rapidly being filled by disenchanted middle-class youth, and armed bands of fascists began to terrorize the principal cities, focusing their attacks on Socialist Party members and other political opponents. The police and military acquiesced in these actions, which bordered on civil war.

In May 1921, a total of 35 fascist deputies were elected to the Chamber, chiefly on a list called the National Bloc (Fascist) (*Blocco Nazionale*; this National Bloc should not be confused with a later National Bloc [Liberal] established by the Italian Liberal Party*). Five of the fascist deputies were later declared ineligible to serve because they had not attained the minimum age of 30 years required of officeholders. But the election of 35 candidates was regarded as a significant breakthrough, and consequently Mussolini's movement was transformed into the National Fascist Party on November 6, 1921. At that time, the party was estimated to have 150,000 members.

Once in the Chamber, the Fascists adopted an intransigent stance and refused to cooperate with any group. A noncooperative attitude pervaded other parties as well, including the then-largest parliamentary grouping, the Italian Socialist Party. Thus Italy was plunged into a series of government crises, with no group able to form a stable governing coalition. By September 1922, the crisis had reached serious proportions, and government authority began to break down.

Mussolini declared his intentions to act outside of the parliamentary sphere, and on October 27, 1922, he organized a mammoth political-military demonstration—the famous "March on Rome." The march was directed by loyal

Mussolini supporters (Italo Balbo, Emilio de Bono, Michele Bianchi, and Count de Vecchi), while Mussolini remained at his newspaper office in Milan. In the face of this action, the caretaker government of Luigi Facta attempted to declare a state of siege on October 28, but King Victor Emmanuel III refused Facta's request. Instead, on October 29, the king appointed Mussolini as prime minister of a coalition government.

Once in power, Mussolini set about to broaden the Fascist Party's parliamentary base by absorbing the Italian Nationalist Association* in February 1923. This move, however, still kept the Fascist representation below 50 deputies. Hence in July 1923, under Mussolini's influence, a new electoral law (Acerbo Law) was passed that modified the system of proportional representation. In future elections, the party that polled at least 25 percent of the total vote would receive two-thirds of the seats in the Chamber. The remaining one-third of seats would be distributed among the other parties in proportion to their shares of the vote. Although opposition was voiced to this change, the parties were compelled to accept it, and new elections were held in April 1924. With the Fascists winning 65 percent of the vote, an all-Fascist cabinet was formed. Once securely in power, Mussolini abolished all other political parties on November 9, 1926.

The National Fascist Party had earlier centralized its organization and authority, following the March on Rome. In early 1923, a Grand Council of Fascism (*Gran Consiglio del Fascismo*) was established and charged with jurisdiction over party organization and policy. Ultimate authority resided with Mussolini himself under his title of *Il Duce* (The Leader). When the last vestiges of intraparty democracy were abolished in 1926 and replaced with the principle of hierarchy, even local Fascist units were denied the right of choosing their own leaders. The National Fascist Party (PNF) also became more integrated with the Italian government until 1938, at which time the PNF was declared to be a civil militia in the service of the state. Party statutes were even promulgated as royal decrees.

In terms of organizational structure, the basic unit of the PNF was the local *Fascio*, which numbered about 7,300 in 1939 (one for each commune). Local *Fasci* were under the leadership of a "political secretary," who was assisted by a local directorate of about five members. The political secretary was appointed by the "provincial secretary," who directed the next-highest level in the hierarchy. Provincial secretaries were appointed by Mussolini himself. They were assisted by a seven-person national directorate. Located at the top of the hierarchy was the "national secretary," who served as the executive officer of the Grand Council and assumed control and direction over the entire party apparatus. The national secretary reported directly to Mussolini.

The most important party assemblage was the Grand Council, which was composed of about 25 members. Membership fluctuated over the 1930s—certain old-time Fascists, such as Balbo, Bono, and de Vecchi, were given life tenure; others were appointed by Mussolini for three-year, renewable terms. There were also several government officials who served ex-officio. Clearly at the top was the figure of Mussolini himself, invested with dictatorial powers, holding the titles of party leader (*duce*) and head of government (*capo di governo*). The titles were combined after 1939 as the boundary between the party and government was eliminated. Italy developed into a self-proclaimed totalitarian society, but practice fell short of proclamation. The regime was no true party-state but rather a broad-based coalition, with large areas of national life outside of direct government control.

The PNF was served by a number of auxiliary organizations. The most important was the Young Fascists (*Giovani Fascisti*). Separate organizations for both sexes of various age groups were formed under this umbrella grouping. Youth organizations were estimated to have had a membership exceeding 7.5 million in 1939. Other auxiliary groupings included the Fascist Militia (about 400,000 members), which was reorganized as a reserve force after 1923, and the National Leisure Time Organization (*Dopolavoro*), a cultural and propaganda grouping among peasants and workers.

Despite periodic purges, the PNF was not an exclusionary party, and membership reached several million in the 1930s. The principal functions of the party were to safeguard the succession of governmental leaders and to indoctrinate the rising generation. However, high offices in the party were often filled with mediocrities, who hobbled efforts to reintroduce Roman severity into national culture. General membership in the Fascist Party was recruited from the Young Fascists organization. Party members were required to undergo an elaborate initiation ceremony known as the Fascist Levy (*Leva Fascista*), which was held annually on May 29 (one of the designated Fascist holidays). Inductees pledged their obedience to the party and its leader. Other members were recruited by cooptation when necessary, or awarded membership as a symbol of gratitude for political services. A large segment of the party's revenue consisted of fees paid for membership cards.

On the eve of World War II, Fascist ideology evolved into a fusion of syndicalism and nationalism: decisive political struggles were taking place, not among classes but among nations, and proletarian Italy would confront the exploiting plutocracies. Fascism had come to mean different things to different Italians; but national unity was the foundation, along with elite direction, class collaboration (corporatism), and greater productivity. An enlightened elite would forge a strong state and build a powerful economy. Mussolini pointed to his achievements: the old church-state conflict was resolved, the Mafia had been driven underground, strikes and lockouts were ended, and an elaborate program of public works and land reclamation was being pursued. Italy's participation in World War II, however, destroyed many of Mussolini's projects (*see* Italy introduction).

On July 25, 1943, following the Allied invasion of Italy, Mussolini was arrested by the king, who was now supported by military plotters, and *Il Duce* was forced to resign as head of the Italian government. Mussolini was replaced by Marshal Pietro Badoglio, who promptly dissolved the National Fascist Party on July 28. Mussolini was rescued from imprisonment by German forces in

September. He reasserted his authority over the party, changed its name to the Republican Fascist Party, and established the "Italian Salò Republic" in the north of Italy, under German protection. The new party pledged a return to the pure republican and socialist roots of the Fascist movement of 1919. The Salò Republic, however, collapsed under partisan attacks and the Allied military advance in early 1945. While attempting to flee an Alpine redoubt, Mussolini was captured by communist partisans and executed on April 28, 1945.

Article 49 of the 1948 Italian constitution specifically prohibits the reorganization under any form whatsoever of the dissolved National Fascist Party. Nevertheless, neofascist tendencies have reappeared in Italy, particularly in the form of the Italian Social Movement,* which has claimed legitimate descent from Mussolini's Salò Republic.

Further Reference. Gerinimo, Dante, *The Italian Fascist Party in Power* (Minneapolis: University of Minnesota Press, 1953); Gregor, A. J., *The Fascist Persuasion in Radical Politics* (Princeton, N.J.: Princeton University Press, 1974); and *The Ideology of Fascism* (New York: Free Press, 1969).

NATIONAL FREEDOM BLOC. *See* MONARCHIST PARTY.

NATIONAL LIBERATION COMMITTEE. *See* DEMOCRATIC LABOR PARTY.

NATIONAL MONARCHIST PARTY. *See* MONARCHIST PARTY.

NATIONAL MOVEMENT FOR SOCIAL DEMOCRATIC ACTION. *See* COMMON MAN FRONT.

NATIONAL RIGHT. *See* ITALIAN SOCIAL MOVEMENT and MONARCHIST PARTY.

NATIONAL VANGUARD. *See* ITALIAN SOCIAL MOVEMENT.

NENNI SOCIALISTS. *See* ITALIAN SOCIALIST PARTY.

NEW ORDER. *See* ITALIAN SOCIAL MOVEMENT.

NEW UNITED LEFT. *See* ITALIAN SOCIALIST PARTY OF PROLETARIAN UNITY (1964-1972).

NSU. *See* ITALIAN SOCIALIST PARTY OF PROLETARIAN UNITY (1964-1972).

NUCLEI ARMATI PROLETARI. *See* ITALIAN SOCIALIST PARTY OF PROLETARIAN UNITY (1964-1972).

NUOVA SINISTRA UNITÀ. *See* ITALIAN SOCIALIST PARTY OF PRO-LETARIAN UNITY (1964-1972).

NUOVO ORDINE. *See* ITALIAN SOCIAL MOVEMENT.

PARTISAN ACTION GROUPS. *See* ITALIAN SOCIALIST PARTY OF PROLETARIAN UNITY (1964-1972).

PARTITO COMUNISTA INTERNAZIONALE. *See* ITALIAN COMMUNIST PARTY.

PARTITO COMUNISTA ITALIANO. *See* ITALIAN COMMUNIST PARTY.

PARTITO COMUNISTA (MARXISTA-LENINISTA) DE ITALIA. *See* ITALIAN COMMUNIST PARTY.

PARTITO COMUNISTA UNIFICADE DE ITALIA. *See* ITALIAN COMMUNIST PARTY.

PARTITO D'AZIONE. *See* ACTION PARTY.

PARTITO D' AZIONE DE SARDEGNA. *See* REGIONAL AUTONOMIST PARTIES.

PARTITO DEI CONTADINI. *See* PEASANT PARTY.

PARTITO DEMOCRATICA ITALIANA. *See* MONARCHIST PARTY.

PARTITO DEMOCRATICO DEL LAVORO. *See* DEMOCRATIC LABOR PARTY.

PARTITO DEMOCRATICO DI UNITÀ PROLETARIA. *See* ITALIAN SO-CIALIST PARTY OF PROLETARIAN UNITY (1964-1972).

PARTITO DEMOCRATICO ITALIANO DI UNITÀ MONARCHICA. *See* MONARCHIST PARTY.

PARTITO DI UNITÀ PROLETARIA PER IL COMUNISMO. *See* ITALIAN SOCIALIST PARTY OF PROLETARIAN UNITY (1964-1972).

PARTITO ECONOMICO. *See* ECONOMIC PARTY.

PARTITO LIBERALE ITALIANO. *See* ITALIAN LIBERAL PARTY.

PARTITO MONARCHICO. *See* MONARCHIST PARTY.

PARTITO MONARCHICO POPOLARE. *See* MONARCHIST PARTY.

PARTITO NAZIONALE FASCISTA. *See* NATIONAL FASCIST PARTY.

PARTITO NAZIONALE MONARCHICO. *See* MONARCHIST PARTY.

PARTITO POPOLARE ITALIANO. *See* ITALIAN POPULAR PARTY.

PARTITO RADICALE. *See* RADICAL PARTY (1878-1921) and (1955-   ).

PARTITO REPUBBLICANO ITALIANO. *See* ITALIAN REPUBLICAN PARTY.

PARTITO SOCIALISTA DEI LAVORATORI ITALIANO. *See* ITALIAN DEMOCRATIC SOCIALIST PARTY.

PARTITO SOCIALISTA DEMOCRATICO ITALIANO. *See* ITALIAN DEMOCRATIC SOCIALIST PARTY.

PARTITO SOCIALISTA ITALIANO. *See* ITALIAN SOCIALIST PARTY.

PARTITO SOCIALISTA ITALIANO DI UNITÀ PROLETARIA. *See* ITALIAN SOCIALIST PARTY and ITALIAN SOCIALIST PARTY OF PROLETARIAN UNITY (1964-1972).

PARTITO SOCIALISTA: SEZIONE ITALIANA DEL INTERNAZIONALE SOCIALISTA. *See* ITALIAN DEMOCRATIC SOCIALIST PARTY.

PARTITO SOCIALISTA UNIFICATO. *See* ITALIAN SOCIALIST PARTY.

PARTITO SOCIALISTA UNITARIO. *See* ITALIAN SOCIALIST PARTY and ITALIAN DEMOCRATIC SOCIALIST PARTY.

PARTITO SOCIALISTA UNITARIO DE LAVORATORI ITALIANI. *See* ITALIAN DEMOCRATIC SOCIALIST PARTY.

PARTY OF ACTION. *See* ACTION PARTY.

PARTY OF PROLETARIAN UNITY FOR COMMUNISM. *See* ITALIAN SOCIALIST PARTY OF PROLETARIAN UNITY (1964-1972).

PAS. *See* REGIONAL AUTONOMIST PARTIES.

PCI. *See* ITALIAN COMMUNIST PARTY.

PC(ML)I. *See* ITALIAN COMMUNIST PARTY.

PCUI. *See* ITALIAN COMMUNIST PARTY.

Pd'A. *See* ACTION PARTY.

PDI. *See* MONARCHIST PARTY.

PDIUM. *See* MONARCHIST PARTY.

PdUP. *See* ITALIAN SOCIALIST PARTY OF PROLETARIAN UNITY (1964-1972).

PDUP. *See* ITALIAN SOCIALIST PARTY OF PROLETARIAN UNITY (1964-1972).

PEASANT PARTY (*Partito dei Contadini*). The Peasant Party, also known as the Italian Farmers' Party, was formed in the early post-World War II period to represent the interests of farmers, especially in rural Piedmont. In 1948 the party obtained one seat, electing its leader Alessandro Scotti, after which the Peasant Party disappeared as a political force.

PER TRIESTE. *See* REGIONAL AUTONOMIST PARTIES.

PLI. *See* ITALIAN LIBERAL PARTY.

PM. *See* MONARCHIST PARTY.

PMP. *See* MONARCHIST PARTY.

PNF. *See* NATIONAL FASCIST PARTY.

PNM. *See* MONARCHIST PARTY.

POPULAR FRONT. *See* ITALIAN COMMUNIST PARTY and ITALIAN SOCIALIST PARTY.

POPULAR MONARCHIST PARTY. *See* MONARCHIST PARTY.

POTERE OPERAIO. *See* ITALIAN SOCIALIST PARTY OF PROLETARIAN UNITY (1964-1972).

PPI. *See* ITALIAN POPULAR PARTY.

PR. *See* RADICAL PARTY (1955-   ).

PRI. *See* ITALIAN REPUBLICAN PARTY.

PROLETARIAN DEMOCRACY. *See* ITALIAN SOCIALIST PARTY OF PRO-LETARIAN UNITY (1964-1972).

PSDI. *See* ITALIAN DEMOCRATIC SOCIALIST PARTY.

PSI. *See* ITALIAN SOCIALIST PARTY.

PSIUP. *See* ITALIAN SOCIALIST PARTY and ITALIAN SOCIALIST PARTY OF PROLETARIAN UNITY (1964-1972).

PSLI. *See* ITALIAN DEMOCRATIC SOCIALIST PARTY.

PSP. *See* REGIONAL AUTONOMIST PARTIES.

PS,SIIS. *See* ITALIAN DEMOCRATIC SOCIALIST PARTY.

PSU. *See* ITALIAN SOCIALIST PARTY and ITALIAN DEMOCRATIC SO-CIALIST PARTY.

PSULI. *See* ITALIAN DEMOCRATIC SOCIALIST PARTY.

RADICAL PARTY (1878-1921) (*Partito Radicale*). Italy's first Radical Party emerged as a progressive democratic group from the parliamentary Left Liberals (*see* Italian Liberal Party) in 1878. At first, the Radicals appeared as a small grouping on the extreme political left that protested against various political and social evils. They accepted the monarchy but insisted on the institution of republican principles. The party's breakthrough occurred in 1895 when it secured 47 seats in the Chamber of Deputies.

The Radicals played an important parliamentary role in defending constitutional liberties in an era of severe suffrage restrictions and electoral manipulation. Very often, they joined with the Italian Republican Party* (another Liberal splinter) and with the Italian Socialist Party* to form a leftist bloc of social reform. The Radicals' political doctrine stressed the role of individualism and the right of the political minority. Furthermore, they expressed their dissatisfaction with the governance of Italy by the older parties (primarily the Liberals), and despite frequent collaboration with the Socialists, the Radicals distrusted collectivist doctrines of the type exposed by the Socialist Party.

Competing with the Socialists for the lower-middle-class vote, the Radicals were especially strong in the provinces of Lombardy, Tuscany, and Venetia. The Radicals reached their electoral peak in 1913 with a total of 73 seats in the Chamber. But the rise of the Socialists after World War I eroded the Radicals' electoral base and reduced them to a mere 12 seats in parliament in 1919. Failing to elect even a single member in 1921, the Radical Party disappeared from the Italian political scene. (A later Liberal splinter readopted the Radical Party name in 1955. See Radical Party [1955-   ].)

RADICAL PARTY (1955-   ) (*Partito Radicale*: PR). Italy's second Radical Party was formed in December 1955 from a dissident left-wing element in the Italian Liberal Party.* (This Radical Party is not to be confused with the historical Radical Party [1878-1921],* another Liberal Party splinter.) The modern Radical Party has emphasized civil and human rights, nonviolence, antimilitarism, and it claims to work for a socialist and democratic society.

The PR has been instrumental in drafting Italy's divorce law and a more liberal abortion law. It has also supported conscientious objection, women's rights, and homosexual rights. It stands opposed to the use of nuclear energy.

The PR first obtained parliamentary representation in 1976 (with four seats) and later increased its strength (to 18 seats) in 1979. With an estimated membership of approximately 5,000, the Radical Party in actuality is a loosely organized grouping composed of many affiliated groups. The present PR leaders are Jean Fabre and Giuseppe Rippa.

RASSEMBLEMENT VALDÔTAIN. See REGIONAL AUTONOMIST PARTIES.

RED BRIGADES. See ITALIAN SOCIALIST PARTY OF PROLETARIAN UNITY (1964-1972).

REFORMIST SOCIALIST PARTY. See DEMOCRATIC LABOR PARTY and ITALIAN SOCIALIST PARTY.

REGIONAL AUTONOMIST PARTIES. In 19th-century Italy, the quest for national unity led to a deliberate policy of national centralized administration that overrode many important regional concerns. Regionalism as a political force remained muted, with only occasional manifestations in the Italian political arena (1896-1905 and 1919-1926). However, the zealous overcentralization that occurred during the fascist period (*see* National Fascist Party) led to an upsurge in regional feelings after World War II. Passions of local pride were coupled with demands for a greater devolution of government authority and increased local and regional autonomy. Five areas were especially troublesome politically to the new postwar Italian government since these areas represented special cultural, geographical, and social problems: Sardinia, Sicily, Friuli-Venezia-Giulia, Trentino-Alto Adige, and Val d'Aosta.

Sardinia and Sicily are large islands removed both culturally and geographically from the Italian mainland. Separatist feelings developed, especially in Sicily, as a reaction to the neglect of these areas from the time of national unification. In 1945 the Sicilian Separatist Movement (*Movimento per L'Independenza della Sicilia*) was formed by Finocchiaro Aprile, a Palermo lawyer. The Movement demanded complete independence for Sicily. Attracting a wide following, it obtained four seats in the 1946 election. The Movement went into decline in 1948 following the provisions of the Italian constitution that granted Sicily special status as an autonomous region.

The Sardinian Action Party (*Partito d'Azione d' Sardegna*: PAS) had its origins in the post-World War I period when it demanded autonomy for Sardinia. The party reappeared after liberation, secured two seats in the 1946 parliamentary election, but then declined as a national force after the special regional provisions of the Italian constitution were put into effect. However, the PAS continues to play a role in the Sardinian Regional Council, where PAS representatives have entered coalition governments with the area's delegations of the Christian Democratic Party* and the Italian Democratic Socialist Party.* Dissatisfied with the partial self-governing provisions for Sardinia, the PAS continues to press for full autonomy for the island; and as such, the party failed to secure any seats at the national level in the 1979 election.

The special statute region of Friuli-Venezia-Giulia encompassed the city of Trieste, which was an area in dispute between Italy and Yugoslavia even after World War II. The region also contains a significant Slovenian population. In 1954 the region was partitioned, with Italy securing Trieste and Yugoslavia obtaining the rural areas surrounding that city. A formal settlement (Treaty of Osimo) was concluded in 1975 and finally ratified in 1977.

The area has produced two important autonomist groupings. The Friuli Movement (*Movimento de Friuli*) has pressed for the autonomy of Friuli within the region of Friuli-Venezia-Giulia. The Movement's program, however, has had little electoral appeal. The grouping has never secured national representation, and it has been able to elect only a few representatives to the Regional Council.

The Movement for Trieste (*Movimento per Trieste*, or simply *Per Trieste*) has demonstrated surprising success as a regional party. It was organized in 1975 to protest certain economic and trade aspects of the Italian-Yugoslav agreement that were deemed detrimental to the city of Trieste. The Movement for Trieste has become the largest party in that city, and in 1979 it managed to elect one representative to the national Chamber of Deputies.

The special statute region of Trentino-Alto Adige contains a large German-speaking population inhabiting the territories Italy acquired from Austria (the Alto Adige area) following World War I. Postwar agreements resulted in considerable administrative autonomy of these territories and in a guarantee by the Italian government to uphold certain linguistic rights for the German-speakers. The region was given special status in 1948. However, the addition of the Italian province of Trentino to the largely German-speaking area of Alto Adige effectively diluted the political voice of the German-speaking population in the Regional Council. Dissatisfaction among the German inhabitants increased in intensity, with numerous acts of terrorism being committed against the symbols of Italian authority. As a result of prolonged negotiations between Austria and Italy, a new statute for the region was instituted in 1971.

The problems of the German-speaking population in Alto Adige led to the creation of the South Tirol People's Party (*Südtiroler Volkspartei*: SVP) in 1948. The party demanded a more equitable treatment of the German population in South Tirol (province of Bolzano), and the SVP received the tacit backing of the Austrian government. Between 1948 and 1979, the SVP was represented by three deputies in the national Chamber of Deputies, and the party's representation increased to four seats in 1979. In nonlinguistic matters, the SVP has essentially followed a conservative Catholic orientation.

Other parties in the South Tirol that have appealed to the German-speaking populations include the Social Democratic Party of South Tirol (*Sozialdemokratische Partei Südtirols*: SPS), which traces its origins to the late 19th century; the Social Progress Party (*Soziale Fortschrittspartei*), a small liberal grouping; and the Trentino Tirol People's Party (*Trentiner Tiroler Volkspartei*: TTVP), which has pressed German linguistic rights in the province of Trentino. All three parties are small local groupings that have limited their activities to the provincial and regional councils.

The special statute region of Val d'Aosta, located at the base of the Pennine Alps, is predominantly French-speaking. It, too, has spawned an autonomist movement in the form of the Val d'Aosta Union (*Union Valdôtaine*). The Union was first represented in the national Chamber of Deputies in 1958 with one seat, which it retained in 1963. The Union was not represented at the national level again until 1979 when the Val d'Aosta Rally (*Rassemblement Valdôtain; Valdostani*)—an electoral alliance formed of several autonomist groupings—secured one seat.

REPUBLICAN FASCIST PARTY. *See* NATIONAL FASCIST PARTY.

REVOLUTIONARY ACTION BANDS. *See* NATIONAL FASCIST PARTY.

ROSA DEI VENTI. *See* ITALIAN SOCIAL MOVEMENT.

SAM. *See* ITALIAN SOCIAL MOVEMENT.

SARAGAT SOCIALISTS. *See* ITALIAN DEMOCRATIC SOCIALIST PARTY.

SARDINIAN ACTION PARTY. *See* REGIONAL AUTONOMIST PARTIES.

SICILIAN SEPARATIST MOVEMENT. *See* REGIONAL AUTONOMIST PARTIES.

SOCIAL DEMOCRATIC PARTY OF SOUTH TIROL. *See* REGIONAL AU-TONOMIST PARTIES.

SOCIAL MASSIMALISMO. *See* ITALIAN SOCIALIST PARTY.

SOCIALIST INITIATIVE. *See* ITALIAN DEMOCRATIC SOCIALIST PARTY.

SOCIALISTI RIFORMISTI. *See* DEMOCRATIC LABOR PARTY and ITAL-IAN SOCIALIST PARTY.

SOCIALIST PARTY: ITALIAN SECTION OF INTERNATIONAL SOCIAL-ISM. *See* ITALIAN DEMOCRATIC SOCIALIST PARTY.

SOCIALIST PARTY OF ITALIAN WORKERS. *See* ITALIAN DEMOCRATIC SOCIALIST PARTY.

SOCIALIST UNITY. *See* ITALIAN DEMOCRATIC SOCIALIST PARTY.

SOCIAL PROGRESS PARTY. *See* REGIONAL AUTONOMIST PARTIES.

SOUTH TIROL PEOPLE'S PARTY. *See* REGIONAL AUTONOMIST PARTIES.

SOZIALDEMOKRATISCHE PARTEI SÜDTIROLS. *See* REGIONAL AU-TONOMIST PARTIES.

SOZIALE FORTSCHRITTSPARTEI. *See* REGIONAL AUTONOMIST PARTIES.

SPS. *See* REGIONAL AUTONOMIST PARTIES.

SQUADRE AZIONE MUSSOLINI. *See* ITALIAN SOCIAL MOVEMENT.

STUDENT MOVEMENT. *See* ITALIAN SOCIALIST PARTY OF PROLE-TARIAN UNITY (1964-1972).

SÜDTIROLER VOLKSPARTEI. *See* REGIONAL AUTONOMIST PARTIES.

SVP. *See* REGIONAL AUTONOMIST PARTIES.

TRENTINER TIROLER VOLKSPARTEI. *See* REGIONAL AUTONOMIST PARTIES.

TRENTINO TIROL PEOPLE'S PARTY. *See* REGIONAL AUTONOMIST PARTIES.

TTVP. *See* REGIONAL AUTONOMIST PARTIES.

UNIFIED COMMUNIST PARTY OF ITALY. *See* ITALIAN COMMUNIST PARTY.

UNIFIED SOCIALIST PARTY. *See* ITALIAN SOCIALIST PARTY.

UNIONE DEMOCRATICA NAZIONALE. *See* ITALIAN LIBERAL PARTY.

UNION OF SOCIALISTS. *See* ITALIAN SOCIALIST PARTY.

UNION VALDÔTAINE. *See* REGIONAL AUTONOMIST PARTIES.

UNITARY SOCIALIST PARTY (1922-1926). *See* ITALIAN SOCIALIST PARTY.

UNITARY SOCIALIST PARTY (1949-1951). *See* ITALIAN DEMOCRATIC SOCIALIST PARTY.

UNITARY SOCIALIST PARTY OF ITALIAN WORKERS. *See* ITALIAN DEMOCRATIC SOCIALIST PARTY.

UNITÀ SOCIALISTA. *See* ITALIAN DEMOCRATIC SOCIALIST PARTY.

UQ. *See* COMMON MAN FRONT.

VAL D'AOSTA RALLY. *See* REGIONAL AUTONOMIST PARTIES.

VAL D'AOSTA UNION. *See* REGIONAL AUTONOMIST PARTIES.

VALDÔSTANI. *See* REGIONAL AUTONOMIST PARTIES.

WORKERS' POLITICAL MOVEMENT. *See* ITALIAN SOCIALIST PARTY OF PROLETARIAN UNITY (1964-1972).

WORKERS' POWER. *See* ITALIAN SOCIALIST PARTY OF PROLETARIAN UNITY (1964-1972).

WORKER'S VANGUARD. *See* ITALIAN SOCIALIST PARTY OF PROLETARIAN UNITY (1964-1972).

YOUNG FASCISTS. *See* NATIONAL FASCIST PARTY.

YOUNG ITALY. *See* ITALIAN SOCIAL MOVEMENT.

YOUNG ITALY MOVEMENT OF THE ITALIAN NATIONAL AWAKENING. *See* ITALIAN REPUBLICAN PARTY.

YOUTH FRONT. *See* ITALIAN SOCIAL MOVEMENT.

Anthony James Joes

TABLE 51. Distribution of Seats in Italy's Chamber of Deputies, 1900-1924

Party	1900	1904	1909	1913	1919	1921	1924*
Catholics[a]	—	—	16	29	—	—	—
Economic Party	—	—	—	—	7	5	—
Ex-Servicemen's Party	—	—	—	—	20	10	—
Italian Communist Party	—	—	—	—	—	15	19
Italian Popular Party[b]	—	—	—	—	100	108	39
Italian Republican Party	29	24	24	17	4	6	7
Italian Socialist Party	33	29	41	52	156	123	22
Liberals[c]	412	415	382	310	197	221	15
National Fascist Party[d]	—	—	—	—	—	35	375
Radical Party (1878-1921)	34	37	45	73	12	0	—
Reformist and Independent Socialists	—	—	—	27	7	1	24
Independents and others	0	0	0	0	5	11	34
Total	508	508	508	508	508	535	535

* The 1924 election was conducted under the Acerbo Law, which awarded two-thirds of the Chamber seats to the party obtaining the largest number of votes (if not less than 25 percent). The remaining one-third of the seats was apportioned among the other parties proportionately, according to their relative shares of the popular vote.

a Prior to the establishment of the Italian Popular Party in 1919, no formal Catholic Party organization existed in Italy. These figures include both those deputies designated as Catholics and Conservative Catholics.

b Became the Christian Democratic Party in 1943 (see table 52).

c Includes various liberal and centrist groupings (including the Constitutional Democrats) that were allied with the Italian Liberal Party.

d In 1921, figure represents those Fascists elected on the National Bloc (Fascist) list.

TABLE 52. Distribution of Seats in Italy's Chamber of Deputies, 1946-1979

Party	1946	1948	1953	1958	1963	1968	1972	1976	1979
Action Party[a]	7	—	—	—	—	—	—	—	—
Christian Democratic Party[b]	207	305	263	273	260	266	267	262	262
Common Man Front	30	—	—	—	—	—	—	—	—
Democratic Party of Proletarian Unity for Communism[c]	—	—	—	—	—	—	—	6	6
Italian Communist Party	104 }	183*	143	140	166	177	179	228	201
Italian Socialist Party	115 }		75	84	87 }	91**	61	57	62
Italian Democratic Socialist Party[d]	—	33	19	22	32 }		29	15	20
Italian Liberal Party[e]	41	19	13	17	40	31	21	5	9
Italian Republican Party	23	9	5	6	6	9	14	14	16
Italian Socialist Party of Proletarian Unity (1964-1972)[f]	—	—	—	—	—	23	0	—	—
Italian Social Movement	—	6	29	24	27	24 }	56 }	35	30
Monarchists[g]	16	14	40	25	8	6 }			0
Radical Party (1955-)	—	—	—	0	0	0	0	4	18
Regional parties:									
Movement for Trieste	—	—	—	—	—	—	—	0	1
Sardinian Action Party	2	0	0	0	0	0	0	0	0
Sicilian Separatist Movement	4	0	—	—	—	—	—	—	—
South Tirol People's Party	—	3	3	3	3	3	3	3	4
Val d'Aosta Union[h]	0	0	0	1	1	0	0	0	1
Independents and others	7	1	0	0	0	0	0	1	0
Total	556	574	590	596	630	630	630	630	630

- An electoral coalition known as the Popular Front, in which the Communists secured 131 seats and the Socialists obtained 52 seats. During 1945-1947, the Italian Socialist Party was known as the Italian Socialist Party of Proletarian Unity (1945-1947).

- • A temporary merger known as the Unified Socialist Party.

a Merged into the Italian Socialist Party in 1947.

b See also Catholics and Italian Popular Party, table 51.

c In 1976 election, known as Proletarian Democracy, an electoral coalition that also included the Worker's Vanguard and the Continuous Struggle (extremist organizations); ran alone in 1979.

d Known as the Socialist Party of Italian Workers, 1947-1951; Unitary Socialist Party of Italian Workers, 1951-1952.

e In 1946, figure represents seats won by the Liberals as part of the National Democratic Union (which also included the Democratic Labor Party and the Action Party); in 1948, the Liberals contested with the remnants of the Common Man Front under the National Bloc (Liberal) label.

f Merged into the Italian Communist Party in 1972; but later the same year, extremist elements of the Proletarian Unity (1964-1972) split off from the Communists and formed the Democratic Party of Proletarian Unity for Communism (see also footnote c).

g In 1946, known as the National Freedom Bloc; in 1948, as the National Monarchist Party. In 1958, there were two monarchist parties: the Popular Monarchist Party (14 seats) and the National Monarchist Party (11 seats). In 1963 and 1968 elections, known as the Italian Democratic Party of Monarchical Unity; in 1972 and 1976, formed an electoral alliance with the Italian Social Movement known as the National Right; in 1979, the monarchists split off from the alliance and contested separately as the National Democracy-Right Constituent.

h In 1979, contested with other regional autonomy groups as the Val d'Aosta Rally.

TABLE 53. Ruling Coalitions in Italy since 1948

Formation Date	Coalition
May 1948	Christian Democratic Party Italian Democratic Socialist Party Italian Republican Party Italian Liberal Party
Jan. 1950	Christian Democratic Party Italian Democratic Socialist Party Italian Republican Party
July 1951	Christian Democratic Party Italian Republican Party
July 1953	Christian Democratic Party
Feb. 1954	Christian Democratic Party Italian Democratic Socialist Party Italian Liberal Party
May 1957	Christian Democratic Party
July 1958	Christian Democratic Party Italian Democratic Socialist Party
Feb. 1959	Christian Democratic Party
Feb. 1962	Christian Democratic Party Italian Democratic Socialist Party Italian Republican Party
June 1963	Christian Democratic Party
Dec. 1963	Christian Democratic Party Italian Socialist Party Italian Democratic Socialist Party Italian Republican Party
June 1968	Christian Democratic Party
Dec. 1968	Christian Democratic Party Unified Socialist Party Italian Republican Party
Aug. 1969	Christian Democratic Party Italian Socialist Party
Mar. 1970	Christian Democratic Party Italian Democratic Socialist Party
Aug. 1970	Christian Democratic Party Italian Democratic Socialist Party Italian Socialist Party Italian Republican Party

TABLE 53. (*Continued*)

Formation Date	Coalition
Feb. 1972	Christian Democratic Party
June 1972	Christian Democratic Party Italian Democratic Socialist Party Italian Liberal Party
July 1973	Christian Democratic Party Italian Democratic Socialist Party Italian Socialist Party Italian Republican Party
Mar. 1974	Christian Democratic Party Italian Democratic Socialist Party Italian Socialist Party
Nov. 1974	Christian Democratic Party Italian Republican Party
Feb. 1976	Christian Democratic Party
Aug. 1979	Christian Democratic Party Italian Democratic Socialist Party Italian Liberal Party
Apr. 1980	Christian Democratic Party Italian Socialist Party Italian Republican Party
Oct. 1980	Christian Democratic Party Italian Democratic Socialist Party Italian Socialist Party Italian Republican Party
June 1981	Italian Republican Party Christian Democratic Party Italian Democratic Socialist Party Italian Socialist Party Italian Liberal Party

Note: First-named party is dominant coalition party.

LIECHTENSTEIN

The PRINCIPALITY OF LIECHTENSTEIN (*Fürstentum Liechtenstein*) is located in a mountainous region between Switzerland and Austria. Although it is one of Europe's smallest independent countries (61 square miles), Liechtenstein is also one of the most industrialized on a per capita basis. The population of approximately 25,220 (1980 census) is mostly Roman Catholic and speaks a Germanic dialect called Alemannic. The nation's economy is primarily based upon the production of industrial goods for export. Principal trading partners are Switzerland, with which Liechtenstein has shared a customs and currency union since 1923, and the European Economic Community, with which Liechtenstein has a special trading agreement.

The Princely Government of Liechtenstein was established in 1719 and has had a representative unicameral legislature (the *Landtag*) since the government became a hereditary constitutional monarchy in 1862. From 1815 to 1866, Liechtenstein was a member of the German Confederation (*see* HISTORICAL GERMANY), after which the state was allied with Austria. The alliance with Austria was abrogated on November 7, 1918, in compliance with the breakup of the Austro-Hungarian Empire as directed by the World War I peace settlements.

Prior to 1918, representatives to the *Landtag* were elected indirectly—eligible male citizens in each community voted for electors (one for every 24 voters) who, in turn, met at a designated location and cast ballots for representatives to the *Landtag*. Direct male suffrage was introduced in 1918; and since 1969, all male citizens over age 20 (approximately 5,000 in 1982) have been eligible to vote directly for representatives to the 15-member *Landtag* assembly. *Landtag* members serve four-year terms, subject to earlier dissolution of the *Landtag* (*see* table 54), and are elected on the basis of proportional representation in two major constituencies: Oberland and Unterland. Female suffrage in *Landtag* elections does not yet exist despite growing popular sympathy for it. However, women were granted the right to vote at the communal level in 1976.

Under the newest constitution, adopted in 1921, executive functions are exercised by the prince and a five-member collegial Board of Councillors whose chairman and members are nominated by the prince with *Landtag* concurrence. The deputy chairman is usually, but not necessarily, a member of the minority coalition party. Since 1938 the government administration has been bipartisan, with both parties sitting in coalition on the Board of Councillors.

Prior to the inception of direct male suffrage in 1918, political parties did not exist in Liechtenstein. Voters and electors simply chose from among preferred personalities in their respective communities. Party development began in 1914 when a trade union movement, supported by workmen in the building and handicraft trades, formed to seek extended rights for the citizenry and a severance of Liechtenstein's pre-World War I economic ties with Austria in favor of new connections with Switzerland. The movement developed a political character during the war years and emerged as the People's Party,* following the movement's success in inducing the introduction of direct male suffrage in 1918.

Seeking to counterbalance possible political domination by the working class, members of the agricultural community and various middle-class elements established their own party—the Progressive Citizens' Party (FBP)*—in that same year. The FBP was essentially a conservative grouping but has had its liberal colorations. For example, the initial 1918 party platform called for: (1) a government executive responsible to both a popularly elected *Landtag* and to the prince, (2) frequent and regular sessions of the *Landtag*, (3) selection of government councillors from among the common citizenry, and (4) the expansion of social welfare benefits for the working class. Both the People's Party and the FBP were nationalistic in outlook and expressed the theme, "Liechtenstein for the Liechtensteiners."

From the very beginning, both the People's Party and the FBP professed allegiance to monarchy as the basis of national government, proclaimed their loyalty to the princely house, and stood solidly behind the principles of democracy, social progress, and Christianity. Consequently, their platforms tended to converge, narrowing both their ideological differences and the gap in their respective numbers. As a further result, since 1938 Liechtenstein's government has consisted of a coalition of these two parties (*see* table 55).

The People's Party maintained a strong majority over the FBP during the ten years following the introduction of direct male suffrage. However, in 1928 electoral sentiment shifted to the right, and the FBP advanced in representation. It continued to build strength throughout the 1930s and remained well entrenched until 1970, holding a parliamentary majority for a record of 42 years. In 1970 the Patriotic Union* (formerly the People's Party) managed to obtain a slight majority over the FBP and held that lead for one term. In 1974 the FBP regained the lead but lost it once more in the *Landtag* elections of 1978. The 1982 elections revealed no change in party strength.

Bibliography

Batliner, Gerard. "Strukturelemente des Kleinstaates: Grundlagen einer Liechtensteinischen Politik—Ein Versuch," *Fragen an Liechtenstein*. Published as *Liechtenstein*

Politische Schriften No. 1. Vaduz: Verlag der Liechtensteinischen Akademischen Gessellschaft, 1972, pp. 11-29.

Constitution of the Principality of Liechtenstein. Vaduz: Presidial Office of the Princely Government, 1965.

Kohn, Walter S. G. *Governments and Politics of the German-Speaking Countries.* Chicago: Nelson-Hall, 1980.

Kranz, Walter, ed. *The Principality of Liechtenstein: A Documentary Handbook.* Vaduz: Government Press and Information Office, 1978.

Pappermann, Ernst. *Die Regierung des Fürstentums Liechtenstein.* Bigge/Rhr, Germany: Josefsdruckerei, 1967.

Raton, Pierre. *Liechtenstein: History and Institutions of the Principality.* Vaduz: Liechtenstein Verlag, 1970.

Seger, Otto. "Political Parties." In *The Principality of Liechtenstein: A Documentary Handbook,* edited by Walter Kranz. Vaduz: Government Press and Information Office, 1978, pp. 202-203.

U.S. Department of State. "Liechtenstein." *Background Notes Series,* no. 8610. Washington, D.C.: Government Printing Office, October 1976.

Political Parties

CHRISTIAN SOCIAL PARTY (*Christlich Soziale Partei:* CSP). The CSP is a small religious-oriented grouping that was formed a few weeks before the 1962 *Landtag* elections. The party's electoral support has been relatively meager, and it has, so far, failed to gain a seat in the *Landtag.* The CSP did not present any candidates in 1978 or 1982. The party publishes a weekly paper, *Der Liechtensteiner Wochenspiegel.*

CHRISTLICH SOZIALE PARTEI. *See* CHRISTIAN SOCIAL PARTY.

CSP. *See* CHRISTIAN SOCIAL PARTY.

FATHERLAND UNION. *See* PATRIOTIC UNION.

FBP. *See* PROGRESSIVE CITIZENS' PARTY.

FORTSCHRITTLICHE BÜRGERPARTIE. *See* PROGRESSIVE CITIZENS' PARTY.

PATRIOTIC UNION (*Väterlandische Union:* VU). The former People's Party* changed its official name to the Patriotic Union in 1936. In 1970 the VU gained a majority position in the *Landtag* for the first time. This majority was lost in 1974 but regained in 1978 and kept in 1982. The Patriotic Union (also referred to as the Fatherland Union) continued to profess its predecessor's liberal social and economic policies and continues to be supported mainly by working-class elements. The VU's current electoral strength resides in the constituency of Oberland. The party publishes a paper, *Liechtensteiner Vaterland*, three times per week.

PEOPLE'S PARTY (*Volkspartie*: VP). The VP was formed in 1918 as a direct outgrowth of the trade union movement in Liechtenstein. Although professing loyalty to the monarchical form of government, the original party platform was based on an expansion of democracy and social progress. In 1936 the VP changed its name to the Patriotic Union.* It continued throughout the century to profess liberal social and economic goals, and it was supported mainly by the working class. It remained the minority party until 1970 when, under its name of the Patriotic Union, it became the majority party in the *Landtag* for the first time.

PROGRESSIVE CITIZENS' PARTY (*Fortschrittliche Bürgerpartie*: FBP). The FBP was organized in 1918 by elements of the middle-class and agricultural community in response to the then recently formed and labor-oriented People's Party.* Although the FBP espouses democratic principles and social progress, its basic orientation reflects the views of various conservative interests in Liechtenstein society. Between 1928 and 1970, the FBP was the dominant government party. The FBP regained its majority status in 1974 but is currently in the minority as a result of losses in the 1978 and 1982 elections. The party's electoral strength resides in Unterland. The FBP publishes the *Liechtensteiner Volksblatt* four times per week.

VÄTERLANDISCHE UNION. *See* PATRIOTIC UNION.

VOLKSPARTIE. *See* PEOPLE'S PARTY.

VP. *See* PEOPLE'S PARTY.

VU. *See* PATRIOTIC UNION.

Joseph H. Rogatnick

TABLE 54. Distribution of Seats in Liechtenstein's *Landtag*, 1922-1982

Party	1922	1926	1928	1932	1936	1939	1945	1949	1953	1957	1958	1962	1966	1970	1974*	1978	1982
Patriotic Union	11	9	4	2	4	7	7	7	7	7	6	7	7	8	7	8	8
Progressive Citizens' Party	4	6	11	13	11	8	8	8	8	8	9	8	8	7	8	7	7
Total	15	15	15	15	15	15	15	15	15	15	15	15	15	15	15	15	15

* The electoral system was changed to one of proportional representation in 1973 in which a vote cast for a candidate was also a vote cast for the candidate's party. Prior to this change, the electoral system was based on party lists with multiple candidates.

TABLE 55. Ruling Parties or Coalitions in Liechtenstein since 1918

Year	Party or Coalition
1918-1928	People's Party
1928-1938	Progressive Citizens' Party
1938-1970	Progressive Citizens' Party Patriotic Union*
1970-1974	Patriotic Union Progressive Citizens' Party
1974-1978	Progressive Citizens' Party Patriotic Union
1978-	Patriotic Union Progressive Citizens' Party

Note: First-named party is dominant coalition party.
* New name of People's Party after 1936.

LUXEMBOURG

The GRAND DUCHY OF LUXEMBOURG (*Grand-Duché de Luxembourg*, French; *Grossherzogtum Luxemburg*, Letzeburgish) is a small but thriving nation of western Europe. Its 999 square miles (a bit smaller than Rhode Island) is nestled between France and Germany, southeast of Belgium. French is the official language of government and business; German is used extensively in the church and schools; and *Letzeburgish*, a West Frankish dialect, is the local language and is spoken by all. Most Luxembourgers speak all three languages, and this complete mixture has precluded the Grand Duchy from ethno-linguistic problems of the type found, for example, in Belgium.

Luxembourg's population of 363,000 (1979 estimate, of which about 25 percent are aliens) is most densely located in the southern region of the country; approximately 75 percent of the Grand Duchy's population resides in this area of heavy industrial concentration and favorable agricultural geography. The forested and slightly mountainous northern region, formerly an area of extensive small-scale farming efforts, has traditionally been less populated than the south; however, since World War II the north has suffered population loss as more than one-half of its farmers have migrated to more profitable industrial employment in the south.

The Grand Duchy enjoys one of western Europe's highest standards of living. Approximately 48 percent of the nation's work force is employed in services, 46 percent in industry, and six percent in agriculture. With large low-grade iron ore deposits in the southwest, iron and steel are the Grand Duchy's core industries—in 1978 accounting for 54 percent of the nation's exports, 25 percent of the GNP, and employing about 33 percent of industrial labor. However, Luxembourg lacks its own sources of industrial fuels and is totally dependent on the importation of coke and rich iron ore for its steel industry. Being thus dependent on international trade, the Grand Duchy has been an active advocate of European political and economic cooperation. To this end, the Belgium-Luxembourg Economic Union (BLEU) was formed in 1921; Luxembourg was a founding member of both NATO (in 1949) and of the European Economic Community (in 1957); and (in 1960) the Grand Duchy joined Belgium and the Netherlands to form the Benelux Economic Union. More recently, the Luxembourg government has sought further economic and political support by creating a favorable environment for foreign investment, primarily through tax incentives. United States multinational corporations, for example, dominate Luxembourg's newer rubber, chemical, and metal-fabricating industries. While the Grand Duchy has long harbored strong pro-U.S. sentiments and policies, the government has also opened the door to Soviet cooperation in certain areas, as indicated by the June 1975 agreement to explore cooperation in air transport, science, and technology.

Luxembourg's political history, like those of most European nations, has been one of mixed autonomy and foreign rule. The founding of Luxembourg is accredited to Count Sigefroid, a descendent of Charlemagne, who in A.D. 963 reconstructed a small Roman fortress called *Lucilinburhuc* (Little Castle) on the site of the present capital city of Luxembourg (same name as the country). Over the next 480 years the fortress expanded into an autonomous feudal estate. In 1443 the land fell to the dukes of Burgundy and eventually passed through marriage to the possession of the Holy Roman Empire; rule for the next 372 years passed among various Spanish and Austrian Habsburgs and to the French.

Luxembourg's modern political history begins in 1815 when the Congress of Vienna, attempting to restore the pre-Napoleonic balance of European powers and to provide a geographic buffer between Napoleon's France and the rest of Europe, assigned Luxembourg its status of Grand Duchy, subject to the king of the Netherlands. Belgium, also assigned to Holland by the Vienna congress, revolted in 1830 and claimed Luxembourg as part of its own territory. The Netherlands formally recognized Belgium's independence in 1839. At that time, under the Treaty of London, Luxembourg was partitioned, with the western, French-speaking section made a province of Belgium and the rest of Luxembourg released back to Holland. Though the Dutch kings continued to rule as dukes of the Grand Duchy, in 1839 Holland granted Luxembourg its own representative assembly. With the second Treaty of London in 1867, Luxembourg was granted total independence as a neutral nation. The Grand Duchy retained its neutral status well into the 20th century; but after German occupation during both world wars, Luxembourg formally abandoned its neutrality in 1949 by participating in the founding of the North Atlantic Treaty Organization (NATO).

Luxembourg is a hereditary, constitutional monarchy with a parliamentary form of national government. The constitution dates from 1868. A grand duke (or duchess) is chief of state but has few political powers beyond the nomination of a prime minister designate. Actual executive power is vested in the Cabinet of Ministers, which acts in the name of the grand duke. The Cabinet is led by the prime minister, who is the leader of the majority political party or coalition. At the local level, the country is subdivided into three administrative districts and 126 communes. The districts function as links between the central and local governments and are headed by commissioners appointed by the national Cabinet. The communes are administered by elected councils, but each is headed by a mayor (*Bürgermeister*) who is appointed by the grand duke and is not necessarily a member of the communal council.

National legislative power in Luxembourg rests with the bicameral parliament, consisting of the Council of State (*Conseil d'État*) and the Chamber of Deputies (*Chambre des Députés*). The Council of State is chiefly an advisory body to the grand duke. Its 21 members receive life-long appointments, with seven members appointed by the grand duke and the others appointed by the Council itself or by the grand duke upon proposals from the Chamber of Deputies. The Council has some legislative authority insofar as it must be consulted in the proposal of all new bills. Furthermore, once the Chamber of Deputies has adopted a law, the Council has three months in which to hand down its final opinion, which also must be considered before the law is formally enacted. Thus the Council's power is primarily that of postponement—its opinion is not binding upon and can be vetoed by the Chamber.

The Chamber of Deputies was introduced as a representative body in 1868. Formerly, the deputies were elected to six-year terms, with partial elections (for one-half of the Chamber seats) being held every three years (for example, *see* table 57). In 1956 the constitution was amended to call for general elections to all seats of the Chamber every five years, if no earlier dissolution occurs (*see* table 58). The deputies are directly elected according to proportional representation. Suffrage is universal and compulsory, beginning at age 18 (lowered from age 21 before the 1974 elections). In 1979, despite the compulsory suffrage, of an eligible electorate of about 210,000 citizens, 188,909 actually went to the polls. Age eligibility to run for office begins at 21 years. Each elector in the four electoral districts (established in 1924) casts a number of votes equal to the number of Chamber seats proportioned to his/her residential district. (For the June 10, 1979, election, the North district was represented by nine seats, the South by 24, the East by six, and the Central district by 20 seats.) Likewise, each political party may run in each district as many candidates as there are Chamber seats available to that district.

Luxembourg permits three methods of suffrage: "list voting," by which the elector votes in a bloc for one party ticket, thereby giving one vote to each candidate on that list; "nominative voting," by which the elector votes on a single party ticket but can selectively cast up to two of his/her allotted votes per candidate; and *panachage* or "variegated voting," by which the elector can cast up to two of his/her allotted votes per candidate but may choose from among different party tickets.

All of Luxembourg's political parties resent the permitting of *panachage* voting, believing it destructive to true proportional (and ideological) representation. The parties urge their respective members to vote instead in party blocs. This is because the seats to each district are proportionally distributed by cumulating the total votes cast for each party ticket. (For a simplified example, consider the East district which is currently allotted six Chamber seats. If Party X has received 50 percent of the total votes cast in that district, then Party X is entitled to three of those Chamber positions and will seat its three top vote-getting candidates. This will occur even if one of those individual candidates has received fewer votes than an individual candidate from some other party. Thus votes cast for an individual may not personally help him or her to get elected.) The most striking feature of this electoral system, therefore, is that it permits the elector to rank his or her preferences with regard both to the individual candidates and to the parties.

A study by Belgium's *Centre de Recherche et d'Information Socio-Politique* showed that in the 1974 election, votes cast in blocs (list voting) represented 58 percent of the national voting pattern, with 15.2 percent of the remaining votes cast nominatively and 26.8 percent cast by *panachage.* The parties that benefit most from list voting are those with a well-defined ideology aimed at a particular social group. Such parties include the Socialist Workers' Party of Luxembourg* and the Communist Party of Luxembourg,* which in the 1974 election received respectively 79.3 and 67.8 percent of their votes from list voting. The parties with open, catchall doctrines and that seek support from a variety of social groups benefit more from the other forms of voting. Hence in 1974, support for the long-ruling Christian Social Party* (*see* table 56) was 50.8 percent from list voting, 19.5 percent nominative, and 29.7 percent variegated; support for the Democratic Party* was 52 percent list, 13.5 percent nominative, and 34.5 percent variegated.

In addition to the seven parties that won seats in the 1979 election, three other parties contested but did not gain representation. These were: the Alternative "Defend Yourself" Ticket (*Defendez-Vous; Alternativ Lëscht-Wiert Iech*), winning slightly less than one percent of the national total votes, primarily in the South and Central electoral districts; the Communist Revolutionary League, winning 0.22 percent of total votes cast, primarily in the South and Central districts; and the Liberal Party, winning 0.20 percent of total votes cast, with support only in the Central district.

Bibliography

Delvaux, Michel, and Mario Hirsch. "Le Grand-Duché de Luxembourg: Aspects de sociologie politique." *Res Publica* (Brussels), vol. 18, no. 1 (1976).

French Embassy (in cooperation with members of the European Community). *European Elections, June 7-10, 1979.* Multilith. New York: French Embassy, May 1979.

Keesing's Contemporary Archives. London: Keesings Publications, volumes for election years.

Luxembourg Embassy. *Results of June 10, 1979, National Elections.* Xerox. Washington, D.C., June-July 1979.

Mackie, Thomas T., and Richard Rose. *The International Almanac of Electoral History.* New York: Free Press, 1974.

Staar, Richard F., ed. *Yearbook on International Communist Affairs 1977.* Stanford, Calif.: Hoover Institution Press, 1977.

U. S. Department of State. "Luxembourg." *Background Notes Series,* no. 7856. Washington, D.C.: Government Printing Office, December 1979.

Weil, Gordon L. *The Benelux Nations: The Politics of Small-Country Democracies.* New York: Holt, Rinehart and Winston, 1970.

Political Parties

ALTERNATIVE "DEFEND YOURSELF" TICKET. *See* LUXEMBOURG INTRODUCTION.

ALTERNATIV LËSCHT-WIERT IECH. *See* LUXEMBOURG INTRODUCTION.

BLOC DE LA GAUCHE. *See* SOCIALIST WORKERS' PARTY OF LUXEMBOURG.

BLOC OF THE LEFT. *See* SOCIALIST WORKERS' PARTY OF LUXEMBOURG.

CHRESCHTLECH SOZIAL VOLLEKSPARTEI. *See* CHRISTIAN SOCIAL PARTY.

CHRISTIAN SOCIAL PARTY (*Parti Chrétien Social:* PCS; *Chreschtlech Sozial Vollekspartei:* CSV). The PCS has been Luxembourg's strongest single party historically, since 1919 dominant in national government coalitions with only one interruption (1974-1979). In a country where 97 percent of the population is Roman Catholic, the Catholic-oriented PCS receives pervasive, natural support in all electoral districts and from moderate-conservative elements in all social groups, including farmers and laborers. Beginning as a Chamber of Deputies faction of the late 19th century, the Catholics organized in 1914 as the Party of the Right.* The change of name to the Christian Social Party occurred officially in 1945.

The PCS has always supported the centralized, monarchical government of Luxembourg. In the 1920s, for example, the PCS began to favor economic cooperation with other western European nations, including support for the 1929 Belgium-Luxembourg Economic Union (BLEU); at the same time, however, the party also strongly declared the maintenance of political autonomy from any of the Grand Duchy's 19th-century rulers. The modern PCS is comparable to other Christian democratic parties of western Europe. In seeking support from a variety of social groups, the PCS advocates progressive labor legislation, a social welfare program, and planned economic expansion through assistance to farmers and small businessmen—but all following a relatively conservative program.

Since World War II, there was only one period during which the dominant PCS did not form a coalition with either the Democratic Party (PD)* or the Socialist Workers' Party of Luxembourg (POSL).* From 1946 to 1948, the PCS prime minister, Pierre DuBong, organized instead his Government of the National Union, with all political parties represented in the cabinet. The 1948 partial elections, however, resulted in the Catholics' loss of three Chamber seats, which were in turn gained by the Socialists (with the other parties retain-ing the same number of seats). DuBong, fearing this shift in electoral sentiment, abandoned his National Union effort and formed the 1948 government coali-tion with the liberals (the PD). The next partial elections of 1951 brought the Catholics a further loss of one seat and a similar loss for the coalition Democrats. The Socialists' additional gain of four seats could not be ignored, and DuBong entered the PCS into coalition with the POSL.

In 1954, Luxembourg's ratification of the European Defense Community Treaty necessitated a new election for all Chamber seats in accordance with that agreement. In this election, the PCS regained five seats versus the Socialists' reduction of one seat. Nevertheless, upon DuBong's death in December of that year when Pierre Frieden assumed the PCS party leadership and the country's prime ministership, Frieden continued the Socialist coalition. Conflict grew between the coalition partners, however, and culminated in late 1958 over an issue concerning a Socialist minister's lack of action in an alleged bribe of a civil servant in his ministry. Criticism was voiced by the Democratic opposition and was joined by the PCS. Following a Chamber vote of no confidence against the minister in question, four POSL ministers resigned from the cabinet. To resolve this conflict in the national interest, Frieden resigned his government in De-cember 1958, and an election was called for February 1, 1959.

In the 1959 election, the Christian Social Party lost the five seats it had previously gained. This loss was attributed to a growing dissatisfaction among the peasantry, who sought greater government protection and therefore shifted their support to the Democratic Party. In response, the new prime minister, the PCS's Pierre Werner (who had been minister of finance and defense under Frieden) formed a coalition with the Democrats. This lasted only until the 1964 election, however, when the PCS and the Socialists, holding a combined total of 43 of the Chamber's 56 seats, formed their "grand coalition."

In 1968, Werner resigned his government due to a disagreement with the POSL coalition partner over the financing of the Grand Duchy's social welfare program. After the election, in which the PCS again emerged dominant, Wer-ner attempted to reinstate the PCS-POSL coalition, but there was still dis-agreement over the Socialists' proposal for increased worker participation in the management of state-controlled firms where they worked. Werner turned to the Democratic Party, which had won fewer seats than the Socialists but with whom the PCS could agree on a coalition program to stimulate the economy through new industries and new employment opportunities.

The 1974-1979 period was the only time since World War I that the Chris-tian Social Party did not participate in a government coalition. The PCS had narrowly won more seats than any other single party. But relative to the previous election, the PCS had lost electoral support, in this instance over the party's conservative stance on the major issues of liberalized abortion, women's rights, inflation control, and agricultural problems. In view of his party's losses at the polls, Werner resigned as prime minister one day after the 1974 election. Grand

Duke Jean asked Gaston Thorn, chairman of the Democratic Party, to form a government. The resulting PD-POSL coalition lasted for only one term, however, and the June 10, 1979, election brought the PCS and Werner back into power.

In 1979 the Christian Social Party captured by far the greatest number of votes won by any single party in that election (34.5 percent; with the next-highest percentage, 24.3, being won the Socialists; followed by 21.3 percent won by the Democratic Party). Negotiations for a coalition partnership began immediately after the election, and four weeks later the PCS formally announced its coalition with the Democratic Party. Shortly thereafter, Prime Minister Werner announced that the coalition program would emphasize the seeking of energy imports in order to avoid construction of a nuclear reactor within Luxembourg; encouragement of further foreign investment in the Grand Duchy; attempts to deal with inflation; and addressing the previous government's liberalization of the nation's abortion and divorce laws.

COMMUNIST PARTY OF LUXEMBOURG (*Parti Communiste de Luxembourg*: PCL; *Kommunistesch Partei*: KP). Founded in 1921, the early history of Luxembourg's Communist Party was somewhat tenuous. Fearing the spread of Communist influence, in April 1937 the Grand Duchy's Chamber of Deputies voted 34 to 19 (with one abstention) to dissolve the PCL for "the maintenance of Public order." An ensuing national plebiscite rejected the dissolution by a slim margin of 50.7 percent to 49.3 percent of votes cast. The Communists gained influence and significance after World War II, however, due in part to the enhanced prestige of the Soviet Union.

The PCL receives its expected electoral support from urban and industrial laborers and from some left-wing intellectuals. The party's bastion is the heavily industrialized Southern electoral district, where it must compete with and sometimes cooperate with the more popular Socialist Workers' Party of Luxembourg. *
The PCL is a highly centralized grouping, with relatively little regional or local organization. Of Luxembourg's 1974 population of approximately 357,000, the PCL claimed 500 to 600 card-carrying members.

The Communists vote as a bloc in the Chamber. The PCL is strongly pro-Soviet; in fact, it was the only western European communist party to approve the 1968 Soviet invasion of Czechoslovakia. There is some indication that the PCL is financially dependent on Moscow. Likewise, the USSR's diplomatic representatives in the Grand Duchy exceed the number normally assigned to a small country. Ideologically, however, the PCL exercises some freedom in choosing its own path. The 1973 Luxembourg party congress declared that socialism could feasibly be constructed on an initial basis of a democratic, parliamentary form of government, and it rejected the goal of a one-party system as incompatible with Luxembourg's conditions and political traditions. Moreover, although the PCL ran (unsuccessfully) two candidates in the June 1979 elections to the

European Community Parliament, the party's stand is against European integration and refusal of Eurocommunism.

In the June 10, 1979, election to Luxembourg's national legislature, the PCL returned to the Chamber of Deputies with two seats (5.8 percent of total votes cast), which constituted a reduction from the five seats (and 10.4 percent of the vote) held from the 1974 election.

COMMUNIST REVOLUTIONARY LEAGUE. See LUXEMBOURG INTRODUCTION.

CSV. See CHRISTIAN SOCIAL PARTY.

DEFENDEZ-VOUS. See LUXEMBOURG INTRODUCTION.

DEMOCRATIC GROUP. See DEMOCRATIC PARTY.

DEMOCRATIC PARTY (*Parti Démocratique*: PD; *Demokratesch Partei*: DP). The PD (also popularly referred to as "the Liberals") traces its history to a liberal faction which dominated Luxembourg's Chamber of Deputies during the late 1800s and which organized as a national party at the turn of the century. Though first known as the Radical Liberal Party, the group has always been at the center of Luxembourg's political spectrum, receiving support from conservative and moderate elements of the business, white-collar professional, and urban middle classes.

The PD has gone through several name changes in its history; it was the Radical Liberal Party until 1937, when moderateness finally rendered senseless the "Radical" part of the party's name and the word was dropped; the Liberal Party until 1945, when World War II brought the return of German occupation and the flight to London of Grand Duchess Charlotte with her cabinet, with the party changing its name to the Patriotic and Democratic Group (*Groupement Patriotique et Démocratique*); in 1954 the liberals campaigned as the Democratic Group (*Groupement Démocratique*); and since 1954, the name has been the Democratic Party.

Regardless of its various historical names, the PD has remained ideologically moderate. It has always offered moderate opposition both to socialism and to religious considerations in politics (though it has sought to protect the nation's nonpolitical Catholic institutions); it is committed to free enterprise, with minimal governmental activity in the national economy, but also supports progressive labor and social legislation. The PD is very strong, however, in its support for European integration, seeing such international cooperation as a means toward improved economic and social conditions in all participating countries.

Since World War II, the PD has been the Grand Duchy's third-largest party in votes received, behind the traditionally dominant Christian Social Party* and the Socialist Workers' Party of Luxembourg.* Most PD support comes from the Central electoral district, which includes the Grand Duchy's largest city (the capital) and surrounding agricultural communities. During the last two elections (1974 and 1979), the PD promoted an image of a dynamic and modern party, a strategy which permitted the PD to increase electoral support in the remaining three districts.

Upon the Christian Social Party's (PCS) resignation from the government one day after the 1974 election, Grand Duke Jean asked PD leader Gaston Thorn to form a new government. The PD had won 14 seats (22.1 percent of votes cast). Thorn, who had been foreign minister in the previous cabinet, formed a coalition with the Socialist Workers' Party (POSL). This government instituted several new programs—most notably the liberalized reforms in Luxembourg's abortion and divorce laws, the introduction of sex education in the schools, and the reduction of adultery from its former consideration as a criminal offense. These issues had aroused much controversy in the 1974 election campaigns and had resulted in reduced electoral support for the traditionally dominant (but Catholic-oriented) Christian Social Party. Other PD-POSL programs included taxation adjustments to reduce burdens on the lower- and middle-income groups, and reforms regarding distribution of governmental incomes.

The June 10, 1979, election, however, ended the PD's control of government when the Christian Social Party was returned to power. In that election, the Democratic Party gained one seat in the Chamber (though its electoral support dropped by 0.8 percent from votes cast in 1974). During the 1979 election campaign, the PD had announced intentions to continue a coalition with the Socialists if the two parties won a joint parliamentary majority (as they had in 1974, winning a combined total of 31 of 59 Chamber seats). The 1979 election, however, resulted in the would-be Democratic-Socialist coalition slightly missing a majority by returning with only 29 of 59 seats. Therefore, when the Christian Social Party resumed government control, the PD entered into coalition negotiations with that party. The two groupings quickly reached an agreement, and the PCS-PD coalition was officially announced just four weeks after the election. Gaston Thorn, outgoing prime minister and continuing PD party leader, was appointed to the position of deputy prime minister under PCS Prime Minister Pierre Werner.

DEMOKRATESCH PARTEI. See DEMOCRATIC PARTY.

DP. See DEMOCRATIC PARTY.

EdF. See FORCED CONSCRIPTS.

ENRÔLÉS DE FORCE. See FORCED CONSCRIPTS.

FORCED CONSCRIPTS (Enrôlés de Force: EdF). The EdF organized for the 1979 election as a pressure group demanding compensation from the West

German government for the forced conscription of approximately 12,000 Luxembourgers into the German Army during World War II. With support in all but the Central electoral district, the EdF won one seat (with 4.4 percent of total votes cast). The EdF deputy is Joseph Weirich, who holds one of 24 seats representing the South electoral district.

GOVERNMENT OF THE NATIONAL UNION. *See* CHRISTIAN SOCIAL PARTY.

GROUPEMENT DÉMOCRATIQUE. *See* DEMOCRATIC PARTY.

GROUPEMENT PARTRIOTIQUE ET DÉMOCRATIQUE. *See* DEMOCRATIC PARTY.

INDEPENDENT SOCIALIST LIST (*Liste Indépendent Socialiste*). The Independent Socialist List was organized for the 1979 election by Jean Gremling (whose name is popularly added to the party title: "Jean Gremlings's Independent Socialist List"). Gremling won the party's one seat on a platform that accused the Socialist Workers' Party of Luxembourg* of compromising socialist ideals while in coalition power during the previous 1974-1979 government. The List received support only in the Central electoral district, resulting in 2.2 percent of the total national vote.

JEAM GREMLING'S INDEPENDENT SOCIALIST LIST. *See* INDEPENDENT SOCIALIST LIST.

KOMMUNISTESCH PARTEI. *See* COMMUNIST PARTY OF LUXEMBOURG.

KP. *See* COMMUNIST PARTY OF LUXEMBOURG.

LËSCHT-WIERT IECH. *See* LUXEMBOURG INTRODUCTION.

LIBERAL PARTY. *See* DEMOCRATIC PARTY and LUXEMBOURG INTRODUCTION.

LISTE INDÉPENDENT SOCIALISTE. *See* INDEPENDENT SOCIALIST LIST.

LSAP. *See* SOCIALIST WORKERS' PARTY OF LUXEMBOURG.

MIDDLE CLASS PARTY (*Parti des Classes Moyennes:* PCM). Formed shortly before the 1954 election, the Middle Class Party polled only 3,645 votes and failed to seat any candidates. The PCM was thereafter dissolved.

MIP. *See* POPULAR INDEPENDENT MOVEMENT.

MOUVEMENT INDÉPENDENT POPULAIRE. *See* POPULAR INDEPENDENT MOVEMENT.

PARTI CHRÉTIEN SOCIAL. *See* CHRISTIAN SOCIAL PARTY.

PARTI COMMUNISTE DE LUXEMBOURG. *See* COMMUNIST PARTY OF LUXEMBOURG.

PARTI DE LA DROITE. *See* PARTY OF THE RIGHT.

PARTI DE LA SOLIDARITÉ NATIONALE. *See* POPULAR INDEPENDENT MOVEMENT.

PARTI DÉMOCRATIQUE. *See* DEMOCRATIC PARTY.

PARTI DES CLASSES MOYENNES. *See* MIDDLE CLASS PARTY.

PARTI OUVRIER SOCIALISTE LUXEMBOURG. *See* SOCIALIST WORKERS' PARTY OF LUXEMBOURG.

PARTI SOCIAL-DÉMOCRATE. *See* SOCIAL DEMOCRATIC PARTY.

PARTY OF NATIONAL SOLIDARITY. *See* POPULAR INDEPENDENT MOVEMENT.

PARTY OF THE RIGHT (*Parti de la Droite*). As the ancestor of the modern Christian Social Party,* the Party of the Right was founded in 1914 in a successful effort to formally organize support for the conservative, Roman Catholic-oriented faction of Luxembourg's national legislature. The Party of the Right took this name to distinguish itself from its socialist-oriented opposition, then known as the Bloc of the Left (*see* Socialist Workers' Party of Luxembourg), and to reflect its stance in favor of the centralized, monarchical form of government. With the onset of World War II and fearing that "Rightism" might be construed as the political polarization identified with naziism and fascism, the party in 1945 formally changed its name to the Christian Social Party.

PATRIOTIC AND DEMOCRATIC GROUP. *See* DEMOCRATIC PARTY.

PCL. *See* COMMUNIST PARTY OF LUXEMBOURG.

PCM. *See* MIDDLE CLASS PARTY.

PCS. *See* CHRISTIAN SOCIAL PARTY.

PD. *See* DEMOCRATIC PARTY

POPULAR INDEPENDENT MOVEMENT (*Mouvement Indépendent Populaire*: MIP). The MIP contested the 1964 election. The party was a right-wing protest movement representing discontented elements in the working and white-collar classes. Though the MIP won two seats in 1964, it had no clear program; and it merged with the Democratic Party* prior to the 1968 election. One MIP deputy sought reelection in 1968, running as a candidate of the Party of National Solidarity (*Parti de la Solidarité Nationale*: PSN); but he was unsuccessful, and the PSN dissolved.

POSL. *See* SOCIALIST WORKERS' PARTY OF LUXEMBOURG.

PSD. *See* SOCIAL DEMOCRATIC PARTY.

PSN. *See* POPULAR INDEPENDENT MOVEMENT.

RADICAL LIBERAL PARTY. *See* DEMOCRATIC PARTY.

SDP. *See* SOCIAL DEMOCRATIC PARTY.

SOCIAL DEMOCRATIC PARTY (*Parti Social-Démocrate*: PSD; *Sozial Demokratesch Partei*: SDP). The PSD was formed in 1971 by a group of moderate dissidents of the Socialist Workers' Party of Luxembourg (POSL).* The split was led by Henry Cravatte, a former POSL party chairman and Luxembourg's deputy prime minister during the Socialists' 1964-1968 minority coalition partnership with the Christian Social Party.* Following the 1968 election, conflict grew within the POSL primarily regarding the issue of cooperation with the Communist Party of Luxembourg* at local levels. Unable to resolve the issue, Cravatte and five other POSL Chamber deputies left the Socialist Party in 1971 and formed the Social Democratic Party, which took five seats in the 1974 election. In the 1979 election, the PSD won only two seats (six percent of total votes cast), with one of those seats continuing to be held by Henry Cravatte.

The PSD is adamantly opposed to any governmental cooperation with the Communist Party. Furthermore, despite its origins in the POSL, the PSD is not a marxist party. It is of some European tendency, stressing the development of the individual European citizen through social solidarity. (*See also* Socialist Workers' Party of Luxembourg.)

SOCIALIST WORKERS' PARTY OF LUXEMBOURG (*Parti Ouvrier Socialiste Luxembourg*: POSL; *Letzeburger Sozialistesch Arbechter Partei*: LSAP). The socialist faction of Luxembourg's Chamber of Deputies first appeared in 1896 and was formally organized as a national party in 1902 under the name Bloc of the Left (*Bloc de la Gauche*). The Bloc adopted its current POSL name in 1924 as the party grew with its natural support base of the organized trade union movement.

POSL platforms are generally built on social welfare and insurance programs, the nationalization of resources, and the separation of religious considerations in the nation's politics and government. The party also favors European integration (as through the European Economic Community), offering as one of its goals a dynamic Europe serving all of its citizens, not a Europe dominated by the politics of multinational corporations. POSL support comes mostly from the heavily industrialized South electoral district and from lower and lower-middle urban classes in the other districts.

The POSL has traditionally been the Grand Duchy's second-largest party, behind only the Christian Social Party (PCS)* in number of votes received. The Socialists have variably participated in government coalitions since 1937. The POSL's "grand coalition" with the PCS was formed during 1964-1968 when the two parties held 43 of the Chamber's 56 seats (POSL-21, PCS-22). Prior to the 1964 election, the Socialists promoted a cooperative image, approaching that of the German Social Democratic Party (see WEST GERMANY). This strategy permitted the POSL to extend its influence beyond its Southern electoral bastion into the rest of the country. However, national support waned as the Socialists exhibited an increasing left-wing orientation; and in the 1968 election, the POSL lost three Chamber seats and its minority partnership in the government coalition.

These losses escalated personal and ideological rivalries within the party, the foremost of which was the issue of cooperation with the Communist Party of Luxembourg.* In the manner it had sought national-level cooperation with the Christian Social Party, the POSL had likewise encouraged compatibility with the Communists at the local level, particularly in the industrialized Southern electoral district where the two labor-oriented parties vie for support from the same electoral base. The conflict culminated in 1971 when six Socialist deputies left the POSL and formed the more socially moderate and adamantly anticommunist Social Democratic Party (PSD).* The impact of this split was felt in the following 1974 election when the PSD won five seats in the Chamber and the POSL lost votes in all districts except in its traditional Southern bastion. Particularly illustrative was the POSL's loss of 12.5 percent of votes in the North district relative to its 1968 support, a loss which corresponded to the PSD's 12.8 percent share of votes received in the same constituency.

The POSL's most recent participation in government control was during 1974-1979 when invited by the appointed Democratic Party (PD)* to enter into coalition. This period marked the only time since World War I that the traditionally dominant Christian Social Party did not participate in the government. The PD-POSL coalition instituted several liberal reforms in Luxembourg's social and economic systems (see Democratic Party for elaboration), some of which had contributed to loss of electoral support for the conservative and opposing PCS at the 1974 polls.

Nevertheless, the PCS was returned to government control in the June 10, 1979, election and formed a coalition with the outgoing Democratic Party. In this election, the POSL dropped from 17 to 14 Chamber seats (with a decrease from 29 to 24.3 percent of total votes cast).

SOZIAL DEMOKRATESCH PARTEI. *See* SOCIAL DEMOCRATIC PARTY.

Sharon Skowronski

TABLE 56.   Ruling Coalitions in Luxembourg since 1926

Years	Coalition
1926-1937	Party of the Right Radical Liberal Party
1937-1940	Party of the Right Liberal Party Socialist Workers' Party
1940-1945	Government flight to London during German occupation
1945-1946	Christian Social Party
1946-1948	Christian Social Partry "Government of the National Union" (all parties represented)
1948-1951	Christian Social Party Democratic Party
1951-1959	Christian Social Party Socialist Worker's Party
1959-1964	Christian Social Party Democratic Party
1964-1968	Christian Social Party Socialist Worker's Party
1968-1974	Christian Social Party Socialist Worker's Party
1974-1979	Democratic Party Socialist Worker's Party
1979-	Christian Social Party Democratic Party

Note: First-named party is dominant coalition party.

TABLE 57. Distribution of Seats in Luxembourg's Chamber of Deputies, 1919-1937

Party	1919	1922	1925	1928	1931	1934	1937
Communist Party of Luxembourg	—	0	0	0	0	1	0
National Party	3	4	8	—	—	—	—
Party of the Right[a]	27	26	22	24	26	25	25
Radical Liberal Party[b]	7	9	9	8	4	7	6
Socialist Workers' Party of Luxembourg[c]	9	7	9	12	14	15	18
Independents and others[d]	2	2	0	8	10	7	6
Total	48	48	48	52	54	55	55

Note: All elections were partial elections for half of Chamber seats. Figures reflect composition of whole Chamber after elections.

[a] Became the Christian Social Party in 1945 (see table 58).

[b] Known as the Liberal Party, 1937-1945; *see also* Democratic Party, table 58.

[c] Known as the Bloc of the Left until 1924.

[d] In 1931, includes 5 Radical Socialists and 5 independents.

TABLE 58. Distribution of Seats in Luxembourg's Chamber of Deputies, 1945-1979

Party	1945	1946*	1948*	1951*	1954	1959	1964	1968	1974	1979
Christian Social Party[a]	24	25	22	21	26	21	22	21	18	24
Communist Party of Luxembourg	5	5	5	4	3	3	5	6	5	2
Democratic Party[b]	8	9	9	8	6	11	6	11	14	15
Forced Conscripts	—	—	—	—	—	—	—	—	—	1
Independent Socialist List	—	—	—	—	—	—	—	—	—	1
Popular Independent Movement	—	—	—	—	—	—	2	—	—	—
Social Democratic Party	—	—	—	—	—	—	—	—	5	2
Socialist Workers' Party of Luxembourg	12	11	14	18	17	17	21	18	17	14
Independents and others	2	1	1	1	0	0	0	0	0	0
Total	51	51	51	52	52	52	56	56	59	59

* Partial elections for half of Chamber seats. Figures reflect composition of whole Chamber after elections.

a Previously known as the Party of the Right (see table 57).

b Known as the Patriotic and Democratic Group, 1945-1954; as the Democratic Group in the 1954 election; as the Democratic Party, 1954-present. (See also Radical Liberal Party, table 57).

MALTA

The REPUBLIC OF MALTA consists of three small Mediterranean islands (Malta, Gozo, and Comino) with a total area of 125 square miles and a population of 352,000 in 1978. The mixed Arab and Italian population stock is almost entirely Roman Catholic, a legacy of 260 years of rule by the Knights of Saint John until Napoleon ousted them in 1798; the Maltese population voluntarily came under British protection soon afterwards, and Malta was formally annexed by Britain in 1814 under the Treaty of Paris. Since that time, the lack of raw materials and agricultural land compelled Malta to become increasingly dependent on Britain, which developed the island as its major defense base in the Mediterranean. This dependence has remained a persistent dilemma of Maltese politics, rendered more acute by the inexorable decline of Britain's imperial role; and the closure of the last British military bases on the islands in 1979 has called into question Malta's future relationship with Britain and perhaps even its continued membership in the Commonwealth.

Two other issues have had a lasting impact upon Maltese politics: the language question and the relationship between church and state. The Maltese language (of Semitic origin) had no place as an official language until 1947; and while English was the language of colonial administration, the Maltese upper classes looked to Italy and the Italian language for their cultural identity. The events of World War II (which resulted in Malta being awarded the George Cross by Britain for bravery in resisting a prolonged Axis siege) served to discredit Italian as a result of its association with fascism; and the Nationalist Party,* which had been identified with the Italian side of the linguistic dispute, shifted its policy to one of promoting Malta's independence and Latin culture. The religious question has not been so easily resolved since Britain did not introduce representative local government until 1887, by which time the Roman Catholic Church had already developed an extensive parish welfare program and tended to view any political activity approved by Britain as a potential threat to its rights and privileges. Both the Constitutionalist Party* before World War II and later the Malta Labour Party* have clashed with the Catholic hierarchy on the issue of secularization of politics in Malta, while the Nationalist Party has tended to support the church. Since 98 percent of the population is Roman Catholic, the attitude of the church hierarchy is of great political importance, so much so that in the 1976 election the church was prohibited by law from engaging in any activities that might influence the outcome of the poll.

Malta's progress toward independence was by no means uninterrupted. From 1921, when the first measure of responsible government was introduced, until independence in 1964, the constitution was suspended no less than three times for internal security and strategic reasons, and Britain imposed direct rule. Even under normal conditions, the dyarchical character of responsible government under the 1921 and 1947 constitutions was a constant source of friction since Britain retained control over all matters relating to defense (Malta's main source of income was the British naval base) and foreign affairs. Even after independence was achieved in 1964 (in 1974 Malta became a republic within the Commonwealth) none of the major political parties were able to put forward a viable method of reducing Malta's economic dependence on Britain, both in the form of direct aid and in the shape of investment and tourism.

Political activity in Malta is based upon strong grass-roots organizations (through party-affiliated social clubs, brass bands, soccer teams, and the like) and the personal following of the leading politicians. The unicameral Maltese assembly consists of a 65-member House of Representatives elected for five-year terms, provided no earlier dissolution occurs. Since 1921, elections for the House of Representatives have been on the basis of proportional representation using party lists and a single transferable vote; this has resulted in a fairly close correspondence between the number of votes cast for and the number of seats obtained by any political party (see table 60), although independent candidates and (in recent years) the smaller parties have not achieved much success. Voter turnout tends to be high despite the complex nature of the voting procedure. In 1962, for example, 91 percent of the electorate voted, and voters had to list numerical preferences for as many as 42 candidates—a process which took illiterate voters about 40 minutes and literate voters about 15. Turnout in 1981 was 94.6 percent. Recent elections have underlined the dominant positions of the Nationalist Party and the Malta Labour Party (see table 59) and have made clear the polarization of Maltese politics between Christian democracy and socialism, while Malta's uncertain economic future seems certain to perpetuate this division.

Bibliography

Austin, Dennis. *Malta and the End of Empire*. London: Frank Cass, 1971.

Barrington, Leo. *Malta, Our Island Home*. London: Macmillan, 1970.

Blouet, Brian. *The Story of Malta*. London: Faber, 1972.

Boissevain, Jeremy. *Saints and Fireworks: Religion and Politics in Rural Malta*. London: Athlone Press, 1965.

Clews, Hilary A. *The Malta Yearbook 1978*. Sliema: De La Salle Brothers, 1978.

Cremona, J. J. *The Constitutional Development of Malta under British Rule*. Malta: University Press, 1963.

Dobie, Edith. *Malta's Road to Independence*. Norman: University of Oklahoma Press, 1967.

Jones, Christopher. "Malta's Assumption to a Republic State," *Contemporary Review*, vol. 227, no. 1317 (October 1975): 206-212.

Lane, John C. "How Malta Votes." In *The Malta Yearbook 1977*, edited by Hilary A. Clews. Sliema: De La Salle Brothers, 1977, pp. 431-438.

Political Parties

ANTI-REFORM PARTY (*Partito Anti-Reformista*: PAR). Organized by Dr. Fortunato Mizzi in 1883, the PAR campaigned for the preservation of Italian as the language of Maltese education, law, and government. It strongly defended the power and prerogatives of the church and drew most of its support from the wealthy urban professional classes who were attracted by its conservative policies. In 1903 the PAR became the National Party (*Partito Nazionale*), pursuing a policy of noncooperation with Britain; and in 1921 it was reformed by Mizzi's son, Dr. Enrico Mizzi, and named the Democratic Nationalist Party (1921-1926). *

CHRISTIAN WORKERS PARTY (CWP). Founded in 1961 by a former secretary-general of the Malta Labour Party, * Anthony Pellegrini, the CWP was a means of attracting support from workers concerned by the anticlerical reputation of Dom Mintoff's Malta Labour Party. The CWP adopted a prochurch, anticommunist stance, calling for independence from Britain through a gradual process of economic development and adjustment. To reduce dependence on British defense expenditure by attracting local and foreign investors, the CWP called for abolition of direct taxation. Although it won four seats in 1962, the CWP had little influence on the independence negotiations and was dissolved after the 1966 election when it lost all its seats.

CONSTITUTIONALIST PARTY (CP). Founded in 1921, the CP promoted the use of English and resisted attempts of the Democratic Nationalist Party (1921-1926) * to achieve primacy of Italian as an official language. CP leader, Sir Gerald (later Lord) Strickland, was a former colonial administrator, and the party drew most of its support from businessmen and landowners attracted by CP opposition to the introduction of direct taxation and to increases in public expenditure. Sir Gerald, with the support of the minority Malta Labour Party, * became prime minister in 1927; but his advocacy of closer links with Britain and separation of church and state caused him to be attacked by the Holy See for anticlericalism. The subsequent dispute caused Britain to suspend the constitution and abandon the election scheduled for 1930. Strickland apologized to the Catholic Church in 1932 but was nevertheless defeated in the election held that year. When Britain reimposed colonial administration in 1933 for economic and defense reasons, the CP (despite gaining a majority in the 1939 election) refused to cooperate until responsible government was restored.

After World War II, the CP went into eclipse and was dissolved in 1946. But the party was revived in 1950 by Professor Robert Galea and Mabel Strickland (Gerald Strickland's daughter) with a platform opposing increases in taxation and public expenditure and accusing the Malta Labour Party of being infiltrated by communists bent on secularizing Malta. After limited success in the 1950 and 1951 elections, the CP rapidly lost support; and in 1953, Ms. Strickland effectively undermined the party by breaking away to form the Progressive Constitutionalist Party. *

CP. *See* CONSTITUTIONALIST PARTY.

CWP. *See* CHRISTIAN WORKERS PARTY.

DAP. *See* DEMOCRATIC ACTION PARTY.

DEMOCRATIC ACTION PARTY (DAP). A revival of the Maltese Political Union, * the DAP was formed in 1947 as a loose association of landowners and professionals to oppose social and economic reform and to promote the interests of the Catholic Church. The party opposed the use of Maltese as a language of education and branded the Malta Labour Party* as a socialistic threat to Catholicism. Although it won four seats in the 1947 election, the DAP did not campaign actively in the 1950 election (in which it retained one seat) and shortly afterwards disbanded.

DEMOCRATIC NATIONALIST PARTY (1921-1926) (*Partito Democratico Nazionalista:* PDN). The PDN was created in 1921 by Dr. Enrico Mizzi to subsume the National Party (*see* Anti-Reform Party). (The PDN should not be confused with the Democratic Nationalist Party [1959-1966]* of the post-World War II era.) The PDN sought to broaden its electoral appeal by adding a program of social welfare legislation to its long-standing demands for the Italian language to be given parity with English. After limited success in the 1921 and 1924 elections, the PDN merged with the Maltese Political Union* in 1926 to form the Nationalist Party. *

DEMOCRATIC NATIONALIST PARTY (1959-1966) (DNP). The DNP should not be confused with the prewar party of the same name (*see* Democratic Nationalist Party [1921-1926]*), which had been one of the original elements in the Nationalist Party (NP). * Dr. Herbert Ganado created this second DNP in 1959 as a progressive offshoot of the Nationalist Party, and he advocated restoration of responsible government after Britain had revoked the 1947 constitution. Unlike the NP, which withheld cooperation with Britain during the period of direct British rule (1959-1962), the DNP advocated cooperation with Britain in order to promote economic development as a means of progress toward independent dominion status within the Commonwealth. The DNP program of social welfare measures and vehement opposition to the Malta Labour Party* enabled the Democratic Nationalists to win four seats in the 1962 elections. But all seats were lost four years later, and the DNP was dissolved.

DNP. *See* DEMOCRATIC NATIONALIST PARTY (1959-1966).

GOZO PARTY (GP). A minor party similar to the Jones Party,* the GP was founded in 1947 to claim more resources and better representation for Gozo, a small island three miles from Malta. Although it won three seats in the 1947 election, all GP candidates were defeated in the 1950 and 1951 elections and the party disappeared.

GP. *See* GOZO PARTY.

JONES PARTY (JP). A minor party similar to the Gozo Party,* the JP was formed in 1945 on the island of Gozo with a platform of development of farmer cooperatives and opposition to the dominance of Malta's interests in the legislature. It won one seat in 1945 and two seats in the 1947 election. The JP was unsuccessful in the 1950 and 1951 elections and disbanded shortly thereafter.

JP. *See* JONES PARTY.

MALTA LABOUR PARTY (MLP). Although not formally established until 1921, the MPL grew out of the labor union movement initiated in Malta in the 1880s. Its first leader, Lieutenant-Colonel William Savona, campaigned in the 1921 election for compulsory education using Maltese, with English to be added in higher grades and Italian as an option in secondary schools only. The MLP also advocated tax reform and improved working and living conditions. Despite these stands, the MLP entered into a coalition, until 1924, with the Maltese Political Union,* an ideological opponent.

   After Dr. Paul Boffa became MLP leader in 1930, the party began to emphasize the need to develop a sound economy less dependent on British defense spending as a precondition for eventual self-government. The expansion of the labor union movement provided increased support for the socialistic MLP, and in 1947 the party gained a majority (24 of 40 parliamentary seats). In 1949, Dr. Boffa was defeated as MLP leader in a party vote of no confidence, and he left the MLP to form the Malta Workers Party.* Dominic (Dom) Mintoff, an Oxford-educated architect, became the MLP leader. This split in the socialist movement effectively prevented the MLP from gaining power until 1955 when Mintoff developed a plan for integration with Britain (analogous to the position of Northern Ireland, *see* UNITED KINGDOM) with substantial local autonomy and representation for Malta in the British House of Commons. The MLP emphasized the need for safeguards to preserve the rights and privileges of the Catholic Church, and the party argued that integration with Britain would lead to improved social services and pay parity with British workers.

The integration proposals aroused considerable opposition from the church hierarchy, which refused to countenance such an arrangement unless Britain guaranteed the interests of the church. As a result, 41 percent of the electorate abstained from the referendum on integration held in 1956 (44 percent approved, 13 percent opposed). Lack of British support rendered the issue meaningless, and the MLP began to campaign for an independent, neutral Malta—a "Switzerland in the Mediterranean." Mintoff's conflict with the church caused the reimposition of direct British rule, 1958-1962; and for a period the Archibishop of Malta interdicted all MLP periodicals, forbidding them to be distributed or read under penalty of mortal sin. However, by the time of the 1971 election, the church had adopted a neutral stance.

In the independence negotiations, the MLP advocated an independent republic with a secular state and a referendum after independence on whether or not to remain in the Commonwealth. After Malta's independence in 1964, the MLP continued to advocate neutral status for the islands and elimination of dependence on foreign military expenditure, using the Socialist International as a forum for pressing Malta's claims for more aid from Britain. Following the MLP's return to parliamentary power in 1971, Mintoff renegotiated the payments for military base facilities made by Britain and NATO, and he endeavored through approaches to France, Italy, Libya, and Algeria to diversify Malta's sources of political and financial support after Malta became a republic in 1974.

This policy was somewhat unsuccessful since only Libya became a substantial provider of aid, and the world economic recession hindered attempts to attract industrial investment and to boost exports. Premier Mintoff has increased his control over MLP supporters by amalgamating the General Workers Union (the island's largest) with the MLP, but Mintoff has not yet developed a satisfactory substitute for British aid—a problem which became more acute when the last British military bases closed down in 1979. By 1981 a rift had developed between Malta and Libya, and Mintoff began to reemphasize Malta's historical ties with Italy. The MLP retained its three-seat majority in the House of Representatives following the 1981 election.

MALTA WORKERS PARTY (MWP). The MWP was established in 1949 by Dr. Paul Boffa after he resigned as leader of the Malta Labour Party (MLP)* following an MLP vote of no confidence. The MWP contested the 1950, 1951, and 1953 elections on a program of cooperation with Britain to promote Malta's welfare and economic austerity, and to divert funds to industrial development. Boffa accused the MLP leader Dom Mintoff of communism and anticlericalism. Although it was a minority partner in the coalition government led by Dr. Borg Olivier of the Nationalist Party* (1951-1955), the MWP's electoral support declined markedly and the party was dissolved in 1955.

MALTESE POLITICAL UNION (*Unione Politica Maltese*: UPM). The UPM was formed in 1920 as a result of a merger of two nationalist groupings, the Malta Political Association (founded in 1905 by Francesco Azzopardi) and the *Comitato Patriottica* (established in 1911 by Mgr. Panzavecchia). The UPM campaigned for parity in education for both the English and Italian languages, defense of the rights and privileges of the Catholic Church, and progress toward Maltese self-government. In the first elections to the legislative assembly under the 1921 constitution, the UPM won a working majority of 14 (out of 32) seats, and the UPM's Joseph Howard became Malta's first prime minister. In the 1924 election, Sir Ugo Mifsud caused the UPM to form a coalition with the Democratic National Party (1921-1926),* and this was made permanent in 1926 when the two groups merged to form the Nationalist Party.*

MLP. *See* MALTA LABOUR PARTY.

MWP. *See* MALTA WORKERS PARTY.

NATIONALIST PARTY (NP). The NP was created in 1926 through a merger of the Maltese Political Union* and the Democratic Nationalist Party (1921-1926),* two parties which had formed a coalition government in 1924 under Sir Ugo Mifsud. The NP became the leading defender of the Catholic faith, as well as of the Italian language and Latin culture against the implicit threat of Protestantism contained in British rule and the dominance of the English language. In 1932 the NP won a sweeping electoral victory (21 of 32 seats); and under Mifsud and his deputy, Enrico Mizzi, a vigorous program of Italianization was instituted in the schools with the intent of eliminating Maltese as the second language. This process was accompanied by increased links with fascist Italy; and in 1933 the British Colonial Secretary declared a state of emergency, suspended the Maltese constitution, and introduced direct British rule to curtail the spread of Italian influence. Italian was eliminated as an official language in 1936 in favor of Maltese, and Mizzi was tried and interned abroad for the duration of World War II.

After World War II, the NP emphasized the need to protect Malta's Latin nationality, and the party protested British interference in domestic affairs, especially when these threatened the privileges and prerogatives of the church. In the 1950 election, the NP won 12 seats and established under Mizzi (returned from wartime internment) a minority government with various welfare programs to ensure the tacit support of the Malta Workers Party (MWP).* After Mizzi's death later in 1950, Dr. Giorgio Borg Olivier became prime minister and continued in office until 1955 in a formal coalition with the MWP.

Under Olivier's leadership, the NP advocated dominion status for Malta and vehemently opposed the plan of the Malta Labour Party* for integration with Britain. The NP's opposition was based on the grounds that integration would undermine Malta's Catholic culture. Instead, the NP continued to campaign for full Maltese self-government and independence within the Commonwealth; and when Dr. Olivier again became prime minister in 1962, he successfully elicited support of the United Nations Special Committee on Decolonization for the principle of Maltese independence. After Malta achieved independence in 1964, the NP policy of continued partial links with Britain did not prevent the steady reduction in British defense expenditure in the island, and the NP's inability to attract more British aid prevented it from reducing income taxes and turning Malta into a tax haven. Dr. Olivier's pro-British and pro-European orientation (the NP developed close links with other Christian democratic parties, particularly the Italian one) did not prevent the NP losing its majority in the 1971 election.

After the NP's failure to regain power in the 1976 election, Olivier retired. He was replaced as party leader by Dr. Edward Fenech Adami, who has attempted to diffuse the somewhat theocratic image of the NP and to reduce the emphasis on continued links with Britain by stressing the NP's commitment to take Malta into the European Economic Community. The NP has also advocated close ties with NATO, and has increasingly criticized Premier Mintoff for what it alleges are his autocratic and authoritarian policies. The NP continued to hold 31 seats following the 1981 election.

NATIONAL PARTY. *See* ANTI-REFORM PARTY.

NP. *See* NATIONALIST PARTY.

PAR. *See* ANTI-REFORM PARTY.

PARTITO ANTI-REFORMISTA. *See* ANTI-REFORM PARTY.

PARTITO DEMOCRATICO NAZIONALISTA. *See* DEMOCRATIC NATIONALIST PARTY (1921-1926).

PARTITO NAZIONALE. *See* ANTI-REFORM PARTY.

PCP. *See* PROGRESSIVE CONSTITUTIONALIST PARTY.

PDN. *See* DEMOCRATIC NATIONALIST PARTY (1921-1926).

PN. *See* ANTI-REFORM PARTY.

PROGRESSIVE CONSTITUTIONALIST PARTY (PCP). Miss Mabel Strickland, proprietor of Malta's leading English-language newspaper and daughter of the founder of the Constitutionalist Party (CP),* created the PCP in 1953 as a protest against the CP's support for the Malta Labour Party's* program of integration with Britain. The PCP was strongly anticommunist and stressed loyalty to the Catholic Church and British crown. The party also called for quasi-dominion status rather than integration with Britain in order to avoid cultural erosion and the secularization which would be involved in adopting British laws on divorce and other matters contrary to Catholic doctrine. Although it contested five elections (1953-1971), the PCP won only one seat (in 1962); and its role in the independence negotiations of 1963-1964 was limited by its advocacy of only minor reforms in the status quo. The PCP did not contest the 1976 election, the first held after Malta became a republic within the Commonwealth, and the party is now defunct.

UNIONE POLITICA MALTESE. *See* MALTESE POLITICAL UNION.

UPM. *See* MALTESE POLITICAL UNION.

Michael Hodges

TABLE 59.   Ruling Parties in Malta since 1921

Years	Party
1921-1924	Maltese Political Union Malta Labour Party
1924-1927	Maltese Political Union Democratic Nationalist Party (1921-1926)
1927-1932	Constitutionalist Party
1932-1947	Nationalist Party
1947-1950	Malta Labour Party
1950-1951	Nationalist Party
1951-1955	Nationalist Party Malta Workers Party
1955-1962	Malta Labour Party
1962-1971	Nationalist Party
1971-	Malta Labour Party

Note: First-named party is dominant coalition party.

TABLE 60. Distribution of Seats in Malta's House of Representatives, 1921-1981

Party	1921	1924	1927	1932	1939*	1945*	1947	1950	1951	1953	1955	1962	1966	1971	1976	1981
Christian Workers Party	—	—	—	—	—	—	—	—	—	—	—	4	0	—	—	—
Constitutionalist Party	7	10	15	10	6	—	—	4	4	—	—	—	—	—	—	—
Democratic Action Party	—	—	—	—	—	—	4	1	—	—	—	—	—	—	—	—
Democratic Nationalist Party (1921-1926)	4	5	—	—	—	—	—	—	—	—	—	—	—	—	—	—
Democratic Nationalist Party (1959-1966)	—	—	—	—	—	—	—	—	—	—	—	4	0	—	—	—
Gozo Party	—	—	—	—	—	—	3	0	0	—	—	—	—	—	—	—
Jones Party	—	—	—	—	—	—	2	0	0	—	—	—	—	—	—	—
Malta Labour Party	7	7	3	1	1	9	24	11	14	19	23	16	22	28	34	34
Malta Workers Party	—	—	—	—	—	—	—	11	7	3	—	—	—	—	—	—
Maltese Political Union	14	10	—	—	—	—	—	—	—	—	—	—	—	—	—	—
Nationalist Party**	—	—	14	21	3	0	7	12	15	18	17	25	28	27	31	31
Progressive Constitutionalist Party	—	—	—	—	—	—	—	0	0	0	—	1	0	0	—	—
Independents	0	0	0	0	0	1	0	1	0	0	0	0	0	0	0	0
Total	32	32	32	32	10	10	40	40	40	40	40	50	50	55	65	65

* House of Representatives suspended; elections were to Governor's Executive Council.
** Nationalist Party formed in 1926 by merger of Democratic Nationalist Party (1921-1926) and Maltese Political Union.

MONACO

The PRINCIPALITY OF MONACO (*Principauté de Monaco*) is located on the Mediterranean coast and is surrounded on three sides by France. It is the smallest fully constituted political state in Europe, comprising 453 acres and approximately 25,000 in population. Monaco is a constitutional, hereditary monarchy with a prince as chief of state.

Founded in 1215 as a colony of Genoa, Italy, by the close of the 13th century Monaco was firmly in the hands of the House of Grimaldi, which became its recognized rulers in 1419. The principality fell briefly under French control during the French Revolution and the First Empire (*see* FRANCE). Monaco was designated a protectorate of Sardinia by the Treaty of Vienna (1815) but regained full sovereignty in 1861. Its independent status was recognized by the Franco-Monegasque Treaty of that year.

Throughout the centuries the prince of Monaco had been an absolute ruler, until a constitution was promulgated in 1911. As a result of pressures demanding constitutional reforms, a completely new and less cumbersome constitution was proclaimed in 1962. It established a Supreme Tribunal to guarantee fundamental liberties, abolished capital punishment, and granted Monegasque females over the age of 25 eligibility to hold political office. Female suffrage had been introduced in 1945. Under the 1962 constitution, the prince began to share his powers with an 18-member, unicameral National Council (*Conseil National*) whose incumbents are elected by universal suffrage for five-year terms (*see* table 61). The eligible electorate (3,647 in 1978) consists only of trueborn Monegasque citizens over the age of 25. The Council usually meets twice per year and gives its approval to laws proposed by the prince through his appointed minister of state.

The bulk of Monaco's residents are foreigners and do not engage in political activity. With a small electorate devoted to the princely house, Monaco functions more like a quasi-familial community. With few minor exceptions, there is widespread support for the political, economic, and social policies of the government. While opposition parties are not formally proscribed, such politics as exist in Monaco tend to be more a matter of personal allegiance than of genuine ideological orientation.

Bibliography

Aureglia, Louis. *Contribution à la Histoire Constitutionelle de Monaco.* 2d ed. Chambery, France: Imprimeries Reunies, 1961.

Gallois, Jean-Pierre. *Le Régime International de la Principauté de Monaco.* Paris: Editions A. Pedone, 1964.

Robert, J. B. *Histoire de Monaco.* Paris: Presses Universitaire de France, 1973.

U.S. Department of State. "Monaco," *Background Notes Series*, no. 8670. Washington, D.C.: Government Printing Office, May 1977.

Political Parties

ACTION MONÉGASQUE. *See* MONEGASQUE ACTION.

AM. *See* MONEGASQUE ACTION.

DEMOCRATIC UNION MOVEMENT (*Mouvement Union Démocratique*: MUD). A small, communist, trade unionist electoral coalition formed in 1963, the MUD is based on elements drawn from the *Union des Syndicats de Monaco.* The group won one seat in 1963 and one in 1973. Its support averaged 1,013 votes in 1978.

END. *See* NATIONAL DEMOCRATIC ENTENTE.

ENTENTE NATIONALE DÉMOCRATIQUE. *See* NATIONAL DEMOCRATIC ENTENTE.

MONEGASQUE ACTION (*Action Monégasque*: AM). A one-time, pre-election coalition of voters, the AM was formed to support a single candidate in the 1973 election. The group's purpose was to introduce a more youthful element into Monaco's political life. The Action's candidate was successful; and as a result of the AM's incursion into Monaco's political arena, a communist candidate was also elected, thereby reducing the dominant National and Democratic Union* to 16 seats and breaking the monopoly the latter had held in the National Council since 1962.

MONEGASQUE SOCIALIST PARTY (*Parti Socialiste Monégasque*: PSM). The Monegasque Socialist Party, a minor left-wing grouping, entered two unsuccessful candidates in the 1978 election. Both candidates obtained an average of 1,058 votes.

MOUVEMENT UNION DÉMOCRATIQUE. See DEMOCRATIC UNION MOVEMENT.

MUD. See DEMOCRATIC UNION MOVEMENT.

NATIONAL AND DEMOCRATIC UNION (*Union Nationale et Démocratique*: UND). The UND represents Monaco's first modern political party. It was formed in 1962 as a result of the merger of two opposing factions in the National Council, the National Union of Independents* and the National Democratic Entente.* Despite both groups' earlier advocacy for constitutional reforms, the UND has strongly supported the policies of the prince and is the dominant government party. It won all 18 seats in the 1978 election.

NATIONAL DEMOCRATIC ENTENTE (*Entente Nationale Démocratique*: END). Prior to the constitutional reforms of 1962, the moderate END was the minority faction in Monaco's National Council. The grouping had obtained seven seats in the 1958 election and was led by Louis Aureglia, a prominent lawyer. It merged with the National Union of Independents* in 1962 to form the National and Democratic Union.*

NATIONAL UNION OF INDEPENDENTS (*Union Nationale des Indépendents*: UNI). Prior to the constitutional reforms of 1962, the UNI was the dominant faction in Monaco's National Council. The conservative-oriented group obtained 11 seats in the 1958 election and was led by Dr. Joseph Simon, who was also Council president. As an outgrowth of a major financial scandal in 1955 (the bankruptcy of the *Societe Monégasque de Banque*, in which the government was a major depositor), the group lobbied strenuously for constitutional reforms, government accountability, and expanded political rights. The UNI merged with the National Democratic Entente* in 1962 to form Monaco's first modern political party, the National and Democratic Union.*

PARTI SOCIALISTE MONÉGASQUE. *See* MONEGASQUE SOCIALIST PARTY.

PSM. *See* MONEGASQUE SOCIALIST PARTY.

UND. *See* NATIONAL AND DEMOCRATIC UNION.

UNI. *See* NATIONAL UNION OF INDEPENDENTS.

UNION NATIONALE DES INDÉPENDENTS. *See* NATIONAL UNION OF INDEPENDENTS.

UNION NATIONALE ET DÉMOCRATIQUE. *See* NATIONAL AND DEM-
OCRATIC UNION.

Joseph H. Rogatnick

TABLE 61. Distribution of Seats of Monaco's National Council, 1958-1978

Party	1958	1963	1968	1973	1978
"National Union of Independents"	11	—	—	—	—
"National Democratic Entente"	7	—	—	—	—
National and Democratic Union*	—	17	18	16	18
Democratic Union Movement	—	1	0	1	—
Monegasque Action	—	—	—	1	—
Total	18	18	18	18	18

* Represents a merger of the National Union of Independents and the National Democratic
Entente after 1962.

NETHERLANDS

The KINGDOM OF THE NETHERLANDS (*Koninkrijk der Nederlanden*, also known as Holland from the name of a former province) is a densely populated, industrialized nation located in the Rhine delta, surrounded by Belgium, West Germany, and the North Sea. The nation's 15,770 square miles are inhabited by slightly more than 14 million people (1980 estimate), almost all of whom are of Germanic ethnicity. While approximately 20 percent of the population claim no religious affiliation, the rest are almost evenly divided between Protestants and Roman Catholics. The nation's official language is Dutch.

Independence from Spain was secured in the 16th century. Until the Napoleonic invasion, the Dutch Republic was a loose confederation of autonomous provinces. In 1813 the country was reorganized as a monarchy. The present constitution dates from 1848, when King William II, reacting to uprisings elsewhere in Europe, acceded to demands for ministerial responsibility to the parliament.

Present-day Holland continues to be a constitutional monarchy, operating under a multiparty parliamentary system. Executive powers at all levels reside with various crown-appointed officials who work in conjunction with their respective legislative bodies. At the national level is the Council of Ministers (*Ministerraad*), which is assisted by an advisory body, the Council of State (*Raad van State*). The administrators of each of the nation's 11 provinces are also appointed by the crown, as are the mayors of all municipalities.

National legislative authority resides in the bicameral States General (*Staten Generaal*). The upper, or First Chamber (*Eerste Kamer*) currently consists of 75 members indirectly elected by provincial legislatures for six-year terms, with half the deputies up for reelection every three years. The lower, or Second Chamber (*Tweede Kamer*) is comprised of 150 members directly elected for four-year terms.

Holland's current electoral system is based on proportional representation and universal adult suffrage (beginning at age 18). Compulsory voting was abolished in 1971. The 1981 electorate totaled approximately ten million, of which about 86 percent voted in that's year's election to the *Tweede Kamer*. Before 1918, members of the Dutch parliament were elected from single or (earlier) multimember districts: in the event that no candidate had a majority of votes, a runoff or second ballot was used to determine the winner. Proportional representation was adopted in 1918. Technically, the country is divided into 18 electoral districts; but by permitting the pooling of votes won in different districts, the electoral law effectively creates one national constituency. To win a seat after 1933, a party had to gain the "electoral divisor" (average number of votes per seat) or 1.0 percent of the national vote. Parties are now required to post a nominal deposit, which is forfeited if the party fails to win 75 percent of the electoral divisor. Seats are allocated according to the d'Hondt or highest-averages formula. The enlargement of the Second Chamber from 100 to 150 seats in 1956 lowered the divisor or threshold to .67 percent of the national vote. Both this and the previous versions of proportional representation in use between 1918 and 1933 are, in contrast to electoral laws in effect elsewhere in Europe, extremely favorable to smaller parties.

Holland's modern-day party system can be traced to the 19th century. Initially, parties were little more than loose clusters of parliamentary deputies. The Liberals* demanded ministerial responsibility, while the Conservatives* defended the prerogatives of the crown. Following the introduction of direct elections to the Second Chamber in 1848, local election societies appeared. The party system was transformed in the latter part of the century by suffrage extension and the emergence of Calvinist, Catholic, and socialist movements (see table 62). Calvinists, and later Catholics, organized in order to demand state support for religious schools, while socialists regarded universal suffrage as a first step toward redress of grievances. As part of their struggle, each group mobilized followers and began to build networks of religious or ideologically based organizations. These included schools, universities, newspapers, trade unions, and social clubs. The result was, by the 1920s, a "pillarized" or segmented social structure.

Although the schools and suffrage questions were resolved by the Pacification Settlements of 1916 and 1917 (providing for universal manhood suffrage, proportional representation, and state support for denominational schools), both the religious parties and pillarized social structure have persisted. Until recently, five major parties or tendencies were usually represented. These were the Liberals (at times grouped in several parties); the socialist Labor Party*; Catholics; and two Protestant parties, the Anti-Revolutionary Party* and the Christian Historical Union.* In addition, an extremely permissive version of proportional representation, in use since 1918, has facilitated the organization of a large number of minor parties expressing differences within or among subcultures. In the interwar period, the number of parties competing in parliamentary elections ranged from 20 to 54, while the number winning seats ranged from ten to seventeen. Some, such as the Revolutionary Socialist Party,* which elected a single candidate in 1933, were essentially one-man splinter groups. Nevertheless, through 1963 the five major parties usually won 88 to 92 percent of the popular vote and seats in parliament.

The large number of parties has complicated the politics of cabinet formation. Cabinets are normally the product of protracted negotiations. Typically, they have been broadly based and nearly inclusive. From 1888 until 1918, cabinets were composed either of Liberals or coalitions of the Catholics, Anti-Revolutionaries, and Christian Historicals. In the interwar period, most cabinets were dominated by the religious parties. Since World War II, most have included the three confessional (religious) parties and either socialists or liberals (the latter, since 1948, represented by the People's Party for Freedom and Democracy*).

Since 1966 the party system has changed considerably. Beginning in the 1960s, the number of parties competing in elections (considerably diminished in the postwar years) began to increase (see table 63) and dissident factions emerged in the major parties. In the late 1960s, the combination of pressure from dissident factions, coupled with major parties' losses and sudden surges of support for new parties such as Democrats '66* or the Farmers' Party,* triggered an extensive debate on the need to simplify the party system. Initially, attempts to reduce the number of parties produced greater fragmentation. But the number of parties has declined again in recent years, and by the late 1970s the Netherlands could be characterized as a four-party dominant system. The greatest changes have been among the religious parties. Extended discussions among the Catholic People's Party,* the Anti-Revolutionaries, and the Christian Historical Union resulted in the fusion of these three parties in the Christian Democratic Appeal,* thus uniting Catholics and Protestants under a common banner.

Similar discussions among the Labor Party, Democrats '66, and the Radical Political Party* explored the possibility of a progressive concentration but resulted only in short-lived electoral alliances in 1971 and 1972. However, Democrats '66, the party that launched discussions on the need to revamp the Dutch party system, has emerged as a left-of-center grouping and a permanent element in the nation's party system. Thus the four major parties, as of the 1981 elections, are the Christian Democrats (with 31 percent of the vote), Labor (with 28 percent), the liberal People's Party for Freedom and Democracy (17 percent), and Democrats '66 (11 percent). However, these four parties continue to be surrounded by a large number of smaller parties whose strength could increase in future elections.

Ironically, because of changes in the style and orientation of Holland's parties, a reduction in the number of parties has not simplified the politics of cabinet formation (see table 64). Following the 1972 election, which produced a 13-party parliament, 165 days were required to form a five-party governing coalition. In 1977 voters began to abandon smaller parties. Nevertheless, because of repeated deadlocks among Labor and the three confessional parties (competing for the first time under the Christian Democratic Appeal banner), 208 days elapsed before a confessional-liberal cabinet took office. In 1981 negotiations for a government of Labor, Democrats '66, and Christian Democrats required only three months, but strains among the coalition partners resulted in the resignation (subsequently withdrawn) of the cabinet only five weeks after that cabinet took office.

Bibliography

Baehr, Peter. "The Netherlands." In *European Political Parties*, edited by Stanley Henig and John Pinder. London: Political and Economic Planning, 1969.

Bakvis, Herman. *Catholic Power in the Netherlands*. Montreal: McGill-Queens University Press, 1981.

Cohen, H. F. *Om de Verneiuwing van het Socialisme: De politieke orientatie van de Nederlandse social-democratie 1919-1930*. Leiden: Universitaire Pers Leiden, 1974.

Daalder, Hans. "The Netherlands: Opposition in a Segmented Society." In *Political Oppositions in Western Democracies*, edited by Robert Dahl. New Haven, Conn.: Yale University Press, 1966.

Houska, Joseph. "The Organizational Connection: Elites, Masses and Elections in Austria and the Netherlands." Ph.D. dissertation, Yale University, 1978.

Irwin, Galen A. "The Netherlands." In *Western European Party Systems: Trends and Prospects*, edited by Peter H. Merkl. New York: Free Press, 1980.

Lijphart, Arend. "The Netherlands: Continuity and Change in Voting Behavior." In *Electoral Behavior: A Comparative Handbook*, edited by Richard Rose. New York: Free Press, 1974.

———. *The Politics of Accommodation: Pluralism and Democracy in the Netherlands*. 2d ed. Berkeley and Los Angeles: University of California Press, 1975.

Lipschits, I. *Politieke Stromingen in Nederland: Inleiding tot de Geschiedenis van de Nederlandse Politieke Partijen*. Deventer, Netherlands: Kluwer, 1977.

———. *De Protestants-Christelijke Stroming tot 1940*. Deventer, Netherlands: Kluwer, 1977.

Oud, P. J. *Honderd Jaren: Een Eeuw van Staatkundige Vormgeving in Nederland, 1840-1940*. 7th ed., updated from 1940 by J. Bosmans. Assen: Van Gorcum, 1979.

Scholten, G. H. et al. *De Confessionelen: Onstaan en Ontwikkaling van de Christelijke Partijen*. Utrecht: Amboboeken, 1968.

Scholten, G. H., and G. Ringnalda. "Netherlands." In *International Guide to Electoral Statistics*, edited by Stein Rokkan and Jean Meyriat. The Hague: Mouton, 1969.

Wolinetz, Steven B. "Party Realignment in the Netherlands." Ph.D. dissertation, Yale University, 1973.

Political Parties

ALGEMENE BOND VAN ROOMS KATHOLIEKE KIESVERENIGINGEN. *See* CATHOLIC PEOPLE'S PARTY.

ANTI-REVOLUTIONAIRE PARTIJ. *See* ANTI-REVOLUTIONARY PARTY.

ANTI-REVOLUTIONARY PARTY (*Anti-Revolutionaire Partij*: ARP). The first Anti-Revolutionary election society dated from 1851. Others followed, and reactions to a new Liberal* school law prompted considerable involvement of Orthodox Calvinists in the Dutch parliament—in 1872 the Anti-School Law League was established. The League provided the nucleus of the Anti-Revolutionary Party, which was established in 1879 under the leadership of a Calvinist minister and newspaper editor, Abraham Kuyper. The ARP was the first mass party in the Netherlands.

Impetus for the organization of the Anti-Revolutionary Party came from a widening gulf between ideas of the enlightenment and Orthodox Calvinism. The Anti-Revolutionaries organized in explicit rejection of secular doctrines of the French Revolution and insisted on the sovereignty of God, as revealed in the Gospels and through history. To the ARP, this meant neither reaction nor conservatism nor an official state religion. Instead, recognizing their minority position in the Netherlands, the Anti-Revolutionaries rallied around Groen van Prinsterer's dictum, "In Our Isolation Lies Our Strength," and they sought to establish conditions under which Orthodox Calvinism could survive, free from the pressures of secularization. This received expression in the establishment of separate denominational schools and a Calvinist university, a religious schism which produced separate Orthodox Reformed (*Gereformeerde*) churches, and the creation of other organizations. The ARP campaigned for state financing for religious schools, Sunday rest, and universal household suffrage as a means of enfranchising its supporters.

Under the leadership of party-founder Kuyper, the ARP supplanted the Conservatives* as the principal opponent of liberalism. However, Kuyper's militancy, his insistence on discipline, advocacy of suffrage extension, and attention to social issues divided the party, and in 1894 the ARP split. Parliamentary leader A. H. de Savornin Lohman, long a rival of Kuyper, left the ARP and established the Free Anti-Revolutionary Party (*Vrij Anti-Revolutionaire Partij*: VAR). This group later formed the nucleus of the Christian Historical Union.*

Although never numerically strong (ARP strength ranged from 12 to 16 percent in the interwar period and nine to 13 percent in the post-World War II period), the Anti-Revolutionaries have been an important element in Dutch politics. The party usually compensated for small size by asserting itself in coalition with the other religious parties. Working in a long-standing coalition with Catholics and, later, with the Christian Historical Union, the ARP was in cabinets during 1888-1891, 1901-1905, and 1908-1913. These "confessional" cabinets were initially able to secure only limited support for denominational schools, but full support was mandated as part of the Pacification Settlements of 1916-1917. In the interwar years, ARP ministers served in all cabinets through 1939; ARP leader H. Colijn was premier of five of these governments. However, under Colijn the orientation of the party changed: while the ARP retained its militant Calvinism, Kuyper's concern with social issues gave way to Colijn's economic conservatism.

The ARP emerged from World War II virtually unchanged. However, in the 1950s and 1960s the ARP leadership began reassessing the implications of the

Gospels for politics. In 1952 the party ended its initial opposition to a welfare state and a managed economy, and the ARP joined the Labor Party,* Catholic People's Party,* and Christian Historicals in government. In the early 1960s, the Anti-Revolutionaries reversed their opposition to decolonization, and the party leaders began more and more to extract a radical egalitarian message from the Gospels. Though the ARP retained a conservative following, party positions in the 1960s and 1970s were slightly left-of-center.

Throughout its history, the Anti-Revolutionary Party remained a cohesive and well-organized group. The party drew support from a small but loyal electorate, consisting primarily of members of Orthodox Reformed Churches, as well as adherents of some more orthodox tendencies within the Dutch Reformed Church. With the exception of periodic attempts to reabsorb the Christian Historical Union, the ARP sought not to broaden its base of support but rather preferred to assert its views in coalition with the other religious parties.

In 1968 the ARP entered discussions with the Catholic People's Party and the Christian Historical Union concerning the desirability of forming one interconfessional party. Though the Anti-Revolutionary leadership viewed the prospect of merger with some skepticism, fearing that its evangelical inspiration might be lost in a larger entity, it sanctioned the formation of the Christian Democratic Appeal* as an umbrella coupling the three parties in 1972 and reluctantly agreed to the submission of a joint list of candidates for the 1977 parliamentary elections. Final agreement on merger was achieved in 1980 when the Anti-Revolutionary Party dissolved itself and joined the Christian Democratic Appeal.

ANTI-SCHOOL LAW LEAGUE. *See* ANTI-REVOLUTIONARY PARTY.

ARP. *See* ANTI-REVOLUTIONARY PARTY.

BOEREN PARTIJ. *See* FARMERS' PARTY.

BOND VAN KIESVERENIGINGEN OP CHRISTELIJK HISTORISCHE GRONDSLAG. *See* CHRISTIAN HISTORICAL UNION.

BOND VAN VRIJE LIBERALEN. *See* LIBERALS.

BP. *See* FARMERS' PARTY.

BRKKV. *See* CATHOLIC PEOPLE'S PARTY.

CATHOLIC NATIONAL PARTY (*Katholieke Nationale Partij*: KNP). A right-wing splinter group from the Catholic People's Party,* the KNP was in existence from 1948 to 1955. Led by C. Welter and supported by many ex-colonials from Indonesia, the Catholic National Party objected to the Catholic People's Party's positions on decolonization and independence for Indonesia. The KNP was temporarily disbanded in 1954 when its leaders yielded to episcopal pressure to restore Catholic unity, and the KNP rejoined the Catholic People's Party in 1955.

CATHOLIC PEOPLE'S PARTY (*Katholieke Volkspartij*: KVP). Until recently, Dutch Catholics were usually organized in one large party, but the party name and organization have changed over time. The first Catholic election societies dated from the 1860s and 1870s. However, until 1896, Catholic deputies in the Second Chamber were divided, and there was little connection between parliamentary caucuses and extraparliamentary organizations. In 1896 a priest, Pater Schaepman, succeeded in uniting Catholic deputies behind a common program. In 1904, Catholic election societies were grouped together in the General League of Roman Catholic Election Societies (*Algemene Bond van Rooms Katholieke Kiesverenigingen*: BRKKV), but this was little more than a loose federation of locally based constituency associations. In 1926 the Roman Catholic State Party (*Rooms Katholieke Staatspartij*: RKSP) was formed with, for the first time, a central-party secretariat. In 1945, the Catholic People's Party succeeded the RKSP as the principal Catholic party in the Netherlands.

Catholic political organization in the Netherlands drew its impetus both from demands for separate denominational schools and from a desire to "emancipate" Dutch Catholics from the second-class status to which they had been relegated since the Reformation and independence from Spain. Until 1795, Dutch Catholics had been barred from public office, and the episcopal hierarchy was banned until 1853. Because of minority status and a sense of inferiority, the Dutch Catholics were anxious to organize in order to defend and enhance themselves. At the same time, however, Catholic leaders were reluctant to use their numbers (which were considerable) or to assert themselves too forcefully, lest they provoke hostile reactions. As a result, Catholic political organization developed more slowly and more defensively than its Calvinist counterparts.

Following the introduction of direct elections in 1848, Catholic deputies allied with the Liberals* under Johan Thorbecke because the latter group sanctioned the reestablishment of the episcopal hierarchy. The increasing secularization of Dutch schools forced the "Papo-Thorbeckians" to break with the Liberals. Even so, until 1896, Catholic deputies were split into liberal and conservative factions. Schaepman, the priest who finally succeeded in unifying Catholic deputies, initially favored an interconfessional party. Only in the 20th century, however, when the Dutch bishops actively promoted Catholic social and political organization and the desirability of Catholic unity in order to advance and emancipate Dutch Catholics, did Catholic party organization flourish.

The Dutch Catholic Church was instrumental in ensuring the unity of party and in mobilizing support. The creation of a large and complex "pillar" of Catholic organizations—schools, newspapers, trade unions, business and farming associations, sport and social clubs—provided a strong base of support for the RKSP and its successor, the KVP. Voting for the Catholic party was an automatic response, albeit one actively promoted by clergy and lay leaders. In contrast to the Calvinist pillar, there were relatively few Catholic splinter parties, and those which organized were short-lived. Until the 1960s, the Catholic party could count on the support of 90 percent or more of Dutch Catholics and, as a result, typically commanded 30 to 32 percent of the popular vote and was both the largest party in parliament and an indispensible element in any cabinet coalition. From 1888 to 1925, Catholics were allied with the Protestant-based Anti-Revolutionary Party* and Christian Historical Union* in *"the* coalition," an alliance of religious parties whose principal goal was state support for denominational schools. This goal was met in the Pacification Settlements of 1916 and 1917. The coalition broke up in 1925 over the issue of Dutch representation to the Vatican; but nevertheless, Catholics usually found themselves in coalition with the Anti-Revolutionaries and Christian Historicals. Also, the Catholics served in every cabinet since the introduction of proportional representation in 1918.

The positions and actions of the Dutch Catholic party, whether the RKSP or the KVP, were strongly influenced by the papal encyclicals, *Rerum Novarum* (1893) and *Quadragisimo Anno* (1933), which stress the necessity of alleviating the plight of the poor and the desirability of avoiding class conflict by uniting all strata of society into one interclass party. This philosophy fitted closely with the church's emphasis on the necessity of Catholic unity in order to advance a backward population. Grouping diverse elements into a single party meant that the party, in some respects, was a "holding company" for Catholic interest groups. Moreover, the need to reconcile the claims of business, labor, and agricultural groups while also keeping the party together meant that the Catholic party usually ended up in the center of the Dutch political spectrum on most issues. This was reflected in postwar preferences for coalition partners: although usually forced to opt for coalition with either liberals or socialists, the Catholic leaders typically preferred an all-party coalition, which would spare them from the necessity of choosing one side or the other.

In 1945 the Roman Catholic State Party was succeeded by the Catholic People's Party. This was largely in response to postwar attempts by other groupings to "break through" confessional lines of division and to establish a broadly based socialist party (*see* Dutch People's Movement). Although some Catholic lay leaders were actively involved in the establishment of the Labor Party,* the Dutch clergy rejected the Labor supposition that because state support for religious schools had been obtained, there was no longer any need for separate religious parties. Instead, the church actively promoted the reorganization of the Catholic party. Although the KVP retained earlier emphases on social integration and Catholic unity, the KVP, in contrast to the RKSP, was established as a programmatic party, open to all who agreed with party positions. Supporters, however, were almost exclusively Catholic. In addition, the KVP was far more open to alliances with the socialists. In the interwar period, the RKSP had been willing to ally with the socialists only "in dire need." After World War II, however, the KVP joined the socialists, as well as Christian Historicals, and Anti-Revolutionaries, in a series of "Red-Roman" cabinets from 1946 to 1958. These cabinets supervised the postwar reconstruction and the elaboration of the Dutch welfare state.

The KVP was seriously affected by changes in the Dutch Catholic Church that surfaced in the 1960s. Caught up in the ecumenical movement, the Dutch Catholic Church withdrew from politics. Free from clerical pressures and seemingly "emancipated" from their former second-class status, many Catholics abandoned the KVP. Until 1963 the party had commanded nearly one-third of the popular vote. However, KVP strength dropped in successive elections: 27 percent in 1967, 22 percent in 1971, 18 percent in 1972.

The changing mood and declining support forced KVP leaders to reconsider the rationale for their party. Although some segments of the KVP advocated transformation into a secularly based party, while others preferred an alliance with the left, the dominant thrust was for merger with the Anti-Revolutionary Party and the Christian Historical Union in order to form a broadly based interconfessional party. However, this strategy met with both internal and external resistance. In 1968 part of a radical faction, which preferred alliance with the Labor Party in a progressive concentration, left the KVP and established the Radical Political Party.* Nor were the Anti-Revolutionaries or Christian Historicals prepared for immediate fusion with the Catholics. Nevertheless, discussions that had begun in 1968 resulted in the 1972 formation of the Christian Democratic Appeal,* a coupling organization linking the three parties. Parliamentary caucuses merged in 1976, and in 1977 the three parties submitted a joint electoral list under the Christian Democratic banner. However, it was not until 1980 that the merger was completed and the constituent party organizations were dissolved.

CDA. *See* CHRISTIAN DEMOCRATIC APPEAL.

CDU. *See* CHRISTIAN DEMOCRATIC UNION.

CHRISTELIJK-DEMOCRATISCHE UNIE. *See* CHRISTIAN DEMOCRATIC UNION.

CHRISTELIJK-HISTORISCHE KIEZERSBOND. *See* CHRISTIAN HISTORICAL UNION.

CHRISTELIJK-HISTORISCHE PARTIJ. *See* CHRISTIAN HISTORICAL UNION.

CHRISTELIJK-HISTORISCHE UNIE. *See* CHRISTIAN HISTORICAL UNION.

CHRISTEN DEMOCRATISCHE APPÈL. *See* CHRISTIAN DEMOCRATIC APPEAL.

CHRISTIAN DEMOCRATIC APPEAL (*Christen Democratische Appèl*: CDA). The CDA resulted from the merger of the Anti-Revolutionary Party,* the Christian Historical Union* (both Protestant-based), and the Catholic People's Party.* Initially established as a coupling organization, the CDA derives its origins from both the ecumenical mood of the 1960s and declining support for the confessional parties, particularly for the Catholics. In 1968, following losses in the 1967 parliamentary elections, the Catholic People's Party launched discussions to explore the possibility of greater cooperation among the three religious parties; and in 1972 the CDA was established as a vehicle to prepare the way for the merger of these three parties.

However, the proposed merger was delayed by disputes about the ideological positioning and religious bases of the new party, particularly whether the new entity should be in the political center or slightly left-of-center, and whether the party should be explicitly based on the Gospels (and thus a party of Christians only) or a party open to all who would subscribe to its political programs. The Catholics preferred an open party, while the Protestants insisted on the importance of evangelical inspiration. The Anti-Revolutionaries, who also favored a left-of-center position, were reluctant to proceed until all issues were resolved.

The actual merger took place in stages. In 1976 the parliamentary caucuses of the three parties began meeting together under a rotating leadership. In 1977 the three parties submitted a combined list of candidates for parliament. However, the extraparliamentary organizations of the parties continued to exist, alongside that of the CDA. The merger was finally completed in October 1980 when the Anti-Revolutionary Party, the Christian Historical Union, and the Catholic People's Party were each formally dissolved. By that time, compromises had been reached on religious, ideological, and organizational issues.

Divided both among its component parts and its ideological wings, the CDA is a party of the political center, leaning to the left on some issues and to the right on others, depending on the strength of groups within the party and opportunities for cabinet coalitions. This latter point is evident in the CDA's choice of coalition partners. During 1977-1981, the CDA allied with the liberal People's Party for Freedom and Democracy* in a coalition under CDA leader Andreas A. M. van Agt. More recently, the CDA has joined with the Labor Party* and Democrats '66* in a center-left cabinet, also under van Agt. The CDA party commands the support of 30 to 31 percent of the electorate.

CHRISTIAN DEMOCRATIC UNION (*Christelijk-Democratische Unie*: CDU). Established in 1926, the Christian Democratic Union was a religiously inspired party which extracted an antimilitarist and anticapitalist message from Christian teachings. The party built on an earlier radical tendency within the Dutch Protestant pillar and drew heavily on the writings of Karl Barth. Never strong at the polls, the CDU won one seat in 1933 and two in 1937. Party positions on many issues were close to those of the Social Democratic Workers' Party (SDAP).* The CDU disappeared as a separate political entity when it joined with the

Radical Democratic League, * the SDAP, and others in the establishment of the Labor Party* in 1946.

CHRISTIAN HISTORICAL ELECTORAL UNION. *See* CHRISTIAN HISTORICAL UNION.

CHRISTIAN HISTORICAL PARTY. *See* CHRISTIAN HISTORICAL UNION.

CHRISTIAN HISTORICAL UNION (*Christelijk-Historische Unie*: CHU). The establishment of the CHU in 1908 institutionalized a long-standing division on tactics and policy within the Dutch Protestant pillar. Issues leading to the division included the degree of militancy with which Calvinist demands should be pressed, the role of the extraparlimentary organization, religious practices and attitudes, and the question of suffrage extension. Divisions centered on A. F. Savornin Lohman, leader of the Anti-Revolutionary Party* group in parliament; and Abraham Kuyper, founder and organizer of the extraparliamentary group. Kuyper favored the militant pressing of Calvinist demands and wanted the franchise extended to include the *kleine luyden* (small men) who supported his movement. Lohman resisted this and stressed the necessity of compromise within the parliament. Proposals to extend the franchise in 1894 led to a split. Lohman and his followers established the Free Anti-Revolutionary Party (*Vrij Anti-Revolutionaire Partij*: VAR) in 1894. In 1903 this grouping joined with the Christian Historical Electoral Union (*Christelijk-Historische Kiezersbond*, established 1896) to form the Christian Historical Party (*Christelijk-Historische Partij*). And in 1908, the Christian Historical Party merged with the Friesian Christian Historical Party (or literally, the League of Electoral Committees Based on Christian Historical Principles, *Bond van Kiesverenigingen op Christelijk Historische Grondslag*, established 1898) to form the Christian Historical Union.

The positions and attitudes of the CHU were best understood in relation to the Anti-Revolutionary Party (ARP). Though seemingly cut from the same cloth, the two parties represented different tendencies within Dutch Calvinism and differed in organization, style, and mentality. The Christian Historical Union drew support primarily from members of Dutch Reformed Churches, while the ARP derived support from both Orthodox Reformed (*Gereformeerd*) Churches and more orthodox elements within the Dutch Reformed Church. In addition, the ARP emphasized discipline and authority and prided itself on strong organization. In contrast, the CHU stressed that it was a union rather than a party and emphasized the autonomy of its branches and elected representatives. Also, CHU members were more favorably disposed to the notion of a state religion and "Christianizing" the Netherlands, in contrast to the ARP emphasis on isolation and purity. This CHU philosophy was paired with a measure of antipapism and hostility toward Catholics.

The Christian Historical Union typically displayed a governmental orientation, being inclined both to serve in cabinets whenever possible and to give sitting cabinets the benefit of the doubt in cases of conflict. The CHU position on left-right issues was difficult to describe. At its inception, the CHU contained many upper-class elements who were opposed to suffrage extension, among other things. In the interwar period, the party could be said to have been to the left of the Anti-Revolutionaries; in recent years, the opposite was the case. The CHU typically won only eight to nine percent of the popular vote and seats in parliament.

After the initial split in 1894, the Anti-Revolutionaries made repeated overtures for the reunification of their party with the CHU. These overtures were resisted by the Christian Historicals on the grounds that their more loosely organized party would be swallowed up by the better organized and more militant ARP. In 1968, however, the CHU joined in discussions with the ARP and the Catholic People's Party* concerning greater cooperation among the three parties. Despite its previous antipapism, the CHU endorsed the merger of these three parties into the formation of the Christian Democratic Appeal,* and formally dissolved itself in 1980.

CHU. See CHRISTIAN HISTORICAL UNION.

COMMUNISTISCHE PARTIJ HOLLAND. See COMMUNIST PARTY OF THE NETHERLANDS.

COMMUNISTISCHE PARTIJ NEDERLAND. See COMMUNIST PARTY OF THE NETHERLANDS.

COMMUNIST PARTY OF HOLLAND. See COMMUNIST PARTY OF THE NETHERLANDS.

COMMUNIST PARTY OF THE NETHERLANDS (*Communistische Partij Nederland*: CPN). The Communist Party of the Netherlands dates from the 1909 expulsion of the left-wing "Tribune faction" from the Social Democratic Workers' Party.* The dissidents (grouped around the weekly publication, *The Tribune*) established the Social Democratic Party (*Sociaal-Democratische Partij*). This party was renamed the Communist Party of Holland (*Communistische Partij Holland*: CPH) in 1917, and the name of Communist Party of the Netherlands was adopted in 1936. The CPN has usually adhered closely to the Moscow line of communist ideology.

The CPN has rarely commanded a large electorate. During the period between the world wars, the Communists won only two to three percent of the votes. In 1946 the Communists, benefitting from their role in the World War II resistance movement, surged to 10.6 percent of the vote. However, CPN support declined in subsequent elections; and by 1959, the party commanded only 2.9 percent. Core support comes from certain working-class neighborhoods in Amsterdam and other cities and from traditionally left-wing rural areas in the north of the country. More recently, the CPN has benefitted from the radical-ization of student movements, and the party has thus improved its position somewhat. The CPN has some—but by no means great—influence in the trade union movement. Party platforms call for abolition of the monarchy, Dutch withdrawal from NATO, and complete socialization of the Netherlands. De-spite sectarian qualities which set it off from other Dutch parties, the CPN has gained a reputation for the quality of its representatives at both the national and municipal levels. Nevertheless, the party has rarely been at the center of Dutch political power.

CONSERVATIEVEN. See CONSERVATIVES.

CONSERVATIVES (Conservatieven). The Conservatives were not an organized political party but rather a loose, 19th-century parliamentary grouping, united by their defense of the prerogatives of the crown. Conservatives were supplanted by religious mobilization and the rise of the Anti-Revolutionary Party* and had all but disappeared by the turn of the century. No other group has appropriated the label. (See also Netherlands introduction.)

CPH. See COMMUNIST PARTY OF THE NETHERLANDS.

CPN. See COMMUNIST PARTY OF THE NETHERLANDS.

DEMOCRATEN '66. See DEMOCRATS '66.

DEMOCRATIC SOCIALISTS '70 (Democratische Socialisten '70: DS'70). Dem-ocratic Socialists '70 was formed in 1970 by right-wing members of the Labor Party (PvdA)* who were unwilling to accept growing "New-Left" influence in that party. Reacting to the increasingly radical posture of the PvdA, DS'70 proposed to offer voters a continuation of the policies which Labor had advo-cated in the 1950s and 1960s. In DS'70's initial campaigns, the emphasis was on responsible fiscal management. Led by Willem Drees, Jr., son of the popular postwar Labor Party prime minister, DS'70 won 6.3 percent of the vote in the 1971 elections and participated in the center-right Biesheuvel cabinet (1971-1972). The resignation of two DS'70 ministers in 1972 brought down this cabinet and forced new elections. The party slipped to 4.1 percent of the vote in 1972 and lost heavily in the 1974 provincial and municipal elections. Poor showings in the 1977 and 1981 national elections (0.72 percent and 0.57 percent) have put the future of DS'70 in doubt.

DEMOCRATISCHE SOCIALISTEN '70. See DEMOCRATIC SOCIALISTS '70.

DEMOCRATS '66 (Democraten '66: D'66). Democrats '66, organized in 1966, originated as a party committed to constitutional reforms and the restructuring of the Dutch party system, but it has since emerged as a left-liberal party. Early D'66 supporters argued that the major parties were based on outmoded doctrines and that the existing party system was undemocratic because voters, confronted with too many choices, had little influence on the actual composition of a cabinet. To rectify this, Democrats '66 advocated the direct election of the prime minister, a district system instead of proportional representation, and a regrouping of parties to create a two-party system.

Competing for the first time in the 1967 elections, D'66 won a surprising 4.5 percent of the vote and seven seats in parliament. This alarmed leaders of other parties and triggered a wide-ranging debate on constitutional reforms and the desirability of electoral alliances and mergers that would reduce the number of parties in the Netherlands. This created a dilemma for the Democrats '66. While D'66 demanded the dissolution of existing parties, it was actively courted by the Labor Party (PvdA),* which saw an electoral alliance as a device for restoring its own sagging strength. Democrats '66 joined the PvdA and the Radical Political Party* in a progressive alliance for the 1971 and 1972 elections. D'66 won 6.8 percent of the vote in 1971 and 4.2 percent in 1972 and served in the center-left cabinet of Labor's Johannes M. den Uyl during 1973-1977.

Severe declines in the 1974 provincial and municipal elections nearly resulted in the party's dissolution in the mid-1970s. However, in 1976, D'66 reorganized. Distancing itself from its previous ally, the Labor Party, and taking advantage of polarization within the Dutch party system, D'66 won 5.4 percent of the vote in the 1977 parliamentary elections and 11.05 percent in 1981. Democrats '66 has deemphasized previous demands for constitutional reforms and now casts itself as a progressive party and one that is particularly concerned with environmental issues and ensuring the livability of Dutch society. D'66 draws support from the secular middle classes and especially from younger and more educated voters. Although stressing its independence from the Labor Party, D'66 still prefers alliances with the left. In 1981, Democrats '66 joined the Labor Party and the Christian Democratic Appeal* in a center-left governing coalition under the Christian Democrats' Andreas A. M. van Agt.

DE VRIJHEIDSBOND. *See* LIBERAL STATE PARTY.

D'66. *See* DEMOCRATS '66.

DS'70. *See* DEMOCRATIC SOCIALISTS '70.

DUTCH PEOPLE'S MOVEMENT (*Nederlandse Volksbeweging*: NVB). Not a political party but rather a movement, the NVB was organized during World War II to promote the renewal of Dutch society and politics. Officially launched in May 1945, following the liberation of the Netherlands, the NVB reflected the spirit of solidarity and cooperation that had developed in detention camps and the resistance movement. Among its principal goals was the breaking down of previous divisions among confessional and secular political forces through the formation of a broadly based, progressive political party. Such a party was to be based on the notion of "personal socialism," a set of beliefs derived from marxist, humanist, or religious perspectives. Although the NVB's larger goals of renewal and change were thwarted by the resurgence of Protestant and Catholic parties, the NVB was instrumental in the formation of the Labor Party,* which resulted from a merger of the Social Democratic Workers' Party,* the Christian Democratic Union,* the Radical Democratic League,* and others in 1946.

ECONOMIC LEAGUE. *See* LIBERALS

ECONOMISCHE BOND. *See* LIBERALS.

FARMERS' LEAGUE (*Plattelandsbond*). The Farmers' League was one of several parties that attempted to represent rural and agrarian interests in the interwar period. Emerging in 1918, the Farmers' League managed to secure at least one seat in parliament between 1918 and 1933 (two seats in 1922). The party declined after 1933 and renamed itself as the National Party of Farmers, Horticulturalists, and the Middle Class (*Nationaal Boeren, Tuinders, en Middenstandspartij*). Nevertheless, the party failed to secure representation in the 1937 elections, after which the party disappeared.

FARMERS' PARTY (*Boeren Partij*: BP). The BP, a protest party similar to the Poujadists of France (*see* FRANCE), initially organized in reaction to the policies of the Dutch Agricultural Board (*Landbouwschap*). Led by Hendrik Koekoek, the party drew support from marginal farmers and shopkeepers and served as a rallying point for protest voters in the 1960s. Founded in 1959, the Farmers' Party won 2.3 percent of the vote in the 1963 parliamentary elections and 4.7 percent in 1967. Growing support for a secularly based protest party alarmed the leaders of the other parties and (along with the proposals set forth by Democrats '66*) helped trigger debate on the shape of the Dutch party system. Aside from this, the BP has not had a great deal of influence. The seven-man caucus elected in 1967 subsequently divided into three groups. Since 1967, the party has not been able to repeat its earlier electoral successes.

FREE ANTI-REVOLUTIONARY PARTY. *See* ANTI-REVOLUTIONARY PARTY and CHRISTIAN HISTORICAL UNION.

FREEDOM LEAGUE. *See* LIBERAL STATE PARTY.

FREE SOCIALISTS. *See* SOCIAL DEMOCRATIC LEAGUE.

FRIESIAN CHRISTIAN HISTORICAL PARTY. *See* CHRISTIAN HISTORICAL UNION.

GENERAL LEAGUE OF ROMAN CATHOLIC ELECTION SOCIETIES. *See* CATHOLIC PEOPLE'S PARTY.

GEREFORMEERD POLITIEK VERBOND. *See* REFORMED POLITICAL LEAGUE.

GPV. *See* REFORMED POLITICAL LEAGUE.

INDEPENDENT SOCIALIST PARTY. *See* SOCIAL DEMOCRATIC WORKERS' PARTY and REVOLUTIONARY SOCIALIST PARTY.

KATHOLIEKE NATIONALE PARTIJ. *See* CATHOLIC NATIONAL PARTY.

KATHOLIEKE VOLKSPARTIJ. *See* CATHOLIC PEOPLE'S PARTY.

KNP. *See* CATHOLIC NATIONAL PARTY.

KVP. *See* CATHOLIC PEOPLE'S PARTY.

LABOR PARTY (*Partij van de Arbeid:* PvdA). The Labor Party (often referred to as the Socialists) is the principal socialist party in the Netherlands. Founded in 1946 by the Radical Democratic League,* the Christian Democratic Union,* dissidents from the Social Democratic Workers' Party,* and members of World War II Dutch resistance groups, particularly the Dutch People's Movement,* the PvdA was intended as a vehicle to "break through" religious cleavages and build a majority for a moderate and not explicitly marxist version of socialism. Based on "personal socialism"—a set of beliefs that could be derived from marxist, humanist, or religious precepts—the Labor Party cast itself as the representative of "all men who labored" and proposed to create "a just order for labor"—in effect, a socialist society. In practice, this meant full employment, a welfare state, and incremental reforms to narrow the gaps in income.

The Labor Party built on trends evident in the Social Democratic Workers' Party (SDAP) and can be considered a continuation of that party. The PvdA leaders argued that because the question of secular versus religious schools had been resolved, religious parties were no longer relevant. However, like the SDAP, the Labor Party has been frustrated by the difficulty of attracting religious voters. The "break-through" attempt was thwarted both by the reemergence of the confessional parties and the post-World War II strength of the Communist Party of the Netherlands.* Instead of the hoped-for majority in the 1946 elections, the PvdA won only 28.3 percent of the vote. Although the Labor Party subsequently advanced to 32.8 percent in 1956 (but then entered a long period of decline), only in recent years has the party been able to win the support of large numbers of Catholics or Protestants.

Inability to command a broader base of support has, in turn, meant that the

PvdA's opportunities to govern are dependent on the predilections of the confessional bloc (primarily the Catholic People's Party* and the two Protestant groupings, the Anti-Revolutionary Party* and the Christian Historical Union*). From 1946 until 1958, the PvdA entered a series of "Red-Roman" coalitions with these religious parties. These cabinets, led from 1948 to 1958 by PvdA leader Willem Drees, supervised the post-World War II reconstruction and built the postwar Dutch welfare state. However, after 1958 the confessional parties opted for coalitions with the liberals (see People's Party for Freedom and Democracy). The Socialists returned to the government in 1965 in coalition with the Catholics and Anti-Revolutionaries, but the cabinet fell about 18 months later when the right wing of the Catholic People's Party withdrew its support.

In the late 1960s, declining support (the PvdA won only 23.5 percent of the vote in 1967), frustration because of the fall of the 1965 cabinet, and the pressure of a dissident faction forced changes in Labor's positions and strategy. Through 1966 the PvdA had been a party of the moderate left, committed to moderate reforms and anxious to govern. In 1966, though, a dissident faction crystallized and gained influence. This group, the New Left, charged that the PvdA was losing support because it had strayed from socialist principles and had been too willing to compromise with other parties. Largely because of New Left pressure, the Labor Party has adopted a more radical posture. In foreign affairs, the PvdA is increasingly skeptical about the NATO alliance and defense commitments. In domestic politics, the party demands greater redistribution and further-going political and social democratization. The party has also embarked on a strategy of alliance and polarization. Rather than waiting until after elections to form coalitions, the PvdA insists that prospective partners form alliances and agree on programs before elections are held. In addition, Labor has insisted on the primacy of its programs in subsequent negotiations. In both 1971 and 1972, the PvdA concluded electoral alliances with the left-liberal Democrats '66* and the Radical Political Party.*

This strategy has produced mixed results. The succumbing to New Left pressure led to a 1970 PvdA split when rightist party members established the Democratic Socialists '70,* a grouping that claims to offer a continuation of Labor policies from the 1950s and 1960s. Although the Labor Party's electoral position has improved (the PvdA won 27 percent of the vote in 1972 and 34 percent in 1977), the PvdA remains dependent on others to govern. From 1969 to 1972, the polarization strategy consigned the PvdA to the opposition. Following the 1972 elections, 165 days were required to form a coalition of Labor, Radicals, Democrats '66, Catholics, and Anti-Revolutionaries under PvdA leader Johannes den Uyl. In office, the den Uyl cabinet was plagued by a series of minicrises, which were partially the result of attempts by the PvdA and its allies to impose reforms on a reluctant confessional bloc. In 1977 the PvdA contested the election without pre-election alliances but was still committed to a distinct program. Although the PvdA gained ten seats, repeated attempts to renew the Labor-confessional alliance failed (this time, with the newly formed Christian

Democratic Appeal*). After 208 days, a confessional-liberal coalition took office. In 1981 the PvdA lost nine seats but was nevertheless able to join a cabinet with the Christian Democrats and Democrats '66.

As was the Social Democratic Workers' Party, the PvdA is a mass party. In the 1950s, PvdA membership reached 140,000, though it is now barely 100,000. The Labor Party retains a working-class membership, but the active party elements are typically young, middle-class, and involved in the service sector of the economy. Some two-thirds of the PvdA electorate is working-class. In recent years, the number of Catholics supporting the Labor Party has increased considerably. Also, there are strong informal ties between the PvdA and the Dutch Federation of Trade Unions (NVV).

LEAGUE FOR NATIONAL RENEWAL (*Verbond voor Nationaal Herstel*). The League for National Renewal emerged in the early 1930s as a small, semifascist party. It won only one seat in 1933 and none in 1937. In 1937 many of its more extreme elements were incorporated into the naziist National Socialist Movement. *

LEAGUE OF ELECTORAL COMMITTEES BASED ON CHRISTIAN HISTORICAL PRINCIPLES. See CHRISTIAN HISTORICAL UNION.

LEAGUE OF INDEPENDENT LIBERALS. See LIBERALS.

LIBERALEN. See LIBERALS.

LIBERALE STAATSPARTIJ. See LIBERAL STATE PARTY.

LIBERALE UNIE. See LIBERALS.

LIBERALS (*Liberalen*). The designation "Liberal" can be applied to a variety of parties and tendencies in the Netherlands. In the middle of the 19th century, the term described a loose formation of parliamentary members. Grouped around Johan Thorbecke, the Liberals were the main protagonists in a struggle to curb the prerogatives of the crown and to secure ministerial responsibility to the parliament. Thorbecke played a major role in the drafting of the 1848 constitution, as well as in subsequent battles which affirmed parliamentary control of the cabinet.

Until 1885 the Liberal organization consisted only of a parliamentary caucus and scattered election societies. In 1885 the Liberal Union (*Liberale Unie*) was established as a federation of Liberal election societies. However, Liberal consensus on parliamentary responsibility and separation of church and state did not extend to social issues or suffrage extension. Divisions in Liberal ranks led to the formation of the Radical League (*Radicale Bond*) in 1892 and to clusters of independent liberals (*vrij-liberalen*) in 1894 and 1896. Efforts to establish greater programmatic unity in the Liberal Union led to further divisions and the formation of the Radical Democratic League* in 1901 as a progressively oriented liberal party. Independent liberals, in turn, grouped themselves in the League of Independent Liberals (*Bond van Vrije Liberalen*) in 1905. In 1921 the Liberal Union, the League of Independent Liberals, and the Economic League (*Economische Bond*, a group which had broken away from the Radical Democratic League) merged to form the Freedom League, later known as the Liberal State Party.* After World War II, the Liberal State Party regrouped as the Party of Freedom, but this group was superceded by the People's Party for Freedom and Democracy* in 1948.

Despite persistent divisions and loose organization, the Liberals have been an influential force in Dutch politics. As noted earlier, under Thorbecke the Liberals were instrumental in curbing monarchial absolutism and establishing the principle of ministerial responsibility to parliament. In 1878 the Liberals were able to pass an education bill, reducing the religious content of education (provoking the formation of confessional, or religion-based, parties). While divisions on the questions of suffrage and social reforms led to fragmentation, the Liberals nevertheless cooperated in electoral alliances (important under the prevailing double-ballot electoral law). Between 1888 and 1913, Liberal strength ranged from 32 to 57 of the 100 seats in the Second Chamber. However, the introduction of proportional representation and universal suffrage in 1918 reduced the number of Liberal mandates and weakened Liberal influence in cabinet politics.

LIBERAL STATE PARTY (*Liberale Staatspartij*: LSP). The LSP was initially known as the Freedom League (*De Vrijheidsbond*). The Freedom League had been formed in 1921 from a merger of the Economic League (*see* Liberals), the League of Independent Liberals (*see* Liberals), and members of the Liberal Union (*see* Liberals). The League renamed itself the Liberal State Party in 1928. Since its inception, this party had represented the more conservative wing of Dutch liberalism, stronger in its endorsement of laissez-faire and classical economics and defense expenditures than the Radical Democratic League.* Following World War II, the LSP regrouped as the Party of Freedom (*Partij van de Vrijheid*: PvdV) but in 1948 joined with some former Radical Democrats in the establishment of the Netherlands' present liberal party, the People's Party for Freedom and Democracy.*

LIBERAL UNION. *See* LIBERALS.

LSP. *See* LIBERAL STATE PARTY.

MIDDENPARTIJ VOOR STADT EN LAND. *See* NETHERLANDS MIDDLE CLASS PARTY.

MIDDENSTANDSPARTIJ. *See* NETHERLANDS MIDDLE CLASS PARTY.

MIDDLE CLASS PARTY. *See* NETHERLANDS MIDDLE CLASS PARTY.

MIDDLE PARTY FOR CITY AND COUNTRY. *See* NETHERLANDS MIDDLE CLASS PARTY.

NATIONAAL BOEREN, TUINDERS, EN MIDDENSTANDSPARTIJ. *See* FARMERS' LEAGUE.

NATIONAAL-SOCIALISTISCHE BEWEGING. *See* NATIONAL SOCIALIST MOVEMENT.

NATIONAL PARTY OF FARMERS, HORTICULTURALISTS, AND THE MIDDLE CLASS. *See* FARMERS' LEAGUE.

NATIONAL SOCIALIST MOVEMENT (*Nationaal-Socialistische Beweging*: NSB). The National Socialist Movement was the principal naziist party in Dutch politics during the 1930s. The party, led by Anton Mussert, began as a lower-middle-class protest movement, but it soon turned radical and imitated the militia aspects of its German counterpart (*see* NATIONAL SOCIALIST GERMAN WORKER'S PARTY, HISTORICAL GERMANY). The Dutch party never had much of a mass following. Electoral support peaked in the 1935 provincial elections when the party won eight percent of the vote. In the 1937 parliamentary elections, the NSB won only four percent of the national vote. During World War II, the NSB collaborated with the German occupying powers. However, although the NSB was the only legal political party after 1941, German authorities kept the party at a distance and never permitted it to govern. The NSB was proscribed by the Dutch authorities in 1945. Attempts to reconstitute the party in the early 1950s were banned by the Dutch courts.

NEDERLANDS MIDDENSTANDS PARTIJ. *See* NETHERLANDS MIDDLE CLASS PARTY.

NEDERLANDSE UNIE. *See* NETHERLANDS UNION.

NEDERLANDSE VOLKSBEWEGING. *See* DUTCH PEOPLE'S MOVEMENT.

NETHERLANDS MIDDLE CLASS PARTY (*Nederlands Middenstands Partij*: NMP). Established in 1971, the NMP won 1.5 percent of the vote in 1971 (two seats) but only 0.9 percent the following year. The party purported to represent the interests of middle-class elements, particularly those of small retailers and shopkeepers. The NMP continues in the tradition of several splinter parties active in the pre-World War II period, such as the Middle Class Party (*Middenstandspartij*) and the Middle Party for City and Country (*Middenpartij voor Stadt en Land*). The former party secured one seat in 1918 and the latter one seat in 1929.

NETHERLANDS NAZI PARTY. *See* NATIONAL SOCIALIST MOVEMENT.

NETHERLANDS UNION (*Nederlandse Unie*). The Netherlands Union was a mass political organization established in July 1940, during the German occupation of the Netherlands. Organized with the consent of the occupying powers, the Netherlands Union embraced corporative doctrines and stressed the need for national solidarity. Although willing to cooperate in the construction of a new political order to replace parliamentary democracy, the Netherlands Union was not a nazi organization. Growing conflicts with the occupying Germans led to the party's dissolution in December 1941.

NMP. *See* NETHERLANDS MIDDLE CLASS PARTY.

NSB. *See* NATIONAL SOCIALIST MOVEMENT.

NVB. *See* DUTCH PEOPLE'S MOVEMENT.

ONAFHANKELIJKE SOCIALISTISCHE PARTIJ. *See* SOCIAL DEMOCRATIC WORKERS' PARTY and REVOLUTIONARY SOCIALIST PARTY.

OSP. *See* SOCIAL DEMOCRATIC WORKERS' PARTY and REVOLUTIONARY SOCIALIST PARTY.

PACIFISTISCHE SOCIALISTISCHE PARTIJ. *See* PACIFIST SOCIALIST PARTY.

PACIFIST SOCIALIST PARTY (*Pacifistische Socialistische Partij*: PSP). The PSP was established in 1957 by individuals seeking an alternative to the pro-NATO policies of the Labor Party* and the pro-Soviet posture of the Communist Party of the Netherlands.* PSP founders included pacifists, former members of the Social Democratic Workers' Party,* and ex-Communists.

As its name indicates, the PSP combines pacifism and socialism in its ideology. Adherents argue that present world problems (such as the armaments race) cannot be resolved in the context of a capitalist economy, and the PSP draws support from students and left-wing intellectuals. Although the Pacifist Socialists were briefly involved in discussions concerning a progressive concentration (with Labor, the Radical Political Party,* and the Democrats '66*), the PSP withdrew when it became apparent that any alliance or merger would involve compromises unacceptable to the Pacifist Socialists.

At the national level, the PSP has avoided government power, preferring instead to use its seats in parliament to advance its views and to present a critique of the established order. In recent elections, the party has been hurt by competition from newer left-wing parties, such as the Radical Political Party. However, many of the PSP's earlier positions have now been adopted by other parties.

PARTIJ VAN DE ARBEID. *See* LABOR PARTY.

PARTIJ VAN DE VRIJHEID. *See* LIBERAL STATE PARTY and PEOPLE'S PARTY FOR FREEDOM AND DEMOCRACY.

PARTY OF FREEDOM. *See* LIBERAL STATE PARTY and PEOPLE'S PARTY FOR FREEDOM AND DEMOCRACY.

PEOPLE'S PARTY FOR FREEDOM AND DEMOCRACY (*Volkspartij voor Vrijheid en Democratie*: VVD). The VVD (also known simply as the Liberals) has been the principal representative of Dutch liberalism in the post-World War II period. The VVD was founded in 1948 when a few former members of the Radical Democratic League* (VDB, amalgamated into the Labor Party* in 1946) found Labor too socialist for their liking and united with the Party of Freedom (*Partij van de Vrijheid*: PvdV, successor to the Liberal State Party*).

Deriving its inspiration from liberalism, the VVD stresses the importance of guaranteeing individual freedom. The VVD recognizes the necessity of a welfare state and the desirability of a managed economy. However, while accepting the major contours of the postwar welfare state, the party generally opposes its extension. In recent years, the VVD has stresed the need to restrain the growth of the public sector in order to allow greater room for private investment.

Although often considered to be at the right of the political spectrum, Dutch Liberals reject attempts to brand their party as right-wing or conservative. Liberals reject the segmentation of Dutch society and would prefer to see the present religious and ideologically segmented media broadcasting arrangements replaced with a national broadcasting system. The VVD also favors greater freedom on moral questions and would like to see abortion removed from the Dutch criminal code.

In post-World War II politics, the Liberals found themselves either in opposition or in coalition with the religious parties. Although the Labor Party and VVD are often in agreement on moral issues such as abortion, the two parties are far apart on social and economic issues. This has been particularly true in the 1970s: socialists, under New Left (*see* Labor Party) influence, have moved to the left; while Liberals, under the leadership of Hans Wiegel, have adopted more vocally liberal positions. The VVD was in coalition with the religious parties from 1958 through 1965 (when the cabinet divided on the broadcasting issues) and during 1967-1972. The VVD recently joined the Christian Democratic Appeal* in the Andreas van Agt cabinet that held office between 1977 and 1981.

While the VVD characterizes itself as a people's party, drawing support from all elements of Dutch society, the party's electorate comes primarily from secular middle and upper classes and from less devout elements of the Dutch Reformed Church. Until 1971, Liberal strength in national elections ranged between eight and 12 percent of the vote. However, in recent elections the VVD benefitted from the weakening of the confessional bloc and the shrinkage of the Catholic People's Party* vote. The VVD advanced to 14.4 percent in the 1972 parliamentary elections, to 17.9 percent in 1977, and fell closer to 17 percent in 1981. Party memberships have increased dramatically: until 1972 the VVD membership ranged between 35,000 and 38,000. In 1977 the total was nearly 88,000.

PLATTELANDSBOND. *See* FARMERS' LEAGUE.

POLITICAL REFORMED PARTY (*Staatkundig Gereformeerde Partij*: SGP). Established in 1918, the SGP is an ultraconservative Calvinist party that draws support from pietistic elements in the Orthodox Reformed Churches. Impetus for the party comes from its rejection of the abbreviation of Article 36 of the Orthodox Reformed Creed (weakening obligations to strive against false gods and the Antichrist). In contrast to the Anti-Revolutionary Party,* the SGP is opposed to alliances with Catholics and demands government in accordance with God's words and laws. The party rejects public welfare and government intervention in the economy, and opposes compulsory vaccinations. The SGP has consistently won two to 2.5 percent of the vote, sufficient for two or three seats in parliament. The SGP has never joined a cabinet.

POLITIEKE PARTIJ RADIKALEN. *See* RADICAL POLITICAL PARTY.

PPR. *See* RADICAL POLITICAL PARTY.

PSP. *See* PACIFIST SOCIALIST PARTY.

PvdA. *See* LABOR PARTY.

PvdV. *See* LIBERAL STATE PARTY and PEOPLE'S PARTY FOR FREEDOM AND DEMOCRACY.

RADICAL DEMOCRATIC LEAGUE (*Vrijzinnige-Democratische Bond*: VDB). Established in 1901, the VDB represented the left or progressive wing of Dutch liberalism. The party was formed when the Liberal Union (*see* Liberals) failed to endorse its own executive's stance in favor of suffrage extension. Dissidents leaving the Liberal Union were joined by the Radical League (*see* Liberals), which had been formed in 1892. Prior to the introduction of universal suffrage in 1918, the VDB held between three and 11 seats in parliament. From 1918 onward, the party controlled from five to seven mandates. Despite its small size, the Radical Democratic League was an influential force in Dutch politics and played a major role in suffrage extension. The VDB disbanded in 1946 when it joined in the establishment of the Labor Party.* However, by 1948 some VDB elements had become disenchanted with the socialism of the Labor Party, and these Radical Democrats defected to help form the Netherlands' current liberal political grouping, the People's Party for Freedom and Democracy.*

RADICALE BOND. See LIBERALS.

RADICAL LEAGUE. See LIBERALS.

RADICAL POLITICAL PARTY (Politieke Partij Radikalen: PPR). The PPR was founded in 1968 and originated from the radical faction of the Catholic People's Party.* This faction had attempted to push the Catholics to the left and in alliance with the Labor Party.* Frustrated in their efforts, part of the faction bolted the Catholics and formed the PPR. They were later joined by some Protestants.

Initially, the PPR attempted to promote the formation of a progressive concentration with Labor, the Pacifist Socialist Party,* and the Democrats '66.* The PPR quickly emerged as a distinctly radical party, demanding extensive social and economic changes, attention to domestic and international inequalities, disarmament, and further political and social democratization. The PPR entered the 1971 and 1972 elections in alliance with the Labor Party and Democrats '66. While the PPR won only 1.8 percent of the 1971 vote, it won 4.8 percent in 1972 and entered the progressive-tinted Johannes M. den Uyl cabinet under the Labor Party. However, the PPR's youthful electorate (half its 1972 support came from voters between the ages of 18 and 21) deserted the party in 1977, at which time the PPR dropped to 1.7 percent of the vote and from seven to three seats in parliament. These three seats were retained in 1981.

REFORMATORISCHE POLITIEKE FEDERATIE. See REFORMIST POLITICAL FEDERATION.

REFORMED POLITICAL LEAGUE (Gereformeerd Politiek Verbond: GPV). Founded in 1948, the GPV is an Orthodox Calvinist grouping which broke away from the Anti-Revolutionary Party* over questions of doctrinal purity and the implications of the Bible for politics. Based on a schism within the Orthodox Reformed Church, the GPV demands greater conformity in public life to God's word and laws.

The GPV won its first seat in parliament in 1963. The party normally wins one to two percent of the vote. While occasionally offering to support government coalitions, the GPV has never been part of the politics of cabinet formation. On religious and political matters, the GPV is, relatively speaking, less conservative than the Political Reformed Party.*

REFORMIST POLITICAL FEDERATION (Reformatorische Politieke Federatie: RPF). A small, right-wing, Orthodox Calvinist party, the RPF was organized in 1980 as a reaction to the merger of the Protestant-based Anti-Revolutionary

Party* and Christian Historical Union* with the Catholic People's Party* to form the Christian Democratic Appeal.* The RPF now joins the Reformed Political League* and the Political Reformed Party* on the right of the Dutch political spectrum.

The RPF won two seats in the 1981 parliamentary elections, and this success was attributed to the willingness of the Christian Democratic Appeal to compromise on a law permitting abortion under certain circumstances. The RPF is strongly opposed to abortion; it is also pro-NATO and advocates cutbacks in the Dutch social welfare system.

REVOLUTIONAIRE SOCIALISTISCHE ARBEIDERS PARTIJ. See REVOLUTIONARY SOCIALIST PARTY.

REVOLUTIONAIRE SOCIALISTISCHE PARTIJ. See REVOLUTIONARY SOCIALIST PARTY.

REVOLUTIONARY SOCIALIST PARTY (*Revolutionaire Socialistische Partij*: RSP). Organized in 1930, the RSP was a small socialist grouping. Rejecting both the reformism of the Social Democratic Workers' Party* and the Soviet doctrine of socialism in one country, the RSP cast itself as a true leninist party. The RSP won one seat in 1933. In 1935 it merged with the Independent Socialist Party (*Onafhankelijke Socialistische Partij*, which had split from the Social Democratic Workers' Party in 1932) to form the Revolutionary Socialist Workers' Party (*Revolutionaire Socialistische Arbeiders Partij*: RSAP). The latter, however, never won a seat in parliament and disappeared by the time of World War II.

REVOLUTIONARY SOCIALIST WORKERS' PARTY. See REVOLUTIONARY SOCIALIST PARTY.

RKPN. See ROMAN CATHOLIC PARTY OF THE NETHERLANDS.

RKSP. See CATHOLIC PEOPLE'S PARTY.

RKVP. See ROMAN CATHOLIC PEOPLE'S PARTY.

ROMAN CATHOLIC PARTY OF THE NETHERLANDS (*Rooms Katholieke Partij Nederland*: RKPN). A splinter of the Catholic People's Party,* the Roman Catholic Party of the Netherlands was established in 1972. The RKPN, which takes a more conservative position on issues such as abortion, won one seat in the 1972 elections but failed to win a mandate in 1977 or 1981.

ROMAN CATHOLIC PEOPLE'S PARTY (*Rooms Katholieke Volkspartij*: RKVP). As a small, progressively oriented party, the RKVP attempted to give voice to

Catholic working-class interests, which the RKVP deemed to be inadequately represented in the Roman Catholic State Party (*see* Catholic People's Party). The RKVP won one seat to parliament in 1925, none in 1929, and one in 1933, after which the party disappeared.

ROMAN CATHOLIC STATE PARTY. *See* CATHOLIC PEOPLE'S PARTY.

ROOMS KATHOLIEKE PARTIJ NEDERLAND. *See* ROMAN CATHOLIC PARTY OF THE NETHERLANDS.

ROOMS KATHOLIEKE STAATSPARTIJ. *See* CATHOLIC PEOPLE'S PARTY.

ROOMS KATHOLIEKE VOLKSPARTIJ. *See* ROMAN CATHOLIC PEOPLE'S PARTY.

RPF. *See* REFORMIST POLITICAL FEDERATION.

RSAP. *See* REVOLUTIONARY SOCIALIST PARTY.

RSP. *See* REVOLUTIONARY SOCIALIST PARTY.

SDAP. *See* SOCIAL DEMOCRATIC WORKERS' PARTY.

SDB. *See* SOCIAL DEMOCRATIC LEAGUE.

SGP. *See* POLITICAL REFORMED PARTY.

SOCIAAL-DEMOCRATISCHE ARBEIDERS PARTIJ. *See* SOCIAL DEMOCRATIC WORKERS' PARTY.

SOCIAAL-DEMOCRATISCHE BOND. *See* SOCIAL DEMOCRATIC LEAGUE.

SOCIAAL-DEMOCRATISCHE PARTIJ. *See* COMMUNIST PARTY OF THE NETHERLANDS.

SOCIAL DEMOCRATIC LEAGUE (*Sociaal-Democratische Bond*: SDB). Established in 1881, the Social Democratic League was the first socialist party of any significance in the Netherlands. Led by a former Protestant minister, F. Domela Nieuwenhuis, the SDB was initially committed to a parliamentary route to socialism. Its program, adopted in 1882, drew heavily on the Gotha Program of the Social Democratic Party of Germany (*see* WEST GERMANY). Although Domela Nieuwenhuis was elected to the parliament in 1888, the SDB was unsuccessful in its attempts to have the franchise extended. As a result, the party and its leader veered toward anarchism and syndicalism. The rejection of parliamentary tactics in the 1890s divided the party and led, in 1894, to the establishment of the Social Democratic Workers' Party.* Although the SDB rejected participation in elections in 1893, followers of Domela Nieuwenhuis, grouped as the Free Socialists (*Vrije Socialisten*), continued to contest elections. The Free Socialists won a single parliamentary seat in 1897, 1901, and 1905. The SDB, however, was disbanded in 1900.

SOCIAL DEMOCRATIC PARTY. *See* COMMUNIST PARTY OF THE NETHERLANDS.

SOCIAL DEMOCRATIC WORKERS' PARTY (*Sociaal-Democratische Arbeiders Partij*: SDAP). The SDAP, established in 1894, developed out of a split in the Social Democratic League.* The adoption of a resolution rejecting parliamentary tactics in 1893 provoked a walkout and the foundation of the SDAP as a party whose doctrines and tactics were closer to those of the Socialist International. Consciously modeled after the Social Democratic Party of Germany (*see* WEST GERMANY)—the SDAP's initial program was a translation of the German party's Erfurt Program—the SDAP grew rapidly and supplanted the Social Democratic League as the principal socialist party in the Netherlands. The SDAP advanced in successive elections so that by 1913 the party had 25,000 members, 18.5 percent of the vote, and 15 seats in the 100-member Second Chamber.

Though committed to eventual revolution, the SDAP was a reformist party for most of its career. SDAP leaders saw no revolutionary situation at hand and concentrated instead on carrying out the class struggle by parliamentary means. While advocating shorter workdays and government-financed pensions, the SDAP also hoped that its advocacy of universal suffrage would produce a socialist majority. This reformist posture produced schisms in the party in 1909 when left-wingers grouped around the magazine *The Tribune* were expelled and eventually formed the Communist Party of the Netherlands.* Further splits developed in 1932 when the left opposition group formed the Independent Socialist Party (*see also* Revolutionary Socialist Party). But only in 1918 did the SDAP stray from reformism. Viewing potential revolutionary developments in Germany, SDAP leader Troelstra stated that the revolution could spread to the Netherlands, and he urged that power be given to the SDAP. The party, however, was totally unprepared for a revolution. When other parties countered by raising a volunteer army and mounting a massive demonstration, the SDAP quickly backed off from Trolestra's pronouncements. As a result, however, the SDAP found itself isolated from other parties for most of the period between the world wars.

Universal manhood suffrage, adopted in 1918, proved to be a severe disappointment for the SDAP. The expected socialist majority never materialized. Instead, because the religious parties were able to mobilize segments of the working class, SDAP growth leveled off at 20 to 23 percent of the popular vote. The SDAP by this time had returned to reformism, but access to power was blocked. In 1913 the SDAP had refused an invitation to join a Radical Democratic League* cabinet. After 1918, the Roman Catholic State Party (*see* Catholic People's Party) refused to ally with the socialists except "in dire need." This kept the SDAP out of cabinets until 1939.

By the 1930s, a new generation of leaders was in control of the SDAP. Increasingly skeptical about the premises of classical marxism and influenced to some extent by the religious socialism of Hendrik de Man, the SDAP leaders began exploring alternative means for establishing socialism in the Netherlands. In 1935 the SDAP and the Dutch Federation of Trade Unions (NVV) issued the *Plan of Labor*, a detailed set of programs designed to alleviate the depression and to lay the groundwork for an eventual socialist society. The SDAP also abandoned its objections to the monarchy and to defense expenditures, and increasingly the party cast itself as the representative of all downtrodden groups in society. Finally, in 1939 two SDAP ministers joined a cabinet.

Like many other socialist parties, the SDAP was a party of mass integration. SDAP membership overlapped with that of the Dutch Federation of Trade Unions (NVV), and joint meetings of the party and trade union directorates were not uncommon. The SDAP and the NVV, in turn, sponsored a socialist press, a broadcasting organization, youth and women's organizations, discussion groups, and a host of other associations. Socialist organizations, especially in the 1920s and 1930s, in effect constituted a separate pillar or segment of Dutch society. The SDAP was dissolved in 1946 when it joined with the Radical Democratic League and the Christian Democratic Union* to form the Labor Party.*

STAATKUNDIG GEREFORMEERDE PARTIJ. *See* POLITICAL REFORMED PARTY.

VAR. *See* ANTI-REVOLUTIONARY PARTY and CHRISTIAN HISTORICAL UNION.

VDB. *See* RADICAL DEMOCRATIC LEAGUE.

VERBOND VOOR NATIONAAL HERSTEL. *See* LEAGUE FOR NATIONAL RENEWAL.

VOLKSPARTIJ VOOR VRIJHEID EN DEMOCRATIE. *See* PEOPLE'S PARTY FOR FREEDOM AND DEMOCRACY.

VRIJ ANTI-REVOLUTIONAIRE PARTIJ. *See* ANTI-REVOLUTIONARY PARTY and CHRISTIAN HISTORICAL UNION.

VRIJE SOCIALISTEN. *See* SOCIAL DEMOCRATIC LEAGUE.

VRIJZINNIGE-DEMOCRATISCHE BOND. *See* RADICAL DEMOCRATIC LEAGUE.

VVD. *See* PEOPLE'S PARTY FOR FREEDOM AND DEMOCRACY.

Steven B. Wolinetz

TABLE 62. Distribution of Seats in the Netherlands' *Tweede Kamer*, 1888-1937

Party	1888	1891	1894	1897	1901	1905	1909	1913	1918	1922	1925	1929	1933	1937
Anti-Revolutionary Party	27	21	15	17	22	15	25	11	13	16	13	12	14	17
Catholics[a]	25	25	25	22	25	25	25	25	30	32	31	30	29	31
Christian Democratic Union[b]	—	—	—	—	—	—	—	—	3	0	0	0	1	2
Christian Historical Union[c]	—	—	0	6	10	8	10	10	7	11	11	11	10	8
Communist Party of Holland[d]	—	—	—	—	—	—	—	—	2	2	1	2	4	3
Farmers' League[e]	—	—	—	—	—	—	—	—	1	2	1	1	1	0
League for National Renewal	—	—	—	—	—	—	—	—	—	—	—	—	1	0
Liberals[f]	46	54	57	48	26	34	24	32	13	10	9	8	7	4
National Socialist Movement	—	—	—	—	—	—	—	—	—	—	—	—	—	4
Political Reformed Party	—	—	—	—	—	—	—	—	0	1	2	3	3	2
Radical Democratic League[g]	—	—	3	4	9	11	9	7	5	5	7	7	6	6
Social Democratic Workers' Party[h]	1	0	0	3	7	7	7	15	22	20	24	24	22	23
Independents and others[i]	1	0	0	0	1	0	0	0	4	1	1	2	2	0
Total	100	100	100	100	100	100	100	100	100	100	100	100	100	100

a Figures represent: 1888-1904, an aggregate of seats won by various Catholic groupings; 1904-1926, the General League of Roman Catholic Election Societies; 1926-1937, the Roman Catholic State Party. (*See also* Catholic People's Party, table 63.)

b During 1918-1925, figures represent seats won by various anticapitalist Protestant predecessor groups. Christian Democratic Union established in 1926. (Helped form the Labor Party in 1946, *see* table 63.)

c Figures for 1894-1903 represent seats won by various local lists of groupings advocating principles based on the Dutch Reformed Church (versus

TABLE 62. *(Continued)*

the more orthodox Calvinist orientation of the Anti-Revolutionary Party and, later, the ultraconservative Political Reformed Party). Consolidated into the Christian Historical Party, 1903-1908; Christian Historical Union formed in 1908.

d Known as the Social Democratic Party, 1909-1917; the Communist Party of Holland, 1917-1936; the Communist Party of the Netherlands, 1936- (*see also* table 63). Party did not contest elections until 1918.

e Known as the Farmers' League, 1918-1933; as the National Party of Farmers, Horticulturalists, and the Middle Class, 1933-1937. (*see also* Farmers' Party, table 63.)

f During 1888-1921, figures include an aggregate of several liberal election societies grouped under the Liberal Union label; from 1905-1921, also includes the League of Independent Liberals and the Economic Union; in 1921, these three groups merged to form the Freedom League, which was then renamed as the Liberal State Party in 1928. (*See also* People's Party for Freedom and Democracy, table 63.)

g Known as the Radical League, 1892-1901. (Helped form the Labor Party in 1946, *see* table 61.)

h For elections of 1888 and 1891, figures represent the Social Democratic League (which then abstained from electoral participation and disbanded in 1900). Social Democratic Workers' Party established in 1894 (and helped form the Labor Party in 1946, *see* table 63). Includes one seat for the Free Socialists in 1897, 1901, and 1905.

i In 1918, includes one seat for the Middle Class Party and one seat for the Middle Party for City and Country.

672

TABLE 63. Distribution of Seats in the Netherlands' *Tweede Kamer*, 1946-1981

Party	1946	1948	1952	1956	1959	1963	1967	1971	1972	1977	1981
Anti-Revolutionary Party	13	13	12	15	14	13	15	13	14	14 ⎫	
Catholic People's Party[b]	32	32	30	49	49	50	42	35	27	27 ⎬ 49[a]	48
Christian Historical Union	8	9	9	13	12	13	12	10	7	7 ⎭	
Catholic National Party	—	1	2	—	—	—	—	—	—	—	—
Communist Party of the Netherlands[c]	10	8	6	7	3	4	5	6	7	2	3
Democratic Socialists '70	—	—	—	—	—	—	—	8	6	1	0
Democrats '66	—	—	—	—	—	—	7	11	6	8	17
Farmers' Party[d]	—	—	—	—	0	3	7	1	3	1	0
Labor Party[e]	29	27	30	50	48	43	37	39	43	53	44
Netherlands Middle Class Party[f]	—	—	—	—	—	—	—	2	0	0	0
Pacifist Socialist Party	—	—	—	—	2	4	4	2	2	1	3
People's Party for Freedom and Democracy[g]	6	8	9	13	19	16	17	16	22	28	26
Political Reformed Party	2	2	2	3	3	3	3	3	3	3	3
Radical Political Party	—	—	—	—	—	—	—	2	7	3	3
Reformed Political League	—	—	—	—	0	1	1	2	2	1	1
Reformed Political Federation	—	—	—	—	—	—	—	—	—	—	2
Total	100	100	100	150	150	150	150	150	150	150	150

a In 1977 and 1981, these three parties contested jointly under the Christian Democratic Appeal label.

b *See also* Catholics, table 62.

c *See also* Communist Party of Holland, table 62.

d *See also* listing for this party's predecessor, the Farmers' League, table 62.

e Formed in 1946 from a merger of the Christian Democratic Union, the Radical Democratic League, and the Social Democratic Workers' Party (for these parties, *see* table 62).

f Modern successor to the pre-World War II Middle Class Party and the Middle Party for City and Country (*see* Independents and others, table 62).

g Known as the Liberal State Party until 1948 (*see* Liberals, table 62).

TABLE 64. Ruling Coalitions in the Netherlands since 1913

Years	Coalition
1913 - 1933	Nonpartisan or extraparliamentary cabinets
1933 - 1937	"National Cabinet"—Anti-Revolutionary Party Christian Historical Union Roman Catholic State Party Liberal State Party Radical Democratic League
1937 - 1939	Anti-Revolutionary Party Christian Historical Union Roman Catholic State Party
1939 - 1940	Christian Historical Union Roman Catholic State Party Social Democratic Workers' Party
1940 - 1945	German military occupation
1946 - 1948	Catholic People's Party Labor Party
1948 - 1952	Labor Party Catholic People's Party Christian Historical Union People's Party for Freedom and Democracy
1952 - 1958	Labor Party Catholic People's Party Christian Historical Union Anti-Revolutionary Party People's Party for Freedom and Democracy
1958 - 1965	Catholic People's Party Christian Historical Union Anti-Revolutionary Party People's Party for Freedom and Democracy
1965 - 1966	Catholic People's Party Anti-Revolutionary Party Labor Party
1966 - 1967	Anti-Revolutionary Party Catholic People's Party
1967 - 1971	Catholic People's Party Christian Historical Union Anti-Revolutionary Party People's Party for Freedom and Democracy

TABLE 64. (*Continued*)

Years	Coalition
1971 - 1972	Catholic People's Party Christian Historical Union Anti-Revolutionary Party People's Party for Freedom and Democracy Democratic Socialists '70
1972 - 1977	Labor Party Catholic People's Party Anti-Revolutionary Party Democrats '66 Radical Political Party
1977 - 1981	Christian Democratic Appeal People's Party for Freedom and Democracy
1981 -	Christian Democratic Appeal Labor Party Democrats '66

Note: First-named party is dominant coalition party.

NORWAY

The KINGDOM OF NORWAY (*Kongeriket Norge*) is a large but sparsely populated country of somewhat more than four million inhabitants (1980 estimate), stretching 125,181 square miles from the North Sea to the Arctic Ocean. Ripples of mountain ranges have made interior communications and economic development a challenge; but the long coastline, inundated with many narrow fiords, has provided alternative pathways. Although among the European states only Iceland is less densely populated, usable land has not been plentiful in Norway. The Gulf Stream prevents genuine Arctic conditions except at the highest altitudes and latitudes; but until the present century, living conditions in much of the land were quite rugged, encouraging the large emigration to North America during the 19th century.

Norway became an independent kingdom only in 1905, but her constitution of 1814 (the Eidsvoll Constitution) is still in force, despite many amendments. It is the oldest written constitution still in force in Europe. The document symbolizes the efforts of the Norwegian elite to establish an independent state after more than 400 years of union with Denmark. The Treaty of Kiel (1814) provided for Denmark's transfer of Norway to the Swedish monarch, but after several hectic weeks a compromise was struck. Norway accepted the Swedish king as her monarch, but she was allowed to keep her own constitutional order.

Patterned after both the American and French constitutions, but reflecting Norwegian and European realities, the Norwegian constitution gave form and continuity to the developing Norwegian polity. For nearly two generations, political power was shared by civil servants, urban and rural economic elites, and their formal representatives in the Norwegian parliament (*Storting*). The cabinet was appointed by and responsible to the Swedish king, but this arrangement was increasingly challenged after 1870. In the first decades of the constitutional order, perhaps only a quarter of the adult male population had voting rights; but by the end of the century, all men (except paupers) had suffrage, and by 1913 this right was extended to women. Between 1919 and 1953, elections took place in multimember constituencies under the d'Hondt system of proportional representation. After 1953, the Saint Lague system was placed in effect with an initial divisor of 1.4. The struggles for suffrage, parliamentary supremacy

(1884), and independence (1905) were the major partisan issues and sources of political organization after the Eidsvoll Constitution was accepted.

Norway today is a constitutional monarchy. Actual executive power resides with the Council of Ministers (*Statsråd*), consisting of the prime minister and 14 deputy ministers. The Norwegian legislature is the bicameral *Storting*, composed of the 39-seat *Lagting* (upper house) and 116-seat *Odelsting* (lower house). The *Storting*, elected by proportional representation (with the voting age having been lowered from 20 to 18 years in 1979), in turn elects one-fourth of its membership to the *Lagting*, with the rest serving in the *Odelsting*. While the two houses consider some legislative matters separately, most activity is carried out by the *Storting* as a whole. Elections are held every four years, and the *Storting* is never dissolved between elections. If the Council of Ministers should resign, the chairperson of the remaining largest party or coalition will form the new government until the next regularly scheduled election.

The origins of Norwegian political parties can most easily be traced back to the battle for ministerial responsibility and parliamentary supremacy, which reached a climax in the early 1880s. The Liberal Party* was the first political group in Norway to constitute itself as a formal political party. For years, there had been a loose coalition of representatives in the parliament who supported the expansion of suffrage and the interests of smaller farmers. Local "associations of farmers' friends" (*Bondevennerne*) had been active in both local and national politics. Early in 1884, the Liberals were established for the showdown on the issue of suffrage and ministerial responsibility. Only a few months passed before their political opponents organized a Conservative Party* to resist these demands. Because the Liberals were successful in significantly expanding male suffrage, parliamentary and eventually local elections were more vigorously contested. The small but rapidly growing urban and rural working class provided the social basis for the third political party. In 1887 the Norwegian Labor Party* was organized by several of the country's labor unions. From the start, the Labor Party has been the political arm of the Norwegian labor movement.

Domestic political quarrels were attenuated in the late 1880s as demands were raised from different political quarters for an end to the union with Sweden. The nationalists had broad support in all of the political parties, and this constitutional question restrained partisan competition until the dissolution of the union was peacefully negotiated with Sweden in 1905. With this question settled, partisanship reappeared with renewed vigor. The economic struggle between employer and employee, as well as regional differences, dominated the domestic political debate.

The economic strains of industrialization, coupled with the sacrifices stemming from World War I (despite lack of direct involvement in the war), sharpened social and political issues in Norwegian politics. Increasingly radical demands were advocated by the Norwegian labor unions, federated since 1889 into the Norwegian Federation of Labor (*Landsorganisjonen*: LO), and by many activists in the Labor Party. Other economic interests were politically mobilized, particularly the farmers, whose interest organization, the Norwegian Union of Farmers, was established in 1896. In 1920 the Farmers' Union organized as the Agrarian Party (see Center Party) to promote the political interests of medium and larger farmers, as well as some fishing interests.

Norwegian politics during the interwar period was characterized by considerable turmoil and stalemate. Many small parties were organized, either as splinters off the older parties or as briefly lived protest movements. The Norwegian Labor Party, for example, split into three wings: a pro-Bolshevik radical group, which formed the basis for the Norwegian Communist Party*; a reformist Norwegian Social Democratic Workers Party (see Labor Party), with pragmatic goals similar to those of the German and Danish social-democratic movements (see SOCIAL DEMOCRATIC PARTY OF GERMANY, HISTORICAL GERMANY; and SOCIAL DEMOCRATIC PARTY OF DENMARK, DENMARK); while the main body of the Labor Party adopted Martin Tranmael's proposals and affiliated with the Russian-dominated Third International between 1920 and 1923. Although the Norwegian Labor Party broke with the Soviet Union, the division of a single Labor bloc into three parties greatly weakened Labor's parliamentary position. In 1927, however, the Labor and Social Democratic Workers parties were reunited on a reformist platform; and with the parliamentary election that year, Labor emerged as the largest political party in Norway, a position it has maintained ever since (see tables 65 and 66).

In the wake of Labor's advance and a deepening economic crisis (which predated the global depression), the Labor Party attempted to fill a political void when neither the rightist nor centrist parties could form a governing coalition. Norway's first Labor government had insufficient parliamentary backing and lasted but 18 days in early 1928. During the ensuing two years, the Liberals managed a partial economic recovery, but the spread of the worldwide depression inevitably enveloped Norway. With soaring unemployment and falling prices, social and labor unrest grew. Antidemocratic movements appeared on the far right and extreme left. An unstable opportunist and former military officer, Vidkun Quisling, appeared on the scene with a nebulous movement to fight domestic radicals and foreign enemies. In 1933, inspired by events in Germany, Quisling formed a political party, the National Union (Nasjonal Samling: NS), with an eclectic mixture of fascist, naziist, and nationalist doctrines. The movement attracted few followers and obtained no seats in the Storting between 1933 and 1936, but some of its doctrines had been echoed by the Agrarian Party (see Center Party), partially in desperation over the agricultural crisis.

In 1935, however, the Labor Party was able to reach a partial accommodation with the Agrarians; and when the latter party provided parliamentary backing, Labor was able to form a government under the premiership of Johan Nygaardsvold. Slowly the national economy began to recover, and the extreme parties failed to make headway. Domestic recovery was abruptly interrupted in April 1940 when the Germans invaded neutral Norway, partially to guarantee their iron ship-ments from Sweden and partially to gain bases for naval and air warfare against Britain. After several weeks of brave but desperate resistance, the Nygaardsvold government was forced to flee to England from where it directed Norwegian exile forces during World War II. With the German occupation established and the constitutional order suspended, Quisling and the National Union could make their reappearance in Norwegian politics.

The war and the relief of liberation in 1945 promoted a lessening of conflict between Norway's democratic parties, and even the Communists gained re-spectability. In the postliberation elections of 1945, the Labor Party won an absolute parliamentary majority (76 of the 150 seats), and their relative strength was increased by the 11 seats won by the Norwegian Communists (their first appearance in parliament). The Labor Party formed a government under the premiership of Einar Gerhardsen; and given the massive reconstruction task facing the war-torn country, Labor's immediate program was broadly supported. The nation's material distress made the introduction of economic planning and strict economic controls less controversial than would otherwise have been the case.

The 1945 elections began a 20-year period of Labor government (*see* table 67). In 1949 the Labor Party improved its majority to an unprecedented 85 mandates, principally at the expense of the Communists who lost all 11 of their seats. Although reduced in the 1953 and 1957 elections, Labor kept its majority until 1961, when the Socialist People's Party,* originally started by two Labor dissenters, won two seats, and Labor found itself two mandates short of a major-ity. Although the Socialist People's Party normally supported the Labor gov-ernment's domestic policies, a mining accident in 1963 caused the two Socialist People's members to join with the nonsocialist parties (Conservatives, Liberals, Center Party, and Christian People's Party*) in a vote of no confidence. The Labor government resigned, and the four opposition parties managed to form a joint government. Although this government lasted only several weeks, it did indicate an alternative to Labor rule. In 1965 the four nonsocialist parties ran separate election campaigns but had a common governing program prepared should they achieve a majority. This they did by a substantial margin; and after two decades of power, Labor was forced into the opposition. The 1969 elections brought substantial gains for Labor (from 68 to 74 seats). At the same time, the Socialist People's Party lost both of their seats, and the nonsocialist government of the Center Party's Per Borten could continue with a one-vote majority.

The Norwegian party system experienced considerable stress during the pro-longed and emotional debate over whether Norway should join the European Communities (EC) (*see* EUROPEAN PARLIAMENT). Although the EC issue had first appeared in 1961, the French veto of British membership (a condition for Norwegian accession) in 1963 stilled the debate. In 1970 the issue reap-peared with the renewed EC applications of Britain, Ireland, Denmark, and Norway. Not only were there substantial differences between the four nonsocialist parties comprising the government, but there were many internal divisions within nearly all of the Norwegian parties. The widening split on the EC question and accusations of parliamentary irregularities forced the resignation of the Borten government in March 1971. Labor took up the reins of power, without a clear parliamentary majority, under Trygve Bratteli. The new government concluded a treaty of accession with the EC and strongly advocated popular approval in the advisory referendum scheduled for September 1972, despite the fact that within the Labor Party there was a vociferous minority calling for rejection of EC membership. However, no party was more dramatically or permanently scarred by the EC debate than the Liberals, who openly split. A majority supporting EC membership formed the New People's Party* with nine mandates, while an anti-EC minority of four remained Liberals.

In the EC referendum of September 1972, a small but clear majority rejected membership, and the Labor government resigned. Since parliamentary elections in Norway may be held only at four-year intervals, the leader of the anti-EC Christian People's Party, Lars Korvald, formed a minority government with the support of the two other anti-EC nonsocialist parties (Liberals and Center). A year later, the two main anti-EC blocs gained dramatically at the expense of the pro-EC parties. Labor lost 12 seats (one Labor member of parliament had already defected to the Socialist People's Party just after the EC referendum), while the pro-EC Liberals in their New People's Party lost eight seats and remained in parliament with but a single member. The anti-EC socialists had formed a broad electoral alliance of anti-EC Laborites (known as the Democratic Socialists-Workers' Information Committee*), joined by the Socialist People's and the Norwegian Communist parties (which had not been represented since 1961). The so-called Socialist Electoral Alliance* won 16 seats in the expanded 155-member *Storting*.

Another new party also made its debut in the Norwegian parliament in the surprising 1973 election. A rightist, Poujadist-type party (*see* UNION FOR THE DEFENSE OF TRADERS AND ARTISANS, FRANCE) organized under the name of its founder and leader, the Anders Lange's Party (*see* Progress Party) and captured four seats with which to promote their campaign of drastic reductions in taxes and social services. Surprisingly, this advance cost the pro-EC Conservatives only some two percent of the vote. Despite the complexity of the postelection parliamentary situation and despite their stunning losses, Labor formed a new government, relying on their ability to organize a majority on an issue-by-issue basis. The EC question was closed by the successful negotiation of a trade treaty between Norway and the EC.

As economic recession gripped western Europe after 1974, Norway's position became anomalous. The discovery of off-shore oil in the late 1960s had attracted little attention because of the high costs to extract the deposits. With the quadrupling of oil prices by the Organization of Petroleum Exporting Countries (OPEC) in 1973-1974, Norway enjoyed an unexpected windfall. The development of a Norwegian oil industry and the drawing upon the expected immense income that these off-shore deposits could be expected to yield allowed Norway to avoid the general economic recession. Norway enjoyed an unprecedented boom, which was reflected in the 1977 parliamentary elections. Labor gained dramatically (14 seats) but did not achieve an absolute majority (76 out of 155), while the Socialist Left Party* (successor to the Socialist Electoral Alliance) lost all but two of its seats. Significant gains (12 seats) for the Conservatives came at the expense of other nonsocialist parties: the Center Party lost heavily, and the New People's Party and the Anders Lange's Party (now called the Progress Party) lost all of their seats. Hence the narrow balance between the socialist and nonsocialist blocs, which had characterized nearly two decades of recent Norwegian politics, was maintained.

The 1981 parliamentary elections saw a significant swing to the right in that the Conservatives gained 13 seats and formed a minority government, while Labor lost ten mandates. The Christian People's Party, however, lost heavily (seven seats), apparently on their rigid antiabortion position. The Center Party lost two more seats, while the rightist Progress Party returned to the *Storting* with four seats. Though the Socialist Left also rose to four mandates, the party's influence will be minimal given Labor's loss. The Liberals kept their two seats. Collectively, the five nonsocialist parties now enjoy a substantial majority (85 of the 155 seats), but whether they can govern together remains to be seen.

Bibliography

Derry, T. K. A *History of Norway, 1814-1972*. Oxford: Oxford University Press, 1973.

Martinussen, Willy. "Politiske skillelinjer og politiske del takelse." In *Det Norske Samfunn*, edited by Natalie Rogoff Ramsøy and Mariken Vaa, vol. 2. Oslo: Gyldendal Norsk Forlag, 1973.

Rokkan, Stein. "Norway." In *International Guide to Electoral Statistics*, edited by Stein Rokkan and Jean Meyriat, vol. 1. The Hague: Mouton, 1969.

———. "Norway: Numerical Democracy and Corporate Democracy." In *Political Oppositions in Western Democracy*, edited by Robert A. Dahl. New Haven, Conn.: Yale University Press, 1966.

Storing, James A. *Norwegian Democracy*. Boston: Houghton Mifflin, 1963.

Torgersen, Ulf. "De politiske institusjonene." In *Det Norske Samfunn*, edited by Natalie Rogoff Ramsøy and Mariken Vaa, vol. 2. Oslo: Gyldendal Norsk Forlag, 1973.

———. *Norske Politiske Institusjoner*. Oslo: Universitetsforlaget, 1972.

Valen, Henry, and Daniel Katz. *Political Parties in Norway*. Oslo: Universitetsforlaget, 1964.

Valen, Henry, and Willy Martinussen. "Electoral Trends and Foreign Policies in Norway: The 1973 *Storting* Elections and the EEC Issue." In *Scandinavia At the Polls: Recent Political Trends in Denmark, Norway, and Sweden*, edited by Karl H. Cerny. Washington, D.C.: American Enterprise Institute, 1977.

Valen, Henry, and Stein Rokkan. "Norway: Conflict Structure and Mass Politics in a European Periphery." In *Comparative Electoral Behavior*, edited by Richard Rose. New York: Macmillan Co., 1974.

Political Parties

AGRARIAN PARTY. *See* CENTER PARTY.

AKP. *See* RED ELECTORAL ALLIANCE.

ANDERS LANGES PARTI TIL STERK NEDSETTELSE AV SKATTER, AVGIFTER, OG OFFENTLIGE INNGREP. *See* PROGRESS PARTY.

ANDERS LANGE'S PARTY FOR A STRONG REDUCTION IN TAXES, RATES, AND PUBLIC INTERVENTION. *See* PROGRESS PARTY.

ANTI-EUROPEAN COMMUNITY MOVEMENT. *See* DEMOCRATIC SOCIALISTS-WORKERS' INFORMATION COMMITTEE.

ARBEIDERDEMOKRATENE. *See* LABOR DEMOCRATS.

ARBEIDERNES KOMMUNISTISKE PARTI. *See* RED ELECTORAL ALLIANCE.

BONDEPARTIET. *See* CENTER PARTY.

CENTER PARTY (*Senterpartiet*: Sp). The Center Party is the modern name for the Agrarian Party (*Bondepartiet*) after a name change in 1959. Although the Agrarians first contested elections in 1915, they were not organized until 1920 as a political party. Sponsored by the Norwegian Union of Farmers (*Norsk Landmandsforbund*) to promote the political goals of that organization, the Agrarians were also known as the Farmers Party. During the prolonged crisis of Norwegian agriculture during the period between the world wars, the Agrarians were active in seeking state assistance and price supports for Norwegian farmers. The party contained strong rightist elements during the 1930s. Nevertheless, it supported cautiously the efforts of Nygaardsvold's Norwegian Labor Party* government to improve the national economy between 1935 and 1940. A complex system of higher prices to farmers, coupled with consumer subsidies on essential foods, was started at that time and continued into the post-World War II period.

The Agrarian Party was weakened in the 1945 election, receiving only ten seats, but the party steadily gained ground in each election through 1973. In 1963 the Agrarians (by this time known as the Center Party) joined the three other nonsocialist parties (Conservative Party,* Liberal Party,* Christian People's Party*) in a common governing program, and in 1965 the Sp leader, Per Borten, became prime minister in the four-party, nonsocialist government. Since the number of people engaged in Norwegian agriculture has declined steadily during the postwar period, the Center Party has sought broader electoral support in urban areas as a pragmatic centrist party (and hence the name change). Although it remains attentive to the needs of farmers, the Center Party has supported the expansion of social services and decentralized industrialization. In the late 1960s, the Sp became an active exponent of environmental protection.

The question of Norwegian membership in the European Community (EC) dramatically affected the Center Party between 1970 and 1973. As a governing party, its leaders participated in the extensive negotiations on the terms of Norwegian entry into the EC, but from the start the party was skeptical of the advantages. The Sp's core support group, the farmers, was alarmed by the threats posed to protectionist Norwegian agriculture by the EC's Common Agricultural Program. The EC's Brussels bureaucracy was perceived as a threat by the Sp's antibureaucratic and anticentralization activists. The Center Party ministers, led by Per Borten, broke with their coalition partners, leading to the government's resignation in 1971. Then the Center Party formed an active core in the nonpartisan Popular Movement Against the EC (*Folkebevegelsen imot EF*). The victory of anti-EC forces in the September 1972 referendum seemed to brighten the Sp's political prospects; and in the 1973 parliamentary elections, the party reached its postwar high of 21 seats (11.03 percent of the vote). Nevertheless, Center's anti-EC stand put it at odds with one of its previous coalition partners, the Conservatives, and the nonsocialist parties no longer seemed as credible as a governing alternative.

These developments, along with Per Borten's retirement as party leader, weakened the Center Party's position in the 1977 and 1981 parliamentary elections. The party won only ten seats in 1981, a loss of 11 since 1973. The distribution of its representatives, mainly from western and central Norway, indicates traditional regions of Center support.

Further Reference. Elder, Neil, and Rolf Gooderham, "The Centre Parties of Norway and Sweden," *Government and Opposition*, vol. 13, no. 2 (Spring 1978): 218-235.

CHRISTIAN PEOPLE'S PARTY (*Kristelig Folkpartiet*: KrF). The oldest and by far the strongest Scandinavian political party specifically committed to the pursuit of Christian ideals in politics, the Christian People's Party was established in 1933 in western Norway. Its founders and many of its voters had previously been associated with the Liberal Party,* and the KrF has contributed to the decline in support for the latter party. The KrF's existence and growing strength during the past half-century attest to the importance of moral and cultural issues in some segments of Norwegian society. Although nearly all Norwegians are Christians and nearly all are at least nominally members of the Norwegian National Church (Lutheran), there continues to be significant cleavages between fundamentalists and more liberal congregations.

Accordingly, the KrF's political program has stressed moral, cultural, and educational matters. It is the principal spokesman for the strong and influential teetotal movement. Also, the party has resisted measures reducing the censorship of pornography and restrictions on abortion. Moreover, the KrF continues to call for stronger emphasis on Christian principles throughout the Norwegian educational system.

In other policy areas, the KrF has been a pragmatic centrist party. It has supported postwar measures vastly expanding social welfare programs, an area in which the KrF has been the most active nonsocialist party. In foreign and defense policy, the Christian People's Party has supported Norwegian membership in NATO and accompanying defense preparedness measures. The KrF was divided on whether or not Norway should join the European Community (EC), and some of the party's leaders were active in the anti-EC campaign. This divisive issue did not, however, significantly weaken party unity.

The KrF's electoral strength increased fairly steadily throughout the post-World War II period from eight seats in 1945 to 22 in 1977. The party's leader, Lars Korvald, was able to form a nonsocialist minority government in October 1972 following the post-EC referendum resignation of the Norwegian Labor Party* government. Korvald's government yielded power to Labor following the September 1973 elections. Although its regional strength remains concentrated in western Norway, the KrF has in recent elections been able to elect representatives in nearly all regions of the country. However, the party's strong antiabortion position cost it seven seats in the 1981 parliamentary elections.

COMMONWEAL PARTY (*Samfunnspartiet*). The Commonweal Party was a small nationalist movement that emerged in the mid-1930s. It was founded by Bertram Dybwad Brochmann, an author and social critic. The party advocated a strengthening of national culture and values and echoed other right-wing themes in Norwegian politics. It appealed primarily to the lower-middle class, shopkeepers, and craftsmen in the towns of some areas along the west coast, and the party's support in the north was among smallholders and fishermen.

Althouth it secured one seat in the *Storting* in the elections of 1933 and 1936, the party was of little political significance. The Commonweal Party reappeared after World War II as New Norway (*Nytt Norge*) and contested the elections of 1945 and 1949 unsuccessfully. It disappeared from national politics after the 1949 elections.

CONSERVATIVE PARTY (*Høyre*: H). Norway's second-oldest political party, the Conservatives (or the Right) was founded late in 1884 in response to the formal establishment of the Liberal Party* on the question of suffrage and ministerial responsibility. The Conservatives were opposed to significant widening of the franchise and rejected the notion that ministers must enjoy the confidence of parliament. In addition, as the party of Norway's political, economic, and cultural elite, the Conservatives supported the union with Sweden until growing strains made that arrangement impossible. Then the Conservatives (known as the Unionist Party [*Samlingspartiet*] between 1903 and 1913) supported the peaceful dissolution of the union. In the following decades, the

Conservatives accepted the principles of parliamentary democracy on the basis of universal suffrage.

Throughout its history, the Conservative Party has supported private property and private enterprise, but the party has generally avoided the extreme moral conservatism of some of the smaller parties. In economic and social affairs, as earlier in political questions, the Conservatives have accepted change after initial opposition. Today, the party supports the principles of welfare capitalism, despite frequent criticism of high taxes, governmental controls, and governmental inefficiency. The party has close political and economic ties to Norwegian industry and serves as the latter's unofficial political spokesman.

The Conservatives are ardent supporters of Norway's membership in NATO and have consistently advocated a stronger defense effort. In addition, the party was an early and strong supporter of Norwegian membership in the European Community (EC). During the EC debate, between 1970 and 1972, no party was more completely and passionately in favor of Norwegian accession; and despite the negative outcome of the 1972 EC referendum, the Conservatives continued to call for Norwegian membership in the 1973 election campaign. Party commitment to the EC was more subdued during the 1977 elections.

In the post-World War II period, the Conservatives have been the second-largest party. Their share of the parliamentary vote rose from 17 percent in 1945 to 21.1 percent in 1965. The party lost ground in 1969 and 1973 but gained greatly in 1977 and 1981, capturing 31.3 percent of the vote and 54 of the Storting's 155 seats in the latter election. In 1963 the Conservative Party leader, John Lyng, formed the brief nonsocialist coalition government; and between 1965 and 1969, the party participated in the four-party, nonsocialist Borten government (see Center Party). Because of its EC position, the Conservatives did not join the brief Korvald government (see Christian People's Party) in 1972. Currently, the Conservative Party possesses a strong organization, particularly its notable youth affiliate. Although strongest in urban centers, the Conservatives are able to elect representatives in all regions of the country.

With the great Conservative advance of 1981 (13 additional Storting seats), the party's leader, Kaare Willock, formed a Conservative minority government in October 1981. The new government will, however, be dependent upon support from the other nonsocialist parties.

DE ENSLIGES PARTI. See SINGLE PEOPLE'S PARTY.

DEMOCRATIC SOCIALISTS-WORKERS' INFORMATION COMMITTEE (*Demokratiske Sosialister-Arbeidernes Informasjon Kommitte*: DS-AIK). Although most of the leadership of the Norwegian Labor Party* supported Norwegian membership in the European Community (EC), there was a significant minority in the party (and in the Norwegian labor movement generally) strongly opposed to that membership. As the EC campaign heated up in early 1972 and the referendum approached, some of the anti-EC Laborites split off to form an agitation movement within the umbrella of the Anti-European Community Movement. Following the success of their campaign and the resignation of the Labor government in that year, the anti-EC group constituted themselves as the leftist DS-AIK. In 1973 they joined with the Socialist People's Party* and the Norwegian Communist Party* in the formal electoral coalition known as the Socialist Electoral Alliance.* This coalition won 16 won seats in the 1973 elections and proceeded to form in 1974-1975 the Socialist Left Party.* The DS-AIK supported these moves and since then has not run independently.

DEMOKRATISKE SOSIALISTER-ARBEIDERNES INFORMASJON KOMMIT-TE. *See* DEMOCRATIC SOCIALISTS-WORKERS' INFORMATION COMMITTEE.

DET LIBERALE FOLKEPARTIET. *See* NEW PEOPLE'S PARTY.

DET NORSKE ARBEIDERPARTIET. *See* NORWEGIAN LABOR PARTY.

DET NYE FOLKEPARTIET. *See* NEW PEOPLE'S PARTY.

DNA. *See* NORWEGIAN LABOR PARTY.

DNF. *See* NEW PEOPLE'S PARTY.

DS-AIK. *See* DEMOCRATIC SOCIALISTS-WORKERS' INFORMATION COMMITTEE.

FF. *See* FREELY ELECTED REPRESENTATIVES.

FOLKEBEVEGELSEN IMOT EF. *See* CENTER PARTY.

FP. *See* PROGRESS PARTY.

FREELY ELECTED REPRESENTATIVES (*Frie Folkevalgte*: FF). The FF was a tiny party established in 1973 as the Women's Freely Elected Representatives (*Kvinnenes Frie Folkevalgte*: KFF), though in 1977 the party participated in the parliamentary elections without specific reference to women. In both 1973 and 1977, the KFF or FF captured less than 0.5 percent of the vote and today remains without political significance.

FREETHINKING LEFT. *See* LIBERAL PARTY.

FREETHINKING PEOPLE'S PARTY. *See* LIBERAL PARTY.

FREMSKRITTSPARTIET. *See* PROGRESS PARTY.

FRIE FOLKEVALGTE. *See* FREELY ELECTED REPRESENTATIVES.

FRISINNEDE FOLKEPARTI. *See* LIBERAL PARTY.

FRISINNEDE VENSTRE. *See* LIBERAL PARTY.

H. *See* CONSERVATIVE PARTY.

HØYRE. *See* CONSERVATIVE PARTY.

KFF. *See* FREELY ELECTED REPRESENTATIVES.

KrF. *See* CHRISTIAN PEOPLE'S PARTY.

KRISTELIG FOLKPARTIET. *See* CHRISTIAN PEOPLE'S PARTY.

KVINNENES FRIE FOLKEVALGTE. *See* FREELY ELECTED REPRESENTATIVES.

LABOR DEMOCRATS (*Arbeiderdemokratene*). The Labor Democrats (or Worker Democrats) grew out of a group of rural workers' associations at the beginning of the 20th century. The party was organized by Johan Castberg as his personal political vehicle. Although somewhat regionally based, the Labor Democrats under Castberg's direction advocated advanced social welfare legislation. Many of the party's policies were eventually enacted into law. The criticism of the left in 1918 reduced the party's support among the electorate; and in 1921 the party was renamed the Radical People's Party (*Radikale Folkeparti*). The party was reduced to one member in 1927 and disappeared from the *Storting* by 1936.

LEFT. *See* LIBERAL PARTY.

LIBERALE VENSTRE. *See* LIBERAL PARTY.

LIBERAL LEFT. *See* LIBERAL PARTY.

LIBERAL PARTY (*Venstre*: V). Norway's oldest political party, the Liberals (or the Left) can trace their roots back to 1884 when Johan Sverdrup and other advocates of parliamentary democracy formally established a political movement to secure these ends. The establishment of the Liberal Party prompted the counterestablishment of an opposing group, the Conservative Party.* The Liberals, however, had existed years earlier as a loose parliamentary and national movement. The Liberals drew supporters from many social groups, but they were especially strong among the farmers of medium-sized holdings in western Norway and in the provincial towns. The Liberals also gained support and leadership from the progressive professionals and intelligentsia of Kristiania (as Oslo was then known). From 1884 to 1918, the Liberals were in the forefront of various political and social reforms measures. In economic matters, they favored free trade and free enterprise, with appropriate adjustments for Norwegian conditions.

The early Liberals were far from being a united party; they actually represented a fragile alliance of fundamentalist and secularist factions. In 1887 the main body of Liberals divided over church-state issues; and a new group, the Moderate Liberals (*Moderate Venstre*), was formed in opposition to the fundamentalist wing of the original party. In 1903 the Moderate Liberals became known as the Liberal Left (*Liberale Venstre*) and later, in 1909, as the Freethinking Left (*Frisinnede Venstre*) and finally, in 1931, as the Freethinking People's Party (*Frisinnede Folkeparti*).

With their basic program of universal suffrage and genuine parliamentary democracy accomplished by the end of World War I, the Liberals found their position in Norwegian politics weakening. The formation of the Agrarian Party (*see* Center Party) in 1920 and the Christian People's Party* in 1933 challenged the Liberals at the center of the political spectrum. Nor was the Liberal laissez-faire economic doctrine popular as the Great Depression hit Norway in the early 1930s.

Between 1935 and 1965, except for the war years, Norwegian politics was dominated by the Norwegian Labor Party.* The Liberals participated neither in the government nor as the leading opposition party. In the first two postwar elections (1945 and 1949), the Liberals polled just under 14 percent of the vote and won 20 and 21 *Storting* seats respectively. During the 1950s they declined, reaching only 8.9 percent of the vote and 14 seats in 1961, but then they gained slightly in the general nonsocialist advance in 1965 (with 10.4 percent and 18 seats). The declining trend resumed in 1969, however, culminating with the splitting of the Liberals in 1972 over the issue of Norwegian membership in the European Community. The party nearly demised in 1973 and 1977.

Postwar Liberal Party programs have been more positive toward an active role for the state in economic planning and growth. Social service programs have also been accepted. The party continues to support measures to reduce restrictions on individual activity, both economic and cultural. The party has supported the general principles of Norwegian foreign policy, though during the 1960s the Liberal Youth Association (*Venstre Ungdom*) became increasingly critical of NATO membership. This skepticism over the advantages of closer Norwegian ties with other Western nations revealed an important split within Liberal ranks. As part of the four-party, nonsocialist government between 1965 and 1971 (*see* Norway introduction), the Liberals participated in the negotiations for Norwegian membership in the European Community. A minority within the Liberal Party found accession unacceptable, either in economic or political terms. This minority in the parliamentary group was supported by many grass-root Liberal organizations, and the result was a party split in 1972. A majority of the parliamentary Liberals, led by former agriculture minister Helge

Seip, created a New Liberal Party, but the name was later changed to New People's Party* to avoid confusion. Both factions did poorly in the 1973 election, with the remainder of the Liberal Party down to 3.5 percent of the vote and two *Storting* seats. The Liberals continued to recede in the 1977 election but managed to hold on to both seats, which were retained in 1981. The New People's Party virtually disappeared from the parliament after 1973, despite efforts to contest elections; and with increased competition for former Liberal voters (now tending to support the Center Party or Christian People's Party), the future of the Liberal Party is in some doubt.

LIBERAL PEOPLE'S PARTY. *See* NEW PEOPLE'S PARTY.

LIBERAL YOUTH ASSOCIATION. *See* LIBERAL PARTY.

MODERATE LIBERALS. *See* LIBERAL PARTY.

MODERATE VENSTRE. *See* LIBERAL PARTY.

NASJONAL SAMLING. *See* NORWAY INTRODUCTION.

NATIONAL UNION. *See* NORWAY INTRODUCTION.

NEW LIBERAL PARTY. *See* NEW PEOPLE'S PARTY.

NEW NORWAY. *See* COMMONWEAL PARTY.

NEW PEOPLE'S PARTY (*Det Nye Folkepartiet:* DNF). The DNF represented the wing of the Liberal Party* that supported Norwegian membership in the European Community (EC). Although the majority of the Liberal parliamentary representatives supported EC membership, a majority of Liberal party members and organizations was opposed. Hence the decision to split the Liberal Party just after the September 1972 EC referendum initially gave the DNF a majority (nine of 13) of the Liberal seats. (Originally called the "New Liberal Party," the name was soon changed to New People's Party to avoid confusion among the voters.) In the 1973 election, the DNF secured only one *Storting* seat. Helge Seip, the DNF party leader and former Liberal minister of agriculture, left Norwegian party politics after 1973; and the DNF failed again in 1977 to attract more than 1.7 percent of the voters, thereby losing its one seat.

In practice, the DNF presented the same basic platform as the Liberals—that of a left-center party committed to the welfare state, to NATO membership, and to international cooperation, but also wary of excessive state regulation. Even more than the Liberals, the New People's Party has failed to make an impression on the modern electorate and is now practically extinct. In 1980, the party adopted the name of the Liberal People's Party (*Det Liberale Folke-*

parti), but in the 1981 elections it captured less than one percent of the votes.

NKP. *See* NORWEGIAN COMMUNIST PARTY.

NORGES KOMMUNISTISKE PARTI. *See* NORWEGIAN COMMUNIST PARTY.

NORGES SOSIALDEMOKRATISKE ARBEIDERPARTI. *See* NORWEGIAN LABOR PARTY.

NORWEGIAN COMMUNIST PARTY (*Norges Kommunistiske Parti*: NKP). The NKP was started in late 1923 when the Norwegian Labor Party* withdrew from the Third International over the question of subservience to the Communist Party of the Soviet Union (*see* SOVIET UNION). Several Laborites remained within the Comintern and founded the Norwegian Communist Party.

The NKP elected representatives to the *Storting* in 1925 and 1927. However, despite its activism in some labor unions and in public during the 1930s, it did not succeed in electing representatives to parliament again until 1945. Strengthened by its World War II role (after 1941) in the anti-German resistance, the NKP received 11.9 percent of the vote (mainly in urban areas) and elected 11 representatives in 1945. That election was also the high water mark of the NKP because with the outbreak of the Cold War, the NKP's electoral strength rapidly disappeared. In 1949 its share of the votes was down to 5.8 percent, and the party lost all of its parliamentary seats. An electoral law reform allowed it to recapture several seats in 1953 and 1957, but once again in 1961 the Communists failed to gain election.

During the 1960s, then facing the election competition of the Socialist People's Party,* the NKP typically gathered less than two percent of the vote. Nevertheless, the Communists enjoyed a brief renaissance in the early 1970s with the mobilization of resistance to Norwegian membership in the European Community. In 1973 the NKP joined the Socialist Electoral Alliance,* and a prominent Communist won a parliamentary seat as part of the Alliance's delegation of sixteen. Discussions within the Alliance to form a broad party of leftist groups provoked vigorous internal debate within the NKP. Efforts at compromise during 1975 were unable to satisfy the majority Communist faction that wished to maintain party identity while continuing electoral cooperation. The result was a split in which the NKP parliamentary delegation, led by NKP chairman Reider T. Larsen, joined the new Socialist Left Party.* The remaining NKP was weaker than ever, though it remains active within the pro-Soviet bloc of communist parties. Running alone again in the 1977 parliamentary elections, the Communists polled merely 0.4 percent of the vote and won no seats. The party fared equally poorly in 1981.

NORWEGIAN LABOR PARTY (*Det Norske Arbeiderpartiet*: DNA). The DNA has been for over half a century Norway's largest party, and it has dominated Norwegian politics throughout the post-World War II era. Founded in 1887, the Labor Party has been the political arm of nearly all Norwegian industrial labor unions. Like other northern European social-democratic parties, the DNA has been reformist, except for the 1918-1927 period when the main DNA body advocated more radical measures and had joined the Comintern (*see* Norway introduction and Norwegian Communist Party). A group of dissidents who opposed Comintern membership and subservience to the Communist Party of the Soviet Union (*see* SOVIET UNION) broke away from the DNA and formed the more moderate Norwegian Social Democratic Workers Party (*Norges Sosialdemokratiske Arbeiderparti*). The latter obtained eight *Storting* seats in the 1921 and 1924 elections. Nevertheless, the Social Democrats rejoined the DNA in 1927.

The Labor Party's era of power began in 1935 when, with support from several center parties, Labor simultaneously tried to relieve the economic distress of the Great Depression and to institute social reforms. Labor's electoral advance in 1945, which gave it an absolute majority of *Storting* seats (76 of 150 seats), began a period of rapid economic and social change in Norway. Influenced by the theories of the socialist economist Ragnar Frisch and by the necessities of rebuilding after wartime destruction and neglect, the Labor government instituted detailed economic planning and controls. Emphasis was placed on the restoration and expansion of the country's capital infrastructure at the expense of consumer goods. Even the nonsocialist parties accepted the necessity and utility of state economic direction during the early postwar years.

The Labor Party's decision to seek closer ties with the Atlantic Powers during 1948-1949 made impossible a Scandinavian Defense Union (with Denmark and Sweden). Labor's foreign minister, Halvard Lange, was responsible for the strong pro-West foreign and defense policy orientation after 1947. Labor's commitment to NATO membership, and after 1961 to European Community membership, strengthened links with the nonsocialist opposition. There was, however, a minority within the Labor Party critical of the pro-NATO foreign policies of the party's leadership. Internal debate became open opposition during the 1950s, and in 1960 two anti-NATO members of the DNA's left wing resigned from the Labor parliamentary group and established the Socialist People's Party. *

The first postwar era of Labor government ended in 1965, when the four nonsocialist parties (Center Party, * Conservative Party, * Liberal Party, * and Christian People's Party*) won a parliamentary majority after an earlier (1963) vote of no confidence in the Labor government. The quiet leadership of Labor premier, Einar Gerhardsen, had changed the political, economic, and social face of Norway. Although the DNA regained its lost seats in 1969 (back to 74 seats, after a decline to 68 seats in 1965), the defeat of both Socialist People's Party representatives made a parliamentary majority impossible. Not until the resignation of the Center Party's Borten government in 1971 over the Common Market issue was Labor able to get back into power. The next 18 months of Labor minority government were devoted entirely to the European Community (EC) debate. Once again, internal dissension led to the secession of some anti-EC members of parliament. These dissidents formed the Democratic Socialists-Workers' Information Committee.* Nevertheless, Labor Premier Trygve Bratteli campaigned hard for voter approval of Norwegian EC membership and was quite disappointed by the narrow defeat in the September 1972 referendum. His government resigned voluntarily in October 1972, and Labor has since accepted the bilateral EC-Norwegian Trade Treaty as the foundation for Norway's European policy for the foreseeable future.

The parliamentary elections of September 1973 were the worst setback for the Labor Party in half a century. The DNA share of the vote fell from 46.5 percent (1969) to 35.3 percent, and the party lost 12 parliamentary seats. Analysis indicates that many Labor voters who had been critical of the party's pro-EC position had deserted primarily to the new Socialist Electoral Alliance.* Despite this defeat, Labor remained by far the largest political party and formed a minority government dependent upon Socialist Alliance votes for domestic matters and nonsocialist votes for foreign policy questions. Although postelection analysis indicated that Labor's loss might be long term, especially in rural districts where the Center Party and Christian People's Party had attracted many former Labor voters, the local elections of 1975 indicated that Labor was again attracting many of its traditional supporters. The internal disputes in the effort to form a Socialist Left Party,* the country's economic prosperity, and the successful transfer of party leadership to Odvar Nordli (who also became premier) and to the more radical Reiulf Steinar as party chairman all contributed to the DNA's surprisingly rapid recovery of electoral strength. The 1977 parliamentary elections brought Labor up to 42.3 percent of the vote (still the second-weakest showing since 1949) and 76 (out of 155) seats. The Labor government continued in power, but it remained dependent upon the two Socialist Left votes.

Early in 1981, Gro Harlem Brundtland became the party's leader and Norway's first woman premier. Campaigning hard, she managed to recoup some of the party's lost popularity, but the 1981 parliamentary elections were still a major setback. The party lost ten seats (dropping to 66) and received 37.6 percent of the vote. Although this was not as dismal as the DNA poll of 1973, Mrs. Brundtland had to resign the premiership in October 1981.

On policy questions, the DNA has shown some evolution in the postwar period. The strict economic controls and quantitative planning of the immediate postwar era have gradually given way to less rigid forms of fiscal policy. Labor has supported measures to increase industrialization, especially in rural and small-town areas. Labor has also supported various forms of European economic cooperation. With the defeat of the EC referendum in 1972, Labor has moved to more pragmatic forms of cooperation, including an associate membership in the

International Energy Agency. Pragmatism has also characterized Labor policies toward Nordic cooperation. Under Labor government, Norway rejected the Scandinavian Defense Union (1944-1949) and regional economic cooperation in the 1950s. The party has supported the Nordic Council and various Nordic arrangements since 1952.

Further Reference. Bergh, Trond, and Helge Pharo, eds., Vekst og Velstand (Oslo: Universitetsforlaget, 1977).

NORWEGIAN SOCIAL DEMOCRATIC WORKERS PARTY. See NORWEGIAN LABOR PARTY.

NS. See NORWAY INTRODUCTION.

NYTT NORGE. See COMMONWEAL PARTY.

POPULAR MOVEMENT AGAINST THE EUROPEAN COMMUNITY. See CENTER PARTY.

PROGRESS PARTY (Fremskrittspartiet: FP). Established in 1973, the FP was originally called the Anders Lange's Party for a Strong Reduction in Taxes, Rates, and Public Intervention (Anders Langes Parti til Sterk Nedsettelse av Skatter, Avgifter, og Offentlige Inngrep), named after its founder, Anders Lange. With Lange's death in 1974, the party changed its name in 1977 to the Progress Party and modeled itself after its Danish example (see PROGRESS PARTY, DENMARK).

With a program calling for sharp reductions in state spending and taxation, the Anders Lange's Party occupied a space to the right of the Conservative Party.* In the 1973 parliamentary elections, the party polled five percent of the vote and won four Storting seats. Excluded from cooperation with the opposition coalition (Center Party,* Conservative Party, Liberal Party,* and Christian People's Party*), the Lange group had little influence on legislation. The party directed its attacks against the social and welfare legislation of the Norwegian Labor Party* government and was the only party to do so in parliament in the post-World War II era. Analysis showed that the Lange Party drew support from a small number of voters across the political spectrum. In September 1977, the party (by then calling itself the Progress Party) polled only 1.9 percent of the vote and lost all four of its Storting seats. In 1981, however, the party regained its four seats with 4.5 percent of the vote.

RADICAL PEOPLE'S PARTY. See LABOR DEMOCRATS.

RADIKALE FOLKEPARTI. See LABOR DEMOCRATS.

RED ELECTORAL ALLIANCE (Rød Valgallianse: RV). Formed in 1973 as an amalgam of small parties on the far left of Norwegian politics, the Red Electoral

Alliance advocates radical change according to what may loosely be called "maoist" revolutionary doctrines. The main force behind the RV has been the Workers' Communist Party (*Arbeidernes Kommunistiske Parti:* AKP), which was originally the youth organization of the Socialist People's Party.* Critical of nearly all domestic and foreign policies, the RV polled only 0.4 percent of the vote in 1973, 0.6 percent in 1977, and 0.7 in 1981. The RV has not been represented in parliament.

RIGHT. *See* CONSERVATIVE PARTY.

RØD VALGALLIANSE. *See* RED ELECTORAL ALLIANCE.

RV. *See* RED ELECTORAL ALLIANCE.

SAMFUNNSPARTIET. *See* COMMONWEAL PARTY.

SAMLINGSPARTIET. *See* CONSERVATIVE PARTY.

SENTERPARTIET. *See* CENTER PARTY.

SF. *See* SOCIALIST PEOPLE'S PARTY.

SINGLE PEOPLE'S PARTY (*De Ensliges Parti*). A small protest group with little electoral support, the Single People's Party stressed the rights of unmarried citizens. It polled about 0.3 percent of the vote in both 1973 and 1977.

SOCIALIST ELECTORAL ALLIANCE (*Sosialistisk Valgforbund:* SV). The SV was formed in 1973 as an electoral alliance among the Socialist People's Party,* the Democratic Socialists-Workers' Information Committee,* and the Norwegian Communist Party.* The Alliance's platform stood sharply against Norwegian membership in the European Community (EC). EC membership had been narrowly defeated in a September 1972 national referendum. However, with the pro-EC stand of the traditionally governing Norwegian Labor Party,* the membership issue continued to be a highly controversial point in the 1973 election campaigns. At the 1973 polls, the newly created Socialist Electoral Alliance received 11.2 percent of the vote and 16 seats to the *Storting*, having campaigned vigorously against EC and NATO membership and calling for decreased governmental defense spending and taxation.

At a party congress in March 1975, the Socialist People's faction of the SV attempted to transform the electoral alliance into a unified political party. While the Democratic Socialists-Workers approved this unification, the SV's Communist constituency became torn in debate over the proposal. In November 1975, the majority of Communist Party members voted against dissolution of their party. Only a small number of Communists, led by their party chairman

Reider T. Larsen, joined with the Socialist People's Party and Democratic Socialists-Workers to form the new Socialist Left Party. *

SOCIALIST LEFT PARTY (*Sosialistisk Venstreparti*: SV). The SV arose from the 1973 Socialist Electoral Alliance* among the Socialist People's Party,* the Norwegian Communist Party,* and the Democratic Socialists-Workers' Information Committee.* The Alliance's electoral success in 1973 (11.2 percent of the vote and 15 *Storting* seats) gave the Norwegian left greater parliamentary strength than ever before. In 1975 the coalition officially became a new political party, the SV, although a number of Communists refused to join the new party and carried forward the Norwegian Communist Party as an independent entity once again.

In program, the SV reflected its origins in the anti-European Community (EC) campaign, as well as the dominant role of the Socialist People's Party on the Norwegian left during the 1960s. Strongly opposed to Norwegian membership in the EC, the Socialist Left Party was equally critical of Norwegian participation in NATO and in the International Energy Agency. Both the United States and, in more muted form, the Soviet Union were criticized for their role in world politics. Foreign and defense policy issues dominated the public profile of the SV as had previously been the case of the Socialist People's Party.

Nevertheless, the SV also has a radical program for domestic political change, with special attention to economic, ecological, and educational issues. In general terms, the party favors income redistribution, greater worker participation in the management of enterprises, and cautious development of Norwegian petroleum resources. In practice, between 1973 and 1977 the SV parliamentary mandates supported the minority government of the Norwegian Labor Party,* particularly in such matters as greater public control of the banking system and in abortion reform.

Already weakened in local and county elections in 1975, the 1977 parliamentary elections were a dramatic setback for the new Socialist Left Party. Its share of the vote was only 4.2 percent, and it won only two seats in the *Storting*. Although this meager result did keep Labor in power, analysis indicates that most of the 1973 SV voters returned to the Labor Party in 1977. Because of its critical role as the supporter of the government, the SV has more clout than would otherwise be the case for so small a party. In foreign and security affairs, however, the SV is isolated. Assuming the role of the Socialist People's Party of a decade earlier, the SV is much reduced in both power and resources from its auspicious start.

The SV did make gains in the 1981 parliamentary elections, winning four seats and 4.9 percent of the vote. With the resignation of the Labor government, however, the SV's influence is likely to be further reduced.

Further Reference. Valen, Henry, "The *Storting* Election of 1977: Realignment or Return to Normalcy?" *Scandinavian Political Science*, n.s. 1, nos. 2-3 (1978): 83-107.

SOCIALIST PEOPLE'S PARTY (*Sosialistisk Folkepartiet*: SF). The SF was established in 1960 by a group of Laborites and independent socialists who were critical of the Norwegian Labor Party's* (and Norway's) strong commitments to NATO. Gradually, the SF's program was broadened into a left-socialist "third alternative" to the reformist and pro-Western Labor Party and the pro-Soviet Norwegian Communist Party.*

Foreign policy issues dominated the small party's debate throughout the 1960s, including attention toward the Third World and anticolonial struggles, disarmament and antinuclear weapons campaigns, and similar themes. Although willing to support the Labor government on domestic policy issues, the SF remained isolated in parliament where it held two seats after the 1961 elections. In 1963 the SF joined with the nonsocialist opposition (the Center Party,* Conservative Party,* Liberal Party,* and Christian People's Party*) in voting no confidence in the Labor government, which led to the latter's resignation and the brief-lived but important four-party, nonsocialist coalition. In 1965 the SF increased its share of the vote to six percent (from 2.4 percent in 1961) but still won only two seats. Internal dissension increased within the SF in the late 1960s as more radical groups appeared, such as the maoist leanings of the SF's youth organization, the Workers' Communist Party, which split from the SF to form the Red Electoral Alliance.* In 1969 the SF's vote fell to 3.5 percent, and both parliamentary seats were lost. During the four years of nonsocialist government, the SF's influence had been negligible.

The reappearance of the Common Market issue in 1970 provided an issue that could unite leftist socialists and could attract many voters who were otherwise uninterested in the sectarian squabbles of the radical left. The SF leaders were prominent in the anti-European Community (EC) movement, and the party's small but committed organization worked hard in the campaign. Following the defeat of the EC referendum in September 1972, the SF took the lead in advocating long-term collaboration with the other two main elements of the Norwegian left fringe: the Communists and disaffected left Laborites organized in the Democratic Socialists-Workers' Information Committee.* In the September 1973 parliamentary elections, these three groups had forged the Socialist Electoral Alliance,* which listed candidates in every constituency. The results were a spectacular success: 11.2 percent of the vote and 15 of the Storting's 155 seats.

On the basis of this advance, preparations were made for uniting the three constituent parties of the Alliance into a new Socialist Left Party* in 1974-1975. The SF spearheaded these efforts, which were successful except for a wing of the Communist Party which wanted to continue only an electoral collaboration. With the formation of the Socialist Left Party in 1975, the Socialist People's Party became defunct as a separate entity.

Further Reference. Stenersen, Øivind, "Venstrekreftene i norsk politikk 1945-65," in *Vekst og Velstand,* edited by Trond Bergh and Helge Pharo (Oslo: Universitetsforlaget, 1972), pp. 372-392.

SOSIALISTISK FOLKEPARTIET. *See* SOCIALIST PEOPLE'S PARTY.

SOSIALISTISK VALGFORBUND. *See* SOCIALIST ELECTORAL ALLIANCE.

SOSIALISTISK VENSTREPARTI. *See* SOCIALIST LEFT PARTY.

Sp. *See* CENTER PARTY.

SV. *See* SOCIALIST ELECTORAL ALLIANCE and SOCIALIST LEFT PARTY.

UNIONIST PARTY. *See* CONSERVATIVE PARTY.

V. *See* LIBERAL PARTY.

VENSTRE. *See* LIBERAL PARTY.

VENSTRE UNGDOM. *See* LIBERAL PARTY.

WOMEN'S FREELY ELECTED REPRESENTATIVES. *See* FREELY ELECTED REPRESENTATIVES.

WORKER DEMOCRATS. *See* LABOR DEMOCRATS.

WORKERS' COMMUNIST PARTY. *See* RED ELECTORAL ALLIANCE.

Eric S. Einhorn

TABLE 65. Distribution of Seats in Norway's *Storting*, 1905 (Independence) - 1936

Party	1906	1909	1912	1915	1918	1921	1924	1927	1930	1933	1936
Agrarian Party[a]	—	—	—	1	3	17	22	26	25	23	18
Christian People's Party	—	—	—	—	—	—	—	—	—	1	2
Commonweal Party	—	—	—	—	—	—	—	—	—	1	1
Conservative Party[b]	36	41	20	20	40	42	43	30	41	30	36
Labor Democrats[c]	4	2	6	6	3	2	2	1	1	1	0
Liberal Party	73	46	70	74	51	37	34	30	33	24	23
National Liberals[d]	—	23	4	1	10	15	11	1	3	1	0
Norwegian Communist Party	—	—	—	—	—	—	6	3	0	0	0
Norwegian Labor Party	10	11	23	19	18	29	24	59	47	69	70
Norwegian Social Democratic Workers Party	—	—	—	—	—	8	8	—	—	—	—
Independents and others	0	0	0	2	1	0	0	0	0	0	0
Total	123	123	123	123	126	150	150	150	150	150	150

a   Known as the Norwegian Union of Farmers, 1915-1920.
b   Known as the Unionist Party, 1903-1913.
c   Known as the Radical People's Party, 1921-1936.
d   A generic term applied to a Liberal Party splinter, which was formally known as: the Liberal Left, 1903-1909; the Freethinking Left, 1909-1921; the Freethinking People's Party, 1931-1936.

TABLE 66. Distribution of Seats in Norway's *Storting*, 1945-1981

Party	1945	1949	1953	1957	1961	1965	1969	1973	1977	1981
Agrarian Party[a]	10	12	14	15	16	18	20	21	12	10
Anders Lange's Party[b]	—	—	—	—	—	—	—	4	0	4
Christian People's Party	8	9	14	12	15	13	14	20	22	15
Commonweal Party[c]	0	0	—	—	—	—	—	—	—	—
Conservative Party	25	23	27	29	29	31	29	29	41	54
Liberal Party	20	21	15	15	14	18	13	2	2	2
New People's Party[d]	—	—	—	—	—	—	—	1	0	0
Norwegian Communist Party	11	0	3	1	0	0	0	1	0	0
Norwegian Labor Party	76	85	77	78	74	68	74	62	76	66
Socialist People's Party[e]	—	—	—	—	2	2	0	15	2	4
Total	150	150	150	150	150	150	150	155	155	155

[a] Known as the Center Party, 1959- .

[b] Known as the Progress Party, 1977- .

[c] Known as New Norway, 1945-1949.

[d] Known as the Liberal People's Party, 1980- .

[e] Known as the Socialist Left Party, 1975- .

TABLE 67.   Ruling Parties or Coalitions in Norway since 1906

Years	Party or Coalition
1906 - 1910	Liberal Party
1910 - 1913	Unionist Party
1913 - 1920	Liberal Party
1920 - 1921	Conservative Party
1921 - 1923	Liberal Party
1923 - 1924	Conservative Party
1924 - 1926	Liberal Party
1926 - 1928	Conservative Party
1928 -	Norwegian Labor Party
1928 - 1931	Liberal Party
1931 - 1933	Agrarian Party
1933 - 1935	Liberal Party
1935 - 1940	Norwegian Labor Party
1940 - 1945	National Union (during German occupation of Norway)
1945 -	All-party coalition
1945 - 1963	Norwegian Labor Party
1963 -	Conservative Party Liberal Party Center Party Christian People's Party (this government lasted only a few weeks)
1963 - 1965	Norwegian Labor Party
1965 - 1971	Center Party Conservative Party Liberal Party Christian People's Party
1971 - 1972	Norwegian Labor Party
1972 - 1973	Christian People's Party Center Party Liberal Party
1973 - 1981	Norwegian Labor Party
Oct 1981 -	Conservative Party

Note: First-named party is dominant coalition party.

VINCENT E. McHALE (Estonia, Latvia, Lithuania, coauthor European Parliament, editor-in-chief) is associate professor and chairman of political science at Case Western Reserve University. He received his Ph.D. from Pennsylvania State University in 1969. His articles on European politics have appeared in *Comparative Politics, European Journal of Political Research, Journal of Common Market Studies*, and the *Western Political Quarterly*. Dr. McHale is coauthor of *Vote, Clivages Socio-politiques et Développement Régional en Belgique* (1974) and coeditor of *Evaluating Transnational Programs in Government and Business* (1980).

SHARON SKOWRONSKI (Luxembourg, coauthor European Parliament, assistant editor) is currently department assistant in political science at Case Western Reserve University. Ms. Skowronski received her B.A. in English from Cleveland State University in 1975.